The Civil War should be seen as America's "bourgeois revolution." So argues Dr. John Ashworth in this novel reinterpretation, from a Marxist perspective, of American political and economic development in the forty years before the Civil War. In this book, the first of a two-volume treatment of slavery, capitalism and politics, Ashworth focuses on the political struggles of the antebellum period and locates them within the class systems of the North and South.

In conjunction with its sequel, this volume will seek to demonstrate that the conflict largely resulted from differences between capitalist and slave modes of production. The sweeping changes in American society unleashed by the rapid development of capitalism in the nineteenth century led to war as the interests of the rapidly developing wage labor system in the North and the slave society of the South diverged. With a careful synthesis of existing scholarship on the economics of slavery, the origins of abolitionism, the proslavery argument and the second party system, Ashworth maintains that the origins of the American Civil War are best understood in terms derived from Marxism.

Slavery, Capitalism, and Politics
in the Antebellum Republic

Slavery, Capitalism, and Politics in the Antebellum Republic

Volume 1: Commerce and Compromise, 1820–1850

JOHN ASHWORTH

University of East Anglia

Published by the Press Syndicate of the University of Cambridge
The Pitt Building, Trumpington Street, Cambridge CB2 1RP
40 West 20th Street, New York, NY 1O11-4211, USA
10 Stamford Road, Oakleigh, Melbourne 3166, Australia

First published 1995

Printed in the United States of America

Library of Congress Cataloging-in-Publication Data
Ashworth, John.
    Slavery, capitalism, and politics in the antebellum Republic /
John Ashworth.
        p. cm
    Contents: v. 1. Commerce and compromise, 1820–1850
    1. Slavery – Economic aspects – United States – History – 19th
century. 2. Capitalism – United States – History – 19th century.
3. United States – Politics and government – 1815–1861. 4. Working
class – United States – History – 19th century. 5. United States –
Economic conditions – To 1865.
E441.A86   1996
331.11'734'0973 – dc20   95-9957
                                                                CIP

A catalog record for this book is available from the British Library
ISBN   0-521-47487-6 hardback
        0-521-47994-0 paperback

Contents

Preface

This is the first of a two-volume study of slavery and capitalism as they relate to the second party system and the origins of the Civil War. The second volume is to be entitled, "Towards a Bourgeois Revolution." The two volumes are divided chronologically in 1850 but when in this volume I consider abolitionism, the proslavery argument and the economic performance of the two sections, I largely ignore this chronology. Similarly, even though most of the direct discussion of the origins of the Civil War will be in the second volume, I shall attribute primacy to long-term causes, operative, that is to say, before 1850 and thus central to the concerns of the first volume.

Nevertheless, my discussion of the political events of the antebellum decades reflects my concern with the collapse of 1860–1861 in that the treatment of each decade is fuller than that of the previous one. What follows is by no means a complete list of the subjects I address but it does indicate my major concerns. For the reader's benefit I have added a reference to the chapters which most directly relate to each of them. In this work and its sequel I maintain the following propositions:

(1) The American Civil War is best understood as a bourgeois revolution; indeed it is one of the world's leading examples of such a revolution. (Introduction and conclusion to this volume but primarily Volume 2.)

(2) The conflict between the sections can only be understood in terms of the differences between capitalist and slave modes of production. (Introduction to this volume, Chapters 1 to 3, also Volume 2.)

(3) Slavery was deeply rooted in American democracy, largely owing to its privileged (albeit unacknowledged) place within the Democratic party and the Jeffersonian tradition. (Primarily Chapters 1, 5 and 6 of this volume.)

(4) In the North the growth of wage labor was crucial in generating new and more militant forms of antislavery (Chapter 3, also Volume 2) and in creating economic imbalances between the sections (Chapter 2).

(5) Slavery is, in certain crucial respects, a weaker form of exploitation than wage labor. (Chapters 2, 4.)

ix

(6) The second party system was a struggle between an essentially pre-capitalist alliance of slaveholders and farmers, on the one hand, and the advocates and allies of merchant capital on the other. (Principally Chapters 5 and 6, but also Volume 2.)

(7) The second party system collapsed primarily because of economic development, national in scope but sectionally variegated. (Chapter 6 but mainly Volume 2.)

(8) The origins of the Civil War are best understood in terms derived from Marxism but existing Marxist historical writing has not yet adequately considered the problem. (mainly Volume 2.)

Acknowledgments

In 1971 I began research on American antebellum politics at the University of Lancaster. One of the reasons I chose to go into American history was the receptivity of Americans to the works of foreign scholars, in marked contrast to the outright hostility – at least at that time – of historians in certain other countries. In hoping for fair and even generous treatment from Americans I have not been at all disappointed and it is a pleasure to acknowledge the help and encouragement I have received from a great many of them.

At the same time, however, I owe a great deal to many British scholars. First and foremost I must thank my one-time supervisor at Lancaster, Professor Michael J. Heale, for his friendship and support. He read this typescript in its entirety and gave me enormous encouragement. The same is true of Professors Howard Temperley and Geoffrey Searle of the University of East Anglia. I must also thank Richard Crockatt, also of the University of East Anglia, for his critical reading of the first two chapters, Richard Carwardine and Richard King (of the Universities of Sheffield and Nottingham respectively) for their readings of the second two, and Martin Crawford, of the University of Keele, who also read the typescript in its entirety. My book has undoubtedly benefited enormously from the criticism of all these scholars.

I have also had the good fortune to have the work read and criticized by a number of outstanding American scholars. Eric Foner, who first helped me in my research more than twenty years ago, read the typescript and offered many invaluable criticisms. Joyce Appleby also gave me much encouragement, not only by reading the typescript but also in many highly stimulating conversations I had with her at the University of California at Los Angeles, where I spent the academic year, 1988–89. At that time I was also greatly helped by discussions with Bob Brenner, whose primary research interests are far removed from mine but whose work presents an outstanding example of Marxist historical writing. I have also benefited from extremely valuable criticisms from three readers employed by Cambridge University Press. Paul Goodman's great knowledge of antebellum America allowed him to make some extremely important points. James Oakes wrote me a lengthy critique which launched what was for me an extremely valuable exchange of views by correspondence. And an anonymous reader also made some very helpful suggestions and observations.

I should also like to thank my editor at CUP, New York, Frank Smith and his staff, together with Alan Hunt and the staff at Keyword Publishing Services, for the invaluable help they have given me. The research and writing of this book were greatly aided by a grant from the American Council of Learned Societies as well as two terms of study leave from the University of East Anglia. Some of that time was spent with Greg and Christy Ludlow, for whose hospitality and friendship I am enormously grateful. It is also a great pleasure to thank my parents, Eric and Freda Ashworth, as well as my children James and Jacqueline. Lastly I wish to record my gratitude to Alyson McLintock for all her support and patience in the many years it has taken to complete this work.

Introduction: Class conflict and the American Civil War

THE experiences of the millions of black Americans who lived in slavery in the United States were extraordinarily varied. Historians have found generalizations difficult. Yet one generalization can be offered. In their millions they disliked being slaves. Abundant evidence exists to show that slaves of all ages, of both sexes, from all parts of the Old South, whether they had attempted flight, insurrection or neither, were united in one sentiment: they wanted to be free. Writing from Liberia in 1857, former slave Daniel Williams reported that in the country which he had made his new home he was able to "enjoy some of that untrammeled liberty, which (as you may well know) my soul has so long and so ardently panted for." Ten years earlier, Jonathan Thomas, an ex-slave, had been asked about his experiences in Kentucky. He acknowledged that he had been well treated. "'Nevertheless,' Thomas said, 'I had from childhood a great wish to be free'." This was also the wish of John Anderson who had run away from Missouri to Canada "determined," according to the interviewer, "to obtain his freedom, which from his youth he seems to have considered his inherent birthright. – He had formed the resolve to sacrifice his liberty only with his life." It is clear that, for these slaves, good treatment did not reconcile them to their condition. In her autobiography, Rosa Barnwell of South Carolina, also a fugitive, declared that "though I did not suffer from cruel treatment, I preferred freedom to slavery; and this desire to reach a land where whips and chains are not found caused me to leave my former home." Likewise William Cornish in 1863 recalled that he "always had a hope that someday I should be free." Cornish too had succeeded in escaping from slavery. James Bradley, on the other hand, had bought his freedom and then moved to Lane seminary. "From the time I was fourteen years old," he related, "I used to think a great deal about freedom. It was my heart's desire; I could not keep it out of my mind. Many a sleepless night I have spent in tears, because I was a slave . . . . My heart ached within me to feel the light of liberty."[1]

---

1. Daniel Williams to Amos Wade, Aug. 16, 1857 in John W. Blassingame (ed.), *Slave Testimony* (Baton Rouge, 1977), p. 110; *ibid.*, pp. 250, 355, 698, 423, 688.

Escape from slavery necessarily involved considerable sacrifice and risk; as C. H. Hall put it, when he made his bid for freedom it was "liberty or death." Self-purchase often required years of grueling labor and involved heart-breaking setbacks. The slaves who achieved their liberation by either of these means were likely to have been driven by a powerful commitment to freedom. But there is ample reason to believe that the same goals were shared by many who simply did not have the opportunity to realize them. William Summerson, a South Carolina steamboatman, was unable to escape until the dislocations of the Civil War occurred. Yet "ever since I knew enough to know right from wrong," he declared in 1862, "I have wanted to get my freedom, but there was no way of escape." He added that "slavery walled me in." Ambrose Headen of North Carolina had to wait for the defeat of the Confederate armies on the battlefields before obtaining his freedom. In his autobiography he recalled that "during all my slave life I never lost sight of freedom." Freedom "was always on my heart." It is of course impossible for historians to know the thoughts and feelings of the millions of slaves of whose lives there is now not the smallest trace. Yet the thoughts of James Curry, who related his experiences in the *Liberator* may not have been untypical. Curry spoke of "the longing for liberty, which, from my childhood, had been the prevailing desire of my heart." Even more poignantly he told his readers how when a slave "I used to wonder why it was that our people were kept in slavery. I would look at the birds as they flew over my head or sung their free songs upon the trees, and think it strange, that, of all God's creatures, the poor negro only was held in bondage." It was a bondage of which John Boggs had had experience in the tobacco fields of Maryland. He told the American Freedmen's Inquiry Commission in 1863 that he would "rather be in the street, and let the wagons run over me every day, than be in slavery."[2]

The same commission attempted to find out how widespread among the slaves was the desire for freedom. The following exchange took place between the commissioners and Robert Smalls, an ex-slave who had achieved fame as a war hero and who would later serve in Congress:

> Q: Do you think the colored people are anxious for their liberty, and if opportunity offered would help themselves to it?
> A: I do, sir . . . .
> Q: Were there any societies among the colored people for discussing the questions of freedom?
> A: No, sir; . . . [but] they pray constantly for the "day of their deliverance."

2. *Ibid.*, pp. 416, 699, 744, 140, 135, 423.

It may be, of course, that Smalls was mistaken or that he was exaggerating. But the opinions he held were shared and expressed by other slaves. According to James Curry the desire for freedom was the slaves' "constant theme." For "no slaves think they were made to be slaves." No matter how "ignorant" their masters kept them, "it is impossible to beat it into them that they were made to be slaves." Curry claimed to "have heard some of the most ignorant I ever saw, say, 'it will not always be so, God *will* bring them to an account'." He was careful to emphasize, however, that when white men were present "no slave would dare to say . . . that he wished for freedom." Ambrose Headen confirmed both the need for secrecy and the prevalence of the aspirations for freedom when he recalled that "we always called freedom 'possum', so as to keep white people from knowing what we were talking about." It was a code which "we all understood."[3]

It is possible that some slaves were content with their situation. Such was not the opinion, however, of James Bradley, who strongly doubted "whether there ever was a slave, who did not long for liberty." It was certainly the case that "slave-owners take a great deal of pains to make the people in the free States believe that the slaves are happy" but, for his part, he "was never acquainted with a slave, however well he was treated, who did not long to be free." Bradley agreed that in front of white men, many slaves would "go so far as to say they would not leave their masters for the world." "But," he continued, "at the same time, they desire liberty more than anything else, and have, perhaps, all along been laying plans to get free." The reason was simple: "if a slave shows any discontent, he is sure to be treated worse, and worked the harder for it; and every slave knows this." Yet as soon as the slaves were "alone by themselves, all their talk is about liberty – liberty!" This was "the great thought and feeling that fills the mind full all the time." Bradley expressed surprise that anyone should doubt the truth of these opinions. "How strange it is," he exclaimed, "that anybody should believe any human being *could* be a slave, and yet be contented!"[4]

Bradley may have been mistaken in assuming that the desire for freedom was universal. Examples can be cited of slaves who declined to be emancipated or even of some free blacks who asked to be enslaved. These examples, however, are few and far between. The problem for the historian, of course, is that no source is entirely impartial. If this generalization can be applied to every subject of historical investigation, it applies with particular force to those connected with slavery. While former slaves had powerful incentives to emphasize the ambitions for freedom of those still

3. *Ibid.*, pp. 376, 135, 744.
4. *Ibid.*, p. 689.

in bondage, the whites who owned them almost always had equally strong reasons for asserting that their slaves were in every way suited to their condition. And other white observers, as we have seen, were generally not allowed to glimpse the true feelings of the blacks on this most explosive of subjects. Nevertheless modern scholarship has been at pains to emphasize black resistance to slavery. This is a comparatively recent development, dating only from the 1940s and it has resulted in the overthrow of the racist assumptions of the Ulrich B. Phillips school of history, whose members saw no reason to doubt that the slaves were docile and "submissive." Most scholars would now agree with Kenneth M. Stampp that the slaves "longed for liberty and resisted bondage as much as any people could have done in their circumstances."[5]

II

For present purposes, however, it is sufficient to make a more modest claim: that a significant number of slaves would have grasped their freedom eagerly if the opportunity had been presented and that many of these slaves offered resistance of various kinds to their oppressors. Again we may quote Stampp. The rebellious slaves, he argues, "when they could, . . . protested by shirking their duties, injuring the crops, feigning illness, and disrupting the routine." Such acts were indeed "in part, an unspectacular kind of day to day resistance to slavery." More spectacular forms of resistance included running away (though this could also be prompted by other motives than a simple resentment of slavery) and, ultimately, insurrection. The relatively small number of servile rebellions in the United States does not seem to have afforded the masters much peace of mind; after the uprising in Santo Domingo they were often haunted by the fear that a new Toussaint L'Ouverture might rise up in the Old South and slaughter them.[6]

5. Kenneth M. Stampp, *The Peculiar Institution: Slavery in the Ante-Bellum South* (N.Y., 1956), pp. 9, 92, 140. According to John W. Blassingame, "there is overwhelming evidence in the primary sources, of the Negro's resistance to his bondage and of his undying love for freedom;" "the slave's constant prayer, his all-consuming hope, was for liberty;" – *The Slave Community: Plantation Life in the Antebellum South* (rev. ed. N.Y., 1979), pp. 192, 193. See also William Green, *Narrative of Events in the Life of William Green* (Springfield, O., 1853), pp. 9–14; Solomon Northup, *Twelve Years a Slave* (London, 1853), p. 260. For examples of works stressing black resistance see Raymond A. Bauer and Alice H. Bauer, "Day to Day Resistance to Slavery," *Journal of Negro History*, XXVII (1942), pp. 388–419; Herbert Aptheker, *American Negro Slave Revolts* (N.Y., 1943); Leslie Howard Owens, *This Species of Property: Slave Life and Culture in the Old South* (N.Y., 1976); Deborah Gray White, *Arn't I A Woman: Female Slaves in the Plantation* (N.Y., 1985).
6. Stampp, *Peculiar Institution*, pp. 108–109.

It will be convenient to follow Stampp and term these varied activities, actions and inactions "black resistance to slavery." This resistance is well known to historians. Or one should perhaps say, it is well known to those historians who have studied the social lives of the slaves. Extraordinary as it may seem, however, it is not well known at all to most students of the economics of slavery, who, as we shall see in a subsequent chapter, often write as though slave labor were not given under duress. Still more remarkable, black resistance is virtually ignored by historians who write about the origins of the Civil War. It is one of the claims of this work that, as a result of this omission, all current interpretations of the war are open to serious criticism.[7]

One way to establish causal significance is to ask whether, in the absence of the proposed cause, the event being explained would still have occurred. We may thus pose the following question: if the blacks had happily accepted slavery, would there have been a Civil War? To answer the question we must, of course, imagine an unreal, a counterfactual past. All such "counterfactuals," as they are termed, are necessarily imprecise and cannot be subjected to empirical testing. To say this, however, is merely to assert the limitations of a purely empirical approach to the study of history. Without pursuing this epistemological question further, we may attempt to justify the use of this particular "counterfactual" by the conclusions which it yields.[8]

Throughout the era of the sectional controversy, southerners were troubled by the prospect that an antislavery majority would come to dominate the nation and take action against the peculiar institution.[9] Such was the principal objection to the abolitionists, whose ultimate goal was apparent to all. Would there even have been a demand for immediate abolition if the blacks had been contented under slavery? It seems unlikely. The abolitionists' task was large enough as it was; if they had not believed that slavery contradicted the wishes of the enslaved, their crusade would have lost much of its passion. The same applies to all those in the Republican party who drew strength from a moral critique of slavery: black support for the institution would have dampened their fervour considerably. Moreover, many of the features of the slave system that most outraged the antislavery forces would have been far less apparent if the blacks had been eager or compliant slaves. Whippings

---

7. An exception is to be found in the work of James Oakes. See Oakes, "The Political Significance of Slave Resistance," *History Workshop*, XXII (1986), pp. 89–107, *Slavery and Freedom: An Interpretation of the Old South* (N.Y., 1990), pp. 139–193.
8. My thinking on these questions has been shaped above all by Roy Bhaskar. See Bhaskar, *The Possibility of Naturalism* (Brighton, 1979).
9. The material in this and the following paragraphs will all be considered at greater length in later chapters. Here my purpose is simply to establish the importance of black resistance to slavery.

would have been far less frequent, separations of families would not have been used so often as a punishment.[10] I shall also argue that the economic dissimilarities of the two sections would have been far less marked if the slaveholders had not been faced with the constraint of a resistant workforce. It is thus difficult not to conclude that the attacks on slavery would have been much weaker if the blacks had been content in their bondage.

More important, however, it seems likely that, in these circumstances, the southern response to the antislavery movement would have been far less fierce than it was. If the slaves had been content, then abolitionism would have lost most of its sting. Southerners would have been able to look on with some degree of indifference, confident that their slaves would have remained loyal. By the same token, free soil, which threatened to doom the South to permanent minority status within the Union, would have been far less threatening, since it would not have portended emancipation. And in these circumstances southerners would not have needed to take the drastic steps which were taken, especially after 1830, to curtail freedom of speech on the slavery question in the South and to ensure that the federal government remained in the hands of those who were "safe" on the subject. These actions, in turn, fueled northern fears of the "slave power," fears that played a major role in creating the Republican party.

Indeed it is not too much to say that behind every event in the history of the sectional controversy, lurked the consequences of black resistance to slavery. In the furore over the gag rule it was the South's vulnerability to abolitionism which prompted the southern militants, while northern hostility both to slavery on moral grounds and to the "slave power" ensured that the question would be enormously controversial.[11] The Mexican war and the crisis that erupted in 1850 had the same roots. All the wrangling which took place over Kansas can be seen in the same light. Most obviously of all, the fugitive slave issue, with all its ramifications, was the product of black dissatisfaction with slavery.

We are thus driven to conclude that black resistance to slavery was a key factor in the Civil War. I shall argue that it was a necessary condition of the struggle, a *sine qua non*. Yet apart from the small number of fugitives who attracted national attention and the leaders of slave insurrections, whose names were equally famous or notorious, the slaves were for the most part unseen players on the political stage. It is, no doubt, for

---

10. It is possible that the southern states might have taken some action to prevent it, if they had not felt that this might have been the entering wedge for abolition.
11. The nullifacation crisis, of course, also derived much of its force from the southern fear of abolitionism. The major work on nullification remains William W. Freehling, *Prelude to Civil War: The Nullification Controversy in South Carolina, 1816–1836* (N.Y., 1965).

this reason that their role has been ignored. Thus while Kenneth Stampp the historian of slavery is, as we have already seen, fully aware of the pervasiveness of black resistance to slavery (and can claim much of the credit for having drawn historians' attention to it), Kenneth Stampp the student of the Civil War and its origins, ignores the subject entirely. Instead he concerns himself with the familiar causes of sectional divergence: economic and cultural rivalries between North and South, the role of agitators in each section, northern majoritarianism clashing with southern minoritarianism, northern predilections for federal power competing with southern attachments to states' rights, northern notions of the "slave power" combating southern images of "black republicanism." I do not in the least intend to deny the significance of any of these factors; indeed these two volumes will pay considerable attention to all of them. For the present it is sufficient to observe that many of them drew their strength from the slavery controversy and the slavery controversy in turn, as I have argued, derived much of its force from the resistance of the blacks to their bondage. In this sense black resistance does not so much compete with as underlie the more familiar list of causal factors. Nevertheless I shall suggest that one can fairly easily imagine a profound struggle over slavery existing in the United States in the absence of many of these factors, and this alone suggests that to ignore black resistance is to present a misleading view of the Civil War and its causes. Nor is Stampp alone in this. In David M. Potter's *The Impending Crisis* and James M. McPherson's *Battle Cry of Freedom* – to name only the two best single volumes on the origins of the Civil War – black resistance to slavery is similarly ignored. One finds in these works ample reference to slavery, but very few references to slaves or the effects of their actions, except where they achieved fame by flight or rebellion.[12]

In both these works the political struggles over slavery in the 1840s and 1850s receive full coverage. This is as it should be. Yet one may again note that a bloody conflict over slavery might well have arisen even if the territorial question, the principal concern of politicians in the 1850s and of the political historians who have studied the decade, had not existed at all. One can imagine a conflict over slavery in, say, Missouri, perhaps in the 1850s, perhaps later, even if there had been no territories to fight over. Indeed if southerners had remained adamant in their refusal to entertain emancipation and if northerners would not have tolerated slavery permanently, then some sort of armed conflict would have been difficult to avoid. In this sense the developments in, for example,

---

12.   Kenneth M. Stampp (ed.), *The Causes of the Civil War* (rev. ed. Englewood Cliffs, N.J., 1974); David M. Potter, *The Impending Crisis, 1848–1861* (N.Y., 1976); James M. McPherson, *Battle Cry of Freedom: The Civil War Era* (N.Y., 1988).

Kansas, on which political historians have spent much time, should perhaps be seen as channels through which the conflict flowed rather than as
fundamental causes in their own right. Yet black resistance to slavery was
not of this nature. In this sense, it was a more profound cause of the
struggle.

III

Let us now consider some objections that might be raised to the argument
as it has so far been presented. First, it might be objected that black
resistance to slavery is of political significance chiefly as it affects pro
or antislavery whites and that an exclusive concern with the latter groups
is thus appropriate. But such an objection carries little weight for while
the premise is true, the conclusion does not follow. Any political history
of the Civil War era must necessarily give most space to the whites who
took the crucial decisions and who wielded political power. But to do so
need not mean denying or ignoring black resistance to slavery. As we
have seen, narrative accounts of the events leading up to the war risk
overlooking such causal factors and leaving the reader unaware of the
role played by the slaves in bringing about the Civil War and thus in
attaining their own freedom. For a variety of reasons, black resistance
came to pose severe problems for the master class. The masters sought
and chose solutions which in effect transferred or displaced these social
and economic challenges into the political arena, an arena from which the
blacks themselves were entirely excluded. The political conflicts that
ensued are of great significance, and will form the subject matter of the
larger part of this book. But this is not to deny the enormous importance
of the behavior of the slaves.

   A more interesting objection might be made along the following lines:
black resistance to slavery played a part in the sectional controversy
primarily as it constrained or provoked the actions of the slaveholders.
But these slaveholders were convinced that the slave was indeed quite
suited to his condition. They denied outright that he desired his freedom.
Again and again they insisted that their bondsmen and bondswomen
were happy and contented and that both masters and slaves were simply
acting in accordance with the divine plan. God intended blacks to be
slaves and their natures were such as to fit them perfectly for their pre-
ordained role. So how can black resistance to slavery be a causal factor if
the people through whose actions it supposedly made itself felt believed
that blacks been placed upon the earth to be slaves?

   One response to this objection would simply be to deny that the slaveholders were speaking the truth. Some historians have argued that the
masters were consumed with guilt about their actions and that deep down

they realized that their slaves ought to be freed. When I discuss the proslavery argument I shall argue against this view. The appropriate response is very different. To say that many of the slaveholders' actions were prompted by black resistance is by no means to claim that the slaveholders themselves identified these prompts correctly. Let us take one or two examples. When the masters railed against the abolitionists, they did not thereby concede that the slave resented his bondage. Instead they claimed that, in the absence of outside influences, he was loyal. But, they charged, when abolitionists poisoned his mind and held out absurd promises of freedom and prosperity, the happy slave of the plantation became the murderous marauder of Santo Domingo. In my opinion we should accept that the masters were, in general, honestly stating their opinions here. Yet to accept their sincerity is not to endorse their judgment. From our own perspective we can instead insist that abolition was a danger to the master because it was impossible to reconcile the slave masses to slavery. Thus the masters – and in this they were no different from most people in most places at most times – failed to achieve a full understanding of the causes of their own actions. Abolition confirmed rather than distorted the ambitions of the slave. Though they did not realize it, the masters, in attacking the abolitionists, were also being driven by the slave's desire for freedom.

The second example is a more subtle one. Another reason for the hatred with which the slaveholders viewed abolitionism derived from their racism. Slaveholders believed that blacks were naturally indolent and intellectually feeble. It followed that abolition, however gradually accomplished, would impoverish the South for ever and doom the blacks themselves, who would simply refuse to work and eventually starve. It also followed that to confer political rights on them would be an act of the greatest folly: blacks simply lacked the capacity for democracy. Once again we may accept the sincerity of these beliefs while, of course, rejecting them and seeking to explain their prevalence. We need to ask why masters believed that so many of their slaves were both ignorant and lazy. There is no need here to attempt a full answer to this question. It is sufficient to note that slaves had an incentive to hide their abilities and their intelligence from their masters, in order thereby to conceal some of their activities. And since so large a proportion of the slaves had no wish to be enslaved, it comes as no surprise that so many of them responded to this incentive and, in consequence, appeared lazy to their masters.[13] Thus

---

13. An opposite incentive was offered, of course, when masters tried to reward their slaves for industriousness or special skills. But to the extent that the attempt was successful, the image of the lazy and ignorant black man – and this was a major ideological support of slavery in the Old South – was challenged. To make the same point a little differently, the masters too had an incentive to underestimate

once again the ideas and the behavior of the master reflected black resistance to slavery, even though the master himself failed to perceive it.

Another objection remains to be considered. At the time of the Civil
War, slavery had existed in the United States for more than two centuries.
Since there is little reason to believe that black resistance was absent in
the early years of the slave regime, why should it bring about a war in
1861? To put it somewhat differently: how can a constant factor explain
the change from peace to war? The answer, of course, is that it cannot.
To recognize this limitation, however, is simply to acknowledge the need
for other causal factors, not to deny the importance of black resistance to
slavery. Chief among these other factors was the shift to wage labor in the
North.

IV

For most of human history the status of the wage laborer has been an
extremely humble one. Americans were heirs to a long and venerable
tradition of hostility to wage labor. Some of its first manifestations
were in Ancient Greece. Aristotle believed that the virtuous citizens
were those "who are freed from necessary services" and explained that
"the necessary [and thus non-virtuous] people are either slaves who minister to the wants of individuals, or mechanics and labourers who are the
servants of the community." For Aristotle "no man can practise virtue
who is living the life of a mechanic or labourer."[14]

These attitudes survived in Europe for hundreds of years. According to
Christopher Hill, in early modern England wage laborers were held to be
inferior to those who possessed even the most minute fragment of land to
farm for themselves. From Francis Bacon's time onwards the word
"hireling" was a term of abuse. What most dismayed observers then
was what had disturbed them in Antiquity: the dependence or servility
of the wage laborer. During the English Revolution Leveller Richard
Overton believed that wage laborers had lost their property in themselves
and thus were in "a condition of servility," while a pamphlet of 1660
declared "servants and laborers" to be "in the nature of vassals." The
most radical English thinker of the seventeenth century, Gerrard
Winstanley, went further and condemned wage labor, especially on the
land, in the most unqualified terms. "Whosoever shall help that man to

        the abilities of the slave, in order to justify his continued enslavement. In these ways
        (and others), the relations between the two impeded the economic performance of the
        slave. See below, Chapter 2. They also obstructed the formation of a coherent
        proslavery argument. See below, Chapter 4.
    14. Aristotle, *Politics*, Book III Chapter 5, in Richard McKeon, *Introduction to Aristotle*
        (N.Y., 1947), pp. 587–588.

labour his proper earth, as he calls it for wages," Winstanley asserted, "the hand of the Lord shall be upon such labourers, for they . . . hold the creation still under bondage." In Winstanley's Utopia "no man shall either give hire, or take hire for his work, for this brings in kingly bondage." Hill also reminds us that in England until 1875 the relations of wage earner and employer were regulated by legislation entitled "Master and Servant" Acts.[15]

On the other side of the Atlantic these, or similar, attitudes found expression, as we shall see, in the Jeffersonian and Jacksonian movements. Jefferson's celebration of the virtue of the independent freeholding farmer is well known. Recently, however, historians have come to recognize that the social ethos of the Jacksonians was far less modern than was once believed. Many Jacksonian Democrats wanted every citizen to be independent, whether of a landlord or of an employer. For them the farmer was the ideal citizen, especially the freeholder who worked his own holding. The general thrust of Jacksonian social philosophy was thus away from wage labor and towards traditional notions of independence – for adult white males at any rate.[16]

The Jacksonian world was thus irretrievably different from our own. Since the early twentieth century, and perhaps even earlier, the modern view of wage labor has prevailed. If we imagine a spectrum ranging from the most complete freedom at one end, to the most complete subjugation at the other, the wage earner would, in the early nineteenth century have been placed close to the slave and the serf, on the subjugation side. By the early twentieth century he would have been placed at the other end of the spectrum. By this time, of course, slavery and wage labor were, in American thought, polar opposites. It would be only a slight exaggeration to claim that in the nineteenth century the United States went from a belief that democracy was incompatible with wage labor (on a large scale) to a feeling that a successful free society and democratic government depend on wage labor and are scarcely possible without it.[17] In my

15. Christopher Hill, "Pottage for Freeborn Englishmen: Attitudes to Wage Labour," in Hill, *Change and Continuity in Seventeenth-Century England* (London, 1974), pp. 219–238. See also David Roediger, *The Wages of Whiteness: Race and the Making of the American Working Class* (London, 1991), pp. 44–49. It may be worth noting that during Reconstruction the freedmen preferred even the smallest landholding to the condition of wage laborer.

16. See, for example, John Ashworth, *"Agrarians" and "Aristocrats": Party Political Ideology in the United States* (London, 1983).

17. This is a slight exaggeration because there is currently no rhetorical appeal to wage labor in the United States or in any other capitalist nation. Instead "free enterprise" is extolled, though it is nonetheless apparent that free enterprise necessarily entails the freedom to engage in economic activities which may well require large numbers of wage laborers. Perhaps too there is a residual unease with wage labor as a term, a lingering doubt about the degree of dependence implied. Signs like "help wanted" in

opinion the crucial stage in this transformation occurred in the 1850s with the rise of the Republican party. It should come as no surprise that so significant a break with traditions that were more than two thousand years old should bring about a major social and political upheaval. The Civil War was such an upheaval.

The ideological transformation followed, of course, a dramatic and continuing increase in the number of wage laborers employed in the antebellum North. It was accompanied by, and helped create, a significant shift in northern attitudes towards the family and towards the conscience. The effect of these ideological and economic changes was to strengthen northern opposition to slavery, which was increasingly viewed as a threat to the North's economic and social progress.[18]

The rise of wage labor meant therefore that a new hostility to slavery was engendered in the North. Let us consider the process a little further. We need to focus, as we did when considering the South, upon the relations at the point of production, in this case between workers and employers. It would be quite mistaken to claim that northern society in the 1850s was wilting under the pressure of the class conflicts between wage laborers and capitalists (though some such conflicts did occur). In fact northern employers could fairly easily contain such hostility as did exist, even though the transition for many of their workers to the status of wage laborer was undoubtedly a highly painful one. But though containment was possible and successful, it entailed momentous consequences, of which the most critical was the enunciation of values (especially concerning the family and the conscience) and a social ethos (emphasizing social mobility), which made slavery increasingly intolerable. The result was as if an alliance had been formed, albeit an unintended and uncertain one, between a northern antislavery phalanx and the slaves themselves. The alliance depended for its power not only upon the growing antagonism of northern society to the South and its peculiar institution, but also upon the continuing resistance of the blacks to slavery. This alliance was scarcely recognized by contemporaries, not even by those who had formed it. But it would effect the ruin of the Old South and of what might be termed the United States' *ancien régime*.

the restaurants of today's America may indicate a desire to appeal to the worker as an independent individual voluntarily offering to assist his employer. The term "help" is noteworthy: does the worker usually see himself each morning setting out to "help" his employer?

18.   See below, Chapter 3.

V

It will by now be apparent that the argument which I am developing here has more in common with Marxist than with conventional approaches to history. It may be appropriate to set out some of the theory that informs the study. First, although I am placing a heavy emphasis on class and class conflict within each section, I am not claiming that the conflicts either in the North or in the South were, in themselves, capable of destabilizing either section. The dominant classes both North and South were, if left to themselves, able to contain their subordinate classes, certainly in the 1850s.[19] And there was no real reason why southern slaveholders and northern employers could not have continued to get along with one another, if each had not been encumbered by a workforce which constrained or helped shape, its actions and beliefs. But the pressures exerted by the subordinate classes restricted the freedom of movement – ideological, economic and political – of the dominant groups and eventually resulted in a conflict between them. It is here, I shall argue in this volume and (at greater length) its sequel, that one finds the origins of the Civil War.

Class and class conflict are, of course, troublesome concepts for historians. Some scholars have argued that class is to be understood above all in terms of class consciousness. According to E. P. Thompson, "class happens when some men, as a result of common experiences (inherited or shared), feel and articulate the identity of their interests as between themselves, and as against other men whose interests are different from (and usually opposed to) theirs."[20] In my view this treatment of class is hopelessly and disastrously flawed. While class consciousness is, in itself, of enormous importance, classes and class conflict can exist without it. For present purposes we may define class relationally, that is to say, in terms of the relationship between two groups at the point of production, where one group is seeking to appropriate to itself some or all of the labor of the other. On this definition slaves and slaveholders comprise classes, whether or not they exhibit class consciousness. It follows that behavior which is consequent upon this relationship and which is the product of a desire to benefit some or all the members of one group at the expense of some or all the members of the other, can be seen as class conflict, whatever the consciousness of the participants. Thus slave resistance may be called class conflict provided that the behavior in question can be attributed to the slave's resentment either of his condition or of its effects. For example we may see the deliberate breaking of a tool as a

---

19. How long the masters could have contained the slaves remains an open question.
20. E. P. Thompson, *Making of the English Working Class* (London, 1963), pp. 9–10.

manifestation of class conflict, provided there is reason to believe that the slave's status *as a slave* led him to break it. The causal links here may be direct and simple or they may be complex and subtle. If the slave broke the tool because he longed for his freedom and accordingly sought a small measure of revenge upon his master, the causal link is a simple one. But if he broke it because, let us say, the master had recently chastised his wife, then the connection may be a more complex one. Let us consider the admittedly unlikely possibility that the slave's resentment was solely provoked by this one action; he had no desire for freedom and no other complaint against the master. Least of all did he exhibit any class consciousness. Nevertheless the act of sabotage was undertaken in response to an action that was itself brought about by the master–slave relation and the antagonism endemic in it.

Several consequences follow from this understanding of class. First it is clear that class conflict may prompt behavior which is undertaken by a single individual, designed only to benefit that individual. Classes or collectivities need not be involved in the behavior at all; it is sufficient that the individual's behavior has, as a significant cause, his membership of a class or collectivity. Nor does it matter that he may fail accurately to perceive the cause. Second, there will be many individual or collective acts which cannot be assimilated unambiguously to the category of class conflict. The breaking of a tool by a slave may, as we have seen, fall into the category but it is also possible that the slave in question is, for reasons entirely independent of his status and condition, like many human beings simply clumsy. No matter what the social structure, such a worker is still likely to break tools. Thus one cannot simply label particular behavioral acts class conflict. The causes of the behavior must be analyzed.

This understanding of class is both wider and narrower than that which historians generally employ. It is wider because acts which are not based upon class consciousness and which are undertaken from a purely individual frame of reference can still be attributed to class. But it is narrower because the power of a class analysis to predict behavior is correspondingly reduced. Thus to emphasize the importance of class in slavery is not at all to predict slave uprisings or even a high degree of class consciousness on the part of the slaves. It is a contingent question as to whether these consequences will follow. Similarly, to stress the role of class in a society of wage laborers and employers is by no means to predict a wave of strikes, still less a social revolution. Again these consequences may well follow, but they are by no means inevitable.

Finally, I should perhaps state that my emphasis on class by no means precludes a concern with ideology. I shall argue throughout this work that ideology – understood simply as a reasonably coherent belief system[21] – is itself causal, in that on all sides of the political spectrum, men and women acted on the basis of convictions that were deeply and most sincerely held. Between 1861 and 1865 millions of them showed that they were prepared to die for these beliefs and principles. I shall also argue that these ideologies are not to be reduced to class interest. Nevertheless I shall also claim that ideology frequently bore the imprint of class interest, sometimes indeed the imprint of a compromise effected between different classes. It will be the principal claim of this work that when one wishes to explain the outbreak of civil war in the United States in 1861 it is to material factors and class conflicts that one must attach primary importance.

21. I do, however, employ the term also in the Marxist sense, which emphasizes the concealed process by which certain sets of ideas serve a particular (and usually dominant) class.

PART I

Context

1

Slavery, sectionalism and the Jeffersonian tradition

The Missouri Crisis (1)

At the start of 1819 Thomas Jefferson, patron saint of American Democracy, remarked that he now had a greater interest in the ancient than in the modern world. Events at Washington were, he declared, of little immediate concern to him. But 1819 was to be a portentous year for the former president. First his financial condition deteriorated sharply, partly as a consequence of the nation-wide economic crisis of that year. Equally important, Jefferson began to voice renewed concern about the imperialistic, centralizing tendencies of the Supreme Court which, he feared, threatened to make the entire constitution a complete *felo de se*.[1] Most important of all, however, were events in Missouri, or rather the reaction to them at Washington. By the end of the year Jefferson was warning his old friend and adversary, John Adams, that a crisis was looming, one more ominous than any the two old men had faced even during the Revolution. What Jefferson had discerned was the specter of sectional conflict and even civil war. The root of the problem was that "a geographical line," had come into existence. "Once conceived and held up to the angry passions of men," he warned, "it will never be obliterated; and every new irritation will mark it deeper and deeper." In the most celebrated phrase of his retirement Jefferson referred to the Missouri Crisis as a "firebell in the night."[2]

Jefferson had not exaggerated the threat. The Missouri Crisis began on February 13, 1819, when congressman James Tallmadge of New York, in Committee of the Whole, moved that slavery be banned from Missouri.[3]

---

1. Paul L. Ford (ed.), *The Federal Edition of the Works of Jefferson* 10 vols (N.Y., 1892–1899), x, pp. 119–122, 140–143.
2. Ford (ed.), *Works of Jefferson*, x, pp. 157, 152, 157–8, 186, 162, 192, 342, 233.
3. On the Missouri Crisis see especially Glover Moore, *The Missouri Controversy, 1819–1821* (Lexington, 1966). Moore is generally highly reliable as an authority but it is still necessary to consult the *Annals of Congress* (hereafter cited as *Annals*) for the 15th and 16th Congresses. See also Philip F. Detweiler, "Congressional Debate on Slavery and the Declaration of Independence, 1819–1821," in *American Historical Review*, LXIII (1958), pp. 598–616.

When it came the southern response was ferocious, anticipating the controversies of the 1840s and the 1850s and also the threats of secession and civil war so frequently voiced in those decades. Thomas W. Cobb of Georgia spoke as many fireaters would speak in the 1850s when he warned that northerners supporting the Tallmadge amendment "were kindling a fire which all the waters of the ocean could not extinguish," a fire "which could be extinguished only in blood." Likewise Philip Barbour of Virginia voiced his fear that "this subject will be an ignited spark, which, communicated to an immense mass of combustion, will produce an explosion that will shake this Union to its centre." Undoubtedly some southerners were alarmed at the prospect of their slaves being incited by northern invocations of the Declaration of Independence to combat their claims to Missouri. Edward Colston of Virginia was fearful that "there might be slaves in the gallery listening to the debate," and even went so far as to accuse one northerner of attempting to incite a servile war.[4] Northerners responded in kind. Tallmadge himself reacted angrily to southern threats of disunion. "If a dissolution of the Union must take place," he declared, "let it be so": "if civil war, which gentlemen so much threaten, must come, I can only say, let it come!" He even added that "if blood is necessary to extinguish any fire which I have assisted to kindle . . . I shall not forbear to contribute my mite."[5] Reactions from politicians both north and south of the Mason-Dixon line made the controversy over the admission of Missouri into the Union the deepest sectional rift that the nation would experience for thirty years.

Yet the year 1819 was significant for the other developments it witnessed. If Jefferson had believed that sectional strife would immediately overwhelm all else, he was of course to be mistaken. The other events of 1819 were to occupy the Republic heavily in the coming decades. The controversy over the judiciary, whose actions Jefferson could see in no other light than as nefarious maneuvers of a subdued but not vanquished Federalist party, anticipated the entire debate over American democracy that would erupt once again in the 1830s and 1840s, pitting Democrats against Whigs, rather as it had once pitted Republicans against Federalists. Moreover the dismay that Jefferson experienced over the economic downturn of 1819 would find echoes in numerous state legislatures in the early 1820s as many Americans began to experience doubts about their involvement in market activities; it would culminate in the desperate struggle waged against first the national then against state and

4. *Annals*, 15 Congress, 2 Session, p. 1437, 16 Congress, 1 Session, p. 107, 15 Congress, 2 Session, pp. 1180, 1205.
5. *Annals*, 16 Congress, 2 Session, p. 1017, 15 Congress, 2 Session, p. 1205.

local banks by Andrew Jackson and his followers. In each of these struggles – the sectional, the democratic, the economic – the Jeffersonian
legacy was crucially implicated. It therefore requires careful consideration.

An egalitarian elite

I

"Those who labor in the earth," wrote Thomas Jefferson in one of his
most celebrated pronouncements, "are the chosen people of God, if ever
He had a chosen people." Here as on so many other occasions Jefferson
waxed lyrical about the farmer's "substantial and genuine virtue" and
dwelt on the impossibility of finding "corruption of morals" among "the
mass of cultivators." The importance of such sentiments in the American
democratic tradition can scarcely be exaggerated and historians have
rightly emphasized the agrarian bias present in so many of the writings
of American democrats, not merely in Jefferson's lifetime but also for a
generation after his death. But these famous and much quoted remarks in
the *Notes on Virginia* cannot be read literally. Jefferson had not the
slightest intention of conferring praise upon all of "those who labor in
the earth." Despite the absence of any explicit disclaimer, the great majority of people engaged in "labor in the earth" with whom the Sage of
Monticello came into contact were men and women whose moral faculties he viewed with contempt or, at best, pity. These were, of course, the
slaves owned in large numbers by Thomas Jefferson and his fellow members of the Virginia landed elite.[6]

It would be quite wrong to dismiss Jefferson's eloquent remarks as
mere hypocrisy. When he made them, the slave had simply disappeared
from his sight. Moreover, many slaveholders who read these and similar
statements were equally likely to forget that they might be taken to apply
to slaves. Yet there was no group in the entire nation which spent a higher
proportion of its time engaged in labor in the earth. Nevertheless, slaveholders like Jefferson, and indeed white non-slaveholders too, knew that,
just as the slave was excluded from the egalitarianism invoked by the
opening words of Jefferson's Declaration of Independence, he was not to
be classified as a noble and virtuous "cultivator of the earth." The slave
had vanished; no-one searched for him.

This absent slave was ubiquitous in the works of Jefferson, of John
Taylor of Caroline, the high-priest of Jeffersonian Democracy, and later
in the writings of the Jacksonian Democrats. Jefferson's agrarianism and

6. Thomas Jefferson, *Notes on the State of Virginia* (new ed. N.Y., 1964), 157.

Jefferson's egalitarianism were heavily implicated in the great political debates of the 1790s and the 1800s, the 1830s and the 1840s. When Republican battled Federalist, when Democrat combated Whig, Jeffersonian principles were at the core of the conflict. Slavery was not the subject of most of these disputes and when Jefferson and his heirs expressed their faith in an egalitarian polity and an agrarian society the slave was again absent from their rhetoric. When they debated the meaning of freedom and equality in the United States, the slave was normally not even mentioned. In this sense his absence from the famous passage in the *Notes on Virginia* was unremarkable. He was absent from almost the entire Jeffersonian democratic tradition. [7]

Moreover, when Jefferson heaped encomia on the cultivators of the earth, he did not pause to consider the place of the slaveholder. Although in the *Notes on Virginia* and elsewhere he praised the husbandman's lack of "dependence" on others, he did not consider the dependence of the slaveholder upon the slave. From almost all of Jefferson's writings and especially those in which he discussed political questions, one would assume that the rural slaveholder was indistinguishable from the farmer. They were alike worthy, industrious, independent, virtuous. They were politically and morally supreme. Thus the farmer and the slaveholder merged into one, the slaveholding plantation became the farm writ large.[8]

Jefferson sometimes criticized slavery, though he rarely translated these criticisms into action. In general, however, as the example of the *Notes on Virginia* suggest, he kept his opinions on slavery and his views on equality in separate compartments. Unfortunately historians have tended to do the same. Without doubt he was sincerely committed to the principles that he enunciated; though as a writer he occasionally saw a contradiction between slaveholding and egalitarianism, more often as a writer and almost invariably as a practicing politician, he saw no relationship between them at all. Perhaps assuming that the actor's own perceptions are the ultimate reality, most historians have done likewise. Hence they have missed some of the essential features of Jeffersonian (and Jacksonian) Democracy. Its egalitarianism rested on the sweated labor of blacks; its agrarianism depended on an alliance of farmers and slaveholders made possible by the expropriation of the fruits of that labor.

For slavery produced a different alignment of classes in the South.[9] It allowed Jefferson to embrace highly egalitarian ideals – but only because

7. As we shall see later in this chapter, Jefferson frequently talked about slavery and his words certainly influenced later generations. But the party political tradition he founded ignored the subject.
8. As we shall see, the famous criticisms of the slaveholder offered in the *Notes on Virginia* – pp. 155–156 – were quite untypical. Moreover they had no effect on the principles upon which Jefferson's Republican party was founded.
9. See below, Chapter 2

those ideals excluded slaves. It allowed him to reach out for the support of the poorer white citizens of Virginia (and other states) – but only because the dominant class in the South, the class of which he was himself a prominent member, exploited black slaves rather than white farmers. Only in these terms can Jeffersonian Democracy be understood. Jefferson and Taylor were members of an elite, an elite of slaveholding planters. Something unusual is happening when well-to-do property holders champion egalitarian views; something extraordinary is happening when they become spokesmen for their class. The extraordinary feature in this case was their ownership of slaves.

II

Since Jefferson is such a familiar figure to American historians, let us consider some of the views of Taylor, whose ideas were in any case much more consistent and coherent. Taylor's writings suffer from a major deficiency in that his prose style was often (though by no means always) heavy and labored and as a result they have been comparatively neglected. His major work, *An Inquiry into the Principles and Policy of the Government of the United States*, was published in 1814, though much of it was a rejoinder to John Adams's *Defence of the Constitutions of Government of the United States* written some thirty years earlier. Taylor's *Inquiry*, and indeed his entire political career, were spent combating aristocracy, which he feared threatened to subvert the new American republic. If, as has been claimed, it is possible to divide human beings into two groups, those who desire more equality and fear inequality and those who desire to maintain or extend inequality and fear a more equal distribution of wealth and power, then there can be no doubt which category Taylor belongs in. His objections to aristocracy were not confined to a titled nobility, which he freely conceded "cannot acquire in the United States the article of wealth, necessary to constitute a separate order or interest." Yet the security which this afforded was a false one; aristocracy was still an ever-present danger. For "nobility and hierarchy" might "be used as feints to cover the real attack." And the real attack would come from an inequality of wealth. In order "to sustain a democratick republick," he asserted, "wealth must be considerably distributed."[10] Taylor's egalitarianism led him to believe that if men were

---

10. John Taylor, *An Inquiry into the Principles and Policy of the Government of the United States* (new ed. London, 1950), p. 255. On Taylor see Eugene T. Mudge, *The Social Philosophy of John Taylor of Caroline: A Study in Jeffersonian Democracy* (N.Y., 1959); Robert E. Shalhope, *John Taylor of Caroline, Pastoral Republican* (Columbia, S.C., 1980).

left to themselves the resulting distribution of wealth would be sufficiently equal to maintain the republic. "A moderate degree of wealth,"
he argued, could be acquired "by a laborious cultivation of [one's] talents
and persevering industry" but if government intervened and aided some
groups or individuals at the expense of others, then an immoderate
degree of wealth would result and inequality would take root. An elite
created and maintained by government – this was what Taylor meant by
aristocracy. As he put it after approximately three hundred and fifty
pages of argument and discussion, "the course of reasoning pursued by
this essay, results in the definition, that *a transfer of property by law, is
aristocracy*, and that *aristocracy is a transfer of property by law*."[11]

Taylor's task was to alert his fellow countrymen to the danger of
aristocracy. "It cannot be forgotten," he insisted, "that aristocracy is a
Proteus, capable of assuming various forms." He addressed his remarks
to the majority in the United States, whose interests, he believed, were
threatened by the wealthy minority. "As power follows wealth," he
argued, "so the majority must have wealth or lose power." Taylor's
fear was that the United States would go the way of all nations that
had sought to establish a "democratick republick" and succumb to the
avarice of the wealthy minority. On one occasion he confronted the
question of leveling and in so doing showed where his priorities lay. A
precise equality of wealth could never exist and so the danger was non-
existent. Far more likely, and infinitely more dangerous, was the possibility of leveling not between individuals but between orders. Taylor
identified three orders, comprising the one, the few and the many, said
to be represented in the British constitution by the monarchy, the House
of Lords and the House of Commons respectively. Leveling between
orders meant each of them possessing a third of the nation's wealth. It
meant, therefore, a highly unequal distribution of wealth. In a sense
Taylor was employing a rhetorical device when he turned the conservative's fear of leveling into an attack upon inequality. But his reading of
history was interesting. Leveling between orders, he maintained, had
existed in all ages, under cover of charging those opposed to it with
seeking to level between individuals, which had seldom been attempted,
would only ever be temporary and was in any case entirely impracticable.
Such was Taylor's principal quarrel with John Adams.[12]

We should also note his highly egalitarian view of humanity. "Talents
and virtue," he claimed, "are now so widely distributed, as to have
rendered a monopoly of either, equivalent to that of antiquity, impracticable." Indeed "had nature been accustomed to produce occasionally rare

11. Taylor, *Inquiry*, pp. 325, 352.
12. Taylor, *Inquiry*, pp. 255, 126.

and extraordinary talents, it is highly questionable whether they would have been beneficial to mankind." Taylor cited Alexander the Great, Julius Caesar and Oliver Cromwell as individuals who were often credited with extraordinary talents but then claimed that even if the assessment were correct, it would have been better to let them live and die in obscurity. "The truth is," he concluded, "that rare talents, like a natural aristocracy, are created by ignorance, and that cunning takes advantage of the opinion to scourge mankind." Americans would be enslaved by "ignorance", freed by "knowledge" because while "the first begets," the other "explodes the errour, that some men are endowed with faculties far exceeding the general standard." As a result Taylor even objected to an unequal distribution of resources for education, intended (as Thomas Jefferson's proposed educational system was) to give to an intelligent elite opportunities to progress further than their fellows. "A power to distribute knowledge or wealth," he declared, "is a power to distribute both." Yet if government refrained from interfering so that "knowledge and wealth are left to be distributed by industry," then the result would be "a beneficent excitement of effort, and a division sufficient to preserve a free government." Once again Taylor's priorities were apparent when he acknowledged that an equality of knowledge was impossible – but insisted that the greater danger was of too much inequality.[13]

The best index of Taylor's egalitarianism was that he constantly saw danger in inequality and safety in equality. The society and the government that he championed depended in no way upon any qualities which were confined to a minority and indeed they would have functioned perfectly if – though he conceded this to be impossible – all men were entirely equal in wealth, power, talents, knowledge and virtue. Taylor warned that those in government, and those in receipt of government favors, would act as all other men in the same situation and seek to enhance even further their unjust privileges. Conservative thinkers wanted instead to employ the superior talents of the elite for the benefit of society as a whole: they projected different roles for different groups, corresponding to the talents that they possessed. The judiciary, in particular, was widely seen as the province of the talented minority. For Taylor, by contrast, it was yet another danger. Judges were simply men and "names cannot change man's nature, and cure him of his passions and vices; if they could, this discovery would have superseded the necessities of all our inventions for curbing the passions and vices of public officers, by calling them judges."[14]

---

13. Taylor, *Inquiry*, pp. 55, 223–224, 532–533.
14. Taylor, *Inquiry*, pp. 206, 199.

Three other features of Taylor's thought need to be emphasized. The first is his agrarianism. Although always present in the *Inquiry*,[15] this theme received its fullest development in *Arator* published in 1818. Here Taylor set out to combat what he called "the manufacturing mania" encouraged by the recent conflict with Britain, by showing that the American republic, American prosperity and American liberty all depended upon agriculture. Indeed whenever Taylor spoke of the majority it was clear that he had in mind the landed interest. In the preface to the work, he wrote that his purpose was "uniting the subjects of agriculture and politics," on the grounds that "agriculture" was "the guardian of liberty, as well as the mother of wealth." The very next line showed the link between his agrarianism and his faith in the majority when he asserted that "as long as the principles of our government are uncorrupted, and the sovereignty of majorities remains, she [agriculture] must occupy the highest political station, and owe to society the most sacred political duty." Taylor's tone became reverential as he referred to "this most useful and virtuous interest" which "from its nature, and also as being generally the employer of a great portion of a nation, cannot be united with power, considered as an exclusive interest." To safeguard the republic it was thus necessary to preserve the agrarian society.[16]

Taylor's faith in the majority is a second important feature of his thought. It rested upon two propositions. First, he claimed that "the general propensity of the whole species, will usually impress its own character, upon a general opinion." Such an opinion "is undoubtedly, less liable to errour, than the conclusions of an individual." Masses were more likely to discern the truth than individuals, however illustrious those individuals might be. But this was only one of Taylor's arguments in favor of the majority. More important were his assertions about self-interest. Again seeing the common features in humanity, he believed that all men were actuated by self-interest. A majority would thus be composed of self-interested individuals. It followed that "the force of self-love is as strong in majorities, as in an individual." But – and here was the crucial difference – "its effect is precisely contrary." Taylor held that the majority could not permanently exploit the minority. Majorities "cannot be lasting tyrants themselves." Self-interest "excites one man to do wrong, because he is surrounded with objects of oppression," but induced "majorities to do right, because they can find none." Taylor never quite explained why the majority could not continue to exploit the minority nor indeed why one minority (and here one cannot help but think of John Taylor and his fellow planters) could not permanently

15. See, for example, Taylor, *Inquiry*, p. 477.
16. John Taylor, *Arator* (new ed. Indianapolis, 1977), pp. 79, 53, 318, 312.

exploit another – the slaves of John Taylor and his fellow planters, perhaps. Nevertheless for Taylor the rule of the majority was the crowning glory of the American republic. Whereas "the old analysis," upon which other governments were built, "intrusts great power to individuals and minorities; and provides no mode of controlling their natural vicious propensities," "our policy," by contrast, "deals out to them power more sparingly, and superadds a sovereign, whose propensity is towards reason, and whose self-interest is an excitement to justice." Taylor even argued that a vicious majority, if allowed to rule, would be impelled by self-interest to end exploitation and thus begin to re-establish virtue in the community.[17]

His discussion of the majority reveals the third feature of Taylor's thought: the absence of the slave. His definition of aristocracy as the transfer of property by law might have led him to condemn laws that facilitated the expropriation of the slave. After all, laws on slavery could be viewed as legalizing the transfer of property from the slave to his master. Needless to say, Taylor's definition did not encompass such laws and he did not even need to say so. As we have already seen, when he spoke of the dangers to be apprehended from a wealthy minority, he might have had in mind the wealthy slaveholding minority. But he did not, and once again he did not need to say so. Moreover, as Duncan MacLeod points out, Taylor subscribed wholeheartedly to the labor theory of value and he could scarcely have found a better principle on which to base an attack on slavery. But once more he not only refrained from such an attack but saw not the slightest antislavery implication in the theory. For him, as for Jefferson, slavery and political economy were two almost entirely separate topics.[18]

III

Jefferson himself shared many of these opinions and attitudes, though he was considerably less consistent in his thinking than Taylor. One of the reasons for his extraordinary influence with later generations, it has been said, was that he could be quoted on either side of every important question.[19] Nevertheless Jefferson's faith in the people, his egalitarianism, and his agrarianism are all sufficiently well known to require no detailed re-examination here. Instead it may be appropriate to approach these subjects indirectly by tracing Jefferson's responses to the political crises

17. Taylor, *Inquiry*, pp. 389–390, 385–386.
18. Duncan J. MacLeod, *Slavery, Race and the American Revolution* (London, 1974), p. 68.
19. Merrill D. Peterson, *The Jefferson Image in the American Mind* (N.Y., 1962), p. 445.

of the early republic and by comparing them with those of his more conservative contemporaries. These responses will then help us to understand the role of slavery in his thought, in Taylor's, and in that of the antebellum democratic tradition that they, more than anyone else, founded.

Not all Americans shared Taylor and Jefferson's faith in the people. The experiences of the 1780s led many members of the nation's elite to revise the high opinion of the people with which they had begun in 1776. Even before the outbreak of the French Revolution John Adams, in the very work which Taylor spent twenty years attacking, argued that popular government was a potent source of evil. In "every page of history," he believed, there were "proofs irrefragable, that the people, when they have been unchecked, have been as unjust, tyrannical, brutal, barbarous, and cruel, as any king or senate possessed of uncontrollable power." Adams's view stood in diametric opposition to Taylor's, as he argued that "the majority has eternally, and without one exception, usurped over the rights of the minority." Whereas Taylor believed that the rich were a threat to the republic, Adams held that the poor presented at least as great a danger and that consequently "the rich . . . ought to have an effectual barrier in the constitution against being robbed, plundered, and murdered."[20] Such a barrier, whatever it might have been, would certainly have constituted the aristocratic influence against which Taylor inveighed. And where Taylor saw similarities between men, Adams saw differences and inequalities. His entire political theory rested upon the assumption that those who possessed superior talents and abilities should be given a special role in government in order to ensure that their talents were used for, rather than against, the nation. As he later wrote, "inequalities of Mind and Body are so established by God Almighty in his constitution of Human Nature that no Art or policy can ever plane them down to a level." Of course neither Taylor nor any other American ever claimed that men were entirely on a level but he rarely if ever made any concession to inequalities. Little wonder then that Adams, responding to Taylor's *Inquiry* in a personal letter to its author, asked the following questions: "Will Mr Taylor profess himself a downright leveller? Will he vote for a community of property? or an equal division of property?" In Adams's view such action would be necessary if the "equality of influence" which Taylor postulated were ever to be attained.[21]

20. Charles F. Adams (ed.), *The Works of John Adams* 10 vols (Boston, 1850–1856), VI, pp. 10, 65. Adams, it should be noted, wanted constitutional safeguards for both the rich and poor.
21. Adams to Jefferson, July 13, 1813 in Lester J. Cappon (ed.), *The Adams–Jefferson Letters* 2 vols (N.Y., 1959), II, p. 355; *Works of Adams*, VI, p. 459.

Adams's doubts about popular government and his limited commitment to equality were apparent in the 1780s if not earlier. Similarly, Alexander Hamilton in 1787 gave vent to traditionally conservative sentiments at the Philadelphia Constitutional Convention when he asserted that "all communities divide themselves into the few and the many." He then explained who formed the two groups. The first, he argued, "are the rich and well born." It was this group whose interests he would later, as Secretary of the Treasury, seek to tie to the federal government. The second were "the mass of the people," who "are turbulent and changing; they seldom judge or determine right." The fears of men like Adams and Hamilton had been aggravated by the social unrest of the 1780s and particularly by Shays' Rebellion in 1786. This event, however shocking it was, paled into total insignificance in comparison with the French Revolution.[22]

The French Revolution had an impact on the eighteenth and early nineteenth century comparable to that of the Russian Revolution in the twentieth. It was viewed by the aristocracies and indeed by conservative or moderate middle class opinion as a cataclysm, an appalling demonstration of the destructive power of a democratic form of government. In Britain it retarded the process of reform by a generation and converted men like Edmund Burke, who had sympathized with the American revolution, into staunch defenders of the *status quo*. The specter of Robespierre and the memories of the Terror gripped the elites of Europe for decades and for half a century every incident of social unrest was feared as a prelude to another 1789.[23]

Many Americans reacted precisely as Burke did. As early as 1790, before the Terror had begun, Adams was complaining that "too many Frenchmen, after the example of too many Americans, pant for equality of persons and property." Many years later he recalled that the very idea of a democratic government in France had always struck him as "unnatural, irrational and impracticable." As he then said, "the French Revolution I dreaded." Its effects reinforced Adams's low opinion of popular forms of government. Writing to Taylor, he insisted that "democracy never lasts long . . . . There never was a democracy that did not commit suicide." Indeed he went further and claimed that "democracy is chargeable with all the blood that has been spilled for five-and-twenty years." Alexander Hamilton, for his part, was even more fearful. In 1794 he described the scene in France as "a state of things the most cruel, sanguinary and violent that ever stained the annals

22. Harold C. Syrett (ed.), *The Papers of Alexander Hamilton* 27 vols (N.Y., 1961–1987), IV, p. 200.
23. Eric J. Hobsbawm, *The Age of Revolution* (London, 1962), p. 138.

of mankind, a state of things which annihilates the foundations of social order and true liberty, confounds all moral distinctions and substitutes to the mild & beneficent religion of the Gospel a gloomy persecuting and desolating atheism." Hamilton looked forward to the day when "it will have been a disgrace to have advocated the Revolution of France in its late stages." He was confident that such a day must come – "if there be any thing solid in virtue."[24]

These reactions were utterly typical of propertied men throughout the world. And the restrictive legislation which Hamilton, Adams and the Federalists passed in the 1790s was comparable to that introduced in Britain at the same time. But in the United States there was a different outcome. The opponents of Federalism rallied, formed the Republican party and won control of the government. In so doing, and in placing Thomas Jefferson at the head of the federal government, they re-structured the American polity and re-established the American democratic tradition.

Thomas Jefferson had always proclaimed a faith in the people and in the decisions of the majority. Late in life he expressed a "most earnest wish" "to see the republican element of popular control pushed to the maximum of its practicable exercise" and subsequently made it clear that this extended to the popular election of the judiciary. What the Federalists and their supporters most disliked about the democratic ethos was the confidence with which it set aside precedent and experience in favor of its own – "visionary" was the common adjective – schemes. Jefferson himself expressed this confidence better than anyone when he wrote that the American people had been the first to try a system of "representative democracy" in which the people delegated power to their agents, but retained complete rights of sovereignty. "The introduction of this new principle of representative democracy," he claimed, "has rendered useless almost everything written before on the structure of government; and in a great measure, relieves our regret, if the political writings of Aristotle, or of any other ancient, have been lost." For the Federalists this was a most dangerous, indeed licentious, theory since it encouraged a demagogic pandering to popular prejudice and emotion. But Jefferson saw little danger in popular government. Throughout his life, he once claimed, he had not been "among those who fear the people." For it was they "and not the rich" who were "our dependence for continued freedom." These statements were made in the security of retirement but they had indeed been the principles of a lifetime. The conserva-

24.   Adams to Richard Price, April 19, 1790, *Works of Adams*, IX, p.564; Adams to Jefferson, July 13, 1813 in *Adams–Jefferson Letters*, II, p. 355; *Works of Adams*, IX, p. 484; *Papers of Hamilton*, XVI, p. 587–588.

tives' fear of popular government arose not so much because they begrudged the people the power to vote as because they feared the policies that would ensue. The ultimate fear was of a division of property, an "agrarian" law such as had been proposed in antiquity. Jefferson, by contrast, while never advocating such a measure, in 1785 argued that "legislators cannot invent too many devices for sub-dividing property." While the conservatives fretted about the egalitarianism inherent in a democratic system of government, Jefferson, like Taylor, instead feared inequality and the power of the elite. In the aftermath of Shays' Rebellion he pondered the problems of social disturbance and unrest and reached some remarkable conclusions. In January 1787 he told Madison that "the late rebellion in Massachusetts" had "given more alarm, than I think it should have done." But he was not content with this observation. To William Smith he wrote: "God forbid we should ever be twenty years without such a rebellion." He then made the extraordinary calculation that since there had only been one rebellion in 11 years in all the 13 states of the Union this amounted to only one in every century and a half for each State. "What country," he then asked, "can maintain its liberties, if its rulers are not warned from time to time, that their people preserve the spirit of resistance?" The contrast with Adams's and with Hamilton's anti-democratic strictures could not have been more acute.[25]

When the French Revolution broke out, Jefferson was among its warmest supporters. In its earliest stages, of course, it commanded widespread sympathy among Americans, who saw it as modeled upon their own. The advent of the Terror, however, quickly turned enthusiasm into horror – for many Americans. But not for Jefferson. In 1793 at the height of the Terror he noted its casualties with regret. However, he added that "the liberty of the whole earth was depending on the issue of the contest." "Was ever," he asked, "such a prize won with so little innocent blood?" While he admitted that his "own affections" had been "deeply wounded by some of the martyrs to this cause," he nonetheless avowed that "rather than that it should have failed, I would have seen half the earth desolated." And Taylor? Even during the Reign of Terror he was, as ever, alarmed about the prospect of aristocracy. It was "evident," he wrote in a pamphlet published in 1794, that "exorbitant wealth constitutes the substance and danger of aristocracy" and that the republic was endangered by "an immense disproportion in wealth." In another pamphlet pub-

---

25. Jefferson to Samuel Kercheval, July 12, 1816 in Ford (ed.), *Works of Jefferson*, X, pp. 37, 41; Jefferson to Madison, Oct. 28, 1785 in Julian P. Boyd (ed.), *The Papers of Thomas Jefferson* 25 vols to date (Princeton, 1950–), VIII, p. 682; Jefferson to Madison, Dec. 20, 1787 in Boyd (ed.), *Papers of Jefferson*, XII, p. 442; Jefferson to William S. Smith, Nov. 13, 1787 in Boyd (ed.), *Papers of Jefferson*, XII, p. 356. See also Jefferson to Madison, Jan. 30, 1787 in Boyd (ed.), *Papers of Jefferson*, XI, p. 93.

lished in the same year he referred directly to the Revolution in France and delivered a warning to his fellow countrymen. It was not the warning that a Federalist would have offered. "Our privileged orders," he noted, "have openly sympathized with privileged orders combined for the suppression of republicanism in France." "Ruminate, fellow citizens upon this fact," he continued, "and if you are republicans, determine whether at this momentous crisis, or at any other period, the commonwealth can be safe in the hands of such a faction."[26]

Why were Taylor and Jefferson able to take so calm a view of the French Revolution? There can be no doubt that each of them believed that their interests were at one with those of the agriculturists and that they had nothing to fear from the farmers, who with their families constituted a clear majority of the nation. Yet we still need to ask why they were so unconcerned about the dangers which the poor presented. After all if the poor were to be enfranchised then what was to prevent them using their political power to divide property and dispossess the rich? As we have seen, it was this prospect that so alarmed the Federalists and which caused them to lament what they took to be the decline of deference within the nation. An expression of faith in the people seemed to men of the Federalist persuasion a dangerous incitement of the poor, an encouragement to mob rule. But such expressions were the stock-in-trade of Jefferson, of Taylor and of many other Virginians. We need to ask why this should have been. Some contemporaries wondered whether the crucial factor was not the existence of slavery. In the first decade of the nineteenth century, when Jefferson himself was President a shrewd English observer, Sir Augustus John Foster, pondered why it was that the South, and especially Virginia, seemed more egalitarian than the North. Then he offered a solution to the problem. The Virginians, he suggested "can profess an unbounded love of liberty and of democracy in consequence of the mass of the people, who in other countries might become mobs, being there nearly altogether composed of their own Negro slaves." Putting it a little differently, the crucial factor was the different alignment of class forces in the slave South, in which the masters, exploiting their slaves, had been able to reach a *modus vivendi* with the non-elite whites. It was this *modus vivendi* which had profound consequences for the development of democracy in the United States.[27]

26.   Jefferson to William Short, Jan. 3, 1793 in Boyd (ed.), *Papers of Jefferson*, xxv, p. 14; [John Taylor], *An Enquiry into the Principles and Tendency of Certain Public Measures* (Phil., 1794), p. 29; [Taylor], *A Definition of Parties: Or, the Political Effects of the Paper System Considered* (Phil., 1794), p. 16.
27.   Richard B. Davis (ed.), *Jeffersonian America: Notes on the United States of America Collected in the Years 1805–6–7 and 11–12 by Sir Augustus John Foster, Bart* (San Marino, Ca., 1954), pp. 163, 307 quoted in Edmund S. Morgan *American Slavery,*

Jefferson and slavery

I

While the area of disagreement separating Virginia Republicans from northern Federalists was a wide one, they shared one conviction whose importance cannot be exaggerated: each group was adamantly opposed to conferring political rights on the most exploited (or even simply the poorest) members of their respective communities. But such an agreement allowed for, and even perhaps encouraged, a bitter conflict over the question of democracy for white men, since the poorest and most exploited groups in Virginia were, of course, black men. To this extent, therefore, the slaves substituted in republican thought for the poorer whites of the North.[28] An examination of the thinking of Jefferson and Taylor on the slavery question reveals this similarity, though it also reveals other important features of their political careers.

Once again we will begin with Taylor since, as always, he displayed less ambivalence than Jefferson. With both Virginians, however, one is struck by the tentative and faltering tone in which their criticisms of the institution were offered. The confidence they possessed in the people and in the possibilities of reform suddenly disappeared when the subject of slavery arose. Their response irresistibly reminds one of an elite faced with a challenge to its vital interests, a challenge whose moral force it could not entirely discountenance but to which it would not or could not submit. For Taylor slavery, or "negro slavery" as he often preferred to term it, was something not to be welcomed. He spent little time on the sufferings of the blacks, however, whom he regarded, as so many Jacksonians would later regard them, as inferior in every respect to the Caucasian, and indeed perhaps even constituting a separate species. Nonetheless he conceded that "negro slavery is a misfortune to agriculture." But Taylor the bold champion of a popular government, willing to set aside all precedent and exulting in the claim that the United States had begun to chart a new course for the whole of humanity, suddenly became defensive, cautious and hesitant. Slavery was "incapable of removal, and only within the reach of palliation." John Adams would have said much the same of aristocracy, which he believed could not be removed, or of

---

American Freedom: The Ordeal of Colonial Virginia (N.Y., 1975), p. 380. As early as 1775 Edmund Burke, of course, calling for conciliation with the colonies, had argued that southerners (and especially southern slaveholders) had a greater attachment to liberty than northerners. See *Speech of Edmund Burke, Esq, on Moving His Resolutions for Conciliation with the Colonies* (London, 1775), pp. 32–33.

28. This is not to say, of course, that the role of slaves in the South was in other ways like that of the poor in the North; on the contrary it is a principal theme of this work that the difference between the labor systems in the two sections was of enormous significance.

inequality, whose worst effects a republic could only palliate. And where Federalists fretted about the possibilities of a political collision of the poor and the rich, encouraged by democracy, so Taylor was terrified by the prospect of a political collision between black and white, encouraged by abolitionism. In this sense, therefore, slavery elicited from Taylor the response which democracy and equality provoked in a Federalist.[29]

Jefferson's view of slavery was more complex and he even has some antislavery credentials.[30] But ultimately he too responded in the same defensive and cautious manner. At the time of the Revolution, like many other Virginians, he was convinced that slavery could not be justified. In his famous *Summary View of the Rights of British America* of 1774 Jefferson made his first attack on slavery in print. He here assailed the slave trade and made the significant if incorrect claim that the abolition of slavery was greatly desired by southerners. Two years later in his original draft of the Declaration of Independence he made similar claims. But the antislavery sections from both documents were struck out and Jefferson never explained the connection between the Declaration and slavery.[31]

In the 1780s his antislavery activities reached their high point. He proposed various schemes for emancipation and supported his state's laws easing manumissions and abolishing the slave trade. Moreover in 1787 came the greatest success of his antislavery career, the Northwest Ordinance, which of course banned slavery from the territory of that region. While one reason for its passage was a southern fear that slave states in the Northwest would compete with the South in tobacco growing, the measure nevertheless linked Jefferson's name and prestige with

---

29. Taylor, *Arator*, p. 115.
30. The best work on Jefferson and slavery is John Chester Miller, *The Wolf by the Ears: Thomas Jefferson and Slavery* (N.Y., 1977) – an unusually rich and thorough survey. See also the discussion in David Brion Davis, *The Problem of Slavery in the Age of Revolution* (N.Y., 1975), pp. 170–184, as well as Davis's inaugural lecture at the University of Oxford, *Was Thomas Jefferson an Authentic Enemy of Slavery* (Oxford, 1970). Much of Davis's argument, however, was anticipated in Robert McColley, *Slavery and Jeffersonian Virginia* (Urbana, Ill., 1964), esp. pp. 115–116, 124, 130, 170, 183. Also of importance in this connection are Winthrop Jordan, *White Over Black* (Chapel Hill, 1968) and MacLeod, *Slavery, Race* . . . . Of course one must still recur to the biographies of Jefferson, especially those by Dumas Malone and Merrill D. Peterson.
31. Miller, *Wolf by the Ears*, p. 279. Jefferson probably hoped that the "self-evident" truth contained in the Declaration would preclude the continued existence of slavery – in the long term. But without doubt he did not concede the right of slaves to demand and secure their own freedom, though it was while Americans were doing precisely this that they had come to recognize these truths in the first place. As Miller observes (p. 279), "From the beginning of his career it was impressed upon Jefferson that he must choose between the preservation of his political 'usefulness' and active opposition to slavery."

opposition to the extension of slavery. It thus created a basis in fact for the Free Soil or Republican Jefferson, whose image was to be so potent in the 1840s and 1850s.[32]

Jefferson's opposition to slavery rested on several claims. In the mid-1780s his famous *Notes on the State of Virginia* appeared and in one of its most celebrated passages he wrote that "the whole commerce between master and slave is a perpetual exercise of the most boisterous passions, the most unremitting despotism on the one part, and degrading submission on the other." He added that "our children see this, and learn to imitate it." Jefferson usually placed the primary emphasis on the evil effects of slavery upon the white slaveholders rather than upon the black slaves but he occasionally acknowledged the paradox of a society of slaveholders fighting for their own liberty but continuing to hold another people in bondage. "What a stupendous, what an incomprehensible machine is man!" he exclaimed, "who can endure toil, famine, stripes, imprisonment and death itself, in vindication of his own liberty, and, in the next moment . . . inflict on his fellow men a bondage, one hour of which is fraught with more misery, than ages of that which he rose in rebellion to oppose." Almost thirty years later he could still call attention to the plight of the blacks. "The love of justice, and the love of country," he declared, "plead equally the cause of these people." He also found, in addition to moral arguments, other grounds for opposing slavery. In the wake of the uprising in Santo Domingo he urged the removal of slavery for the sake of self-preservation. Otherwise, he warned, "the revolutionary storm, now sweeping the globe, will be upon us." The problem was, moreover, an urgent one, for "every day's delay lessens the time we may take for emancipation."[33]

Jefferson continued to believe until the end of his life that emancipation or insurrections was the choice facing the South.[34] Yet, taken in its entirety, his record on slavery was not as impressive as some of his early actions might suggest. From his first involvement in politics he had learned that to engage in wholesale denunciations of slavery was to incur the implacable hostility of Virginia's planter class. It is thus significant that the *Notes on Virginia* were at first not intended for anything other than private publication since Jefferson was extremely

32. Miller, *Wolf by the Ears*, pp. 21–22, 26–30. See also Robert T. Berkhofer, Jr., "Jefferson, the Ordinance of 1784 and the Origins of the American Territorial System," *William and Mary Quarterly*, XXIX (1972), pp. 231–262; Peterson, *Jefferson Image*, 189–209.
33. Thomas Jefferson, *Notes on Virginia*, p. 155; Jefferson to Jean Nicolas de Meunier, June 26, 1786 in Boyd (ed.), *Papers of Jefferson*, X, p. 63; Jefferson to Edward Coles, Aug. 25, 1814 in Ford (ed.), *Works of Jefferson*, IX, pp. 478–479; Miller, *Wolf by the Ears*, p. 133.
34. Miller, *Wolf by the Ears*, pp. 100–103.

anxious about the effects on his reputation of the antislavery passages. The book was originally written in 1781–1782 at the request of the French *chargé d'affaires* in Philadelphia and Jefferson wanted it to be read by French *philosophes*, not American slaveholders. When the appearance of a poorly translated French edition forced his hand he still tried to have it published anonymously. At this moment he used an argument that he would call upon again and again in the future: slavery ought to be attacked when the time was ripe but that time had not yet arrived. He even professed to believe that inaction was in the interests of the slaves. Would not an "unsuccessful effort," he wondered, "as too often happens, . . . only rivet still closer the chains of bondage?"[35]

As Duncan MacLeod has demonstrated, for him the evils of slavery had to be measured against the dangers of abolition. Since he could not tolerate the prospect of blacks as equal citizens, mass colonization was the only solution.[36] In his last years the American Colonization Society began to attract considerable support from northerners and southerners alike. But Jefferson perceived that the scale of the problem was simply too vast for the Society and he instead gave some encouragement to the plan of his son-in-law, Thomas Mann Randolph. In 1820–1821, when Randolph was Governor of Virginia, he put forward a plan by which the state government would each year buy, manumit and then send to Haiti, a proportion of the young slaves of the state. But the legislature gave the plan short shrift. Jefferson, convinced that compensation would have to be paid to the slaveholders, now realized that the problem was too great also for a single state. He concluded that the federal government would have to be involved and suggested that the revenue from western land sales be used to finance the project. Clearly this would have necessitated a huge expansion of the role of the federal government and Jefferson acknowledged that a constitutional amendment would be required. Even then the costs, he soon realized, would be prohibitive and so he modified his plan so that it closely resembled the one he had advanced many years previously in the *Notes on Virginia*. At the age of five, slave children would be taken from their parents, raised as wards of the states, trained in skills that would later be of use to them, and then shipped off to Haiti. Thus the United States would gradually lose its black population. But there were many problems in this scheme, quite apart from the injustice involved in a forced separation of black families. Chief amongst them was the huge increase in the power of government that would be required. Though the financial costs were probably less than would have been entailed if adults and children were all to have been transported, the role of government in raising hundreds of thousands of black children was one which was extremely difficult, if not impossible, to reconcile with Jeffersonian principles. Nonetheless, Jefferson continued to believe that abolition was feasible. As late as August 1825 he declared that it was "not impossible" and "ought never therefore to be despaired of." But surely colonization of all the nation's slaves, whether done gradually or not, was utterly impracticable. And since Jefferson's racism meant that colonization had to accompany abolition, then the conclusion was inescapable: abolition was indeed "impossible." Was there any reason why a realistic observer should not conclude that it was, in truth, a project which "ought therefore to be despaired of?"[37]

II

One reason for Jefferson's poor record as an opponent of slavery was his racial prejudice. At no time did he express a conviction that blacks were the equal of whites (in the way that Alexander Hamilton, for example, did). Like many slaveholders he easily assumed that they were lazy and slow, without ever considering that this might be part of an elaborate charade, a pretence of incompetence or of ineptitude assumed by slaves for their own protection. On several occasions he declared flatly that blacks were unequal and it is not even clear that he believed in monogenesis. Certainly a belief that blacks were a separate species would explain his utter horror of miscegenation, as well as his utter indifference to the plight of free blacks in Virginia and the nation as a whole. He even claimed that racial prejudice had been ordained in order to prevent intermarriage.[38]

As President, and indeed at all times after the 1780s, Jefferson's actions in support of the slave were few and far between. For more than thirty years he refused to do anything other than talk about antislavery. And his words were almost always in private letters. As Merrill Peterson notes: "while he continued to favor the plan of gradual emancipation . . .

37. Miller, *Wolf by the Ears*, pp. 268–270, 276. As Miller observes (p. 269), in 1819 Madison estimated the value of the slaves at 600m dollars. This plus the cost of transportation, would mean a bill of a billion dollars. In 1791 he had taken the view that a national debt of 90 million dollars would be virtually impossible to repay. In Miller's words, "the execution of this plan required the expansion of the powers of the federal government and its intervention into the private affairs of American citizens far beyond anything dreamed of in the philosophy of Alexander Hamilton."

38. Jefferson, *Notes on Virginia*, pp. 133–137; Foster, *Jeffersonian America*, pp. 155–156; Jefferson to Edward Coles, Aug. 25, 1814 in Ford (ed.), *Works of Jefferson*, IX, pp. 478–479; Miller, *Wolf by the Ears*, pp. 24, 76–78, 255–256; 87–88, 128–129.

neither he nor any other prominent Virginian was ever willing to risk friends, position, and influence to fight for it." Yet the rationalizations for his inactivity were feeble in the extreme – if one views them in purely intellectual terms. Once again they are the words of a ruling class faced with a proposal whose justice it would like to acknowledge but whose effects upon its vested interests it cannot tolerate. As David Brion Davis has pointed out, Jefferson employed a variety of circumlocutions and struck attitudes that were entirely at odds with his thinking on other issues. As early as 1786 and in the very letter in which he had acknowledged the irony of demands for freedom on the lips of slaveholders, he immediately undercut his own observation. "But," he cautioned, as if to dampen any reforming zeal which he might have aroused, "we must await, with patience, the workings of an overruling Providence, and hope that that is preparing the deliverance of these, our suffering brethren." When would this be? Jefferson did not fix a time. He merely opined that it would be "when the measure of their tears shall be full, when their groans shall have heaven itself in darkness." At this portentous but carefully unspecified moment, "doubtless a God of justice will awaken to their distress."[39] But for Jefferson the God of justice would always operate by persuading the slaveholders of the South that emancipation was either necessary or desirable; action had to be initiated by them, not by northerners, still less by foreigners, least of all by the slaves themselves. As we shall see later, during the Missouri Crisis he made it clear he would tolerate no "interference" from northerners on the subject of slavery. Many years earlier, at the time of the revolutionary war, he was outraged when the British offered freedom to slaves who would join them and as Secretary of State in Washington's cabinet he sought compensation for Virginians who had lost their "property" in this way. And when he heard in 1800 of Gabriel Prosser's attempted slave revolt his first words were: "we are truly to be pitied!" Once again the welfare of the exploiters took precedence over that of the exploited.[40]

Of course where the rights of white Americans were concerned, Jefferson like Taylor was energetic and intrepid, exhorting Americans to the boldest acts. But on the slavery question, he was timid and diffident, inviting a passive acquiescence in the *status quo*. By the 1780s he had begun to trust to time. He was still trusting to time at his death in 1826. In between he had carefully dissociated himself from all antislavery organizations, maintained while president a careful silence on the subject

39. Merrill D. Peterson, *Thomas Jefferson and the New Nation: A Biography* (N.Y., 1970), p. 153; Davis, *Problem of Slavery in Age of Revolution*, pp. 169–184; Jefferson to Jean Nicolas de Meunier, June 26, 1786, in Boyd (ed.), *Papers of Jefferson*, x, p. 63.
40. Miller, *Wolf by the Ears*, pp. 115–118, 127.

of slavery and failed to endorse measures which would have excluded slavery from the new territories of the Southwest or the District of Columbia. As leader of the opposition to the Federalists, he had proposed that holders of government securities and of bank stock be prohibited by federal law from sitting in Congress. Slaveholders, of course, would face no such prohibition. Similarly foreigners, before becoming citizens, must renounce all titles; they need not, of course, renounce their slaveholding. It is hard to disagree with John C. Miller's conclusion about Jefferson; he was indeed "more concerned with the wrong done to slave-owners than with the wrongs done by them."[41]

To the end of his life Jefferson was still announcing his readiness to "make any sacrifice which shall ensure their [the slaves'] complete retirement from the States, and effectually, at the same time, establish them elsewhere in freedom and safety." He even complained that young southerners had not responded as they should have done, though this did not prevent him from rebuffing a young antislavery Virginian, Edward Coles, when he sought endorsement of antislavery proposals.[42]

Yet in retirement Jefferson did once publicize his views on the slavery question. This departure came at the time of the Missouri Crisis. But as we shall see, his influence was used on behalf of, not against, the slaveholders. This was not the first nor the last time that Jeffersonian democracy was of great benefit to the slave interest. And it is here that we encounter the greatest problem with current historical assessments of Jefferson and slavery. Historians now recognize that Jefferson's record is not as good as was once believed. And they have found valid explanations for the poor performance. Winthrop Jordan is surely correct in emphasizing the extent to which racism undermined his antislavery convictions.[43] One must also agree with David Brion Davis that his class position as a slaveowner and a leader of a slaveholding society played a vital role too. Yet slavery was more important even than this. It was not simply the cause of the flaws within the Jeffersonian credo; it played a key role in the formulation, the development and the triumph of that credo itself. I have already suggested that slavery allowed key members of the southern elite to espouse highly egalitarian, even radical ideas. But the relationship between slavery and democracy was still more complex. Just as slavery facilitated the adoption of Jeffersonian ideology, so that ideology continuously served the interest of the slaveholding class. The two

---

41. Miller, *Wolf by the Ears*, pp. 143, 122, 274. Miller is speaking here of the 1820s but the conclusion seems equally applicable to Jefferson's entire career.
42. Miller, *Wolf by the Ears*, pp. 204–205, 208, 250–251. It should perhaps be added that insolvency was a part cause of these remarks.
43. As Davis points out, Jordan's explanation is essentially Jefferson's – Davis, *Problem of Slavery in Age of Revolution*, p. 172.

progressed together. Historians know that neither Jefferson nor Taylor had this objective in mind. The task then is to show that this unplanned, unintended and indeed often unrecognized connection was neither arbitrary nor random.

The advancement of class interests (1)

I

It is tempting to argue that the advancement of class interests requires intent. A common-sense approach might lead us to think that unintended events are necessarily the product of chance. And such a conclusion is often valid. Indeed sometimes human activity is not meaningfully involved at all in producing unintended events. Let us take by way of illustration the case of a motorist, who, driving along a road, is suddenly hit by a tree falling upon his car. The tree has been struck by lightning. As long as no individual or group of people intended that there should be a thunderstorm, that lightning should suddenly strike the tree in question, that the tree should fall, or that the motorist should be injured we may reasonably conclude that chance played a major part in producing the motorist's misfortune. An unsought outcome is here attributable in large part to chance.

But this will by no means always be the case. Suppose we now consider an economic recession. While there may be some individuals or groups who benefit from an economic slump, in general recessions are not sought by the population at large, nor by those charged with the management of the economy. Yet they happen periodically. A full explanation of this tendency is not required here. It is merely sufficient to note the probability that recessions are *unwilled yet non-random*. Many wars, though by no means all, can be similarly viewed. And so can the mutually supportive relationship between Jeffersonian ideology and the interests of the slaveholding class.

A problem immediately arises. If the historian wishes to establish a causal relationship, the demonstration of intent will often strengthen his case.[44] Alternatively he may seek to demonstrate the existence of what are sometimes termed "constant conjunctions" – whenever A happens, B follows. The discovery of such conjunctions or correlations is frequently the task of the natural scientist who may be able, in laboratory conditions, to isolate the key variables. Such is the essence of positivism.

---

44.   Yet even though one has shown intent and shown that the outcome was identical to the intent, it is still possible that the outcome is attributable to other causes than that intent.

Similarly the historian or social scientist may seek to establish such connections, though isolating the key variables may now be far more difficult. Even when a correlation has been demonstrated, however, there is still no guarantee that a causal relationship exists. Nevertheless the existence of "constant conjunctions" is often an indication of causality.

Yet no such conjunction exists in the case of Jeffersonianism and slavery. Just as an intent to promote slavery cannot be demonstrated, so it would be quite wrong to suggest that Jeffersonian ideology was the inevitable concomitant of slaveholding. One must guard against reductionism.[45] I am in no way suggesting that Jeffersonian Democracy was a simple reflex of, and is thus reducible to, the self-interest of slaveholders. It is surely evident that the self-interest of this class cannot be adduced as a full and complete explanation of the Jeffersonian movement. To explain Jeffersonian (and Jacksonian) ideology one must pay considerable attention to the legacy from Europe and especially England. Indeed it may be argued that there is a resemblance between the ideas of Americans like Jackson, Taylor and Jefferson on the one hand, and radical English groups of the seventeenth century like the Levellers, on the other. It follows that these ideas can exist in a society that does not contain a single slave. A full explanation of American democratic thought must then accord full weight to the English heritage. It seems safe to argue that without this heritage there would have been no Jeffersonian movement, no Jeffersonian Democracy, no Jacksonian Democracy. There are other causes at work besides slavery.[46]

Nor is it plausible to claim that all slaveholders in the United States embraced the democratic theories we have been considering. The reaction of George Washington, for example, to the threat of the French Revolution was akin to that of Adams and Hamilton, rather than to that of Jefferson and Taylor. Washington also sounded out warnings to his countrymen about the dangers of democracy. So slave ownership by no means guaranteed support for the Jeffersonian movement or sympathy with Jeffersonian ideals. Even more significantly, slave ownership was no more a universal characteristic of Jeffersonians or Jacksonians than it was

45. If we "reduce" A to B then we claim that an explanation of B contains a complete explanation of A. Thus a reduction of Jeffersonian Democracy to the slaveholding interest denotes that the former is entirely explicable in terms of the latter. Note, however, that historians sometimes mistakenly imply or assume that an argument for primacy is a reduction. In this work I shall frequently argue for the primacy of material factors, never for a reduction.

46. The correspondence between American democratic thought and that of, for example, the Levellers is striking, though there is no evidence of a direct influence. Rather it would appear that American thought had inherited many of the general attitudes and beliefs of English popular radicalism.

of seventeenth-century Levellers, for example. The Democratic party from the time of its creation until the Civil War was a truly national organization, able to recruit support and win elections in every section of the Union. As we shall see later, it even contained within its ranks men who professed hostility to slavery.

It follows that there is no simple empirical test for the hypothesis that links slavery to the development of American democracy by way of Jefferson, Taylor and the Democratic party. There was no "constant conjunction" of slaveholding and Jeffersonianism and it is not possible to "control" for the influence of other variables.[47] Since the claim is that slavery was an *unrecognized* or *invisible* underpinning, an unacknowledged condition of Jeffersonian and Democratic thought, certain other empirical tests would be inappropriate. Even if we were fortunate enough to have at our disposal a time machine which would enable us to travel back to the 1790s, a questionnaire to allow us to ask all the right questions, and even a truth drug to ensure the veracity of all the responses, we could still not resolve the problem. We would then find in all likelihood a genuine indignation on the part of the Jeffersonians at the attempt to devalue their commitment to liberty by connecting it with the interests of a slaveholding elite. But only if we accept that men and women are fully conscious of all the forces that operate upon them would this response be conclusive.[48]

It is thus not possible to test the hypothesis directly. Although Sir Augustus John Foster, Edmund Burke and others could be cited in its support, a larger number of equally intelligent contemporaries or observers could be cited against it. Another way of resolving the issue needs to be found. What is this way? It can only be in terms of explanatory power. We must consider some of the phenomena that are difficult or impossible to explain in any other terms.[49]

---

47. The hypothesis is thus not open to simple positivist verification.

48. The notion that individuals *do* possess a complete understanding of their own ideas and the antecedents of those ideas is a curious one. It is analogous to the claim that possession of a body makes every man as knowledgeable about physiology as his doctor. It would seem, however, that the claim has much to do with the fear of the nefarious political purposes to which the alternative view may be put: the danger that an ostensibly all-seeing elite (in government) may impose upon a community its "real" interests, regardless of its wishes.

49. The hypothesis is not amenable to "falsification" in the sense in which Karl Popper used the term. But these positions in the philosophy of science are, in my view, dubious. A better criterion concerns explanatory power. If we postulate the existence of a mechanism without which certain observable phenomena are inexplicable then even if the mechanism itself is not observable, it is logical (and scientific) to accept its existence. Needless to say, however, such a conclusion is tentative and open to challenge in the light of further evidence or argument.

There are many such phenomena and they will recur throughout this book and its sequel. Some of them, such as the tendency for Democrats, northern as well as southern, to favor slavery more than their opponents, will be considered more fully later. For the present we will merely note three facts or tendencies that are in need of explanation. The first is simply the extraordinary confidence which Jefferson, Taylor and many others of their class had in the people at a time when elites everywhere were haunted by the specter of revolution. How else can this be explained? There is a tendency for this question not even to be posed for such has been the triumph of democratic thought in the United States that it is all too easy to assume that it was in some way inevitable. The magnitude of the Jeffersonian triumph, therefore, has diverted attention away from the causes of the triumph. Some answers, however, have been offered. Historians have argued that it is the availability of land in early America which, by placing property ownership within the grasp of so many white males, allowed republicanism to develop.[50] The republican idyll after all emphasized independence, and independence, in republican thinking, was secured primarily by ownership of property and especially land. Other scholars have claimed that colonial Virginia, at least after Bacon's rebellion, was marked by a high degree of social cohesion and political stability and that these characteristics continued to be present into the 1780s and 1790s. As a result democratic ideals could flourish, since those to be enfranchised had already demonstrated their dependability.[51]

Yet these interpretations complement and strengthen, rather than compete with the argument offered here. After all, it is striking that the elites of the North, unlike those of the South, did not eulogize the farmer. It is equally striking that it was Jefferson who purchased Louisiana, almost doubling the size of the nation in so doing while Adams and most of the Federalists wanted to diversify the economy and restrict rather than increase the availability of land. We must also ask where the cohesion and stability of early Virginia originated. We are then forced back to a consideration of the role of slavery. As Edmund Morgan has noted in relation to the revolutionary struggle, the existence of slavery meant that the Virginia elite exploited blacks, not whites and so a considerable degree of political unity among the whites was much easier to attain. In the North (as we shall see in a future chapter) the elite, apart from the large landowners who lived off their rents, were drawn increasingly into non-agricultural forms of activity. In the South this also happened

50. An extreme statement of this view is to be found in Robert E. Brown, *Middle Class Democracy and the Revolution in Massachusetts* (Ithaca, 1955).
51. For example, Morgan, *American Slavery, American Freedom*, p. 367, though Morgan himself takes pains to link this stability to the existence of slavery.

but to a considerably lesser degree. Hence the potency of the agrarian idyll in the South. The pre-capitalist vision of a democratic state was one in which government allowed all men to retain the full fruits of their labor. So long as blacks were excluded from the community, with the proceeds of their labor going not to them but to their masters, then this vision had a strong appeal to the slaveholder. As we shall see, Democrats from the time of Jefferson onwards did indeed think of blacks as non-members of the political community – in some cases, indeed, as non-members of the human race. Thus the rallying cry of early modern radicalism, the demand that all should enjoy the full fruits of their labor, which to northern elites was simply the crudest demagoguery, had a strong appeal to many slaveholders. While northern elites looked to government to foster growth and facilitate capital formation so that an increasingly diversified economy could develop, the southern slaveholders for whom Taylor and Jefferson spoke, confident that they had a market in Europe for their goods, and possessing good natural means of transportation, had little need for this kind of governmental activity. Hence they enlisted instead in the defense of the landed interest and made common cause with the farmers of North and South.[52]

The second phenomenon in need of explanation is closely linked to the first. It is the remarkable strength of republicanism in the South. Opposition to the Federalists began and was always strongest in the South. Let us consider the presidential election of 1796. The result of this contest was truly astonishing. Adams carried the whole of New England, together with New York, New Jersey and Delaware. Maryland and Pennsylvania's votes were divided, with Jefferson obtaining all but one in the latter, and Adams obtaining 7 out of 11 in the former. Taking the North as a whole, one would have to say that Jefferson's performance was poor. In the South, however (and also in the West), the results were reversed. Here Adams obtained a mere two electoral votes, while Jefferson amassed fifty.

Of course each party had supporters in every section of the Union. But the balance of forces was different in North and South. By 1800 the Republicans were stronger in the North than they had been four years previously, although Adams again carried the whole of New England. It is tempting to speculate on the development of the United States if the nation's boundaries had ended at the Mason-Dixon line. The Federalists would presumably have continued in office and they would have

---

52. My debt to Morgan is evident here. But I do think that his thesis better explains the course of events *after* the Revolution than the events leading up to it. To put it somewhat differently, it explains the creation of American democracy rather than the creation of American republicanism.

attempted to lead the nation in approximately the direction which Britain had taken, so far as politics and political economy were concerned. But the power of the South changed all this. Indeed its importance may have been even greater than the figures suggest. After all the problem for the Republicans in the North was that they lacked leaders of the fame or stature of the Federalists. They probably needed the enormous prestige of Thomas Jefferson, a man whose role in the revolutionary struggle was second only to George Washington's and whose patriotism could not be successfully impugned. As I have tried to argue, the ideas of the Republicans would have been considered disreputable by the leaders of most communities; indeed the Federalists would dearly have loved to fasten such a label on their opponents. But the role that the elite of Virginia had played made this a difficult strategy – indeed, outside of New England, an impossible one.

This imbalance in the political geography of the nation was by no means limited to the 1790s. The Federalists continued to decline but remained strongest in New England. It was their opposition to the War of 1812, of course, which ultimately sealed their fate. Yet even this should not be seen in isolation from the question of slavery. The New England elite was, in large part, a mercantile elite, and the merchants were the principal opponents of Jefferson's Embargo and the group most hostile to the Anglophobic policy of the Republicans. But can we separate this from slavery? Can we really believe that the concentration of mercantile activity in the non-slaveholding section of the Union was for reasons unconnected to slavery? Here we confront the fact that slavery generates a different kind of elite and propels a society along a different developmental path.[53]

In the aftermath of the War of 1812, the Federalists gradually expired and the Republicans eventually became the sole party in the nation. But the election of 1828 witnessed the rebirth of party conflict. A comparison of the outcome with that of 1796 is illuminating. This time Adams's son swept New England, while his opponent, Andrew Jackson, carried every state south and west of Maryland. Again Pennsylvania opposed an Adams and this time New York did the same. Once more a predominantly southern party had defeated a candidate who was clearly linked with the North. Indeed the presidential election of 1828 saw a wholly southern ticket (Jackson and Calhoun) opposed by a wholly northern one (Adams and Rush). Thus Jacksonian like Jeffersonian Democracy derived its initial momentum from the South. And under the Jacksonians the ideas of Jefferson, and still more of John Taylor of Carolina, would once again be in the ascendant.

---

53. See below, Chapter 2.

Thirty years later, in the final decade of the antebellum republic, the identification of the Democratic party with the South would be still more apparent, although in the intervening years, and especially for the decade or so after the Panic of 1837, the political parties enjoyed good support in every section of the Union. However, if we treat the years from the 1790s to the Civil War as a single unit, and characterize the antebellum republic as a single regime, then a clear pattern is apparent. In that regime the Democratic party was dominant. And the South was dominant within the Democratic party. And the slaveholders were dominant within the South.[54]

This is not to say, of course, that the issues of 1796 were those of 1828 or those of 1856. (It is probably for this reason that historians rarely comment on the secular tendency that we are considering.) Most important, slavery, the crucial issue in 1856 had no real salience in 1796 and was of limited significance in 1828. But we should be very reluctant to believe that the South, which had been the mainstay of the Democratic party from the very beginning, in the 1850s suddenly had the good fortune to find the party an effective shield for slavery. Here we encounter the third phenomenon in need of an explanation. The slaveholders in the 1850s united under the Democratic party as never before and in so doing they helped modify its ideology. Nevertheless many of the principles with which it had traditionally been associated were retained. These proved highly advantageous to the slaveholders. Without the hypothesis I am proposing this is yet another coincidence. But if instead we recognize that Jeffersonianism, without Jefferson (or Taylor) ever being aware of it, always bore the imprint of the class interest of the planters, it comes as no surprise that it should be of benefit to that class when a crisis developed. As we shall see, the price would be that the hitherto concealed class interest became increasingly visible so that by the 1850s the Democracy was seen by all and sundry as the party of the southern slaveholder, the party, to use the then-current phrase, of the Slave Power.

Before we consider those principles yet another qualification is in order. It would be quite erroneous to suggest that Jeffersonian democracy was the only creed that could have furthered the interests of the slaveholding class in the United States. Nor does it follow that the creed was necessarily the best way for those interests to be promoted (though such a claim might well be made).[55] The proposal here is a more modest one: that Jeffersonian Democracy benefited the slaveholders and the benefits reaped, while not the result of any premeditated plan, were not the prod-

---

54. The argument stated here will be defended in subsequent chapters and in the sequel to this volume. My purpose here is merely to state it.
55. I am thus not making a functionalist argument here.

uct of chance either. Hence in the 1850s, when the party which Jefferson had founded was faced with a deadly threat from the antislavery forces, it provided a highly comfortable home for the slaveholding classes.

We may begin with the doctrine of states' rights. Decentralized government with its corollary of local control was a primary goal of the Levellers, for example, in the seventeenth century.[56] It thus need not be associated in any way with the defense of slavery. And both Taylor and Jefferson often defended the doctrine without reference to slavery. In a pamphlet of the 1790s Taylor asked how "the national judgment or will" should be expressed. His first answer was "by cautiously electing members of Congress, of a similarity of interests – of burthens – of benefits – and of habits with the electors." His second answer led to a full exposition of the role of the state in his and his party's thinking. For the state governments offered "a security for liberty of the happiest texture which could have been devised." "The State Legislatures," he continued, "are the people themselves in a state of refinement, possessing superior information, and exhibiting the national suffrage in the fairest and safest mode." Here Taylor's confidence in the people re-emerged. "Holding their power by an annual tenure," the state legislators were "frequently accountable to the people, often changed, and incapable of forming combinations for their private emolument, at the public expense." The advantage of the state governments lay in the fact that their officers were "more immediately within the view of their constituents," and thus exposed, should they "misrepresent the public mind," to "a detection, or a contradiction," which would be "almost instantaneous." Jefferson's view was very similar. In his first Inaugural he referred to the state governments as "the most competent administrations for our domestic concerns and the surest bulwarks against anti-republican tendencies."[57]

When Jefferson referred to "our domestic concerns" it is possible but by no means certain that slavery was one of the subjects he had in mind. In general when he and Taylor spoke about states' rights it was not in the context of the slavery question. After all, the debate over the proper extent of federal power was one that went beyond the concern of southern slaveholders for their chattels and some ardent defenders of states' rights both in the 1790s and for decades afterwards, had not the slightest desire to defend human bondage. Nevertheless the doctrine of states' rights proved enormously beneficial to the slave interest and indeed became one of the principal justifications for secession in 1860–1861.

The doctrines implanted in American politics by slaveholders in the 1790s thus came to the aid of their slaveholding descendants two generations later. If this is not to be dismissed as mere coincidence then we may note that there were certain factors common to both eras. Both in the 1790s and in the 1850s southerners were confident that from within their own states, there was no real threat. At each time the slave interest was safe. In the 1790s slavery helped remove the fear of the people and the fear of radicalism which so tormented the northern elites; there was a harmony of interests between the southern elite and the southern farmer that had no precise counterpart in the North. It followed that as long as there continued to be no internal threat to their power from an indigenous antislavery movement, states' rights would continue to possess great appeal for the planters. In the 1790s those who wished to augment federal power did not, in general, seek to move the federal government against slavery. But in the 1850s, after more than twenty years of abolitionist and later free soil pressure, this was precisely the goal of the Republicans. Hence in the latter decade it was clear to any discerning observer, in a way that it had not been in Jefferson's time, that the doctrine of states' rights was being used primarily to protect slavery. Yet in each decade an elite of slaveholders had formed an alliance with the non-slaveholding whites in its own section, against a predominantly northern opposition; in each case the different configuration of class interests brought about by slavery was crucial.

Second, we may consider again the problem of race. While there is no need to reduce racism to slavery, it is a minimal claim to suggest that racism supported slavery and was a great impediment to antislavery activity in the South, and indeed (notwithstanding the examples of some racist abolitionists and free-soilers) in the nation as a whole. So a subtle process was operating. Jefferson and Taylor's racism clearly derived some of its strength from slavery. By the time of the Missouri Crisis, as we shall see, identifying oneself with, and enlisting under the banner of, the party of Jefferson meant for most northern and virtually all southern Democrats, endorsing the racism of the party's founders. Party membership thus entailed the adoption of a racist outlook that militated against concern for the slaves in the South. So yet again, the Jeffersonian creed offered support for the slaveholder of the South. And even though such had not been Jefferson's goal, the outcome was in no way a random one.[58]

58. The reason events may be both unwilled yet non-random has to do with the *relations* between individuals and groups of individuals. The opposite view, by contrast, reduces society to the individuals composing it.

Lastly we must reconsider the role of agriculture, of agrarianism and of radicalism in Democratic thinking and in the Democratic party. As I have already suggested, the eulogies which Taylor and Jefferson offered to the farmer cannot be divorced from slavery. And I shall suggest that the presence of slavery in the South retarded the development of industry and of cities there.[59] As a result, northern opponents of urbanization and of industrialization frequently looked with great favor upon the South. Militant labor leaders in the 1830s and 1840s, for example, found the pre-capitalist ideals of southerners like John C. Calhoun most attractive. What they most welcomed was the demand that all white men should enjoy the full fruits of their labor, a demand which in turn implied an agrarian society of property-owning farmers or small craftsmen. This demand, as we have already seen, had great appeal to southern slaveholders, so long as slaves were considered as property. Another subtle process was at work. Slavery allowed Jefferson and Taylor to make radical demands for an egalitarian and agrarian society. These demands had considerable appeal in the North. But if northern radicals were to secure the support of the southern elite and fully to identify themselves with the nation's democratic tradition, they had to acquiesce in slavery in the South.

This is not to say that all northern radicals tolerated slavery, though it is notable that most did. Rather it is to make a more general point concerning the power of the slaveholders. By the Jacksonian era the Federalists had been discredited to the extent that it was electorally disastrous for a party in public to claim any affinity with them. Instead the nation's democratic tradition was closely identified with the Democratic party. And since the image of America was closely associated with its democratic forms of government, the Democratic party had around it a strong aura of nationalism. Federalist opposition to the War of 1812 as well as the Democratic party's responsibility for the extension of the nation's boundaries first by the Louisiana Purchase and later as a consequence of the Mexican war, reinforced the association between the party and the nation. This was a source of great strength to Democrats and, as we shall see, it gave party members a deep conviction that the nation had been established on correct principles so that their task was merely to remain true to them. As a result traditional Jeffersonian principles acquired additional legitimacy; the mantle of nationalism was wrapped around them. For radicals in the North the effect was to sanction their opposition to capitalist development there; they were furnished with a powerful set of arguments and with a potent oppositional tradition. But absent, of course, was any real concern with slavery. As we shall

---

59. See below, Chapter 2

see again and again, the Jeffersonian tradition, with its racism, its emphasis on states' rights and its tolerance of southern slavery, worked to disable northern antislavery sentiment.[60] Indeed, as we shall also see, many Jeffersonians (and Jacksonians too) followed the Sage of Monticello in viewing abolitionism as Federalism in disguise. Jefferson's achievement was to establish afresh the meaning of the nation; but his achievement had depended upon, bore the imprint of, and thus helped perpetuate, slavery in the South.

II

This advancement of class interests requires careful specification and theorization. Clearly it should be distinguished from the naked forms of control that some dominant groups in history have been able to establish and which, indeed, many planters enjoyed in their dealings with their own slaves. The social thinker who gave most thought to this question, at least in the twentieth century, and to whose work it is most appropriate to turn, has probably been the great Italian Marxist, Antonio Gramsci. One of Gramsci's key concepts was "hegemony." Though it had been used previously by Lenin (and other Marxists), Gramsci began to use the term in the 1920s in order to explain the failure of revolution in the West following the Bolshevik seizure of power. At its core is the idea of leadership, intellectual, moral and cultural – exercised by a class so as to produce a significant measure of consent on the part of those governed and dominated by that class. Gramsci himself did not specify the necessary conditions for hegemony and it is clear that he recognized that the extent to which hegemonic values pervade a society can vary. In an extreme case the entire population might embrace the dominant values as ideal ones; at the other extreme people might believe them to be deficient but acquiesce in them out of a fear that any alternative would surely be worse. There are thus different degrees of hegemonic control and only rarely will hegemony lead to the complete ideological incorporation of the lower classes.[61]

The concept of hegemony was designed to shed light on the failure of revolution; the goal was to explain the stability of certain regimes. Gramsci did not believe that hegemony was a characteristic of all societies and it is probable that he doubted whether it existed before the rise of the bourgeoisie. Yet there is good reason to describe the slaveholders' power

---

60. Some of these features of Jeffersonianism, however, such as its racism, fueled the free soil movement. See below, Chapter 6.
61. It is thus important not to exaggerate the degree of consensus implied by the notion of hegemony.

in the politics of the antebellum republic (though not on their own plantations) as hegemonic. In a sense this example goes beyond Gramsci's normal use of the term, which generally implied a greater degree of purposive action on the part of the hegemonic class, a fuller political self-awareness as it were, than I have found within the Jeffersonian slaveholders. But Gramsci's task was to undermine mechanistic models, derived from Marxism, of the relationship between economic and political power, in which the latter was simply reduced to the former. He insisted that a hegemonic class was able to transcend its immediate, narrowly conceived, economic interests and present itself, with a reasonable degree of plausibility, as acting in the general interest.

Such was the manner in which the slaveholders of the South advanced their interests. Their hegemony manifested itself in various forms. It operated so as to foreclose certain options, to make some more attractive than others, to predispose Americans to view events within a specific framework. It encouraged certain actions by clothing them with the respectability of tradition or by identifying them with the prestige of the nation. The slaveholders' interests were thus furthered in a variety of complex and subtle ways, and sometimes merely by undermining or disabling ideas that might serve antagonistic interests. In effect this southern elite had insinuated itself and its interests into not merely the economic structure of the nation but also its political system, its institutions, and its social practices; above all perhaps it had penetrated deep into the realm of what large numbers of Americans simply took for granted. The special subtlety of the American example arises from the fact that the ideas of this hegemonic group were most clearly associated with a man who believed himself not the champion but instead the enemy of that class interest. This cloak itself, though a cause of future difficulty, would remain for many years yet another source of hegemonic power.[62]

Sectionalism before 1820

The relationship between slavery and the party of Jefferson became manifest when the state of Missouri, with its constitution which tolerated slavery, applied to join the Union. The climactic events that followed make the Missouri Crisis worthy of careful consideration. But we need first to consider the relations between North and South in the earliest decades of the Republic. At the time of the American Revolution, slavery had, of course, existed throughout the nation. But it never possessed in

62. John Urry, *The Anatomy of Capitalist Societies: The Economy, Civil Society and the State* (London, 1981), p. 23.

the North the importance it had at the South so that even though some individual northerners were dependent for their wealth upon their slaveholding, no northern state's economy rested upon it. For a variety of reasons (which do not need to be considered here) the North in the aftermath of the revolution gradually moved against the institution.[63] It is important not to exaggerate the hostility of the North to slavery. Abolition proceeded in many states quite slowly and even as late as 1820 there were fears that Illinois, for example, might yet succumb and allow slaveholders to enter with their slaves.[64] Nevertheless there was by 1820 a firm and widespread conviction in the North that slavery was undesirable for a variety of reasons, both economic and moral.

This conviction fueled the Missouri Crisis. What made it different from previous conflicts over slavery, however, was a general realization that the time had come for action against the South. Ever since the founding of the Republic there had been clashes between northerners and southerners over the question and it is almost certain that without the safeguards and guarantees given by the founding fathers (especially the three-fifths clause) Georgia and South Carolina, at least, would not have remained in the Union. Sometimes in the 1780s and 1790s, debates over slavery were conducted with great bitterness and acrimony. Yet there was no sustained or concerted antislavery campaign waged by northern politicians in these years. Politics in the 1790s, for example, did not revolve at all around the slavery question and when northern opponents of the peculiar institution did seek to drum up support, their attempts invariably ended in failure. One reason for this was that northerners were able, quite plausibly, to believe that time was on their side. The antislavery cause was still, it seemed as late as 1810, making considerable advances. In New Jersey, for example, abolition had triumphed as recently as 1807. Even more important, the slave trade had just been abolished and it was still possible to hope, as northerners had long hoped, that without the trade, slavery itself was doomed. More important still, the economic problems afflicting the Upper South made the prospect of abolition in Maryland a realistic one. And if Maryland got rid of her slaves, might not Virginia, the largest and most important of all the slave states, follow suit? In these circumstances a northern opponent of slavery could afford to sit and patiently wait.[65]

63. See Arthur Zilversmit, *The First Emancipation: The Abolition of Slavery in the North* (Chicago, 1967).
64. MacLeod, *Slavery, Race* . . , pp. 12, 102. It should perhaps be noted that Illinois had a large southern population at this time.
65. MacLeod, *Slavery, Race* . . , pp. 103–105.

Ten years later, however, the situation had been transformed. In the aftermath of the War of 1812 came a cotton boom and suddenly an institution that had looked outmoded and obsolete now seemed fresh and dynamic. In the deep South huge fortunes were being made and the new states of the Southwest, acquired by Jefferson's purchase of Louisiana, threatened to offer a permanent and safe future for the slaveholders. The alarming conclusion was that while the international slave trade had obviously depended upon slavery, the converse was not true. Slavery had sunk its roots deep into American soil.

Many northerners were affected by a sincere moral repugnance against slavery that was deepened by the wave of benevolence and philanthropy which was sweeping over the country at this time and which would peak in the 1820s and 1830s. But they were concerned too by an issue which appealed to a larger constituency in the North: the political power of the South in the Union. After 1800 many New England Federalists had watched the Republican electoral triumphs with increasing dismay and had concluded that New England was now a permanent and exploited minority in the nation. The Louisiana Purchase opened up the prospect of an indefinite future of Republican victories, effected principally by the states of the South, though in conjunction, of course, with their northern allies. In the first decades of the nineteenth century it was the New England states which were contemplating secession. Nor was dissatisfaction confined to New England. Other northerners were resentful at southern possession of the offices of government. In 1812 De Witt Clinton of New York, though himself a Republican, ran for President against Madison. Although he lost, opposition to southern dictation was a major campaign issue. Federalists and Clintonians were to be the two most militant groups in the North during the Missouri Crisis. Both would point repeatedly to the danger that an increase in the number of slaveholding states would upset the balance of power between the sections in the federal government, and especially in the Senate.[66]

What then was the southern view of slavery before 1820? In fact it would be more appropriate to speak of views rather than of a view, and still more accurate to refer to a spectrum of opinion. At one extreme, defenses of slavery had been offered in Congress prior to the debates over Missouri, defenses which were largely unqualified and which anticipated those which Calhoun and other southerners would present from the late 1820s onwards. At the other extreme there were many antislavery societies south of the Mason-Dixon line; indeed as late as 1827 the South could boast more such societies than the North. Yet these were entirely

66. Moore, *Missouri Controversy*, pp. 10–17.

in the Upper South and the great majority were either in east Tennessee or in the Quaker counties of North Carolina. Neither antislavery nor an explicit proslavery was typical in the South in the first two decades of the nineteenth century. In reconstructing southern opinion on the subject, it is important to distinguish sharply between the slave trade and slavery itself. Many southerners, especially from the Upper South, favored a speedy abolition of the slave trade yet would have been unwilling to take any action at all against slavery itself. In some cases, indeed, abolition of the trade was advocated precisely to safeguard and protect slavery, since it was feared that an excess of slaves, consequent upon continued importations from Africa, would render the entire labor system uneconomic as well as unsafe. Yet northerners often failed to appreciate the distinction and assumed that an attack on the slave trade was a declaration of war on slavery itself. The South Carolinians and Georgians who defended both, encouraged this mistake. And the confusion was increased by those southerners like George Mason who, at the constitutional convention of 1787, made a series of remarks which seemed to condemn slavery only to advocate abolition of the trade as a means of protecting the institution.[67]

Other prominent Virginians, like Thomas Jefferson and George Washington, had expressed serious reservations about slavery, though as we have seen, Jefferson did little to carry them into practice. In the era where the slave trade had been a principal subject of concern, Virginians had blamed the British Crown for the trade and often given the impression that they had had inflicted upon them, entirely without their consent, an unjust labor system. But in the most strategic parts of the state antislavery sentiment never had deep roots. Especially in the politically dominant east, it withered or flourished with the economic prospects of the slaveholders themselves. During the Missouri Crisis, northerners were to be surprised and alarmed at Virginia's determination to ally herself with, indeed to give leadership to, the slaveholding South.[68]

Yet it is doubtful whether northerners were justified in concluding that most Virginians, or southerners generally, had revised their opinions about slavery. The significance of the Missouri Compromise was rather different: it compelled many in the South to establish their priorities. Previously it had been possible for them to acknowledge the evil of slavery, while at the same time noting the dangers and impracticalities of emancipation and insisting that climatic factors made black labor essen-

67. Moore, *Missouri Controversy*, pp. 30–32; MacLeod, *Slavery, Race . . .* , pp. 34–38.
68. For Washington's views see MacLeod, *Slavery, Race . . .* , pp. 131–135; Davis, *Problem of Slavery in Age of Revolution*, pp. 165, 170–171.

tial.[69] So long as there was no federal assault upon the institution a painful assessment of priorities had been avoidable. Yet even before 1820 the question of the extension of slavery – the thorniest one raised in the debate over Missouri – had been aired. Even at that time many southerners had claimed that to exclude slaveholders from the West would be an act of gross injustice and would moreover worsen the condition of the slaves (since western lands were superior) and thereby increase the dangers of servile insurrection. As early as 1798, for example, southerners had offered fierce resistance when northerners had attempted to abolish slavery in the Mississippi territory. Nonetheless southern, and especially Virginian, opposition to what would later be called the free soil doctrine came as a profound shock to many northerners.[70]

Their disappointment flowed from their perception or, it might be more accurate to say, their misperception of the Northwest Ordinance of 1787. The sixth article of that enactment had barred slavery from the Old Northwest and had in the North acquired enormous symbolic importance by 1820. (In the 1850s its symbolic importance would rise even higher.) As Duncan MacLeod points out, it had become such a potent symbol as a result of its timing and the unanimity with which it was passed. It served as a reminder of the harmony that had characterized North and South at the time of the Revolution. It reaffirmed the nation's commitment to liberty. It seemed to demonstrate that there had been a time when all Americans, whether living in a slave society or not, had agreed that the nation's future lay with freedom and not with slavery. The role of Virginia, in ceding the territory in question and in providing the statesman, Thomas Jefferson, who inspired the legislation, was particularly significant. It meant that Virginians who later opposed a policy of free soil would be regarded as apostates, traitors to the glorious and selfless tradition established by their revolutionary forebears.[71]

The reality was somewhat different. Jefferson's role was indeed an important one and it probably represents the high-water mark of his antislavery actions, as opposed to his antislavery rhetoric. As he originally drafted it in 1784, the bill that would become the basis of the Ordinance three years later stipulated that slavery would be eliminated from all the western lands held by Congress by 1800. This delay was an implicit recognition of the property rights invested in slavery since some slaveholders had already migrated to the territories in question with their slaves. Yet even in this form the act was voted down by southerners with

69. It was also said that unless enslaved the blacks would not work.
70. MacLeod, *Slavery, Race* . . . , p. 12; Moore, *Missouri Controversy*, pp. 29–30.
71. This and the following paragraph are based entirely upon MacLeod, *Slavery, Race* . . . , pp. 47–61.

Jefferson himself one of only two southern delegates to support it. Three years later, however, the Ordinance was passed unanimously. One reason for the reversal of fortune may have been that there was now no attempt to free the small number of slaves already in the territories, not even at a remote date in the future. But more important was a southern fear that slave states in the Northwest might compete successfully with southern states in the production of staple crops, especially tobacco. By the time it had become apparent that these fears were illusory, the Louisiana Purchase had created considerably better opportunities for slaveholders in the Southwest both in cotton and sugar, a new crop for the United States. As a result there was no pressure from southerners to reopen the question. Thus the unanimity with which the Ordinance was passed and upheld was largely fortuitous and the impression of southern sentiment which it conveyed was highly misleading. And its author, Thomas Jefferson himself, in 1820 repudiated outright the claim that the Ordinance had established a precedent for Missouri.

But even if their reading of the Northwest Ordinance had been correct, northerners still erred in assuming that what the South would concede for the Northwest it would concede for the Southwest or for the territory of Missouri. One problem in determining the fate of that territory was that while the Ohio river provided an obvious boundary between slave and free territory east of the Mississippi, there was no such natural boundary to the west. In retrospect it is clear that whether the line were placed on the southern or northern border of Missouri one of the two sections would feel highly aggrieved, especially since with the admission of Alabama into the Union each section now had eleven states. Slavery had existed under French and Spanish law throughout the area of the Louisiana Purchase and slaveholders had taken their slaves into Missouri. As a result, when Missourians petitioned Congress for admission into the Union, they assumed that slavery would be left untouched. But as we have seen, northerners had reason to react differently.

The Missouri Crisis (2)

I

The Missouri Crisis was the most important event in the conflict between North and South until the controversy over the Wilmot Proviso engulfed the nation at mid-century. Its significance was threefold. First, it clarified many issues which had hitherto remained obscure and demonstrated in the most vivid way where the key points of sectional controversy now lay. Second, it served as a curtain-raiser to the debate over the territories which would erupt in the late 1840s and which would ultimately precipitate secession and the Civil War. Many of the arguments used on each side of that debate were aired in the struggle over Missouri between 1819 and 1821. Third, and perhaps most important, it offered a clear example of the power of the slaveholding class in American politics, exercised as it had been before, and would be so many times in the next forty years, through the party which Thomas Jefferson had founded in the 1790s.

The Congressional debate began immediately after Tallmadge introduced his portentous amendment. It is important to consider the arguments presented by both sides, since they anticipated in important ways those employed a generation later. Let us begin with the North. Northerners were alarmed and genuinely disconcerted by the vehemence with which the South asserted the rights of slaveholders present and future in Missouri. Two days after Tallmadge's resolution his close ally, John W. Taylor of New York, reminded southerners of their traditional criticisms of slavery. He recalled "their own declarations on the subject of slavery" and remembered "how often and how eloquently," they had "deplored its existence among them." He noted that they had previously evinced not merely "willingness" but "solicitude" to be rid of the burden. Southerners, he continued, had blamed Great Britain for inflicting the evil upon them. Now they had an opportunity to ensure that future generations could be rid of it in the western territories. Otherwise those future generations would be compelled to resort to a similar argument: they too would blame their forebears, the evil would persist and the opportunity for eradicating it would be gone forever.[72]

Undoubtedly Taylor was challenging the southern delegation. But it was not merely a taunt. He almost certainly felt genuine surprise and dismay at southern attitudes. Similarly Arthur Livermore of New Hampshire showed how for him southern insistence on the extension of slavery into Missouri had suddenly discredited not merely the notion of gradual abolition but also the colonization society, the Bible societies of the South and even the motives for which the African slave trade had been abolished:

> Let us no longer tell idle tales about the gradual abolition of slavery; away with colonization societies, if their design is only to rid us of free blacks and turbulent slaves; have done also with bible societies, whose views are extended to Africa and the East Indies, while they overlook the deplorable condition of their sable brethren within our own borders; make no more laws to prohibit the importation of slaves; for the world must see that the object of such laws is alone to prevent the glutting of a prodigious market for the flesh and blood

72. *Annals*, 15 Congress, 2 Session, p. 1174.

of men, which we are about to establish in the West, and to enhance the price of sturdy wretches, reared like black cattle and horses for sale on our own plantations.

Southern attitudes to slavery were clarified during the Missouri Crisis and northerners now began to see clearly what they had previously only glimpsed. Slavery, they now realized, threatened to become a permanent feature of the American landscape.[73]

The result was a critical commentary upon southern society, the southern economy and southern politics such as the nation had never before witnessed. Some northerners focused on the injustice done to the enslaved blacks. Arthur Livermore of New Hampshire, Walter Lowrie, John Sergeant and Jonathan Roberts of Pennsylvania, Charles Rich of Vermont and Timothy Fuller of Massachusetts all noted the effects of slavery upon the slave family.[74] William Plumer of New Hampshire argued that the domestic slave trade was as pernicious as the African trade since in each case the result was "the breach of every tender and every domestic tie – the separation of parents from their children, of husbands from their wives, and of friends and connexions from those with whom, from infancy, they have been united." Arthur Livermore added that slaves were unable to acquire knowledge and made the rather dubious claim that they were denied all knowledge of the Bible. Other northerners recurred to the Declaration of Independence and claimed that its explicit egalitarianism was at war with slavery. John W. Taylor of New York cited this "first truth declared by this nation, at the era of its independence," and asked whether it had now become "a solemn mockery" in the light of southern demands for slavery. Northerners were of course on difficult ground here, since they had to show that republican values proscribed slavery, without going so far as to deny that the existing slave states were actually in possession of a republican form of government. But the debates show that for many northern congressmen, the ideals of the nation had some application to blacks, whether slave or free.[75]

Yet in 1819–1821 concern for the enslaved was, as it would remain throughout the antebellum era, subordinate to concern for the white race. When northerners engaged in criticism of slavery, they spent more time on its effects upon white society than on the injustices done to the slave. A resolution sent to Congress by the State Legislature of Vermont succinctly

73. *Annals*, 15 Congress, 2 Session, p. 1194.
74. *Annals*, 15 Congress, 2 Session, p. 1191, 16 Congress, 1 Session, pp. 207, 343, 1215, 1432–1433, 1486.
75. *Annals*, 16 Congress, 1 Session, pp. 1432–1433, 15 Congress, 2 Session, p. 1191; Detweiler, "Congressional Debate on Slavery," p. 607.

complained that slavery "paralyzes industry," to the detriment, of course, of the entire economy. A common stratagem was to compare the economy of the North with that of the South. This was an approach favored by John W. Taylor of New York. Taylor lamented the introduction of slavery into Maryland and claimed that in its absence her "numerous and extensive old fields, which now appear to be worse than useless, would long since have supported a dense population of industrious freemen, and contributed largely to the strength and resources of the State." More explicitly, he entered into a lengthy comparison of Maryland with Pennsylvania:

> Who has travelled along the line which divides that State from Pennsylvania, and has not observed that no monuments are necessary to mark the boundary; that it is easily traced by following the dividing line between farms highly cultivated and plantations laying open to the common and overrun with weeds; between stone barns and stone bridges on one side, and stalk cribs and no bridges on the other; between a neat, blooming, rosy-cheeked peasantry on the one side, and a squalid, slow-motioned, black population on the other?

As Taylor later argued, it was surely the height of folly for Congress to hesitate a moment in deciding the fate of Missouri. So long as "improved lands" were "more valuable to a State than barren wastes," so long as "a compact population of freemen" was "better than hordes of slaves," the choice was obvious: Missouri must be free.[76]

A more detailed analysis of the economic effects of slavery was offered to the House by William Plumer of New Hampshire. Plumer began by noting that agriculture, commerce and manufacturing were "the three great sources of national wealth." Manufactures, he asserted, hardly existed "in countries where slavery prevails to any great extent." As far as commerce was concerned, the damaging effects of slavery were so obvious that "not a word need be said" on the subject. Plumer nevertheless could not resist the temptation to say a few more words. "Who ever heard of a mercantile people," he asked, "engaging in the pursuits of commerce with the labor of servile hands?" He continued by noting that "the commerce and navigation of the United States belong principally to the non-slaveholding States." He then added that American seamen, who had triumphed on all the seas of the world, "were not only freemen themselves, but born and nurtured in a land where slavery is unknown." Finally, Plumer considered agriculture. Here too he found the record of the slave South lamentable. It was in the fields, of course, that slave labor

76. *Annals*, 16 Congress, 2 Session, p. 78, 15 Congress, 2 Session, p. 1178, 16 Congress, 1 Session, p. 953.

was most commonly employed. But while such labor appeared to be cheap, costing only the "subsistence" of the slaves, it was "in effect the dearest and least profitable of all kinds of labor." Plumer now drew attention to one of the chief failings of slavery, one that would be emphasized by antislavery spokesmen as long as slavery existed in the nation: the slaves' lack of incentive. "Feeling no other motive than the fear of punishment," he declared, the slaves "labor slowly and with great reluctance, and seek only how they may escape with the least possible exertion from their daily, and to them unprofitable tasks." As a result slavery failed in agriculture, just as it failed in commerce and manufacturing. "The slave and his task-master," Plumer concluded, "placed in a land flowing with milk and honey, would convert even the garden of Eden into a desert and a waste."[77]

Even this, however, did not exhaust the economic arguments against slavery. Some northerners revived the traditional charge that slavery encouraged idleness on the part of the slaveholder and a debilitating love of luxury. The corollary was still more important: labor was not esteemed in slave societies in general and in the South in particular. John Sergeant argued that the effect of slavery in Missouri would be either to "banish free labor" or to "place it under such discouragement and opprobrium as are equivalent in effect." Timothy Fuller of Massachusetts concurred and claimed that in a slave society "those who are obliged to earn their subsistence by their own exertions and labor, are in a state of hopeless subservience." The problem was that, as John W. Taylor explained, easterners would not go to a Missouri in which slavery was tolerated. They wished to contribute to a society in which labor was esteemed, not degraded and "you cannot degrade it more effectually than by establishing a system where it shall be performed principally by slaves." "The business in which they are generally engaged," he asserted, "be it what it may, soon becomes debased in public estimation." "It is considered," he noted, "low and unfit for freemen."[78]

Taylor then went on to offer a political indictment of the South which other northerners endorsed and which anticipated the northern attacks of the 1850s upon the "Slave Power." As a result of the degradation of labor in the South, non-slaveholders, he complained, were not elected to office. "When have we seen a Representative on this floor, from that section of the Union," he asked, "who was not a slaveholder?" Only slaveholders were elected to Congress or the state legislatures of the South, and only they were appointed to high executive or judicial office. Other north-

---

77. *Annals*, 16 Congress, 1 Session, p. 1427. See also 16 Congress, 1 Session, p. 1487.
78. *Annals*, 16 Congress, 1 Session, pp. 1213, 1484, 15 Congress, 2 Session, pp. 1176–1177.

erners rounded upon the three-fifths clause of the constitution and claimed that it violated true republican principles. (One congressman claimed that it was never intended to apply to new states in any case, only the original slaveholding states.) James Tallmadge himself, who had of course launched the entire debate over slavery in Missouri, made a charge that would in later decades feature prominently in the sectional controversy and which would form part of the arraignment of the "Slave Power." Edward Colston of Virginia had already interrupted one northern congressman to warn him that his references to the Declaration of Independence might be overheard by slaves working in Congress itself. He had also accused another of seeking to incite a servile war. Tallmadge now complained of this challenge to free speech. "Has it already come to this," he asked, "that in the Congress of the United States . . . the subject of slavery has become a subject of so much jealousy – of such delicacy – of such danger, that it cannot safely be discussed?" How absurd it was to consider extending slavery into Missouri and thus extending a power which was already at war with the principle of free speech. At this moment the debate anticipated that which would occur in the 1830s and early 1840s over the gag rule.[79] Of course, some of the northern charges against slavery derived their force from recent events. Northerners claimed, and southerners denied, that slavery left the country vulnerable to foreign invaders. Here memories of the War of 1812 were very much in evidence. But in general the arguments made by northerners between 1819 and 1821 would reappear again and again in the final decades of the antebellum republic. And as we have already seen, the debate in 1820 looked ahead too to secession and war between the sections.

II

We have already noted that some southerners believed that civil war was high on the northern political agenda. But it is probable that a larger number of them feared that the North was engaged in a longer campaign, a war of attrition which would begin by denying southerners their equal rights within the Union and end, perhaps much later, in a direct assault upon the peculiar institution. Hence they insisted upon southern rights in the West. And neither for the first nor the last time they equated the rights of southerners with the rights of slaveholders. If slaveholders were banned from Missouri, this constituted an affront to the entire South.

---

79. *Annals*, 15 Congress, 2 Session, pp. 1177, 1213, 16 Congress, 1 Session, p. 217, 15 Congress, 2 Session, pp. 1205–1206.

Such reasoning was explicit when Philip Barbour argued that the master was attached to, and needed the labor of his slave in Missouri. "Under these circumstances," Barbour concluded, "a prohibition of slaves would, in almost every instance, be tantamount to a prohibition of the emigration of the Southern people to the State of Missouri." On other occasions the reasoning was implicit, as when Felix Walker of North Carolina reminded northerners that the South had already given up the Northwest. Since she had nonetheless contributed her share to the purchase of Louisiana, it was entirely unjust to deny her access to Missouri. Even though only a very small number of southern spokesmen had now arrived at the conclusion that slavery was a positive good, a much larger number clearly assumed that the rights of the South were synonymous with the rights of the slaveholder.[80]

Many southerners were therefore faced with a difficult problem. They had to acknowledge that slavery was an evil and at the same time demand that it be allowed to spread. An obvious solution to the problem was to claim that an extension of slavery would actually mitigate its evils. This was the strategy employed by Felix Walker of North Carolina:

> Slavery is an evil we have long deplored but cannot cure; it was entailed upon us by our ancestors; it was not our original sin, and we cannot, in our present situation, release ourselves from the embarrassment; and, as it is an evil, the more diffusive, the lighter it will be felt, and the wider it is extended, the more equal the proportion, of inconvenience.

Some southerners argued that the extension of slavery would improve the lot of the slave. John Scott, the delegate from Missouri itself, claimed that the climate in Missouri was more congenial for the slave. But in comparing his own territory with the Deep South he unwittingly confirmed the fear of northern humanitarians concerning the treatment received by many slaves. If the blacks were confined to "Southern latitudes," he warned congressmen, they would be consigned "to long scorching days of labor and fatigue" in "swamps and morasses." He was thus one of many southerners who endorsed the view that the "diffusion" of slavery was desirable. Other southerners developed the "diffusion" argument in what may have been a safer manner when they claimed that the alternative was an ever denser slave population in the original southern states. They then made the further claim that smaller slaveholdings, in general, meant milder treatment for the slave. Hence the extension of slavery, once again, was in the interest of the slave himself.[81]

80.　*Annals*, 15 Congress, 2 Session, pp. 1188, 1226.
81.　*Annals*, 15 Congress, 2 Session, pp. 1227, 1202, 1187, 1234.

How valid was the "diffusion" argument? It is easy to appreciate the force of the northern rejoinder that an evil should not be allowed to spread. "Diffusion," as Daniel Raymond neatly put it, "is about as effectual a remedy for slavery as it would be for the small pox, or the plague." But we should be reluctant to conclude that southerners were simply being hypocritical. Apart from anything else, the well-being of the slave was sometimes presented as a factor which was of desperate concern to the whites – and for the least altruistic of reasons. Thus Philip Barbour endorsed the "diffusion" argument and confirmed that the slaves would indeed benefit. But he also claimed that "their motives to insurrection" would accordingly "diminish." Senator Freeman Walker of Georgia echoed Barbour's words when he declared that if the slaves "should ever do us harm, it will be by their dense population: when they can act in concert at short notice." "But," he added, "this is a topic too delicate to touch."[82]

Perhaps the major effect of the Missouri Crisis was to encourage some southerners to clarify their views on slavery. In the past it had been relatively easy for them to ignore the tension, if not the outright contradiction, between the ideals of the Declaration of Independence and the fact of slaveholding. So long as the peculiar institution was not being challenged, the problem was containable and the Declaration need not be reinterpreted so as to exclude the slave. It was possible for southerners to express nebulous hopes for the future, to trust, as the author of the Declaration himself was trusting, to time. The northern assault upon slavery unleashed by the Missouri Crisis, however, prompted a reappraisal. John Tyler of Virginia, later of course to become President of the United States, developed one line of thought when he expressed an affection for the Declaration "as an abstract truth." But "can this proposition," he asked, "admit of application to a state of society?" Tyler's next question showed his doubts: "does not its fallacy meet you in every walk of life?" Abandoning the rhetorical mode, he asserted that "distinctions will exist" and listed "virtue and vice, wealth and poverty, industry and idleness" as the qualities which operated as "barriers, which human power cannot break down," but "which will ever prevent us from carrying into operation, *in extenso*, this great principle." The principles enshrined in the Declaration "although lovely and beautiful," could not "obliterate those distinctions in society which society itself engenders and

---

82. *Annals*, 15 Congress, 2 Session, p. 1190, 16 Congress, 1 Session, p. 174. For a recent interpretation of the South that takes the diffusion argument very seriously see William W. Freehling, *The Road to Disunion: Secessionists at Bay* (N.Y., 1990).

gives birth to." Only as an abstract truth, then, but not as a guide to practical action, could the Declaration be read and understood.[83]

Tyler's understanding of the Declaration was problematic, however. If it had no practical application in 1820, why should it have had one in 1776? And if it had no practical application in 1776 then its importance as an event in world history shrank accordingly. Perhaps mindful of this problem, other southerners instead re-interpreted the Declaration and insisted that it was a proclamation of the liberty and equality of whites. Otherwise, Nathaniel Macon of North Carolina asked, why did Thomas Jefferson himself not advocate abolition? To those northerners who sought to enlist Jefferson in the antislavery cause, primarily by citing his famous remarks in the *Notes on Virginia*, Macon retorted that "what ought to be inferred from Mr Jefferson's notes and life, is that he thinks slavery is a curse, but thinks it a greater curse to emancipate, in his native Virginia." Macon concluded that "his democracy appears . . . to be of the white family. The implications for the Declaration were obvious.[84]

Southerners were indeed awkwardly placed in 1820. Their attitude to slavery was in a transitional phase, uneasily poised between the revolutionary generation's acknowledgment of a "necessary evil" and the advocacy, increasingly widespread in the final antebellum decades, of "positive good" theories. A striking feature of the debates of 1819–1821 is that neither southerners nor northerners were quite able to describe sentiment accurately. Northerners were wont to assert, quite incorrectly, that all Americans agreed that slavery was an evil. Louis McLane of Delaware, who was actually committed to the southern position, expressed a conviction "that there was no quarter of the country in which slavery is more seriously deplored than in the South." This was a highly dubious claim and an extremely misleading one, since he ought to have added that in no section was it more warmly embraced than in the South. But the errors of the congressmen were understandable; many southerners continued to assert that slavery was indeed an evil. A typical attitude was perhaps that of James Barbour, one of Virginia's Senators. After praising the great slave societies of antiquity, he disavowed any intention to defend slavery as a positive good. "Let it not be supposed," he explained to the Senate, "that in the abstract I am advocating slavery." For "like all other human things, it is mixed with good and evil – the latter, no doubt, preponderating." Barbour subscribed to the centuries-old view that slavery was a consequence of the sinful nature of man or,

83. *Annals*, 16 Congress, 1 Session, p. 1384.
84. *Annals*, 16 Congress, 1 Session, pp. 227–229. See also Detweiler, "Congressional Debate on Slavery," *passim*. Some southerners in fact used the Declaration to justify an insistence on southern (slaveholders') rights.

alternatively, a God-given institution which man ought not to challenge. In practice these two possibilities merged into one since the inevitable consequence was that slavery was sin but also ineradicable: it was truly a "necessary evil." Barbour had here moved some way from Thomas Jefferson. Whereas in practice, for by far the greater part of his career, Jefferson acquiesced in slavery, in theory he remained committed to the goal of abolition. Barbour, on the other hand, claimed that slavery was in harmony with God's will and used historical precedent to deny the feasibility of abolition:

> Whether slavery was ordained by God himself, in a particular revelation to his chosen people, or whether he has merely permitted it as a part of that moral evil, which seems to be the inevitable portion of man, are questions I will not approach. I leave them to the casuists and the divines. It is sufficient for us, as statesmen, to know that it has existed from the earliest ages of the world, and . . . no remedy, even plausible, has been suggested; though wisdom and benevolence united have unceasingly brooded over the subject.

While he acknowledged the evil of slavery, Barbour thus placed little emphasis upon it.[85] And here his attitude was undoubtedly typical of those southerners who asserted the rights of slaveholders in Missouri while conceding that slavery was an evil. Yet an observer in Congress listening attentively to the debates would have found it difficult to say which of the criticisms of slavery these men accepted. Usually the acknowledgment was cursory and vague. It is probable that most of them rejected the arguments about the effects of slavery upon the southern economy, or the claim that slavery made labor dishonorable. Undoubtedly they repudiated the charge that the non-slaveholders were dishonored in the South. Nor (like Barbour) did they accept that slavery was in conflict with the Bible in general or the Golden Rule in particular. And the claim that slaves were badly treated failed to move many southerners. Nathaniel Macon of North Carolina, without endorsing the "positive good" argument, nonetheless asserted that aged slaves were better cared for "than any poor in the world." Similarly Feeman Walker of Georgia, again without adopting an explicitly proslavery position, claimed that, to the best of his knowledge, the slaves were "well clothed, well fed, and treated with kindness and humanity." Moreover, they were "cheerful and apparently happy." So what was it about slavery that made it an evil? In a general sense, these southerners merely

---

85. *Annals*, 15 Congress, 2 Session, p. 1228. Barbour's speech was published in full as *Speech of Mr. Barbour, of Virginia, on the Restriction of Slavery in Missouri ... in the Senate, Jan. 31, 1820* (n.p., n.d.). See especially pp. 14–15, 23–25.

acknowledged that the United States would have been better off without any slaves within her borders. Slavery was sin but southern slaveholders were not on that account sinners.[86]

A small minority of southerners did, however, move beyond their colleagues and closer or even onto ground that would later be occupied by the proslavery theorists. Surprisingly perhaps, since his later career took him away from such positions, Richard M. Johnson of Kentucky, a future Vice-President of the United States, was one of those who made a lengthy and favorable comparison of southern slave society with the free labor system of the North. Johnson recounted his surprise when he first came to Congress at the spectacle of "citizens from the non-slaveholding States . . . riding in a coach and four, with a white servant seated before, managing the reins, another standing behind the coach, and both of these white servants in livery." These servants, who possessed the vote and "on whose voice the liberties of the country" might consequently "depend," were, in Johnson's view, in a "degraded condition." He explained that he "could not reconcile it" with his "ideas of freedom" because "in the State where I received my first impressions, slaves alone were servile." The result was that "all white men there are on an equality, and every citizen feels his independence." The equality to which Johnson referred was not, of course, an equality of wealth; rather it was the absence of class divisions coupled with an equality of esteem. As a result, in the South "we have no classes – no patrician or plebeian rank." The conditions of white men might differ but this did not modify the operation of the egalitarian creed. "Whatever may be the condition of a citizen with us," Johnson insisted, "you must treat him as an equal."[87]

In the North, however, Johnson observed a different and much less satisfactory condition of society. There "ranks and distinctions, the precursors of aristocracy, already begin to exist." He then went a little way to confirming northern suspicions about the status of labor in the South. But he added a crucial qualification, one that would be made repeatedly by southerners over the coming decades: manual labor was not itself dishonorable but menial labor was. "They whose business it is to perform menial offices in other states," he declared, "are as servile as our slaves in the South." Between the servant "who keeps your stable," who "blacks your boots," who "holds your stirrup, or mounts behind your coach when you ride," he claimed, and the actual slave, there was "a nominal difference" only. "In the one case," he continued, the dependence "is called voluntary, because it is imposed by its own necessity," whereas in the other it was dubbed "involuntary, because imposed by the will of

---

86. *Annals*, 16 Congress, 1 Session, pp. 226, 173.
87. *Annals*, 16 Congress, 1 Session, pp. 347–349.

another." But "whatever difference there may be in the principle, the effects upon society are the same." Johnson also went on to argue that the material condition of the slave was in many respects superior to that of the northern servant.[88]

Johnson's derogatory remarks about northern society anticipated those which would be made by the proslavery thinkers of the late antebellum decades. But there was a significant difference. His comparison was apparently with the landed or perhaps the mercantile elites of the North; he attacked the practices of those who had servants, who kept horses and who rode in carriages. In later years the comparison would instead be between slaves and northern wage laborers employed not primarily as domestic servants but in production, and especially factory production. The southern emphasis thus shifted from consumption to production and reflected the increasing importance of wage labor in the northern economy.[89]

This and other characteristics of Johnson's argument were apparent in a speech by a fellow Kentuckian, William Brown. Brown criticized northern society for the inequalities which it fostered between rich and poor. The poor, he claimed, stood in awe of the rich and he cited the example of cooks, shoe-blacks, and scullions. Once again domestic service was the assumed form of dependence. Like Johnson, Brown asserted that in the North "the miserable, poor, and laboring white man is degraded and dishonored," whereas in the South, "he is saved and redeemed by the intervention of blacks." Inequalities of wealth were inevitable in human society and had existed "since the days of Adam to the present time" but the crucial difference between the slaveholding and the non-slaveholding states "upon this subject is, that the former has degraded their black, and the latter their white brethren, to those servile duties." For "where slavery is tolerated, slaves perform, for others, the servile and menial duties of the stable, the kitchen, and the house." (Brown explained that it was not the performance of these tasks themselves that was dishonorable. The house-wife was not dishonored by doing her own house labor. The stigma attached instead to the performance of such labor for others.) The result was an equality of esteem within the white race: the poor man visited the rich man and was "a welcome guest at his smoking board." Hence it was quite mistaken to claim that slavery made labor dishonorable in the South. With the exception of – and indeed because of – the menial work of slaves, labor was accorded a more respected place in the South than in the North.[90]

---

88. *Annals*, 16 Congress, 1 Session, pp. 349–351.
89. See below, Chapter 4.
90. *Annals*, 16 Congress, 2 Session, pp. 1202–1205.

Johnson and Brown of Kentucky, however, were not the most ardent defenders of slavery in Congress at this time. Although Charles Pinckney of South Carolina, one of the founding fathers, sought to enlist the authority of the Bible in its defense, this distinction belongs to William Smith, also of South Carolina. According to Smith, slavery was an ever-present feature in human history and would remain so as long as human nature was what it was. Smith announced to the Senate that it had "been the lot of man, in this shape or that, to serve one another from all time." By this he meant that "slavery has prevailed in every country on the globe, ever since the flood," and he cited the Romans and the Greeks as highly enlightened peoples who had held slaves. Like Pinckney he found not the slightest challenge to slavery in the Bible; indeed he argued that "the Scriptures teach us that slavery was universally indulged among the holy fathers." Turning his attention to the material condition of southern slaves, he did not claim that they were better off than northern wage workers but he did insist that there was no other "class of laboring people in any country upon the globe" (except the United States) who were "better clothed, better fed," were "more cheerful," "more happy," and "indeed have more liberty and indulgence" than the slaves "of the Southern and Western States." In exempting northern workers, Smith did not take the final step in the proslavery argument. Nevertheless there was little ambivalence in his attitude. He explicitly rejected Jefferson's criticisms of slavery in the *Notes on Virginia*, claiming that they were "the effusions of the speculative philosophy of his young and ardent mind," effusions "which his riper years have corrected." Besides, he added (quite accurately), they were written "to gratify a foreigner, at his own request." Jefferson's specific charges against slavery, he insisted, were entirely unjust: the master had no motive for the "boisterous hostility" to which Jefferson had referred: it was "at war with his interest, and it is at war with his comfort." Instead, he claimed, "the entire commerce between master and slave is patriarchal." In Smith's thought there was clearly no vestige of the "necessary evil" argument. Little wonder that one northerner remarked that he had never heard anyone go so far in defence of slavery.[91]

III

However bitter the clash over the slavery question, moderate opinion in both sections ultimately triumphed, at least so as to ensure the passage of the famous compromise measures. The so-called Missouri Compromise

91. *Annals*, 16 Congress, 1 Session, pp. 1324, 266–270, 279.

subsequently came to be regarded, especially in the North, as a sacred and inviolable compact, but it is important to be clear about the manner in which it was passed and the alignments that the voting revealed. Tallmadge himself had attempted to introduce not one but two crucial amendments to the Missouri bill which Congress had been considering. The first prohibited the further introduction of slaves into the territory; the second freed the children of existing slaves there once they had reached the age of 21. Both measures passed the House of Representatives in February 1819 after a vote that was almost entirely sectional. Every southern representative except two voted against the amendments. Northern opinion was almost as uniformly in favor; 86 northern representatives supported the first amendment, with 10 against; 80 supported the second, with 15 against. But in the Senate the amendments had no chance. Here the southern senators stood firm and managed to attract enough support from the North to ensure the defeat of the amended House bill. Thus the events of 1819–1821 anticipated those of the late 1840s and 1850s with a northern majority in the House of Representatives constantly being frustrated by the power of the South and her allies in the Senate.[92]

In another respect the Missouri Compromise anticipated later controversies between the sections. By the terms of the agreement Missouri was admitted into the Union as a slave state, while in the future slavery was prohibited in the Louisiana Purchase above the 36° 30′ line of latitude. At the same time and in order to maintain the sectional equilibrium Maine was admitted into the Union as a free state. But the compromise resembled the other great settlement of the antebellum years, the Compromise of 1850, in failing to command a majority in Congress in its omnibus form. That is to say, agreement was only secured by taking the items one at a time.[93] The key vote came in the House on the elimination of Tallmadge's antislavery amendments. Fourteen northerners now voted with the South and a further four were absent. These eighteen provided the essential margin of victory. Nevertheless they were only a small minority of northern congressmen; a further 87 refused to remove the antislavery clauses, even after all the dire threats which southerners had uttered. By this time, however, southerners were more willing to compromise. The measure that they were being asked to swallow was, of course, the prohibition of slavery north of 36° 30′. A small majority of southern representatives (39 out of 76 who voted) gave the restriction, and thus the compromise as a whole, their support. (In the Senate the

92. Moore, *Missouri Controversy*, pp. 55–64, 94–111.
93. This applies to the voting in the House of Representatives; in the Senate the situation was different.

majority was larger.) In time the Missouri Compromise came to be regarded in the North as sacrosanct and irrepealable but at the time it secured a majority of southern, but not of northern votes in each chamber of Congress. Indeed at the time it was widely viewed in the North as a southern measure. Nor did it possess at that time any special status. While some statesmen already saw it as a compact between the sections, others considered it instead as an ordinary, repealable legislative measure.[94]

Both these features of the Compromise – its status and its southern orientation – came under scrutiny in the very next session of Congress when Rollin C. Mallary of Vermont introduced an amendment providing for the gradual abolition of slavery in Missouri. This amounted, of course, to a complete repudiation of the Compromise and it received the votes of two-thirds of northern congressmen. Clearly northerners were unhappy with the Compromise struck at the last session, on the grounds that it leaned excessively towards the South. It was for this reason that they challenged the constitution which Missourians now submitted to Congress, citing as unacceptable a provision that prevented free blacks and mulattos from entering the state. The result, of course, was a reopening of the entire controversy and a lengthy debate over the rights of blacks and mulattos within the nation, culminating in a promise by the new state to honor the rights of the citizens of all other states within her borders. Northerners were dissatisfied with the Compromise, even though the North obtained the lion's share of the Louisiana Purchase, perhaps because they felt that as a majority within the nation, they had a clear right to rule.[95]

Similar reasoning led most southerners to accept the Compromise: it was the best a minority could hope to obtain. As Senator Montfort Stokes of North Carolina wrote: "All that we from the slave holding states can do at present is to rescue from the rapacious grasp of these conscientious fanatics a considerable portion of Louisiana, including all the settled parts of that extensive country." Stokes explained that he could see "no means either now or hereafter, of accomplishing this object but by consenting that slavery may be prohibited in the northern portion of the Louisiana purchase." As a result many southerners swallowed their scruples about federal power and set aside their doubts about the constitutionality of Congress's actions regarding slavery in the territories, doubts and scruples that had been in evidence time and time again during the debates of 1819–1821. The state displaying most concern about states' rights at this time was Virginia. South Carolina, by contrast was quieter

94. Moore, *Missouri Controversy*, pp. 89, 107–128.
95. Moore, *Missouri Controversy*, pp. 142, 149.

and her leading statesman, John C. Calhoun gave a cordial welcome to the Compromise. It would not be long, however, before many of the South's leaders, and especially John C. Calhoun and his disciples, would bitterly regret this surrender of states' rights principle.[96]

IV

While the Missouri controversy offered a portent of later sectional strife, the resolution of the controversy was equally revealing of the nature of American antebellum politics. More clearly than ever before the Jeffersonian democratic tradition came to the aid of the slaveholders of the South and enabled them to consolidate their power within their region and within the Republic as a whole. To understand this process we must look first at the response of Jefferson (and Taylor) to the crisis, and then at the way in which their northern allies were in effect induced to surrender any antislavery convictions they might have had in the interests of what they already viewed as the American democratic tradition.

Jefferson was, of course, anything but indifferent to the Missouri Crisis. One might have expected the great opponent of slavery to rejoice that its spread might be stopped. But such was not his concern. Instead, his loyalties were found to lie precisely where a member of the slaveholding elite's loyalties would be expected to lie: with his fellow slaveholders. Yet here as ever there was no direct defence of slavery, instead a series of maneuvers and stratagems whose effect was to disable the opponents of slavery and to empower its defenders. Once again there is no reason to doubt Jeffersons sincerity; but nor is there reason to doubt the *functionally* proslavery cast of Jeffersonian democracy.

Jefferson did not view the conflict as one between the defenders and the opponents of slavery. On the contrary, he insisted that antislavery was no more than a pretext to cover the ambitions of designing northerners. Who were these designing northerners? Jefferson saw the specter of Federalism. "The leaders of federalism," he announced, "defeated in their schemes of obtaining power by rallying partisans to the principle of monarchism, . . . have changed tack, and thrown out another barrel to the whale." As a result of the controversy, he declared, "Hartford convention men" had obtained power "under the auspices of morality." The Missouri dispute was "a mere party trick."[97]

Jefferson took it so seriously, however, not merely because it threatened to revive Federalism but also because of the immediate threat it

96. Moore, *Missouri Controversy*, pp. 113–114.
97. Ford (ed.), *Works of Jefferson*, x, pp. 157, 152, 157–158, 186, 162, 192, 253, 342, 233.

offered to the slaveholders. "The real question," he told John Adams in
January 1821, "as seen in the states afflicted with this unfortunate population, is, are our slaves to be presented with freedom and a dagger?"
Nevertheless the fear of Federalism was undoubtedly sincere and it rested,
in turn, on a deep suspicion of the social and economic interests for which
Federalism stood. Taylor at this time published another work, entitled
Construction Construed, and Constitutions Vindicated in which he
reduced the antislavery sentiment witnessed during the Missouri debates
to the interests that stimulated and were stimulated by, Federalist legislation:

> The great pecuniary favour granted by congress to certificate-
> holders, begat banking; banking begat bounties to manufacturing
> capitalists; bounties to manufacturing capitalists begat an oppressive
> pension list; these partialities united to beget the Missouri project;
> that project begat the idea of using slavery as an instrument for
> effecting a balance of power; when it is put in operation, it will
> beget new usurpations of internal powers over persons and property,
> and these will beget a dissolution of the union.

Once again Jefferson and Taylor were at one in their political perceptions.[98]

Though this was a distorted view of northern antislavery principles, it
was plausible enough to convince not only Jefferson, Taylor and their
southern supporters, but also many northerners. And some of the actions
of Federalists and their supporters seemed to confirm the analysis beyond
all reasonable doubt. Rufus King, for example, who was as prominent as
any northerner in his criticisms of slavery, was notorious to Republicans
as an arch-Federalist and while he probably had no hope of reviving the
fortunes of his ailing party he may well have hoped to establish a new
northern party, one powerful enough to defeat the South in national
elections and in Congress. Indeed some Federalists said as much publicly.
A writer in the Boston *Daily Advertiser*, for example, a Federalist newspaper, rejoiced at "the weapon [antislavery] which has at length placed
itself in our hands," and at the prospect of "the new parties, which this
question is likely to produce." One reason for the hostility of men like

98.   Jefferson to Adams, Jan. 22, 1821 quoted in Dumas Malone, *The Sage of Monticello*
      (Boston, 1981), p. 341; John Taylor, *Construction Construed, and Constitutions
      Vindicated* (Richmond, 1820), pp. 293–294, 298: Jefferson went so far as to insist
      that only men sound on the Missouri question should be employed at the University
      of Virginia. As Davis observes, Jefferson "bequeathed to the South the image of anti-
      slavery as a Federalist mask for political and economic exploitation" – Davis,
      Problem of Slavery in Age of Revolution, p. 184. See also Robert E. Shalhope,
      "Thomas Jefferson's Republicanism and Antebellum Southern Thought," *Journal
      of Southern History*, LVII (1976), pp. 529–556.

King to the South was their resentment of the uses to which southern political power was put. In 1820 a large number of southerners combined to defeat the Baldwin tariff bill; a majority of southerners at this time were also opposed to federal internal improvements. Northerners who objected to slavery were often those who were conspicuous in their support of tariffs and internal improvements. This correlation was no coincidence. Many argued that slavery in the South had created an interest prejudicial to the continuing development of the northern economy and the legislation necessary to promote it. It was a common belief that a lasting policy of protection could not be established until southern political influence were checked and the obvious means to this end was a refusal to countenance any new slave states. Thus in Harrisburg, Pennsylvania, in 1820 a toast was offered in the wake of the defeat of the protective tariff to "National Industry" which, it was claimed, "is held in fetters by the iron grasp of slavery."[99]

It did not follow that when these northerners expressed concern for the welfare of the slave they were being hypocritical; there was no reason why they should not condemn slavery on grounds of morality as well as political economy. But hypocrisy was precisely what Jefferson and his disciples discerned. The problem was that the same Federalists (or Clintonians) who were professing a humanitarian concern for blacks were those who were in Connecticut in 1817, for example, defending the union of church and state, or in New York in 1821 opposing the attempt to extend the suffrage to poorer whites. In these circumstances it was all too easy to conclude that a group which had little interest in the freedom or equality of white men in its own locality could scarcely be moved by a sincere concern for the plight of enslaved black men, women and children thousands of miles away.[100]

This logic soon struck staunchly Republican northerners as well as southerners. Initially many of them had sympathized with the desire to limit the spread of slavery but soon it became clear that this was not compatible with other goals. They simply could not have antislavery and the Republican party as they had known it. Perhaps they could not even have antislavery and the Union as they had known it. When they read Federalist newspapers like the Salem *Gazette* advocating that "the Union be dissolved rather than extend slavery," they were irresistibly reminded of the Hartford Convention. Thus like Jefferson they easily discerned base motives lurking behind northern antislavery utterances. John Parrott, for example, a Republican from New Hampshire dismissed the antislavery movements as "a Federalist plot to undermine the Democratic

99. Moore, *Missouri Controversy*, pp. 183, 322–329.
100. Moore, *Missouri Controversy*, p. 185.

party," while Isaac Hill's *New Hampshire Patriot*, having initially warned against the spread of slavery, soon changed tack and condemned northern antislavery agitators as men whose goal was "not so much to put a stop to slavery, as it is to create a Northern and a Southern interest; not so much to further the Union and happiness of this Republic, as to effect sinister and party purposes." Even more explicitly, the Franklin *Gazette* in November 1820 recalled the enormous political debt that all northern republicans owed to the South. "We believe," wrote the editor, "that the agitators of the Missouri question *now* are actuated by a desire to sever the union, if they cannot otherwise obtain the reins of power." Why did these agitators "hate the southern states?" Answering his own question, the editor declared that it was "not for their slavery, but for their republicanism." He recalled that "it was with their aid that we upset the fabric of federal folly and tyranny in 1800; and they never have and never will forgive them and us for it."[101]

Here was the crucial point. The democratic orientation of the southern states, and their key role in the destruction of Federalism and the establishment of the American democratic tradition were crucial in 1820 precisely as they had been in the 1790s and would continue to be for the next thirty or even forty years. To sustain their party and indeed the Union as they had known it, northern Jeffersonians in 1820 were impelled to denounce antislavery agitators from their own states as hypocrites. Thus in the crucial House vote on the elimination of the antislavery proviso in the constitution of Missouri, fourteen northerners voted with the South and another four were absent. These eighteen were denounced in some quarters in the North – all were Republicans except three, and two of those were neutral between the two parties. In the northern press the Compromise was either ignored or praised by Republican papers, condemned by Federalists. In the words of one historian, a majority of northern Federalists "were much more militant and uncompromising toward the South than the Democrats."[102]

It was not, of course, that the northern Jeffersonians explicitly defended slavery. Instead it was the hidden inscription on the party creed, an inscription that made its supporters rally to the defence of the slaveholding interest in the South, even if they disliked slavery itself. In 1820 a fault line running through the American political system became visible as it had not previously been and would not be again for many years. The conflict over slavery came to the forefront of federal politics and it produced a political earthquake that revealed the foundations of the Republican party, itself the dominant political force in the nation. At

101. Moore, *Missouri Controversy*, pp. 144, 150–151,187, 189–196, 198, 233.
102. Moore, *Missouri Controversy*, pp. 105, 160, 184.

the moment of crisis, the special relationship between slavery and Jeffersonianism was exposed and the special and quite disproportionate power of the slaveholders was suddenly revealed. The crisis revealed an important truth about Jefferson: although he was in no sense a proslavery thinker, Jeffersonian thought and Jeffersonian democracy were *functionally* proslavery. But the moment of crisis was relatively brief, the tremor subsided and the familiar political landscape was restored. Missouri had been a portent of things to come.

Compromise and commerce

To some contemporaries and some historians the Missouri Compromise demonstrated or confirmed that an alliance existed within the Republican party. It was an alliance, they observed, between, in contemporary parlance, "the planters of the South" and "the plain republicans" of the North.[103] Though this was an acute observation, the formulation was misleading in two respects. First there were many plain republicans in the South too. Indeed as we have seen, the key to the dominance of the Republican party was the redefinition, in rhetoric and in ideology, of the planter so as to obliterate any difference between planters and plain republican farmers. The second inaccuracy follows from the first. The term "alliance" is inappropriate to the extent that it implies a formal agreement or contract between two or more individuals or groups. The support which other groups would bring to the party of Jefferson and later of Jackson was the consequence of a relationship both narrower and wider than an alliance, narrower because no formal agreement had been reached, wider because there was an affinity based on political experience, common aspirations, general beliefs. As we shall see, merely by subscribing to the principles of Jefferson and Taylor – principles that did not even mention slavery – northern Democrats were led repeatedly to support the South and the interests of the slaveholding elite.

To find a term to describe the elements uniting under the Republican banner we can once more look to the work of Antonio Gramsci. Gramsci introduced the notion of a "historic bloc," a configuration or alignment of social forces, which when formed allows a class to maintain its dominance not simply or even primarily by the use of force but instead

---

103. The classic contemporary statement was that of Martin Van Buren in his famous letter to Thomas Ritchie of January 1827 and the classic historiographical statement is Richard H. Brown, "The Missouri Crisis, Slavery, and the Politics of Jacksonianism," *South Atlantic Quarterly*, LXV (1966), pp. 55–72. I discuss Brown's thesis more fully in Chapter 5 below.

"because it is able to go beyond its narrow, corporative interests, exert a moral and intellectual leadership, and make compromises (within certain limits) with a variety of allies."[104] This bloc was never completely united and its composition was never static. But a strong case can be made to say that this bloc ruled the United States at the time of the Virginia dynasty. Many of the actions taken by the federal government at this time can be seen in this light. As one historian has observed:

> Flaunting [sic] Britain, sacrificing the interest of New England commerce when necessary, and cajoling or threatening France and Spain as the occasion demanded, the Jeffersonian Republicans grasped control of the entire Mississippi Valley, the Floridas, and the vital entrepot of New Orleans, guaranteeing the security of slavery in the vast Louisiana territory and promoting the greatest and easiest possible access to foreign markets for the rising planters of the deep Southwest.[105]

The ideological cement for this bloc was provided by the demand that all white men should enjoy the fruits of their labor and should be protected in this enjoyment by the possession of political rights. In the North this doctrine had immense appeal to the small farmers and craftsmen who resented the elitist aspirations of Federalism and who applauded all efforts to democratize the nation's institutions. In the South it appealed to the same groups but also to many among the planting elite, whose right to the fruits of the labor of their black bondsmen would go unchallenged by a party which ignored the inequalities produced by slavery, and which indeed, in its political economy and its political theory, ignored the slave altogether.

Yet this "historic bloc" was not united in its opinions. Not only was there the disagreement which briefly emerged over slavery in Missouri and which would re-emerge in the future, there was also an older, more lasting disagreement. The party which Jefferson had led to victory in 1800 was united on the desire to oust the Federalists but it was seriously divided on other matters. We have examined some of the opinions of its radical wing, whose chief spokesmen were John Taylor of Caroline, Nathaniel Macon of North Carolina and (though in some key respects his opinions were markedly different) John Randolph of Roanoke. These men were the heirs of the Antifederalists, deeply suspicious of government, and especially of the federal government, and profoundly hostile to banks, corporations and funding systems. They hoped that Jefferson's

---

104. A.S. Sassoon in Tom Bottomore *et al.* (eds), *A Dictionary of Marxist Thought* (Oxford, 1983), p. 201.
105. McColley, *Slavery and Jeffersonian Virginia*, p. 181.

election would merely be the first stage in a much needed process of constitutional restoration. Federalists must be purged, Hamilton's financial system dismantled, and the egalitarianism of the Revolution confirmed by a thorough democratization of the judiciary, the last bastion of Federalist power. At many stages of his career Jefferson himself acted with the radicals and was never unsympathetic to their views.[106]

But there was another wing of the Republican party, one which ultimately triumphed. James Madison who, far from being an Antifederalist had actually inspired the federal constitution, was the leader of the moderate republicans and can himself be described as an arch-moderate. While the radicals (apart from the eccentric Randolph) retained considerable respect for Jefferson, they frequently condemned Madison. Other moderate Republicans included Albert Gallatin, Alexander J. Dallas, and James Sullivan. These men looked with disfavor on the antidemocratic utterances of the Federalists, but they were distrustful too of the populism of most of the radicals. While they might dislike the Anglophilia of the Federalists, they were unwilling to countenance the anti-commercial animus of the radicals. So far as the election of 1800 was concerned, they believed the result demonstrated that proper political and constitutional principles had been re-established. There was no need to uproot the Hamiltonian financial system and no need either to bring the judiciary under greater popular control. Indeed such projects were to be strongly resisted. In his desire to end party strife and recruit the support of the Federalist voters and in his refusal to dismantle the Hamiltonian system, Jefferson acted with the moderates. When the succession passed to Madison in 1809 it was clear that the moderates had triumphed.[107]

When war came with Britain, the Federalists suffered further reversals. Yet as their party crumbled, many of their policies were resuscitated. The Republicans introduced a protective tariff, showed themselves willing to embark on a program of road and canal building, re-chartered a national bank and in fact created more state banks than the Federalists had ever managed. Yet the moderate Republicans had not simply converted to Federalism. Instead they had created a new synthesis. Like the radicals the moderates believed wholeheartedly in majority rule and were appalled by the unabashed elitism of Federalism. But like the

---

106. By far the best work on the divisions within the Republican party is Richard E. Ellis, *The Jeffersonian Crisis: Courts and Politics in the Young Republic* (N.Y., 1971) – a book which deserves to be far better known than it is. See also, however, Charles Sellers, *The Market Revolution: Jacksonian America, 1815–1846* (N.Y., 1991).
107. On Madison, see Drew McCoy, *The Elusive Republic: Political Economy in Jeffersonian America* (Chapel Hill, 1980). In my view, the insights in Joyce Appleby's *Capitalism and a New Social Order* apply to the moderate wing of the Republicans rather than to the party as a whole.

Federalists, they sought to accelerate the commercial development of the nation and did not shrink from using the power of government, and especially the federal government, when appropriate – despite the cries of anguish emanating from the radicals. A reconciliation of commerce and democracy was being attempted.[108]

Thus by the time Andrew Jackson was embarking on his presidential campaigns of the 1820s, the nation's unity had been confirmed by one compromise – that struck between North and South at the time of the Missouri Compromise – and its political economy shaped by another – that founded on the moderate Republican synthesis. In a sense, the key to both was commercial development, essential to the moderate Republican synthesis and also a source of national unity in that it seemed to promise growing prosperity for Americans on both sides of the Mason-Dixon line. Unfortunately, however, both these compromises would be undermined by the commercial success on which they depended and which they facilitated.

First to come under strain was the compromise effected by the moderate Republicans. Indeed the growing pains of the new economic order were already being severely felt by 1820. At the very time congressmen were debating the slavery question, their constituents were probably far more concerned with the effects of the financial Panic which had set in the previous year and which, as we have seen, had a disastrous effect upon Thomas Jefferson's personal finances.[109] The instabilities and insecurities, above all, perhaps, the inequalities, entailed by an increasingly market-oriented economy would send many Americans scurrying back to the doctrines – if not necessarily the books – of John Taylor of Caroline. As we shall see, Andrew Jackson himself, partly under the pressure of events during his presidency, became the most powerful exponent of Taylorean principles the nation had ever seen and in response to another financial Panic (that of 1837) agrarian radicalism would reach its high tide. Simultaneously these conflicts would do much to reopen the debate over political democracy. Alarmed at the recrudescence of agrarian radicalism and perturbed by the accompanying political egalitarianism, many Americans would seek to shore up the nation's commercial and political structures by ensuring that a "natural aristocracy" would rule. Such men would form the Whig party. Thus the Jeffersonian legacy would split and the moderate/radical division would re-emerge. Not for nothing would radical Democrats of the Jacksonian era honor the name of John Taylor;

---

108. Ellis, *Jeffersonian Crisis*, pp. 283–284. See also the early chapters of Sellers, *Market Revolution*, for an excellent discussion of the entrepreneurial thrust of (moderate) Republicanism.
109. Moore, *Missouri Controversy*, pp. 170–172.

not for nothing would so many Whigs (and conservative Democrats) revere the name of James Madison above all other statesmen.[110]

But the problems brought by commercial development did not end here. While the often bitter party conflicts witnessed in the Jacksonian era owed much to the unevenness of the growth process and to the dissatisfaction of its victims, its very successes drove a wedge between North and South. For while both sections prospered together, the effect was to confirm the attachment of each to its own labor system. In the North the growth of wage labor, an inevitable effect of the market revolution, necessitated significant ideological shifts. Once these momentous changes had occurred, there would no longer be room for an accommodation with slavery and the days of sectional peace and national unity would be numbered. It is here that one finds the origins of the American Civil War.

---

110. The argument of this and the following paragraph will be central themes of the remainder of this book (and its sequel).

2

Free labor, slave labor, wage labor

Slavery and free labor: The traditional view

On visiting the South, William Seward, the leading figure in the Republican party before the election of Lincoln, recorded his impressions:

> It was necessary that I should travel in Virginia to have any idea of a slave State . . . . An exhausted soil, old and decaying towns, wretchedly-neglected roads, and, in every respect, an absence of enterprise and improvement, distinguish the region through which we have come, in contrast to that in which we live. Such has been the effect of slavery.

By the 1850s many northerners shared Seward's view of the South. According to Republican Senator Henry Wilson of Massachusetts, free labor was so utterly superior to slavery that it could entirely offset the natural advantages of the South. "Freedom," he told the Senate, "took the rugged soil and still more rugged clime of the North, and now that rugged soil yields abundance to the willing hands of free labor." By contrast "slavery took the sunny lands and the sunny clime of the South, and it has left the traces of its ruinous power deeply furrowed on the face of your sunny land." Since slaves had no incentive to work well, their labor was of poor quality and reluctantly given. Since they performed the menial tasks and were a degraded class, the tendency was for all manual labor to be despised. As a result the South with its stagnant economy and leaden social system lagged hopelessly behind the North in population, in income, in wealth, and in all the elements of modern civilization.[1] It is no exaggeration to say that Republicans fought the Civil War primarily because they deplored the economic effects of slavery.

1. Frederick W. Seward (ed.), *William Seward: An Autobiography* (N.Y., 1891), p. 268; Henry Wilson, *Are Working Men Slaves: Speech in the Senate, March 20, 1858* (Washington, D.C., 1858), p. 7; Eric Foner, *Free Soil, Free Labor, Free Men: The Ideology of the Republican Party Before the Civil War* (N.Y., 1970), pp. 40–72.

At one time most economists and economic historians shared the Republican view. Yet much recent economic history has purported to discredit the northern critique of slavery, not of course the moral indictment, but instead the more frequently voiced criticisms derived from political economy. On this view, the War becomes a struggle brought about not by the real differences between a slave and a free-labor economy but instead by the perceived, indeed misperceived, differences. The destruction of slavery, wrought above all by the conviction that slavery impeded economic development, was effected by a series of fortuitous misjudgments. Justice was served not by truth but by error.[2]

Some of the objections to the traditional, neo-Republican view are quite valid; we should not conclude that northerners were able to describe the South accurately. Yet these criticisms have been pushed too far. The northern critique was closer to the mark than is generally recognized. And when it missed the target it was because of socially generated crosscurrents. In other words, the northern view of slavery was a socially mediated one. We need to establish the extent of the distortion and then to explain it. The first task is the object of this chapter. Although the economics of slavery covers a wide variety of subjects I shall confine myself to the three most important: the development of cities in the South, the development of industry, the growth and efficiency of the southern economy.

Assumptions

The great majority of economic historians currently studying slavery are wedded to concepts and assumptions derived from neo-classical theory. Although there are, needless to say, important differences between scholars, it is safe to say that in most economic history the basic unit of analysis is the individual. Often this individual is seen to be a profit-maximizer; it is assumed that this is the characteristic form of behavior of humans, certainly in societies with a considerable degree of market orientation. Analogous to the profit-maximizing impulse is what might be termed the utility-maximizing tendency: individuals set out to maximize

2. The best known work is, of course, Robert W. Fogel and Stanley L. Engerman, *Time on the Cross, The Economics of American Negro Slavery* 2 vols (London, 1974). Of at least equal importance is Robert W. Fogel, *Without Consent or Contract: The Rise and Fall of American Slavery* (N.Y., 1989). A vigorous reply to Fogel and Engerman is Paul David (*et al.*), *Reckoning With Slavery: A Critical Study in the Quantitative History of American Negro Slavery* (N.Y., 1976). The conclusion that slavery was destroyed because its economic strength was misperceived is also reached by Howard Temperley in his discussion of British antislavery. See Temperley, "Capitalism, Slavery and Ideology," *Past and Present*, LXXV (1977), pp. 94–118.

the benefit or utility they derive from specific goods or services. Of course, no economic historian believes that these impulses are universally present; deviations from the norm are frequently noted, and then (though less frequently) explained.

In its purer form (as found for example in the work of Robert Fogel and Stanley Engerman), this approach in turn leads to specific claims about the American antebellum economy. First it is said that southern slaveholders, who were undoubtedly profit-conscious, were more similar to, than different from, northern businessmen. Plainly both groups were market-oriented. Hence it is permissible to regard both as capitalist. Of course this does not mean that there are no differences between slave-holding capitalists and capitalists who own no slaves. But there is no *a priori* reason to expect a superior economic performance (by capitalist criteria) from northern employers of free labor than from southern owners of slaves. Indeed some economic historians have claimed that by these very criteria the southern performance was outstandingly good. A second assumption follows from the first: the differences between free labor and slave labor, while of considerable importance, are not such as to invalidate the assumptions upon which orthodox economic analysis rests. Hence the methodological approach and the analytical tools appropriate to the analysis of even a modern capitalist economy will be found equally serviceable when the southern slave economy is being considered.

There are important variations within this school and these need to be considered. However, it is fair to say that there is only one fully elaborated alternative to the neo-classical approach and that is derived from Marxism. Unfortunately Marx wrote no formal treatise on slavery and, although he did comment at some length on the American Civil War and its causes, his ideas cannot be simply dusted down and employed in their existing form. It is more fruitful to look instead at the foundations of his political economy and then test their explanatory power in a concrete historical situation.[3]

One of the problems confronting all students of Marx is to grasp that his approach to the study of society is emphatically relational. Thus rather than focus upon things, individuals or even groups of individuals, Marx begins with the relations between men. This has many consequences, one of which is that he develops a more restrictive definition of capitalism than is generally adopted by economists or economic historians. For Marx (though it must be said that he was not always con-

---

3. I shall make no attempt here to discuss the inconsistencies which are apparent in Marx's work. My purpose is not to defend him but instead to use those aspects of his thought which are of value. I might add, however, that in my view this entails the greater part of his work.

sistent here) capitalism entails a specific set of *social relations* between the owner of capital and the employee who works for him for wages. Capitalism does not exist merely because capital exists. As he put it in *Capital*, "means of subsistence, machines and other means of production does not yet stamp a man as a capitalist if the essential complement to these things is missing: the wage labourer." For "capital is not a thing, but a social relation between persons . . . ." In slavery this relation does not exist, since the slave is not a wage laborer. Nor is a society of independent farmers, each working for himself on his own land, capitalist, even if production is, to a considerable extent, for the market.[1]

This analysis immediately implies a different approach to the economic history of the antebellum United States. As we shall see, it leads us to expect that the pursuit of self-interest will frequently be mediated or structured by concerns that grow out of the key relations, whether between slave and master, or between employer and wage laborer. Since these concerns are in certain crucial respects, dissimilar, the pursuit of self-interest will have significantly different consequences in slave and wage labor economies. We would therefore not be surprised to find that such economies have different trajectories of development. But first we should note that Marx's definition of capitalism suggests that the straightforward distinction between free labor and slave labor that is familiar to all scholars, requires a crucial modification. For we need to distinguish between a capitalist free labor system and one that I have already referred to as pre-capitalist commodity production.[5] In the latter labor is free but not for wages; producers are independent farmers or self-employed craftsmen. It is true that this mode of production is unlikely to survive for very long and may indeed never have existed in a pure form (that is to say unaccompanied by wage or slave labor) anywhere. Nevertheless, an approximation to it existed in the antebellum United States. Thus whereas orthodox – one might say bourgeois – economics finds "capitalism" throughout antebellum America, Marxist theory implies the co-existence of three modes of production: pre-capitalist com-

---

4. Karl Marx, *Capital* Vol. I (London, 1976), p. 932. Anyone who is interested in the theoretical foundation of my discussion of political economy will find it in this, the 33rd chapter of *Capital* entitled, "The Modern Theory of Colonization," pp. 930–940.

5. An alternative term sometimes employed is "simple commodity production." There are two problems with these terms. One is that "pre-capitalist commodity production" exists only where much of what is produced is not for the market at all – and thus not strictly speaking in commodity form. The second, and more important, objection is that there is clearly a temporal overlap between capitalist and "pre-capitalist" production. I am aware of the issues raised in this connection by Eugene D. Genovese in his *The World the Slaveholders Made* (rev. ed. Middletown, Conn., 1988), esp. p. vi but I shall not discuss them until the second volume of this work.

modity production, slavery, and (wage-labor) capitalism. Of course, these alternative approaches are politically loaded: the political aspirations of Marxism are well known, the commitment of neo-classical economists to the existing order (whether reformed or not) is also apparent. But this is not to say that the choice between them is to be made as a result of political preference. Rather we must pose the vital question: which has the greater analytical power?

Growth and efficiency in the antebellum South

I

There is now much evidence available on regional growth rates in antebellum America. Although conceptual and empirical problems are by no means absent from the data, I shall nevertheless follow the practice of most economic historians of treating them as offering the best available summary of southern economic performance. Originally assembled by Richard Easterlin, these data are reproduced in Table I. At first glance it is apparent that southern per capita income before the Civil War, while below that of the North as a whole, was significantly higher than that of the Northwest. Moreover, southern income between 1840 and 1860 was actually growing faster than that of the North. Such figures suggest a thriving economy, for in the entire history of the world "only a handful of countries have been able to sustain long-term growth rates substantially in excess of that achieved by the antebellum South between 1840 and 1860."[6] The importance of this conclusion can hardly be exaggerated: if valid, it refutes the Republican analysis of southern society entirely and means that the perception of southern economic inferiority was a misperception. The implications for the origins of the Civil War are unmistakable.

This analysis must be resisted, however. Let us recur to the Marxist categories. Although the data is difficult to obtain, there can be no doubt that capitalist production in this sense was a characteristic not of the antebellum North so much as of the Northeast. The West was still overwhelmingly agricultural and as late as 1860 there was only one wage laborer for every two farms in the North. There is abundant evidence that farmers, especially in the West, simply could not get wage laborers in any

6. Richard A. Easterlin, "Interregional Differences in Per Capita Income, Population and Total Income, 1840–1950," in *Trends in the American Economy in the Nineteenth Century* (Princeton, 1960); "Regional Income Trends, 1840–1950," in Seymour Harris (ed.), *American Economic History* (N.Y., 1961), pp. 525–547; Fogel, *Without Consent or Contract*, pp. 88, 109; Fogel and Engerman, *Time on the Cross*, I, pp. 255–257. See also Robert E. Gallman, "Slavery and Southern Economic Growth," *Southern Economic Journal*, XLV (1979), pp. 1007–1022.

Table I. *Per capita income and regional economic growth, 1840 and 1860 (1860 dollars)*

Region	1840	1860	% Average annual growth
United States	96	128	1.4
North	109	141	1.3
Northeast	129	181	1.7
Northcentral	65	89	1.6
South	74	103	1.7
Southeast	66	84	1.2
East South Central	69	81	1.3
West South	151	184	1.0

Source: Table reproduced from Robert W. Fogel and Stanley L. Engerman, *Time on the Cross*, I, p.248

quantity. Even in the Northeast the proportion of wage laborers was almost certainly far lower than in England. Of course throughout the North capitalist and non-capitalist labor coexisted but the balance was obviously different in, say, Massachusetts from Iowa. In the South, however, we may assume that wage labor was of far less significance than in the Northeast or, perhaps, the Northwest.[7]

In this light, Table I merits the closest attention. As previously noted, it shows the South performing very adequately, especially in comparison with the Northwest (Northcentral). But the fastest growing subregion is the Northeast which by 1860 was far ahead of all parts of the South except the states of the West South Central which had the benefits of sugar production in Louisiana and the exceptionally fertile alluvial soil of that state. Even so, the Northeast by 1860 had almost closed the gap with the West South Central. Using our tripartite analysis we would conclude that the slave states as a whole could compete effectively in the growth

7. Wright, *Political Economy of the Cotton South*, p. 46. Stanley Lebergott has supplied the following data about wage labor – Lebergott, "The Pattern of Employment Since 1800," in Harris (ed.), *American Economic History*, pp. 281–310, esp. 290–291:

The US labor force in 1800 and 1860

	1800	1860
Self-employed	57%	37%
Slaves	31%	23%
Wage earners	12%	40%

stakes with the North where free labor took the pre-capitalist form. But where wage labor was well developed, it outpaced slavery.

This analysis also helps us to make sense of the more rapid growth of the South as a whole compared to the North as a whole. The paradox is that each subregion of the North was growing faster than each subregion of the South. The paradox dissolves when we note that there was a redistribution of people and resources from East to West in both sections. But in the North this meant a redistribution to a less prosperous area, while in the South it meant the opposite. The aggregate data make it easy to conclude that the South was faring better than the North. Yet the conclusion would be erroneous. For the Northwest would, in time, approximate the Northeast; in 1860 it was simply at an earlier stage of development. Capitalist relations would eventually predominate there and the gap with the Northeast would rapidly close. But the advantage of the Southwest depended on soil and climate; there was no prospect of the Southeast ever matching it in these respects. Looked at in this light, the Republican critique of the South, heavily oversimplified though it was, begins to re-acquire some validity.

II

Although growth and efficiency are fundamentally different concepts, those who have found a high level of one in the South have often found an equally high level of the other. Thus Fogel and Engerman have claimed that southern agriculture, far from being backward, was actually more efficient and, in this sense, more advanced than northern. They claim – and the claim has been reiterated in Fogel's more recent work – that, in 1860, southern agriculture was 35 percent more efficient than northern. Moreover, economies of scale were operative, bringing the biggest gains on plantations with over fifty slaves. According to Fogel, the South's lead in agriculture was almost entirely attributable to slavery; the free white farms there had efficiency ratings that were much closer to those of northern farms. The impact of the gang system was decisive. When the crops and the number of slaves available permitted its use, then "on average, about 39 percent more output" could be produced "from a given amount of input" than was possible "either on free farms or slave farms that were too small to employ the gang system." Efficiency calcula-

8. Fogel, *Without Consent or Contract*, pp. 74–76; Fogel and Engerman, *Time on the Cross*, I, p. 192. See also Fogel and Engerman, "Explaining the Relative Efficiency of Slave Agriculture in the Antebellum South: Reply," in Fogel, *Without Consent or Contract: The Rise and Fall of American Slavery: Markets and Production* technical papers Vol. I (N.Y., 1992), pp. 266–303, *Without Consent or Contract: The Rise and Fall of American Slavery* Evidence and Methods (N.Y., 1992), pp. 278–282.

tions are notoriously difficult and, as we shall see, Fogel and Engerman's have been questioned. But in their calculations they sought to take account of differences in crops, soil, and hours worked.[8]

In fact there is reason to believe that these comparisons are simply inappropriate. The empirical problems are not insignificant; the conceptual problems probably insurmountable. The key fact is that southern slave farms and plantations were governed by a logic different from that which operated in northern agriculture. It is as yet unclear whether economies of scale, at least in the orthodox sense of the term, were available to southern slaveholders. However, they did enjoy at least two major advantages. First, slavery both permitted and necessitated a greater degree of production for the market. In order to obtain a return on capital invested in slaves, market production was required. Free farms lacked an equivalent incentive. Moreover, free farmers were, in the ante-bellum years as they had been for centuries, risk averse. That is to say, they were willing to sacrifice some potential income in order to increase their chances of retaining their farms. Rather than maximize profits and risk the loss of everything if market conditions turned against them, they would instead meet a considerable portion of their subsistence needs and then market their surplus. (Hence the phrase "marketable surplus.") Such a strategy cannot be dismissed as unintelligent or irrational since land supplied so many needs in the antebellum years. (Furthermore, farmers tended to buy more land than they could farm, since land prices were relatively low. This offered the prospect of windfall gains if their locality boomed, but without the risks attendant on complete subjection to the market.) Slave farms, however, possessed a different logic. Planters could and did meet their subsistence needs relatively easily and this left a higher proportion of production for the market. Their larger size allowed them to incur the risk of cotton production on a larger scale since they would be much more easily able to weather any economic storm. They would thus combine subsistence and cash crops in different proportions. This may be termed the "crop mix" effect.[9]

The second advantage enjoyed by slave farms involved the use of female labor. While it would be absurd to suggest that on free farms women did not work, it is nonetheless true that fewer women worked in the fields. For a variety of reasons, planters were very willing to put slave women into the fields. Moreover, a relatively high proportion of fieldwork, as compared with domestic labor, resulted in production for the market. Once again, therefore, slave farms allowed a greater market

9. Wright, *Political Economy of the Cotton South*, pp. 44–55, 74–86; "Prosperity, Progress, and American Slavery," in David (*et al.*), *Reckoning With Slavery*, pp. 302–336, esp. 316–320. See also Lacy Ford, Jr., *The Origins of Southern Radicalism: The South Carolina Upcountry, 1800–1860* (N.Y., 1988), p.73.

orientation than free farms.[10] Thus the effect of the crop mix and of female labor gave slavery a significant advantage and it is at least arguable that it is this, rather than any economies of scale,[11] which explains the apparently greater efficiency of the larger plantations. The goals of self-sufficiency might well be common to both the free farm and the large plantation but "this common pattern of self-sufficiency implied an extremely high payoff to the reallocation of 'marginal' labor from the household to the fields." It is significant that after emancipation black family labor moved to a more conventional pattern – with predictably damaging effects. One conclusion, drawn by the historian Gavin Wright, is that "the efficiency of slavery is historically specific to an era in which free households chose to sharply limit their participation in the market economy."[12]

In other respects the efficiency comparisons with non-slave agriculture, and especially with northern agriculture are still more problematic. To begin with, there are considerable problems with data. It is necessary to calculate the numbers of hours worked by slaves and northern farmers respectively and then make allowances for the inclusion in the southern figure of the less productive workers (children, the aged, and women) whom the planters were able to use. Fogel claims that, although slaves worked more intensely than free white farmers, they worked fewer hours. This, however, is highly contentious yet in any calculation of efficiency the number of hours worked per annum is clearly of major importance. And, on the output side, the use of data from the year 1860 may bias the calculation in favor of the South, since that year produced a bumper cotton crop at least in certain parts of the South, but was an indifferent one for northern agriculture.

Even more important is the procedure used to measure land as an "input." Fogel and Engerman use land value here, since otherwise no allowance could be made for differences in quality of soil or climate. Northern farms could not grow cotton and so the calculation must assume that this disadvantage was reflected in the price. But land values also reflect locational advantages which, in the North, with its denser population and thus greater dependence on local markets, could be very considerable. The price of land reflects, in part, the opportunity its owner enjoys of participating in a given network of local exchange relations. If

10. See, in addition to Wright, Jacqueline Jones, *Labor of Love, Labor of Sorrow: Black Women, Work and the Family, from Slavery to the Present* (N.Y., 1985), pp. 11–43.
11. Though the crop mix and female labor effects could be seen as the consequences of a larger-scale operation and in this (unorthodox) sense as "economies of scale."
12. Wright, *Political Economy of the Cotton South*, pp. 82–83, "The Efficiency of Slavery: Another Interpretation," in *American Economic Review*, LXIX (1979), pp. 219–226, esp. 225.

these exchange relations are relatively well developed, the value of the land will rise, no matter what the quality of the soil or climate. As a result, the "inputs" into northern agriculture will increase and its apparent "efficiency" will decline. In other words, the more mature the economy, the more inefficient it will appear to be! Such figures thus tell us absolutely nothing about the relative efficiency of free and slave labor. Two conclusions are in order here. First we may doubt whether an efficiency comparison is possible between northern and southern agriculture; the empirical problems are formidable, the conceptual ones still more so. Second, the agnostic position to which we are driven nevertheless places at the minimum a question mark against the notion that northern agriculture enjoyed an efficiency advantage in the way that virtually every northern opponent of slavery in the antebellum era assumed. Modern scholarship simply does not confirm this view.[13] Once again we are left wondering whether northern superiority was not specific to sectors in which wage labor, rather than merely free labor, were prominent.

On the other hand, the ultimate source of southern economic growth remains unclear. Supposed efficiency gains as a result of the gang system and economies of scale have not been conclusively demonstrated. The "crop mix" and "female labor" advantages are more plausible but one may object that, like virtually every feature of the southern antebellum economy, they depended upon the continuing high demand for southern staples, and especially cotton. Yet there is reason to believe that cotton brought both triumph and tragedy to the southern economy. From 1830 to 1860 the Industrial Revolution in Britain, specifically the mills of Lancashire, created an almost insatiable appetite for cotton, with demand increasing at 5 percent per year. On the eve of the Civil War three-quarters of US cotton was exported and the nation supplied no less than 70 percent of Britain's need. The land and climate of the South, and especially of the Southwest, were exceptionally suitable for the crop. As a result planters were fortunate indeed in being in the right place at the right time with the right product. But this success concealed structural weaknesses in the southern economy. For the British textile industry was, it has been argued, on the brink of a major downturn in 1860 and never again would demand increase at the pace of the antebellum years. The consequences for the South, even without war and emancipation in the

---

13. Fogel, *Without Consent or Contract*, pp. 77–79; Wright, "Efficiency of Slavery," pp. 219–222, "Prosperity, Progress, and American Slavery," pp. 313–314. As Paul David and Peter Temin point out (p. 213), this also assumes a perfectly competitive national capital market for land in which buyers would move indifferently to free or slave states. No historian has ever demonstrated that this existed – David and Temin, "Slavery, the Progressive Institution?," in David (*et al.*), *Reckoning with Slavery*, p. 215.

1860s, would have been extremely painful. Slave prices would have plunged and an attempt to turn more slaves into industrial workers might well have generated the kinds of abolitionist pressure in the cities which were fatal to slave regimes elsewhere. There may well have been a crisis of overproduction looming in the South in 1861 but it has been obscured by the tumultuous events and social upheavals of that decade.[14]

Industry in the South

I

It is important to note that industrialization and urbanization were by no means the same process in antebellum America, since many factories were located in rural areas and since urban economies were frequently commercial rather than industrial. We may begin therefore by looking at manufacturing, at the distribution of manufacturing within the nation and specifically at the performance of the South. One problem with the data is that the census records are notoriously incomplete, or fragmentary, especially before 1850. There are also problems of classification. Should a sugar mill located on a cotton plantation be included under manufacturing? A case can be made but such was not the practice of the census officials. Table II indicates estimated output of manufactured goods in 1810 while Table III supplies fuller information for 1850 and 1860.

The South was being outpaced by the West in manufacturing, though both sections were far behind the Northeast. On the assumption that wage labor was concentrated in the Northeast, we can conclude, once again, that the slave economy was increasingly diverging from a free labor economy, as free labor came to mean wage labor.

The data on industrialization demonstrate that a gap was opening up between the sections. This conclusion indeed is shared by all scholars, even those most firmly committed to the view that the South had a successful capitalist economy.

Correlations, however, are not causes and we need to establish the reasons for the slower pace of southern industrialization and urbanization. According to the neo-classicists, the reason is simple: the South's comparative advantage lay in agriculture and thus it was entirely rational for southerners to concentrate on farming rather than commerce or industry. Unfortunately this view now lacks empirical foundation.

14. Wright, "Prosperity, Progress, and American Slavery," pp. 328, 309, 332–333, *Political Economy of the Cotton South*, pp. 90–97. It should be noted, however, that there is no agreement on the extent to which British demand for cotton might have grown in the absence of war and emancipation from the 1860s.

Table II. *Estimated output of manufactured goods, 1810*

Region	Manufactured output ($000)	Population (000)	Output per capita ($)
North	128,570	4,002	32.1
Northeast	128,566	3,965	32.4
Northcentral	4	37	0.1
South	40,831	3,005	13.6
United States	169,401	7,007	24.2

Source: Reprinted from *A Deplorable Scarcity: The Failure of Industrialization in the Slave Economy*, by Fred Bateman and Thomas Weiss. Copyright © 1981 by the University of North Carolina Press.

Table III. *Manufacturing in the United States, by region, 1850–1860*

Region	Capital ($000,000)	Employees (000)	Output ($000,000)	Output per capita ($)
1850				
North	465	845	902	61
Northeast	402	734	756	81
Northcentral	63	111	146	27
South	67	110	101	12
United States	532	945	1003	43
1860				
North	866	1127	1618	78
Northeast	692	938	1271	111
Northcentral	174	189	347	38
South	116	132	193	19
United States	982	1259	1811	59

Source: Reprinted from *A Deplorable Scarcity: The Failure of Industrialization in the Slave Economy*, by Fred Bateman and Thomas Weiss. Copyright © 1981 by the University of North Carolina Press.

According to the most definitive work on southern manufacturing, rates of return in manufacturing in the South were extremely good. "The average for all southern manufacturing," according to historians Fred Bateman and Thomas Weiss, "was 28 percent in 1860 and 25 percent in 1850." And prospects did not vary greatly from subregion to subregion. Moreover, these rates of return "were not simply high, they were substantially above the returns earned from slavery and slave-based farming." Why did southerners not engage in manufacturing to a greater degree? There can be only one answer (though it is one which Bateman and Weiss will not accept): they were not profit-maximizers in the way that neo-classical economics postulates. This is no small matter; it suggests a catastrophic weakness in the entire neo-classical approach to the southern economy. For it reinforces the possibility that a slave-based economy cannot industrialize. And if this is correct, how appropriate can it be to label such an economy "capitalist"?[15]

Let us now see if the Marxist approach fares better. Is there reason to believe that the pursuit of self-interest was mediated or structured by the exigencies of the master–slave relation? Indeed there is. For manufacturing posed special problems for the masters, problems that had no real equivalent on the plantation or in an agrarian society generally and which were also less severe (or absent altogether) in a wage labor economy. An overwhelming amount of evidence can be cited in support of this proposition. Before we examine this evidence, however, we should note the root cause of the master's difficulties. As we shall see, the problems stemmed from the fact that so many slaves did not wish to be slaves, did not wish to see the fruits of their labor appropriated by another and therefore attempted, in various ways, to resist this exploitation. Insofar as the evidence demonstrates that slave resistance (in its many forms) constrained southern economic development, it compels us to acknowledge the vital importance of class interests. In inhibiting the development of industry (and of cities) in the South, the slaveholder was simultaneously advancing a class interest.

As we shall see, the southern failure to industrialize or to urbanize cannot be explained without reference to this class interest. Of course such an interest was, to a considerable extent, an economic one, since the slaves were themselves the source of the economic well-being of the masters. But it was not an economic interest of the kind which modern neo-classical economics envisages: it was not a profit-maximizing impulse. For the slaveholders' pursuit of wealth and prosperity was subject to a complex series of mediations. Here the relations between the contending classes assume the utmost importance. The desire to maintain their slaves and thus their class position constrained the slaveholders' response to commercial opportunities, allowing and encouraging certain activities at the expense of others. And the need to take account of the non-slaveholding whites, whose loyalty was essential to the maintenance of their regime, in turn constrained the defense of slavery, again encouraging certain activities rather than others. The problem with the neo-classical

---

15. Bateman and Weiss, *A Deplorable Scarcity*, pp. 106, 113. See the appendix to this work for a more extended critique of their work.

approach is not its assumption that slaveholders were acquisitive or self-interested but its refusal to accept the existence of these filters, as it were, through which self-interest was perceived or interpreted and then pursued.

II

What then were the problems slavery faced in an industrial environment? One claim, made by Eugene Genovese among others, is that southern slaveholders displayed "a notable tendency toward aristocratic consumption" which "inhibited the rise of new industries." This interpretation is quite consistent with the relational approach favored by Marx; as Genovese puts it, "the high propensity to consume luxuries, for example, has always been functional . . . in aristocratic societies, for it has provided the ruling class with the facade necessary to control the middle and lower classes." Such consumption is obviously highly self-interested not only in itself but also in its tendency to strengthen the master's hold over his slaves, the source of his wealth and income. But it is, of course, a different kind of self-interest from that pursued by a profit-maximizer. Here is an example of the process by which the key relationship between the exploiter (the master) and the exploited (the slave) mediates self-interest or directs it into certain channels rather than others. But the problem is that Genovese presents little evidence of conspicuous consumption while evidence can be found of the contrary phenomenon: that is to say, of wealthy slaveholders living in rather rude conditions. Of course, there was some conspicuous consumption in the South, especially perhaps in the exceptionally wealthy areas close to the Atlantic and Gulf Coasts or by the Mississippi river. But northern societies displayed similar tendencies, particularly among the so-called merchant princes of the urban centers. While it is certainly possible that slaveholders engaged in this to a greater extent than rich northerners, it has yet to be demonstrated. Hence we must look elsewhere to explain the southern failure to industrialize.[16]

In a more general sense, there is a danger of attempting to deduce the characteristics of a slave society, without paying sufficient attention to the specifics of southern slavery. For southerners had not merely their slaves

---

16. Genovese, *Political Economy of Slavery*, pp. 245–246, 18. In this work the only evidence of conspicuous consumption cited is a reference to Thomas R. Dew's defense of the practice (p. 18). See also James Oakes, *The Ruling Race* (N.Y., 1982), pp. 84–85. The same conclusion – that the evidence has not yet been assembled to prove the point – can be drawn regarding claims about soil erosion and poor management practices.

to take into account; if the slaves had been the only factor to consider then a large measure of conspicuous consumption might indeed have served to intimidate them or instill respect for their owners. But the South of the nineteenth century was also the South of the yeoman farmer, who had the vote and who was highly responsive to the cries of "aristocrat" hurled at those who claimed social superiority. The Jacksonian democratic movement was at least as strong in the South as in the North; indeed one can argue that it functioned in part to defend the southern way of life. But its egalitarianism frowned upon conspicuous consumption on the part of slaveholders.[17]

Here was a dilemma which southerners were never able to resolve. Slave ownership constrained the master's freedom of maneuver; the existence of a large number of non-slaveholding whites did likewise. But the problem for the slaveholder was that the constraints were frequently quite different, indeed contradictory. In strengthening his relationship with one group, the slaveholder all too often aggravated his problems with the other. The southern attitude to the work ethic reflects both sets of constraints. On the one hand slavery, especially when it had a racial underpinning, encouraged a tendency to despise the labor performed by slaves. As a result slaveholders throughout history have had an interest in claiming to be above such forms of work. In Antiquity, for example, manual labor was held to be degrading, except when performed voluntarily as a recreation.[18] Some southerners noted this tendency in the South and complained about it. For example James Martin of Alabama, writing in *De Bow's Review* in the late 1850s referred to "the strange notion that our young men have, in believing that the training of the mind and hand to any kind of handicraft, causes them to lose caste in society", while De Bow himself in 1860 complained that "it is the great fault of Southern people that they are *too proud to work*."[19]

---

17. Genovese argues for paternalism on the part of slaveholders to non-slaveholding whites but this, it seems to me, is the weakest part of his entire analysis. Very little evidence is presented and almost the entire southern political tradition runs in the opposite direction. Again see Oakes, *The Ruling Race, passim*. Though the point cannot be discussed here at any length, I believe Genovese is on far stronger ground in arguing for paternalist relations between slaveholder and slave. Now it is true that there were tensions between the two roles: in his relationship with his slaves the master might wish to magnify the distance between himself and the poorer whites; in his relationship with the poorer whites he might wish to minimize it. But this problem is more fundamentally a function of the uneven distribution of slaves in an egalitarian political community and, most fundamentally of all, a function of the weaknesses of slavery as a system of exploitation. See below, Chapter 4.
18. G.E.M. De Ste. Croix, *The Class Struggle in the Ancient Greek World* (London, 1981), pp. 116–122. On southern attitudes to work, see Chapter 4 below.
19. *De Bow's Review*, XXIV (1858), p. 383, XXIX (1860), pp. 74–75, XIX (1855), p. 15.

Yet there was another tendency at work in the Old South. Southern masters had the non-slaveholders to consider. These whites performed manual labor, sometimes precisely the same tasks as the slaves. This checked the tendency to despise such labor, though it did not entirely obliterate it. As we shall see in a future chapter, the result was a permanent tension in southern thought. Some southerners were scornful of manual labor, others insisted that it was highly respected in the South. A third and perhaps more common position introduced a distinction between manual labor, which was deemed to be respectable, and menial labor, which was not. Did these views serve to inhibit industrialization? This is a hard question, since there is no way directly to test the thesis. But it may be significant to note that in the industrializing North a heavy emphasis was placed on the work ethic, and almost all forms of gainful employment were extolled. No distinction was made between manual and menial labor.[20]

Slaveholders faced other problems when it came to using slaves in industry. Even on plantations they frequently complained about the use or rather misuse of tools by their slaves. An example is the following complaint from a South Carolina planter in 1855:

> The wear and tear of plantation tools is harassing to every planter who does not have a good mechanic at his nod and beck every day in the year. Our plows are broken, our hoes are lost, our harnesses need repairing, and large demands are made on the blacksmith, the carpenter, the tanner, and the harnessmaker.[21]

Contemporaries and travellers to the South were often shocked by the slaves' treatment of tools. Why should a slave misuse tools? Marx offered one possible answer in a little known passage in *Capital*:

> Under slavery, according to the striking expression employed in antiquity, the worker is distinguishable only as *instrumentum vocale* from an animal, which is *instrumentum semi-vocale*, and from a lifeless implement, which is *instrumentum mutum*. But he himself takes care to let both beast and implement feel that he is none of them, but rather a human being. He gives himself the satisfaction of knowing that he is different by treating the one with brutality and damaging the other *con amore*. Hence the economic principle, universally applied in this mode of production, of employing only the

---

20. A contrary view is provided in Jonathan Glickstein, *Concepts of Free Labor in Antebellum America* (New Haven, 1991). Although I have found this work immensely stimulating, I do not think this thesis has been demonstrated. I shall return to this question in the second volume of this work.

21. Quoted in Genovese, *Political Economy of Slavery*, p. 55.

rudest and heaviest implements, which are difficult to damage owing to their very clumsiness.[22]

It is of course impossible to know whether the thought processes which Marx describes here were common among the slaves of the Old South. But what is not open to question is the frequency of the masters' complaints about the poor work of the slaves. While all men might be "indolent and have a disinclination to labor," this propensity, according to one southerner, was "a great deal stronger in the African race than in any other." This view accorded nicely with the racism upon which slavery in the South rested but here as elsewhere that racism extracted a high price. Ironically, it encouraged masters to accept poor work. Hence the same southerner noted, with a sad resignation, that the slaves would not work "except to avoid punishment," they would "never do more than just enough to save themselves from being punished," and, most important of all perhaps, "no amount of punishment" would prevent their working "carelessly and indifferently."[23]

Did this make masters reluctant to place slaves in industrial employment, where the dangers or the financial losses arising from the misuse of equipment might be much higher? In 1850 the average value of capital employed to each worker in US manufacturing was $558; in 1860 it was $780. Unfortunately this figure includes not only implements but also the capital invested in land and buildings whereas the figures for southern agriculture do not. Nevertheless the contrast with slave labor in agriculture could not be sharper. In the slave states the value of implements per worker in 1860 was between thirty and forty dollars, regardless of the size of the plantation. Even allowing for the fairly high price of northern land (of which relatively little was needed for manufacturing), the slave in agriculture had far less capital to work with than the industrial worker. The equipment which the industrial worker had at his disposal made that with which the slave in agriculture worked seem cheap indeed. Whether a reluctance on the part of the masters to entrust slaves with more expensive equipment played a role is difficult to say with any certainty. As we shall see, some masters did in fact employ slaves in industry, but the evidence here does not preclude the possibility that across southern society as a whole a real constraint existed.[24]

22. Marx, *Capital*, I, pp. 303–304.
23. Frederick Law Olmstead, *A Journey in the Seaboard Slave States* (N.Y., 1861), pp. 104–105. See also Kenneth M. Stampp, *The Peculiar Institution: Slavery in the Ante-Bellum South* (N.Y., 1956), pp. 99–109.
24. I have derived these figures on capital per employee from the data in Bateman and Weiss, *A Deplorable Scarcity*, p. 17. For the South see Wright, *Political Economy of the Cotton South*, p. 53. See also Stampp, *Peculiar Institution*, pp. 102–103.

The more general problem was that many forms of industrial work enhanced the slave's opportunities for resistance. As a result, many southerners warned that it was too dangerous to allow slaves to become either skilled mechanics or even mere factory laborers. Some commentators feared that in an industrial environment there was an increased risk that slaves would be taught to read and write, perhaps by free blacks, perhaps by sympathetic whites. But the problem was wider than this. Illiteracy by no means precluded the acquisition of skills in an agricultural or an industrial setting but one difficulty was again that many whites were predisposed to doubt the capacity of blacks to acquire skills. "As a general rule," observed the editor of one southern journal in 1860, "it requires more intellect to make a good mechanic than the negro possesses." "The sons of Ham," he explained, "are peculiarly fitted for menial service and the heavier duties of the field, while the manual labor of the white man is better adapted to the mechanic arts, which have, in all ages, occupied a high position." According to one of the delegates at the Southern Commercial Convention held at Montgomery in 1858, "the negro" was simply "not skillful in the mechanic art." But the complexities of the situation became apparent when the same delegate argued that even if this were not so, it would be unwise to teach him this art, since the effect would be to encourage him to resist his enslavement. It was not, he asserted "for our interest that our negroes should be so employed, because such employment gives the negro an opportunity for brooding and meditation, and the fermentation of discontent." The conclusion was that "the field is the proper sphere of the negro." This conclusion was shared by James Hammond of South Carolina. In the early 1840s Hammond had urged the use of slaves in industry but ten years later he had changed his mind. He now insisted that "whenever a slave is made a mechanic, he is more than half freed, and soon becomes, as we too well know, and all history attests, with rare exceptions, the most corrupt and turbulent of his class." Similarly James H. Taylor in *De Bow's Review*, warned that if we "fill our factories and workshops with our slaves . . . we shall have in our midst those whose very existence is in hostile array to our institutions." In this way the fear of servile rebellion once again may have affected the character of southern economic development.[25]

According to Robert Starobin, "industrial slaves usually sought either the fruits of their own labor for their own use and satisfaction, or resentfully tried to cripple their industrial work places," Starobin, *Industrial Slavery in the Old South* (N.Y., 1970), p. 78.

25. *The Plantation*, I (1860), p. 267; *De Bow's Review*, XXIV (1858), p. 581, VIII (1850), pp. 25–26. I have followed the general interpretation of the passage from Taylor but it is possible that he believed it was the white artisans whose "existence" would be "in hostile array to our institutions."

Alongside the fear of the slave, however, was the danger posed by white artisans faced with competition from slave labor. This problem was as prominent when industrialization was discussed as when the growth – or slow growth – of southern cities was under consideration. A writer in *De Bow's Review* (possibly De Bow himself) argued that "in placing the negro in competition with white mechanics – a superior intellectual power – we drag the latter down to a level with the former." The unfortunate result was that the latter were "regarded by some as being no better than the former." This situation was in turn extremely dangerous since "it is well calculated to breed a discontent and hatred on the part of the white mechanic, and make him an enemy to an institution which should be the means of promoting the interests of the very pursuit in which he is engaged." Hence many southerners could not endorse industrialization on the basis of slave labor.[26]

The alternative was for the South to industrialize but using white labor. Such a policy had a definite appeal since it would perpetuate and even confirm the division of labor along race lines. But other southerners were not persuaded of the wisdom of this policy. Once again the exigencies of the master–slave relation created problems. Christopher Memminger of South Carolina, later to be the Secretary of the Treasury in the Confederacy, in 1849 wrote a private letter to James Hammond in which he warned of the danger of creating a white working class. According to Memminger a party was gaining ground in South Carolina, and especially in Charleston, which advocated the exclusion of slaves from all activities except agriculture. (Perhaps Memminger did not know that Hammond was an illustrious member of this "party.") But this group comprised "the only party from which danger to our Institutions is to be apprehended among us." For if negro mechanics were "driven out" of manufacturing and out of the cities then who would take their place other than "the same men who make the cry in our Northern Cities against the tyranny of Capital?" Such men would soon "raise hue and cry against the Negro, and be hot Abolitionists." Moreover, "every one of those men would have a vote." Memminger argued that already "in our Cities, we see the operation of these elements" but if "Barnwell District," for example, were to be filled "with some hundred Lowellers," there would be great scope for a demagogue to "foment division among us." For "even in our lower Country, there are many that could be Marshalled against the Planter, upon the idea that they were fighting against the aristocracy." Though Hinton Helper's volume had not yet appeared, Memminger in effect argued that a white

26. *De Bow's Review*, XXVI (1859), pp. 477–478. See also *De Bow's Review*, XXVI (1859), p. 477, XXIV (1858), p. 581.

working class would furnish the materials which the explosive doctrines of Helperism could ignite.[27]

Other southerners agreed with this judgment.[28] But a more subtle threat was also identified. In a brilliant article published in 1854 in the *Southern Quarterly Review*, an anonymous writer questioned whether the planter actually had any stake in the commercial and industrial development of the South. Then he argued that slavery would only be recognized as a positive good if "the ruling class declare it to be right." The problem was that if industrialization progressed and the "planter class" came to "feel itself inferior to the merchant and the manufacturing class" then "it will no longer dare to defend an institution condemned by them." In effect slavery would be marginalized in the South. The writer then condemned cities and industry alike as a mortal threat to the South and her institutions:

> Every city is destined to be the seat of free-soilism. It is undoubtedly making its appearance in Charleston, and it is destined to increase with every fresh arrival of European immigrants. Whites are driving our slaves from their old employments – all fostered by the cities.[29]

As we have seen, these views were by no means universally accepted in the South. Some southerners claimed that immigration and industrialization on the basis of white labor posed no threat to the South; others insisted that black labor could be safely employed. But these difficulties had no counterpart in the North, simply because slavery did not exist there.[30]

The result was a widespread concern about industrialization, a fear that it might prove incompatible with the maintenance of southern slave society. Even those southerners who went ahead with the use of slaves in industry tacitly recognized the greater freedom of an industrial environment when they arranged the housing of the slaves so as to prevent the occupants from running away, a precaution rarely taken on the plantation. More explicitly, William Gregg, one of the South's foremost industrialists, as late as 1855 admitted that "there are misgivings in the public mind with regard to manufacturing at the South." The widespread

27. Memminger to Hammond, April 28, 1849 quoted in Starobin, *Industrial Slavery*, pp. 209–210.
28. Chancellor William Harper in *De Bow's Review*, x (1851), p. 57. See *The Second Annual Report of the Board of Directors of the South Carolina Institute* (Columbia, S.C., 1850), p. 6 for a warning that the working class might become antislavery.
29. "The Prospects and Policy of the South, as they Appear to the Eyes of a Planter . . . ," *Southern Quarterly Review*, xxvi (1854), pp. 431–457. This article anticipates many of Gavin Wright's arguments.
30. De Bow himself took no consistent line here. See *De Bow's Review*, viii (1850), pp. 75–76, xi (1851), p. 319, xii (1852), pp. 183–185, xvii (1854), p. 182.

suspicion of manufacturing also found expression in the lack of esteem with which manufacturers were viewed in the South. Daniel Pratt of Alabama was perhaps, along with Gregg, the best-known southern industrialist but a series of essays published in the Montgomery *Atlas* "reminded Pratt that his industrial reputation was no evidence of [his] ability to mark out a path for the Southern people" and that his wealth "acquired through manufactures rather than agriculture has made you step above your station." Similarly candidates for high political office in the South were generally required to demonstrate not merely their dedication to slavery, but their attachment to the agrarian way of life.[31]

Finally, industrialization was constrained by another factor. Dependence on the land was in a sense self-reinforcing in that it encouraged a particular form of development in the South, or rather a lack of it. For the exploitation of land and slaves encouraged its own forms of economic behavior. Most importantly it allowed a considerable degree of self-sufficiency on the plantations. Robert Gallman, among others, has shown that cotton and corn were fairly complementary crops in that the time when labor was needed for one was the time when it was not needed for the other. Corn allowed a plantation to feed itself and this self-sufficiency had major consequences for southern development. It meant that there was no specialization in food production by those who were not involved in cotton or crops for export. Hence the markets which these farmers encountered remained local. Many pockets of subsistence or semi-subsistence farming remained in the South even as late as 1860, by which time they scarcely existed in the North. And the final link in this causal chain emerges when we compare northern industrial development with southern. For in the North the displacement of eastern farmers by (especially) western foodstuffs played a key role in providing the labor for the factories of the Northeast. In the South the displacement process was much weaker. The land and climate encouraged the use of slave labor, but once established, slave-based agriculture inhibited diversification and economic development.[32]

---

31. Starobin, *Industrial Slavery*, p. 93; *De Bow's Review*, xvii (1855), p. 780; Bateman and Weiss, *A Deplorable Scarcity*, p. 162.

32. Robert Gallman, "Self-Sufficiency in the Cotton Economy of the Antebellum South," in Parker (ed.), *Structure of Cotton Economy of the Antebellum South*, pp. 5–24; Diane Lindstrom, "Southern Dependence on Interregional Grain Supplies," in Parker (ed.), *Structure of Cotton Economy*, pp. 101–113; Wright, *Political Economy of the Cotton South*, p. 120. Lacy Ford found that in the area of South Carolina he surveyed, 85 percent of plantations were until the 1850s self-sufficient in basic food crops – Ford, *Origins of Southern Radicalism*, p. 58. See also Bill Cecil-Fronsman, *Common Whites: Class and Culture in Antebellum North Carolina* (Lexington, 1992), pp. 18, 106.

For a variety of reasons, then, southerners clung to the more familiar ways of agriculture. The problems in generating a work ethic, a possible reluctance to entrust slaves with expensive tools and machinery, the difficulties of controlling them in an industrial environment, the higher status attached to the plantation life, and the tendency towards local and plantation self-sufficiency in agriculture – some or all of these factors constrained southern industrialization. Of course it is difficult or impossible to subject them to quantitative analysis but this is not a reason to deny their existence. We know that southerners expressed fears of industrialization, for the reasons already mentioned. So only the extent of these fears can be open to question. Although modern economic historians resist the conclusion there is not the slightest reason to doubt that these fears – themselves ultimately attributable to the class conflict between master and slave – played a major part in constraining southern industrialization.

Cities in the South

I

Just as all scholars agree that the South lagged behind the North in industrialization, so it is undisputed that southern urbanization proceeded more slowly. Table IV shows the proportion of Americans living in urban areas, by region in 1810, 1850 and 1860. Urbanization in the South was below that of the Northwest and far below that of the Northeast. Again the real discrepancy emerges with the growth of wage labor and it may be that the key contrast is between slavery and wage labor rather than slavery and free labor.

Slaves were used throughout the antebellum era in both cities and in industry. Moreover, the cities of the South played a key role in the

Table IV. *Percentage of population living in urban areas, 1810, 1850, 1860*

Region	1810	1850	1860
New England	10.1	28.2	36.6
Middle Atlantic	11.5	25.5	35.4
East North Central	0.1	9.0	14.1
West North Central	0	10.3	13.4
South Atlantic	4.5	9.8	11.5
East South Central	0.6	4.2	5.9

Source: Table from Douglas C. North, *The Economic Growth of the United States, 1790–1860* (N.Y., 1961), p.258.

regional economy. Without attempting to theorize the antebellum city either north or south of the Mason-Dixon line, one may suggest that cities functioned to allow a deeper division of labor, to provide the supporting infrastructure for the rural economy, and to facilitate forms of social and commercial intercourse which would be difficult or impossible elsewhere.

If such were the advantages and opportunities offered by cities, they were also the source of the masters' problems. City life required large numbers of small commercial transactions (as well as larger ones), from the buying and selling of goods on the local market or from local retailers to the carrying of the luggage of those newly arrived in the city. Some cities were also industrial centers, though we should remind ourselves that this was by no means a universal characteristic. The problem for the slaveholder was that the network of commercial relations which not only existed within the city but was virtually its *raison d'étre*, gave a degree of autonomy to slaves which many commentators insisted, quite plausibly, was unhealthy. That slavery operated profitably in cities (and in industry) did not remove this problem; on the contrary it aggravated it. For it opened up the real possibility that what was advantageous for individual masters was disadvantageous for the masters as a class.

The commercial opportunities offered by the city resulted in a number of practices that struck many observers as dangerous. In the first place, the hiring of slaves developed. Although this was by no means rare in the country areas, it was far more common in the urban environment. Moreover, in many cities, slaves were allowed to hire out their own time. In these circumstances the master insisted on a portion of the slave's earnings but left him in all other respects alone, not always obliging him even to live in close proximity. Although self-hire and living out were generally banned by city ordinances, the laws proved quite impossible to enforce, as the complaints of many white city dwellers attest.[33] (Some slaves even went so far as to hire other slaves to work for them!) Thus in 1845 a grand jury in Savannah observed that self-hire was "an evil of magnitude," one which "is striking directly at the existence of our institutions." "It is but the beginning of the end," the jury warned, "and unless broken up in time, will result in the total prostration of existing relations." The problem was that self-hire gave the slave too much freedom. "More than any other cause," the *Savannah Republican* complained, the practice was destroying "in fact, if not in name, the relation of master and servant." Although no-one knew how widespread self-hire was, one Charlestonian in 1850 calculated that many thousands

33. Richard C. Wade, *Slavery in the Cities* (N.Y., 1964), pp. 38–54.

of slaves in his city were so situated. But the evil did not end there. For, as the New Orleans *Picayune* pointed out, their example "was contagious upon those who do not possess these dangerous privileges." It is quite conceivable that self-hire was very much in the master's financial interest, but many southerners believed that it created in the slave a love of freedom, a degree of autonomy and a sense of self-esteem that were incompatible with his lowly status. As the Governor of Louisiana observed in 1860, the "pernicious" practice of self-hire gave blacks "liberties and privileges totally inconsistent with their proper condition and good government."[34]

But even this did not exhaust the problems of self-hire. For it profoundly antagonized the white workers forced to compete with the slaves. In 1858, for example the Mechanics Association of Charleston petitioned for the enforcement of the laws passed against self-hire. But the problems were, in reality, insuperable. By the standards of the Old South the mechanics had a real grievance and no amount of tinkering could remove it. If the slaves were hired out at very low rates then whites would be unable to compete; if the rates were higher then the possibility would arise of whites and blacks doing similar work, an affront to the race pride of the whites and a repudiation of one of the fundamental principles of the slaveholders' regime. Only an outright ban could resolve the problem. But a ban presented great problems. A Committee of the South Carolina state legislature wrestled with this problem in a Report published in 1858. The committee observed that "the evil" of self-hire is that the slave "avoids the discipline and surveillance of his master and is separated from his observation and superintendance." As a result "slaves are permitted to go at large, exercising all the privileges of free persons, making contracts, doing work and in every way being and conducting themselves as if they were not slaves." They assumed an air of "freedom and independence." To this extent the committee demonstrated its sympathy for those seeking an outright ban. But unfortunately, the labor thus performed by these slaves was highly useful to the community. Slaves worked in cities as laborers, as porters, as dockers and in many other capacities. The white South was "accustomed to black labor and it would create a revolution to drive it away." Moreover, it was impossible to have a contract with the owner for every specific job (for example carrying a passenger's trunk) done by a slave. The committee concluded that "the subject, therefore, is full of difficulty, and until you can change the direc-

---

34. Savannah *Republican*, Oct. 28, 1845, Charleston *Courier*, Sept. 12, 1850 and New Orleans *Picayune* all quoted in Wade, *Slavery in the Cities*, pp. 50, 52, 49, 51–52; Governor Robert C. Wickliffe quoted in Paul D. Lack, "Urban Slavery in the Southwest" (Ph.D. dissertation, Texas Technical University, 1973), pp. 53–54.

tion of the public prejudice, presuppositions and habit, you can never enforce a law which conflicts with them." Though self-hire was an evil, it was apparently a necessary one.[35]

Moreover, many of the problems associated with self-hire were actually endemic in any hiring system, however carefully supervised by whites. White laborers were, in general, bitterly resentful whenever they had to compete with slave labor, whether it was hired, self-hired, or owned by their employer. In Little Rock in 1858, for example, the labor movement claimed that the "mechanic arts" which should receive the utmost respect, were instead degraded if slave labor was allowed to engage in them. "If the negro is fit for the mechanic arts," the workers asserted, "he may aspire to belles lettres . . . languages, mathematics . . . the graces and accomplishments of music, drawing, dancing . . . ." Such a prospect could not be tolerated. Slave competition affected their material interests, of course, but the Little Rock workers emphasized that this was not their major grievance:

> What is still worse – we find ourselves *morally* degraded by seeing ourselves yoked with hired slave mechanics in the public streets and thoroughfares in the towns of our state, or being confined in the same rooms (shops) with a lot of sweating and puffing hired black slave buck mechanics . . . How humiliating for us to be yoked with hired slave mechanics . . . in towns and crowded cities, in full view of all passers-by. How painful must it be to a noble wife, a loving mother, an adoring daughter or a tender-hearted sister to see the well-cultivated, high-minded husband, the devoted father, the noble son, the kind brother, yoked with hired slave mechanics, on '*the corners of the streets,* and in the market-places.'

The city and state legislatures of the Old South did not move to prohibit hiring out or the use of slaves alongside white labor. Once again they were on the horns of a dilemma. For to concede so important a restriction on the power of the master was to risk further demands from the non-slaveholders and to weaken the moral and political authority of the individual master accordingly. In Little Rock when the skilled mechanics argued that slaves were "better adapted to the labor of the plantation" and sought to ban them from other activities, a local newspaper replied that such a ban would be a precedent for similar demands from those in any pursuit – even farming – and would thus threaten to "abolish

35. South Carolina Mechanic Association of Charleston quoted in Claudia Goldin, *Urban Slavery in the American South 1820–1860: A Quantitative History* (Chicago, 1976), p. 29; South Carolina Committee on Colored People, Report, December 7, 1858 quoted in Wade, *Slavery in the Cities*, p. 52. See also *De Bow's Review*, xxvi (1859), p. 600.

slavery in the South."[36] At Joseph Anderson's Tredegar iron works in Richmond, a group of skilled white workers in 1847 struck to get slave labor removed. But the result was that they themselves were removed. Anderson, in a letter to the Richmond *Enquirer* argued that "such combinations are a direct attack on slave property; and, if they do not originate in abolition, they are pregnant with its evils." Anderson insisted that this was "a matter in which the whole community was concerned" and the *Enquirer*, in declaring that a reversal of his decision would "render slave property utterly valueless," apparently concurred. [37]

The alternative was simply to do nothing and deplore the actions of white workers. On some occasions these actions were quite drastic. Thus in Wilmington in 1857 a group of carpenters burned a building recently erected by slaves and threatened to repeat the action if the use of slave labor were not discontinued. Less dramatically the Mechanical Association of Jackson, Mississippi, sought to strike a responsive chord when it argued that the "suppression of the practice of making public mechanics of negroes would" not merely "operate advantageously not only to the white mechanics," but also "would tend to strengthen the institution of slavery itself." Yet this appeal fell on deaf ears and here as elsewhere urban labor was allowed to harbor grievances against both slavery and slaveholders.[38]

Yet southerners faced a more general problem in the cities. The very essence of the urban environment was the opportunity it gave for mixing with a larger number of people. Moreover, not all of them were, or were ever likely to become, slaveholders themselves and of these some were out-and-out undesirables – from the slaveholders' standpoint. Conspicuous here were the free blacks. A large proportion of the total free black population of the South lived in cities and slaveholders feared the friendships they naturally formed with the slaves. Indeed intermarriage was quite common. In the words of the New Orleans *Daily Picayune*, free blacks were "a plague and pest in the community" because they brought "the elements of mischief to the slave population." In particular they were thought to harbor runaways. More generally they demonstrated the capacity of black men and women for freedom and thus were a living affront to the slaveholders' regime.[39]

But it was not only fraternization with blacks that disturbed the slaveholders. While hostility from urban whites was a real problem, the

---

36. Arkansas *State Gazette and Democrat*, Oct. 16, 1858, Arkansas *True Democrat*, Sept. 29, 1858 both quoted in Lack, "Urban Slavery in the Southwest," pp. 61, 64.
37. Starobin, *Industrial Slavery*, pp. 126–127; Goldin, *Urban Slavery*, p. 30.
38. Starobin, *Industrial Slavery*, p. 212; *Mississippian*, Jan. 7, 1859.
39. *Daily Picayune*, March 8, 1856 quoted in Wade, *Slavery in the Cities*, p. 251; Wade, *Slavery in the Cities*, p. 248.

danger of excessive familiarity between the races was, if anything, still more alarming. Within the interstices of the urban social system a range of dubious activities developed. Backroom bars, grog shops and gambling establishments emerged, which often catered to whites, free blacks and slaves alike. The availability of liquor, in particular, created a whole raft of social problems. In the first place it fostered conviviality between slaves and the various "undesirables" who might frequent the grog shops. Second, it gave rise to drunkenness with resulting insubordination among the slaves. Third, it gave a powerful incentive to pilfering, since many of the owners of grog shops were prepared to accept payments in kind for liquor. The urban environment almost certainly made pilfering easier. Finally, the pilfering might instead result in slaves bringing to market their produce and thus incurring the wrath of local traders and retailers, who were bitterly resentful of slaves selling on the local market goods that were (as a group of butchers in Savannah quaintly phrased it) "unfairly acquired."[40]

One solution was to limit the number of commercial activities in which slaves could engage. Some cities required masters to give passes to slaves whenever they had been authorized to engage in a transaction. But this process was highly cumbersome and indeed it undercut the benefits of slavery in the urban environment. Thus in Camden, South Carolina, in 1817 merchants and storekeepers petitioned the state legislature for the revision of a statute requiring slaves to have written permission before they could buy goods for their owners. Other cities required passes for all slaves who were out after nightfall, but once again such laws proved highly inconvenient for the masters and were extremely difficult to enforce.[41]

If the essence of the urban environment was the complexity of the social arrangements that it facilitated, the inevitable result was greater opportunities for slave resistance in its various forms. Runaways found the city a hospitable environment, not merely because free blacks might offer aid, but because of the more attenuated and impersonal relationships between owner and slave. Another form of protest was the attempt to acquire literacy skills, fiercely resisted by the masters, especially after 1830, but more difficult to prevent in an urban setting. Similarly opportunities for acquiring goods illegally and for disposing of them were, as we have seen, enhanced in the city; pilfering was harder to detect and more richly rewarded. The city, by virtue of the advantages it offered to the master, gave enhanced opportunities for slave autonomy and, potentially therefore, for slave resistance.[42]

40. Goldin, *Urban Slavery*, p. 29.
41. Goldin, *Urban Slavery*, pp. 31–32.
42. Wade, *Slavery in the Cities*, p. 215.

II

These problems were frequently noted by southerners. The Louisville *Public Advertiser* in 1835 noted that in the cities "negroes scarcely realize the fact that they are slaves." Instead they became "insolent, intractable, and in many instances wholly worthless." All too often they would "make free negroes their associates, . . . imbibe feelings and imitate their conduct, and [become] . . . active in prompting others to neglect their duty and to commit crime." Even more important, many southerners feared that abolition was fostered in the cities. Edmund Ruffin in 1857 emphasized the threat abolitionists posed "in the Southern cities, especially, where they may be safe even from suspicion in their various ostensible or real employments of traders, mechanics and laborers, or sailors."[43] Over twenty years earlier, in 1835, a group of eminent South Carolinians met at Calhoun's invitation and reviewed the effect which abolitionism had had upon southern opinion. Although these southerners were confident that the odious doctrines had made little progress in the South, they specifically exempted the cities. "The minds of our Slaves," the report claimed, "are totally uninfected" by abolitionism – but only, it transpired, "out of our commercial cities." These slaveholders expressed a confidence "that a very large majority of the Slaves would support their masters and die by their sides, even in a servile contest" but once again qualified their remarks with the telling words "out of the cities." In New Orleans the *Daily Delta* in 1854 drew attention specifically to the grog shops of the city "within the precincts of whose damned halls, at the dead hour of midnight, heaven knows what plots are hatched against our peace."[44]

In these circumstances it was scarcely surprising that many southerners were convinced that slavery and cities simply did not go together. As one Kentuckian observed in 1848, "there are two things that always, and under all circumstances, abrogates [sic] slavery. The first is a dense population, . . . the next the intelligence of slavery." Hence it was, he concluded, that "slavery exists in Louisville and St. Louis only in name." A South Carolinian in 1822 observed that slavery required "fear" as well as a "strong sense of inferiority" on the part of the blacks. When these requirements were present, the slave was "happy and contented." The writer then added that "that is almost universally the case among the

43. Louisville *Public Advertiser*, Nov. 30, 1835 quoted in Wade, *Slavery in the Cities*, p. 245; *De Bow's Review*, XXIII (1857), p. 547.
44. "Report and Resolutions of a Public Meeting at Pendleton, Sept. 9, 1835" in Clyde N. Wilson (ed.), *The Papers of John C. Calhoun* (Columbia, S.C., 1959–), XII, pp. 549, 87. On the fear of servile rebellion see also the New Orleans *Daily Delta*, Sept. 10, 1854; Wade, *Slavery in the Cities*, p. 158.

country Negroes." A Louisiana planter similarly observed that "slavery is from its very nature eminently patriarchal and altogether agricultural." In other environments "the slaves become dissipated, acquire the worst habits" and are generally "corrupted." Hence the conclusion: slavery "does not thrive with master or slave when transplanted to cities." More bluntly, one southerner simply declared that "the cities is [sic] no place for niggers!" For "they get strange notions into their heads and grow discontented." It followed that "they ought, everyone of them, be sent back onto the plantations."[45]

Of course, not all southerners shared these views. If they had been universal, then the proportion of slaves living in cities would have been even smaller than it was. But there can be little doubt that such opinions were widespread. Can there be any doubt that they therefore fed into, and reinforced, a general anti-urban sentiment within the South, or that this sentiment was a powerful constraint on the urbanization process itself?[46]

The Richmond experience

Before leaving the subjects of urbanization and industrialization, let us look in more detail at Richmond, Virginia, probably the city in the South where slaves were most used in industry. The use of slave labor in the city's manufacturing has been the subject of at least two recent studies.[47] At first glance the Richmond experience seems to give comfort to those who wish to assimilate slavery to capitalism. In 1860 it was the wealthiest southern industrial city, ranking thirteenth in manufacturing in the United States and twenty-fifth in population. The final antebellum decades saw an important trend towards industrialization. Metal working and flour milling were important sectors of the economy but tobacco

---

45.   Louisville *Daily Journal*, Feb. 22, 1848 quoted in Wade, *Slavery in the Cities*, p. 3; [A South Carolinian], *A Refutation of the Calumnies Circulated Against the Existence of Southern and Western States, Respecting the Institution of Slavery, Etc.* (Charleston, 1822), p. 55; Diary of Samuel Walker quoted in Wade, *Slavery in the Cities*, p. 245. See also Wade, *Slavery in the Cities*, p. 209, *Governor Hammond's Letters on Southern Slavery: Addressed to Thomas Clarkson* (n.p., n.d.), p. 9 (for the claim that miscegenation was most common in the cities where a majority of the offenders were said to be northerners or foreigners).

46.   A contrary conclusion is reached by Goldin. See the appendix to this work for a critique.

47.   Suzanne G. Schnittman, "Slavery in Virginia's Tobacco Industry – 1840–1860" (Ph.D. dissertation, University of Rochester, 1986); Rodney D. Green, "Urban Industry, Black Resistance, and Racial Restriction in the Antebellum South: A General Model and a Case Study in Urban Virginia" (Ph.D. dissertation, American University, 1980).

manufacturing was most important of all, employing by 1860 over half the industrial workforce. The tobacco industry was highly profitable for its owners and from 1820 factories grew larger and more numerous, employing by the time of the Civil War, on average, more than sixty workers. Tobacco manufacture required a variety of skilled and semi-skilled, as well as unskilled tasks. What makes Richmond and its tobacco industry so interesting is that slaves were employed there on a large scale. In the 1850s, while the slave population of most cities was declining, Richmond's was increasing, with a marked increase in the number of slaves in industry, and especially tobacco. Indeed by 1860 almost all the labor in the tobacco industry was black, some of it free but most slave. Thus the example of Richmond shows that industrialization and urbanization could both proceed in the South, and on the basis of slave labor.[48]

We need to ask, however, how this slave labor functioned. In 1850 approximately half of the slaves in the tobacco industry were hired; by 1860 the proportion had risen to at least two-thirds. Often urban and rural inheritors of slaves could not afford to support them, especially if their land was relatively infertile and thus turned to the hiring agencies that were prominent in Richmond and other southern cities. The usual hire period was one year, but if the employment arrangement was acceptable to all parties, the hired slave in later years could often renew it himself. In this way, self-hire developed, though it is impossible to say how widespread it was.[49]

It was the fact of hiring, together with the scale of operations in tobacco manufacturing, that generated the problems with the slaves in Richmond. In some southern cities, slaves who were domestic workers or even the property of artisans operating small workshops lived with their masters. In the iron and mining industries, sometimes located in rural areas, they were confined either in barracks or in what were effectively company towns. But the sheer scale of the Richmond tobacco industry made such arrangements impossible. The factory owners found it instead to their advantage to pay 75 cents or a dollar a week to their slaves for board money. So small an amount available for rent necessarily restricted the choices available to the slaves, who often ended up in the same areas of the city as those inhabited by the free blacks, also a highly disadvantaged group. This spatial segregation in turn necessarily limited the amount of control that the employers possessed and also limited the

---

48. Schnittman, "Slavery in Virginia's Tobacco Industry," pp. 30, 22; Green, "Urban Industry, Black Resistance . . . ," p. 209. In 1860 Richmond's population was 38,000, comprising 62 percent white, 7 percent free black, and 31 percent slave.
49. Schnittman, "Slavery in Virginia's Tobacco Industry," p. 114.

sanctions they could apply. Or rather, the sanctions were increasingly characteristic of a wage labor system. The slaves were able often to play off master and hirer. Sometimes the master seems to have taken account of the preference of his slaves when selecting the hirer. The effect would, of course, be to strengthen the slave's power at the workplace. And the hirer could not threaten to sell or break up the slave's family. Slaves who felt ill-treated often ran off to their masters, who of course had their own reasons for objecting to harsh punishments inflicted by the hirer, and who did not share the hirer's concern with industrial output. Owners would sometimes take hirers to court for ill-treatment of their slaves. In consequence whippings were not often imposed and when they were, slaves could respond with a cessation of singing, which the factory owners knew meant low morale and low productivity. More extreme forms of retaliation included physical attacks on overseers, usually under cover of darkness, or even arson.[50]

In these circumstances the factory owners instead devised other means of control. They relied heavily on cash bonuses to provide their workers with incentives. The slaves themselves had ample reason to respond to these incentives, given the considerable autonomy which they enjoyed outside the workplace. In the busy seasons "overwork" rates of three to five dollars per week would be paid. Incentives and rewards were not uncommon in plantation slavery, but it was far less common for them to be given in cash. The result was that the slaves in Richmond's tobacco industry had an unusual degree of purchasing power as well as an unusual degree of independence. They spent their money on liquor, on gambling and in brothels. Drink was both cause and consequence of lawbreaking, with much stealing of food or of tobacco. The slaves' purchasing power gave opportunities for some whites to cater to their needs or to act as receivers of stolen property. Despite being illegal, miscegenation was not uncommon.[51]

50. Schnittman, "Slavery in Virginia's Tobacco Industry," pp. 114, 274, 268, 337, 185. As she observes (pp. 184–185): "When physical punishment was inflicted on slaves by overseers and masters, the result was slave demoralization, manifested by an increase in runaways, work slowdowns, accidents, misuse of equipment, theft, arson, self-inflicted bodily harm, and other acts of sabotage. Both owned and hired slaves indulged in these activities but hired slaves had an additional advantage. If they felt misused, they could flee to their owners and place employers in economic and legal jeopardy. In consequence, employers thought twice before inflicting punishment on slaves."

51. Schnittman, "Slavery in Virginia's Tobacco Industry," pp. 142–143, 171–172, 174–178, 181–182, 217, 251, 338. It is incorrect to argue, as Robert Starobin did, that "if owners of hired slaves felt that bonuses corrupted them or represented a threat to the slaves' lowly status, they surely would not have permitted them to be paid," see Starobin, "Disciplining Industrial Slaves in the Old South," *Journal of Negro History*, LIII (1968), pp. 111–128. As Suzanne Schnittman notes (pp. 222–223):

In the 1850s Richmond's white citizens unleashed a storm of protest against the increased presence and nuisance of blacks, especially the tobacco hands. The slave hiring process which by the 1850s lasted nearly three weeks annually was described as a "boisterous brawl" which disrupted the entire city. Self-hire, illegal in Virginia since 1811, was also outlawed by a city ordinance in 1857, but the practice continued, despite mounting resentment from the white community. At the heart of the problem was what whites took to be the constantly increasing unruliness and insubordination of the slaves (and the free blacks). Attacks were made on the board and bonus system with one newspaper, the *Richmond Republican*, expressing a common attitude when it complained that the system encouraged drinking, gambling, theft, burglary and arson. Throughout the decade newspapers "were filled with accounts of individuals who resisted their enslavement in urban industrial jobs." These anxieties reached a peak in 1852 with the furore surrounding the Jordan Hatcher case.[52]

Hatcher was a slave in a tobacco factory who, in resisting punishment, killed his overseer. The tobacco manufacturers at first wanted him hanged. They argued that "a growing spirit of insubordination amongst the negroes of this city has been manifested for several years and particularly amongst those employed in the Tobacco Factories; who number some two or three thousand." At present, they continued, "this evil" was "so great that the managers of those establishments can now rarely correct the negroes for the greatest offences, without hazarding their lives." Hatcher received a death sentence but a successful campaign was nevertheless launched to have the sentence commuted. The Hatcher case created an uproar in Richmond to rival the one following Nat Turner's rebellion some twenty years earlier. In its aftermath resolutions to bar living out and board money payments were passed by the city authorities though with only limited success. By now the tobacco manufacturers, however, concerned about the loss of production that might follow the ending of incentive payments, were denying that the slaves were a threat to public order. Their political power, together with the city's dependence on the industry, allowed them to contain reforming pressure for some

---

"They knew that slaves needed bonuses to survive and probably would not work without them. They certainly recognized that the bonus had come to be seen by slaves as a right rather than a privilege, as a necessity rather than an option subject to the whim of the employer." The fundamental point is that individual factory owners might have an interest in maintaining the bonus system, however much it might damage the interest of the slave regime as a whole.

52. Material in this and the following paragraph is from Schnittman, "Slavery in Virginia's Tobacco Industry," pp. 121–122, 3–4, 234; Green, "Urban Industry, Black Resistance . . . ," pp. 576–605.

years. The newspapers complained that the manufacturers defended the system in order to be "lenient" with the slaves (who preferred it to any alternative that was available). Many whites felt that the problems were intensifying. By the time of the Civil War draconian black codes were in place in Richmond, as in other southern cities. In the 1850s visitors to the city were "astonished to encounter guards with bayonet-tipped rifles around the Capitol" and other extensive security measures to control the city's large black population.[53]

What does this tell us about slavery, urbanization and industrialization? In 1857 the *Richmond Examiner* drew the following conclusion about slavery in an urban or industrial environment:

> In the South we do an immense injury to the institution of negro slavery by employing our slaves in the mechanical arts in competition with white mechanics, and allowing them to leave the plantation in the country to congregate in towns, in factories, and in the trades. If our legislature were to enact laws prohibiting the employment of negroes in any capacity except as house servants and agricultural laborers, they would do more to strengthen the institution than if a dozen Oregons, Nebraskas, Kansases and embryo territories, containing some dozen or two negro species were brought into the union as slave states.

But what could the slaveholders do? They above all others insisted that the rights of the master should not be questioned. Hiring out was not illegal. It was not illegal to employ slaves in industry, or to give them incentive payments, or to allow them to live apart from their owners. And the system was profitable to the urban industrialist. The only recourse was to extol the virtues of the agrarian life and hope that such values, coupled with a concern about the deleterious effects of urbanization and industrialization on slaves, kept enough of them in the countryside. Some slaveholders, of course, responded to market signals, and put their slaves in industry. Sometimes there were no adverse consequences. But the Richmond experience, at first glance so damaging to the theory that slavery constrains urbanization and industrialization, helps us to see why the South had its "deplorable scarcity," both of industry and of cities.[54]

53. The Black Codes forbade blacks to smoke, carry a cane, use offensive language in public, sell or barter agricultural products without written permission from a white person, or to keep restaurants or any business through which they could sell alcohol. In addition blacks had to give up space on the sidewalks if needed by whites; they might not congregate in numbers of five or more in any location, and were required to disperse from church locations within thirty minutes after the services.
54. *Richmond Examiner* quoted in Green, "Urban Industry, Black Resistance . . . ," p. 573. The tobacco manufacturers professed themselves ardent defenders of slavery, as no doubt they were. Yet the total cost to the employer of hiring and rewarding his

The advancement of class interests (2)

I

How can we explain the growing divergence between the economies of the North and the South in the decades prior to the Civil War? I have argued that the slow pace of development in the South, as measured by conventional indices of urban growth and manufacturing output, cannot be explained without reference to the constraints imposed by slavery. There are simply no other plausible explanations. Both an urban and an industrial environment offered enhanced opportunities for slaves to translate their resentment of their condition into action. Many of the actions they took were clearly attributable to their desire not to be slaves; they can therefore only be seen as illustrations of the class struggles endemic within a slave society. If the slaves had been fully reconciled to their condition, then the masters could have looked upon economic development in the South with complete equanimity.

Of course not all the actions that slaves took in cities or in industry which were alarming to masters proceeded from the same cause. The slave who took advantage of the facilities available in the grog shop, for example, might well have used those facilities had he been a free man. But the problem for the whites was that they themselves had to prevent such action regardless of the cause. If the behavior of the slave flouted the conventions the masters thought essential to their own safety they had to respond, regardless of his precise motives. In other words the masters were compelled to react in a manner that would strengthen their control over their bondsmen. This too is the quintessence of class struggle.

Finally, we should note two other characteristics of the class conflict in the Old South. First it was apparent, as it were, even in its absence. To a considerable extent, the low level of industrialization and urbanization in the South were a function of the masters' desire to maintain full control over the class they exploited and the fear of the *potential* conflict that would otherwise erupt. This potential class conflict between slave and master in an industrial or urban environment constrained southern economic development. To this extent the masters were able to strengthen their system of class rule and exploitation. But of course they paid a heavy price for this success. Here is a second characteristic of the class struggle in the Old South. When northerners looked southwards they

slave workers was higher than he would have had to pay even for free white workers. (Whites would not work in the factories, for reasons of pride rather than money.) And the employer could not fire his slaves in the way that he could fire a free worker. Thus he was acquiring a direct economic interest in emancipation.

were struck by the slow pace of economic development and quickly concluded that the South was backward both economically and socially. The Republican victory of 1860 and the refusal to compromise in the winter of 1860–1861 were directly attributable to this conviction. Hence the slaveholders did not solve the problems of class conflict endemic in slavery; in helping slow down the developmental process in the South, they merely displaced them. Nemesis would come not from slaves in an industrial or urban setting, but instead from northerners, to whom the "deplorable scarcity" of cities and manufacturing in the South was a vivid and irrefutable confirmation of southern divergence from the American mainstream.

II

When describing the United States in the middle of the nineteenth century most historians are struck by the contrast between the free labor system of the North and the slave-based labor found in the South. In dubbing the northern economy a free labor economy, they gloss over the differences between what I have termed capitalist and pre-capitalist commodity production. There are, of course, good reasons to conflate the two, especially when they are being contrasted with slavery. In the modern world wage labor has become dominant in all developed countries so that those who are in the labor force but not working for wages are referred to as the "self-employed," a term that would have been meaningless before the nineteenth century. Wage labor is now entirely respectable, as is self-employment, whereas slavery has been stigmatized throughout the world. Hence in the antebellum United States southern slavery, an ultimate form of unfree labor, naturally contrasts sharply with northern free labor.

Nevertheless in certain respects a more important contrast is between pre-capitalist commodity production on the one hand, and either slavery or wage labor on the other. For most of human history, wage labor has been perceived as something akin to slavery and American democratic thought up to and including the Jacksonian era was heir to this pre-capitalist perception. In this sense the southern apologists for slavery who compared the wage slavery of the North so unfavorably with the chattel slavery of the South were, in dubbing both "unfree," continuing an ancient and venerable tradition, no matter how novel their specific formulations might have been. It was the Republicans themselves who made the dramatic break with the past in assimilating wage labor to "freedom." This ideological shift had momentous consequences and will be the subject of future chapters.

In yet another sense, however, wage labor is the odd man out. There are a number of extremely important similarities between pre-capitalist commodity production and slavery. Both imply agriculture, in slavery for the reasons already discussed, in non-capitalist free labor because a relatively shallow division of labor is necessary. Otherwise complete dependence on market production will force out the inefficient or the unfortunate and convert them into wage laborers. Both imply also a relatively low level of investment. High investment means commercialization, specialization and a process of competition that will again tend to force out the unfortunate or the inefficient. At the ideological level the similarities are no less important and these will also be the subject of future chapters. The home tends to remain the center of production, with the characteristic family farm, or plantation. This contrasts sharply with a capitalist social formation where production instead tends to shift outside the home. As we shall see, a capitalist society is apt to place a heavy emphasis on the distinction between the public and the private, to perceive the family as a refuge, even a "haven in a heartless world." One effect is crucial: a society which views the family in this light is increasingly intolerant of slavery, especially if, as in the American South, the slave is denied the right to a legal marriage. I shall argue that these processes played a key role in bringing about the American Civil War.

It is in the political sphere that the impact of wage labor is most apparent. The principal thesis of this work is that it was possible for southern slavery and pre-capitalist free labor in the North to coexist, but increasingly difficult, and finally impossible, for slavery and capitalism to coexist. For the moment the economic effects are our principal concern. We have found that the Republican and abolitionist attacks on the southern economy were, to some degree, misdirected, as the modern economic historians, often using the techniques of cliometrics, have demonstrated. But we have also found that the contrasts drawn by Republicans between free labor and slave labor are remarkably accurate if one substitutes "wage labor" for "free labor" in the formulation. This difference is certainly crucial, and we must seek to explain it. Nevertheless the conclusion which emerges is that the growth of capitalism in the North generated the economic critique of southern slavery. And this critique, it will be argued, was the principal source of antislavery sentiment. It was thus a principal cause of the American Civil War.

III

In this discussion of political economy I have suggested that class struggle played a more central role in the shaping of southern economic development than most scholars (especially those writing outside the Marxist tradition) have allowed. I have argued that the differences between capitalism and slavery are crucial and that as free labor in the North became wage labor, so the differences with the southern economy became increasingly marked. To some extent these differences derived from a reluctance on the part of many slaveholders to plunge into non-agricultural economic activities even when the market invited them to do so. This reluctance itself was partly the product of "custom," a traditional and perhaps largely unquestioned desire to maintain the agrarian way of life and a refusal to bestow the highest social status on those whose actions threatened it.[55] But it was also attributable to a clear and explicit recognition of the problems involved in maintaining control over slaves in an urban or industrial environment. Although orthodox economic historians can scarcely bring themselves to accept this possibility, the consciousness of a wider class interest almost certainly led many southerners to shun some of the economic opportunities that beckoned and thus to modify the goal of profit-maximization.

Is this any real reason why we should not accept this proposition? The political history of the antebellum republic is replete with examples of southerners detecting in what were apparently the most innocuous measures a threat to their class interests. For example, many of them believed that an increase in the tariff was to be resisted even to the point of nullification (or secession), not merely because of its direct effects but because of the precedent it offered for abolition. A larger number of slaveholders did not even want Congress to be allowed to discuss antislavery petitions, again because such discussions in various ways threatened their control over their slaves. So are we really to believe that they ignored the danger signs visible in their own midst when slaves were employed in industry or when large urban centers developed?

This form of class conflict contrasts sharply with that which we found in the Jeffersonian democratic tradition. In the latter we found an ideology functioning to serve a class interest, even though those who formulated it were not aware of the function. By contrast those who identified in economic development a threat to their class power were acting in strict accordance with class consciousness. Yet once again a simple equation between class consciousness and class conflict is unsatisfactory. As we have also seen, the effect of the class consciousness of the masters was to constrain southern economic development and thus to prevent the full emergence of the conflicts which many southerners feared would accompany industrialization and urbanization. In other words class

---

55. One should not make too much of "custom," since northerners too were heirs to the view that agriculture was the preferred form of economic activity.

consciousness served to mute class conflict. The final twist came when the conflict expected and feared by the masters as a consequence of economic development was displaced into a sectional conflict, as northerners reacted to the slow pace of change in the South.

Yet we have encountered another example of an ideology inscribed with a class interest, and, moreover, a class interest that is undeclared and even unrecognized. This is the ideology which lurks behind the neo-classical approach to economic history. This approach has dominated mainstream economics since the last quarter of the nineteenth century and one of its effects has been to obliterate the distinction between what I have termed capitalist and pre-capitalist commodity production. Of course in practice the distinction between the two is inevitably blurred since there are many intermediate forms that defy easy classification. Indeed it is a principal argument of this work that the North was an economy in transition. While the factories of the Northeast or the semi-subsistence farms which existed in the West in, say, 1840 present no problem, the increasingly commercialized farm of 1860 which employed one or two laborers on a seasonal basis is much harder to categorize, especially if its main reliance was upon the labor of the immediate family. Yet the distinction in principle is straightforward and one may wonder why it has eluded most economic historians. A complete answer to this question is not possible here but some explanation can be offered.

The key is to be found in the history of economic thought itself. The founder of modern economics, Adam Smith, had laid considerable emphasis upon the labor theory of value, asserting (albeit inconsistently) that the value of goods was determined by the labor time taken to produce them. This emphasis was continued in the work of David Ricardo, Karl Marx and others and has indeed proved a central, if still controversial, feature of radical and socialist economics. For the same reason it soon proved politically troublesome. In a non-capitalist free labor economy the doctrine provided powerful ammunition against the owners of landed wealth, whose extraction of high rent from the producer could be seen as a form of exploitation. However, with the development of wage labor, awkward questions arose. The problem was that the profits of the capitalist now had to be explained and the danger was that they too would be seen as an unjustified deduction from the product of labor. Smith had seen this pitfall and had developed, side by side with his labor input theory of value, an alternative labor commanded theory, in which the value of the labor was to be determined by the goods produced. The two theories were not really compatible and Smith never resolved the contradiction.[56]

From the 1860s, however, a shift in economic thinking occurred and economists began to move away from the labor input theory and towards the labor commanded approach. In the early 1870s, economists like William Stanley Jevons, Carl Menger and Leon Walras, each working independently of the others, stressed the role of individual "utility," in determining the value of commodities. Individuals derived different degrees of "utility" from specific commodities and this determined aggregate demand for them. Producers responded to this demand and the price of the commodity was given by the point at which supply and demand intersected. Consumers were thus "utility"-maximizers. But – and this was the key claim – so were producers. Workers decided how much time to work, and in so doing they balanced the desire for leisure with the desire to consume (or save). This balance was itself determined by their own subjective preferences, which allocated different degrees of "utility" to leisure or consumption.

Here was a very considerable triumph for defenders of the capitalist order. The value of labor, the wage rate, was determined impersonally by the market value of the goods produced. Orthodox economics elaborated and refined this theory over many decades. The employer, it was argued, paid the worker according to the marginal product of his labor. The worker chose whether and where to work. Some economists even went so far as to argue that the distribution of wealth was a matter of choice. The poor had chosen to be poor![57]

This is not the place for a discussion or critique of neo-classical, as it came to be termed, economic theory. What is important, however, is to grasp the nature of the neo-classical achievement. Its essence lay in the assimilation of production to consumption and of both to exchange. Producers responded to market signals and maximized "utility", precisely as consumers did. Let us consider the act of consumption more closely. In a market economy it will generally be preceded by an exchange; the seller receives money, the buyer receives the commodity. The exchange is an equal one. No coercion is present; each party both gives and receives. According to the neo-classicists, the wage-relation entails an identical process. The employer and the wage-laborer meet as supplier and consumer of labor. The wage-laborer sells his labor to the employer; in return

---

56. A good discussion of the development of political economy is Ken Cole, John Cameron and Chris Edwards, *Why Economists Disagree: The Political Economy of Economics* (London, 1983).
57. In case this should seem a gross exaggeration, consider the following passage: "The most important conclusion that emerges from the economic analysis of the personal or family distribution of income is that in a broad sense, and subject to inequalities of initial circumstances . . . the distribution at a point in time is determined by individual choice." – H. G. Johnson, *The Theory of Income Distribution* (London, 1973), pp. 220–221, quoted in Francis Green and Peter Nore (eds), *Economics: An Anti-Text* (London, 1977), p. 89.

he receives an equivalent in the form of wages. Another exchange relation has been established.

At the time Marx was writing *Capital* the full flowering of neo-classical economics lay in the future. But he was very much aware of the efforts of contemporary economists to assimilate the wage relation to an act of exchange. He gave the following ironic restatement of the theory:

> The sphere of circulation or commodity exchange, within whose boundaries the sale and purchase of labor-power goes on, is in fact a very Eden of the innate rights of man. It is the exclusive realm of Freedom, Equality, Property and Bentham. Freedom, because both buyer and seller of a commodity, let us say of labor-power, are determined only by their own free will. They contract as free persons, who are equal before the law. Their contract is the final result in which their joint will finds a common legal expression. Equality, because each enters into relation with the other, as with a simple owner of commodities, and they exchange equivalent for equivalent. Property, because each disposes only of what is his own. And Bentham, because each looks only to his own advantage. The only force bringing them together, and putting them into relation with each other, is the selfishness, the gain and the private interest of each. Each pays heed to himself only, and no one worries about the others. And precisely for that reason, either in accordance with the pre-established harmony of things, or under the auspices of an omniscient providence, they all work together to their mutual advantage, for the common weal, and in the common interest.[58]

The deficiency in this approach, of course, lay in the refusal to consider the inequality – of power, income, and wealth – likely to obtain between the employer and the worker. The formal equality at the point of exchange, while of considerable importance, contrasts sharply with, and indeed masks, the inequality at the point of production. Marx drew attention to the contrast:

> When we leave this sphere of simple circulation or the exchange of commodities, which provides the "free trader *vulgaris*" with his views, his concepts and the standard by which he judges the society of capital and wage-labor, a certain change takes place, or so it appears, in the physiognomy of our *dramatis personae*. He who was previously the money-owner now strides out in front as a capitalist; the possessor of labor-power follows as his worker. The one smirks self-importantly and is intent on business; the other is timid

58. Marx, *Capital*, I, p. 280.

and holds back, like someone who has brought his own hide to market and now has nothing else to expect but – a tanning.[59]

The neo-classical tradition in the late nineteenth century answered to many of the needs of the existing capitalist order. An emphasis on the formal equality of exchange served to displace from economic theory, and thus legitimize, the glaring inequalities at the point of production. At a time when unfree labor systems throughout the world were being dismantled and when the social order was being challenged by radicals and socialists, neo-classicism, ostensibly value-free and scientific, gave powerful ammunition to the defenders of the *status quo*.

As a result orthodox economic theory scarcely considers the relationship between the wage-earner and the capitalist except as an act of exchange. This emphasis on exchange means that slavery contrasts dramatically with free labor, since it denies the producer the right to enter freely into contracts, and consequently the right to sell either his goods or his labor on the market. But wage labor and non-capitalist free labor merge into one since the distinction between the sale of goods and the sale of labor on the market appears trivial by comparison. And economic history bears the imprint of neo-classical theory. Indeed the recent work of cliometric historians, who have borrowed the econometric techniques of modern neo-classicists, bears this imprint perhaps even more clearly than the older economic history.

A glance at any economic history textbook illustrates the effect. The development of market production is invariably perceived to be of far more importance than the growth of wage labor. Once market production has been established, the major index of economic change is the proportion of the workforce employed in industry as opposed to agriculture, or, alternatively, the proportion of the population living in cities as opposed to the countryside. The textbooks reflect the priorities of the subject as it is now studied. Little wonder then that one cannot at present find detailed information about the proportion of the workforce employed for wages.

Of course, not all who have embraced mainstream economics share these political goals. This is because the class interest inscribed on neoclassicism is invisible even to some of its devotees. But the effect of neoclassical assumptions, as we have seen, is to concentrate attention on certain aspects of economic behavior rather than others and to bias the economist in favor of certain explanations and against others. Unfortunately the economist is oblivious to these biases if, without necessarily sharing the goals of its founders, he perceives the neo-classical

59. Marx, *Capital*, I, p. 280.

approach to be scientific, value-free and objective. As Marx himself put it:

> Political economy confuses, on principle, two different kinds of private property, one of which rests on the labour of the producer himself, and the other on the exploitation of the [wage] labour of others. It forgets that the latter is not only the direct antithesis of the former, but grows on the former's tomb and nowhere else.[60]

Where Marx wrote "political economy," may we not substitute "the economic history of slavery"?[61]

60. Marx, *Capital*, I, p. 930.
61. A scholar whose work is at least partially exempt from these weaknesses is Gavin Wright. See the appendix to this work for a critique of his interpretation of the southern antebellum economy.

PART II

Slavery versus capitalism

3

Abolitionism

The impact of abolitionism

I

The nineteenth century, and especially its middle decades, was the great era of western capitalism. Its greatness lay not in its material achievements, which, however impressive to contemporary observers, seem modest indeed by the standards of the twentieth century, but instead in the courage and confidence that inspired some of its spokesmen. In these years the challenges that would later undermine the political, economic and intellectual certainties of the mid-Victorian era were as yet scarcely glimpsed and mankind seemed finally to have found the path to everlasting material and moral improvement. It was above all the nations and the classes which were most obviously benefiting from this material change where the gospel of progress took firmest hold. This meant the bourgeoisies of the more developed economies – in particular Britain and the United States, the two most advanced industrial nations in the world in 1860. In some quarters the confidence of the era shrank into a smug self-congratulation, a myopic complacency about a future whose character was assured. But among other groups the notion of progress was energizing: there was evil and malpractice in the world and the reformer must not hesitate to war against them, whatever the cost in inconvenience or unpopularity, however great the risk of financial or physical hardship.[1]

The great crusade against slavery, triumphing first in Britain but culminating in the emancipation proclamation and the American Civil War, was initiated by bourgeois reformers who displayed precisely this combination of bravery and self-sacrifice. Antislavery in both countries, but especially in the United States, attracted many adherents. Some did not claim that their concerns were altruistic or that they wished in any way to

---

1. I hope this paragraph expresses some of the admiration which I feel for many of the reformers, and most of the abolitionists, of the antebellum North. While I do not share their confidence either in "progress" or – which was much the same thing anyway – in capitalism, I am struck by their dedication, their self-sacrifice and their commitment to a set of, on the whole, highly laudable goals.

improve the condition of the enslaved; instead they embraced an economic critique which dwelt upon the injustices done to the non-slave-holding whites in slave society. This analysis was extraordinarily powerful by the eve of the Civil War.[2] But in parallel there ran for over thirty years a concern with the immorality of slavery, an insistence that it was utterly evil, that it should not be tolerated, and that even to compromise with it was to perpetrate evil. Immediatists, as these anti-slavery reformers have been termed, were dedicated reformers who insisted that the moral question be kept uppermost. Their dedication would lead some of them to reject their churches, their religions, their government, and their nation's constitution.

Antislavery had become prominent in the western world in the last quarter of the eighteenth century. But historians are agreed that a new era opened with the first issue, on January 1, 1831, of William Lloyd Garrison's *Liberator*. In the prospectus of that first issue Garrison set out the terms on which he would engage in the struggle with slavery:

> I will be as harsh as truth, and as uncompromising as justice. On this subject, I do not wish to think, or speak, or write with moderation . . . . I am in earnest – I will not equivocate – I will not excuse – I will not retreat a single inch – AND I WILL BE HEARD.[3]

Soon there were many abolition societies. Apart from the Garrison circle, the most famous groups were those headed in upstate New York by the wealthy philanthropist Gerrit Smith, in New York city by Arthur and Lewis Tappan and in Ohio by Theodore Dwight Weld. In Boston the group around Garrison included Wendell Phillips, one of the greatest orators of the nineteenth century. Although the question of women's rights would soon split the abolitionist movement irrevocably, women like Elizabeth Cady Stanton, Sarah and Angelina Grimké and Lydia M. Child played major roles. Not all abolitionists, of course, shared the same views even of the slavery issue; in particular there were sharp differences over the question of political involvement, with the Tappans and Smith prepared to take their principles into the political arena, and Garrison and Phillips insisting that such involvement would inevitably sully the

2. It was, as I shall argue in the sequel to this volume, at the heart of the Republican party's appeal.
3. *Liberator*, Jan. 1, 1831. For samplings of the different political positions see *Annual Report of the American and Foreign Anti-Slavery Society* (N.Y., 1849), p. 11; almost any issue of *Principia*, or the *Radical Abolitionist*; William Lloyd Garrison, "Disunion," *The Anti-Slavery Examiner no. 12* (N.Y., 1845); Charles E. Hodges, "Disunion our Wisdom and Our Duty," *Anti-Slavery Tracts*, no. 11 (n.p., n.d.); "The United States Constitution," *Anti-Slavery Tracts*, no. 1 (n.p., n.d.); Wendell Phillips, "Can Abolitionists Vote or Take Office Under the United States Constitution," *The Anti-Slavery Examiner no. 13* (N.Y., 1845), p. 7.

movement and blunt its moral force. Garrison himself came not only to repudiate the US constitution but to embrace a form of Christian anarchism that was anathema to many, perhaps most, abolitionists. As we shall see, abolitionists claimed the right for all men and women to follow the dictates of their consciences. Conformity would never characterize their ranks.

The differences within abolitionism are of great interest but they are not of primary concern here. Instead my goal is to relate the movement to the emerging capitalist order of the North.[4] But since this is itself part of a discussion of the origins of the Civil War, a prior question presents itself: what was the role of abolitionism in intensifying the sectional controversy in the years after 1830?

II

While it is impossible to determine with accuracy the impact of abolitionism upon the northern people, there is no doubt that in its early years the movement was extremely unpopular. On October 21, 1835 Garrison was attacked by a mob which placed a rope around his neck and led him through the streets of Boston. He was then imprisoned by the authorities for his own protection. The previous year a mob entered Lewis Tappan's house and destroyed the furnishings, while two years later another mob in Alton, Illinois, murdered Elijah Lovejoy, an abolitionist editor. Henry

4. My understanding of reform movements has been considerably influenced by Paul Johnson, *A Shopkeeper's Millennium* (N.Y., 1978) and, though its subject is a much larger one, by Stephanie Coontz, *The Social Origins of Private Life: A History of American Families, 1600–1900* (London, 1988). The work upon abolitionism that I have found most useful is Ronald G. Walters, *The Antislavery Appeal: American Abolitionism After 1830* (Baltimore, 1976). One must still refer, however, to older works like Gilbert Hobbs Barnes, *The Antislavery Impulse, 1830–1844* 2nd ed. (N.Y., 1964). See also Louis Filler, *The Crusade Against Slavery, 1830–1860* (N.Y., 1960). Only in the 1960s did the abolitionists begin to receive a favorable press from historians generally. See the essays in Martin Duberman (ed.), *The Antislavery Vanguard: New Essays on the Abolitionists* (Princeton, 1965). Since that time scholars have given very careful consideration to their opinions and to the differences within their ranks. Especially valuable here is Aileen S. Kraditor, *Means and Ends in American Abolition: Garrison and His Critics on Strategy and Tactics, 1834–1850* (N.Y., 1970), which corrects the anti-Garrison bias found in some of the earlier works. On abolitionist thought see, in addition to Walters, Lawrence J. Friedman, *Gregarious Saints: Self and Community in American Abolitionism, 1830–1870* (Cambridge, UK, 1982); Lewis Perry, *Radical Abolitionism: Anarchy and the Government of God in Antislavery Thought* (Ithaca, 1973); Peter F. Walker, *Moral Choices: Memory, Desire and Imagination in Nineteenth-Century American Abolition* (Baton Rouge, 1978) – valuable studies all. A good collection of essays is Lewis Perry and Michael Fellman (eds), *Antislavery Reconsidered: New Perspectives on the Abolitionists* (Baton Rouge, 1979). On the whole it is safe to say that historians have been more successful in explicating abolitionist thought than in elucidating the social origins of the movement.

B. Stanton later recalled that he had been mobbed one hundred and fifty times before 1840.[5] These mobs did not, however, necessarily reflect the spontaneous reactions of the people. Many were organized, comprising negrophobes of low social standing but led by, as contemporaries and historians have described them, "gentlemen of property and standing." Yet hostility to blacks was endemic in northern society and undoubtedly many northerners were repelled by a movement that would apparently jeopardize the Union in order to improve the conditions of an inferior race. The Ohio legislature, for example, passed a resolution condemning the abolitionists as "wild, delusive, and fanatical," and even a sincere opponent of slavery like Abraham Lincoln signed a resolution in Illinois stating that the effect of abolitionism was to increase the evils of slavery, rather than to eliminate them. When in the 1840s Garrison began to burn the US constitution in public, on the grounds that it sanctioned slavery in the South, he again incurred bitter hostility. As David Potter points out, northerners wanted both to be antislavery and to retain the Union. Garrison challenged the cosy assumption that the two were easily reconciled and reaped a considerable unpopularity as a result.[6]

An agitator, however, invariably provokes hostility and resentment and such hostility may even be a measure of his success. Garrison himself announced that "there shall be no neutrals . . . . Men shall either like me or dislike me." Both reactions were widespread. Despite its unpopularity in many quarters, abolition undoubtedly made large advances in the 1830s. Newspapers and periodicals were established, pamphlets published, agents enlisted. Theodore Weld, for example, met with considerable success in Ohio. An area covering several counties was already organized as the Paint Valley Antislavery Society before he arrived, but by the time Weld left it had 4,000 members and was the largest in the country.[7]

The abolitionists soon had an impact on national politics. In 1835 at the second annual meeting of the American Anti-Slavery Society, Lewis Tappan proposed that a massive pamphlet campaign be launched with the pamphlets sent all over the country, but in particular into the South. Tappan's suggestion was accepted and the circulation of the pamphlets

5. Merton L. Dillon, *The Abolitionists: The Growth of a Dissenting Minority* (DeKalb, Ill., 1974), p. 76; Leonard L. Richards, *"Gentlemen of Property and Standing": Anti-Abolition Mobs in Jacksonian America* (N.Y., 1970).
6. Russel B. Nye, *Fettered Freedom: Civil Liberties and the Slavery Controversy 1830–60* (Urbana, 1972), pp. 14, 18; David M. Potter, *The Impending Crisis, 1848–1861* (N.Y., 1976), pp. 47–48.
7. Garrison quoted in Russel B. Nye, *William Lloyd Garrison and the Humanitarian Reformers* (Boston, 1954), pp. 50–51; Dwight L. Dumond, *Antislavery: The Crusade for Freedom in America* (N.Y., 1961), pp. 183–184.

immediately caused a furore. They greatly increased the fame – or the notoriety – of the abolitionists. In the mid- and late 1830s the American Anti-Slavery Society took up and extended the practice, common since the time of Washington, of petitioning Congress. The House in 1836 adopted the famous gag rule (which remained in force until 1844) by which antislavery petitions would be received but then immediately laid upon the table, without discussion. This action, however, merely encouraged the abolitionists to greater efforts. In the third session of the twenty-fifth Congress, for example, petitions on no fewer than eight different slavery-related topics were submitted. They requested the abolition of slavery in the District of Columbia and in the territories, the repeal of the gag law, the prohibition of the interstate slave trade, the recognition of the Republic of Haiti, and the removal of the federal government to a free state. In addition they opposed the annexation of Texas and the admission into the Union of any more slave states. In all there were 1,496 such petitions presented to the House of Representatives, containing more than 100,000 signatures. These petitions probably reached a wider audience than any other form of antislavery literature.[8]

It is impossible to say how many Americans became abolitionists. In 1838 James Birney estimated that there were more than fourteen hundred societies with at least 112,000 members. Birney explained that the true figure might be closer to 150,000 and he claimed that, in any case, an equal number were waiting for the opportunity to join a society as soon as one was founded in their locality. Of course as a proportion of the US population (approximately seventeen million in 1840) or even of the northern population, this number was small. But it did indicate a rapid growth in support over the decade.[9]

By the late 1830s, however, abolitionism had reached an impasse. The initial hope that slaveholders themselves could be induced to free their slaves had proved to be quite illusory. Partly as a result of this failure, Garrison in particular had begun to question more and more of the fundamental values of the nation, and to challenge its religious leaders in the North as well as the South. He began to cast doubt upon the value of some passages in the Bible, he embraced a feminist position that was a century or more in advance of most of his countrymen, and after 1842 he launched a direct assault upon the federal constitution. The movement accordingly began to fragment and never again would there be the concerted action that had produced the petition campaign of the 1830s. Many abolitionists reached precisely the opposite conclusion to Garrison about politics and urged antislavery men and women to take

8. Dumond, *Antislavery*, pp. 245–246.
9. Dumond, *Antislavery*, pp. 257–258.

their case to the voters. In 1840 and 1844 the Liberty Party ran Birney himself for president. In the first of his campaigns he obtained fewer than 7,000 votes but four years later his support had increased almost tenfold to 62,000. Undoubtedly there was some moderation of the antislavery message but it was clear that the party was becoming a force to be reckoned with. Even among political abolitionists, however, there were disagreements about the federal constitution with some arguing that it was an antislavery document which authorized the federal government to take action against slavery wherever the state governments were not sovereign. This meant an attack on slavery in the District of Columbia, for example, abolition of the interstate slave trade and the repeal, on the grounds of unconstitutionality, of laws for the return of fugitive slaves. This position later became associated with Salmon P. Chase and with the radical wing of the Republican party in the 1850s. Other abolitionists, like Lysander Spooner, William Goodell and Gerrit Smith, instead claimed that the constitution authorized even the abolition of slavery in the southern states where it existed. This view was, of course, the antithesis of Garrison's.[10]

As slavery began to occupy the center of the nation's political stage in the mid- to late 1840s, abolitionists added their voices to the chorus of anti-southern and antislavery sentiment that was emerging in the North. They deplored the annexation of Texas, the war with Mexico, the gains resulting from that war and the concessions to the South that were made in the Compromise of 1850. Many, though by no means all, of the Liberty party men joined the Free Soil ranks in 1848 and this brought them closer to the mainstream of national politics even if it entailed a further dilution of antislavery principles. By the 1850s it was even more difficult to measure the impact of the abolitionists since parts of their message were being transmitted by many who were quite separate from, indeed often bitterly opposed to, the movement. The extent of antislavery and anti-southern sentiment in 1860 cannot, of course, be taken as an index of the success of abolitionism, since many Republicans, probably a large majority, were explicitly opposed to the doctrine of immediate abolition.

On the other hand, the abolitionists had themselves helped to educate and convert many of the leading Republicans, especially those on the radical wing of the party. In the 1830s Weld converted Joshua Giddings, Ben Wade and Owen Lovejoy to antislavery, while in Massachusetts Charles Sumner and Henry Wilson freely acknowledged their debt to Garrison. All these men played major roles within the Republican party in the 1850s. Salmon P. Chase was perhaps the leading

10. On these divisions, see esp. Kraditor, *Means and Ends.*

example of a Liberty party man who achieved national prominence and high office as a Republican. In 1853 Wendell Phillips gave a public oration in which he assessed the impact of the abolitionists. He listed a dozen well-known Republicans and claimed that the "antislavery cause," by which he meant the abolitionists, had had a major, though unacknowledged, effect in facilitating their careers:

> The antislavery cause . . . converted these men; it gave them a constituency; it gave them an opportunity to speak, and it gave them a public to listen. The antislavery cause gave them their votes, got them their offices, furnished them their facts, gave them their audience. If you tell me they cherished all these principles in their own breasts before Mr Garrison appeared, I can only say, if the antislavery movement did not give them their ideas, it surely gave them the courage to utter them.

Of course Phillips was anything but a dispassionate observer and a possible rejoinder would be to claim that it was not simply the abolitionists but an entire series of events, over which the abolitionists themselves had no control, that created the antislavery constituency in the North and prepared the way for the rise of the Republican party. This objection has some, but only limited, validity.[11]

The process by which abolitionism affected northern sentiment was a complex one. In the first place, it had a direct effect in convincing some northerners of the rank injustice of slavery. Those who were thus persuaded might well join the movement but their numbers, as we have seen, were limited, especially in comparison with the much larger numbers who were willing to support the far more moderate antislavery of the Free Soil and Republican parties. However, the most important effect of abolitionism on northern opinion was an indirect one. The movement caused the deepest alarm and anger among many southerners. Their reactions propelled them and their northern allies into a series of defensive moves which in turn generated the currents of anti-southern sentiment that swept the North from the late 1840s and which would ultimately erupt in Civil War and culminate in the abolition of slavery. Let us examine this process in more detail.

III

To understand the southern response to abolitionism we must recall the situation in the southern states in the early 1830s. In 1831 Nat Turner's

---

11. Wendell Phillips, *Speeches, Lectures, and Letters* 1st series (Boston, 1863), pp. 136–137. The best discussion of the relationship between abolitionism and radical republicanism is chapter 8 of Friedman, *Gregarious Saints*, pp. 225–252.

revolt in Virginia sent a shock wave through the South. The attempted insurrection made many southerners feel highly vulnerable and filled them with anger and anxiety at the prospect of a militant attack by northern opponents of slavery. Equally important, however, were the events taking place in Britain where the pressure for abolition was mounting. The British abolitionists finally triumphed in 1833 and for southerners their victory was ominous indeed. Although other slave regimes remained, a principal ally in the form of the West Indian slaveholders had been lost. Even more alarming was the encouragement given to American abolitionists. Southerners concluded that they must take every possible action to prevent a repetition of the events that had transpired in Britain.

Thus the initial unpopularity of abolitionism in the North gave many southerners no comfort. They noted with Arthur P. Hayne of South Carolina that "for the first 25 years, Mr Wilberforce was repeatedly mobbed in the Streets of London for his fanatical doctrines." Yet "in less than 25 years" he and his men had "guided" the English people to embrace this "their darling abstraction:" "that as liberty . . . was sweet – so slavery must be 'a bitter draught.'" Southerners also noted that at first Wilberforce had claimed only to oppose the slave trade. As soon as this goal had been realized, however, he had changed tack and come out against slavery itself. So how seriously could southerners take abolitionist claims that they wanted slavery to be ended by the voluntary action of slaveholders? Agitation meant the risk of falling slave prices, a collapse of public confidence in slavery, and a further fall in prices. Before long the federal government would be able to buy the slaves and effect the ruin of the planters. Alternatively they or their northern converts would abandon any commitment they acknowledged to the constitution or claim that it permitted congressional action against slavery in the states. As the *Charleston Mercury* argued in 1833, if a northern majority ruled, the southern states would be "as virtually colonies as the British West Indies – as much at the mercy of knavish and fanatical speculators, and with no greater security for their liberty and property."[12]

Hence southerners watched the progress of abolitionism with fear and trepidation. They soon appreciated that the movement was expanding. Future president John Tyler in 1835 observed that whereas two years earlier when he had been in Washington, the abolitionists had been a ridiculed handful, now they had 250 subordinate societies with four presses in New York alone. Three years later in 1838, after receiving some abolitionist pamphlets, a group of southern congressmen in a committee headed by F. H. Elmore of South Carolina, wrote to James Birney

12. William W. Freehling, *Prelude to Civil War: The Nullification Controversy in South Carolina, 1816–1836* (N.Y., 1965), pp. 307–308, 123.

and asked him a series of questions about the abolitionists. Elmore asked how many abolition societies there were, how many members they had, what their strategy was, how and how well they were funded as well as a whole host of additional questions. It was apparent that these southerners took the abolitionists very seriously indeed.[13]

Although Franklin Elmore was at the head of this committee, its guiding spirit was his leader and fellow South Carolinian, John C. Calhoun. Calhoun had begun his career as a nationalist, but he had responded to the shifts of opinion within his state in the 1820s and had become an ardent defender of states' rights. The principal change of policy concerned the protective tariff, which Carolinians now saw as the cause of all their economic woes. By 1830 Calhoun too was preoccupied with the tariff and this was indeed the issue that precipitated the nullification crisis. But as William Freehling has shown, behind the tariff question lay the larger issue of federal power. And the concern with federal power was prompted above all by fears for slavery. Hence even the empowerment of the tariff as an issue among southern militants depended to a considerable extent upon the slavery question. Calhoun himself made it clear where his priorities lay. "Of all questions, which have been agitated under our government," he reminded a group of Georgians in 1836, "abolition is that in which we of the South have the deepest concern." For (unlike the tariff) "it strikes directly and fatally, not only at our prosperity, but our existence, as a people." [14]

Throughout the 1830s and 1840s Calhoun took the utmost care to monitor the progress of the abolitionists in the North. In 1836 he announced to the Senate that the antislavery cause was "no longer in the hands of quiet and peaceful . . . Quakers," but instead had been taken up by, and was "under the control of," "ferocious zealots." These fanatics were "organized throughout every section of the non-slaveholding States," they had "almost unlimited funds" at their disposal, and were "in possession of a powerful press, which, for the first time, is enlisted in the cause of abolition." In January 1836 he warned of the "rapid advances in the Northern states" which the abolitionists were making and one year later he claimed that they had "already succeeded in a great measure, in bringing the public mind under their control in

13. Allan Nevins, *Ordeal of the Union: Fruits of Manifest Destiny* (N.Y., 1947), p. 140; Dumond, *Antislavery*, pp. 257–258.

14. Freehling, *Prelude to Civil War, passim.* Calhoun to A.S. Clayton and others, Athens, Ga., Aug. 5, 1836 in Clyde N. Wilson (ed.), *The Papers of John C. Calhoun* (Columbia, S.C., 1959–) XIII, p. 263. The best biography of Calhoun is still Charles Wiltse's multivolume work, though it errs in failing to recognize that the constraints under which Calhoun was operating made the kind of consistency which Wiltse finds (and so admires) impossible. On the early years see Wiltse, *John C. Calhoun, Nationalist, 1782–1828* (Indianapolis, 1944).

many of the States" of the North. Little wonder then that he dubbed the movement "the mightiest evil that has ever threatened our Government." By now he was convinced that if abolitionism were not arrested, the Union would not survive. The next few years brought no respite; on the contrary, the power of the abolitionists continued to grow. In 1838 he noted that the current number of abolition societies represented an increase of 500 percent within three years. They were "increasing at the rate of one a day." By the early 1840s he perceived a further accretion of strength. "Whatever doubt might have existed of the tendency of the Abolition movement at its origin," he told the Senate in 1842, "there [can] . . . be none now, that it . . . [will] end in the dissolution and overthrow of the Government." Already the zealots "wield power sufficient to govern the legislatures of some of the States." The South must therefore take action.[15]

Calhoun's view of the abolitionists was more fully thought out than that of many southerners. He was quick to label them fanatics and associated them with the religious zealotry of the seventeenth century which "tied the victim that it could not convert, to the stake." This spirit of persecution, "after lying long dormant," he declared, "is now resuscitated in another form, with no abatement of its blind fury or thirst for blood." This analysis was the standard southern polemic. But Calhoun also tried to analyze the reasoning of the abolitionists. They began with the abstract notion that slavery was an evil and then with "the blindness of fanaticism" leapt to the conclusion that it was "their duty to abolish it, regardless of all the disasters, which must follow." He himself of course by now subscribed wholeheartedly to the view that slavery was a positive good, but he nevertheless argued that, even if it were an evil, the abolitionist conclusion was erroneous. Government itself, for example, could be dubbed an evil yet should it on these grounds be abolished? This was a more interesting analogy than he knew. For William Lloyd Garrison himself was soon to reach the same conclusion. Indeed the two men saw eye to eye on many questions. Both believed that the constitution explicitly protected slavery within the states; both believed that to extirpate evil, not only the constitution but government itself must be challenged.[16]

Calhoun's most interesting observations, however, were on the growth of the movement. He realized that the abolitionists could, of course, advance simply on the basis of a successful appeal to public opinion

---

15. *Papers of Calhoun*, XIII, p. 163; Calhoun to Littleton W. Tazewell, Jan. 24, 1836, in *Papers of Calhoun*, XIII, p. 50; *Papers of Calhoun*, XIII, pp. 366, 497, XIV, p. 71, XVI, pp. 110–111.
16. *Papers of Calhoun*, XIV, pp. 58–59, XIII, p. 62.

or, if necessary, by reshaping public opinion. This was the process he described to the Senate in 1836. While the "enlightened of all parties at the North" were "with little exception" as yet "sound," yet the "ample means possessed by the abolitionists" would allow them to "poison" the minds of "the young, the thoughtless, and the enthusiastic." "The incessant action," he warned, "of hundreds of societies, and a vast printing establishment, throwing out daily, thousands of artful and inflammatory publications, must make, in time, a deep impression" on "the young, the inexperienced, the ignorant and thoughtless." But to his credit he also developed a political theory that, without specific reference to the abolitionists, could explain how they were able to advance. In his *Disquisition on Government* he argued that a political system based upon the rule of the numerical majority would inevitably degenerate into anarchy or tyranny since the prospects for gain were too great: the majority would plunder the minority by the use of the power of taxation. So far his theory was of general applicability and it did not specifically relate to abolition. However, the key fact was that the lure of the spoils would induce each major party to make reckless appeals to various interest groups in order to manufacture the all-important majority. Hence, as he explained to the Senate, northern partisans, in the heat of the party battle, would be forced to bid for the support of the abolitionists, with a reckless disregard of the consequences for the South and the nation. "In the hot contest of party in the Northern section," on which the control of both state and federal government might depend, he began, "all the passions are roused to the greatest height in the violent struggle, and aid sought in every quarter." As a result the parties will "forget us in the heat of battle; yes, the success of the election, for the time . . . [will] be more important than our safety." It was therefore of limited significance that "the great mass of both parties of the North are opposed to Abolition." Their fear of "incurring the displeasure" of the abolitionists and thus inviting electoral defeat would pervert their principles, to the ruin of the South. "Of this," he concluded "we may be perfectly assured."[17]

In pursuit of a remedy, Calhoun first alighted upon nullification, an attempt to unite the South behind a constitutional theory that sharply limited the power of the numerical majority. Nullifiers insisted that a majority of the representatives of all the principal interests must concur before legislation could be agreed. But the strategy required a widespread conviction that abolition and the tariff already portended doom for the

---

17. *Papers of Calhoun*, XIII, pp. 275, 65, XV, pp. 103, 101, XIII, p. 263; John C. Calhoun, "A Disquisition on Government and a Discourse on the Constitution and Government of the United States," in Richard K. Crallé (ed.), *The Works of John C. Calhoun* 6 vols (Columbia, S.C., 1851–1855), I, pp. 373–376.

South, and outside South Carolina this view was not held by most southern statesmen in the early 1830s. Calhoun fully appreciated the need for
unity in the South. "It is time," he wrote in 1833, "that the South should
overlook all minor differences and unite as one man in the defense of
liberty." But nullification failed (though Calhoun himself was loath to
admit it) and a change of strategy was required.[18]

Central to his strategy of the 1830s was the creation of unity within the
South. To his enemies this was a disgraceful objective, since it meant
breaking down the attachments to party, which they believed produced
harmony between the sections by defusing explosive questions like slavery. But for reasons we have already examined, Calhoun felt unable to
rely upon public opinion in the North and he argued that Congress, since
it ultimately reflected majority opinion, was no more reliable. As a result
the South had only herself to depend upon. Fortunately, in the federal
constitution lay the salvation of the South and thus of the Union. "The
Constitution," he declared in 1836 "has placed in our power ample
means, short of secession, or disunion, to protect ourselves." "All we
want," he concluded, "are harmony and concert among ourselves to
call them into effectual action, when the necessity comes."[19]

The crucial task was to re-educate the electorate, first of the South and
then perhaps of the North too, into a correct understanding of the constitution. Too many of his countrymen had assumed that "this was one
great national republic, to which the States bore the same relation that
counties do to a State, and in which, of course, the voice of an absolute
numerical majority was without any practical restraint." So heretical a
view, however, did violence to the rights of the States. And although
abolitionism had been created by the spirit of persecution and bigotry,
it had been "excited into action" by this very illusion. Hence "the antidote was to be found in the opposite view of our system; that it was a
federate republic; that the States composed its parts, and that the Union
was formed and entered into for the purpose of their mutual advantage
and security." It followed that the states' rights principle, correctly understood and correctly applied, was "the only one that could interpose an
effectual check to the danger, and restore harmony and concord to the
Union."[20]

Calhoun set out to restore the government to its original purity and
thereby vanquish the abolitionists. He repeatedly urged southerners to
refuse to make any concessions. "The very ground on which we are asked

18. Calhoun to Bolling Hall, March 25, 1833, quoted in William J. Cooper, Jr., *The
     South and the Politics of Slavery, 1828–1856* (Baton Rouge, 1978), p. 109.
19. *Papers of Calhoun*, XIII, p. 263.
20. *Papers of Calhoun*, XIV, p. 37.

to make the first concession," he warned, "will be urged on us with equal force to make the second, the third, and every intermediate one till the last is consummated." First on the abolitionist agenda was the demand that their petitions be received in Congress. If this were granted, the next demand would be for abolition in the District of Columbia. Next would come an attack on slavery in the territories, then on the interstate slave trade, finally on slavery in the States. "At every step," he concluded, "they would become stronger, and we weaker, if we should be so infatuated as to make the first concession."[21]

Such reasoning led Calhoun to scrutinize every piece of congressional legislation, every congressional action, to ensure that the rights of the states were not infringed. Little wonder, then, that he soon became known as John Crisis Calhoun. His policy on the petitions was rejected and a compromise was struck by which they were accepted but tabled without further discussion. Nevertheless he continued to seek commitments from northerners and southerners alike on the slavery question. In 1837, in direct response to abolitionist pressure, he introduced six resolutions into the Senate. They were designed to force a confrontation on the slavery question, to put northerners, and especially northerners who claimed to be friendly to the South, to the test. The resolutions declared that slavery was a local institution which nonetheless must be protected by the federal government and condemned abolitionism as "a direct and dangerous attack on the institutions of the Slave-holding States." Calhoun's goal, once again, was to break down the allegiance to party which, he believed, divided the South fatally even as it offered opportunities to avaricious spoilsmen in the North. Despite the success of the resolutions, he again failed in that for the next five years or so party issues relegated sectional questions to second place. But even in 1837 Calhoun succeeded in embarrassing many southerners. They had not wished the resolutions to be introduced but found it impossible not to support them, once they had appeared. This earned Calhoun considerable unpopularity, even in the South. Many dedicated supporters of slavery took the view that agitation of the question by proslavery men as well as by abolitionists was dangerous and to be condemned. They believed that the best way to combat abolitionism was to ignore it, and not allow it to become a subject of political debate.[22]

Some historians, especially those of the "revisionist" school, have applauded these sentiments and argued that agitation of the slavery question, by extremists of either North or South, was indeed a key cause of sectional strife. But Calhoun's position was no less logical or

21. *Papers of Calhoun*, XIII, pp. 75–76.
22. I shall return to this question in Chapters 5 and 6.

sensible, if one grants his initial premise. He realized, in fact, that his course of action was likely to arouse antagonism in the North. "We are told," he acknowledged to the Senate, "that the right of petition is popular in the North, and that to make an issue, however true, which might bring it in question, would weaken our friends, and strengthen the abolitionists." Such an outcome was most regrettable; he, for one, "would not do any thing, willingly, which would weaken them at home." But the issue was not so simple. If a concession – and here he was referring to the petition controversy but the argument applied to all the points of sectional conflict – would ease northern pressure on the South, then it should indeed be considered. But this result could not be guaranteed and "nothing short of the certainty of permanent security can induce us to yield an inch." As we have seen, Calhoun believed that the antislavery movement in the North needed no aid from outside to advance and that concession would encourage rather than discourage it. Such a view was certainly plausible, probably correct. And according to Calhoun, "if there must be an issue, now is the time." "We never can be more united or better prepared for the struggle," he declared, and "I, for one, would much rather meet the danger now, than to turn it over to those who are to come after us." Again his argument is difficult to challenge. Time was indeed on the side of the North. In industrialization, in urbanization and in population growth the North was outstripping the South and when the conflict did come, these factors would prove decisive. In these respects Calhoun's position was well formulated and well considered. He would knowingly risk strengthening the abolitionists in the North in order to establish what he took to be the constitutional rights of the southern states.[23]

In the 1830s Calhoun experienced one failure after another. In the 1840s, however, he triumphed, at any rate in the short term. When the unfortunate death of William Henry Harrison in 1841 propelled John Tyler into the White House, a rupture between the Whig party and its new president soon occurred. Tyler had never been an orthodox Whig but as Vice-President this would scarcely have mattered. Now the effect of Harrison's death was to create a president without a party. Moreover, Tyler and his Secretary of State, Abel P. Upshur, shared many of Calhoun's opinions. Indeed Tyler had left the Democratic party with Calhoun over the nullification controversy. By 1843 he was searching for an issue with which to challenge the hold of party. As he put it in a letter of 1844, "the great point is to rouse the South and to unite it." The

23. *Papers of Calhoun*, XIII, pp. 106–107.

death of Upshur in a steamboat accident was yet another fortuitous development. Calhoun entered Tyler's cabinet as Secretary of State.[24]

As early as 1837 Calhoun had been talking of the desirability of annexing Texas. By the winter of 1843/4 there was intense interest in the project. It was seen as a way of strengthening slavery but others, chiefly Democrats, like Robert J. Walker of Mississippi and John L. O'Sullivan, editor of *Democratic Review* and originator of the phrase "manifest destiny," believed in the measure for reasons quite independent of slavery. Here was Calhoun's chance. He had hoped to win the Democratic nomination in 1844 but it seemed almost certain that it would go instead to Martin Van Buren, in his view the archetypal spoilsman. At a stroke he would be able to damage Van Buren, improve his own presidential prospects and deal a blow to abolitionism. Calhoun seized the opportunity. He drafted his famous letter to Richard Pakenham, British minister in Washington, in which he took strong ground not only in favor of the annexation of Texas, but also on behalf of slavery. The effect was to associate in the public mind the annexation with slavery and to make it difficult for northerners who were mindful of antislavery sentiment in their own states, to support. As a result, Van Buren was overthrown, James Polk was elected and Texas was annexed. Calhoun did not get everything he wanted; he was denied the presidency himself, for example. But he did succeed in strengthening the connections between the Democratic party, slavery and the South.[25]

The cost, of course, was a reaction in the North, with the build up of free soil sentiment. But Calhoun, as we have seen, was willing to pay this price. In the 1840s and the 1850s the Democratic party would become increasingly tied to slavery and the South, to the growing discomfort of its northern members. Calhoun's strategy was working. But in a sense it empowered the abolitionists even as it sought to emasculate them. By reacting so intensely to their propaganda, Calhoun and his supporters took actions which would add immensely to the strength of antislavery and anti-southern sentiment in the North.

IV

Calhoun was one of many southerners who believed that abolitionists sought to incite the slaves to rebellion. There was at best only a modicum of truth in the claim but no number of denials would convince southern militants. Governor Floyd, of Virginia, for example was convinced that

---

24. Calhoun to H.W. Conner, July 3, 1844 quoted in Clement Eaton, *The Freedom-of-Thought Struggle in the Old South* rev. ed. (N.Y., 1964), p. 151.
25. For a fuller discussion of these events, see below, Chapter 6.

the Nat Turner rebellion was attributable to abolitionist writings, and especially to the *Liberator*, while William Gilmore Simms in the *Southern Literary Messenger* wrote that, owing to the nature of the blacks, slave insurrections "have been singularly infrequent, and perhaps would never have been dreamed of, were their bad passions not appealed to by the abolitionists or their emissaries." He believed the blacks to be "not a warlike people . . . indeed, a rather timid race" – until acted upon by designing abolitionists. Twenty years later, during the election campaign of 1856, the South was again gripped by the fear of slave revolts. According to the *Mississippian*, "the conspiracies detected among the slaves in Tennessee, Kentucky, South Carolina, and Texas show that the vile emissaries of abolition, working like moles under the ground, have been secretly breathing the poison of insubordination into their minds."[26]

The combination of abolitionist pressure and the Nat Turner revolt made southerners from the early 1830s increasingly intolerant of all criticism of slavery. In Virginia laws were passed forbidding blacks from preaching or from circulating incendiary pamphlets; in North Carolina, Alabama and Tennessee the laws were directed also against assemblies of blacks. Except for Kentucky, every southern state passed laws controlling and limiting freedom of speech and of the press. In 1836 Maryland imposed a penalty of between ten and twenty years imprisonment for anyone arguing in favor of abolition and Virginia did the same. Both Maryland and Tennessee made it a felony for any free black to receive an abolitionist newspaper. In the cotton South such legislation was by then already in place. Throughout the South newspapers, books and magazines were all carefully watched. By 1840 discussion of slavery had more or less ceased in southern schools and educational institutions and by the late 1850s across most of the South even ownership of Hinton Helper's *The Impending Crisis of the South* constituted treason.[27]

Abolitionist activity in the 1830s produced a whole series of responses from southerners.[28] To combat the pamphlet campaign the Virginia

---

26. Eaton, *Freedom-of-Thought Struggle*, pp. 121, 125–126; *Southern Literary Messenger*, III (1837), p. 657; *Mississippian*, Dec. 19, 1856. Abolitionists began by repudiating violence utterly but by 1859 many of them were applauding John Brown – his means as well as his ends. See Haven, *Sermons*, p. 172, *National Sermons*, pp. 169–177; *Principia*, Nov. 26, 1859; Friedman, *Gregarious Saints*, pp. 196–222.

27. Eaton, *Freedom-of-Thought Struggle*, pp. 122–143; Nye, *Fettered Freedom*, pp. 91, 161.

28. In addition to the pressure of white abolitionists, black revolutionaries like Nat Turner and, equally important, David Walker, played major roles in creating the climate of fear in the South of the 1830s. Unfortunately the role of black abolitionists is beyond the scope of the present work.

legislature passed a law whose effect was to have the addressee arrested. President Jackson was eager to use federal law against the pamphlets but, largely owing to the fear of centralized power, the South opted instead to leave the matter to the states. Censorship of the mails by postmasters and Justices of the Peace now became common, in spite of a federal law that forbade the practice. In Charleston former Governor Robert Hayne led a mob which invaded the post office and destroyed sacks of the offending pamphlets. In the state legislatures of South Carolina, North Carolina, Georgia, Alabama and Virginia, resolutions were passed asking northern states to make it a felony even to publish abolitionist materials. (Such legislation was proposed but never adopted in the North.) It was at this time that prices were placed on the heads of the abolitionists. Georgia offered $5,000 for the trial and conviction "under the laws of this state, [of] the editor or publisher of a certain paper called the *Liberator*," while Governor George McDuffie of South Carolina in 1835 told the state legislature that those who published abolitionist material should be put to death without benefit of clergy![29]

Yet the official southern response to abolitionism was one that did not satisfy large numbers of southerners. Extra-legal action was also recommended, and taken, by members of the southern elite. In Congress Joshua Giddings, Owen Lovejoy and John P. Hale were all threatened with hanging by southerners. Governor James Hammond of South Carolina told the South Carolina state legislature that abolitionism could be "silenced in but one way – *Terror–Death*." He further observed that a group of citizens cooperating to suppress abolitionism was "no more a mob than a rally of shepherds to chase a wolf out of their pastures." In 1836 he warned the abolitionists, "ignorant and infatuated barbarians as they are, that if chance shall throw any of them into our hands, they may expect a felon's death." From the mid-1830s, Committees of Vigilance were formed in many localities of the Deep South. In the words of the committee of Barnwell District, South Carolina, "where the laws of the land are insufficient to meet the emergency, the laws of natural justice and self-preservation shall supply the deficiency." The members of the committee avowed themselves "deliberately and advisedly determined that the guilty *shall not escape!*" Some committees regularly inspected hotels and taverns and checked the baggage of travellers, as well as offering rewards for the capture and conviction of famous abolitionists.[30]

29. Eaton, *Freedom-of-Thought Struggle*, pp. 198–199, 201; Nye, *Fettered Freedom*, pp. 139, 67, 154–155; Fawn M. Brodie, "Who Defends an Abolitionist?" in Duberman (ed.), *Antislavery Vanguard*, pp. 57–58. See also W. S. Savage, *The Controversy Over the Distribution of Abolition Literature* (Washington, D.C., 1938).
30. Nye, *Fettered Freedom*, pp. 177, 179; Brodie, "Who Defends an Abolitionist?", p. 57.

While the heyday of the mob was probably the 1830s, such extra-legal action continued to be advocated up to the time of the Civil War. By the 1850s southerners had observed the rise of free soil sentiment in the North. Many of them failed to distinguish it from abolitionism. Like Benjamin M. Palmer of Louisiana they now perceived a continuous growth in northern antislavery sentiment, from the 1830s when it was represented by "a few fanatics, who were at first despised," to the "gigantic proportions" which it assumed in 1860, with Abraham Lincoln its "high-priest." In the mid-1850s many southerners were terrified by the prospect of abolitionism in Kansas. The main impact was felt in Missouri and, addressing a proslavery convention there, one speaker was frank in recommending the treatment that should be meted out:

> the practical abolitionist, who labors to impair a vested right of property in slaves, is a negro-thief. And a negro thief should be regarded and treated as a horse-thief, a burglar, or any other sort of thief; and those who give them aid and comfort should be regarded and treated as their accomplices in guilt. An organized band of such persons, and for such ends, should be treated as an organized band of conspirators against the lives and property of the citizens, enemies alike to God and man; and, therefore, slaveholding communities have just the same right to take all necessary measures of defence, whether legal or extra-legal, judicial or extra-judicial against a negro thief, or an organized band of negro thieves, as they have a right to take, and are universally acknowledged to have a right to take, against horse thieves or house-thieves.

The actions of proslavery Missourians in Kansas outraged northern opinion in the mid-1850s. In conjunction with the other actions taken at least in part to combat abolitionism, they confirmed the allegations of a "slave power."[31]

---

31. Rev. Benjamin M. Palmer, *Thanksgiving Sermon, Delivered at the First Presbyterian Church N. Orls, . . . Nov 29, 1860* (N.Y., 1861); [James Shannon], *An Address Delivered Before the Pro-Slavery Convention of the State of Missouri . . . July 13, 1855 on Domestic Slavery* (St. Louis, 1855), p. 28. Southerners continued to review the past and continued to find evidence of a rapid growth of abolitionist sentiment. As one of them put it on the eve of the Civil War: "Scarcely thirty years ago, the abolition party was so small and insignificant that it was greeted, even in New England, with derision and ridicule. Now, it has overspread fifteen States of this Union; taken possession of their political power; wields it to its own purposes; has thoroughly sectionalized the country; and at the last Presidential election gave to its sectional candidate, although a mere adventurer without any claims to statesmanship, 1,301,812 votes, and that, too, against a man irreproachable in character, and one of the most experienced statesmen in the Confederacy" – [John Townsend], *The South Alone, Should Govern the South . . .* (Charleston, 1860), p. 13. See also George S. Sawyer, *Southern Institutes, or , An Inquiry into the Origin and Early Prevalence of Slavery and the Slave-Trade . . .* (Phil., 1858).

This charge became the stock-in-trade of Republicans in the 1850s but by then it had been central to the abolitionist critique of slavery for more than twenty years. The abolitionists had claimed from the outset that, in order to maintain so unnatural an institution as slavery, southerners were compelled to take desperate actions which would jeopardize the liberties of all Americans, northerners and southerners, blacks and whites. The petition campaign was, in this respect, a masterstroke. It showed the South willing to sacrifice the right of petition on the altar of slavery. So important a figure as John Quincy Adams, who did more to publicize abolitionism in the 1830s than any other congressman (except perhaps Calhoun) avowed that his primary concern was with the right of petition, not the abolition of slavery. From the time of the introduction of the gag rule to its repeal in 1844 congressmen maneuvered to avoid or sustain it and the result was additional publicity for the antislavery cause and further evidence of the existence of a "slave power."[32]

In the mid-1830s southerners were able to count upon some northerners to aid them in their war against the abolitionists. Again, however, the consequence was to strengthen the forces of antislavery. The pressure on northern legislatures to act against abolitionists alarmed many northerners who were themselves quite unconcerned about the plight of the slave but very concerned to maintain freedom of speech. The anti-abolition riots of these years, conducted by men who were taking their cue from the leaders of southern opinion, also created deep disquiet and tended to confirm the abolitionist claim that slavery disorganized the entire nation. Charles Sumner in 1836 wrote that "we are becoming abolitionists at the North fast: riots, the attempts to abridge freedom of discussion, and the conduct of the South generally, have caused many to think favorably of immediate emancipation who have never before been inclined to it." But it was the murder of Elijah Lovejoy in Alton, Illinois, which did most to enlist support for the abolitionists in the North. In the words of one historian, "the Alton tragedy rocked the North to its foundations. With it abolitionism and freedom of the press merged into a single cause." After it, according to future Republican Senator Henry Wilson, "large accessions were made to the ranks of pronounced and avowed abolitionists." (One convert was none other than Wendell Phillips.) William Channing, for example, had once deprecated the abolitionist movement as almost "wholly evil" but now said he looked upon it "with unmixed respect."[33]

32. Good examples of abolitionist emphasis on the "slave power" are Parker, *The Slave Power, passim*; Burleigh, "Slavery and the North," pp. 10–11.
33. Nye, *Fettered Freedom*, pp. 41–85, 149–150, 136–137. Abolitionists also made the point that their enemies were threatening the civil liberties of all northerners. See "To the People of the United States," *The Anti-Slavery Examiner* no. 1 (n.p., 1836), p. 7.

Though the abolitionists had begun with the hope of convincing southerners, they had soon realized that this goal was unattainable and focused
all their energies upon the North. Some of them, at least, were fully aware
that they had pushed southerners into increasingly drastic actions.
Wendell Phillips, who had a clear vision of his role as agitator, in 1853
declared that "to startle the South to madness, so that every step she
takes, in her blindness, is one step more toward ruin, is much." And
"this", he claimed, quite accurately, "we have done."[34]

The origins of abolitionism

While it is relatively easy to show the impact which abolitionism had both
upon the North directly and upon northerners as a result of southern
responses to the movement, its origins present a greater challenge.
Historians should not ignore the debate over British antislavery, since
some of the vital questions have been raised there. The issues are indeed
complex and they concern, above all, the relationship between ideas and
economic interests.

Initially historians paid no attention to economic factors when explaining the rise of abolitionism. They instead saw the movement in the same
terms as the abolitionists themselves; indeed the very first historians had
actually been abolitionists. Thomas Clarkson's *History of Abolition* is a
good example. Clarkson, a prominent British abolitionist, believed that
antislavery began as early as the sixteenth century with prominent individuals like Queen Elizabeth I and gradually spread until it attained the
influence which enabled it to dismantle slavery in the British Empire.
Such an account accorded well with the Whig interpretation of history,
which invoked a concept of progress to explain historical change. Often,
as in Clarkson's case, progress itself was attributed to Providence, though
more secular versions of the Whig interpretation were also advanced. As
Howard Temperley has noted, this may be termed the "intellectual diffusionist" account of the origins of antislavery. It is an essentially idealist
approach.[35]

In American historical writing a variant of this idealism has been very
much in evidence, even in comparatively recent times. We may take as an
example Dwight L. Dumond's *Antislavery: The Crusade for Freedom in*

34. Phillips, *Speeches, Lectures, and Letters*, p. 153.
35. Thomas Clarkson, *The History of the Rise, Progress and Accomplishment of the
     African Slave Trade by the British Parliament* 2 vols (London, 1808); Howard
     Temperley, "The Ideology of Antislavery," in David Eltis and James Walvin (eds),
     *The Abolition of the Atlantic Slave Trade: Origins and Effects in Europe, Africa, and
     the Americas* (Madison, Wis., 1981), pp. 21–35.

America, first published in 1961. This book has been highly influential and its arguments merit a brief examination. Dumond discussed the origins of abolitionism in a chapter entitled "Impulses for Reform." He gave the Whig interpretation an American, Turnerian twist by emphasizing the role of the West. "History," he wrote, "does not reveal another migration of people equal to that which poured *no less* than six million souls across the Alleghenies in three decades after 1810." Dumond then contrasted the West, "truly a land of promise and opportunity," with the eastern states and "particularly the cities," where a "deep depression had settled." Without in any way demonstrating the relevance of these activities to the growth of antislavery sentiment, he then described the processes of community and state-building in which the newly arrived westerners engaged. Roads, railroads and canals joined the West to the East. And in the East there was a "startling increase in crime, intemperance, and poverty in the cities," to combat which a host of benevolent and reform societies sprang up. Nevertheless it was again the challenge of the West that proved decisive. Politicians, financiers, industrialists and religious leaders all knew its "strategic importance," and all "came to realize that here would be fought to conclusion the battle between slavery and freedom." Dumond also gave attention to the changes in evangelical religion, spearheaded by Charles Finney, and to the political reform movements in the North which brought universal manhood suffrage, abolition of imprisonment for debt, and the growth of public schools. These in turn he attributed to "man's fierce passion for individual freedom and equality of opportunity."[36]

Finally, Dumond described the activities of the American Tract Society, which would serve as a model for other benevolent movements, including abolition, and again stressed the role of political democracy. He concluded his chapter with a series of questions. "Need one wonder," he asked, "why an institution at war with the natural rights of man, the cardinal principles of the Christian faith, and the ideals of individual freedom and social progress was swept away?" "Is it necessary," he continued, "to labor over the source of opposition to the extension of slavery beyond the Mississippi and to colonization?" This question, like the one which preceded it, seemed rhetorical but, in case there were any readers still in doubt, Dumond answered it: "the answer, of course, is an emphatic no!"[37]

Dumond's explanation for the rise of abolition was little more than another invocation of the notion of progress. Migration to the West, as the example of the southwestern states shows, implies nothing about

36. Dumond, *Antislavery*, pp. 151–157.
37. Dumond, *Antislavery*, pp. 151–157.

slavery. Nor was universal manhood suffrage, if, as even in the North, it was usually for whites only, incompatible with the most dogmatic forms of proslavery. Undoubtedly there were links between the abolitionists and other reform movements and Dumond is correct to emphasize the extent to which abolition was modeled on those movements. To this extent he is adopting a viable idealist, indeed "intellectual diffusionist" position. But this cannot be anything like a complete explanation. To explain abolitionism in terms of the general reform impulse merely displaces the question: what accounts for the reform impulse itself?

As his concluding remarks imply, Dumond applauded the abolitionists (and especially the non-Garrisonian abolitionists). Other historians, often though by no means always from a southern background, have been far more critical. Many have denied that abolitionism can be attributed to "progress". Drawing attention to the highly emotive, indeed often violent rhetoric of the abolitionists, their refusal to compromise, and their demand for "immediate" emancipation (qualified though this may have been), these scholars found the explanation for the movement in the psychological problems experienced by its members. David Donald in the 1950s argued that abolitionists were experiencing acute status anxieties. They were "a displaced class in American society," members of a formerly elite group now experiencing "profound social and psychological dislocation," and participating in the movement because it offered the only opportunity for "personal and social self-fulfillment." He even went so far as to claim that "the freeing of the slaves ended the great crusade that had brought purpose and joy to the abolitionist" with the result that "for them Abraham Lincoln was not the Great Emancipator; he was the killer of the dream." Similarly Avery Craven, in a work first published in 1942, believed that "the modern psychologist," with his emphasis on "youthful experiences, maladjustments, inferiority complexes, and repressed desires," had much to contribute to an understanding of the origins of abolitionism. Other historians have also spoken of the need to ease tension and especially the tension produced by guilt, as a key characteristic of the abolitionist.[38]

The objections to this approach are many, varied and well-known. First, the tendency was to confine the psychoanalysis to the abolitionists. Even proslavery extremists were often spared. But the "moderates" on the slavery question were assumed to be entirely healthy, psychologically. This leads to the second objection. It was taken for granted that the centrist, compromising approach of the majority was viable, even perhaps morally supreme. In making this assumption, these historians often

---

38. David Donald, *Lincoln Reconsidered* (N.Y., 1956), pp. 28–36; Avery Craven, *The Coming of the Civil War* (Chicago, 1957), p. 117.

showed how low a priority they gave to the victims of these compromises, the slaves. The notion that the mainstream opinion on slavery might itself be pathological was never considered, let alone refuted. Third, the attempt to link abolitionism with declining status lacked empirical foundation. It has never been shown that the abolitionists as a group were declining in status, still less that this was the reason they joined the movement. Fourth, the assumption that the aggressive posture which the abolitionists often adopted was a sign of maladjustment is itself highly value-laden. It simply ignores the reality of the situation in which the abolitionists found themselves. They were surrounded by intransigence, hostility and hatred; in these circumstances an aggressive response, it can be argued, was entirely natural and "normal."[39]

Recent historiography has sought to deploy some of the insights of psychology, though in a far less tendentious form. Yet in general historians have not recently confronted the question of the origins of American abolitionism. Instead they have considered the principles, values and attitudes of the abolitionists, and, in particular, the meaning of the movement to those who participated in it. These works have been, for the most part, highly suggestive; by implication they shed light upon the question of origins. But we need to glance in addition to the literature on British antislavery.

The essential starting point is Eric Williams's *Capitalism and Slavery*. According to Williams, economic forces built up, sustained and finally dismantled slavery in the British Empire. Economic self-interest was the key at each stage. Slavery was intimately related to the West Indian sugar monopoly, it was established when the sugar monopoly required it and destroyed when the sugar monopoly found it burdensome. Williams concluded that "the rise and fall of mercantilism is the rise and fall of slavery."[40] As a result he played down the role of British abolitionists in the destruction of slavery, even while rather grudgingly conceding the idealism and sincerity of at least some of them.

Williams's empirical work has drawn heavy criticism. Some scholars have challenged his claim that the destruction of West Indian slavery promoted the interests of a capitalist class; indeed abolition has been described as an act of "econocide." Yet even if these criticisms are valid, they do not invalidate his work. For Williams's achievement was to assign to material factors a larger role than they had traditionally played and he placed at the top of the agenda the question of the relation-

---

39. Some of these points are made in Gerald Sorin, *The New York Abolitionists: A Case Study of Political Radicalism* (Westport, Conn., 1971), pp. 3–17. See also Brodie, "Who Defends an Abolitionist?"
40. Eric Williams, *Capitalism and Slavery* (Chapel Hill, N.C., 1944), pp. 169, 136.

ship between capitalism and antislavery. Although a severe critic of Williams, Howard Temperley has observed that "if our reasoning leads to the conclusion that 'capitalism' had nothing to do with . . . [the destruction of slavery], then the chances are that there is something wrong with our reasoning." Williams can take some of the credit for the creation of the modern historiographical agenda.[41]

On the other hand, like many other Marxists of his generation, Williams faltered when it came to the role of moral issues. He tended (like Charles Beard) to reduce morality to self-interest, though in practice he realized that this was not always possible. What eluded him was a more sophisticated theory of the relationship between ideas and material interests. In recent years other scholars have tried to make good this deficiency;[42] what follows is an attempt to further this process.

Material change and class interest

I

I wish to suggest that material changes – together with class interests – played a key role in fostering the abolitionist movement in the United States. But some general remarks are in order. First, it is clear that there can be no set of material conditions which automatically and singly generate antislavery sentiment at any time and in any place. Thus the North abolished slavery in the late eighteenth century. We cannot cite the same material factors to explain both this wave of emancipation and the growth of immediatism in the 1830s for the simple reason that material conditions were strikingly different. Hence there can be no simple formula connecting economic change and antislavery sentiment. However, this is a problem for *all* interpretations of antislavery that seek to connect

41. Howard Temperley, "Capitalism, Slavery and Ideology," *Past and Present*, LXXV (1977), pp. 94–118, esp. 105; Seymour Drescher, *Econocide: British Slavery in the Era of Abolition* (Pittsburgh, Pa., 1977).

42. Two key works are David Brion Davis, *The Problem of Slavery in the Age of Revolution, 1770–1823* (Ithaca, N.Y., 1975); Thomas Haskell, "Capitalism and the Origins of the Humanitarian Sensibility," 2 parts, *American Historical Review*, XC (1985), pp. 339–361, 547–566. See also Davis, *The Problem of Slavery in Western Culture* (N.Y., 1966). I gave an initial critique of Haskell's thesis in "The Relationship between Capitalism and Humanitarianism," *American Historical Review*, XII (1987), pp. 813–828. Davis also responded in "Reflections on Abolitionism and Ideological Hegemony" in *ibid.*, pp. 797–812, and Haskell in turn replied in "Convention and Hegemonic Interest in the Debate over Antislavery: A Reply to Davis and Ashworth," *ibid.*, pp. 829–879. The entire exchange, together with additional contributions from Davis and from me is to be found in Thomas Bender (ed.), *The Anti-Slavery Debate: Capitalism and Abolitionism as a Problem in Historical Interpretation* (Berkeley, 1992). I shall not therefore repeat my objections to the Davis and Haskell theses here.

it with economic developments. Only a return to the discredited Whig view can overcome this problem.

Second, abolitionists perceived their struggle in highly moralistic terms. As we shall see, they insisted that moral rather than economic considerations be kept uppermost. In the absence of any reason to doubt their sincerity, we must immediately acknowledge that a materialist interpretation takes issue with the participants' understanding of their own movement. Some may find this objectionable but otherwise we are again back to the idealism of the Whig view.

Third, a distinction needs to be drawn between two questions. The first is why American society generated a movement calling for the immediate abolition of slavery. The second is who joined that movement. It is all too easy to assume that the answer to the second will provide the answer to the first but this is not so. We may explain the movements of iron filings by reference to a magnetic field, but this explanation will not itself tell us which iron filings were the first to move, which moved more slowly and which did not move at all. When we are dealing with human beings, explanations of actions are, of course, even more difficult. Why did two Tappan brothers support antislavery and temperance while another became a drunkard? Plainly, the factors that explain why American society generated abolitionism are unlikely to be able to explain the contrasting behavior of members of the same family.

The crucial question is why thousands of men and women were impelled to create afresh an antislavery movement in the years after 1830. Even if it were possible to acquire data on each of these individuals, even if each had left a record of his or her reasons for opposing slavery, the historian's task would still have hardly begun. A reconstruction of the individual's motives would all too quickly, one suspects, return us to the Whig view, and we should end where Clarkson began, with the abolitionists' view of the abolitionists. Nor, as we have seen, have attempts to establish a personality type been successful. But even if a common personality type could be shown to have existed, we would still need to know why that personality type at that time behaved in that way. Explaining who was attracted to the movement will not explain the emergence of the movement itself.

Throughout the remaining part of this discussion of abolitionism, I shall argue that the development of wage labor was a key cause of immediatism. I am not suggesting, however, that abolitionists themselves necessarily either employed or directly profited from wage labor. Of course, some connections exist between ideology and class position. Thus few abolitionists had been manual laborers. Most were "middle class" and some were from patrician families. Their inability to understand the problems of the poor no doubt had much to do with this. But ideas cannot be read off from class position; human beings have more freedom of action than such a deterministic model would suggest.

Nonetheless, the interpretation I am proposing accords primacy to material factors. Unless we invoke chance, divine intervention or some quasi-religious notion of progress, the only non-materialist interpretation is one which interprets the growth of abolitionism in terms of other changes at the level of ideas, that is to say, an idealist approach. More plausibly, one can claim that ideas and material interests are interdependent. In my view, however, a materialist approach is more powerful. Let us look more closely at this.

II

Historians generally assume that the events that they study are to be attributed to a combination or conjunction of material and non-material factors. A typical historical analysis finds a profound interdependence of the two, notes that neither can exist without the other, and then concludes that it is arbitrary and ahistorical to assign priority to either. Without doubt this is the most widespread objection to materialist interpretations of history, and specifically, of course, to Marxism. Although I cannot hope to do justice to this question here, I should nonetheless like to indicate my reasons for rejecting this orthodoxy.

Let us for a moment make an impossible distinction. Let us imagine ideas existing entirely separate from material forces. In the real world, of course, this is impossible; when either material forces or ideas change, the other is likely to change too. But the impossible case we are postulating reveals an important asymmetry between the two. In an otherwise static economy (that is say one that remains constant except in response to a change in ideas), we need to determine where the driving force for change is to be found. What is there in the realm of ideas which effects change? Again, except by recourse to divine intervention or a quasi-Hegelian notion of history as "progress in the consciousness of freedom," to my knowledge no-one has shown that ideas contain within themselves the seeds of their own destruction, transformation or supersession. This inertia, as it may be termed, of ideas is strengthened by the tendency of the ideologue to perceive and present his own views as "natural," hence timeless and unchanging.

It may be otherwise with the economy. Let us consider an economy where there is some dependence on the market but where individual producers are eager to remain landholders. A supporting ideology exists, which encourages independence and autonomy while at the same time not forbidding market production. Such an economy contains within itself the seeds of its own transformation. If some producers, whether by chance or by their own failings, are unable to produce at competitive prices, they may be forced off their land entirely. If alternative supplies of land are not available they may be forced to join the ranks of wage labor, even if the supporting ideology frowns upon such a course. Of course such change is not inevitable: other factors may be present. But the key point is that in a capitalist economy, there are pressures for change that often prove irresistible however much men and women yearn for continuity and stability.

Hence in certain kinds of economy, there are profound structural causes of change. In a modern economy such structures are still more evident. Economic transformations occur without anyone necessarily willing them, without anyone necessarily intending to effect them, either consciously or unconsciously. Yet such transformations are not random. Neither are they necessarily neutral in their impact upon different classes. As I shall argue, class interests may be furthered in this way. But the key point here is that there is an asymmetry between ideas and material forces. While neither is likely to change without the other, it does not follow that there is an equally powerful *autonomous* dynamic for change in both. An automobile cannot move along the road without both front and back wheels revolving. When one set of wheels spins, the other one (normally) must. But this does not allow us to conclude that each is playing a comparable role in propelling the vehicle. The engine may drive only one pair of wheels, which in turn forces the other pair to move. Though there is interdependence between the two axes, the interdependence is asymmetric. So, in my view, with historical change. The historian who concludes that ideas and material forces are interconnected and inseparable is correct. He is right to emphasize interdependence. Where he is wrong is in assuming that such interdependence is necessarily symmetrical.

III

The interpretation of abolitionism I shall advance emphasizes class interests. Although I have already discussed the advancement of class interests in previous chapters, a definition is now appropriate. Class interests lie in the preservation or betterment, either directly or indirectly, of the material conditions enjoyed by a class relative to another class. Such interest may be furthered indirectly by political or ideological means or even by conceding a material loss so as not to suffer a larger one. Thus we are dealing with a broad category of activities and processes and only rarely will an emphasis on class yield predictions. That is to say, we are concerned with explanatory rather than predictive power. And even if we are able to conclude that class interest is a major causal factor, the

explanation will not then be at an end. For we need also to identify the
process by which those interests come to be advanced and then go on to
explain the process itself.

There are several ways in which class interests can be furthered. First
and most obviously, they may be promoted as a result of the conscious
intention of the agent. One example will suffice. As we have already seen,
many southerners observed that cities and industry posed a control problem for slaveholders. Some of the many southerners who refrained from
investing in industry, or who refused to allow their slaves to be employed
in a city, may have been responding to this imperative. Of course other
reasons may have been present and one can cite the explicit and deliberate pursuit of class interest only as a possible motive. As I have already
argued, however, there is every reason to believe it was a real and powerful factor. Little more needs to be said on this subject.

Second, an agent may realize a goal which he believes to be unrelated
to class but which is nonetheless a function of an ideology structured by
class interest. To take an example. When Marie Antoinette told the
impoverished citizens of Paris (never mind that the story is probably
apocryphal) to eat cake when there was no bread, she was not seeking
to deceive them. Nor is there any reason to believe that she was deceiving
herself. Instead her position in society (amongst other things) caused her
failure to understand that the Parisian poor could not afford cake. The
deception was not a self-deception but a socially induced one.

Let us pursue this imaginary story a little further in order to get to grips
with the problem of the unintended promotion of class interests. We are
in the Paris of 1789 and the disgruntled masses, still seeking bread, take
violent action. Marie Antoinette, baffled by their refusal to alter their
eating habits, concludes that they are quite unreasonable men and
women with whom nothing can be done and reluctantly orders the
National Guard to open fire upon them. She wishes to preserve order
and sees her action as in the interests of all classes and not especially of
her own. She has no conscious or unconscious intent to further a class
interest. Nonetheless we can still say that she is, in good part, moved by
class interest. In the first place her original error, attributable largely to
class position, is uncorrected partly because it is her interest to retain that
position. She tends to discountenance evidence which might rectify the
error but which at the same time might raise disturbing questions about
the nature of the society she wishes to preserve. In the second place, the
decision to open fire upon the rebellious crowd is caused by a commitment to "order" that is, to say the least, heavily impregnated with class
interest. For it is clearly in Marie Antoinette's interest to define social
disorder in terms of rebellious peasants, whereas the interest of the poor
might well lie in defining it in terms of mass hunger and starvation. All of

which is to say that an individual can act in accordance with an ideology that bears a clear imprint of class interest but perceive his or her actions as being in the general interest or even in no particular interest at all. Such actions are common; indeed one might argue that the most successful tyrants are those who rule primarily in the interests of a dominant class but whose propaganda asserts that they serve the general interest. And the most successful of all are often the ones who, without any self-deception, believe their own propaganda.

The story I have just cited is, of course, a fictional one. Let us take as a second example the anti-union propaganda so prevalent in Britain, the United States and indeed throughout the western world in our own times. Let us imagine a situation in which certain groups take the lead in condemning the pursuit of self-interest collectively by union actions such as strikes. They argue that such action is morally indefensible since it results in coercion of both employers and of those workers who would prefer not to strike. The anti-union campaign is successful and strikes are banned. The campaigners believe that they have advanced the general interest and actually benefited all groups, including labor. There is no intention of furthering a class interest. Nevertheless it is easy to see that the attempt to confine self-interest to individualist channels is part of a morality which in turn is heavily structured by class interest. It benefits those whose power can be asserted individually rather than those whose power depends upon collective assertion. The example is akin to that of Marie Antoinette. Once again the values concerned bear the imprint of class interest and whether this is or is not recognized by the actor is a separate and subordinate question.

A third and final example is one that I have already outlined in this work. It comes from the politics of antebellum America. The ideology of the Democratic party, as developed in the writings of Jefferson and of John Taylor of Caroline, extolled the yeoman farmer. It did not accord privileged status to the slaveholder. Nonetheless those who adopted it were, as I have already argued, driven to defend positions which weakened the antislavery movement and thus protected the interests of the slaveholder. Racism, limited government and states' rights could all be espoused by northerners who had not the slightest desire to further the slaveholding interest but who nonetheless were captivated by the agrarian egalitarianism of the creed. Yet all three sapped the potential of antislavery. This was not a chance occurrence. I have argued that Jefferson, Taylor and others extolled the yeoman in large part because slavery encouraged the formation of a racial alliance between farmers and slaveholders. Though they did not realize it, the different balance of class forces in the South was crucial in generating the ideology in the first place. In this way the class interests of the slaveholders were promoted unwittingly by both the recruits to the party and its founders, none of whom were necessarily guilty of self-deception.

It is perfectly true that the actions of Marie Antoinette, of the anti-union campaigners, or of Democratic partisans are not the only ones compatible with class interest. But this will only count against a class interest interpretation if it is assumed that such interests dictate a single course of action. And such an assumption can be seen to be unfounded as soon as we recognize that it is not predictions but explanations after the event which we are seeking. A full explanation would need to show how and in what way the actions chosen were based on a set of values that were impregnated with class interest. In other words we need to proceed from interests to ideas and values and then to actions.

There is a third route by which class interests may be furthered. Certain outcomes may be unsought by anyone yet benefit one class at the expense of others. The benefit might be entirely fortuitous but it might, alternatively, have a structural cause. Let us consider an example of this process. Overseas demand for a product suddenly falls and unemployment ensues. While a minority of employers suffer, wages fall and the strength of employers relative to employees increases. This outcome was not what anyone intended, nor is it inherent in any individual's goal. Yet it is not a random one. It proceeds instead from the greater structural power of the employer, which protects him from adversity and allows him to augment his power still further. Society can be viewed as a prism through which intentionate actions pass on their way to becoming outcomes. Some are blocked entirely, some are refracted and transformed, others pass through undisturbed. This is obviously a complex process but in each case the interest of various classes can *sometimes* play a decisive role.

When we consider outcomes, we find similarly that, whether they are intended or unintended, the social structure frequently plays a vital role. And all too often, class is a central, structuring force in society. Let us return for a moment to Marie Antoinette. Her decision to employ the National Guard against the peasants results not in the re-establishment of order but instead in a full-blown revolution. One consequence of the revolution is the execution of certain aristocrats, one of whom is none other than Marie Antoinette. With hindsight it becomes apparent to all that her action was not optimal either for herself or for her class. Similarly, one might argue that the actions of the slaveholders in federal politics from the 1840s onwards, since they helped precipitate Civil War and emancipation, were not optimal for their class (though it is not clear that there was a better alternative). An important conclusion follows. Just as class interest may be advanced intentionally or unintentionally, so actions taken may be functional or dysfunctional for the class that takes them.

Thus it is indeed the case that beliefs produced by class interest may or may not further that interest.[43] As we have seen, there is no reason to assume that classes (and in this they resemble individuals) always succeed in promoting their own interest even when they set out to do so. Yet outcomes are not quite so indeterminate as this line of reasoning might suggest. There is a likelihood of some "fit" between actions and outcomes, especially where a dominant class is concerned. Why is this? Clearly a full answer is impossible here but some suggestions can be offered. First there will generally be a tendency for a social system to reproduce itself *ceteris paribus*. Thus the intention of a dominant class will be to sustain itself and its disproportionate power will help here. Second, there will be feedback if the intended goals are not attained or if outcomes have the unexpected consequence of diminishing that interest. As a result actions will be altered and practices revised. Again the disproportionate power of a dominant class will help. Third, the dominant class can present itself as the defender of the general interest and thus of values like "order," and this posture will help it to secure its goals. The question of the consequences of antislavery and abolition for the bourgeois order is a vital one and I shall return to it later.

Before leaving this subject let us consider both ideology and outcomes a little further. When considering the growth of antislavery, I shall argue that the abolitionists espoused a set of values or an ideology which was clearly associated with, but not to be reduced to, or read off from, class interests. Such is frequently the case with ideology. It is often deeply influenced by past traditions, by the state of technology, by chance, by climate, by religion and by many other factors as well as by class. Some of these influences are, in turn, connected to class interest, others are not. Even those which are so connected can hardly ever be *reduced* to class interest. Finally, ideology is deeply influenced by the interests of other groups besides classes. Yet I shall argue that, when all these qualifications have been made, any attempt to explain antislavery without a heavy emphasis on class interest is doomed. The values of the reformer, I shall claim, were structured by the interests, and rooted in the practices of, an emerging bourgeois class.

At this point we may turn to Marx's definition of ideology. Marx stresses the manner in which certain ideas or values promote the interests of particular groups and classes but in a covert manner. A good example is the much proclaimed belief that all human beings are greedy, self-interested and ambitious. At face value this assertion seems to be neutral between the interests of different groups or classes. However, it qualifies

43. As Haskell argued – Haskell, "Convention and Hegemonic Interest in the Debate over Antislavery," p. 872.

as an "ideological" utterance in that it tends to undermine opposition to the existing order. (Why seek to supplant capitalism if it accords with basic human instincts?) It thus functions to advance the interests of the dominant class. Let us note a frequent characteristic of ideological utterances of this type: the claim that certain characteristics (or it may be, events or practices) are "natural," when they may instead be the product of specific historical processes. To the extent that an event, idea or practice is believed to be "natural," then opposition to it is, of course, disabled.

Yet Marx did not believe that ideological beliefs are generated conspiratorially. That is to say, he did not argue that a dominant class was deliberately setting out to propagate views which it knew to be in its interest but which purported to be universally valid. Instead the creation and diffusion of ideological views is a highly complex process. In the first place the propagators may themselves be sincerely and deeply committed to their own "ideological" utterances. Second, there may be mechanisms in the real world that make it appear to the observer as something other than it actually is. The real world thus tends to conceal itself. We have already seen an example of this in the realm of political economy. Thus many defenders of capitalism are impressed with the freedom and equality that it bestows. Individuals are free to make contracts and as capitalist and worker they exchange on an equal basis: each gives and receives an equivalent. But of course, for Marx this conceals the massive inequality that so often prevails in the sphere of production. Hence the "bourgeois ideologue" who perceives a free and equal relation has seen a genuine and vitally important feature of capitalist relations but erred in ignoring the deeper and less obvious inequalities that may well vitiate the freedom and equality which are formally present. We now see the inadequacy of historians' reliance upon self-deception. As one theorist has put it, "it is not the subject who deceives himself, but reality which deceives him."[44]

Finally, this misperception may itself be functional for the continued operation of a society, economy or polity. Belief in the formal equality and freedom of capitalism plainly act as a social, economic and political lubricant. This effect cannot be overemphasized. Nevertheless (though this has not been recognized sufficiently by theorists), there may well be only a partial "fit" between ideology and the needs of a particular society or class. Precisely because there is no individual or group exercising the kind of control postulated by a conspiracy theory, the ideas themselves may come to be employed in ways that do not, strictly

---

44. M. Godelier, "System, Structure and Contradiction in Capital," quoted in Nicholas Abercrombie, *Class, Structure and Knowledge* (Oxford, 1980), p. 77. One of those who has relied most heavily upon self-deception is David Brion Davis.

speaking, continue to further the original class interest. To legitimate particular practices by dubbing them "natural," is, as we have seen, to bestow great authority upon them. However, the very success of this process creates the possibility that other practices will now appear to be unacceptably "unnatural." This, I believe, happened with abolitionism in the United States and it is here, I shall argue, that one finds the relationship between capitalism, class interest and antislavery.

It will not be possible to do justice here to abolitionist thought by analyzing its every aspect. Instead I shall concentrate on three subjects, each of which is vital to understanding the origins of the movement and its relationship to capitalism in the United States.[45] I shall begin with abolitionist views of the economy. Later I shall turn to the abolitionists' understanding of the conscience and its functions. Finally, I shall consider their perception of the family.

The abolitionist economy

I

It is widely known that the abolitionists insisted upon keeping the moral critique of slavery uppermost. It is less widely known that they gave considerable attention to the economic arguments against slavery. As we shall see, they responded to economic development in the North with considerable enthusiasm and their economic indictment of slavery derived from a comparison of the northern and southern economies that found the South woefully inadequate.

Central to the economic critique was the argument that the slave lacked the incentive to work. This claim would be common among the Republicans in the 1850s but here, as elsewhere, the abolitionists were decades ahead of them. As Lydia Maria Child argued in 1836, "the slave does not care how slowly or carelessly he works." Whereas it was "the free man's interest to do his business well and quickly," the slave, by contrast, "is indifferent how many tools he spoils." He lacked the free man's "motive to be careful." This lack of incentive affected all aspects of his work and behavior. His clothing might be "cheap" but it ended by being more costly to the slaveholder than the initially more expensive clothes of the free worker, since it was "of no consequence to him how fast it is destroyed – his master *must* keep him covered." Hence the "hired laborer" typically made his clothes last "three times as long." Nor did the slave have the same reason to be honest as the free worker,

---

45. I shall therefore omit some key questions, such as the abolitionist attitude to race. An excellent discussion is to be found in Friedman, *Gregarious Saints*, pp. 160–195.

since in his case a reputation for honesty would make him "none the richer." Indeed incentives would operate in precisely the opposite way – "his poverty", together with "his sense of wrong," would "urge him to steal from his master." The lack of incentives meant that an overseer was essential; at best, however, he could only produce the work which in a free man would derive from "the desire of increasing the comforts of himself and family." Even then the overseer, of course, must be paid. More often he would fail to motivate the slaves sufficiently. As a result, Child concluded, the typical slave could only do two-thirds or perhaps even a half of the work of the "hired laborer." Other abolitionists concurred. Addressing the Worcester, Massachusetts Antislavery Association, George Allen asked rhetorically whether "that system, parcel or part," could be "good for him who uses it, which coercing labor and taking away its proper stimulus, makes it shiftless and thriftless, unprogressive in its meager skill, and without motive or tendency to improvement by him who yields his sweat for another's bread?"[46]

The evil effects, however, did not end here. To keep the slaves in slavery they had to be kept in ignorance too. As a result all their faculties were, according to Child, "stupefied." The skilled labor which abolitionists believed necessary in manufacturing was thus difficult to obtain from slaves. The result was a dearth of manufacturing in the South. Nor could the deficiency be made up by the labor of free whites. For in a slave society "manual labor is a degradation to white people." This was an old criticism of slave societies, one heard at the time of the Missouri Crisis, and one that would also re-emerge in Republican propaganda of the 1850s. It was, perhaps, universally endorsed by abolitionists. Lydia M. Child, George Allen, William Lloyd Garrison, the Tappans and their American and Foreign Anti-Slavery Society, Charles Burleigh, Alvan Stewart, Gerrit Smith – all stated unequivocally that slavery degraded labor, and especially manual labor.[47]

46. Lydia Maria Child, *An Appeal in Favor of Americans Called Africans* (N.Y., 1836), pp. 76–77; [George Allen], *A Report on American Slavery read to the Worcester Central Association, March 2, 1847* (Boston, 1847), pp. 18–19.

47. Lydia Maria Child, *The Right Way the Safe Way, Proved by Emancipation in the British West Indies, and Elsewhere* (N.Y., 1862), p. 5; Child, *Appeal in Favor of Americans*, pp. 76–77, 22; Charles Burleigh, "Slavery and the North," *Anti-Slavery Tracts*, no. 5 (n.p., n.d.), p. 10; "Influence of Slavery Upon the White Population," *Anti-Slavery Tracts*, no. 9 (n.p., n.d.), p. 5; "Letter of Gerrit Smith to Rev. James Smylie," *The Anti-Slavery Examiner*, no. 3 (N.Y., 1837), p. 46; Alvan Stewart, *The Cause of the Hard Times* (n.p., n.d.), p. 1; *Address to the Inhabitants of New Mexico and California on the Omission by Congress to Provide them with Territorial Governments, and on the Social and Political Evils of Slavery* (N.Y., 1849), p. 14; Theodore Parker, *The Slave Power* (reprint: N.Y., 1969), p. 60; [George Allen], *A Report on American Slavery*, pp. 18–19; *National Anti-Slavery Standard*, Jan. 27, 1855.

The result was not only a lack of manufacturing in the South but also a general absence of economic and social development. Navigation and commerce were "locked up" by the slave system, the soil itself was ruined, there was no incentive to promote labor-saving technology. Instead "indolence" and "dissipation" ruled in the South. Wendell Phillips in 1861 contemptuously described South Carolina as a state in which one half of the population – the slaves – were doing "only half the work of a freeman" and in which the other half – the whites – were "idlers." The result was as if only "one quarter of the population" was "actually at work." Again like the Republicans in the 1850s, the abolitionists delighted in statistical comparisons between North and South. These seemed to show that the North was pressing ahead with common schools, academies and lyceums with a population highly literate, progressive and educated. The South meanwhile was stagnating; in all these areas, it was claimed, as well as in the publication of magazines, newspapers, and books, in population growth, and in the development of commerce and manufacturing, she was far behind. In the words of Charles Beecher, "slavery degrades labor, discourages education, science, art; enfeebles commerce, blights agriculture, and continually works society towards barbarism." The disastrous fate of the Roman Empire, he claimed, illustrated these effects in the most dramatic manner.[48]

Abolitionists were not, however, entirely uncritical of the northern economy. Theodore Parker, for example acknowledged in 1847 that "there is suffering enough among the weak and poor in the cities of the free laborious North," though he quickly added that it was not on the scale seen in the South. Some years later he warned that prosperity, which many in his congregation were doubtless experiencing, frequently injured men morally. In the very early days of the *Liberator* William Lloyd Garrison told his readers how the sight of factories in a northern village caused him some "pain," on the grounds that too much labor was required of the workers and their education was neglected. Garrison avowed himself in favor of the ten-hour day. He also exhorted "our rich capitalists" to "beware how they grind the face of the poor." "Oppression," he warned "injures the value of labor, begets resentment, produces tumults, and is hateful in the sight of God."[49]

Yet these reservations were of only minor importance. The tinge of "pain" which Garrison felt, did not alter the fact that, overall, the sight

48. [George Allen], *A Report on American Slavery*, p. 19; Phillips, *Speeches, Lectures, and Letters*, p. 367; *Liberator*, Nov. 21, 1856; Rev. Charles Beecher, "The God of the Bible Against Slavery," *Anti-Slavery Tracts*, no. 17 (n.p., n.d.), p. 3.
49. Parker, *Slave Power*, p. 116, *Sins and Safeguards of Society* (Boston, n.d.), p. 233; Garrison to *Liberator*, Sept. 13, 1832 in Walter M. Merrill (ed.), *The Letters of William Lloyd Garrison* 4 vols (Cambridge, Mass., 1971–), II, pp. 167–168.

of those same factories gave him "no inconsiderable pleasure." A more serious doubt arose in the minds of abolitionists after it became clear that many amongst the very rich were extremely hostile to the antislavery crusade. In *The Liberator* of November 21, 1856, Garrison noted that the "commercial and manufacturing classes" in the North were the first to rally to the defense of the South. Their attitude fueled the resentment that was vividly expressed by the reference, common in the 1850s, to the unholy alliance between the "Lords of the Loom" and the "Lords of the Lash." The response of the northern manufacturing and mercantile elites to abolitionism thus deepened the suspicion of the rich that was already, one suspects, present among many antislavery zealots.[50]

If they had pressed these arguments further, the abolitionists might have ended by endorsing the critique of northern society that radical labor leaders and some Democrats were advancing. But while they were prepared to acknowledge imperfections in the northern social order, the abolitionists ended not merely by accepting it in all its essential features, but by glorifying it. The contrast with radical Democrats was sharp indeed. In 1840, *The Emancipator* took Orestes Brownson to task for grossly misrepresenting northern society. That year Brownson had called attention to the plight of the northern wage laborer and had actually expressed the desire to abolish the wage relationship. Joshua Leavitt acknowledged that Brownson's analysis "may find a semblance of reality in some manufacturing places in New England." This was a typical abolitionist utterance. Even more typical was the comment that immediately followed. "Nothing can be more unjust," Leavitt insisted, "than to assume such to be the general condition of that portion of the people of New England who labor for wages." Leavitt then painted a glowing picture of northern society, one that highlighted social mobility. The picture was similar to that which northern Whigs were offering to the electorate; it was identical to the one that would inspire the Republicans in the 1850s; it was the one which Lincoln would use to present the Civil War itself. "The truth is," Leavitt declared, "that the *great body* of the young men of New England, and a large portion of the young women, work for wages, acquire the means of becoming either employers or operatives in their own shops or on their own farms." It followed that "to assume the existence of a distinction between employers and paid workmen, as a permanent state, is either to dream or to deceive." In the United States, he continued, "the wheels of fortune revolve too rapidly, and the rich and poor change places too frequently, to allow a foundation for such an agitation as this."[51]

50. Garrison to *Liberator*, Sept. 13, 1832 in *Letters of Garrison*, II, p. 167; *Liberator*, Nov. 21, 1856. See also Parker, *The Slave Power*, pp. 369, 381.
51. *Emancipator*, Dec. 31, 1840.

Many abolitionists would have endorsed this analysis in its entirety.[52] In the very first issue of the *Liberator* Garrison noted, with unmistakable dismay, that "an attempt has been made – it is still making – we regret to say, with considerable success – to influence the minds of our working classes against the more opulent, and to persuade them that they are contemned and oppressed by a wealthy aristocracy." Again Garrison acknowledged that "public grievances" "unquestionably" exist. But these "affect all classes" and it was "in the highest degree criminal, therefore, to exasperate our mechanics to deeds of violence, or to array them under a party banner." A few weeks later he expounded orthodox conservative social philosophy when he emphasized "the mutations" that characterized American society. "In a republican government, especially," he argued, "where hereditary distinctions are obsolete, and the people possess unlimited power; where the avenue to wealth, distinction and supremacy are open to all; it must in the nature of things, be full of unequals." Inequality, however, did not mean injustice; inequalities "can exist without even the semblance of oppression." Unfortunately, he continued, "there is a prevalent opinion, that wealth and aristocracy are indissolubly allied, and the poor and vulgar are taught to consider the opulent as their natural enemies." Garrison left his readers in no doubt of his own views. "Those who inculcate this pernicious doctrine," he asserted, "are the worst enemies of the people."[53]

Garrison professed himself unable to comprehend the reasoning of the radical labor leaders. He recognized the existence of some abuses but asked for "the evidence that our wealthy citizens as a body, are hostile to the interests of the laboring classes." Where could such evidence be found? Not "in their commercial enterprises, which whiten the ocean with canvas, and give employment to a useful and numerous class of men," nor "in their manufacturing establishments, which multiply labor and cheapen the necessities of the poor," nor "in the luxuries of their tables, or the adornments of their dwellings, for which they must pay in proportion to their extravagance." Perhaps the source of the complaint was mere envy. For it was "a miserable characteristic of human nature to look with an envious eye upon those who are more fortunate in their pursuits, or more exalted in their station."[54]

Wendell Phillips shared Garrison's opinions. After the Civil War he would become a convert to the labor movement but in the 1830s, 1840s and 1850s he took orthodox conservative ground. In 1847 he declared

52. Some radicals, for example William Leggett, were also staunchly antislavery, but this was very much a minority position. See also *Liberty Party Paper*.
53. *Liberator*, Jan. 1, 29, 1831.
54. *Liberator*, Jan. 29, 1831.

flatly that in the United States "the laborers, as a class, are neither wronged nor oppressed." But even if they were, he continued, they had the vote, the right to choose where to work, as well as "habits of economy" with which to improve themselves. The American social order, or rather the northern social order, was essentially just and like all others "the laboring class" must rely upon "economy, self-denial, temperance, education, and moral and religious character" for "its elevation and improvement." Without these qualities "political and social changes are in vain and futile" and with them all political questions "except the equality of woman, sink into comparative insignificance." Phillips deployed a common strategy when he contrasted the North with European society. "Many of the errors on this point," he observed, "seem . . . to proceed from looking at American questions through European spectacles, and transplanting the eloquent complaints against capital and monopoly, which are well-grounded and well applied there, to a state of society here, where they have little meaning or application, and serve only for party watch-words." The demands of the labor movement, acceptable in Europe perhaps, were improper and incongruous in the United States.[55]

The abolitionists could not help comparing the condition of the working classes with those of the slaves. Whereas labor leaders used the comparison to generate support for their own movement, to the abolitionists it served only to concentrate attention still more firmly upon the plight of the slave. Garrison deemed it "disgraceful" to argue that the slave's condition was better even than that of the English operative, let alone his American counterpart. Among the many advantages enjoyed by the free worker, the opportunity for mobility was perhaps paramount. According to Joshua Leavitt, every man in the free states "sees a chance to rise, either himself or his children." Did not everyday experience confirm this? Leavitt explained that when he "look[ed] around for the families of those men who were day-laborers in my native place thirty or forty years go," he found "with the exception of here and there an imbecile or a drunkard . . . none of them now in the condition of day-laborers." These opportunities, together with the vote and the availability of free land in the West, meant that in a conflict between labor and capital "the laborer always gets the advantage".[56]

The excellence of northern society derived from the incentives it offered to labor. These were not only material but also cultural. In sharp contrast to the South, the North extolled labor. Theodore Parker declared that "in the free States the majority work with their hands, counting it the natural

55. *Liberator*, July 9, 1847.
56. *Liberator*, Dec. 24, 1841; *Emancipator*, Oct. 10, 1839.

business of a man, not a reproach, but a duty and a dignity," while Louis Tappan for the American and Foreign Anti-Slavery Society proclaimed that in the North "no poor man is deterred from seeking a livelihood by honest labor from a dread of personal degradation" – unlike, he did not need to add, the situation in the South. The result was that even poverty could be socially benign. Wendell Phillips argued that poverty, or at least "wholesome poverty" (he did not stop to describe "unwholesome" poverty), was "no unmixed evil." It was in fact "the motive power that throws a man up to guide and control the community," "the spur that often wins the race," "the trial that calls out, like fire, all the deep, great qualities of a man's nature." Once again the comparison with slavery, which deadened ambition and stultified labor, could not have been sharper.[57]

Despite the importance they attached to the ending of slavery, the abolitionists did not spend time discussing the mechanics of abolition. Instead they insisted that emancipation would allow the South to be remade in the image of the North. Some of them seem to have believed that the transformation would take place overnight. "The moment slavery ceases," according to Alvan Stewart, "labor will be honorable in all at the South." As a result "the amount of labor there, then, would be instantly doubled." In 1833 Garrison explained the effect of abolition upon the southern economy. "It will banish the poverty of the South," he claimed, "reclaim her barren soil, and pour new blood into all her veins and arteries." Emancipation would effect "the transformation of two millions of slaves into free laborers, animated in view of a just recompense for their voluntary toil," and this would "renovate the whole frame of society." "There is not a slave State," he assured his audience, "but will exhibit the flush of returning health, and feel a stronger pulse, and draw a fresh breath." In the words of a Connecticut abolitionist newspaper, with free labor "our whole Southern country would spring into a new existence."[58]

57. Parker, *Slave Power*, p. 60; *Address to the Inhabitants of New Mexico and California*, p. 17; Phillips, *Speeches, Lectures, and Letters*, p. 503. For a lengthy discussion on the causes and consequences of poverty see the series of articles in *The Principia*, Aug. 25, Sept. 1, 8, 15, 22, 29, 1859. For a telling contrast between slavery and poverty – the latter inevitable, the former not – see *The Liberty Bell*, XIII (Boston, 1853), pp. 166–172.

58. Stuart, *Cause of Hard Times*, p. 4; *The Abolitionist: Or Record of the New England Anti-Slavery Society* (Boston, 1833), p. 22; *The Charter Oak*, September, 1838. One would have thought that the results of emancipation in the West Indies (where sugar production fell on some islands catastrophically) would have given the abolitionists some doubts. In fact these failures were either denied or excused – see e.g. Richard Hildreth, "The 'Ruin' of Jamaica," *Anti-Slavery Tracts*, no. 6 (n.p., n.d.); James A. Thome and J. Horace Kimball, "Emancipation in the West Indies, A Six Months Tour in Antigua, Barbados, and Jamaica in the Year 1837," *The Anti-Slavery Examiner* no. 7 (N.Y., 1838), p. 207.

II

This faith in the power of free labor is highly significant, for it offers a further clue to abolitionist thought. But perhaps we should first return to the question whether abolitionism should be seen as a class ideology. The temptation to label it "middle class" is irresistible but we need to be clear what this label means. If we say that abolitionism was middle class we may mean several different things. In the first place we might mean that it consciously set out to promote the interests or values of the middle classes above all others. To some extent this was indeed the goal of the abolitionists but of course, they believed – indeed insisted – that abolition would benefit all classes. Second we might mean that the movement had an especial appeal to the middle classes. In absolute terms this was not, of course, true. Only a tiny portion of the middle class of the North had any connection with abolitionism, and there is no evidence that more than a small portion of that class sympathized with its goals. Third, we might mean that of those who did join or support the movement a majority were middle class. Not surprisingly perhaps, this is true of the leadership. As far as New York state was concerned "abolitionism tended to draw its leadership . . . from the highly educated, moderately prosperous segments of society," and there is no reason to believe that New York was atypical in this respect. The social composition of the rank-and-file is more difficult to ascertain and it has been claimed that artisans, at least in New York city, played a larger role than has been recognized. But the most famous abolitionist groups – the Tappans, the Garrison circle, the Gerrit Smith wing – had around them an unmistakable middle class aura. They themselves believed their supporters were from that class, as an editorial in the *Emancipator* in October 1839 makes clear:

> The abolition movement begun [sic] among the middling class of society, those who live by their own earnings and think their own thoughts, who daily offer Agur's prayer, and who deem the privilege of working with *their own* hands, and eating *their own* bread, and choosing *their own* rulers, and doing good unto all men as they have opportunity, as infinitely surpassing in value the pride of wealth, or the advancement of 'the manufacturing and banking' interests, or any other exclusive aggrandisement.

While it would be desirable to know more about the composition of the abolitionist movement, such information would not really resolve the question about the connection between abolitionism and middle class interests.[59]

59. Sorin, *New York Abolitionists*, p. 119; John B. Jentz, "Artisans, Evangelicals, and the City: A Social History of the Labor and Abolitionist Movements in Jacksonian New

To call abolitionism "middle class" or "capitalist" we need to refer again to the beliefs of its proponents and to establish whose interests they reflected. In fact, when they discussed the economy, almost every idea and assumption was such as to legitimate capitalist production. While poverty and suffering might exist, they were seen as first, inevitable, second, on so small a scale as to be trifling, or third, actually benign. In each case it followed that the social order should not be challenged on behalf of the poor. The abolitionists tended also to reduce economic questions involving northern society in its entirety, to moral ones, involving only individuals. In 1841 in the depths of the economic recession, Garrison actually calculated, in dollars and cents, the costs of the various sins of which Americans were guilty. He found that the cost was "an amount sufficient to fill the land with prosperity" and concluded that the way to end the recession was by "the moral regeneration of the people." Garrison also, as we have seen, assumed that poverty and oppression could be relieved by an appeal to the better natures of the employers – an assumption which again undercut political opposition to the *status quo*.[60]

As we have also seen, abolitionists strongly endorsed the work ethic and believed that it was one of the glories of the North that labor was universally respected there. Whether this was entirely true or not is less important than the social consequences of the belief. Traditionally some forms of labor have been seen in western thought as dishonorable, at least if pursued out of necessity rather than for recreation. As we have seen, this is especially true of wage labor. Throughout this book I argue that "capitalism," properly defined, requires the existence of a market for labor power, that is to say, it requires wage labor. If the abolitionists believed that employment for wages (except of course in such morally unacceptable activities as the rum industry or prostitution) was honorable, there would be still more reason for calling their economic thought "capitalist."

Unfortunately, when they spoke of "free labor," they did not always distinguish the wage labor form. Yet there can be no doubt that they believed such labor honorable, natural and desirable. Indeed they often simply assumed that free labor meant wage labor. As we have seen, when Lydia Maria Child complained that slavery removed incentives, she compared the slave's attitude with that of the "hired laborer." In making the

York" (Ph.D. dissertation, City University of New York, 1977); *Emancipator*, Oct. 10, 1839. For similar statements by Garrison see *Proceedings of the State Disunion Convention, Held at Worcester, Mass, Jan 15, 1857* (Boston, 1857), pp. 32–33. See also Dumond (ed.), *Letters of Birney*, I, p. 363; Phillips, *Speeches, Lectures, and Letters*, p. 369.
60. *Liberator*, Nov. 15, 1841.

comparison, moreover, she clearly believed she was offering a generalization about prevailing or characteristic labor forms in both societies.
What is still more striking is the way in which she seemed to employ the
terms "free man" and "hired laborer" as though they were synonymous.
In the following extract she moves from one to other without acknowledging a distinction between them:

> A salary must be paid to an overseer to compel the slave to work; the
> free man is impelled by the desire of increasing the comforts of
> himself and family. Two hired laborers will perform as much work
> as three slaves; by some it is supposed to be a more correct estimate
> that slaves perform only *half* as much labor as the same number of
> free laborers.

For Child no stigma attached to wage labor. Instead working for wages
was an entirely natural economic activity. In 1836, opposing the colonization society, she asked why the repatriation of free blacks should be
advocated when "labor is greatly needed, and we are glad to give good
wages for it." Many years later, in 1862, she made a still more unmistakable comment on the desirability of wage labor by introducing a telling
analogy. "We should question the sanity of a man who took the mainspring out of his watch and hired a boy to turn the hands round," she
noted. "Yet he who takes from laborers the natural and healthy stimulus
of wages, and attempts to supply its place by the driver's whip, pursues a
course quite as irrational." Wages were thus "natural and healthy." For
Child the regeneration of the South would be the result of the introduction not merely of free labor, but of wage labor, into the region on a large
scale. "It is often asked," she acknowledged, 'what is your plan.'" The
answer was that her plan was "a very simple one . . . It is merely to
stimulate laborers by wages, instead of driving them by the whip." The
results would be rapid and dramatic. "When that plan is once adopted,"
she assured her readers, "education and religious teaching, and agricultural improvements will soon follow, as matters of course."[61]

Other abolitionists made similar utterances. It was generally believed
that once freed, the former slaves would work for wages. Such employment would not mean oppression. We have already seen that the
Emancipator rejected out of hand Brownson's demand for the abolition
of the wage labor relationship and the social analysis upon which it was
premised. Joshua Leavitt, its editor, believed that there was no danger
that wage laborers would be oppressed. A slightly more complex, if

61. Child, *Appeal in Favor of Americans*, pp. 76, 128, *The Right Way the Safe Way*, pp.
     95–96; *Correspondence between Lydia Maria Child and Governor Wise and Mrs
     Mason, of Virginia* (Boston, 1860), p. 26.

equally naive view was advanced by William Lloyd Garrison. "The evil in society is not that labor receives wages," he affirmed, "but that the wages given are not generally in proportion to the value of the labor performed." This remark would have puzzled radicals like Brownson for whom the unjust payments received by wage laborers were inherent in the system itself. Garrison's concession that they were too low seemed to confirm this analysis. The only way to make sense of his remark is on the assumption that he had once again reduced a social problem to one of individual morality. With the proper moral outlook the employer would remunerate his workers adequately and the problem would disappear. Thus even when they recognized that the existing conditions of some contemporary wage workers were unsatisfactory, abolitionists assumed that such flaws were incidental to, rather than inherent in, the wage system.[62]

The classic defense of wage labor was made, however, by reference to social mobility. Like some Republicans in the 1850s, some abolitionists believed that only those who lacked talent, industry, luck or some combination of these attributes would remain wage laborers for life. As we have seen, Leavitt believed that of those who had been wage laborers thirty years earlier in his youth, only the "imbecile" or "drunkard" remained in this condition now. Such progress out of the ranks of wage labor was clearly desirable. Nevertheless the suspicion that fell upon such men was a consequence of their imbecility or drunkenness, not their status as wage workers. Still less were they to be compared with the slave. Other abolitionists did not emphasize the desirability of movement out of wage labor. Their attitude thus contrasted still more sharply with traditional views of liberty and independence. Contrary to the traditionally accepted view, freedom did not require the ownership of property, or of means of production. Instead it required self-ownership, which in turn implied the right to sell one's labor power for wages. Theodore Parker in 1847 described the free society of the North and the mechanisms of social mobility in terms identical to those which Abraham Lincoln would use in the late 1850s and during the Civil War:

> In the free States the farmer buys the land and his cattle; hires men to aid him in his work – he buys their labor. Both parties are served – this with labor, that with employment. There is no degradation, but reciprocal gain. In a few years the men who at first sold their labor will themselves become proprietors, and hire others desirous of selling their services. It requires little capital to start with.

62. *The American Anti-Slavery Almanac for 1839* (Boston, 1839), pp. 37–38, 48; *Emancipator*, Oct. 10, 1839; *Liberator*, March 26, 1847.

Parker added that the same process operated in manufacturing.[63]

Hence for abolitionists wage labor played a central role in a thriving economy. They recognized its importance in the North and wished to see it introduced into the South after emancipation. The wage laborer was in no sense degraded; his labor was honorable; his very existence facilitated the process of social mobility that was one of the crowning glories of northern society. As we shall see, abolitionists embraced a view of human nature that was entirely consonant with the existence of wage labor on a considerable scale and even developed a religious faith structured by it. The opposition to slavery, I shall thus argue, derived much of its force from a comparison between slavery and wage labor. According to Theodore Weld, God thundered "anathemas against those who 'used their neighbor's service without wages.'" Like other abolitionists, Weld took wage labor for granted and thus reflected its growing acceptance in the northern states. This was an ideology attuned to the needs of an emerging capitalist order.[64]

The conscience and the soul

A reconstruction of abolitionist views on the economy, however, threatens to obscure an important point: in their writings and their speeches against slavery the abolitionists insisted that the moral critique was primary. The milder antislavery that characterized moderate Republicans in the 1850s would emphasize the economic case against slavery and some Republicans, at least, were uneasy about the introduction of apparently uncompromisable moral demands into politics. (For this very reason, militants like Garrison refused to operate within the political system.) Abolitionists, however, considered the economic indictment worthy of less emphasis. To some extent this was a tactical matter. They recognized that their opponents in the North especially, where outright proslavery thought was of negligible importance,[65] preferred to discuss political economy rather than morality. For however widely it was accepted that free labor was more productive than slave, an opponent might still challenge the specifics of emancipation. In 1834 such fears prompted Arthur Tappan, then Chairman of the Executive Committee of the American Anti-Slavery Society, to warn Theodore Weld of the danger of being "drawn away from the main object" into "a detailed PLAN of abolition."[66]

---

63. Parker, *Slave Power*, p. 63.
64. [Theodore Weld], *The Bible Against Slavery* (N.Y., 1838), p. 79.
65. By this I mean the belief that slave labor was better than free so that the North was disadvantaged by its absence.

The danger that arose with the discussion of specific details was that those being addressed might find objections to them and thus relieve their consciences. The alternative approach, recommended by Tappan and followed by all the abolitionists, was to appeal instead to the conscience of the listener. Ironically, of course, this refusal to enter into such discussion, and the moral absolutism upon which it rested, only served to confirm the enemy suspicion that abolitionists were indeed "fanatics."

Yet this appeal to the consciences of the North (and in the early years of the movement to the consciences of the South as well) was no mere tactical choice. Lydia Maria Child, whose economic indictment of slavery we have already considered, described the analysis of slavery derived from political economy as one proceeding "from a lower point of view." A clue to abolitionist thought is provided by an editorial in the *National Anti-Slavery Standard* of March 1849. The writer assessed Henry Clay's career, and especially his position on slavery. Not surprisingly, Clay was heavily criticized. But what is of interest is the grounds of complaint. The problem with Clay, it was argued, was that "he takes the case out of the Court of conscience where alone it can be decided absolutely and without appeal, and puts it at the mercy of the never-ending litigation of political economy." From the court of political economy, it seemed, there might be an appeal; from the court of conscience there could be none.[67]

Abolitionists never doubted that men's consciences were on their side. According to Gilbert Haven, slavery was "opposed by the Conscience of every man." This meant southerners as much as northerners. According to Lydia Maria Child, "the conscience" of the slaveholders, "whispers to them that the system is wrong." She added that it "is not sufficiently revered to overcome the temptation of apparent interest." Harriet Beecher Stowe, author of *Uncle Tom's Cabin*, reflects this view in the novel when she makes it clear that all slaveholders are afflicted by attacks of conscience, to escape from which they resort to drink or other diversions. The thoroughly evil slaveholder like Simon Legree rejects his conscience outright, precisely as he rejects antislavery.[68]

66. Arthur Tappan to Weld, Feb. 20, 1834 in Gilbert H. Barnes and Dwight L. Dumond (eds), *Letters of Theodore Dwight Weld, Angelina Grimké Weld and Sarah Grimké 1822–1844* 2 vols (N.Y., 1934), I, p. 126.

67. *Correspondence between . . . Child and Governor Wise . . .* , p. 10; *National Anti-Slavery Standard*, March 22, 1849.

68. Gilbert Haven, *Sermons, Speeches and Letters on Slavery and Its War, From the Passage of the Fugitive Slave Bill to the Election of President Grant* (Boston, 1869), p. 23; Child to Francis and Sarah Shaw, Aug. 17, 1838 in Milton Meltzer and Patricia Holland (eds), *Lydia Maria Child: Selected Letters* (Amherst, 1982), p. 86; Harriet Beecher Stowe, *Uncle Tom's Cabin: Or, Life among the Lowly* (1852: reprint London, 1981), p. 528.

Yet it soon became clear to the abolitionists that an appeal to the conscience of the slaveholder would not succeed – because it would not be permitted. So attention switched to the North. But the target remained the conscience. "From the beginning," declared the American and Foreign Anti-Slavery Society in 1847, "we have been sensible that the first thing to be done, is to enlist the consciences of men, on the side of the slave." This would be done "by producing a general conviction of the inherent injustice of slavery, and the consequent sinfulness of the act of holding a fellow-man in that condition." The American and Foreign was, of course, the anti-Garrisonian organization. But the Garrison wing fully shared this view. "Our strength," according to one of its adherents, "all lies in a single force – the conscience of the nation." The writer admitted that "all else is on the side of the oppressor." But this was no cause for despondency, since "conscience, that force of forces when properly instructed, is all, and always, on our side." In effect the human conscience was itself an abolitionist.[69]

The abolitionists were not content, however, to rest only their anti-slavery convictions upon the conscience. Instead they argued that conscience should be the arbiter of all moral questions. According to Theodore Parker, "it is the function of conscience to discover to men the moral law of God." Lydia Maria Child lamented that "few men ask concerning the right and wrong of their *own* hearts. Few listen to the oracle *within*, which can only be heard in the stillness." What Child referred to as "the oracle within" was what other abolitionists termed the conscience or, occasionally, the soul. The implicit exhortation in her words was identical to that which William Lloyd Garrison offered explicitly when he urged every reader to "settle it as a principle that his conscience, and not his lay or spiritual leaders, must be his commander."[70]

As Garrison's words suggest, the realm over which the conscience was to rule was a wide one. It would be accurate to say that it would encompass not simply moral questions, but political, economic and social ones too. It would be still more accurate to say that political, economic and social questions were to be made into moral ones and resolved accordingly by the conscience. In any event, the results were startling. The conscience was not simply a necessary, but virtually a sufficient, guide

69. *Remonstrance Against the Course Pursued by the Evangelical Alliance on the Subject of American Slavery* (N.Y., 1847), p. 2; "Revolution the Only Remedy for Slavery," *Anti-Slavery Tracts*, no. 7 (n.p., n.d.), p. 16. Wendell Phillips argued that "Virginia did not tremble at an old gray-headed man at Harper's Ferry; they trembled at a John Brown in every man's conscience" – *Speeches, Lectures, and Letters*, p. 273.

70. Parker, *Slave Power*, p. 292; Lydia Maria Child, *Letters from New York* (N.Y., 1843), pp. 148–149; *Liberator*, Jan. 26, 1833.

to action, even in – perhaps especially in – the political arena. According to Henry C. Wright, "God, in making human beings, has given to each a power of self-government, which needs, which admits of, no other rule – a conscience, to govern the movements of both soul and body." Such a view had far-reaching consequences. Faced with immoral laws, the conscientious citizen was compelled to take extreme action – and disobey the laws. Theodore Parker, noting that conscience was "relatively perfect," and thus "the last standard of appeal," reasoned that all men must follow it regardless of society's approval. "Nothing," he declared, "can absolve me from this duty." Parker was speaking in the aftermath of the Fugitive Slave Act of 1850, which required northerners to aid slaveholders in recovering their runaways. For many in the North as well as in the South, laws passed by any legally constituted government must be obeyed, unless the right of revolution were being invoked. For Parker, however, laws were only as valid as the moral principles inspiring them. He did not hesitate to advocate disobedience. Indeed he poured scorn upon those who would not disobey such legislation. "If a people has this notion," he began, "that they are morally bound to obey any statute legally made, though it conflict with public morals, with private conscience, and with the law of God," "then", he concluded, "there is no hope for such a people, and the sooner a tyrant whips them into their shameful grave, the better for the world."[71]

Such opinions were far from rare in New England in the 1850s. One of the fullest statements of abolitionist thought on this subject was made by Gilbert Haven in 1850, again in response to the Fugitive Slave Bill. Haven, like Parker, believed that civil government must be judged on moral principles. These principles in turn were derived from conscience. Hence "before the judgment seat of the Conscience" government must "stand." If the conscience "condemns it," then "must it plead guilty." If the conscience "forbid obedience to its wrong behests, they must be disobeyed" and if the conscience "demands that it should repeal its laws and make them conformable to the law of God, it must hasten to obey on pain of the righteous displeasure and sure judgements of God." The conscience was nothing less than God's "vice-regent".[72]

Such a view was highly alarming to conservatives, in the North as well as in the South. It appeared utterly anarchic and indeed it is no accident that abolitionists like William Lloyd Garrison ended by espousing a form of Christian anarchism. Conservatives feared that this appeal to the

71. Henry C. Wright, *Marriage and Parentage: Or, The Reproductive Element in Man, as a Means to His Elevation and Happiness* (Boston, 1855), pp. 249–250; Parker, *Slave Power*, pp. 292–293, *Sins and Safeguards of Society*, p. 64.
72. Haven, *Speeches and Letters*, p. 7.

conscience would destroy the possibility of civilized life itself, since in any community concession and conciliation were necessary and some moral principles had to be compromised. They assumed that different people could and would conscientiously hold differing views. But the abolitionists believed that the danger from a clash of consciences, as it were, was negligible. Indeed they simply ignored the problem. Gilbert Haven argued that the conscience "however perverted" was attracted "towards the true and the excellent" and introduced an interesting metaphor which compared it to the needle on a compass. While acknowledging that "the needle may be drawn by wrong attractions, for the moment, from its true direction," he nonetheless insisted that "still within it dwells the force that is ever pressing it against all temptations to point to its pole." Here the implicit assumption was that morality was a single fixed entity; the task was to locate it. Moral principles were absolute, timeless, unchanging. Implicit too in Haven's words was the premise that, for all practical purposes, every conscience advocated a similar course of action.[73]

Haven's view becomes somewhat less surprising when we recall that the abolitionists believed that even slavery, the most contentious issue of the entire antebellum era, provoked only a single response from the conscience. Every conscience, even that of the southerner, was in reality antislavery. Of course they recognized that, in the short term, the conscience might be led astray, just as the needle on a compass might be diverted by a closer, though ultimately weaker, magnetic force. Yet "however much beguiled from its steadfastness by the force of education, custom, fear, or flattery," the conscience "cannot be wholly perverted." It was no less than man's means of communication with God, it was "employed," as Haven put it, "by our Creator as His representative in the soul." It followed that "the Conscience sits sovereign." To disobey it and to "yield to what we know to be wrong," was, according to Lydia Maria Child, to close "the avenues by which heaven communicates with our own souls."[74]

Ironically, the careers of the abolitionists themselves tended to confirm conservative fears. Following the dictates of their consciences, many of them came to be deeply suspicious of the various churches, to say nothing of the political parties, in the nation, all of which, it seemed, had made sinful compromises or concessions. The Garrisonians took these views furthest but the example of William Goodell shows the extent to which even those who did not renounce organized religion or political parties,

73. Haven, *Speeches and Letters*, p. 9.
74. Gilbert Haven, *National Sermons* (Boston, 1869), p. 9; Lydia Maria Child, *Good Wives* (Boston, 1833), pp. xi-xii.

shared their opinions. Writing in the *Radical Abolitionist*, Goodell asserted that he "could not belong to a party," – and he made it clear that the same applied to a church – "further than it belongs to universal justice and truth." "So far as the church is right," he continued, "it belongs to me." The use of the word "belongs" here suggests a highly individualistic attitude. Still more individualistic was his conclusion. "When the party and the Church do not belong to me," he averred, "I excommunicate both."[75]

Even more remarkable was the demotion of the Bible which some abolitionists effected. By the mid-1840s Garrison and Henry Wright had repudiated those parts of it that did not accord with their principles. More generally, and more importantly, they and others insisted that the individual's sense of Truth and Right should be employed to evaluate the Bible, rather than the Bible be used to inculcate the sense of Truth and Right. In a similar if more temperate vein, Lydia Maria Child, in a letter written in 1856, acknowledged that "Most devoutly do I believe in the pervasive and ever-guiding Spirit of God." But she added that "I do not believe it was ever shut up within the covers of any *book,* or that it ever can be." While "the words of Christ" seemed to her to be "*full* of it [the Spirit of God], as no other words are," nevertheless she cautioned that "if *we* want truth, we must listen to the voice of God in the silence of our *own* souls." To do so was, after all, to do "as *he* did." Child expressed a fear that "Protestants, in their blind hereditary worship of the Bible, worship an *image* as truly as the Catholics do."[76]

In the name of the individual conscience, therefore, the abolitionists claimed the right to scrutinize laws, political parties and churches, together with the nation's constitution (found by the Garrisonians to be utterly corrupt) and even the Bible. This was indeed the enthronement of the individual. But if we recognize – as surely we must – that aboli-tionists espoused an extreme form of individualism, we must also recog-nize that the individual was not the single person we might expect. Behind the solitary figure who wielded his conscience in the battle against sin stood the family. Without it the individual simply could not function.

75. *Radical Abolitionist*, I (July, 1856), p. 100. For examples of abolitionist attacks on the clergy, see Stephen S. Foster, *The Brotherhood of Thieves; Or, a True Picture of the American Clergy* (Concord, 1886), pp. 9, 15; Allen, *A Report on American Slavery*, p. 24; *Platform of the American Anti-Slavery Society and Its Auxiliaries* (N.Y., 1855), p. 21. The growing dissatisfaction and disappointment with the church is explained in Charles K. Whipple, "The Relations of Anti-Slavery to Religion," *Anti-Slavery Tracts*, no. 19 (n.p., n.d.); Garrison, "The Infidelity of Abolitionism," *Anti- Slavery Tracts*, new series, no. 10 (N.Y, 1860), p. 90.
76. Child to Lucy Osgood, Feb. ? [date unknown], 1856 in Meltzer and Holland (eds), *Child: Selected Letters*, pp. 277–278.

Home and family

"In their power over the organization, character and destiny of human beings," Henry C. Wright announced, "the Church is nothing, the State is nothing; religion, government, priests and politicians, are nothing, compared to marriage and parentage, to the husband and wife, the father and mother." It followed that "those who make marriage an appendage to commerce, to government or religion, to pecuniary or educational institutions, sacrifice the substance of life to the shadow." It also followed that all the other relationships into which men and women entered, whether religious, political, social, or commercial, "should be measured and valued by their adaptation and their power to fit men and women for true marriage and parental relations, and to aid them to enter into, and to perform rightly and nobly, all the obligations, and duties inherent in them." "Marriage," Wright concluded – and he made it clear once again that he included parenthood – "is the central, vital relation of our being."[77]

Wright was not alone among abolitionists in attaching such significance to the family. Indeed they were unanimous in agreeing on its importance. According to Theodore Parker, "the family" would "last forever," since "its roots" were "in the primeval instincts of the human race." "Home," he observed in 1843, "is the oldest of all human institutions. It is foreordained in the nature of man's body and soul. It represents an indestructible want, and satisfies that want." For Charles Beecher, the Bible confirmed that God was "the Author of the family state, and the jealous defender of its purity." He concurred in the general estimate of its importance. "The family," he declared, "is the oldest, simplest, strongest and most sacred institution of God on earth." Similarly, James Birney proclaimed that the family was "a divine institution for the maintenance, comfort and improvement of the human race on earth, and its due preparation for heaven." For his part, William Lloyd Garrison wrote rhapsodic passages on the importance of marriage and the family, while Charles K. Whipple believed that "society at large" was "but an aggregate of families." William Goodell, writing in the *Principia* again managed to outdo other abolitionists when he offered an estimate of the family's role. He argued that it was "the first institution of society," preceding both Church and State in time as well as in importance, and then went on to claim that "had the family relation been duly honored and preserved in fidelity for its original ends, there is little reason to think that any church or any other state would ever have been needed."[78]

77. Wright, *Marriage and Parentage*, p. 276.
78. Parker, *Lessons from the World of Matter* . . . , p. 187, Parker, *Sins and Safeguards of Society*, p. 207; Beecher, "God of the Bible Against Slavery," p. 3; [James G.

As we have seen, the abolitionists rejected or criticized many of the social and political institutions of their country. The family was the great exception. They looked forward to the creation of a society without institutions like slavery, they believed that the conscience within was a better guide to action than any church, some of them could even imagine the nation functioning without any organized government. But they could not imagine any remotely healthy society without the family. "Break it down by violence or corruption," said Garrison, "and the nation will become as Sodom and Gomorrah." "Without the relations of the family state," Gerrit Smith warned, "the world would be nothing better than one scene of pollution and wo."[79]

Smith's words offer a clue to the role the family was expected to play. At the same time as the movement for immediate abolition began, that is to say in the 1830s, a cult of domesticity was also emerging in the United States. Domesticity emphasized the qualities which home and family fostered, contrasted them with those which were promoted at work and, in its most idealistic variants, insisted that the values of the home could spread outwards and conquer society as a whole. This ideology reflected, though in a complex and highly mediated form, the major changes which the family itself was undergoing in the final three decades of the antebellum era. In the colonial era, as one historian has put it, Americans had "had little sense that emotional interactions among people were qualitatively different within the family than outside it." Hence there had been no need to require that the family teach social behavior which "might conflict with that fostered by other institutions," and which could not be learnt elsewhere. Far from being a refuge from society, the family was coterminous with the community. Work of course, was centered in the household, a tendency that was actually strengthened in the early decades of the Republic for all but the very rich or the very poor by the putting out system and the growth of what was known as "domestic industry."[80]

Birney], "The Family and Slavery," *American Reform Tract and Book Society Tract* no. 37 (n.p., n.d.), p. 1; Garrison to George W. Benson, Sept. 4, 1835 in Merrill (ed.), *Letters of Garrison,* I, p. 494; Charles K. Whipple, *The Family Relation, As Affected By Slavery* (Cincinnati, 1858), pp. 23–24; *Principia,* Nov. 24, 1859.

79. Garrison to George W. Benson, Sept. 4, 1835 in Merrill (ed.), *Letters of Garrison,* I, p. 494; *Letter of Gerrit Smith to . . . James Smylie,* p. 43. For other examples of abolitionists extolling the family see *The Family and Slavery by a Native of the South-West* (n.p.,n.d.), pp. 1, 5; "White Slavery in the United States," *Anti-Slavery Tracts,* no. 2 (n.p., n.d.).

80. Coontz, *Social Origins of Private Life,* pp. 87, 88, 119–120. The literature on domesticity is now very considerable. See, for example, Mary Kelley, *Private Woman, Public Stage* (N.Y., 1984); Mary Ryan, *The Empire of the Mother: American Writing about the Domesticity, 1830–1869* (N.Y., 1984).

But this economy contained within it the seeds of its own destruction. The spread of new commercial opportunities and the inability of fathers to pass on a viable farm (especially in New England) pushed more and more young men in the years following the Treaty of Ghent towards work outside the home. A simultaneous decline in the number of apprentices working within the household paved the way for the new ideology of domesticity, especially since men could now less easily combine moral, religious and domestic tasks with work outside the home. What could be more natural than to assume a God-given division of labor between the sexes and to conclude that the family was the source of values needed for, but not necessarily acquired in, the outside world? The family was no longer the community in microcosm; instead it was a refuge from the outside world, "a defense against some elements of the community."[81]

In fact there is reason to doubt whether the separation between work and home was as complete as the ideology of domesticity and the notion of "separate spheres" for men and women would suggest. In practice even middle-class urban women were more heavily involved in money-making activities than propagandists of the new domesticity generally conceded and this was even more true of rural and working-class women. The home was thus less insulated from market activities than the rhetoric suggested.[82]

Abolitionists, however, were apparently unaware of these complexities; certainly they were amongst the most enthusiastic proponents of the new ideology. They believed that without the influence of the home and family, highly dubious practices and highly immoral standards would prevail. Theodore Parker was perhaps most explicit in describing the social function of the family. He believed that "a man's home" was "to him the most chosen spot of the earth." For here he was allowed "a rest from the toils of life." "Here," Parker continued, employing a telling phrase, "he can lay off the armor wherewith he is girt for the warfare of this world." The picture which Parker painted of the world beyond the

---

81. Coontz, *Social Origins of Private Life*, pp. 166, 193.
82. Works which stress the separation between home and market activities include Nancy F. Cott, *The Bonds of Womanhood: 'Woman's Sphere' in New England, 1780–1835* (New Haven, 1977); Mary P. Ryan, *Cradle of the Middle Class: The Family in Oneida County, New York, 1790–1865* (N.Y., 1981); Carroll Smith-Rosenberg, *Disorderly Conduct: Visions of Gender in Victorian America* (N.Y., 1985). Works which qualify (or even reject) this notion include Jeanne Boydston, *Home and Work: Housework, Wages, and the Ideology of Labor in the Early Republic* (N.Y., 1990); Thomas Dublin, "Women and Outwork in a Nineteenth-Century New England Town: Fitzwilliam, New Hampshire, 1830–1850," in Stephen Hahn and Jonathan Prude (eds), *The Countryside in the Age of Capitalist Transformation: Essays in the Social History of Rural America* (Chapel Hill, 1985); Joan M. Jensen, *Loosening the Bonds: Mid-Atlantic Farm Women, 1750–1850* (New Haven, 1986); Christine Stansell, *City of Women: Sex and Class in New York, 1789–1860* (N.Y., 1986).

family circle was a grim one. It was characterized by "strife" and it demanded "hardness," together with "habitual restraint and self-conceal-ment." The effect of "sad intercourse with the selfish" was to make even the altruistic "selfish" too. "The sphere of a man's daily business, as things commonly go," he warned, "is but a place for the exercise of his understanding, shrewdness and skill." While "it often sharpens the lower qualities of the mind to a high degree," "it does not make the same demands on his affections, on the loftier and better sentiments of his nature," since "these he finds not necessary to attain his private ends."[83]

Fortunately, however, home provided the necessary antidote. Parker subscribed fully to the Victorian view of the home as a "haven in a heartless world." "A man's home," he declared, " – it is to him the most chosen spot of the earth." At home a man could forget the "strife" of the world, "living quietly once more." At home he could "speak as he thinks and think as he feels, not fearing to be misunderstood and censured." Thus home could be "likened to a little conservatory or glass house, so formed as to keep in the sun and to keep out the cold, and create a milder atmosphere, where delicate plants may grow into hardi-hood, till they can bear the bleak exposure of the common field." Home was "the place wherein we must cultivate all the narrow virtues which cannot bear the cold atmosphere of the outside world."[84]

In no sense did the effect of home and family challenge the role of the conscience and the soul. Instead they were entirely complementary. "Only in a true home," Wright asserted, "can the soul attain its full development in all directions." Only there could "the conscience become a universe of light to guide the soul onward and upward." The aboli-tionists believed that men were made in God's image but, for Wright at least, it was "in that hallowed retreat, and no where else," that "men and women truly reveal the beauty and glory of their nature." "The pure in heart," he concluded, "must be created and developed, not in the market, nor the school, nor the church, nor in halls of legislation, but in the true home of freedom and of rest, where all the elements and functions of soul and body can be called into healthful activity."[85]

Abolitionists frequently tried to explain how the effects of home were to operate. Here there were significant differences of emphasis between

83. Parker, *Sins and Safeguards*, pp. 208–209, 211–212. As Henry C. Wright put it: "In commercial, social, political or religious life, conscience becomes seared, reason obtuse, affection chilled, and the soul altogether bewildered by unnatural excitement in pursuit of that which, if obtained, can give no rest. Only in a true home can the soul attain its full development in all directions" – Wright, *Marriage and Parentage*, p. 291.
84. Parker, *Sins and Safeguards*, pp. 209, 212, *Lessons from the World of Matter*, p. 197.
85. Wright, *Marriage and Parentage*, pp. 291, 299.

them. The most direct effect would, of course, be upon children who, it was believed, in a loving home would be taught "a reverential obedience to the voice of conscience in the smallest as in the greatest affairs of life." At the same time, however, children themselves were thought to be redemptive, "a savior . . . to the parents," as Wright put it. In *Uncle Tom's Cabin* St Clair's daughter plays precisely this role, and her Christ-like qualities are all the more apparent when her death is presented as if in necessary atonement for the sins of the society and the family into which she has been born. Lacking the formal education which adults have received, for this very reason she is able to perceive the truth about slavery. She alone among the whites in the St. Clair household is able to listen to and obey the voice within. Such a view of childhood represented a reversal of the traditional belief that the child was willful and in need of strict discipline. In the past physical punishment had been advocated as a means of will-breaking. Lydia Maria Child in her books on child rearing began by advocating physical punishment but by 1843 she had repudiated this opinion and was firmly opposed to all corporal punishment.[86]

Despite the importance attached to children, however, the vital role in the family was to be played by the wife and mother. In northern society at large the ideology of domesticity was accompanied by a "cult of true womanhood," which emphasized the qualities that the true woman, in contrast to the true man, was supposed to possess.[87] Abolitionists agreed on the importance of the woman's role in the family and agreed too that her duty was to inculcate religious values into her children and also, when necessary, into her husband. In *Uncle Tom* St Clair observes that his mother had been "all that stood between me and utter disbelief for years" and added that "she was a direct embodiment and personification of the New Testament." Her achievement had been to make him aware of "the dignity and worth of the meanest human soul," and he "might have been a saint, reformer, martyr," had she not died when he was still a child. Yet many abolitionists, and especially those who followed Garrison, challenged the notion of femininity which "true womanhood" required. They doubted whether women should inhabit a separate sphere and demanded that they be accorded full civil and political rights. But they did not repudiate the cult of domesticity – the vision of the family

86. Wright, *Marriage and Parentage*, pp. 317, 134; Compare Lydia M. Child, *The Mother's Book* (N.Y., 1835) with Child, *Letters from New York* 2nd series (N.Y., 1845), p. 106. Garrison also asserted that children were naturally antislavery – *Liberator*, April 2, 1831.

87. Barbara Welter, "The Cult of True Womanhood: 1800–1860," *American Quarterly*, XVIII (1966), pp. 151–174, *Dimity Convictions: The American Woman in the Nineteenth Century* (Athens, Oh., 1976).

and its social function – nor did they deny the role of the mother within the family. Lydia Maria Child, for example, complained bitterly about the plight of women in her own times. But she argued that men were destined to become more like women and even she referred to home as "that blessed world, which opens to the human heart the most perfect glimpse of Heaven, and helps to carry it thither, as on an angel's wings." The feminist abolitionist thus endorsed the general opinion of woman as the repository of moral and religious values even while seeking to strengthen her political role and secure her economic rights.[88]

The family and the home, in conjunction with the conscience and the soul, were to supply the necessary foundations for the social order. "A man without a home," Wright observed, "is without a centre to his life . . . his thoughts, affections, hopes, aims and aspirations, gather fondly and permanently around no fixed centre." He believed that properly constituted homes and families might actually effect a redemption of American society as a whole. "Only in the home," he announced, "can marriage and parentage perform their perfect work in the regeneration and redemption of the race." The family was thus the school for altruism. In *Uncle Tom's Cabin*, the head of one highly virtuous family spells out this function: " 'Thee uses thyself only to learn how to love thy neighbor, Ruth,' said Simon, looking, with a beaming face, on Ruth. 'To be sure. Isn't it what we are made for? If I didn't love John and the baby, I should not know how to feel for her.'" In Stowe's words, the "mothers of America" had "learned, by the cradles of . . . [their] own children" "to love and feel for all mankind."[89]

Nevertheless, abolitionists had such high hopes for the family that they were gravely disappointed by its contemporary manifestations. Even Theodore Parker acknowledged that many northern families failed to fulfill their true functions. Others went further. "Among the dislocations of the age," wrote Theodore Weld to Angelina Grimké, his wife-to-be, "the relations of husband and wife are perhaps as they now are the most horrible perversions of all," while Elizabeth Cady Stanton believed that "the right idea of marriage is at the foundation of all reforms." Such a conclusion was perhaps inevitable. If social evils were to be seen in moral

88. Stowe, *Uncle Tom's Cabin*, pp. 332, 337, 338; Child, *Letters from New York*, p. 238. The extent to which Garrisonian abolitionists departed from the (highly sexist) orthodoxy of their times is still a subject of debate amongst historians. See Kristin Hoganson, "Garrisonian Abolitionists and the Rhetoric of Gender, 1850–1860," *American Quarterly*, XLV (1993), pp. 556–595; Jean Fagan Yellin, *Women and Sisters: The Antislavery Feminists in American Culture* (New Haven, 1989); Karen Sanchez-Eppler, "Bodily Bonds: The Intersecting Rhetorics of Feminism and Abolitionism," *Representations*, XXIV (1988), pp. 28–59.
89. Wright, *Marriage and Parentage*, pp. 305, 299; Stowe, *Uncle Tom's Cabin*, pp. 623, 220.

terms, and the family were the source of moral values, then northern families would always be given much of the blame for any imperfections that were visible within northern society.[90]

Yet the many criticisms that could be leveled against the northern family shrank into insignificance when compared to the family under slavery. "The worst abuse of the system of slavery," in Harriet Beecher Stowe's opinion, "is its outrage upon the family." According to George Allen, slavery had the effect of "abrogating domestic relations, and forbidding the comfort and solace of wife or children," which were available to the free man "whatever may betide him in this rugged world." Southern slaveholders insisted on the right to buy and sell slaves at pleasure and to break up families when necessary. As a result "that original law, inscribed deep in the nature of man, 'for this cause shall a man cleave to his wife,' – this law to which such might is given, to keep the world from being a wilderness, and to save it from the ferocity of man, is shattered and dissolved throughout the dominion of slavery." Was it not evident that slavery "breaks into the sanctuary of the home."? For Gerrit Smith it had been "abundantly proven, that slavery is, essentially and inevitably, at war with the sacred rights of the family state." To James Birney it was equally apparent that "the Family," which was no less than "the head, the heart, the fountain of society," did not possess "a privilege that slavery does not nullify, a right that it does not violate, a single faculty for improvement it does not counteract, nor a hope that it does not put out in darkness." The principal effects were, of course, upon the family of the slave. But abolitionists also charged that the power of the slaveholder allowed him to take advantage of his female slaves – an occurrence whose frequency was shown by the number of mulattos in the South. The effect of this outrage was to undermine not only her family but his too. The family in a slaveholding community was thus inevitably in a perilous condition.[91]

Since they expected so much from the family, the abolitionists naturally emphasized its abuses under slavery. In a letter to George Benson written in 1835, Garrison dwelt upon the holiness of marriage and the family. This immediately brought him back to the issue of slavery. "In this mirror," he continued, "how is the terrific image of the monster Slavery

90. Parker, *Sins and Safeguards*, p. 210; Weld to Grimké, April 15, 1838 in Barnes and Dumond (eds), *Letters of Weld . . .* , II, p. 637; Theodore Stanton and Harriet Stanton Blatch (eds), *Elizabeth Cady Stanton as Revealed in her Letters, Diary and Reminiscences* (N.Y., 1922), II, p. 48.

91. Harriet Beecher Stowe, *The Key to Uncle Tom's Cabin* (London, n.d.), p. 257; [George Allen], *Report on American Slavery*, pp. 13–14; Allen, *Mr. Allen's Report of a Declaration of Sentiment on Slavery Dec. 5, 1837* (Worcester, 1838), pp. 7, 9; *Letter of Gerrit Smith to . . . James Smylie*, p. 41; [Birney], "The Family and Slavery," p. 23.

reflected!" The abolitionist differed from other northerners not so much in his estimate of the importance of the family as in his insistence that its values should be honored among all races, throughout the nation, indeed throughout the world.[92]

Conclusion: abolitionism and capitalism

I

It is appropriate now to consider the way in which abolitionists perceived the individual as a social and political entity. A brief comparison with the views of their contemporaries in the major political parties will serve to show the distinctiveness of abolitionist perceptions.[93] The Whigs (especially in the North) shared many of the abolitionists' views on economic questions. They too emphasized social mobility, the privileged condition of labor in the United States, the salutary effects of technological development and industrial and commercial growth. The similarities would be still more apparent if we were to consider liberal, antislavery Whigs like William Seward. In the 1850s, of course, Seward would be the best-known and leading Republican in the North but in the era of the second party system it was Whigs of the Webster stripe who were closer to the mainstream of the party. These men were repelled by abolitionist individualism. They believed the appeal to the conscience to be a dangerous absurdity and instead looked to the community and especially its social and political leaders, to foster a collective moral sense. They believed, in short, in an organic society. Where abolitionists tended to see society as little more than an aggregate of individuals – and, as we have seen, of families, Whigs compared society itself to a family.

Individualism clearly bulked much larger in abolitionist than in Whig thought. But the Democrats also espoused "individualism," of a no less intense but very different kind. They even shared the abolitionist view that on moral questions, such as temperance, men should be allowed to follow the dictates of their conscience. But here the resemblance ends. For the Democrats it was the utmost folly to rest the social and political order upon the conscience, even if supplemented by the family. In certain circumstances the conscience would be overwhelmed. Whenever men possessed the opportunities for self-aggrandizement, the conscience would be utterly unable to provide the necessary restraint. Thus an appeal to the

92. Garrison to George W. Benson, Sept. 4, 1835 in Merrill (ed.), *Letters of Garrison*, I, p. 494.
93. Here I am merely summarizing Whig and Democratic ideology. For a fuller discussion, see below, Chapter 5.

conscience of legislators (who possessed the power to enrich certain groups at the expense of others), or of bankers (who possessed precisely the same power) was futile. Instead political constraints (laws, checks and balances) must be established in order to prevent the predatory minority from filching the proceeds of the labor of the majority. Only when this had been achieved would the virtuousness of human nature flourish. Thus the Democrats insisted that men should be allowed to follow their consciences over questions like temperance, precisely because such questions were deemed to belong outside the political arena. The primary task of politics was to ensure that men received a just reward for their labor.

The Democrats assumed a particular social and economic order, one in which a fair reward for labor was forthcoming, in the absence of "artificial" government activity. This social order was overwhelmingly agrarian. They insisted that freedom be grounded in the ownership of productive property. Here the contrast with the abolitionists could not be sharper. Democratic individualism was rooted in the ownership, on the part of the mass of the citizenry, of the means of production. Even if – and this was problematic – those who owned no property possessed the necessary independence, they did so only because most of their fellow citizens were property holders. Hence Democratic individualism rested upon individual ownership of property. Abolitionist individualism was quite different. It referred to a set of values that allowed the individual to become an economic actor regardless of his or anyone else's ownership of property. The conscience, supported by the family, was to perform the function which for the Democrats would be performed by the ownership of property, and especially landed property.

In a pamphlet entitled *The Chattel Principle the Abhorrence of Jesus Christ and the Apostles* Beriah Green argued that "every child of America," had the right of "wielding, within reasonable limits, his own powers, and employing his own resources, according to his own choice." He then added a *caveat*: "But mark – HIS OWN powers and resources, and NOT ANOTHER'S are thus inalienably put under his control." The Democrats might have assented to this doctrine but they would have construed it quite differently. Plainly it was incompatible with slave status, unless the slave was denied the title "child of America." This a Democrat would have done. But the doctrine placed the slaveholder too beyond the pale, unless the slave was denied the title "another." This too a Democrat would have done. Yet the Democrats would have had serious doubts whether the doctrine was compatible with wage labor. Did the employer control the "powers and resources" of the wage laborer? The Democrats feared that he did. The abolitionists thought otherwise. When they wrote about the conscience, they did not privilege the wage laborer. But abolitionist thinking here, as elsewhere, obliterated the difference between the wage worker, the employer, and the self-employed. It thus assimilated the wage laborer into the mainstream of American society.[94]

A central problem for Whig, Democrat and abolitionist alike concerned the pursuit of self-interest. Insofar as a society allows the market to prompt individuals, the force of self-interest is legitimized. But self-interest is a highly dissolvent force. If its pursuit is universal, it undermines its own foundations. Why should self-interested individuals not seek to buy the law? Why should they not sell the nation itself for gain? Why should they not rob, kill or maim their competitors? It might well be in their interest to put an end to the system by which everyone else's freedom can be pursued. This of course, is the paradox of freedom. If all are free, will not some use their freedom to end the freedom of others? A similar paradox of self-interest exists. A society based upon self-interest needs certain institutions, certain practices that must remain outside the area in which self-interest can operate. For self-interest to operate, there must be a sphere from which it is barred.

The Democrats' solution to this problem lay in their view of human nature. In the absence of government interference, a just reward for labor would both cater for and, as it were, discharge men's self-interested impulses and the knowledge that they were members of a just society would then allow an innate altruism to flourish. Self-interest would be properly confined because, in these circumstances, human nature would itself impose a check. The Whigs, by contrast, were highly sceptical about Democratic appeals to the self-interest of, for example, the majority. But at the same time, they were the apologists for commercial development in the United States. In effect they recognized the paradox of self-interest. Their solution was to emphasize the need for restraint, for the inculcation, perhaps by government but also by schools, churches and other institutions, of values which would counterbalance that of self-interest or channel it into socially benign activities. Here again was an organic view of society, a perception of society as a family. The abolitionist, on the other hand, claimed for every individual the prior right to judge those institutions himself. Unlike a Whig, he denied the legitimacy of outside social constraints; unlike a Democrat, he denied the need for individual ownership of property. Where then did the necessary constraints lie?

For the abolitionist they lay, quite simply, within the individual himself. All men possessed within themselves the necessary restraint. All men

---

94. [Beriah Green], *The Chattel Principle the Abhorrence of Jesus Christ and the Apostles* (N.Y., 1839), pp. 22–23.

had within themselves a spiritual quality which, if cherished, would be an unfailing guide to good behavior and virtuous action. This was none other than their conscience or soul, nourished and protected by the family. The abolitionist thus resolved the paradox of self-interest by making a part of the individual – his conscience or soul – in effect his own policeman. He believed that these faculties existed within all men, regardless of race or class. And just as the pursuit of self-interest is threatened by those who, in order to advance their own interest, "buy" a policeman, so the buying and selling of an individual, and thus of an individual's own private policeman, was utterly unacceptable. The abolitionist could countenance the buying and selling of labor power, and the huge extension of market activities that this entailed. But for this very reason he insisted upon a rigid separation between the buying of labor power, which made no claim upon the conscience of the laborer, and the buying of the man himself, which did.

We are now in a position to appreciate one of the abolitionist's central objections to slavery. He had invested the conscience and the soul with the most transcendental qualities, qualities he viewed as holy and God-given but whose secular role was of enormous importance. The slaveholder, he argued, in buying and selling the slave, was not only disobeying the holy voice within, he was also buying and selling the holy part of another. Such an action was simply outrageous. According to Henry C. Wright it was "diabolical impiety" to seek to traffic in a person. In one of the most powerful passages in *Uncle Tom's Cabin*, Harriet Beecher Stowe commented upon the blasphemy inherent in a slave warehouse:

> Then you shall be courteously entreated to call and examine, and shall find an abundance of husbands, wives, brothers, sisters, fathers, mothers, and young children, to be 'sold separately, or in lots to suit the convenience of the purchaser'; and that soul immortal, once bought with blood and anguish by the Son of God, when the earth shook, and the rocks rent, and the graves were opened, can be sold, leased, mortgaged, exchanged for groceries or any goods, to suit the phases of trade, or the fancy of the purchaser.

In terms which also did not seek to conceal its sense of outrage, the American and Foreign Anti-Slavery Society complained that some clergymen in the North "have announced from their pulpits that HE has sanctioned the conversion into articles of merchandise of beings charged with no crime, made a little lower than the angels, and redeemed by his own blood." "How," asked William Alger in 1859, "can there be room for further wrong, when a soul is made a thing?"[95]

95. [George Bourne], *Picture of Slavery in the United States of America* (Middletown, Conn., 1834), p. 35; Stowe, *Uncle Tom's Cabin*, p. 467; *An Address to the Anti-*

We ought perhaps to remind ourselves at this point that, while Christianity has, for two millennia, emphasized the importance of the soul and of the conscience, for all but a small portion of that time, the buying and selling of men has not been thought to be at all immoral. Yet, at the very moment when more commodities than ever before – and especially the crucial commodity of labor power – were being bought and sold, the abolitionists discovered that it was impious in the extreme to sell human beings. One reason, I have argued, concerns what I have termed "the paradox of self-interest."

But it was not merely the conscience that was to be religiously guarded from commercial transactions. An identical role in supporting the market was to be played by the home and the family. Accordingly, they too had to be kept apart from commerce. It was the sin of the slave system that it engulfed the family within the market economy. What should have been an external support was instead incorporated into the system. This was another of the ultimate perversions of slavery. Little wonder, then, that abolitionists stressed its impact on the family. The individual, supported by his family and fortified by his conscience, was able to tread a virtuous path through the pits and snares of commerce only when both family and conscience were kept outside the realm over which commercial transactions held sway and the market ruled.

II

The relationship between abolitionism and capitalism thus needs the most careful analysis. First it is necessary to distinguish causes from consequences. Let us begin with consequences. Here it is necessary, in turn, to distinguish between the consequences of abolitionism and the consequences of the abolition of slavery itself. I shall consider the latter

---

Slavery Christians of the United States (N.Y., 1852), p. 3; William Alger, *The Historic Purchase of Freedom, An Oration Delivered in . . . Boston, December 22, 1859 . . .* (Boston, 1859), p. 8. As Theodore Weld put it: "ENSLAVING MEN IS REDUCING THEM TO ARTICLES OF PROPERTY – making free agents, chattels – converting person into *things* – sinking immortality into *merchandise* . . . . In a word, the profit of his master is made the END of his being, and he, a *mere means* to that end – a mere means to an end into which his interests do not enter, of which they constitute no portion. MAN, sunk to a *thing*! the intrinsic element, the *principle* of slavery; MEN, bartered, leased, mortgaged, bequeathed, invoiced, shipped in cargoes, stored as goods, taken on executions, and knocked off at a public outcry. Their *rights*, another's conveniences; their interests, wares on sale; their happiness a household utensil; their personal inalienable ownership, a serviceable article or plaything, as best suits the humour of the hour; their deathless nature, conscience, social affections, sympathies, hopes – marketable commodities" – [Weld], *Bible Against Slavery*, p. 8. See also Weld to J. F. Robinson, May 1, 1836 in Barnes and Dumond, (eds), *Letters of Weld . . .* , I, p. 296.

question in the sequel to this volume. But what of the impact of abolitionism on northern capitalism? Clearly the abolitionists celebrated the northern social order, or rather the potential within that social order. Northern society either was, or could be made, classless and harmonious. More specifically, wage labor was, or could be made, benign and progressive, both morally and materially. To this extent, those who were influenced by the abolitionist crusade were presumably propelled towards or confirmed in a conservative view of the North. To this extent abolitionism was hegemonic in its effects.

Yet this hegemonic effect was surely very limited. As far as can be judged, only a small proportion of the northern electorate was sufficiently influenced by the abolitionists to convert to their view of the northern social order. More important, the demands which abolitionists made for the northern social system were extraordinarily high. They demanded much because they believed much was possible. Abolitionism unsettled its devotees, even as it unsettled its enemies, north and south of the Mason-Dixon line. To call this a conservative influence would surely be stretching words too far. Nor did the abolition message confer any prestige upon northern financial or busir ders, most of whom were severely censured for their indifferer e antislavery crusade.

So abolitionism gave only modest support to capit the United States. There is not the slightest reason to think that t support was a necessary, still less a sufficient, cause of northern economic development, nor that it was necessary to establish or maintain capitalist hegemony in the North. Nevertheless, when we consider the limited, but still significant success enjoyed by this movement, as opposed to some others, an emphasis upon hegemony is more appropriate. If we wish to explain why antislavery had far greater success than the radical schemes of some labor leaders, or Orestes Brownson's call for the abolition of wages, then the hegemonic influence of the financial and industrial elite is surely a significant factor.

This brings us to the question of causes. Plainly capitalism cannot be anything like a total cause of abolitionism. Other factors are of great importance and must be noted. First, the continuing strength of slavery in the South. Slavery did not, as many Americans had once expected, wither and die and its expansion into the Southwest, together with its central role in supplying cotton for the industrial revolution in Britain discredited traditional assumptions that it was moribund. If it had indeed been on the way out, then either the abolitionist demand for immediate action would never have been heard or the movement would have provoked far less controversy. Second, and very much related, the southern defense of slavery played a key role in increasing the impact and fostering the growth of abolitionism. Southern resistance tended to polarize northern opinion, to force even reluctant northerners to determine where their priorities lay. Proslavery thought and abolitionist pressure grew together, each feeding off the other. Finally, the blatant inability of the American Colonization Society to solve the problem, and the feebleness of its efforts spurred many who had been more moderate in their antislavery to embrace the new militancy. Indeed this was the route by which William Lloyd Garrison himself arrived at immediatism.

But the vital question concerns the relationship of abolitionism to northern society and the extent to which material changes in the North can be cited as causal. Why did the immediate abolitionist find slavery so odious? Far more than previous opponents of slavery, he stressed its effect on the family[96] and the conscience; far more than those who advocated gradual abolition or colonization, he assumed that an economy in which wage labor played a key role was "natural," easily established and necessarily superior to one in which labor was coerced. Above all he assumed that the necessary controls needed to create social harmony, moral and material progress, were within the individual, not within external institutions. He viewed with impatience those traditional social practices which, because they had been slowly evolving and maturing, seemed to the conservative to be either beyond reproach, or at least, delicate and unamenable to change. And first among such practices was slavery.[97]

The abolitionist lived in a world of rapid change, one in which material development was occurring at a faster pace than at any time in history. In common with many other northerners, he made sense of his world [98]by revising traditional notions of the family, the conscience, the sources of economic growth and individual betterment. Having made sense of this world, he was left with a set of principles and values which implied the immediate abolition of slavery. Not all northerners who agreed with his estimate of the family, the conscience or the economy became immediatists; the hallmark of the abolitionists who followed Garrison, Tappan, Smith and others was their willingness to pursue their principles to the

---

96. As Ronald Walters observes, "Abolitionists after 1831 took slavery's impact on the family more seriously than their ancestors had, because society, economy, and demographic alterations made family life an issue of concern in the three decades before the Civil War" – Walters, *Antislavery Appeal*, pp. 95–96. As for the appeal to conscience, it could even be argued that it was this which made abolitionists abandon gradualism. The demand for gradual emancipation, it was claimed, actually retarded the cause "by soothing the public conscience with the hope of a wise and well digested measure of relief" – *Anti-Slavery Reporter*, I (1833), p. 67.

97. David Brion Davis, "The Emergence of Immediatism in British and American Antislavery Thought," in Davis, *From Homicide to Slavery: Studies in American Culture* (N.Y., 1986), pp. 256–257.

98. I do not mean to imply, however, that this process of "making sense of the world" was unrelated to class interests or neutral between classes.

utmost lengths, pressing their ideals to their ultimate conclusion. They were unmindful of the disruption that might ensue precisely because they believed the reforms they advocated were "natural" and thus in no way disruptive.

Let us consider the role of wage labor in this process. Its impact in generating the comparison between North and South in economic development is most obvious. The immediatist made it clear that he expected wage labor and not merely free labor to regenerate the South, just as he rejected the traditional notion that the wage laborer was excessively dependent and servile. Nothing is more striking than the severing in abolitionist thought of the traditional connection between wage labor and slavery. Whereas they had once both been perceived as conditions of "unfreedom," the abolitionist now explicitly contrasted the two in order to explain differential growth rates and contrasting patterns of economic (and moral) development.

No less important is the role of wage labor in generating the abolitionist perception of the family. As production increasingly left the home,[99] it became plausible to postulate a contrast between the values of home and those of the workplace – a contrast that would have been meaningless for previous generations. The separation of home and work did not necessarily mean that the male householder who went out to work was either an employer or an employee (though such was likely) but it did necessitate, at the societal level, a deepening division of labor, itself only possible on the basis of wage labor.[100] The view of the family that emerged both facilitated and legitimated this process. As Stephanie Coontz in her brilliant history of the American family notes, the new image of womanhood that emerged in the generation before the Civil War derived "from a decisive change in patterns of social and personal reproduction following the spread of wage labor." She adds that in these years new "subjective, personal mechanisms had to be forged" which would serve "to channel people into the new roles and behaviors required for successful adjustment to the spread of wage labor." Moreover, as Amy Dru Stanley has noted, the traditional association of wage labor with dependency (a female condition) created, at least in theory, the possibility that the wage worker would be himself feminized. To avert this dire outcome, it was urgently necessary to "disrupt" the "analogy between wives and hired men." And "separate spheres fulfilled this

---

99. Although the home remained the site of many market-oriented activities, there can be no doubt that the proportion of goods and services produced outside the home was rising in this period.
100. See the discussion above in Chapter 2 and the appendix to this volume.

ideological purpose." As Stanley emphasizes, it was the spread of wage labor that set this process in motion.[101]

Equally important is the abolitionist perception of the individual and his moral faculties. At the very time when traditional links between worker and employer were being attenuated (as a result of larger units of operation as well as the shift of production outside of the home), the abolitionist, in common with many other northerners, found that the moral sense was innate within all who chose to listen to the voice of conscience. The wage laborer was not, as had previously been thought, so dependent as to be unable to discover and adhere to his own moral principles. Instead, his conscience, unsullied by his relationship with his employer, was a sufficient guide to action so that, in normal circumstances at least, employer and employee alike could heed the voice within.[102]

III

It remains to consider the question of class interests. Clearly the abolitionists did not set out merely to further the interests of any single class, except perhaps the slaves. They did not intend consciously to further middle class interests, especially not to the detriment of labor, and there is little reason to believe that this was an unconscious intention. Nevertheless, the ideals they promulgated bore the imprint of capitalist interests. This was most obviously true concerning the economy. The insistence that the wage laborer was free and independent, enjoying almost unlimited opportunities for financial betterment, clearly served the interests of American capitalism and American capitalists. To the extent that abolitionists were deceived here, it was not by themselves but partly by their class position, which made it hard for most of them to understand the situation confronting the wage laborer, and partly by the fact that reality itself encouraged this view. The formal equality between worker and employer, together with the real possibility of upward mobility (even if only for a minority) lent plausibility to the abolitionist view of the economy. This process was complex and for this very reason it should not be reduced to self-deception.

101. Coontz, *Social Origins of Private Life*, pp. 162, 179; Amy Dru Stanley, "Home Life and the Morality of the Market," in Melvyn Stokes (ed.), *The Market Revolution in America: Social, Political and Religious Expressions, c1800–1880* (University of Virginia Press, forthcoming). I believe that Ms Stanley's piece in this volume is a major contribution to the literature on the relationship between capitalism, antislavery and gender.
102. Johnson, *Shopkeeper's Millennium, passim.*

It is essential to determine in what ways abolitionist perceptions of the family and the conscience promoted a class interest. We should note that the cult of domesticity did not explicitly extol capitalist competition. But as we have seen, the new perception of the family smoothed the way to an accommodation with the spread of market relations. The task of the family, and especially of the wife, was to provide a counterbalance so that the working male would neither withdraw from the market nor yield too completely to it. Either eventuality would be highly damaging. (In effect, too complete a submission would reveal the paradox of self-interest.) Moreover, as wage earners experienced a decline in their control over their working lives, they were encouraged to find consolation in the enhanced freedom possible in family life, now less subject to the direction of the employer or the community at large.[103]

Although the abolitionist sincerely believed that his were the values of humanity, timelessly and universally valid, some of them were in fact quite class specific. For example, it was extremely difficult if not impossible for working class parents to lavish attention upon their children in the recommended way, still less to benefit from their allegedly redemptive innocence. Similarly, the ideology of domesticity ignored the increasing numbers of women who as servants "often worked gruelling hours to create this middle class oasis." Finally the emphasis on the family helped provide an explanation for the evils in society and thus served to prevent a deeper analysis. It was all too easy to reduce complex social problems to inadequate families, to assume that they could be conquered by proper behavior within the family home.[104] Much the same applies to abolitionist notions of the conscience. If the necessary restraints were within the individual and original sin did not exist, it followed that the more impersonal relations established by the cash nexus, and especially the relationship between worker and employer, were acceptable. Indeed, excessively impersonal relations at work need not be feared since the conscientious, family-oriented worker was sure to make a good citizen.[105]

In these ways abolitionist thought bore the imprint of capitalist values and interests. In northern society an ideological adjustment was being made to the spread of wage labor. Abolitionism took its cue from this shift in values. Most of the northerners who subscribed to these new values were nonetheless restrained from following them to their logical conclusion. No doubt many of them shrank from the personal dangers which abolitionism could entail or from the disturbing consequences

103. Coontz, *Social Origins of Private Life*, pp. 173, 193.
104. Coontz, *Social Origins of Private Life*, pp. 201, 212–214, 218. The middle class assumptions of abolitionists are sometimes glaringly apparent. In *The Mother's Book* (p. 153) Lydia M. Child assumes her readers have servants.
105. Johnson, *Shopkeeper's Millennium, passim.*

which it so often had for membership of churches, political parties, even loyalty to the nation's constitution. The abolitionist possessed unusual courage, together with a dedication to principle and a refusal to compromise that set him apart from most of his countrymen. Yet in one sense he was the quintessential northerner. He took views that were, or were in process of becoming, hegemonic and applied them with unchallengeable logic – but to subjects where the leaders of northern opinion insisted they were inappropriate or irrelevant. As a result the acceptance of wage labor and the consequent redefinition of family, conscience and the role of the individual meant that slavery, long disliked in the North, was now, for those who embraced the new values most enthusiastically and unreservedly, utterly unacceptable. Hence it must be abolished – and immediately.

4

The proslavery argument: Dilemmas of the master class

Introduction

I

Under the regime that had been established in 1776 and modified by the election of Thomas Jefferson in 1800, slavery had acquired a powerful place in American politics. In the first decades of the nineteenth century, political debate was conducted between the major parties without reference to slavery and the Republicans had achieved a position of dominance within the nation as a whole. Slavery was secure not because a majority of Americans believed it good but because other issues generated real divisions within the nation along party and not sectional lines. It had thus been removed, to a considerable extent, from the political arena. The slaveholders had in Thomas Jefferson and James Madison the two most important and imposing figures in the Republican party; as we have seen, antislavery formed no part of their politics. And the election of Andrew Jackson in 1828 was in a sense a continuation of the Republican triumphs of earlier years. Like Jefferson, Jackson was at the head of what would soon be seen as an egalitarian though highly racist organization, one which would champion the rights of white men against the advocates either of "aristocratic" forms of government or of corruptly generated social and economic inequalities, while maintaining a discreet silence on the subject of slavery.[1]

The parties which Jefferson headed and which Jackson led did not claim that slavery was a desirable institution. Indeed a striking feature of Republican and, later, Democratic political economy was the invisibility of the slave. Jefferson, Madison and John Taylor of Caroline wrote and argued as though the plantation were merely the farm writ large. In their politics the distinctiveness of the South was, in effect, that farmers (thus defined) had a greater social and political weight than in the North. This left much for the political parties to argue about: the nature and the extent of popular participation in government and the future profile of

1. See above, Chapter 1, and below, Chapters 5 and 6.

the nation's economy were very much at issue in these years. Nevertheless slavery was conspicuously absent from the list of partisan issues. When they discussed it at all, the Republicans generally argued that slavery was a "necessary evil" which would in the future be removed from the United States.[2]

Protected by this political silence, slavery in the first decades of the nineteenth century advanced rapidly. Indeed one can argue that the most effective defense for slavery was offered in these years: it consisted in offering no defense at all. Under these circumstances Americans could trust to the future, to the hand of Providence or to the workings of one or other law of political economy, as they pleased, to remove slavery at some time, usually left carefully unspecified, in the future. Although there had been rumblings of dissent earlier, the first major challenge to this consensus came, as we have seen, in 1819–1821 when the crisis over Missouri erupted. The successful resolution of this crisis once again took slavery out of the political arena for some years. And when in the 1830s it re-emerged it was not a subject over which the political parties clashed. Indeed most statesmen believed it ought to be absent from federal politics. In these circumstances, slavery continued to thrive, even as politicians struggled to keep it outside the boundaries of political debate.[3]

But while such a strategy offered a valuable protection for slavery, it could do so only on one condition: that attacks upon it were either absent or innocuous. Once they reached larger proportions, then southerners had to clarify their views. For reasons which we shall consider later, the only possible outcome was the articulation, or rather continued development, of a proslavery argument. There had been earlier defenses of slavery as a "positive good" from maverick figures in the South but from the 1830s such a position became increasingly common. The rise of a militant antislavery in the North, together with the ever greater role of slavery and especially of slave-produced cotton in the southern economy, meant that more and more southerners reassessed their attitudes to the "peculiar institution." The state of South Carolina now assumed the leadership of the proslavery forces in the South, a role it maintained throughout the remaining decades of the antebellum republic. Slavery did not immediately become a major partisan issue but by the 1850s at the latest it had clearly attained this status. By now proslavery theorists,

2. To repeat the argument of Chapter 1: slavery was not ignored politically; rather, it lay outside the sphere of partisan controversy. See Duncan J. MacLeod, *Slavery, Race and the American Revolution* (Cambridge, UK, 1974); John C. Miller, *The Wolf By the Ears: Thomas Jefferson and Slavery* (N.Y., 1977); Donald Robinson, *Slavery in the Structure of American Politics* (N.Y., 1970).
3. For the Missouri Crisis, see above, Chapter 1. For the views of Democrats on the slavery question, see below, Chapter 5.

who had once been frustrated observers of the drama of American politics, were players in their own right.

II

Historians have encountered many problems with the proslavery argument.[4] The first concerns definition. No southern writer denied that some evils attended the institution so one cannot define "proslavery" in an absolute sense. The extent to which southerners and indeed Americans in general can be termed "proslavery" clearly depends on a closer definition of the term. Large numbers of northerners and southerners found some good in it but without claiming even that it should be retained. I shall adopt, therefore, a more restrictive definition. I shall consider as proslavery spokesmen only those who argued that, as a labor system, slavery was preferable to the alternatives found in Europe, in Britain and, most of all, in the northern states.[5] Even subject to this restriction, proslavery thought was far from monolithic. Not surprisingly, different writers concentrated on different features of slavery: some dwelt on the moral aspects of enslavement, some pressed for a recognition of its political benefits, some concentrated on the economics of slave as compared to free labor. But proslavery was diverse in more respects than this. Some writers advanced arguments which others would undoubtedly have rejected. Unanimity no more characterized the defenders of slavery than its opponents. These differences of opinion warrant careful consideration if we are to get to grips with the ideology of the South in the late antebellum era.

Historians have encountered additional problems. Since the twentieth century finds slavery so repulsive, it has been tempting to see guilt, hypocrisy or some combination of both, in the pronouncements of these militant southerners. The effect has been a rejection of the proslavery

---

4. The starting point for all students of the proslavery argument remains William S. Jenkins, *The Pro-Slavery Argument in the Old South* (Chapel Hill, N.C., 1935). The two historians who have recently done most to encourage study of proslavery sentiment are Eugene Genovese and Drew Faust. See Drew G. Faust, "A Southern Stewardship: The Intellectual and the Proslavery Argument," *American Quarterly*, xxxi (Spring, 1979), pp. 63–80; Faust, *A Sacred Circle: The Dilemma of the Intellectual in the Old South, 1840–1860* (Baltimore, 1977); Eugene D. Genovese, *The World the Slaveholders Made: Two Essays in Interpretation* (rev. ed. N.Y., 1988). Faust's concerns are somewhat different from mine. Genovese's are not.
5. A much wider definition is offered in Larry E. Tise, *Proslavery: A History of the Defense of Slavery in America, 1701–1840* (Athens, Ga., 1987) – and it is this which accounts for most of the apparently startling conclusions which Tise reaches. See esp. p. xv. Note that this definition makes not only almost every southerner in the late antebellum era, but also most northern Democrats, "proslavery."

argument as weak or feeble.[6] I shall argue against the view that slave-holders were either guilt-ridden or hypocritical. Here I am following those who have written on the subject in the last twenty or thirty years, most notably Eugene D. Genovese. It is he, more than anyone else, who has insisted that the proslavery theorists be taken seriously. I shall also argue, however, that the proslavery position was indeed a weak one, but for a very different reason. I shall claim that the weaknesses of the proslavery argument derive from the weakness of slavery itself, when it is contrasted with free labor systems. But it is only by taking the argument with the utmost seriousness that these weaknesses can be identified. In the long perspective of human history, the destruction of slavery was achieved with remarkable rapidity. A close examination of the intellectual defenses that were offered by those who sought to retain it can perhaps help explain its comparatively swift demise.[7]

III

The first sign of slavery's weakness emerged at the very moment that the abolitionist assault began. In theory at least, southerners had a choice. They might have continued to acknowledge that slavery was an evil, while also continuing, perhaps, to insist that it was necessary. Some southerners – initially they were almost certainly a majority – did indeed adopt this strategy. But as we have seen, abolitionism grew rapidly in the 1830s and it was inevitable that, with so much at stake, some southerners should begin to anticipate a future in which antislavery dominated north-ern opinion. Now this in itself would have been a far less alarming

6. A good example of a historian who has found it difficult to take the proslavery argument seriously is David Donald. See Donald, "The Proslavery Argument Reconsidered," *Journal of Southern History*, XXXVII (1961), pp. 3–18. Among the works which have found guilt at the heart of southern views of slavery are W. J. Cash, *The Mind of the South* (N.Y., 1941), pp. 59–98; Charles G. Sellers, Jr., "The Travail of Slavery," in Sellers (ed.), *The Southerner as American* (Chapel Hill, 1960), pp. 40–71; William W. Freehling, *Prelude to Civil War: The Nullification Controversy in South Carolina, 1816–1836* (N.Y., 1965); Ronald T. Takaki, *A Pro-Slavery Crusade: The Agitation to Reopen the African Slave Trade* (N.Y., 1971); Kenneth M. Stampp, *The Imperilled Union: Essays on the Background of the Civil War* (N.Y., 1980); James Oakes, *The Ruling Race: A History of American Slaveholders* (N.Y., 1982). See also Gaines M. Foster, "Guilt Over Slavery: A Historiographical Analysis," *Journal of Southern History*, LVI (1990), pp. 665–694.
7. Other works which are useful on the proslavery argument include Wilfred Carsel, "The Slaveholders' Indictment of Northern Wage Slavery," *Journal of Southern History*, VI (1940), pp. 504–520; George M. Fredrickson, *The Black Image in the White Mind: The Debate on Afro-American Character and Destiny, 1817–1914* (N.Y., 1971); Ralph E. Morrow, "The Proslavery Argument Revisited," *Mississippi Valley Historical Review*, XLVII (1961), pp. 79–93; Robert Shalhope, "Race, Class, Slavery and the Antebellum Southern Mind," *Journal of Southern History*, XXXVII (1971), pp. 557–574.

prospect if the North, and not the South, were in a minority. A numerically dominant South would not have needed to worry about the federal government so much. But, as we have also seen, intelligent southerners like John C. Calhoun were able, quite plausibly, to predict a future in which abolitionist (or at least antislavery) sentiment would dominate the dominant section. Originally, of course, the two sections had been roughly equal in population and their rates of natural population increase were also not very different. But the big northern advantage lay in immigration. The inability of the South to attract immigrants, as I have already argued (and as contemporaries recognized), owed much to the existence of slavery. As a result, even the early growth of antislavery at the North would be of vital concern to southerners. Slavery could not compete demographically with free labor and this limitation severely constrained southerners' freedom of action.

Yet there was a second, more pressing problem. Southerners felt they could not be indifferent to antislavery propaganda. They were infinitely more anxious about it than northerners were about assaults on the northern labor system. Orestes Brownson in 1840 delivered a stinging attack on northern society and the northern labor system when he called for the abolition of inheritance, the ending of the wage system and the elimination of the priesthood. Northern conservatives were anything but pleased. But no price was placed upon his head. Nor were restrictions upon free speech considered. Similarly, when southern proslavery theorists condemned the wage slavery of the North, many northerners often actually welcomed the attacks, since they provided ammunition to use against the southerners themselves. Antislavery northerners even publicized the southern criticisms and took pains to ensure that northern wage laborers knew how southerners viewed them. The contrast with the southern response to abolitionism, at once rational but frenzied, could not have been sharper. When the two systems were under attack, it immediately became evident that slavery was a far less secure foundation for a society than the free labor system of the North.

As a result increasing numbers of southerners concluded that to acquiesce in antislavery was to hand over their destiny to a society increasingly hostile to their peculiar institution and increasingly convinced that its abolition was possible. Resistance, however, meant sacrifices. To curtail freedom of speech was to make a significant departure from American tradition and to risk confirming the stigma which slavery placed upon the South. If the slaveholders themselves were to rally in defense of slavery, could they continue to believe that it was an evil, however necessary? Would such a belief not undermine their morale, their capacity to resist? Would they be able to continue to demand an equal share of the West if, on their own admission, a slave West would be inferior to a free West? The original purpose of the proslavery theorists was to convince their fellow slaveholders that the institution was very much worth defending. In the context of the abolitionist assault of the 1830s, and given the economic viability of slavery in these years, a reappraisal was inevitable. And it was inevitable that increasing numbers of southerners would find slavery a positive good.

The weakness of slavery

To claim that slavery, as a system of exploitation, is weak is not to claim that its victims can easily avoid or overthrow it. In the South relatively few slave rebellions broke out, for the very good reason that the slaves faced hopeless odds. The chance of success was infinitesimal, the likelihood of death extremely high. Flight from slavery offered better opportunities but was still highly dangerous and the losses which the great majority of masters suffered from runaway slaves were modest or even non-existent. The weaknesses of slavery lie elsewhere.[8]

They become apparent when we compare it with wage labor. In a brilliant passage Marx drew attention to a key difference between the two systems. "On the basis of the wages system," he wrote, "even the unpaid labor seems to be paid labor." But "with the slave . . . even that part of his labor which is paid appears to be unpaid."[9] From this simple difference most of the weaknesses of slavery ultimately spring. However modest the educational attainment of the slave, he is able to perceive that the fruits of his labor are being appropriated by the master. However impressive the educational attainment of the wage laborer, there is still a chance of convincing him that his wages are the result of a contract freely and equally entered into by both parties. Thus history records no example of a people who have chosen to be enslaved, or even accepted their enslavement as just and necessary, whereas much of western social thought over the last two centuries has rested upon the assumption, or has sought to demonstrate, that freedom is to be equated with the ability to engage, uncoerced by another, in market transactions. This does not mean, of course, that a wage labor system is necessarily unopposed by the wage laborers. But the weakness of slavery derives from the impossibility of fully reconciling the slave to his condition and the consequences of this dissatisfaction. By comparison, a wage labor system has two advantages. First the proportion of dissatisfied workers is likely to be much lower.

8. On slave revolts see especially Herbert Aptheker, *American Negro Slave Revolts* (N.Y., 1943); Eugene D. Genovese, *From Rebellion to Revolution: Afro-American Slave Revolts in the Making of the New World* (N.Y., 1979).
9. Karl Marx and Friedrich Engels, *Selected Works* 3 vols (Moscow, 1969–1970), II, pp. 59–60.

Anyone who doubts this need only reflect on the prevalence of the view that wage labor is "normal" and characteristic of free citizens. Second, and more important, the forms which resistance to exploitation take, are different and, from the standpoint of the exploiting class, preferable.[10]

I do not wish to claim that the development of wage labor in the United States was a smooth or uncontested process. On the contrary, it is a principal argument of this work that it was not. Considerable resistance was offered by those who faced what was often seen as a demeaning dependence on an employer. This resistance had vitally important effects. But the key point is that northern society was able to make the necessary adjustments. In the South the resistance of the slaves to their condition also compelled adjustments on the part of their masters. But ultimately these adjustments themselves proved ruinous.

Let us compare slavery and wage labor a little more systematically. There are five principal differences. First the mere continuation of market transactions in a free labor economy creates, without anyone necessarily willing it, wage laborers. Hence the process seems impersonal, inexorable, and "natural." By contrast, the power of the master over the slave appears anything but impersonal, and anything but inevitable. The victims of slavery can rarely, if ever, be convinced that their enslavement is "natural." Second, some of the essentials of simple (pre-capitalist) commodity production – with each agent free to contract, to observe the operations of the market and to pursue his self-interest – are retained in a wage labor system, though not in a slave system. The very essence of slavery is the inability of the slave to enter freely into contracts. Once again therefore, the nature of exploitation within a wage labor system is so much more difficult to detect. Third, the wage laborer may well wish to advance beyond his status and become an independent producer or an employer of others. But such an aspiration can often be welcomed and encouraged by the employing class, since it will result in better work as a wage-earner. It is true that the slave may also be offered the opportunity to transform his status and some slave regimes have held out the prospect of manumission to those in bondage. Such an incentive is, of course, extremely powerful but it was one which the slave South increasingly rejected – for the best of reasons, as we shall see. Fourth, the potential hostility between wage laborer and employer can be mitigated by appeals to shared values and by attempts to enhance the esteem of the worker.

---

10. Historians have not considered the proslavery argument in this light. A partial exception is Lawrence Shore, *Southern Capitalists: The Ideological Leadership of an Elite* (Chapel Hill, 1986). I wish to acknowledge my indebtedness to this book, though I should perhaps add that I believe Shore's evidence and arguments powerfully sustain the opposite thesis from the one he proposes. His book, in my view, shows that the southern elite was anything but capitalist.

The wage laborer may be addressed as one who has been dignified by his labor. Inter-class agreement on the work ethic and the dignity of labor, or the sanctity of the home may well function to bridge the gap between the employer and the worker. But in a slave society, certain types of labor are likely to be regarded as servile. Moreover a high social status for the slave challenges the very fact of his enslavement. A large gap in status is likely to separate master and slave; it may or may not exist in a wage labor system.

On the other hand, it might be argued that a weakness of a wage labor system is that the laborer is highly vulnerable, especially in times of crisis. He risks unemployment and even starvation. Southern defenders of slavery were quick to point out this danger. But while they were able to score a point here, they could not press home the advantage. For they had nothing to put in the place of wage labor. To offer the workers of the North enslavement would have been absurd. Instead they could only seek to recruit support for certain policies which appealed to northern workers, in return for acquiescence in slavery. This was the strategy some of the South Carolinians pursued and it was not without success. An alternative was to appeal to the northern elite on the grounds that otherwise their workers would rebel against the northern social order. This strategy was also pursued by southerners – and sometimes the same southerners – once again with some success. But both these strategies could be accommodated within the northern political system, even in times of economic trouble, let alone in prosperous times. So the North did not need to curtail freedom of speech in the interests of any group or class.

Here is a fifth advantage of a wage labor system. It was comparatively easy for northerners to suggest an alternative to southern slavery. Even colonization, impracticable as it was, was easy to contemplate by comparison with the uprooting of every wage relationship in the North. But antislavery militants did not, in the main, advocate colonization. Instead they simply demanded that free and, if necessary, wage labor replace slavery in the South. Undoubtedly they underestimated the difficulties of such a readjustment. But again, compared with the abolition of wage labor, the process was easy to envisage. Critics of southern slavery had only to see a northern free black behaving as a responsible member of society to confirm the feasibility of emancipation. No such threat could be offered by southern critics of the northern social order. As we have already seen, while northern society could easily absorb the criticisms levelled against it by the defenders of slavery, southerners could not be so tolerant of northern attacks. Ironically, it was this very weakness, as we have seen, which helped call forth the direct defense of slavery. It was also responsible for the restrictions on freedom of speech and of the press in the South – which further antagonized the North. Such restrictions should be seen as a reflection or outgrowth of the deep structural antag-onism between slave and master.[11]

It may be worth repeating that this analysis does not depend on the claim that southern slaves were constantly on the verge of insurrection nor upon a denial of the savagery of the sanctions at the master's dis-posal. Instead the claim is that the dissatisfaction of the slave with slavery had many consequences which, taken together, produced serious weak-nesses for the regime as a whole. Some of these we have already encoun-tered in our discussion of political economy. First, the risk of antislavery propaganda reaching the slaves was one which masters in any slave regime could not afford to run. Second, and equally important, in the South the relationship of the slaveholders to the non-slaveholders became highly problematic. Southern masters recognized from the first that their regime was doomed if it were attacked from within as well as from with-out. Again a comparison with a wage-labor society is appropriate. The non-slaveholders posed a far greater potential threat to slavery than the independent farmers and craftsmen in the North posed to wage labor there. The northern employer could afford to be quite indifferent to the nature of the relationship between an independent farmer and a wage laborer. Whether they fraternized together or cordially disliked one another was of little moment. But the slaveholder could not allow the non-slaveholder, except in isolated cases, to become friendly with the slave. There must be no closeness between them lest the non-slaveholder begin to believe that the slave's condition was unjust or the slave become excessively familiar with whites. But the master's problems did not end there. If the non-slaveholder resented the slave, there was an equal danger that his resentment might be turned against the master too. Thus a further set of constraints operated on the slaveholder. The pressures from the slave himself, in conjunction with those imposed from the North, spilled over into the master's relations with the non-slaveholder. We have already seen the deleterious effects of these constraints upon the southern economy. They were also registered in the proslavery argument, which, as we shall see, reflected the problems and dilemmas of the master class. The last decades of the antebellum republic witnessed the efforts of the slaveholder to maneuver between the obstacles that increasingly sur-rounded him and limited his freedom of movement. The Civil War and the destruction of slavery witness the final and ultimate failure of the strategy he had been impelled to adopt.

---

11. Thus they are the products of class conflict in its most fundamental sense: the conflict between exploiters and exploited over the distribution of the proceeds of the latter's labor.

John C. Calhoun and the political system

The first southern leader of national stature to embrace the proslavery argument was John C. Calhoun. We have already seen that the growth of abolitionism filled him with horror and that he responded with a series of actions whose unsought, though not entirely unforeseen, effect was to deepen sectional hostilities. We have seen too, that he set out to unite the South behind him, if necessary at the expense of the party system. Let us now return to his thought and to his career to illustrate the problems which the defense of slavery entailed within the political system.

According to Calhoun, slavery was "the most safe and stable basis for free institutions in the world." Like most proponents of the proslavery argument, he insisted that it was the destiny of the North to be racked by social conflict. But slavery made the South different – and better. "With us," he claimed, "it is impossible . . . that the conflict can take place between labor and capital, which makes it so difficult to establish and maintain free institutions in all wealthy, and highly civilized nations." The reason was that master and slave had a common interest in securing to labor the full fruits of its toil, the master because he owned the title to that labor, the slave because he himself would benefit from the resulting generosity of the master. And such generosity was itself underpinned by self-interest; the master had an interest in securing the welfare of the slave. The employer had no reason to care about the well-being of his employee, but the master had a strong motive for maintaining the health and welfare of the slave, since a failure to do so would diminish the value of his capital.[12]

Such reasoning depended, of course, on the conviction that blacks were naturally suited to slavery. As a result Calhoun attempted to show that free blacks fell victim to pauperism, deafness, blindness and idiocy whereas under slavery the race "enjoys a degree of health and comfort which may well compare with that of the laboring population of any country in Christendom." Yet even as he made this claim – and it was made in part to repel the danger of abolition – Calhoun unwittingly underlined the central weakness of slavery. In South Carolina for example, he and a group of his followers claimed, slavery "resembles in a great measure a happy and patriarchal state in which the benevolence of the master, and the fidelity and affection of the slave, combine in the most bland and harmonious manner."[13] But Calhoun was unable to derive any security from this supposedly secure relationship. More than anyone he emphasized the dangers of abolition. The slaves, even though they should

---

12. *Congressional Globe*, 25 Congress, 2 Session, Appendix, p. 62, 25 Congress, 1 Session, p. 514.

have appreciated their blessed condition, in fact could not be trusted to do so; they would succumb to the insidious campaigns of the abolitionists. Here Calhoun was responding in practice to the central weakness of slavery – the slave's cause for dissatisfaction – even as he sought to deny it in theory.

There were two consequences, which in our discussion of the proslavery argument we shall encounter again. One was a curiously dualistic view of the blacks. The simple and contented child of the well-ordered plantation could be suddenly transformed by abolitionist propaganda into the bloodthirsty zealot who followed Denmark Vesey, Nat Turner or even Toussaint L'Ouverture. The tension in this view of the blacks itself had effects which we shall examine later. The second consequence was an inability on the part of Calhoun and the other proslavery theorists to understand the problems facing the slaveholders. Never could they recognize that hostility to slavery was endemic to the regime; invariably they perceived an exogenous cause, usually in the form of northern, but sometimes British, antislavery pressure when the root cause was actually endogenous. This failure necessarily limited their ability to defend their own class. But it was a failure that followed inevitably from their insistence on the naturally harmonious relations between master and slave.

When we return to Calhoun the political partisan, we find additional signs of slavery's weakness. As we have seen, no-one was more aware that the South could not be indifferent to the growth of abolition, both for its inherent program and for its potential support in the dominant section. Slavery's vulnerability and its inability to compete demographically with free labor made Calhoun a determined minoritarian (though this was not the reason he would have given). The threat was from the federal government; the remedy was to ensure that minority rights were protected, as the Constitution stipulated. But Calhoun had an erratic career as a partisan and his political wanderings reveal a crucial dilemma which he and others faced, a dilemma that also had its roots in the deficiencies of slavery, as a form of exploitation.

Calhoun longed for allies in the North. Even a united South would be helpless within the Union unless at least some northerners acquiesced in the peculiar institution and resisted the abolitionists. Of course secession was always possible, but throughout his career Calhoun endeavored to make the Union safe for the South. Only if this proved impossible should it be dismantled. Hence the need for allies.

After having been elected Jackson's Vice-President, he soon broke with his leader. Jackson's firm response to nullification propelled Calhoun into

13. Richard K. Crallé (ed.), *The Works of John C. Calhoun* 6 vols (Columbia, S.C., 1851–1855), v, pp. 337–338; Clyde N. Wilson (ed.), *The Papers of John C. Calhoun* (Columbia, S.C., 1959–), xii, p. 550.

a defensive co-operation with the nascent Whig party, which found unity in its opposition to the President's use of executive power. Behind Whig attacks on "King Andrew" lay a profound distrust of the new party structures that were emerging and behind this distrust, in turn, lay an equally profound suspicion of the claims which Democrats were making for the virtue and wisdom of the people.[14] Calhoun was able to unite with Webster and Clay in opposition not only to presidential power but also to Democratic theories of party, to Democratic majoritarianism and to Democratic egalitarianism. We shall consider these views later. What we need to consider now is the reason the alliance with the Whigs collapsed.

By the end of 1837 Calhoun had in effect rejoined the Democratic party. The ostensible cause was Van Buren's adoption of the Independent Treasury proposal, which Calhoun claimed to have himself advocated some years earlier. The support he gave to the Independent Treasury was real enough but it was a symptom rather than a cause of his break with the Whigs. The Whigs made poor allies for Calhoun, for several reasons. To begin with, it was not merely the Independent Treasury that divided them. On all aspects of economic policy he and they were poles apart. The Whigs, like the National Republicans, it would soon become evident, championed the protective tariff; Calhoun had actually originated the theory of nullification to combat the tariff. The Whigs believed in federal internal improvements; Calhoun did not. Finally, the Whigs continued to advocate a national bank; Calhoun continued to oppose one.[15]

Yet these policy differences were merely the tip of a large ideological iceberg. Calhoun's strategy – or rather, one of them – was to propose an alliance of conservative property holders, North and South. He sought to unite conservative interests in the defence of property rights. In a speech in the Senate in 1836 he explained the rationale for such an alliance:

> The sober and considerate portion of citizens in the non-slaveholding States, who have a deep stake in the existing institutions of the country, would have little forecast not to see that the assaults which are now directed against the institutions of the Southern States may very easily be turned against those which uphold their own property and security. A very slight modification of the arguments used against the institutions which sustain the property and

14. See John Ashworth, *"Agrarians" and "Aristocrats": Party Political Ideology in the United States, 1837–1846* (London, 1983).
15. Ashworth, *"Agrarians" and "Aristocrats,"* pp. 240–244. A valuable recent work on Calhoun's thought is Lacy K. Ford, Jr., "Inventing the Concurrent Majority: Madison, Calhoun and the Problem of Majoritarianism in American Political Thought," *Journal of Southern History*, LX (1994), pp. 19–58.

security of the South would make them equally effectual against the
institutions of the North . . . [16]

With the economic instabilities of the 1830s and early 1840s this alliance
was not entirely unattractive, in that many northern Whigs believed that
Jackson's regime, with its appeal to the self-interest of agrarian interests,
threatened to tear apart the nation's commercial fabric. There was thus
some scope for the alliance Calhoun sought to create.

Yet in reality he had little to offer northern conservatives beyond a
purely defensive strategy that would block federally launched attacks on
property rights. They wanted and needed more. Having long since learnt
that a mass electorate would not respond to so narrow an appeal, they
stressed instead the benefits to the entire community of economic growth
and of diversification. In an economy that was chronically short of capital, they reasoned, the federal government had a key role to play. Hence
the need for the Whig economic program – which Calhoun opposed in its
entirety. So even though agreement between the two was possible on the
question of inequality, southern proslavery men could not forge an alliance of conservative property holders because, by the dictates of their
own theories, the South was too different from the North. Northern
conservatives hoped to incorporate potential dissidents into their social
order by offering them enhanced commercial opportunities. Southerners
could hardly make a similar offer to the abolitionists. Nor could they
hope to overcome the dissatisfaction of the slaves, a dissatisfaction they
could not even recognize, by building canals, factories, schools or banks,
least of all under the auspices of the federal government. The exigencies
of the master–slave relationship once again created problems for the
South; the defenders of a free-labor *status quo* had a far easier time of it.

A further problem existed. Although in the 1830s and the early 1840s,
many conservatives in the North were overtly critical of the increasingly
populistic tone of American politics and anxious about a perceived threat
to property rights, continued economic development gradually eased
their anxieties. As a result Calhoun had even less to offer them. Yet
slavery in the South continued to be threatened by northern antislavery
opinion; the return of prosperity did nothing to diminish the threat and
perhaps even augmented it. Northern wage labor relations probably
became increasingly secure; southern slave labor relations were subject
to an at least constant threat from within and a growing challenge from
without.

Hence northerners refused to enter into the alliance which Calhoun
offered. They continued to reject the offer when made by Calhoun's

16. Crallé, *Works of Calhoun*, v, p. 207.

successors. On the eve of the Civil War Jefferson Davis, himself very much a Calhoun disciple, sought to associate abolitionism with socialism and once again hinted at the need for a conservative alliance of property holders:

> In fact, the European Socialists, who, in wild radicalism, . . . are the correspondents of the American abolitionists, maintain the same doctrine as to all property, that the abolitionists do as to slave property. He who has property, they argue, is the robber of him who has not. *"La propriété, c'est le vol,"* is the famous theme of the Socialist, Proudhon. And the same precise theories of attack at the North on the slave property of the South would, if carried out to their legitimate and necessary logical consequences, and will, if successful in this, their first stage of action, superinduce attacks on all property, North and South.[17]

But northern business interests, concerned though they might be about some of the labor unrest of the late 1850s, did not believe that antislavery, especially in its moderate, free-soil form, posed a challenge to all property rights. Instead they believed that slavery itself impeded the processes of political, economic and ideological adjustment that economic development necessitated.

The core of Calhoun's problem was that slavery could not be assimilated to other forms of property. It did not matter that the slaveholding interest was as large as any in the nation, it was subject to attacks different from those leveled against property in a free labor economy. Its points of weakness were different, its needs were different. Even if the southern elite was as acquisitive and as commercially minded as its northern counterpart, the fundamental differences between slavery and free labor, which a proslavery theorist as much as anyone emphasized, undermined the possibility of co-operation between them. The Whig program had its supporters in the South, of course, but they were not proslavery spokesmen.[18] Slavery made the South too different from the North for Calhoun and his followers to join the Whigs in an inter-sectional conservative alliance. Calhoun himself in 1838 stated the problem quite clearly. He acknowledged that "the great mass" of the Whig party "was sound and averse to the dangerous projects of the fanatics [the abolitionists]," but this was not enough. "Candor compelled him," he informed the Senate, "to declare that he could not look to them in this hour of danger." For "when we touched the Constitution and asked them

---

17. Rowland Dunbar (ed.), *Jefferson Davis, Constitutionalist, His Letters, Papers and Speeches* 10 vols (Jackson, Miss., 1923), IV, p. 183.
18. See below, Chapters 5 and 6.

what barrier, according to their conception, that instrument contains against their [the abolitionists'] incendiary and mad projects, they are silent." The problem was that their very "political creed not only admits of none, but, in fact," by virtue of its emphasis on federal power, "rouses into action that dangerous spirit of fanaticism which threatens to subvert our institutions." The Whigs could not be relied upon.[19]

Many of these difficulties vanished once Calhoun turned away from the Whigs and back to the Democrats. Unfortunately, however, they were replaced by a different set of problems. Nevertheless, in many respects the Democrats were far more suitable as partners than the Whigs. They believed in states' rights and in limited government, they were far less committed even in the North to the protective tariff. Moreover, the party had traditionally looked to the South for support and throughout the country its members, with but few exceptions, were thoroughgoing racists, even though northern Democrats did not believe that slavery was a positive good. So after the crisis of nullification had passed, and Calhoun had led his small band of supporters back into the Democratic party, on most issues the two groups were able to work together quite harmoniously. By the early 1840s Calhoun even entertained ambitions for the Democratic nomination in 1844.[20]

Yet his hopes were entirely illusory. The agreement on policy masked huge disagreements on the most fundamental principles. Calhoun was an out-and-out inegalitarian. He believed that inequality of condition was "a necessary consequence of liberty." Other Democrats might have concurred but where Calhoun differed from them was in believing this inequality desirable. "It is, indeed," he wrote in his *Disquisition on Government*, "this inequality of condition between the front and rear ranks, in the march of progress, which gives so strong an impulse to the former to maintain their position, and to the latter to press forward into their files." Here was "the greatest impulse" which was given to "progress." As a result Calhoun utterly repudiated the Declaration of Independence as well as the Jeffersonian (and Jacksonian) notions of equality and liberty. Far from being a natural right or "a blessing to be gratuitously bestowed on all alike," liberty was "a reward to be earned . . . a reward reserved for the intelligent, the patriotic, the virtuous and deserving." Least of all was it "a boon to be bestowed on a people too ignorant, degraded and vicious, to be capable of appreciating or of enjoying it."[21]

19. Wilson (ed.), *The Papers of John C. Calhoun*, XII, p. 58.
20. Ashworth, *"Agrarians" and "Aristocrats"*, pp. 243–244.
21. Crallé, *Works of Calhoun*, I, pp. 55–57.

When Calhoun spoke in this way, it was not always clear which people he had in mind. If he had merely meant the people of other lands, the departure from Democratic orthodoxy might have been less significant (though it would still have had important implications for immigration, amongst other questions). But in fact he clearly had the people of the United States very much in mind when he made these observations. Unfortunately for him, events in 1842 in Rhode Island exposed the gulf that separated him from the party mainstream.

The events of the Dorr rebellion do not concern us here.[22] What is significant is that Thomas Dorr and his supporters invoked the original rights of the people to rule and set aside the existing and highly undemocratic constitution of the state of Rhode Island. In the nation as a whole the political parties responded as one might have predicted. The Whigs denounced Dorr as a traitor to his country, even though some of them agreed that the franchise in Rhode Island needed widening. To the Democrats, however, Dorr became a hero. Or rather, one should say, outside the Calhoun ranks, he became a hero. Calhoun himself wrote a public letter condemning the theory of sovereignty upon which the Dorrites had based their case and of which virtually the entire Democratic party had expressed approval.

Important though the Dorr war was, it merely revealed a more fundamental divergence between Calhoun and the Democrats. The party's principal spokesmen were deeply committed to the notions of equality and liberty that they had inherited from Jefferson. They were restated again and again in party publications and partisan speeches. For Calhoun to have won the nomination in 1844 he would have had to have re-educated the entire party. Not surprisingly, it soon became clear that his candidacy was hopeless, whereupon he joined the Tyler administration and began to work for the annexation of Texas.[23]

Yet it was not only northerners about whom Calhoun entertained doubts. His statements about liberty and equality did not exclude the South. It comes as no surprise to learn that slaves and free blacks were hopelessly wanting; more surprising is the suspicion of the whites. In fact Calhoun had strong doubts about the political capacity of large numbers, perhaps even a majority, of whites in the South. He rejected majoritarian democracy not merely for the federal government but also for South Carolina itself. Indeed one might argue that his goal was to create at the federal level a set of political structures or practices modeled upon those operating in his native state. In South Carolina, he announced, with

---

22. For a brief discussion see Ashworth, *"Agrarians" and "Aristocrats,"* pp. 225–230.
23. For a discussion of the maneuverings for the Democratic nomination in 1844, see below, Chapter 6.

unmistakable pride, the numerical majority was not in control. He rejoiced that there was not a single state-wide direct election and argued strongly against those who wished to place the election of the Governor in the hands of the people. The effect of such a change, he asserted, would be to transform "our State Government," from "a beautiful and well adjusted Republick, protecting the interest of all, and uttering the voice of the whole Community," into "a wild, factious and despotik Democracy under the control of the dominent [sic] interest."[24]

Here was the strength but also the weakness of Calhoun's position. In South Carolina the prevalence of slaveowning, together with the state's remarkably undemocratic political system, gave Calhoun a strength within his native state that no other politician in the land could equal. From this base he could plan a strategy to combat abolition untrammeled by the party considerations which intruded upon those who made similar attempts in other states. South Carolina was truly different and the differences here redounded to Calhoun's advantage. But at the same time the very uniqueness of the state made it difficult for him to forge the alliances he knew were essential in the fight to sustain slavery. He tried to reach out for support to northern Democrats and enjoyed a measure of success. In 1837, for example, he rounded upon the nation's banking system. "Never was an engine invented better calculated," he declared, "to place the destiny of the many in the hands of the few, or less favorable to that equality and independence, which lies at the bottom of all free institutions." Such sentiments were the purest form of radical Democratic thought and some northern labor leaders found in Calhoun and the other southern militants, champions of the rights of the northern worker. But, by his own admission, Calhoun was neither radical nor even a believer in democracy. Instead he was, as he announced in the same year, "a conservative in its broadest and fullest sense." And while he had no designs on the laboring classes of the North, it was as much as he could do to defend the interests of the masters of the South. An alliance between the two groups foundered on the question of majority power and there was a fundamental clash between the egalitarianism of radical northern Democrats and the unabashed elitism of Calhoun and his disciples. For those who wished to intensify the struggle with the banks Martin Van Buren was the obvious candidate. Though Van Buren failed to win the nomination in 1844, he ran far ahead of Calhoun.[25]

24. Calhoun to A. H. Pendleton, Nov. 19, 1838 in "The Correspondence of John C. Calhoun," *Annual Report of the American Historical Association for 1899* (ed. J. Franklin Jameson, Washington, D.C., 1900), p. 421.
25. *Congressional Globe*, 25 Congress, 1 Session, Appendix, p. 507; Crallé, *Works of Calhoun*, I, p. 614.

It was not easy to square Calhoun's calls for an alliance of elitist property holders with his appeal to antibank sentiment across the nation. The very labor leaders who responded most warmly to Calhoun were precisely those whom northern conservatives most feared. This is why characterizations of Calhoun as a man driven by logic and principle are so wide of the mark. On the other hand, it was not that he was, by nature or temperament, an "opportunist," but rather that his position was so desperate that he had to cast about for allies, on whatever terms he could find them.[26] Indeed he also undertook a third strategy. Since the master class could not easily ally itself with either labor or capital in the North, perhaps it could instead serve as an impartial regulator or umpire of the struggle that was already waging between them, and that with luck would intensify in the future. "When wages command labor," he informed the Senate in 1847, "as in the non-slaveholding States, there necessarily takes place between labor and capital a conflict, which leads, in process of time, to disorder, anarchy and revolution, if not counter-acted by some appropriate and strong constitutional provision." The constitutional provision would be provided in some way by the slave-holding states which, "in all conflicts which may occur in the other por-tions of the Union between labor and capital," would always "be found to take the conservative side." The conclusion was a familiar one: "thus regarded, the non-slaveholding States have not much less interest, fairly understood, in upholding and preserving the equilibrium of the slave-holding States, than the latter themselves have." Once again Calhoun was searching for a stick with which to beat back abolitionism.[27]

Nothing is so apparent in this strategy as its haziness. How would southern slaveholders come to be recognized as having this crucial role to play? How would they actually play it? Calhoun never answered these questions. Once again his strategy depended on a recognition from north-erners that their social system was inherently unstable, that the subordi-nate classes could not be reconciled to their inferiority – the very conditions which he himself refused to acknowledge in the South. In one sense Calhoun saw deeply into northern society; the class conflicts he predicted did become a feature of late-nineteenth-century America, though without the apocalyptic finale which, with a barely concealed relish, he anticipated. In another sense, however, he was utterly naive. Just as slave rebellions would not have altered (and had not affected) his conviction that the slaves were, left to themselves, happy and contented in

26. Charles Wiltse's biography of Calhoun takes Calhoun at his own evaluation, Gerald Capers, *John C. Calhoun – Opportunist: A Reappraisal* (Gainesville, Fla., 1960), does not.

27. Crallé, *Works of Calhoun*, IV, pp. 360–361.

their bondage, so northern employers would not have been converted by labor unrest to the southern view of free society. Just like the slave-holders, but with much greater plausibility, they would have found extra-neous or exceptional forces at work. So Calhoun's strategy failed yet again. Neither the working classes of the North, nor their employers wished to look to the southern slaveholder either as an ally or as an umpire. The needs of these groups were simply too different.

Finally, we should note the absence from Calhoun's thought of any specific appeal to the non-slaveholders of the South. Insofar as they were addressed at all, it was as potential slaveholders, on the one hand, or as respectful and deferential followers of the slaveholding elite (led of course by Calhoun), on the other. Only in the 1850s would the question of the non-slaveholders fully engage South Carolinians. Thus Calhoun was unable to become the spokesman of conservative property-holders throughout the nation, or the dependable ally of northern labor, or the honored and honorary umpire of the struggle between labor and capital in the North. He was not even the spokesman of the white South. His views cut across the party system and cut him off from potential support even in the South. The very factors that gave South Carolina its unique sensitivity to the politics of slavery made it hard to accommodate her leading statesman into the political system.

In the late 1840s and the 1850s, however, the Democrats moved some-what closer to the Calhoun position. But the shift was never complete and the cost would be a hemorrhage of electoral support in the North. In the South, meanwhile, the Calhoun legacy split. Some proslavery men went off in an ever more inegalitarian direction and celebrated the inequalities within the white race as well as those between the races. This process culminated in the writings of George Fitzhugh, who insisted that slavery was desirable, in theory at least, for large numbers of whites, as well as for blacks. By contrast, others sought to develop what has been aptly termed a "*Herrenvolk*" conception of the social and political order which asserted a highly racist white egalitarianism. As we shall see, both stra-tegies brought insuperable problems.[28]

Slavery, race and the Bible

Whatever the differences between the elitists and the "*Herrenvolk*" ega-litarians, both groups looked to Christianity, and specifically to the Bible, to buttress their arguments for slavery. While a modern reader might

---

28. The term "*Herrenvolk*" has been employed, of course, by George Fredrickson. See Fredrickson, *Black Image in White Mind*.

expect the slaveholders to be on weak ground here, in fact the reverse was true and appeals to the Bible and to traditional Christian values were among the strongest weapons in the proslavery arsenal. They help demonstrate the sincerity of proslavery sentiment in the South and remind us that the proslavery argument must not be dismissed as the product of guilt or hypocrisy. Yet even here, southern ideologues encountered problems.

The proslavery theorists unhesitatingly claimed that the Bible supported them. As one writer in the *Presbyterian Review* for 1849 put it, "Christianity undoubtedly sanctions slavery." The general reappraisal of slavery which took place in the South in the thirty years before the Civil War prompted many scholars to scrutinize the Bible closely, in order to rebut the claims made by antislavery spokesmen. One writer freely acknowledged that his purpose was to help southerners "form correct views of their rights and of the rectitude of their Institution as appointed by God and sustained by the Bible." By implication he was also acknowledging that in the past many incorrect views had been taken. [29]

Southerners examined in great detail both the Old and the New Testaments. From the Old Testament they concluded that many of the Patriarchs, including Abraham, Moses, and Jacob were slaveholders. Since Abraham, for example, was explicitly termed the father of the chosen people, there could be little doubt that God sanctioned slavery. Moreover, the Mosaic law was equally explicit in distinguishing between the slavery of a Hebrew and that of an alien, which alone was to receive legal protection. As if this were not enough, southerners continued, the Decalogue, which laid down the moral code for all time, again referred directly and without criticism to slavery. The Fourth Commandment

---

29. *The Christian Doctrine of Human Rights and of Slavery in Two Articles from the Presbyterian Review for March 1849* (Columbia, S.C., 1849), p. 13; [Iveson L. Brookes], *A Defence of Southern Slavery against the Attacks of Henry Clay and Alexander Campbell . . . by a Southern Clergyman* (Harrisburg, S.C., 1851), p. i. For typical southern discussions of slavery and the scriptures see Peter G. Camden, *A Common-Sense, Matter-of-Fact Examination and Discussion of Negro Slavery in the United States...* (St. Louis, Mo., 1855); Rev. George D. Cummins, *The African a Trust from God to the American: A Sermon Delivered . . . Baltimore, Jan. 4, 1861* (Baltimore, 1861); Herbert Fielder, *The Disunionist: A Brief Treatise Upon the Evils of the Union Between the North and the South* (n.p., n.d.), pp. 42–44; *Governor Hammond's Letters on Southern Slavery: Addressed to Thomas Clarkson* (n.p., n.d.), pp. 4–5; Reverend Leander Ker, *Slavery Consistent with Christianity* (Weston, Mo., 1853); [James Shannon], *An Address Delivered Before the Pro-Slavery Convention of the State of Missouri . . . July 13, 1855 on Domestic Slavery* (St Louis, Mo., 1855), pp. 12–18; *Slavery in the South: A Review of Hammond's Letters, and Chancellor Harper's Memoir on that Subject, from October 1845 Southern Quarterly* (n.p., n.d.); Thornton Stringfellow, *A Brief Examination of Scriptural Testimony on the Institution of Slavery* (n.p., n.d.).

likened the relationship of master to slave with that of father to son, while in the Tenth slave property again received direct and unqualified protection. Nowhere in the Old Testament, southerners concluded, was the abolition of slavery suggested; nowhere was the institution even criticized.[30]

The same was true, they maintained, of the New Testament. Slavery was widespread in the Christian era, as it had been earlier, but nowhere did He condemn it. On one occasion He healed a slave, without in any way criticizing his enslavement. Slaveholders were warmly welcomed into the Christian faith, on many occasions the Apostles exhorted slaves to obey their masters and most unequivocally of all, Paul urged Onesimus, a runaway slave, to return to his master, Philemon.[31]

Some of these interpretations were challenged by antislavery spokesmen. As we have already seen, some abolitionists – and some historians have endorsed this view – claimed that antislavery could be inferred from general Christian precepts such as the Golden Rule. But these arguments were, and are, easily refuted.[32] Another tactic was to claim that the Bible was referring not to slaves but to servants and many northerners pursued this point. A lively etymological debate ensued. However, since it was possible for southerners to point out that these "servants" were actually bought and sold, they had much the better of the argument. The most that can be said against them is that slavery in Biblical times was in certain respects less rigid than its antebellum counterpart, with some slaves being allowed to inherit from the master and even marry the master's children. On the other hand, it is not at all clear that the material

30. For discussions of slavery and the Old Testament see Mathew Estes, *A Defence of Negro Slavery as it Exists in the United States* (Montgomery, Al., 1846), pp. 13–30; George Junkin, *The Integrity of Our National Union versus Abolitionism* (Cincinnati, 1843), pp. 16–44; Alexander McCaine, *Slavery Defended from Scripture, Against the Abolitionists, in a Speech Delivered before the General Conference of the Methodist Protestant Church in Baltimore, 1842* (Baltimore, 1842); George S. Sawyer, *Southern Institutes or, An Inquiry into the Origin and Early Prevalence of Slavery and the Slave-Trade . . .* (Phil., 1858), pp. 29–50; Reverend Thornton Stringfellow, *Slavery: Its Origin, Nature and History* (Alexandria, 1860), pp. 11–18; Stringfellow, *Scriptural and Statistical Views in Favor of Slavery* (Richmond, 1856), pp. 7–30; John B. Thrasher, *Slavery A Divine Institution* (Port Gibon, Miss., 1861), pp. 6–16.
31. For discussions of slavery and the New Testament see Estes, *Defence of Negro Slavery*, pp. 30–48; Junkin, *The Integrity of Our National Union*, pp. 44–70; McCaine, *Slavery Defended*, pp. 22–24; Sawyer, *Southern Institutes*, pp. 99–132; Stringfellow, *Slavery: Its Origin*, pp. 19–32; Stringfellow, *Scriptural and Statistical Views*, pp. 35–55; Rev. J. H. Thornwell, *The Rights and Duties of Masters: A Sermon . . .* (Charleston, 1850), pp. 15–16; Thrasher, *Slavery A Divine Institution*, pp. 16–18.
32. See Thomas Bender (ed.), *The Antislavery Debate: Capitalism and Abolitionism as a Problem in Historical Interpretation* (Berkeley, 1992), p. 269.

conditions of slaves in the Old South were worse than those which pre-vailed in Christ's times.[33]

When abolitionists like Garrison announced that they were prepared to set aside certain passages in the Bible entirely, southerners felt that the battle was won. Peter G. Camden, for example, was one of those who noted, quite correctly, that some abolitionists actually placed man's con-science above the Bible. From this he concluded, not quite so correctly, that even they conceded that the Bible approved of slavery. In the course of one of the fullest discussions of slavery and the Scriptures, Thornton Stringfellow presented as evidence a list of Biblical quotations and ended with a rhetorical question which captures the confidence that southerners felt about their biblical claims: "Now, I ask, can any man in his proper senses, from these premises, bring himself to conclude that slavery is abolished by Jesus Christ?" On another occasion Stringfellow offered to renounce slavery and slaveholding entirely if the Bible could be shown to be against it. There is not the slightest reason to doubt that these sentiments were common amongst slaveholders in the final years of the Old South. As one clergyman put it, only a few years before the Civil War, "the Southern slaveholder is now satisfied, as never before, that the relation of master and slave is sanctioned by the Bible; and he feels, as never before, the obligations of the word of God." Of course we need not assume that the typical southern slaveholder was greatly concerned with biblical exegesis, but those who experienced a need to reconcile slavery with Christianity were provided with powerful weapons.[34]

Nevertheless the slaveholders faced two problems in this connection. First, they were unwilling to allow slaves unimpeded access to the Bible. Though they were able to claim that Christianity in no direct way under-mined slavery, they were troubled by the interpretations that could be given to certain passages. Christ's appeals were primarily to the poor and dispossessed and this, in conjunction with the emphasis on the equality of men before God and the Old Testament invocation of vengeance against the oppressor, gave southerners cause for concern. We should not

33. On the attitude of the Bible to slavery and race see, for example, the entry under "slavery" in the Oxford Dictionary of the Christian Church which concedes that "in the Old Testament . . . a mitigated form of slavery was tolerated by the Mosaic Law," that "in New Testament times it was an integral part of the social system whose sudden abolition would have reduced the Roman Empire to chaos," and that "there is no explicit teaching on the subject [of slavery] in the gospels." Though this work (quite implausibly in my view) seeks to claim that the spirit of Christianity opposes slavery, its exegetical conclusions fully vindicate southern claims – *The Oxford Dictionary of the Christian Church* (2nd ed. London, 1974).

34. Camden, *Common-Sense . . . Examination*, p. 8; Stringfellow, *Scriptural and Statistical Views*, p. 43; Stringfellow, *Brief Examination*, p. 17; Reverend Fred A. Ross, *Slavery Ordained of God* (Phil., 1857), p. 101.

conclude that they doubted whether the Bible supported slavery, though such was the conclusion which abolitionists immediately drew. Instead southerners feared that the meaning of certain passages could be tortured to serve unscrupulous and even diabolical ends. Once again it was the potential for unrest among the slaves themselves that could not be ignored.

The second problem was of an entirely different order. It involved the not merely thorny but ultimately intractable problem of race. Let us begin by considering the one principal remaining argument derived from the Scriptures. In Genesis a curse is placed upon Canaan for the sin (perpetrated by Ham) of looking upon his naked father, Noah:

> And he said, Blessed be the Lord God of Shem; and Canaan shall be his servant.
>
> God shall enlarge Japheth, and he shall dwell in the tents of Shem; and Canaan shall be his servant.

Southerners made much of this passage. As William Jenkins has pointed out, it led them to claim that God had decreed the enslavement of African blacks. But at this point they encountered difficulties.[35] Once again there were semantic questions concerning the status of "servant." More important, it became necessary to demonstrate that all black peoples were descended from Ham. Even then the southerners' problems were not at an end. The curse was delivered not upon Ham, the progenitor, so it was claimed, of all black races, but upon Canaan. He then had to be seen as the representative of all Ham's posterity. At each point southerners had to offer an interpretation, rather than a literal reading, of the Bible. Nevertheless many southerners pursued this strategy. Typical were the claims made by an anonymous "Marylander" who claimed that "all labor" was "the result of sin" and "the entail of the curse of God" (a view which contrasted sharply, of course, with the northern emphasis on the dignity of labor). Then the writer turned to the curse of Canaan:

> So do we learn from the Bible, that when the human race began a new career in the posterity of Noah, that for the first sin of one of his sons, God renewed the curse of labor, and made it more onerous than it was originally, by connecting with it the degradation of servitude; the second curse was servile labor, and it was instituted by God for the sin of irreverence of an Earthly Father; it was designed to be perpetual until the end of time; and to be compulsory, that portion of the earth might be brought into cultivation, which otherwise would have remained forever unproductive.

35. Jenkins, *Pro-Slavery Thought*, p. 201.

This was a possible interpretation of a passage in the Bible but it was open to serious challenge.[36]

The Curse of Ham was of obvious value to southerners. It strengthened their tendency to justify southern slavery by reference to the alleged racial inferiority of blacks. But the problem was that the rest of the evidence adduced from the Scriptures, and especially the crucial claims about the New Testament, could not be forced into this mold. Many southerners – and especially those who pursued the *Herrenvolk* defence – wanted to make two separate claims. First they wanted to show that slavery had existed if not throughout history, then at least in all the most glorious eras of the past. Biblical evidence was very pleasing in this connection, as were the practices of slaveholding Romans and Greeks in Antiquity. But second, they wished to show that the enslavement of blacks by whites was divinely inspired. Unfortunately the slavery of biblical times and of Antiquity was highly inconvenient in this respect. However one might trace the ancestors of the different races, one could scarcely claim that these eras witnessed the enslavement of blacks by whites. As we shall see, George Fitzhugh took his fellow proslavery theorists severely to task for their failure to confront this difficulty. As he reminded them, too many of the precedents they cited involved the enslavement of whites by whites, a practice which the egalitarian or *Herrenvolk* defenders of slavery condemned as vehemently as the abolitionist.

Nevertheless, we must allow that the southerner was able to deploy a formidable range of arguments to counter the view that Christianity in general and the Scriptures in particular outlawed slavery. This alone should make us doubt whether he experienced anything like the level of guilt over slavery which some historians have claimed. Indeed the guilt thesis, one might suggest, implies a northern view of the Bible, rather than the southern one (though its adherents appear to ignore the question). But avoiding guilt was the easiest problem faced by the proslavery writer. A greater difficulty came when he tried to justify from biblical or indeed any other historical precedent, a theory of racial inequality in which blacks, unlike whites, were said to be biologically suited to enslavement. Though he could scarcely do without an appeal to race and racism, here as elsewhere the defender of slavery found that such appeals severely constrained his own freedom of intellectual and political maneuver.

36. *Slavery, By A Marylander* (n.p., n.d.), p. 1.

A racist egalitarianism

I

The problems raised by the attempt to ground the proslavery argument upon race and racism are visible not only in the discussion of biblical and historical precedents for slavery, but also in the widely made appeal to racist egalitarianism. The proslavery theorists who espoused egalitarian ideals (for adult white males) were prominent within the South – and in all parts of the South – throughout the antebellum era. Their arguments need the fullest consideration primarily perhaps because of the difficulties they experienced in maintaining an egalitarian stance. Ironically this egalitarianism was challenged not so much by southern critics, still less by northern enemies, but instead by the implications of other ideas which its adherents either had to adopt or at least could not renounce. Undoubtedly the attempt to ground slavery in a racist egalitarianism was of fundamental importance in the maintenance of the hegemonic power of the slaveholding class, but it was a complex process, fraught with difficulty and never attended with anything approaching complete success.[37]

The basic egalitarian premise was nevertheless a simple one: slavery permitted a greater equality outside the ranks of the enslaved than was possible in free society. In the South this meant an equality among whites, regardless of slaveownership, achieved in contrast to, and in part as a result of, the inequality between the races. According to Albert Gallatin Brown of Mississippi, "nowhere on the face of the globe, in or out of Christendom, are white people so near on a footing of equality as in the slave holding states of this Union!" "Nowhere," he continued, "in this broad Union but in the slaveholding states is there a living, breathing exemplification of the beautiful sentiment, that all men are equal." For "in the South all men are equal." Lest anyone commit the egregious error of thinking that "all men" denoted all men, Brown quickly added that he meant "of course, white men," reminding his audience that "negroes are not men, within the meaning of the Declaration [of Independence]." Thus the visitor to Mississippi could see there "what he never will see in a free state – a whole community standing on a perfect level, and not one of them the tithe of a hair's breadth higher in the social scale than

---

37. While historians have of course recognized this tendency in southern and especially proslavery thought, they have on the whole failed to recognize the problems inherent in it. The appeal to racist egalitarianism is thus viewed as a highly effective, though of course highly pernicious, means of securing planter dominance. This is the general position of Fredrickson's *Black Image in the White Mind*. By contrast, I wish to argue that the South was in fact unable to explain itself even, and especially, to itself, and that the appeal to racist egalitarianism was extremely problematic.

another."[38] For Brown this "social equality" was "the equality to which all men were born."

Similarly R. M. T. Hunter of Virginia, a Calhoun disciple, boasted that "with us, so far as the white class is concerned, there never was any organization of human society in which the equality between all the members of that race was so complete and so perfect." He then rebutted the charge that manual labor was degraded in slave society and claimed instead that the laborer – so long of course as he were white – "in the slaveholding States is more nearly on an equality with every other man in the community, than every white laborer in the North is on an equality with every other man in the North." In the words of John Townsend of South Carolina, "in no country in the world does the poor white man, whether the slaveholder or non-slaveholder, occupy so enviable a position as in the slaveholding states of the South."[39]

These claims were easy to make, more difficult to substantiate. Southerners were by no means agreed on the precise nature of the equality which slavery promoted. Abel P. Upshur of Virginia was one who claimed that slavery produced a greater equality of wealth than was otherwise possible. He conceded that "there is no form of government which can preserve an equality of wealth among individuals, even for a day," and acknowledged that "it would be absurd to say that domestic slavery can produce any such result." But the advantage of slavery was that "it approaches that result much more nearly than any other civil institution, and it prevents, in a very great degree, if not entirely, that gross inequality among the different classes of society from which alone liberty has anything to fear." Southerners were consequently "equal in our rank" and "equal in our fortune." Republican government could flourish in their midst since "the spirit of levelling sees nothing to envy," "the spirit of agrarianism sees nothing to attack."[40]

Though Upshur was not the only southerner to make such claims, the equality that most proslavery theorists emphasized was rather different. It was an equality of esteem or status which slavery was thought to promote. (The contrast with equality of wealth, however, was by no means

38. Albert Gallatin Brown, *Correspondence to J.Z. George et al, Sept. 27, 1860* (n.p., n.d.), p. 6; Albert Gallatin Brown, *Speeches, Messages, and Other Writings of the Hon. Albert Gallatin Brown, A Senator in Congress from the State of Mississippi*, M.W. Cluskey (ed.) (Phil., 1859), pp. 336–337.
39. *Speech of R. M. T. Hunter, of Virginia, on Invasion of States, Delivered in the Senate of the United States, Jan. 30, 1860* (Washington, D.C., 1860), p. 14; John Townsend, *The Doom of Slavery in the Union: Its Safety Out of It* (Charleston, S.C., n.d.), p. 22. Townsend, however, did not explicitly claim that whites were especially equal in the South.
40. Abel P. Upshur, "Domestic Slavery," *Southern Literary Messenger*, v (1839), pp. 677–687, esp. 678, 687.

complete since equality of esteem, one suspects, required relatively narrow inequalities of wealth.) Sometimes this equality was merely implicit. When Felix Huston argued that "it is only where there is slavery that all white men who are honest and worthy are really equal," it was probably an equality of status which he envisaged. Albert Gallatin Brown likewise noted that white men only lost their equality "by dishonesty or immorality of some sort."

Other proslavery writers, however, were more explicit. They made it clear that slavery allowed all whites to share certain "social and civil privileges, which the white man enjoys nowhere else." John Campbell of South Carolina in effect enumerated some of these social privileges when he insisted that in a society that lacked slavery the poor were "necessarily . . . to some extent . . . excluded as companions upon terms of equality at the tables, and in the parlors, of the rich." In the South, by contrast, the poor non-slaveholder was able to associate upon equal terms with the wealthy owner of a large plantation.[41] J. G. B. De Bow, whose *Review* was the most important journal of the antebellum South, also insisted that the poor man in the South could expect, and was given, a seat at the wealthy slaveholder's table. Other southerners made the same claim. Herbert Fielder of Georgia explained that "these privileges" were available to all southern whites. Nevertheless, as Fielder explained, this equality had its limitations:

> We do not mean that the most ignorant clown in a community would be considered an eligible companion for a refined and polished scholar, or that a ragged and dirty vagabond would feel easy in a parlor of fashionable gentlemen and ladies, but that, so far as social privileges are concerned, the poorest white man in the land, is equal to the richest. Whether he has prepared himself to enjoy those privileges is another question.

The qualifications that Fielder here introduced were not in themselves, perhaps, of great significance. Yet they reflect a general characteristic of proslavery thought which we shall encounter again in more distinct form: even when it stressed equality, it betrayed definite inegalitarian tendencies.[42]

Although some proslavery thinkers emphasized equality of esteem or status, others contented themselves with observations upon the general

---

41. *Address of Gen. Felix Huston, To the Members of the Southern Convention, To Be Held at Nashville, 3 June 1850* (Natchez, n.d.), p. 7; Brown, *Speeches, Messages . . .* , p. 337; *Speech of John Campbell of South Carolina in the House of Representatives, April 15, 1842* (Washington, D.C., 1842), p. 17.

42. J. G. B. De Bow, *The Interest in Slavery of the Southern Non-Slaveholder* (Charleston, S.C., 1860), p. 9; Herbert Fielder, *The Disunionist: A Brief Treatise Upon the Evils of the Union between the North and the South* (n.p., n.d.), p. 46.

egalitarian effect of slavery on the collective psychology of the white South. Superiority of race and color, it was claimed, gave the non-slave-holding poor white an enhanced self-respect, a confidence in his own worth that was difficult to create in a free labor society. According to Townsend, "the poorest non-slaveholder . . . except . . . he be debased by his vices or his crimes, thinks and feels and acts as if he was, always intended to be, superior to the negro." Benjamin Stringfellow of Missouri declared that in southern slave society, "the white man, however poor, whatever be his occupation, feels himself a sovereign." As a result, he could deal with other white men "as his equals," for example exchanging "his labor for their money, not honored by their service, but reciprocating the favor of equal to equal." Stringfellow also claimed that northern mechanics who came to the South immediately "felt this vast difference" and could "bear witness to it." The white southerner was, in the words of George Sawyer, "inspired with the just pride of a freeman, a sovereign." He was imbued with a love of liberty, and of the equality upon which it depended.[43]

Nevertheless, when they sought to relate this equality to the economic practices of southern society, proslavery theorists found that their troubles began. Some of them placed great stress upon the distinction between manual labor, allegedly respected in the South, and menial labor, necessarily and properly regarded as degraded there because associated with slave status. The claim was that southern white society was made more equal because menial labor was performed by slaves. In the North, by contrast, it was said to be performed by whites who had accordingly lost all entitlement to equality of esteem or status. This argument, or a variant of it, received its most forceful expression in James Henry Hammond's famous "mudsill" speech of 1858 in which he argued that all societies needed a lower stratum or "mudsill" and that the only difference between North and South in this respect was that the South was fortunate enough to have an inferior race, ideally equipped to perform this function, whereas in the North whites themselves comprised the "mudsill."[44]

Other southerners made identical claims. Felix Huston, a few years earlier argued that a "lower substratum must necessarily exist in all countries, some must perform the menial offices and be the servants of others, and when that is the case, social equality cannot exist." "But," he continued, "when this substratum is composed of an inferior class,

43. Townsend, *Doom of Slavery*, p. 23; B. F. Stringfellow *et al.*, *Negro Slavery No Evil: or The North and the South: A Report Made to the Platte County Self-Defence Association* (St Louis, Mo., 1854), pp. 27–28; Sawyer, *Southern Institutes*, p. 374. See also Brown, *Speeches, Messages* . . . , p. 336.
44. *Congressional Globe*, 35 Congress, 1 Session, p. 963.

different in color, the line of demarcation is plainly marked, and all above that line can unite in social equality with no other distinction than that of intelligence and worth." In the South, he concluded, "this is the prevailing rule." John Townsend was still more explicit:

> In countries where negro slavery does not exist, (as in the Northern States of this Union and in Europe), the most menial and degrading employments in society are filled by the white poor, who are hourly seen drudging in them. Poverty, then, in those countries, becomes the badge of inferiority, and wealth of distinction. Hence the arrogant airs which wealth there puts on, in its intercourse with the poor man. But in the Southern slaveholding States, where these menial and degrading offices are turned over to be performed exclusively by the negro slave, the status and color of the black race becomes the badge of inferiority, and the poorest non-slaveholder may rejoice with the richest of his brethren of the white race, in the distinction of his color.

We should note that Townsend's indictment of menial labor came close to being a more general indictment of drudgery. As we shall see, it was here that the problems intensified.[45]

Some writers enumerated the tasks or occupations that necessarily brought degradation. The jobs of boot-black, carriage driver, waiter or chambermaid were placed firmly in this category. Albert Gallatin Brown boasted to the Senate that "it would take you longer to find a white man, in my state, who would hire himself out as a boot-black, or a white woman who would go to service as a chambermaid, than it took Captain Cook to sail round the world." He avowed that he himself "in thirty years" had "never found a single one." Hence there was more equality in the South because "we have no WHITE MENIALS." Other southerners made identical claims. According to De Bow, "no white man in the South serves another as a body servant, to clean his boots, wait on his table, and perform the menial services of his household;" indeed the white southerner's "blood revolts against this, and his necessities never drive him to it." Herbert Fielder similarly affirmed that "the poorest and most dependent white man in Georgia would resent it as an insult if commanded to hold a horse or black a shoe for the most opulent man in the State." "Nor," he added, "does he like to be hired to perform menial services."[46]

Yet this apparently enticing egalitarianism was more problematic than it seemed. There is an ambiguity in the word "menial," which literally

45. *Address of Huston*, p. 7; Townsend, *Doom of Slavery*, pp. 22–23.
46. Brown, *Speeches, Messages . . .* , p. 336; De Bow, *Interest in Slavery of Southern Non-Slaveholder*, p. 9; Fielder, *Disunionist*, p. 45.

means "household" or "domestic." We shall term this the first meaning. By extension, however, the word comes to possess a second meaning: "of a servant" (or slave). By further extension, a third meaning is obtained: menial work is "of the nature of drudgery" because performed by one of low status, probably a servant or slave. In principle these meanings are distinct (though not unrelated); in practice the distinctions are not always apparent. Southern usage concentrated on the second: menial labor was that appropriate only to "slaves."

The problem was, however, that it was in the South impossible to limit slaves to "menial" labor in this sense of the term. While slaves could certainly be employed as domestic servants, or carriage drivers, the South did not need millions of such workers. What it did need, of course, was a productive workforce, especially in agriculture. Such work did not in any way fit southern notions of "menial labor." We have seen that those proslavery theorists who specified the tasks that were "menial" excluded agricultural field work, even of an unskilled type. This was scarcely surprising. If such work were indeed "menial," where did this leave the hundreds of thousands of white farmers who owned no slaves, but who in order to raise their crops – among which might be the same crops as those raised on the large plantation – had to perform the same labor as the slave? Thus a wider definition of "menial" labor was impossible since it would have undermined the racist egalitarianism for whose support the term had been initially introduced. In effect, therefore, southerners were forced to combine the first two meanings of the word. "Menial" labor was that performed by slaves, but it tended to be only their domestic labor.[47]

The problems involved here were even greater than might at first sight appear. The slaveholder himself often needed to work alongside the slave in the field, especially if he owned only a small number of slaves. Such labor had an ideological as well as an economic pay-off in that it reaffirmed the identity of interest and reinforced the putative equality with the non-slaveholding white farmer. Southerners quite explicitly stated that this labor was natural and honorable. According to Albert Gallatin Brown it was "a gross slander" to say any man "loses caste at the South because he works in the same field or in the same shop with a slave." Brown was especially emphatic on this point. "Nothing is more

---

47. The historian who has done most to draw attention to the problems associated with the proslavery theorists' investigation of the labor process is Laurence Shore in his book *Southern Capitalists*. In my view, however, the problems derive precisely from the fact that slavery is not capitalism, that southern slaveholders are not capitalists and that these problems – discussed with great ability by Shore – are not experienced by defenders of capitalism.

common in the South," he insisted, "than to see the master and his slave working together at the same trade." Such behavior was so normal that "the man who would breathe a suspicion that the master had sunk one hair's breadth in the social scale in consequence of this kind of contact would, by general consent, be written down an ass." Brown also asserted that this sharing of labor was not confined to agriculture: "in the South . . . all the mechanic arts are treated as honorable, and they are not the less so because practised by blacks."[48]

Hence there was in the South no clear division of labor along race lines, merely a small number of tasks performed only by blacks. When Brown told northerners that "the line that separates menial from honorable labor with you is not marked by a caste or distinct color, as it is with us," he was only partly correct. Only a comparatively few tasks were reserved for blacks and, however important these might be, they were clearly subordinate to the principal economic function of slave labor, which was in agriculture and which involved labor that might be indistinguishable from that performed by whites. Moreover there were – or should have been – two aspects to the complaint about the inegalitarian tendency of menial labor performed by one person for another. The effect southerners considered was the diminished status of the menial worker. They utterly ignored the effect on the employer or master. For there was surely a danger that he would assume a superiority not merely over the servant, slave or worker who performed the menial tasks for him, but also over those who had to perform such tasks for themselves. Southerners acknowledged that the master or employer was likely to feel superior to the slave or servant who blacked his boots, but what they were most reluctant to acknowledge, in this context at any rate, was the danger that he would also feel superior to the non-slaveholding white man who blacked his own boots. The egalitarians could scarcely countenance this possibility, since it highlighted an aspect of slavery which ran counter to the alleged egalitarian tendency they were at pains to emphasize. The problem was, once again, that despite their common racial identity, slaveholders and non-slaveholders might confront fundamentally different situations.[49]

A major reason for this difficulty derived from the distribution of slaves in the South. If every white family had owned slaves (or if there had been a collective ownership of all blacks by all whites), then the egalitarian

---

48. Brown, *Correspondence to J.Z. George* . . . , p. 4; Brown, *Speeches, Messages* . . . , p. 336. As one writer put it in *De Bow's Review*, "no southern man could be induced to black his employer's boots or attend at his table, while he might not have the slightest objection to work in the field or in the shop, even by the side of the negro" – "Reply to Abolitionist Objections to Slavery," *De Bow's Review*, xx (1856), p. 662.

49. Brown, *Speeches, Messages* . . . , p. 336.

argument derived from menial labor would have been far more powerful – and consistent. But slaves were not owned by all white families and
indeed the proportion of slaveholding families in the South was actually
shrinking. Some Southerners recognized this tendency and, as we shall
see, the campaign to reopen the African slave trade was an attempt to
address the problem. As we shall also see, however, this "solution" created as many problems as it removed.[50]

II

Equality of whites thus rested, it was claimed, upon a sentiment prevalent
in the South, an equality of esteem or status that conferred a dignity upon
the poor that was absent in free society. When they sought to explain this
equality, southerners emphasized the exemption of whites from menial
labor. As we have seen, however, they were forced to define such labor
not simply as that which the typical slave performed but instead as that
which no white person would perform for another. This meant domestic
labor. Unfortunately this was a narrow base upon which to build an
argument for equality of esteem throughout southern society. "Menial"
labor was in fact performed by only a minority of slaves and even these
specific (household) tasks were identical to those carried out by whites,
even if for themselves rather than for others. The closer one looks at
southern claims, the more unsatisfactory they become. Indeed one
could argue that the evidence cited could have been employed more
effectively in favor of the opposite claim: most slaves were engaged
most of their time upon (agricultural) tasks that were not very different
from those which most whites performed – a highly distressing conclusion for the racist egalitarian.

Of course, proslavery men were free to argue that such labor was
performed very differently by the two groups. But, as we shall see, this
possibility was constrained by other considerations. The slaves could not
be said to be working under significantly harsher conditions, since this
militated against the claim that slavery was benign for blacks. An alternative strategy, pursued by some proslavery theorists, was to claim slave
labor was organized so as to produce economies of scale. But as we shall
see this claim was equally problematic and in fact threatened once again
to undermine the egalitarian claims that had initially inspired the distinctions between honorable and menial labor.

When they looked at the labor process in the South, therefore, proslavery writers experienced considerable difficulties. The reality they

---

50. By 1860 only a quarter of white families owned slaves; in 1830 the proportion had
been 36 percent.

perceived and needed to explain – above all to themselves – was not consonant with the claims made by the devotees of white egalitarianism. For this reason, perhaps, some proslavery thinkers opted for a different strategy. In effect they reverted to the third meaning of "menial" and characterized the labor of the slave as that which was not merely servile but also based on drudgery.

Such was James Henry Hammond's position. "This idea," he declared, "that Slavery is necessary to the performance of the drudgery so essential for the sustenance of man, and the advance of civilization, is undoubtedly the fundamental ground on which the reason of the institution rests." Similarly, Edmund Ruffin asserted that it was "this institution, which, by confining the drudgery and brutalizing effects of continued toil, or menial service, to the inferior race, . . . gives to the superior race leisure and other means to improve mind, taste, and manners." This theme nevertheless received its fullest expression in the work of Mathew Estes, who in his *Defence of Negro Slavery as it Exists in the United States* insisted that drudgery was incompatible with refinement, or a high level of intellectual attainment. "A man who is daily engaged in a certain kind of hard drudgery," he declared, "cannot possibly devote much time to the cultivation of his mental powers." He was prepared to "state it as a fact, which is confirmed by the whole history of mankind – that there is a certain kind of hard drudgery which is incompatible with any high degree of mental improvement." Estes took pains to emphasize that he was here describing not simply manual labor, but instead "the hardest labor – that which is commonly performed by slaves." Thus the advantage of slavery was that it enabled society's need for drudge labor to be met, while at the same time permitting the elite to avoid it and concentrate instead upon more noble activities.[51]

This argument was in many respects more satisfactory than those developed by writers who dwelt instead on the alternative definitions of "menial" labor. It served to explain, for example, the South's preeminence in national politics, proudly noted by virtually every proslavery writer. The southern slaveholder had the time to devote to the study of statecraft, since menial tasks and drudge labor were done by his slaves.[52] But there was, of course, a fatal flaw in this approach which ruined it – or ought to have ruined it – for proslavery egalitarians: it was utterly inegalitarian in its thrust. After all, non-slaveholding whites had to

---

51. Hammond to Mathew Estes, in Estes, *Defence of Negro Slavery*, p. viii; Edmund Ruffin, *The Influence of Slavery, or of its Absence, on Manners, Morals – Intellect – : Address to the Virginia State Agricultural Society, Dec. 16, 1852* (n.p., n.d.), p. 26; Estes, *Defence of Negro Slavery*, p. 25.
52. Hammond, *Letters on Southern Slavery*, p. 8.

perform drudgery too. The inegalitarian assumptions in Estes were unmistakable:

> The great mass of white laborers in the Union are such poor readers, that they really derive little benefit from it; and such must necessarily be the case with persons whose whole time is given to hard manual drudgery. A man who is compelled by his necessity to work from twelve to fifteen hours a day, has but little time, and less disposition, to read. Such persons, therefore, never profit much by reading.

Here we should note that Estes was referring not simply to the North but to the "great mass of white laborers" in the Union. He was even more explicit when he declared that "intense agricultural toil in a southern climate . . . and a thousand menial offices in society, are totally incompatible with any high degree of mental culture." Thus the slave's performance of drudge labor could be adduced in favor of slavery, but it could scarcely be adduced in favor of white egalitarianism.[53]

Estes recognized that his criticisms applied to farmers who lacked slaves, whether north or south of the Mason-Dixon line. Other southerners voiced the same criticisms but without confronting – perhaps even without recognizing – the fact that in the process they were undermining their own egalitarian claims. Whenever proslavery theorists derided the lot of the northern farmer, they almost invariably fell into this trap. Edmund Ruffin described the condition of a farmer in Pennsylvania or New York and insisted that even if he possessed moderate means (enough to secure his independence), he would nevertheless "be compelled to be one of his own continual laborers." Moreover "his sons, and not less his daughters, would be brought up to continued labor, in the lowest and most repulsive employment, and without any improving social intercourse, because its cost could not be afforded."

Similarly George S. Sawyer, who wrote appreciatively of the egalitarianism that flourished in the South, contrasted the lot of the agriculturist North and South. The southern slaveholder was well informed, cultured, a man of wide experience and enlarged views. The northern farmer, by contrast, was "compelled to live within a more limited sphere":

> However commendable may be his industry, honesty, and frugality (and we would not say a single word disparagingly of the same), it is a necessary economy to keep his expenses within his means. His daughters, as soon as they are capable, must share the burdens and labors of the household affairs; hence neatness in cooking, washing, ironing, chamber-work, &c., is, by the force of necessity, held up as a very requisite and fashionable accomplishment for a young lady. His

---

53. Estes, *Defence of Negro Slavery*, pp. 123, 170–171.

sons, from the age of fifteen to twenty-one, are thoroughly drilled in the exercise of the crow-bar, the hoe, axe, spade, &c., to fit them for the duties of citizens, and their sphere of usefulness in after life. From two to three months' cessation from labor during the inclemency of winter, affords them an opportunity to attend a common country school. Here, by improving their opportunities, they may learn to read and write, something of Geography, of English Grammar, and of Arithmetic as far as Interest of the rule of Three. At the age of twenty-one, they have read their Bible, some religious family newspaper (the *Liberator, Emancipator, et hoc genus omne*), and have been to mill and to meeting. And this they call education.

Ruffin and Sawyer agreed with Estes that too much physical labor prevented refinement. Unlike Estes, however, they failed to note that the same objections were applicable to southern farmers.[54]

This problem was acute. In effect there had been since Jefferson's time an implicit (and sometimes) explicit alliance between the planters and the non-slaveholding whites of the southern upcountry areas. The very basis of this alliance was localism: the non-slaveholding areas would be left untouched by state government; the non-slaveholding farmers would be given a very considerable degree of freedom, equality (understood in Jeffersonian terms) and autonomy. Slavery, as we now know, tended to preserve these upcountry areas in their subsistence or semi-subsistence agriculture. By mid-century the South had far more farms that were outside the market economy (on any but the most local scale) than the North. Hence the objections which men like Sawyer could make to northern agriculture in fact applied with still greater force to the South.[55]

Despite his claims about the importance of racial identity in securing equality in the South and bridging the gap between those who did and those who did not own slaves, the proslavery writer easily slipped into the assumption that the southerner was a slaveholder. As he attacked northerners, he often implicitly condemned the non-slaveholder of the South. This was the effect of Sawyer's and of Ruffin's strictures against the lot of the ordinary farmer. Ruffin's indictment, however, went further. He dwelt on the predicament of the farmer's wife. She was necessarily "the most unceasing drudge on the farm;" indeed even if her husband were worth $30,000 she would be "still the most laborious domestic drudge." Ruffin never explained why these observations should not apply equally to the non-slaveholding southern farmer, who indeed at this point had

---

54. Ruffin, *Influence of Slavery*, p. 28; Sawyer, *Southern Institutes*, p. 377.
55. Life in these areas is exceptionally well described and analyzed in the work of Stephen Hahn. See, for example, Hahn, *The Roots of Southern Populism: Yeoman Farmers and the Transformation of the Georgia Upcountry, 1850–1890* (N.Y., 1983).

disappeared entirely from his analysis. In this sense, his writings were antithetical to those of Jefferson, Jackson and John Taylor in whose work the slaveholder and the slave had disappeared.

Benjamin Stringfellow, having lingered fondly on the alleged egalitarian effect of slavery upon all white men, also considered the position of women. After claiming that slavery "elevates the character not only of the master, the actual owner of slaves, but of all who wear the color of the freeman," he added that it similarly "ennobles woman." At this point, however, the non-slaveholder of the South once again suddenly vanished:

> Relieved by the slave from the abject toil, the servile condition to which the white woman is so often subjected by necessity where negro slavery does not exist, and which strip her of woman's greatest charm, modesty; which make of her the rude, drudging despised servant of a harsh master; the white woman becomes, as she is fitted to be, not the slave, but the queen of her household, fit mate for a sovereign.

Stringfellow even added that slavery protected the white woman by offering instead the female slave as a target for the aggressions of the lewd and lascivious. He did not even refer specifically to the non-slaveholding white woman but the implications of his observations would scarcely have pleased an audience of southern non-slaveholders.[56]

His failure, however, and that of other proslavery writers was not simply a failure to argue consistently. The problem was less in the contradictory defense of slavery, than in the contradictions of slavery itself, which, though they did not realize it, mystified even its defenders and made any fully consistent defense impossible. In order to shore up the peculiar institution, proslavery men needed to appeal for the support of the non-slaveholding whites, who made up the majority of voters in the Old South. The salience and potency of the democratic tradition, the tradition of Jefferson, Taylor and Jackson, made an appeal on the basis of equality both logical and superficially easy to formulate. But Jefferson, Taylor and Jackson, who had never distinguished between farmers, North or South, and slaveholders, had not defended slavery either. They had generally ignored the effect of slavery on the labor process; indeed they had scarcely considered the division of labor between races at " The proslavery theorists, however, were less fortunate. They were compelled to look more closely into these matters. But as they emphasized the benefits which slave labor brought to the men and women who were supposedly exempted from either drudgery or menial labor they necessarily underlined the differences within the South between those

---

56. Ruffin, *Influence of Slavery*, p. 28; Stringfellow, *Negro Slavery No Evil*, p. 27.

who had slaves and those who did not. The pattern of slaveownership was such as to generate a class of masters who comprised only a minority of white southerners but who were unwaveringly committed to the defense of their own power and of the society they dominated. But as they reached out for the support of the entire white South, they, or those who formulated their theories, invoked egalitarian principles that were undermined if not contradicted by the realities of their own class power. The more closely they examined and justified the material foundation of their society, the more difficult it became to maintain these egalitarian claims. At their best the proslavery theorists were educated, sophisticated and highly vocal but the cause of slavery had been more effectively promoted in an earlier age, when a generation of slaveholders had been able to maintain a discreet but exploitative silence on the subject.

A critique of George Fitzhugh

I

The problems encountered by the racist egalitarian were undoubtedly responsible, in part at least, for the existence of a strand of proslavery thought which delighted in repudiating virtually all notions of equality. Traditional exponents of the "necessary evil" theory had of course claimed that the relations between slave and master were merely one expression of the inequalities which necessarily separated man and man but this attitude would no longer suffice in the final decades of the Old South. Slavery had to be shown to be different from, and superior to, other forms of social organization.

No writer met this challenge more squarely than George Fitzhugh of Port Royal, Virginia. Indeed of all the southern writers who engaged in speculation about slavery, capitalism and race in the United States, none reached conclusions more startling. With great force and insistence Fitzhugh argued that slavery was desirable in itself, not because the South was fortunate enough to have a black population within her borders, but because, regardless of race, slave labor was superior to free labor. Such a conclusion, of course, implied slavery for some whites, if not in the United States then certainly elsewhere, and it thus completely contradicted the claim, made by most proslavery theorists, that enslavement was appropriate for blacks but not, in the nineteenth century at least, for whites. Fitzhugh argued, moreover, that the superiority of slavery over free labor was moral and economic, political and social. For him the opprobrium that was attached to slavery belonged in reality to free societies, in which most citizens were reduced to the status of slaves without masters and in which humans, like cannibals, consumed one another. Fitzhugh pressed the inegalitarian aspects of the proslavery argument to their logical conclusion. His most famous work was entitled "Cannibals All!" and subtitled "Slaves Without Masters."[57]

Like all southern slaveholders, however, Fitzhugh was a racist. He did not doubt the inferiority of blacks and indeed became increasingly rigid in his racism as he imbibed the sentiments of the late antebellum South. But his departure from what we might call the path of proslavery orthodoxy resulted from his refusal to rest slavery upon racism. As a consequence he challenged many of the assumptions of his fellow southerners and exposed some of the tensions and contradictions in their thought. Fitzhugh prided himself on his refusal to engage in abstract philosophizing, his stern insistence on practicalities rather than abstractions, his recognition of the imperfections and limitations inherent in human nature. Yet the truths he told were in part vitiated by a curious tendency towards utopianism in his own thought. It is perhaps not so surprising that he himself failed to discern this tendency; what is more surprising is that historians have ignored it too.

II

From their vantage point as defenders of an alternative labor system, proslavery theorists were able to draw attention to all the evils of free society. Where northern or European commentators were constrained by the fear of unleashing radical protest movements on the one hand, but alarmed that inaction would perpetuate the social conditions fueling such movements on the other, the proslavery men felt no such ambivalence. Fitzhugh was somewhat more extreme than most, but his prognosis for capitalism in general was not very different from that of other southern ideologues. His view of free society was clearly expressed in his two major works, *Sociology for the South* and *Cannibals All!* as well as in numerous articles which he published from mid-century onward. The Fitzhugh reading of modern history was distinctive. The Reformation cleared away much of the rubbish of medieval society and released an

---

57. Fitzhugh's two books are *Sociology for the South, or the Failure of Free Society* (N.Y., n.d.) and *Cannibals All! or, Slaves Without Masters*, new ed., C. Vann Woodward (ed.) (Cambridge, Mass., 1960). One must also, however, consult his articles in *De Bow's Review*, two of which are in part reprinted in Drew G. Faust (ed.), *The Ideology of Slavery: Proslavery Thought in the Antebellum South, 1830–1860* (Baton Rouge, 1981), pp. 274–299. Among secondary works, the essential starting point is Genovese, *World the Slaveholders Made*, pp. 115–244. See also Woodward's introduction to *Cannibals All!* Useful for biographical data is Harvey Wish, *George Fitzhugh: Propagandist of the Old South* (Gloucester, Mass., 1962), though, as Genovese points out, Fitzhugh was not really a propagandist at all.

enormous amount of talent and capital. The aggregate wealth of society
increased rapidly. But unfortunately the process went too far. The individualism inherent in Protestantism contaminated all it touched and as a
result the natural sociality of human nature was thwarted. Above all, men
were left on their own, to compete as best they could with their fellows.

The winners in this competition of course received rich prizes: they had
all the pleasures of wealth and power without any of the responsibilities.
But for the losers, life was grim indeed. Bereft of the protection which
feudalism (or slavery) had provided, they were at the mercy of those
richer, wiser, more intelligent or simply more ruthless than themselves.
They experienced all the disadvantages of the new system and none of its
advantages. According to Fitzhugh free societies, unless there were special
mitigating factors, produced a hundred or even a thousand losers for
every winner.[58]

Fitzhugh then rounded upon Adam Smith as the primary apologist for
free society. He accused him of generalizing from his own narrow experience. As a winner himself, Smith too easily assumed that his experience
was typical. He recommended the pursuit of individual self-interest,
oblivious to its disastrous effects upon the majority. Moreover, Smith
made the same error in his discussions of international trade. Once
again he recommended as objectively and universally benign, a system
which benefited only the strong, in this case, Great Britain, against the
weak – her trading partners. Anticipating the objections to free trade
made in the twentieth century, Fitzhugh argued that it operated to confirm the international division of labor, with the most productive pursuits
monopolized by the stronger nations.[59]

At this point we see the similarities between Fitzhugh's thought and
that of socialists, both in his time and in ours. He was contemptuous of
contemporary political economy and of political economists, since "the
morality which they teach is one of simple and unadulterated selfishness," whose effects could be seen in the impoverishment of the masses
in Europe. Fitzhugh delighted in quoting at length from radicals, especially if they were also antislavery radicals, on the evils in free society.
Such evidence was, he claimed, his "trump card," since it amounted to an
eloquent denunciation of free society from the lips of those who wished to
convert the South to it.[60] He also delighted in citing conservative British
commentators on the dangers they perceived from the British working
classes (whose activities occasioned considerable fear, especially in the

58. *Sociology for the South*, pp. 8–15, 20–23, 239; *Cannibals All!*, p. 72.
59. *Sociology for the South*, pp. 12–14.
60. *Sociology for the South*, p. 20; *Cannibals All!*, p. 85. These critics of free society of
    course always insisted that slave labor was still worse.

1840s). Observing the effect of the labor unrest in Britain and the revolutions of 1848 in Europe, and ever mindful of the still greater upheaval of 1789, he concluded that free society necessarily produced a war of rich against poor, of capital against labor.

Fitzhugh departed immediately from the socialists, of course, when it came to remedies. And underlying his concrete proposals lay a view of human nature that was in certain key respects the antithesis of theirs. Like the socialists he believed that free competition was destructive of true human happiness, but unlike them (or at least most of them) he found and celebrated irrepressible inequalities within the human race. Here he went beyond some proslavery theorists (the *Herrenvolk* contingent) in insisting that such inequalities were not merely between races (though undoubtedly the races were highly unequal), but also within the white race. "Laissez-faire," he maintained, or "free competition, begets a war of the wits, which economists encourage, quite as destructive to the weak, simple and guileless as the war of the sword."[61]

He added to his catalogue of inequalities, that which existed between the sexes. Here he was able to score heavily over those who defended both free society and the domestication of women. Many defenders of free society insisted that the family in particular and the relationships between men and women in general, must not be governed by the logic or the sentiments of the marketplace. But they gave no guarantee that such would not in fact occur and relied on little more than exhortation. Fitzhugh, however, was able to assimilate the family and indeed the relations between the sexes, to his general anti-individualist, inegalitarian scheme. Within the household, inequality and interdependence would prevail. Family and gender relationships would thus be those of society in microcosm. Since "woman fares worst when thrown into this warfare of competition," the solution was simple: women, along with blacks, lunatics and the many others for whom competition was inappropriate, would not compete.[62]

Hence for Fitzhugh, the modern world was askew. The Reformation had gone too far; Protestantism in religion, Smith in political economy, Locke in political and moral science, had made the catastrophic error of enthroning individual man, in so doing tearing him out of society and community. "An isolated man," he wrote in one of his more memorable sentences, "is almost as helpless and ridiculous as a bee setting up for himself." Pursuing his zoological analogies, he observed that competition had been going on in nature for thousands of years. Yet there was not the slightest reason to believe that the animals (or the plants) were better now

---

61. *Sociology for the South*, p. 21.
62. *Sociology for the South*, pp. 23–24.

than heretofore. What was true of plants and animals would be found to be true for man.[63]

Fitzhugh's perspective allowed him to swipe out at the defenses of free labor offered by northern conservatives. On one occasion he confronted the claim that concentrations of wealth did not disadvantage those who started poor, nor undermine equality of opportunity, since inherited wealth was enervating and, consequently, a barrier to future accumulation. He neatly turned the claim against the claimants. "In Heaven's name," he exclaimed, "what is human life worth with such prospects ahead?" And what of the effect on the initial motive for accumulation? "Who would not rather lie down and die," he asked, "than exert himself to educate and make fortunes for his children, when he has reason to fear that by so doing he is to heap coals of fire upon their heads?"

In general, however, Fitzhugh acknowledged that free society supplied incentives to individual aggrandizement; indeed this was its principal deficiency. Offering the prospect of universal gain, it stimulated greed and avarice and created a society in which Christian values were overwhelmed. "Christian morality," he observed, "can find little practical foothold in a community so constituted that to 'love our neighbor as ourself' or 'to do unto others as we would they should do unto us' would be acts of suicidal self-sacrifice." And the gross inequality of outcomes similarly violated Christian principles. Free society, he complained, "hides with a veil the agonies of the vanquished, and only exhibits the vulgar mirth of the victors." In a moment of self-congratulation, he added that "we have lifted the veil."[64]

As a result, Fitzhugh insisted that free society was a "small experiment," both in the scope of its moral vision and in its place in history. On one occasion he referred to "the little experiment of universal liberty that has been tried for a little while in a little corner of Europe," and on another he claimed that "the English Poor Laws and the English poor constitute its [free society's] only history; for only in England has the experiment been made on a large scale for several centuries."[65] The case of the North, however, was somewhat different. Here Fitzhugh drew an important distinction, one commonly made by southern apologists for slavery. While the doom of free societies was, in the long term, sealed, in the short and medium term, special factors might intrude. Fitzhugh did not always make it clear what these special factors were. Sometimes he referred simply to the denseness or sparseness of population, implying that so long as sparseness prevailed, free society could

---

63. *Sociology for the South*, pp. 25, 31–32.
64. *Sociology for the South*, pp. 238–239; *Cannibals All!*, p. 30.
65. *Sociology for the South*, pp. 70–71; *Cannibals All!*, p. 118.

survive. This in turn meant that new countries were more suitable to free labor than older ones, and even, he conceded, better suited to free labor than to slavery.

Yet sparseness of population clearly was a proxy in his thought for land ownership. It was this which he believed would give the North its breathing space. Society would fail in the Northeast, he predicted, when the West was settled. But "till then, the despotism of skill and capital, in forcing emigration to the West, makes proprietors of those emigrants, benefits them, peoples the West, and by their return trade, enriches the East." "The North is now doing well," he acknowledged; "her poor are not the slaves of capital, and never will be while there are vacant lands . . . ." So there would be a delay before the region met its doom. On one occasion Fitzhugh hinted that the delay might be a long one indeed:

> Until the lands of America are appropriated by a few, population becomes dense, competition among laborers active, employment uncertain, and wages low, the personal liberty of all the whites will continue to be a blessing. We have vast unsettled territories; population may cease to increase slowly, as in most countries, and many centuries may elapse before the question will be practically suggested, whether slavery to capital be preferable to slavery to human masters.

Nevertheless, this concession did not weaken Fitzhugh's indictment of free society. For "the situation of the North is abnormal and anomalous." In effect, like most of the proslavery theorists, he directed almost all his attacks against not free labor but rather wage labor. The secret asset of the North was not simply unsettled land, but the effect this would have in giving labor the opportunity to escape the clutches of capital. Like many other contemporaries in the North as well as in the South, and in common with future commentators like Frederick Jackson Turner, Fitzhugh viewed the West as a safety valve for eastern discontent.[66]

III

Despite this concession, Fitzhugh clearly underestimated the staying power of western and especially European capitalism. Moreover the twentieth century has demonstrated that his emphasis on the importance of land in maintaining northern capitalism was misplaced. Yet we should note that conditions in Europe in Fitzhugh's era – and especially in the "hungry forties" – led others, whether radicals, reformers or

---

66. *Cannibals All!*, pp. 11, 199, 40; Fitzhugh, "Southern Thought," *De Bow's Review* XXIII (1857), p. 345.

conservatives, to venture the same predictions, albeit with widely varying degrees of enthusiasm. Furthermore, this error in no way undermined the contributions which Fitzhugh made to the growth of proslavery sentiment, nor does it diminish his importance for the historian as a commentator upon the antebellum South.

Like many other southerners, Fitzhugh emphasized the superiority of slavery, for slaves, slaveholders and non-slaveholding whites alike. He devoted considerable attention to its impact upon the slave himself. Under free labor, he noted, the worker's income shrank as his needs expanded, for example, in the event of the birth of a child. But the enslaved worker experienced the opposite, since the master had an incentive to care for slave children. Indeed the contrast between the conditions of the wage laborer and the slave was stark. The slave enjoyed "a consciousness of security, a full comprehension of his position, and a confidence in that position," with the result that "the absence of all corroding cares and anxieties, makes the slave easy and self-assured in his address, cheerful, happy and contented, free from jealousy, malignity, and envy, and at peace with all around him." "The free laborer," on the other hand, "rarely has a house and home of his own; he is insecure of employment; sickness may overtake him at any time and deprive him of the means of support; old age is certain to overtake him, if he lives, and generally finds him without the means of subsistence; his family is probably increasing in numbers, and is helpless and burdensome to him." The consequence of "all this" was that "there is little to incite to virtue, much to tempt to crime, nothing to afford happiness, but quite enough to inflict misery." Fitzhugh concluded that "man must be more than human, to acquire a pure and a high morality under such circumstances." The conditions, both material and moral, of the slave were far superior to those of the wage laborer.[67]

Here Fitzhugh was serving up the standard fare of proslavery writing. But he went far beyond it when he considered the role of race in slavery and denied that racial inequality was a sufficient or even a necessary condition. Here his writings present exegetical problems. His meaning is not always as clear as one would wish, a weakness accentuated by his delight in paradox, the shifting meanings of some of his key terms, and a desire to startle his readers. On one occasion he actually declared that whites made the best slaves.[68] But by this he merely meant that they were the most easily civilized of peoples; in this context "slavery" was infinitely better than "freedom" since it entailed a wholly desirable subjection to

67. *Sociology for the South*, pp. 27–29, 37–38.
68. "Origin of Civilization – What is Property? – Which is the Best Slave Race," *De Bow's Review*, xxv (1858), pp. 653–664, esp. 654.

the essential restraints of civilization. Nevertheless, when he referred to "slavery", he usually had a different and more common meaning in mind. In *Sociology for the South* he announced that "we have introduced the subject of negro slavery to afford us a better opportunity to disclaim the purpose of reducing the white man any where to the condition of negro slaves here." This was, of course, the standard meaning of "slavery", as well as the standard emphasis upon racial differences.

These linguistic inconsistencies do not, however, prevent us from determining the precise role of race in Fitzhugh's thought. Indeed we obtain an important clue in his very next line: "it would be very unwise and unscientific to govern white men as you would negroes." Fitzhugh contended that in those countries where white slavery was needed (and the United States was not among them, at least not yet), a different form of slavery should be established. Whether this concession would have given solace to the working classes in Europe or not, the form of slavery Fitzhugh intended for them would be "much milder than negro slavery."[69]

His position was unusual and complex, but, if we make allowances for the shifting terminology, it was also coherent and consistent. He insisted that the defense of slavery must go beyond race. "We deem this peculiar question of negro slavery," he remarked, "of very little importance." For "the issue" must be "made throughout the world on the general subject of slavery in the abstract." The South was fortunate in having in its midst a race whose enslavement was always appropriate and whose presence removed the need for white slavery, but slavery itself did not require an inferior race. "Domestic slavery," he wrote in *De Bow's Review*, "must be vindicated in the abstract, and in the general, as a normal, natural, and, in general, necessitous element of civilized society, without regard to race or color."[70]

Fitzhugh now set about explaining how the alternative erroneous view had arisen. He acknowledged that "the temptation to confine the defence of slavery to mere negro slavery is very strong," since "it is obvious that they require masters under all circumstances, while the whites need them only under peculiar circumstances." Moreover "those circumstances" were "such as we can hardly realize the existence of in America." He expressed the hope that "the day" might "never arrive when our lands shall be so closely monopolized, and our population become so dense, that the poor would find slavery a happy refuge from the oppression of capital." Thus the unusual conditions prevailing in the United States, in

69. *Sociology for the South*, pp. 94–95.
70. *Sociology for the South*, p. 94; "Southern Thought," p. 347.

conjunction with the obvious inequality of the races, had operated so as to confuse southerners and northerners alike.[71]

Especially confused were the more orthodox defenders of southern slavery. Fitzhugh was at his most powerful not when analyzing free society, nor even when he was considering slave society, but instead when he was criticizing mainstream proslavery thinkers. With great incisiveness he pointed to the problems inherent in their racist defense of slavery. In the Bible, he reminded them, enslavement was not of blacks to whites. The same was true both of the great slave societies of Antiquity and of the various forms of unfree labor in the Christian era, at least until the settlement of the Americas. The consequences were extremely serious. Since "the Jewish slaves were not negroes," and since "we read of no negro slavery in ancient times," it must follow that "to confine the justification of slavery to that race would be to weaken its scriptural authority, and to lose the whole weight of profane authority." This seemed to Fitzhugh to provide ample justification for white slavery. It surely followed that "if white slavery be morally wrong, be a violation of natural rights, the Bible cannot be true." His principal goal was thus to establish that both experience and the Scriptures demonstrated that slavery was the normal condition and so-called free society the temporary aberration. But it was "white slavery, not black," which "has been the normal element of civilized society." Once again Fitzhugh acknowledged that in the South only black slavery was necessary. Indeed both Scriptures and experience, in approving white slavery, were "still stronger authorities in favor of negro slavery, for the principles and the practices of mankind in the general have been to make inferior races and individuals slaves to their superiors." But while the South was extremely "fortunate" in having "this inferior race, which enables her to make the whites a privileged class, and to exempt them from all servile, menial and debasing employments," it did not alter the fact that slavery must be defended without reference to race.[72]

From Fitzhugh's perspective the orthodox defense of slavery was little less than absurd. Those southerners who had defended black slavery while admitting its inapplicability to whites, he maintained, were guilty of the most spurious reasoning. "With singular inconsistency," he charged, "after making this admission, which admits away the authority of the Bible, of profane history, and of the almost universal practice of mankind – they turn round and attempt to bolster up the cause of negro slavery by these very exploded authorities." Once again it followed that "if we mean not to repudiate all divine, and almost all human authority

---

71. "Southern Thought," p. 348.
72. *Sociology for the South*, p. 98; *Cannibals All!*, p. 200; "Southern Thought," p. 338.

in favor of slavery, we must vindicate that institution in the abstract." Not to do so, to confine oneself instead to "the defence of mere negro slavery, will, nay, has involved us in a thousand absurdities and contradictions." Fitzhugh was unsparing in his criticism. "What a ridiculous and absurd figure," he declared, "does the defender of mere negro slavery cut, who uses this argument." The conclusion was a severe one: "he who justifies mere negro slavery, and condemns other forms of slavery does not think at all – no, not in the least."[73]

The final step in the argument was taken when he actually managed to criticize orthodox proslavery theorists not merely for exaggerating the importance of race but also for exaggerating racial inequality itself. At first glance it would seem that the inequalities between the races could never be too great for the purposes of the southern slaveholder but Fitzhugh argued otherwise. In a quite brilliant passage, though one in which his penchant for the startling overstatement was quite apparent, he argued that "the strongest argument against slavery, and all the prejudice against it, arise from the too great inferiority of race, which begets cruel and negligent treatment in the masters, who naturally feel little sympathy for ignorant, brutal savages." "Inferiority of race," he concluded, "is quite as good an argument against negro slavery as in its favor."[74]

Here he had encountered one problem in the standard justification of slavery. If they were to be considered so unequal as to be expelled from the human family, blacks would not be given the humane and considerate treatment to which they were entitled, and upon which many proslavery theorists also in part rested their defense. In other words there was a tension between paternalism and racism: if racism went too far, it would undermine the scope for paternalism. On these grounds, Fitzhugh rejected polygenesis (though he subsequently changed his mind on the question). "The argument about races," he observed in reference to the theories of Samuel Nott and his school, "is an infidel procedure." Not only did it challenge the Scriptures, it also tended to encourage maltreatment of the slaves by, once again, building up insuperable barriers between the races. If differences of race were elevated to the rank of differences of species, the danger to paternalist relations between master and slave was obvious. The extended family of the plantation could include different races; it was far from clear that it could include different species.[75]

73. *Cannibals All!*, p. 99; "Southern Thought," pp. 348, 339. See also Fitzhugh, "The Conservative Principle," *De Bow's Review*, XXII (1857), p. 423.
74. "Southern Thought Again," *De Bow's Review*, XXIII (1857), p. 451.
75. "Southern Thought," p. 347; *Sociology for the South*, pp. 95, 147. Later Fitzhugh reversed himself and embraced polygenesis wholeheartedly.

Fitzhugh's primary object was to demonstrate that slavery, or at least unfree labor, was the "natural" condition of human beings. The stakes were very high, for success would simultaneously strengthen southern resolve and disable northern opposition. His goal was not to ignore race but to transcend it, to bring southern society with its slaveholding base into the mainstream of human history by associating it with exclusively white societies in other eras. Success would have clothed the South with the mantle of legitimacy. Fitzhugh knew all of this. He set out the ideological agenda for the planters on the eve of the Civil War:

> We must take high philosophical, biblical, and historical grounds, and soar beyond the little time and space around us to the earliest records of time, and the farthest verge of civilization. Let us quit the narrow boundaries of the rice, the sugar and the cotton field, and invite the abolitionists to accompany us in our flight to the tent of Abraham, to the fields of Judea, to the halls of David and of Solomon, to the palaces and the farms of Athens and of Rome, and to the castles of the grim Barons of medieval time. Let us point to their daily routine of domestic life. Then, not till then, may we triumphantly defend negro slavery.[76]

IV

Though he did not put it in these terms, what Fitzhugh was groping towards was a defense of slavery that rested unambiguously upon class. Men were sufficiently different to justify an explicitly inegalitarian social order, one that removed from the less talented the need to compete with their superiors. Under normal conditions, free labor (which meant wage labor) did not qualify, hence forms of unfree labor, and especially slavery, were indispensable. Whether in Fitzhugh's desired form of slavery, opportunities for movement out of (or into) slavery existed, he did not say. In any event, humanity was divided into two classes: those who had the right to be masters and those who had the right to be slaves. "Men are not," as he put it, "born entitled to equal rights!" Indeed "it would be far nearer the truth to say, 'that some were born with saddles on their backs, and others booted and spurred to ride them,' – and the riding does them good." He added that "they need the reins, the bit and the spur."

This graphic statement, typifying the Fitzhughian desire to startle, was highly misleading in that he expected slavery to be paternalistic and benign, not harsh and punitive. But it did convey the inegalitarian

76. "Southern Thought," p. 348.

convictions that suffused his thinking. Men were divided by nature into classes. When these divinely ordained class distinctions corresponded to differences of race, so much the better, but such a correspondence was merely fortuitous. Slavery was a system that rested upon innate differences, differences which necessarily and properly placed men into distinct relationships with their fellow men and with the material world.[77]

It is thus easy to see how Fitzhugh's views have been attractive to a Marxist scholar like Eugene Genovese. While taking pains to repudiate the social purpose to which his writings were put, Genovese has found much to applaud in them. First, though least important, the attacks on the bourgeoisies of the North and of Europe were, as we have seen, similar in certain respects to the socialist indictment of capitalism, both then and now. Second, Fitzhugh's critique of capitalism itself accords with the Marxist characterization of slavery as a non-capitalist form. His writings give valuable support to the view of slavery as pre-capitalist, especially when he combated, and vanquished, those southern apologists who in effect maintained the contrary. Third, and for present purposes most important, Fitzhugh's insistence on the primacy of class and his depreciation of the role of race find a warm response among those historians who make the same claim. Let us consider this in more detail.[78]

Genovese argues that Fitzhugh's ideas represent "the logical outcome of the slaveholders' philosophy." He contends that in Fitzhugh's work one can trace a shift in the proslavery argument "from a focus on racial caste to a focus on social class." More than anyone else, Fitzhugh exposed the assumptions which the masters held, stripped away many of the contradictions and hesitations in their thought and "in so doing, . . . took a major step toward the formation of a coherent slaveholders' world view." Genovese argues that Fitzhugh's "primary task" was of overwhelming importance: it was "to reshape the South in the image of the best of its ruling class." However untypical his views may have been, his thought thus occupies "a central place in the development of the ideology of the master class." Since he "loomed large in the story of . . . developing class consciousness," he deserves to be seen as a "central figure" in the history of the Old South.[79]

Just as Genovese finds much to applaud in Fitzhugh's analysis of the South, so we can find much to applaud in Genovese's analysis of Fitzhugh. Historians too easily forget that an atypical thinker or theorist can still play a crucial role in demonstrating the tensions, contradictions, or hidden assumptions in the thinking of his contemporaries. Genovese

77. *Sociology for the South*, p. 179.
78. Genovese, *World the Slaveholders Made*, *passim*.
79. Genovese, *World the Slaveholders Made*, pp. 118, 129, 189.

reminds us of this fact. Moreover, it is to Genovese that much of the credit belongs for the resuscitation not merely of Fitzhugh but of proslavery thought as a whole. Nevertheless, there is reason to doubt his principal conclusions.

Some of the claims which Genovese makes for Fitzhugh are, at least in part, undermined by the concessions which he (Genovese) himself makes. First, he argues that Fitzhugh, aware that slavery and capitalism were in the final analysis irreconcilable, called for the South to abandon "free trade," and, moreover, in so doing, "to insulate itself from the world market, to strive toward autarky, and ultimately to help overthrow the capitalist system everywhere." Yet Genovese also acknowledges that Fitzhugh was unable to turn his back upon, or repudiate, the enormous material gains which capitalism had made possible. Here Genovese is undoubtedly correct. Indeed the dilemma is even more apparent than he acknowledges, when we compare the passages in which autarky is recommended with those like the following:

> It is important that we should write our own books. It matters little who makes our shoes. Indeed, the South will commit a fatal blunder, if, in its haste to become nominally independent, it loses its present engines of power, and thereby ceases to be really independent. Cotton is king; and rice, sugar, Indian corn, wheat, and tobacco, are his chief ministers.

> We should not jeopard this great lever of power in the haste to become, like Englishmen, shop-keepers, cobblers, and common carriers for the universe. Our present pursuits are more honorable, more lucrative, and more generative of power and independence than those we fondly aspire to. We cannot do double work. If we become a commercial and manufacturing people, we must cease to be an agricultural one, or at least we shall cease to have an agricultural surplus. We should become as feeble, as isolated and contemptible as Chinese or Japanese. Actual independence would be bartered off for formal independence, which no one would respect.

One can, of course, agree with Genovese, that Fitzhugh was in a difficult position. But the point is that Fitzhugh merely registered the problem; he could not resolve it. Thus Genovese goes too far when he claims that Fitzhugh alone "saw the last step in the [proslavery] argument, which was that slavery could not survive without the utter destruction of capitalism as a world system." Fitzhugh's message was far more tentative and contradictory than this.[80]

---

80. Genovese, *World the Slaveholders Made*, p. 166; "Southern Thought," p. 341; Genovese, *World the Slaveholders Made*, p. 131, see also pp. 157, 173–174.

More important, however, are Fitzhugh's remarks on the relative importance of race and class. As we have seen, Genovese applauds these observations on the grounds that they show Fitzhugh's grasp of the problems confronting the Old South. In making them, Genovese argues, Fitzhugh was leading the planter class towards a deeper understanding of its own tasks, its own role, its own responsibilities. This, I shall argue, is only partly true and in any case highly misleading. The problem concerns our understanding of "class." For some Marxist historians, class requires class consciousness. It is not entirely clear whether Genovese endorses this view or not. What does seem clear is that he assumes, in this case at least, a fairly unproblematic relationship between reality and perception. Fitzhugh, having perceived the central role of class, offers a more truthful and accurate picture of slavery to the slaveholders. The gifted observer thus penetrates to the essence of the problem.[81]

The alternative view proposed here maintains instead that class conflict in the South between master and slave operated in such a way as to conceal itself from the master class. We know from the studies of slavery that have been carried out in the last twenty or thirty years – not least by Genovese himself – that the slaves did not wish to be slaves. Their disaffection took many forms, from feigning illness or incompetence, to flight, to rebellion. All these forms of resistance, insofar as they stemmed from a dislike of slavery, constitute in the most literal sense, class conflict: they are the product of antagonisms generated by one class's attempt to exploit another. The severity of this conflict, in its multiple forms, constitutes the first weakness of slavery.

Yet especially after the northern attack on slavery had gathered momentum, the masters had to decide whether or not they believed slavery beneficial to the slaves. As we have seen, for a variety of reasons they concluded that it was. To have done otherwise would have been a major defeat. It consequently became impossible for them to understand the nature of the conflict surrounding them. The second weakness, in short, was the inability to perceive the first.

Nevertheless they saw its effects. Disobedience, laziness, flight, rebellion – all these phenomena had to be explained. The abolitionist was, of course, an excellent scapegoat and there is no doubt that southerners were quite sincere when they attributed slave misconduct to his influence.

---

81. Genovese, *World the Slaveholders Made*, p. 237. Genovese also argues, however, that "the necessity to defend simultaneously a system of class rule and one of caste privilege created enormous difficulties, which could only be hidden so long as no attempt was made to bring rigor to the ideological defense of either." With this I wholeheartedly agree. I am not convinced, however, that Genovese has satisfactorily elucidated the problem.

But the other – complementary rather than competing – explanation was found in racism. Blacks responded to abolitionist propaganda, it was held, because they were genetically incapable of seeing its nefarious intent. Slaves worked slowly and badly because they were black; blacks were congenitally lacking in the necessary self-discipline to work properly. Some slaveholders even argued that sullen apathy on the part of their slaves, which in reality often indicated a profound discontent with slavery coupled with a realization that rebellion was hopeless, was proof that, unlike white men, they were simply unfit for liberty and did not even aspire to it. The roots of racism are many and complex but one cause was the need to explain resistance on the part of the slaves to their enslavement. The true reasons for resistance could not be, and were not, acknowledged.

Other forces intensified racism in the South. The terrifying possibility of an alliance between the slaves and the non-slaveholding whites gave a further incentive to the masters to emphasize race. They needed to forge bonds with the non-slaveholders. Of course the fatal alliance never materialized and was never even close to materializing; the non-slaveholders responded warmly to the racist appeal. But if the slaves had welcomed slavery in the way that proslavery ideologues claimed, the relations between slave and poor white would have been of little consequence to the master. Once again, therefore, class conflict generated racism.

We are now in a position to appreciate Fitzhugh's contribution. It arose from a profound paradox in his thought. Even as he moved towards a defense of slavery based upon class, he, more than any other southern ideologue, denied the conflict between classes which in fact suffused all slave societies. Let us recall his description of the slave's condition. "A consciousness of security," he wrote, "a full comprehension of his position, and a confidence in that position, and the absence of all corroding cares and anxieties, makes the slave easy and self-assured in his address, cheerful, happy and contented, free from jealousy, malignity, and envy, and at peace with all around him." He even argued that the Young England movement sought to produce the sympathy between rich and poor which slavery alone could effect.

Other southerners might have made similar claims but they differed from him in attending to the consequences of the conflict between master and slave, even if they refused to grant or could not see that it was in any way endemic in the regime. Racism was their rationalization for class conflict, the intellectual category that expanded in order to explain what was otherwise inexplicable. In some quarters fears for the at least potential instability of the master–slave relationship found expression in a reluctance to opt for industrialization and urbanization. James Hammond, for example, as we have seen, had a healthy fear of the effect of factory work upon the slave. But Fitzhugh failed utterly to see such dangers. Hence he opened fire upon the agrarianism which was one mechanism operating to control the slaves. "Farming," he informed his readers, "is the recreation of great men, the proper pursuit of dull men." He added that he was "very sure" that "the wit of man can devise no means so effectual to impoverish a country as exclusive agriculture." From a narrowly economic point of view, he may have been correct. But here, as elsewhere, he utterly failed to confront the arguments of those who feared for the stability of the master–slave relation.[82]

Similarly, he entirely ignored the problems in the relationship between the slaveholders and the non-slaveholding whites. Many southerners feared that to build up a white working class in the cities would be to court disaster, but Fitzhugh ignored these problems. His faith in slavery knew no bounds. On one occasion (though it must be said he was not consistent here) he actually dismissed abolitionism as "a harmless humbug," far less to be feared than negrophobia! Fitzhugh was a great admirer of Don Quixote but he had acquired more of the eponymous hero's characteristics than he knew. In an appendix to *Sociology for the South* he recounted the following incident

> We tried to persuade, some days since, a young negro man, who, with his young wife, were desperately poor, that he would be better off as a slave, as he might expect soon to have a large family to support, and could now scarce support himself. He quaintly replied, "that he then would hire out his children and live easy."

He took this reply to be proof of the free black's innate propensity to vice. This was Fitzhugh at his most foolish. Other southerners knew that one could not hope to convince free men to become slaves. Fitzhugh did not. The slavery he championed had never existed and would never exist. It was a utopian dream.[83]

This utopian tendency was his strength as well as his weakness. It allowed him to perceive the flaws in the racist defense of slavery. Ironically, his denial of conflict between classes enabled him to emphasize class where other southerners were driven to stress race. But contrary to Genovese's claims, this did not make him a satisfactory spokesman for the class interests of the slaveholders. He was far too reckless to be given this role. Just as no self-respecting bourgeoisie entrusts its destiny to those who see not the slightest danger in the relationship between capital and labor, so Fitzhugh could never be allowed to speak for the master class, still less an "advanced fraction" of it. Thus Genovese errs when he argues

82. *Sociology for the South*, pp. 37, 43, 156, 15.
83. *Sociology for the South*, pp. 147, 274.

that Fitzhugh "more than any other man saw the direction in which his world was moving and perceived what was needed to bring it safely to its destination." This, we might suggest, is precisely what he did not perceive. Nor was his "greatest achievement . . . to bring order to the incoherent philosophy of the slaveholding class." Fitzhugh's thought is indeed important but it is important because it illustrates the intractable problems inherent in the defense of slavery, not because it provided viable solutions to those problems.[84]

Orthodox proslavery thinkers saw, if not the conflicts within slavery, then at least their effects, but were compelled to deny their class nature. Fitzhugh, by contrast, saw the class nature of the regime and wished to reshape the world view of the planters accordingly. But he could do so only because he was utterly blind to the conflict inherent in the class relationships he identified. Racism may well have been an unsatisfactory defense for slavery in the South. Fitzhugh saw the problems but could resolve them only by positing a conflictless slavery, a veritable utopia of unfreedom.

V

Before leaving Fitzhugh, it is important to consider another of Genovese's claims. On one occasion he asserts that "the equation of slavery and white supremacy was a fraud," since racism could not provide an adequate foundation for a proslavery position. It is not entirely clear what "fraud" means here. If the term is to be interpreted literally it implies dishonest deception, insincerity, faithlessness. It is possible, though extremely unlikely, that Genovese means to suggest that the slaveholders employed racist appeals hypocritically, in order to reach out for nonslaveholder support. There is, of course, not the slightest evidence for such a claim. It is far more likely that he is instead implying that racism was functional for slavery in the South, that it helped the planters to create and maintain their hegemony, and that once enunciated, racist utterances convinced masters and poor whites alike. This far more sophisticated position is much more tenable.[85]

It is, however, still highly problematic. An important theoretical issue is involved here. Following Gramsci, Genovese attaches great importance to "hegemony" and the process by which a ruling class achieves social and political leadership. (Indeed more than any other historian in the English-speaking world, he can claim the credit for having introduced Gramsci

---

84. Genovese, *World the Slaveholders Made*, pp. 131, 151.
85. Genovese, *World the Slaveholders Made*, p. 238.

and "hegemony" to historians.) For Gramsci hegemony was established not merely by a dominant class persuading another of the propriety of its rule. Instead, as he himself put it, "undoubtedly the fact of hegemony presupposes that account be taken of the interests and the tendencies of the groups over which hegemony is to be exercised, and that a certain compromise equilibrium be formed – in other words, that the leading group should make sacrifices of an economic-corporate kind."[86] One would like to ask Genovese precisely what he believes the role of racism to have been in establishing the hegemony of the slaveholders. Is it a concession to the non-slaveholders? Is it a "fraud" perpetrated on them in order to secure their loyalty to the regime? If so, in what sense does Fitzhugh, who shifts the emphasis away from race and onto class, and whom Genovese hails as a key spokesman of the master class, contribute to its hegemonic rule? Genovese's position is far from clear.

The alternative view proposed here is as follows. The first and most important function of racism was to assist in explaining to the masters themselves the world in which they lived. Racism allowed them simultaneously to deny that slaves naturally resisted their enslavement and to take all necessary steps to check that resistance. Both the denial and the preventative action were essential to maintain their class rule. Hence racism was vital not merely to secure the loyalty of the non-slaveholders, but to ensure the masters' will and ability to exploit their slaves and thus to survive as a class. In comparison with this, all other questions were unimportant, even those concerning relations with the non-slaveholders. While misperceptions are involved here, there is no trace of "fraud."

Once again therefore, as in the case of equality under capitalism, a misperception was functionally necessary. The failure to perceive black resistance and the tendency to ascribe it to racial failings, were both serious errors but also necessary ones, given that the masters both needed to explain its effects and deny its true causes. There are two conclusions, one specific the other more general. The specific one relates to Fitzhugh, whose example suggests that the inadequacy of the solution could be exposed but only by one who ignored the problem and thus felt no need to provide an alternative solution. Thus his thought does more than point towards the tensions in the thinking of his contemporaries; it suggests that the problem they identified but which he ignored, in truth had no viable solution. His writings thus underline the weaknesses of slavery.

---

86. Antonio Gramsci, *Selections from the Prison Notebooks* (ed. Q. Hoare and G. Nowell-Smith, London, 1971), p. 161 quoted in Nicholas Abercrombie, *Class, Structure, and Knowledge: Problems in the Sociology of Knowledge* (Oxford, 1980), pp. 115–116.

The more general conclusion is that a ruling class, despite its superior power and even its ideological leadership, its hegemony, is unable to guarantee a complete "fit" between its interests and the belief system or ideology which it seeks to propagate. Whatever its impact upon others, such a class is itself, to some extent, the victim of the flaws contained within that ideology.[87]

The southern economy

I

If southerners were to mount an effective defense of slavery, they had to be sure of the claims they were making for the peculiar institution and for the social structure of which it was part. Without a clear understanding of its strengths and weaknesses they could not be sure how to marshal their defense, how to mount a counterattack upon the North, how to explain their society not only to the world at large but, even more important, to themselves. In this context some fundamental economic questions emerged. Unfortunately for the South they admitted of no easy answers.

The two principal questions which came to dominate southern thought upon the economy concerned productivity and development. How productive was slavery compared with a system based upon free labor? Along what path should it develop in the future? These questions were, of course, linked but for convenience they can be separated. Each was vital to the South, to the proslavery argument and to the defense of slavery. Yet each brought problems that proved irresolvable.

II

When a defender of slavery asked whether his cherished system was more or less productive than one based upon free labor, he had, in theory at any rate, a number of possible answers available. One was simply to concede that slavery was less productive and, as a result, less profitable. As we shall see, those who made this concession were then obliged to find powerful alternative benefits to compensate for this huge liability. A second response was to claim that the two systems were the same, or rather that the differences between them somehow cancelled out so that neither could be said to have an advantage. Admirably even-handed, this

---

87. It is perhaps unnecessary to add that I do not here intend to endorse a pluralist position (in which the dispersal of power and influence among different groups is thought to safeguard liberty and justice), still less to deny that other groups are more disadvantaged.

approach was for that very reason unsuited to the political climate of the late 1840s and 1850s. Moreover it posed very considerable problems. No southern writer even attempted to show how slavery came to be the precise equivalent of free labor, let alone succeeded in the task. We need not therefore consider this possibility further.

A third option was to insist that slavery was at least as profitable as free labor in certain circumstances and given certain conditions. Many southerners developed this argument but as we shall see it conflicted at certain points with other requirements that the proslavery theorist had to meet. A fourth response was to claim that slavery was in fact more productive potentially but to recognize or protest that special factors had prevented this potential from being realized. This too was a popular option, especially since exploitative federal legislation inspired by the North was so easily adduced as the special factor. But if this response was congenial to southern militants in the late antebellum years, it too, as we shall see, brought problems in its wake. Finally a fifth response consisted of the claim that slavery was unambiguously and unreservedly superior in economic terms to free labor. In a way the most "proslavery" of all these proslavery stances, this one was, as we shall also see, no less problematic as a strategy.

For about a quarter of a century before 1850 there had been a consensus that the North was more prosperous than the South. This did not mean, however, that southerners conceded the inferiority of slave labor. Men like John C. Calhoun discoursed interminably on northern privations against the South but rarely assessed the productivity of slave as opposed to free labor. In the late 1840s and 1850s, however, the economic indictment of slavery began to assume greater prominence (though as we have seen it had always been present in abolitionist thinking). With the battle for the territories economic questions began to assume a new urgency and southerners were not slow to sense it. However, it was not always easy for them to do battle with abolitionists and free-soilers at the same time. Arguments effective against the former were often disastrous against the latter.

Thus Albert Bledsoe took issue with the many northerners who insisted on comparing pairs of northern and southern states, always of course to the detriment of the South. Bledsoe argued that whether Kentucky and Virginia, for example, had fallen behind Ohio and Pennsylvania was irrelevant, even if the case could be proven and the responsibility fixed upon slavery. Instead the appropriate comparison was between southern states with slaves and those same southern states with millions of freed blacks. The evidence from the West Indies, he claimed, showed the disastrous effect of emancipation upon production. Then, apparently unmindful of the debate over the territories, he added that "if the question were, whether slavery should be introduced among us, or into any non-slaveholding State, then such facts and explanations [provided by the abolitionists] would be worthy of our notice." Yet Bledsoe's book appeared in 1856, the very time when the conflict over Kansas was at its peak and posing precisely the "question" to which he referred. He thus conceded the relevance and legitimacy of much of the free soil position.

This was a huge concession. The central issue of the 1850s was the fate of the territories and a crucial question was whether the establishment of slavery in the new West would hinder or facilitate economic growth there. Moreover, most southerners insisted that free soil and abolition were in effect one and the same, each aiming at the same result even if by different processes and according to different timetables. By this logic, defeat on the territorial question spelt abolition and thus total ruin. As he sought to vanquish the immediatists, Bledsoe capitulated before the free-soilers and thus cleared the way for an alternative route to a more gradual abolition.[88]

Other southerners were also prepared to concede defeat on the economic question. Among them was George Fitzhugh. Even though he did not discuss the question directly, Fitzhugh noted that "slaves work so little that, if the laborers of England were slaves, we fear that the products of their labor would not suffice to support half the present population," thus implying that slavery was in general less productive than free labor. Such a view was of course entirely compatible with his insistence that the lot of the slave was preferable to that of the wage laborer. Fitzhugh, however, was not a typical defender of slavery. Far closer to the southern political mainstream were Jefferson Davis who admitted that "slave labor is a wasteful labor," or Edward Shepard of North Carolina who acknowledged that "slave cultivation is an exhausting and impoverishing one to the soil," that "this must always necessarily be more or less the case," and that except on the best lands "his labor is not remunerative."

More explicitly and at greater length, James Henry Hammond of South Carolina compared free and slave labor and concluded that "as a general rule, . . . it must be admitted, that free labor is cheaper than slave labor." Like Fitzhugh, Hammond emphasized the impact which population density had upon the wage level. With a dense population, competition for jobs would reduce wages to the subsistence level whereas the slave, meanwhile, would remain well fed, well housed, well cared for. Hammond insisted that the employer's costs were much lower than those of the slaveholder and even offered to free his slaves if he could obtain free labor at this cheap rate (and provided he could dispose humanely of

88. Albert T. Bledsoe, *An Essay on Liberty and Slavery* (Phil., 1856), p. 228. Bledsoe was a Professor of Mathematics in the University of Virginia.

his former slaves). He thus conceded that slavery generated lower profits than free labor. Yet once again this position was not only compatible with, but actually strengthened, the other standard proslavery claim: that slavery benefited the slave. As Hammond put it, southerners have "the consoling reflection that what is lost us, is gain to humanity; and that inasmuch as our slave costs us more than your free man costs you, by so much is he better off." In order to develop the argument that slavery benefited the slave, Hammond, like Fitzhugh and in common with many other southerners, gave ground on the economic question.[89]

The chief source for southern thought on economic questions, however, was not the writings or speeches of prominent politicians but instead the pages of *De Bow's Review*. For the decade and a half preceding the outbreak of hostilities at Fort Sumter, J. G. B. De Bow's *Review* kept up a constant stream of commentaries, by prominent southerners in all walks of life, upon all matters of concern to the South. Inevitably the *Review* concerned itself increasingly with political questions, even though such had not been the founder's original intention. But its prime interest was economics. Despite the talents of its editor and founder, however, no consistent line was taken. On the eve of the Civil War one contributor, writing on "Plantation Life – Duties and Responsibilities," acknowledged that slavery might be less profitable than free labor. "Let it be so," he conceded, "as some political theorists have boasted, that slave labor is not as profitable as free labor."

This admission was perhaps surprising in that some years earlier De Bow himself had taken strong exception to a similar concession made in the *Southern Quarterly Review*. In 1856 a writer in that journal had argued that questions of political economy should not be given a high priority by defenders of slavery. If economics showed the superiority of free labor then the South should not lose heart but should instead rest her defense elsewhere. In his own journal De Bow condemned this reasoning in the strongest terms. "For ourselves," he began, "it is sheer madness to throw away our armor at the very moment when we should be girding it on to the defence." Indeed, he continued, "this is precisely what our antagonists would desire, and already we can imagine those of them who may have noticed our review triumphantly chuckling over an opponent who just as the fight thickens offers them so palpable an advantage." De Bow recognized that the concession was too great. It amounted to "the absolute hoisting of a signal to the enemy," and the result would be that "every gun will be pointed at the wavering ranks." He implied that if slavery were inferior in economic terms, then southerners themselves

---

89. *De Bow's Review*, xxx (1861), p. 403; *Mississippian*, May 17, 1850; Raleigh *Standard*, Dec. 14, 1850; Hammond, *Letters on Southern Slavery*, pp. 10–11.

could be targets for northern propaganda. For "a master's interest must be in his slave – must be identified with the comfort of the slave." De Bow recognized a crucial dilemma. While Hammond and others were prepared to claim that the slaveholder in effect sacrificed his own interest to secure that of the slave, De Bow instead insisted that slaveholders could not, and should not, be expected to show such altruism. Slavery must promote the interest of both; more precisely, it must be the master's interest to promote the interest of the slave. "It must be more profitable to him to have healthy and happy slaves than sick and wretched ones," he observed. "It must be more profitable," he continued, "to him that they should live than that they should die; and this can only be, so long as the slave's labor is more profitable to him than any other which he can attain." Thus De Bow argued strongly that even from basic motives of self-interest southerners could not afford to concede the economic inferiority of slavery.[90]

He was not the only southerner to see how high the stakes were. The *Augusta Chronicle* in 1851 declared that "slaveholders must demonstrate in a large way, and by visible results, that slave labor in Georgia, is as profitable to you and as useful to the world, as free labor is at the North or can be at the South." This meant showing that it was "not inimical to common schools, the improvement of the soil and the progress of manufactures." Like De Bow the editor believed that "our sectional movements are taken for weakness in this regard" and even added that the entire controversy between North and South "will turn in the end on the pivot of dollars and cents." Southerners could only "prove our view by attaining prosperity."[91]

Some southerners who conceded the economic superiority of free labor nevertheless insisted that it was an illusory superiority. If the North were on the road to social revolution, caused by the growing antagonism of labor and capital, and if this were to be followed by economic breakdown, then in the long term slavery might still prove more productive. As we have seen, this was Fitzhugh's view. But as we have also seen, Fitzhugh found it extremely difficult to predict the timing of the northern apocalypse and on some occasions at least, implied that it was many decades away. The Panic of 1857 raised southern hopes, since it hit certain parts of the North with greater severity than the South, and by the same token the labor unrest of the 1850s gave southerners considerable satisfaction. But neither the northern economic downturn nor the

90. *De Bow's Review*, xxix (1860), pp. 357–368, esp. 361, xxi (1856), pp. 331–349, esp. 337, xxi (1856), pp. 443–467 esp. 453–454.
91. Augusta *Chronicle*, quoted in Robert H. Shryock, *Georgia and the Union in 1850* (Phil., 1926), pp. 34–35.

disputes in which some of its workforce engaged were on anything like the scale needed. The problem for southerners was that to stake all on an explosion in the North was hazardous; each year without one widened the gap between the sections and risked the creation of further doubts in the minds of their own supporters.

The first answer to the question of slave productivity was thus fraught with difficulty. To concede that slavery was less productive was to hand northern antislavery forces a formidable weapon. At a time when both North and South were in competition for the territories of the West, the dangers were acute. Of course it was possible for southerners to concede the overall inferiority of slavery while claiming that for a large portion of the population the economic benefits were in fact greater than those obtained by the beneficiaries of a free labor system. The obvious claim to make was that southern whites were better off than northern whites. But on this reasoning it followed that black slaves were, by a larger margin, worse off and this contradicted the proslavery argument at its heart. Southerners had to argue that wage workers were the most deprived group in the North but if slaves were far worse off than even these workers, it followed that there was far more deprivation, not to mention oppression, in the South than in the North. According to this logic, wage labor was less oppressive than slave labor, the United States would be a more equitable nation if slavery did not exist, and slavery was once again merely a "necessary evil."

III

An alternative answer to the riddle of southern productivity was provided by those southerners who argued that given certain special conditions slavery could at least equal, and perhaps even outperform, free labor. Among these conditions by far the most important were those relating to climate. Slave labor, it was claimed, performed by black men and women, could match or better free white labor if both had to work in the inhospitable climate of the South, and especially the deep South. Theodore Clapp, Leander Ker, Mathew Estes, James McDowell and James Henry Hammond all argued along these lines.

Hammond, for example, asserted that "in their appropriate sphere," and engaged upon "the cultivation of our great staples, under a hot sun and arid miasma, that prostrates the white man, our negro slaves admit of no substitute, and may defy all competition."[92] We have already seen,

92. Theodore Clapp, *Slavery: A Sermon Delivered in the First Congregational Church in New Orleans, April 15, 1838* (New Orleans, 1838), p. 5; Ker, *Slavery Consistent With Christianity*, p. 12; James McDowell, *A Lecture, by the Late Hon. James McDowell . . .* (Phil., 1851), p. 25; Estes, *Defence of Negro Slavery*, p. 154;

of course, that Hammond conceded the overall economic inferiority of slave labor and we should acknowledge that his claims for slave labor in a sub-tropical climate did not conflict with that assessment. For Hammond, like other southerners who made this claim, did not suggest that in a hot climate slaves were more productive than whites in a more temperate zone. The claim was a much more modest one: in unsuitable conditions for whites, black slaves might work better. One writer in *De Bow's Review* boasted that slave labor had "explored regions under whose miasmatic influences the white man sickened and died," while another explained that white men could not, owing to the climate, cultivate cotton, rice or sugar. This argument, of course, accorded nicely with the standard proslavery emphasis on race: racial differences made slave labor preferable in hot climates. Also writing in *De Bow's Review*, an "Alabama Planter" even went so far as to estimate that in such a climate twenty negroes would do as much hard labor on, for example, the railroads, as thirty whites.[93]

Yet at this point the proslavery theorist began to encounter problems. The argument derived from climate was too crude to meet his needs. In the first place, to restrict slavery to intemperate climates was to abandon much of the West to the North especially if, as some of these writers asserted, the negro was ill-suited to more temperate zones. This signaled a retreat from the high ground which many southerners believed it essential to occupy. Slavery was not the norm for society, as Fitzhugh among others insisted, merely an expedient in bad weather. Second, and more important, non-slaveholding whites, to say nothing of some small slaveholders, worked throughout the South on the same fields, in the same industries, and under the same hot sun as the slaves. The distribution of slaves, in short, did not reflect differences of climate to anything like the required degree.

This problem was recognized by Dr Samuel Cartwright of New Orleans, a physician who had achieved some fame as an authority on ethnology. Cartwright argued strongly in favor of polygenesis and thus was naturally attracted to arguments emphasizing racial differences. In an article published in *De Bow's Review* and entitled "How to Save the Republic, and the Position of the South in the Union," he argued that natural laws would confine slavery to areas where the climate made negro labor "more efficient, cheaper, and more to be relied on than white labor." He then raised a key issue. "The question is," he asked, "shall the white man bring disease and death upon himself by performing

"Governor Hammond's Address before the South Carolina Institute," *De Bow's Review*, VIII (1850), pp. 501–522, esp. 518.

93. *De Bow's Review*, XXI (1856), p. 455, XX (1856), p. 661, XIX (1855), p. 729.

drudgery work in the sun, or make the negroes do the work – the sun, which sickens and kills him, being a luxury to them?" The correct arrangement, he insisted, would place the white slaveholder "in the shade, laboring and managing for their benefit as well as his own," and put the black slaves "in the sun, working for the benefit of the common household."

At this point Cartwright, like many other writers appeared to have forgotten the non-slaveholding whites of the South. In fact, however, he was fully mindful of them and thus condemned explicitly what would otherwise have merely been criticized implicitly. Looking carefully at the existing work practices of many non-slaveholding whites, he made it clear that he did not like what he saw. "Here, in New Orleans," he complained, "the larger part of the drudgery-work requiring exposure to the sun, as rail-road making, street-paving, dray-driving, ditching, building, etc., is performed by white people." In accordance with his theories about race, Cartwright stressed the effects of this labor, which he believed brought "sickness and mortality" on a large scale, upon whites. Even more interesting, however, was his reference to these workers as a "class of persons who make negroes of themselves in this hot climate." He went so far as to conclude that the high mortality rate in the city of New Orleans was "mainly owing to a large class of persons in this city violating nature's laws by making negroes of themselves." We should remember that this charge was extraordinarily insulting in the South. Cartwright pressed his racist assumptions to their logical conclusion. He realized that the distribution of labor in the South was, according to the principles of the confirmed racist, profoundly unsatisfactory but as he sought to correct the problem he was driven to insult, and challenge the livelihood of, tens of thousands of non-slaveholders, whose race pride most proslavery theorists took the utmost pains to flatter and upon whose loyalty the slaveholding regime ultimately depended.[94]

IV

If the emphasis on climatic differences was as unsatisfactory as the concession of southern economic inferiority, other options were still available. A popular strategy was to claim that slavery was in fact more productive than free labor and would be seen by all to be so, except when extraneous factors intruded. Southerners who pursued this argument found two sets of impediments preventing the realization of southern economic potential. One set were internal to the South and we shall

94. *De Bow's Review*, XI (1851), pp. 184–197, esp. 195.

consider these when we examine the debate about southern development. The other set, however, were external. Northerners, it was claimed, had succeeded in seizing control of the federal government and using its powers to transfer the wealth of the South to the North, thus concealing the inferiority of their own system.

This argument was extremely attractive to southerners, from the time of John C. Calhoun onwards. As late as 1860 it was the theme of two lengthy treatises, one by Thomas Prentice Kettell, a former editor of the *Democratic Review*, entitled *Southern Wealth and Northern Profits*, and one by John Townsend entitled *The South Alone Should Govern the South*. Northerners welcomed accretions in federal power because they allowed them to exploit the South:

> How enormous have been the pecuniary advantages, which the North has extracted from the South, by the Union. No wonder then that they should threaten us with fire and sword, if we attempt to leave them . . . . Hundreds of millions of dollars taken from the agricultural industry of the South, and transferred as a tribute through the oppression of unjust laws, to the industry of the North! Is any one surprised, that the South thus robbed, is left poor; while the North, the robber, overflows with wealth, and "strengthened himself in his wickedness." Thousands of millions, – the lawful earnings of the South, added, during the progress of the Government, to Northern accumulation!

The result, according to Townsend, was that "the North . . . overflow[s] with capital, to enable her to undertake any, the most gigantic schemes of public improvement, or private enterprise" while the South, "thus stripped bare of her profits, and left destitute of capital, is unable to build a ship to establish Direct Trade, or to start one enterprise of Domestic manufactures." The conclusion was of course, a simple one. Secession would allow slavery and the southern economy to flourish and southerners would then enjoy unrivalled prosperity.[95]

But this argument was highly problematic. To begin with, it was doubtful whether the actions of the federal government could really be construed in this light, especially after the Walker tariff of 1846. In the 1820s and early 1830s the tariff had indeed been of great concern, and the Whig tariff of 1842 also provoked considerable resentment in the South. But the Polk administration responded to this resentment and most southerners were pleased with the Walker tariff of 1846. Indeed for the next

---

95. Thomas Prentice Kettell, *Southern Wealth and Northern Profits, As Exhibited in Statistical Facts and Official Figures* (N.Y., 1860), pp. 146, 161–163; John Townsend, *The South Alone Should Govern the South* . . . (Charleston, 1860), p. 62.

fifteen years opposition to it was mainly from northerners who wanted higher duties. In reality, however, the tariff had ceased to be a major issue, as northerners recognized that their prosperity did not seem to be dependent upon the protective principle. Outside of South Carolina, there were few southerners who complained about high tariffs after 1846. Similarly with internal improvements. Clay's American system, which had called for an entire network of federally funded improvements, was dead by the late 1840s. Polk and his Democratic successors in the 1850s were not advocates of federal improvements, to the chagrin of many northerners. This issue too ceased to be of great importance, partly because the individual states expanded their operations so that the role of the federal government became far less critical. Finally the federal banking system was even less suitable as a target of southern hostility. The Whig attempts to recharter a bank in the early 1840s had failed and the Polk administration successfully reintroduced the Independent Treasury. Thus there was not a single federally chartered bank between 1836 and the Civil War (except of course the purely local ones in the District of Columbia). Contemporaries recognized the passing of these issues. By 1852 at the latest, there was little to choose between the parties on economic matters and few southerners were able to make capital out of attacks on federal economic policy. Indeed the general consensus North as well as South was that the federal government under Democratic leadership was unusually sensitive to the needs of the South when determining its economic policy.[96]

Moreover, many dedicated exponents of the proslavery argument recognized that it was unrealistic – and indeed dangerous – to blame the North or the federal government for southern economic difficulties. Those wanting change to come from within the South realized that reform would be frustrated if northerners were made the scapegoats. This was not the major difficulty, however, in the position taken by Calhoun, Kettell, Townsend and others. Their principal problem was explaining the potentially high productivity of slavery, a problem experienced in even more acute form by those who proclaimed the outright and unqualified superiority of slave labor.

V

Although it was bold to claim that slavery could outperform free labor, a considerable number of southerners were prepared to take the plunge. Sometimes the context was a general assertion of southern superiority.

---

96. See below, Chapter 6. These points will also be developed in the sequel to this volume.

Some militants simply declared that the South was better than the North economically as in virtually every other respect. Thus Benjamin Stringfellow argued that despite "the cramping influence of oppressive legislation," despite "the very laws of nature," "the people of the slave-holding States" were "more religious, healthier and happier, multiply faster, live longer and better, and are far richer than the people of the North." More specifically his namesake, Thornton Stringfellow, claimed that slave states enjoyed greater wealth per capita. Iveson Brookes and Edmund Ruffin made the same claim and Ruffin added that he was counting slaves as people and not merely property. Of course the effect of this assertion was to undercut complaints about northern exploitation of the South and also to undermine the efforts of those southerners who were insisting on economic reform within the South. The conclusion which might well be drawn from the reasoning of men like Brooks and Ruffin was that there was little need for change.[97]

To explain southern superiority, however, was not easy. One possible explanation focused on the work of the slaves. If the slaves were forced to work harder than white men in the North, then a plausible explanation for the southern economic triumph had been located. Yet few southerners were prepared to pursue this argument. For it conflicted, of course, with the most cherished claim of the proslavery theorists: that slaves did not have to work harder, and indeed normally worked less hard, than free laborers. Iveson Brooks himself claimed that "no country on the globe presents three millions of laboring peasantry better fed, clothed and pro-tected" and "no section of the earth exhibits the same number of laborers so little overworked." Furthermore, the great majority of southerners were committed also to the notion that slaves were congenitally lazy. Ruffin himself asserted that "it is the general characteristic of the negro race to prefer idleness to labor" and as we have already seen, this con-viction had an important function in the South and could not lightly be discarded. It explained slave resistance while retaining the claim that slavery in fact suited blacks. Hence the rationale for southern success had to be sought elsewhere.[98]

A second possible explanation centered not on the quantity of work performed by the slaves but its quality. Thus Samuel M. Wolf, of Virginia, in attempting to rebut the charge of southern economic back-

97. Stringfellow, *Negro Slavery No Evil*, p. 26; Stringfellow, *Scriptural and Statistical View*, p. 132; Brookes, *Defence of Southern Slavery*, p. 31; Edmund Ruffin, *Slavery and Free Labor Described and Compared* (n.p., n.d.), p. 28. Ruffin, himself, however, did urge changes in the agricultural practices of the South.
98. Brookes, *Defence of Southern Slavery*, p. 31; Ruffin, *Two General Evils of Virginia, and Their One Common Remedy* (n.p., n.d.), p. 7.

wardness leveled by Hinton Helper, endorsed the claim of another southerner (Lamar of Mississippi) that the slaves were now "the finest body of
fixed laborers that the world has ever seen." Yet this argument was, if
anything, even less satisfactory than that which stressed the quantity of
slave labor. For proslavery theorists were also committed to the belief
that blacks were irredeemably inferior to whites. This belief was, as we
have also seen, important in securing the loyalty of the non-slaveholding
whites in the South. Thus extravagant claims about the quality of slave
labor were difficult to sustain. Wolf himself felt compelled to add that the
negro "has not the capacity for becoming, under any circumstances, an
enlightened man." He did not trouble to explain the discrepancy between
his two claims.[99]

The problem for southerners was to explain how, with a workforce of
racial inferiors, congenitally lazy, lacking in intelligence and without the
incentives possessed by free laborers, the South had outperformed the
North. Since the slaves alone could not be credited with the triumph it
was only possible for proslavery theorists to give the credit to the slaveholders themselves. This in turn meant an emphasis on the relations either
between slave and master or between slave and slave, as supervised or
organized by the master. The two possibilities merged into one. Some
writers, including Edmund Ruffin, argued in effect for economies of scale.
Anticipating the work of modern cliometrics, Ruffin claimed that large
plantations could allocate cooking and child-minding activities to a small
proportion of the female slaves, releasing the remainder to work on
marketed output. The fullest discussion of this issue, however, came in
a Lecture given by Georgia's Robert Toombs in Boston, Massachusetts.
Toombs acknowledged that "the truth itself needs some explanation, as it
seems to be a great mystery to the opponents of slavery, how the system is
capable at the same time of increasing the comforts and happiness of the
slave, the profits of the master, and do no violence to humanity." He then
pointed to the role of the highly educated, highly intelligent master, who
prevented the black man from falling victim, as he most assuredly would
if freed, to "his own folly and extravagance . . . his ignorance, misfor-
tunes and necessities." In this way Toombs suggested that the racial
inadequacies of the slave could be mitigated by the master. He also
claimed, however, that the master's key function was to provide
"capital," which when united with labor, and "directed by skill, forecast
and intelligence," would be "capable of the highest production" and yet
at the same time would leave "a margin both for increased comforts to
the laborer and additional profits to capital." "This," he concluded, "is
the explanation of the seeming paradox."[100]

99. Samuel M. Wolf, *Helper's Impending Crisis Dissected* (Phil., 1860), pp. 200, 219.

Toombs's answer was at least the equal of that provided by any southerner. But it left a key problem. If slave labor could be used so produc-
tively by the master, how could the non-slaveholder compete? How could
he produce, for example, a few bales of cotton for the market at a price
competitive with the slaveholder but without the enormous advantages
conferred, in the form of economies of scale, by slaveownership? Toombs
and Ruffin in effect drove a wedge between those in the South who
owned slaves and those who did not. As he built up the role of the
slaveholder as the key figure in southern economic performance, the
proslavery theorist once again threatened the racist egalitarianism upon
which so much of the case for slavery rested.[101]

VI

Proslavery theorists thus experienced the greatest difficulty in explaining
the southern economy, not merely to northerners and outsiders, but also
to southerners. Understandably many of them lapsed into serious inconsistencies. De Bow, for example, was probably the leading advocate of
diversification and economic reform in the entire South but on one occasion he published a lecture in which it was claimed that "we have in the
South more wealth per capita than the population of the North possess,"
regardless of the damage this claim did to his own campaign for change.
Nevertheless, those who pressed for reform, including De Bow, were
normally driven to emphasize the weaknesses of the southern economy.
Partly as a consequence of this tendency, the debate over economic development in the South was as problem-ridden as the disagreement over
economic growth.[102]

In making their case, the advocates of change often reiterated and
endorsed point by point the accusations leveled by the most steadfast
critics of slavery. De Bow himself constantly warned that the South
was economically backward. In the very first year of the *Review* he
complained of the South's "humiliating" dependence on the North and
pleaded for diversification. The following year he noted that there had

100. Ruffin, *The Political Economy of Slavery; Or the Institution Considered in Regard to
Its Influence on Public Wealth and the General Welfare* (Washington, D.C., 1858),
pp. 9–10, 25–26; Robert Toombs, *A Lecture Delivered in the Tremont Temple,
Boston, Massachusetts on 24 Jan. 1856* (Washington, 1856), p. 15.
101. Sometimes the proslavery writer failed to discern the problem. George Sawyer, for
example, made frequent reference to the South's economic superiority but also
stressed the racial inadequacies of its slave workforce, without perceiving the need
to reconcile the two ideas – Sawyer, *Southern Institutes*, p. 363.
102. "The Development of Southern Industry: Address of James Orr at the South Carolina
Institute for the Promotion of Agricultural, Mechanical Arts and Manufactures," in
De Bow's Review, XIX (1855), pp. 1–22, esp. 19.

been much talk on this subject but little action and as late as 1860 he was still lamenting the failure to act. "Is it not," he asked, "a notorious fact, that, in the face of the measures projected, the resolutions adopted, and the testimony adduced in favor of Southern industrial independence, we are almost as far off as ever from a due appreciation of its importance?" Moreover, on various occasions De Bow and those who contributed to his journal set about explaining the South's failure; they once again confirmed much of the antislavery indictment of the South. Planters were guilty, it was charged, of "sloth and idleness;" they had failed to display even "one half the energy and enterprise of the Yankees." On another occasion De Bow remarked that it was "the great fault of Southern people that they are too proud to work! and very often they perform the work that they do in such a manner that they are half ashamed of it." He also insisted that it was an error to blame the North for the South's weaknesses. "Tariffs," he conceded, "may have had their influence," and equally, "government legislation may have had some effect," but these were not the key factors. Instead it was "our own supineness and lack of energy."[103]

Many northern opponents of slavery would have applauded these utterances and would have been quick to attribute these acknowledged failures to the influence of slavery. Of course De Bow and those who felt as he did refused to take this final step and so their explanations were often cast in terms of defects of the southern character, themselves left entirely unexplained. On at least one occasion De Bow actually likened the deficiencies of the South to those of the slaveholding Republics of Antiquity, while still refusing to admit the influence of slavery. Like the "haughty Greek and Roman," the southerner, he wrote, doubted the worth of commerce and manufacturing. All three were accustomed to "class the trading and manufacturing spirit as essentially servile," in contrast to the work of the planter or professional. As a result, he lamented, northerners did not need to proscribe southern manufactures: "no code could be more stringent than that which the planter has himself practically enacted." De Bow concluded bitterly that "the COLONIAL SPIRIT still adheres to the South."[104]

The pages of his journal were filled with complaints about the planters and with criticisms of the southern economy. James Orr of South

103. *De Bow's Review*, II (1846), pp. 407–408, 426, IV (1847), p. 209, XXIX (1860), p. 217, I (1846), p. 436, V (1848), p. 190, XXIX (1860), pp. 74–75, XII (1852), p. 299.
104. *De Bow's Review*, XII (1852), p. 556, VIII (1850), p. 99. De Bow added that "only now" [in 1850] were these attitudes "passing away," and lamented that it might be "too late." On one occasion he observed that "we are poor and miserable whereas we should be great" – *De Bow's Review*, XII (1852), p. 500.

Carolina in an Address which De Bow chose to republish complained
that in his home state (which was of course the heartland of proslavery
sentiment), "some of our villages can boast of no higher attainment in the
mechanic arts than the possession of a blacksmith who can shoe a horse
and lay a plough; or a house carpenter who can jack plank and saw
lumber." Orr referred glumly to "our decaying prosperity." At the
same time James Henry Hammond, another South Carolinian whose
words De Bow believed should reach a wider audience, insisted that
unless reforms were swiftly introduced the South would be utterly impoverished. He then endorsed a principal antislavery charge against the
planter-dominated South in the course of a recommendation that white
labor be used to industrialize. For in South Carolina alone, he calculated,
there were 50,000 poor whites who had a precarious living, and who did
little more than trade with slaves and encourage them to plunder. In effect
this was the shiftless class of non-slaveholding whites, who stalked the
pages of Republican and abolitionist propaganda, but whose existence
most defenders of slavery in most contexts took the utmost pains to
deny.[105]

Not surprisingly these complaints about the southern economy were
more often made in reference to the South Atlantic states than to the
newer, more prosperous states of the Southwest. Thus Clement Clay of
Alabama, speaking before a horticultural society, warned that Alabama
must "prevent the shameful decadence of agriculture so palpable in
Virginia and the Carolinas." But slaveholders from the Southwest –
like De Bow himself – were clearly alarmed that a similar fate awaited
their own states. "Our system [of agriculture]," one of them observed, "is
of the most exhausting character." He invited those among his readers
who wished to see its results to "ask central Georgia, where once the
cotton field spread out its white luxuriant beauty, where now red hills,
gullies and broom sedge alone vary the landscape" or alternatively
"South Carolina and her vanishing population." Even Virginia, "once
the high seat and centre of agricultural wealth," was "but lately almost
desolate in her ten thousand abandoned farms." According to the writer,
similar problems were already afflicting the Southwest; "already around
our towns and villages fenceless old fields are spreading like diseased
spots, and the time will one day be when even our deep canebrake soil
will refuse to yield food or clothing."

Another of De Bow's contributors offered a portrait of the poor whites
of the Southwest which corresponded precisely with that offered by

---

105. "The Development of Southern Industry," in *De Bow's Review*, XIX (1855), pp. 6, 12;
      "Governor Hammond's Address before the South Carolina Institute," *De Bow's
      Review*, VIII (1850), p. 519.

Hammond for South Carolina – and with that painted by the most deter-mined antislavery militants. In an article calling for the industrial regen-eration of the South this writer urged economic diversification on the grounds that "our *poor, degraded, half-fed, half-clothed, and ignorant population, without Sabbath-schools, or any other kind of instruction – mental or moral – or without any just appreciation of the value of char-acter* [emphasis added]" could only be improved by the enhanced oppor-tunities for employment offered by industrialization.[106]

Many northern opponents of slavery insisted that the South was not merely inferior in its per capita wealth but was also afflicted by a general torpor paralysing all classes. They believed the southern economy not only insufficiently diversified but also devoid of any impulse for devel-opment even in agriculture. Again De Bow's journal, had they taken the trouble to study it, would have provided them with valuable ammunition. Looking at the profits made from cotton, one writer remarked that an observer would expect to find opulence in the home of the wealthy plan-ter. But a different spectacle confronted him: "habitations of the most primitive construction, and these so inartificially built as to be incapable of protecting the inmates from the winds and rains of heaven." "Instead of any artistical improvement," he would find a "rude dwelling . . . sur-rounded by cotton fields, or probably by fields exhausted, washed into gullies and abandoned." Rather than canals and turnpikes, he would find "navigable streams . . . unimproved, to the great detriment of transpor-tation," and "common roads" that were "scarcely passable." As if this were not enough the writer added that all too often in the South "edifices erected for the accommodation of learning and religion" were "frequently built of logs and covered with boards". It was unfortunately true that in the southern states "the fine arts were little encouraged or cared for."[107]

The proponents of diversification in the South were quite certain that slavery was not the problem, though they were able to marshal few arguments in support of this contention. Their indictment of the present reality, often based on the most minute observation, contrasted sharply with their hopes for the future, often based on little more than whimsy. They noted that their states possessed very considerable reserves of raw materials. Yet these were of little value unless a suitable workforce could be found; here additional problems arose. As we have already seen,[108]

106. "Address of Clement C. Clay, Jr., Delivered before the Chunnenuggee Horticultural Society of Alabama," *De Bow's Review*, xix (1855), pp. 725–728, esp. 727; *De Bow's Review*, xviii (1855), p. 26, xii (1852), p. 49.
107. *De Bow's Review*, iii (1847), p. 200.
108. See above, Chapter 2.

many southerners believed that slaves should not be given this task, because they were racially disqualified, because they would then become difficult to control, or because the resentment of white workers, itself fatal to the prospects for slavery in the South, would be incurred. As we have also seen, however, other southerners were equally certain that a white workforce was just as dangerous since it would promote the values of free labor, to the ultimate ruin of the slaveholding class. The proponents of diversification were unable to resolve this question. Some wanted to use white labor, others the labor of the slaves.

Those who recommended the latter were sometimes driven to extol slave labor in the most glowing terms. One of De Bow's contributors sought to dispel the notion that slaves could not become skilled workers. "It is a fact well established," he declared, "that negroes learn blacksmithing, carpentering, boot and shoe making, and in short all the handy craft trades with as much facility as white men." But such sentiments, of course, threatened to undermine the racism on which the entire regime depended and which in other contexts proslavery men were eager to reaffirm. *De Bow's Review* took no consistent line here. The claims of the writer who extolled slave labor were, for example, difficult to reconcile with the sentiments expressed, and reported favorably by De Bow, at the Commercial Convention held at Montgomery in 1858. "The negro," one delegate argued, "is not skillful in the mechanic art." De Bow the following year announced that he agreed with the notion "that the true functions of the slave are menial, or are to be exercised in the fields." On the whole the advocates of diversification felt it somewhat safer to recommend the use of white labor, until by the 1850s many of them reached the conclusion that the South had an insufficient supply of such labor. De Bow himself arrived at this point. Hence he began to look elsewhere for a solution. The campaign to reopen the African slave trade now engaged his attention.[109]

Reopening the African slave trade

I

As proslavery sentiment developed in the final decades of the antebellum South, so many southerners began to re-examine their history and to review past utterances, traditional assumptions and previous legislation on the peculiar institution. Since leaders of the 1840s and 1850s generally perceived slavery very differently from the generation of Jefferson and

---

109. *De Bow's Review*, III (1847), p. 196, XXIV (1858), p. 581.

Washington, they not surprisingly found much to criticize in the southern past. Some of them began to cast doubt upon the Declaration of Independence and upon democratic forms of government, as well as upon free labor and free society. All these revisions provoked dismay in the North. But of all the campaigns originating in the late antebellum South, the one that caused greatest revulsion and outrage was the agitation to reopen the African slave trade.[110]

The African slave trade had been closed since 1807 and indeed in 1820 had been branded piracy by the federal government itself. Early proslavery men like John C. Calhoun had not questioned this judgment and before 1850 the issue was believed irrevocably settled. Indeed in that year Jefferson Davis told the United States Senate that "there is no man in the United States who would be willing to revive it." It was "odious among us now, as it was with our ancestors." The trade was thus scarcely a source of sectional discord.

In 1853, however, Leonidas W. Spratt, a young South Carolinian, published in the newspaper he edited an article which called for the reopening of the trade. Within two years the Governor of South Carolina, James H. Adams, in his Annual Message was urging the measure upon the state's legislature. As the decade wore on, more and more southerners debated the question. To take only one example: the Southern Commercial Conventions, which had been meeting since the 1830s, became increasingly preoccupied with the topic, a process culminating at Vicksburg in 1859 when the slave trade was the only important question under discussion.[111]

Nevertheless, for a variety of reasons which we shall shortly examine, the South did not unite behind the movement. Even with complete unity, northern opposition would certainly have prevented the necessary legislation but without it the slave trade men had no chance of success. To their great chagrin, even the Confederacy did not opt for reopening. Thus

110. The best work on the campaign to reopen is Takaki, *Pro-Slavery Crusade*, though in my view the work is a little marred by the author's insistence that many southerners were consumed with guilt. Also of great value is Shore, *Southern Capitalists*. These works largely supersede the older treatments. See, however, W. J. Carnathan, "The Proposal to Reopen the African Slave Trade in the South, 1854–1860," *South Atlantic Quarterly*, xv (1926), pp. 410–429; James P. Hendrix, Jr., "The Efforts to Reopen the African Slave Trade in Louisiana," *Louisiana History*, x (1969), pp. 97–124; Daniel P. Mannix, *Black Cargoes, A History of the Atlantic Slave Trade, 1839–1865* (N.Y., 1962); Harvey Wish, "The Revival of the African Slave Trade in the United States," *Mississippi Valley Historical Review* (1941), pp. 569–588.

111. Davis's speech is in *Mississippian*, May 3, 1850. Adams's message, together with the majority and minority reports of the South Carolina legislative committee to which it was referred, can be conveniently found in *Report of the Special Committee of the House of Representatives of South Carolina on ... the Message of Gov. Jas. H. Adams as relates to Slavery and the Slave Trade* (Columbia, S.C., 1857).

if the drive for southern independence was to prove a lost cause, the agitation to reopen the African slave trade was a lost cause within a lost cause. It was one of several dreams cherished by proslavery enthusiasts, dreams that were to come crashing down in ruins along with so much of the South itself by the time of Appomattox.

The slave trade agitation, however, should not be dismissed as a quixotic failure. Like Fitzhugh and those who contributed to the debate over diversification which took place in *De Bow's Review*, Spratt and his allies (among whom were Fitzhugh and De Bow) illuminated some of the problems of southern society even as they offered unworkable solutions to them. The slave trade men focused on some key issues, and though they could not resolve them, the debate, taken in its entirety, suggests that their opponents could not resolve them either. The campaign, and the response to it, help us understand the difficulties entailed in the proslavery position.

II

In the United States Senate in 1859 Benjamin Wade, Ohio's radical Republican Senator, responded with characteristic sarcasm to a long and moving description offered by a southerner of the relationship he held with an old house servant. The occasion was the exclusion of slavery from Kansas and Wade remarked that "nobody wished to forbid his taking his old mammy with him to Kansas – we only sought to forbid his selling her after he got her there." It was a neat rejoinder, humorous as well as biting, and it derived its force from the tension between the paternalism which southerners claimed – not without some justice – characterized their relations with their slaves, and the commercialism which, from time to time at least, inevitably intruded upon that relationship.

At a still deeper level the exchange revealed the contradiction at the heart of slavery: the slave was simultaneously a person, with whom the master could forge real human relations, and a piece of property, to be disposed of at will. When slavery was being defended from abolitionist assaults, southerners not surprisingly emphasized the former aspect. More surprising, perhaps, are their frequent references, even in private correspondence, to their family "white and black."[112] In this context the buying and selling of slaves, especially when it resulted in the break up of families, was an embarrassment to many proslavery men. The internal

---

112. *Congressional Globe*, 35 Congress, 2 Session, p. 1354; Genovese, *Roll, Jordan, Roll: The World the Slaves Made* (N.Y., 1976), pp. 70–75.

slave trade had, of course, flourished with the growth of the slave economy but many southerners acknowledged that even though slavery itself was a positive good, the domestic slave trade was no more than a necessary evil.

The international slave trade, of course, was even more disturbing to contemplate. Its effects in stimulating wars in Africa were frequently commented upon, the horrors of the Middle Passage well known, the disease and suffering among the blacks, to say nothing of the death rate, too high to escape notice. The trade was hard to accommodate to southern notions of paternalism. One simply did not subject future members of "the family", however humble, to such an experience. Little wonder then that even ardent proslavery men in the 1830s and 1840s wasted no time lamenting the demise of the African slave trade.[113]

On the other hand, the very process of defending slavery required a defense of the master's title to his property. This meant asserting his right to dispose of it with as few restrictions as possible, certainly it meant maintaining his right to buy and sell slaves. Indeed the prosperity of the South was both cause and consequence of the flourishing slave markets dotted all over the region. The men who followed Spratt's lead in agitating for the African slave trade were able to seize upon two of the central features of slavery within the South, each of which was fully recognized in southern thought. The first was the claim that slavery was itself a positive good. If slavery were truly desirable, and the internal slave trade essential to it, it surely followed that southerners ought not to apologize for it. And if it were acceptable to buy a black man in, for example, Virginia, why should it be unacceptable to buy one in Africa? By the lights of orthodox proslavery theory, one could in fact claim that the second action was especially meritorious.

Here the advocates of reopening seized upon a second, and crucial, tenet of the proslavery faith. If, as southern militants insisted, slavery benefited the slave and elevated him far above the condition of the blacks in Africa – materially, culturally and spiritually – it surely followed, once again, that it was the duty of southerners to take more Africans and confer similar benefits upon them. For many southerners this logic was highly compelling.

Leonidas Spratt was one such southerner. Reflecting the confidence felt by many southerners in the superiority of their social system, he began by asserting that "the civilization we possess" was no less than "a trust for all the human race." The slaves introduced into the South had plainly

---

113. Few, if any southerners, in these years called for the reopening of the trade, though of course illegal importations of slaves continued. See Takaki, *Pro-Slavery Crusade*, pp. 200–226.

benefited enormously; it was "indeed to be doubted whether there have been other savages born in the wastes of Africa, or upon the wastes of any other savage country, so truly blessed as have been the 400,000 Africans who, during the continuance of the slave trade, were transported to the South." Hence closing the slave trade was scarcely less than a sin: "it was not for us to shut its light from those who, in no other way, could take its brightness."

The *Charleston Mercury* likewise argued that the trade could "rightfully claim for itself an origin higher than mere avarice," partly on the grounds that it had had the effect of "bringing the savage within the pale of civilization and Christianity." Most proslavery men agreed that slavery was beneficial for the slaves; to have done otherwise would have been to offer a major concession to antislavery sentiment. Most of them also engaged in comparisons between blacks in slavery and blacks, whether in the North, the South or in foreign countries, out of it and the conclusions were always the same. But to the extent that such conclusions were valid, they cast doubt upon the outlawing of the African slave trade.[114]

The advocates of reopening all looked carefully at the legislation concerning the slave trade. Some southerners, among them William Yancey, argued that the restrictions should be repealed, while doubting whether actual importations from Africa should resume. The legislation in force was a stain on the South, it was argued. If the slave trade were piracy, men like Spratt and Governor Adams reasoned, then the slave himself must be plunder. "If it be a crime to take him," Spratt argued, "it is a crime to keep him." "Sense and reason," he insisted, "tell us we abandon slavery, when we admit a wrong in the means to its formation."[115]

These considerations were part of a wider concern with the position the South occupied in front of the civilized world. Spratt demanded that the South give to slavery "the moral strength of an aggressive attitude – a position in which there could be no admission of a wrong – no implication of a sense of shame in its condition." Slavery, he argued, should become far more assertive. "It is time," he told the Legislature of South Carolina, "that slavery should be roused to a consciousness of its own

---

114. Leonidas W. Spratt, *The Foreign Slave Trade the Source of Political Power and of Material Progress, of Social Integrity, and Social Emancipation to the South* (Charleston, 1858), pp. 8, 23; Charleston *Mercury*, in *De Bow's Review*, XVII (1854), p. 612.

115. Leonidas W. Spratt, *Speech upon the Foreign Slave Trade, Before the Legislature of South Carolina* (Charleston, S.C., 1858), p. 9. Some of the constitutional and legal aspects of the slave trade were thoroughly discussed by southerners. See, for example, Richard S. Coxe, *The Present State of the African Slave Trade* (Washington, 1858); Henry Hughes, *State Liberties: Or, the Right to African Contract Labor* (Port Gibson, 1858), p. 3.

preservation; that it should become an actor in the drama of its own fate." For Spratt reopening the African slave trade would simultaneously remove a stigma attached to the South and place slavery where it belonged – on the offensive in the war against free labor.[116]

Some southern militants endorsed Spratt's proposals, not so much because they believed in the merits of the slave trade, nor even because they were concerned to repeal legislation which affronted them, but simply because they felt that reopening would hasten secession and southern independence. Some heeded the warnings of northern Democrats that the party would split hopelessly if an attempt were made to commit it to the scheme but drew the conclusion that the attempt should therefore be made. Edmund Ruffin, of Virginia, was one who wished to see the Democracy wrecked and hoped that the slave trade might be the appropriate means. Others like Spratt himself argued that the North would not dare to resist reopening, if it were presented as the only alternative to secession, and added that if he were mistaken, and secession ensued, there would be no cause for regret.[117]

At the heart of the case for reopening, however, lay a series of economic and social considerations. A relatively minor concern – minor because it did not receive great attention – was with the future of the South's near monopoly of cotton production. Governor Adams, for example, argued that the South could not meet the demand for cotton, because she lacked an adequate labor supply. Consequently Britain would continue to encourage attempts to grow the staple in other parts of the world. Adams insisted that since free labor could be used in cotton growing, it was only a question of time before other countries were able to mount a dangerous challenge to what was, after all, the foundation of southern prosperity. The solution was to increase the South's labor supply by importing Africans. Another argument, occasionally advanced by the slave trade campaigners, held that with less money spent on labor, more would be available for fertilizers and land improvements, both of which were essential to the long-term success of southern agriculture. More important was the claim that with a renewed supply of free labor, the South would be able to expand geographically, either into the western territories, or, more likely, into Latin America.[118]

Yet these concerns were not uppermost in the minds of men like Leonidas Spratt. Spratt was instead preoccupied with a different question: the pattern of slaveownership within the South and the position of

---

116. *De Bow's Review*, XXVII (1859), p. 208.
117. Takaki, *Pro-Slavery Crusade*, pp. 28–30; Spratt, *Foreign Slave Trade Source of Political Power*, pp. 28–29.
118. *Report of the Special Committee of the House of Representatives of South Carolina*, pp. 46–48; Charleston *Mercury*, Aug. 6, 11, 1858.

the non-slaveholding whites. Ironically, it was the very success of slavery that created the problem. As slavery demonstrated its profitability, so in the boom years of the late 1840s and 1850s the price of slaves rose dramatically. In 1845 a prime field hand could be bought on the New Orleans slave market for $700. But by 1850 the price was $1,000 and by 1860 it was $1,800. This trend deeply perturbed most of the slave trade advocates. They reasoned that the cost of a slave was now far beyond the means of millions of southern whites, and perceived, quite correctly, that the proportion of southern families owning slaves was falling.[119] Reopening was, above all, intended to address this problem.

Southerners were only too aware of the activities of opponents of slavery in the South like Cassius M. Clay, Daniel Reeves Goodloe, Henry Ruffner, and above all Hinton Rowan Helper. The publication in 1857 of Helper's volume, *The Impending Crisis of the South*, with its attacks upon the slaveocracy and its appeal to the non-slaveholders of the South, sent a shock wave throughout the South and the book was quickly outlawed. The efforts of these men may have produced few concrete results but they helped spread alarm among many of the Old South's leaders. Historians do not know the potential or actual support which such doctrines commanded within the South. Nor did the slaveholders themselves. Their suppression of virtually all debate on the subject in the 1830s had driven most opposition underground. It surfaced occasionally in the form of petitions to state legislatures protesting against the use of slaves in cities or in industry. Though such protests were usually accompanied by the most vigorous denunciations of abolitionism and the most fulsome affirmations of the virtues of slavery, the masters were not always reassured. In this context, the high price of slaves and the increasing proportion of non-slaveholders in the southern population took on additional importance.[120]

Warnings were sounded by the slave trade advocates. One Louisiana editor feared that if "things go on as they are now tending," then "the days of this peculiar institution of the South are necessarily few." He then identified the problem: "the present tendency of supply and demand is to concentrate all the slaves in the hands of the few, and thus excite the envy rather than cultivate the sympathy of the people." Another Louisiana newspaper was even more unequivocal: "that minute you put it out of the power of common farmers to purchase a negro man or woman to

119. The absolute number of slaveholding families was, of course, increasing. See Gavin Wright, *The Political Economy of the Cotton South: Households, Markets, and Wealth in the Nineteenth Century* (N.Y., 1978), pp. 11–42.
120. I shall consider hostility to the slaveholders within the South more fully in the sequel to this volume.

help him in his farm, or his wife in the house, you make him an abolitionist at once."

Such fears were present in every slaveholding state, even South
Carolina. Some (though not all) of that state's leaders were highly
alarmed by the failure of many of the non-slaveholding counties to support secession in 1850 and even more fearful of the doctrines taught by
"Brutus," who had published in 1851 an appeal to the non-slaveholders
denouncing the aristocracy that ruled the state. In 1854 the *Charleston
Mercury*, then in favor of reopening, warned that continued high prices
for slaves would give the non-slaveholders little cause to defend slavery so
that "the idea and spirit of that infamous pamphlet 'Brutus'" would
spread.[121]

These fears persisted in the South to the very eve of secession. In 1860
J. G. B. De Bow wrote a famous article asserting that the non-slaveholders were indeed fully committed to slavery but his private opinions
were almost certainly rather different. At almost the same time, his
Review published the equally famous articles by "Python" (probably
former president John Tyler's son) which utterly contradicted the editor's
bland assurances. According to "Python", the mechanic trades in the
South had been degraded by the presence of slaves. As a result "the
no-property men of the South" shared "a feeling of deep-rooted jealousy
and prejudice, of painful antagonism, if not hostility, to the institution of
slavery." High wages in the South, consequent upon high cotton prices,
aggravated the problem, in that they gave an added incentive to masters
to lease their slaves for use in the factories. As we have already seen, this
caused considerable friction in cities like Richmond.[122]

There was further irony. Economic historians have pointed out that
slavery permitted what has been termed "allocative efficiency:" the supply of slaves could be allocated to places where it was most profitable.
This meant, of course, the Southwest and the migration of slaveholders to
the West in large numbers was one of the southern economy's great
success stories. But there was, of course, also an impact upon the states
they had left. The 1850s witnessed a series of challenges to slavery in
border states like Kentucky, where Cassius Clay remained active, in

121. Ouachita *Register*, quoted in Takaki, *Pro-Slavery Crusade*, p. 63; Sparta (La.,)
      Jeffersonian, quoted in Roger W. Schugg, *Origins of Class Struggle in Louisiana:
      A Social History of White Farmers and Laborers during Slavery and After* (Baton
      Rouge, 1939), p. 88; Takaki, *Pro-Slavery Crusade*, pp. 64–65. See also Edward B.
      Bryan, *Letters to the Southern People Concerning the Acts of Congress and the
      Treaties with Great Britain in Relation to the African Slave Trade* (Charleston,
      1858), p. 35.
122. De Bow, *Interest in Slavery of the Southern Non-Slaveholder*; *De Bow's Review*,
      XXVIII (1860), pp. 254–255; Takaki, *Pro-Slavery Crusade*, p. 62.

Maryland where "controversy over the free black question brought to the surface . . . the conflict between [large slaveholders] and non-slave-holders," and above all in Missouri, where a bill for abolition was actually presented in the legislature. Here was additional food for proslavery thought.[123]

Among those who agitated for the slave trade it was Leonidas Spratt who was most outspoken on this question. As we have seen, Spratt was utterly convinced of the moral superiority of southern slave society. Yet this confidence existed side by side with the utmost anxiety about the non-slaveholders. "Gentlemen may disguise the fact if they will," he told the Knoxville Commercial Convention, "but there is no fact clearer to my mind than that in the Southern states, those men who own slaves, and those who do not, stand in antagonistic positions as regards the institution of slavery." Writing in the *Charleston Standard*, he was even more explicit. There were, he argued, in the South, some three million whites who owned no slaves and who were thus, as he quaintly put it, "unfixed in the social compound." "To that extent," he declared, "the system of our country is disintegrated and to the order and efficiency of slavery, perhaps, to its existence as a distinct order of society, it is of the last importance that its integrity shall be restored."

Very few southerners ever spoke this way, especially in public and Spratt acknowledged the fact. "I know," he conceded, "that it is common to pass this subject lightly, for it is not thought best to arouse the slumbering spirit of Democracy." Even though the non-slaveholders had shown themselves dependable in 1856, when Frémont's election had seemed possible, it was nevertheless a fact that "in many sections of the South, there is free labor in competition with slave labor – free sentiment in competition with slave sentiment and . . . this is a condition dangerous, if not to the South, at least to slavery as a living system at the South." The stakes were high. At issue was a question "about which it would be madness to be mistaken."[124]

Spratt then surveyed the entire South and discussed each state's commitment to slavery:

> In Delaware and Maryland there is scarce the effort to defend slavery. In Virginia the proposition to receive a colony of abolitionists is not exceedingly offensive. In Kentucky it has been proposed to

123. Barbara J. Fields, *Slavery and Freedom on the Middle Ground: Maryland during the Nineteenth Century* (New Haven, 1985), p. 82. I shall deal at some length with Missouri in the sequel to this volume.

124. Spratt quoted in Shore, *Southern Capitalists*, p. 53; Spratt, *Foreign Slave Trade Source of Political Power*, pp. 11–12 (this pamphlet was reprinted from the Charleston *Standard*).

emancipate their negroes. In Missouri there is a Free-soil party to contend for power, and there is the disposition to transport their slaves farther South. In Tennessee it is not so popular to speak of slavery as of equality and fraternity. In Georgia, Alabama, Mississippi, Louisiana, and Arkansas, there are more whites than blacks; and there, also, while all parties would whip the North, it is abundantly evident that many of them even there would strike rather for the South than for Slavery at the South.

Spratt believed that only in South Carolina, where there was "an excess of slaves" (by which he probably meant a majority of slaves in the population), was "the slave sentiment composed and steady." In a sense, therefore, he wished to use the African slave trade to remake the entire South in the image of South Carolina.[125]

He was well aware that slavery was leaving many of the cities of the South. This he attributed to the growth of free labor, which sought to restrict the slave and to impose taxes upon his master. At the Montgomery convention, when Spratt argued that the non-slaveholders of western Virginia were not all "true to the best interests of the South," a Virginian, Roger Pryor dissented. Spratt then asked whether these non-slaveholders were "willing that slave labor should come in competition with them in the mechanic arts." Pryor replied that they were, and Spratt dryly observed that "in western Virginia there was a degree of magnanimity on the subject that there was not elsewhere." Spratt's views were easily summarized. As he put it himself, "the basis of slave labor . . . is too narrow for all to stand on."[126]

It would be quite wrong to assume that Spratt was expressing the secret fears of the entire leadership of the South. Undoubtedly there were doubts about the non-slaveholders in some quarters but the simple fact is that no-one knew how loyal they would be. The doubts were probably more widespread than the record suggests, since those on both sides of the slave trade question acknowledged the delicacy of the subject and the tendency to pass over it quickly. One senses that even some of those who followed Spratt felt that this was a dangerous question: to acknowledge reservations about the non-slaveholders seemed almost to legitimate them. Thus C. W. Miller of South Carolina, an advocate of reopening, appeared to claim at one and the same time that the non-slaveholders were and were not sufficiently loyal to the regime. "It cannot be disguised," he began, "that the man who is shut out by poverty and the high price of negroes

---

125. Spratt, *Foreign Slave Trade Source of Political Power*, p. 12. See also Edward B. Bryan, *Letters to the Southern People*, p. 36.
126. Spratt in *De Bow's Review*, XXIV (1858), p. 602; Spratt, *Foreign Slave Trade Source of Political Power*, p. 13.

from holding and enjoying this property, now held only by the rich and fortunate, will not have the same sympathy with slaveholders which interest would inspire." Apparently fearing that he had said too much, Miller then went some way towards a retraction. "Nevertheless," he reassured his audience, "I believe that the patriotic poor man, though not a slaveowner, who sees his country's power and glory dependent, as they are, on the continued existence of slavery, will arm and fight side by side with the rich in its defence." The conclusion was, however, that, no matter how "patriotic," the "poor man" needed to be given an additional stake in the regime: "if, therefore, his condition and that of the country, may be benefited by re-opening the slave trade, it is due to him, it is right, and imperatively demanded by justice and the common good, that all classes in the South, should unite to institute so desirable a measure of public policy."[127]

Since the advocates of reopening had their doubts about the indigenous non-slaveholding whites of the South, it comes as no surprise to discover that they were even more suspicious of the immigrant. Spratt was one of many who observed that millions of immigrants had gone to the North, swelling its population and disturbing the balance between the sections. He wanted an influx of Africans to rectify the balance and he preferred Africans for a variety of reasons, one of which was a fear of the consequences of free white immigration. "Europeans," he asserted, "will not come . . . but if they should, it is to be feared they would not come to strengthen us, or to extend slavery, but to exclude the slave." Such, he argued, had been the effect in Maryland, Delaware, and the northern counties of Virginia, as well as most of the larger cities of the entire South. If immigrants entered on the scale seen in the North, and were unable to purchase slaves cheaply, "they would abolitionize the States they came to strengthen and would break the very centres of our institution." On the other hand, if, as a result of reopening, the price of slaves fell to an affordable level, "we could draw an army of defenders from every State in Europe."[128]

Adams likewise referred to white immigrant labor as "a species of labor we do not want, and which is, from the very nature of things, antagonistic to our institutions." Like Spratt, he wanted to see slaves employed in a wider variety of occupations than was currently the case. "It is much better," he told the South Carolina Legislature, "that our drays should be driven by slaves – that our factories should be worked by slaves – that our hotels should be served by slaves – that

127. C.W. Miller, *Address on Re-Opening the Slave Trade . . . at Wylde-Moore, Aug. 29, 1857* (Columbia, S.C., 1857), p. 8.
128. Spratt, *Speech . . . Before the Legislature of South Carolina*, pp. 5–6.

our locomotives should be manned by slaves." The alternative was that "we should be exposed to the introduction . . . of a population alien to us by birth, training and education, and which, in the process of time, must lead to [a] . . . conflict between labor and capital." Thus more blacks were needed for "the full development of our whole round of agricultural and mechanical resources." As C. W. Miller, also of South Carolina, put it: "it is a proposition too well proved, that no nation can attain the highest degree of liberty, independence and power without the trinity of agriculture, manufactures and commerce." To those who questioned the suitability of slave labor outside agriculture, he replied that "slave labor may well be employed in manufactures and in the preparatory departments of commerce."[129]

At first glance, it appears that these slave trade enthusiasts possessed great confidence in slavery as the basis for the southern economy. Indeed Spratt asserted that "both theory and experience concur in showing that a number of negroes, under the discipline of slavery, will accomplish more than will an equal number of laboring whites without it." "Slave labor," he observed on another occasion, "is too efficient . . . to permit of hireling labor in competition with it." It was thus quite logical to seek to increase both the number of slaves in the South, and the range of economic activities in which they were employed.[130]

Yet anyone looking for evidence that slavery had distorted the operation of the southern economy needed to look no further than the utterances of men like Leonidas Spratt. Miller in effect conceded that the South suffered from a severe shortage of labor for railroads, manufacturers, and the mechanic arts, while Spratt himself argued that the price of slaves, being determined by productivity levels in the Southwest, denied opportunities to southern entrepreneurs. He then painted a bleak picture of the reality of economic life in South Carolina, the only state, we may recall, whose commitment to slavery he believed unimpeachable:

> Without such opportunity, there is no advancement in population; without advancement in population there is no profit in lines of Railroads and Steamboats; no increase in the value of lands and other permanent property, and so it is therefore, that beyond the cultivation of the soil and the sale and transportation of its products to a foreign market, it is hard to say what business there is in which enterprise and capital can be invested with the certainty of success;

129. *Report of the Special Committee of the House of Representatives of South Carolina*, p. 48; Miller, *Address on Re-Opening the Slave Trade . . .* , p. 8.
130. Spratt, *A Series of Articles on the Value of the Union to the South* (Charleston, 1855), p. 16; Spratt, *Foreign Slave Trade Source of Political Power*, p. 4.

and while we teem with enterprise, while we pour millions into
undertakings that never pay, and at the call of public spirit, are
ready to pay many millions more, we do not stagnate . . . for the
reason that we have not enterprise, or fail for the reason that we are
simpletons and sluggards, but we stagnate for the want of opportunity, and we fail for the reason, that we have hoped against hope and
have staked our fortunes upon the achievement of success, where
success was never possible.

At the time of the slave trade, he claimed, Charleston and its surrounding
districts had boomed. But in recent decades the "splendors" of those
areas "waned." Again the picture was a dismal one:

Progress left them for the North; cultivation ceased; the swamp
returned; mansions became tenantless and roofless; values fell;
lands that sold for $50 per acre now sell for less than $5; churches
are abandoned, trade no longer persecuted – of twenty tanyards, not
one remains . . . and Charleston, which was once upon the road
from Europe to the North, now stands aside, and while once the
metropolis of America, is now the unconsidered seaport of a tribu-
tary province . . . .

Spratt added that "the experience of that District, to a greater or less
extent, has been the experience of other sections of our Southern seaboard."[131]

Of course, Spratt believed that reopening the slave trade would cure
these evils. But, as we shall see, there were powerful counter-arguments
that he was unable to dispose of. Behind his confidence in slavery, lay a
bleak description of southern slave society. Its economic development
was being retarded and distorted; it contained within it millions of potential enemies who must be appeased if it were to survive. Spratt was utterly
convinced of the superiority of slavery and of the beneficial effects of
reopening. But his scheme takes on some of the qualities of a panacea,
given the diseases it was designed to cure. Moreover, his critical analysis
of the slaveholding present contrasted sharply with his hopes for an
imagined slaveholding future. From the mouth of one of its most ardent
defenders, came a recognition that slavery had had some extraordinarily
damaging effects.

An even more striking contrast was between Spratt's concern for the
non-slaveholding whites and his relative neglect of the slave himself. It
was scarcely surprising that proslavery southerners should insist upon the
benefits conferred upon the blacks and, as we have already seen, Spratt

---

131. Miller, *Address on Re-Opening the Slave Trade . . .* , *passim*; Spratt, *Speech
. . . Before the Legislature of South Carolina*, p. 6.

placed great emphasis upon this claim. Nevertheless, he was blind to the problems which slaves themselves posed to the South and, as we shall see, it was here that he was most vulnerable to the arguments of his opponents.

III

The opponents of reopening lost no time in combating the new proposal when it was first aired. By the end of 1856 a congressional resolution, introduced by a southerner, had condemned the trade as "horrid and inhuman." The House of Representatives passed the resolution by a large majority. Yet this vote is highly deceptive. A large majority of southerners voted against the motion, and although this cannot be taken as an index of support for reopening, it is enough to confirm what many southerners already knew: if they opposed the new campaign, they needed to deploy solid argument.[132]

One strategy was simply to deny the central claims made by Spratt and his followers regarding the non-slaveholders and simply insist that they were utterly loyal to the South. Albert Gallatin Brown, whose power base in Mississippi was in the poorer areas of the state, wrote a public letter in which he affirmed that they were even more committed to slavery than the slaveholders themselves, such was the fate that awaited them if the blight of abolition should ever descend. Brown was an opponent of the African slave trade. From a different standpoint William Gregg, one of the best known industrialists in the South, denied that immigrants were in any way hostile to slavery. He refused to countenance the notion that those southerners who did not own slaves, were in any way a threat to the regime. Undoubtedly many in the South agreed with him.[133]

More important, however, some of Spratt's opponents were able to cast doubt upon the efficacy of the remedy he was offering. If large numbers of importations reduced the price of slaves in the South, would this not cut the value of the master's property, and thus weaken his attachment to slavery? Henry Foote of Mississippi argued that high prices for slaves were needed to keep slaveholders true to the South. But it was in the border states that these arguments had most force. Ironically,

132. Takaki, *Pro-Slavery Crusade*, p. 7.
133. Albert Gallatin Brown, *Letter of Hon. Albert Gallatin Brown, On the Interest of Non-Slaveholders in the South in the Perpetuation of African Slavery* (n.p., 1860), *passim*; William Gregg, "Southern Patronage to Southern Imports and Domestic Industry," in *De Bow's Review*, XXIX (1860), pp. 623–624. See also *De Bow's Review*, VIII (1850), p. 510; XXIV (1858), pp. 579–582; Herbert Wender, *Southern Commercial Conventions* (Baltimore, 1930), p. 215.

these were the very states about which Spratt had most doubts and whose commitment to slavery he was seeking to strengthen. But there can be little doubt that a majority of border state southerners believed that his plan would have the opposite effect. "What is there in such a policy," one Virginia newspaper asked, "for slave-holders of Rockbridge: For several years the State Revenue of the country has been paid by the sale of her slaves. Open the Slave Trade and what will our Negroes be worth?" Competition from Africa, if it did indeed reduce slave prices, seemed an unattractive prospect for border state southerners and their politicians increasingly absented themselves from the commercial conventions of the 1850s, in the knowledge that they would be preoccupied by the question of the African slave trade. No Virginians even attended at Vicksburg. Many of them had by then concluded that reopening would simply encourage abolition in Virginia.[134]

Spratt's opponents were therefore able to claim that reopening would aggravate the regional differences between the Upper and Lower South. Moreover, it was far from clear that a lower price for slaves would help the Southeast and prevent the drain of slaves to the West. Spratt insisted it would but others were highly sceptical. With a cut in prices, might not the advantages of soil and climate allow an even greater concentration of slaves in the Southwest, facilitating ever larger economies of scale there? No-one knew the answer.[135]

As if these doubts were not enough, there was still the problem of the white laborers already in the South. The very argument used by the advocates of reopening was that slaves would do many of their jobs, especially the unskilled ones. Slaves would then enter cities in large numbers. The effect on wages, however, was at best problematic. In Texas, Sam Houston fought and won a gubernatorial election by insisting that the slave trade be made a key campaign issue. Houston argued that reopening was directly against the interests of the working man. If the trade were resumed, he warned, "not a poor man would be able to stay in the country, because labor would be so cheap that he would not be able to get bread for himself and family." A conflict would then occur between rich and poor whites, the very conflict which reopening had been intended to obviate.

Robert Harper of Georgia pressed this point further when he deployed the familiar argument that slaves should be kept to agricultural activities. Reopening, followed by a diversification based on slave labor, was highly dangerous, since "the tendency would be to make enemies instead of

---

134. *De Bow's Review*, XXVII (1859), pp. 214–221; Lexington *Valley Star* quoted in Takaki, *Pro-Slavery Crusade*, p. 119.
135. Las Casas, *The Charleston Courier and the Slave Trade* (n.p., n.d.), pp. 15–17.

friends to the institution even in the heart of the South." Harper then testified to the delicacy with which southerners treated this question. "Upon this train of thought," he remarked, "much might be said – but there are some points on which it is perhaps wiser to reflect than to write."[136]

Spratt's opponents had by no means refuted his arguments about the danger posed by the non-slaveholders but they had succeeded in showing that his remedy was highly problematic. In truth no-one knew, or could know, what the pattern of slaveownership would be, if a large influx of Africans occurred. Whether it would increase or diminish social mobility and regional equality was impossible to say. In a sense, however, Spratt's opponents did not need an outright victory. A draw was sufficient. They could therefore turn to other arguments, in the belief that they had at least neutralized Spratt's principal appeal.

Of course, those southerners who were avowed Unionists lost no time in announcing that an attempt to reopen the slave trade would inevitably be resisted by the North, and would thus further divide the nation. But by the eve of the Civil War, many secessionists too had concluded that the campaign was dangerously divisive. Robert Rhett, editor of the *Charleston Mercury*, reversed his previous position and came out against the trade on the grounds that it tended to divide not the nation but the South. A third contingent of southerners, who could not be called out-and-out Unionists, nevertheless followed James Henry Hammond in arguing that the Democracy offered the best prospects of safety, both for slavery and the South, and thus heeded the warnings of their northern allies that reopening would doom the party in the North.[137] Finally, some southerners who were unambiguously proslavery nevertheless continued to insist on the immorality of the slave trade.[138]

These were not, however, the principal concerns of those in the South who opposed the African slave trade. While Spratt and many of his supporters focused on the relationship between slaveholders and non-slaveowning whites, their opponents instead concentrated on the relations between master and slave. Spratt's scheme implied that a relatively large number of Africans were to be brought into the South, for otherwise

---

136. Takaki, *Pro-Slavery Crusade*, pp. 180–184; Robert G. Harper, *An Argument against the Policy of Re-Opening the African Slave Trade* (Athens, Ga., 1858), pp. 71–72. See also *Speech of Wade Hampton, on the Constitutionality of the Slave Trade Laws Delivered in the Senate of South Carolina, Dec. 10, 1859* (Columbia, S.C., 1860), p. 15.
137. Takaki, *Pro-Slavery Crusade*, pp. 103–133, 228, 230.
138. See *The Revival of the Slave Trade*, p. 18. The writer argued that the property rights of the entire European aristocracy would collapse if such reasoning were employed, since their property had often originated in fraud or theft.

the impact on slave prices would be slight. But how would the South absorb these Africans? In what ways would southern slavery change? Again no-one knew. In a sense, Spratt's diagnosis of the ills within southern society called for what the twentieth century has termed "social engineering." But the tools at the disposal of the mid-nineteenth century were crude, clumsy and unpredictable in their effects. Importing thousands of Africans, even if it could be done, was the most unpredictable course of all.

Some of the advocates of reopening explained that the new slaves would be socialized into the South by means of a "couple-working" system. A "civilized" slave would be placed alongside a "savage" African, in order to accustom him to his new role and his new responsibilities. Nothing is more remarkable than the faith exhibited by these southerners in the slave. While they harbored, as we have seen, the most corrosive doubts about the non-slaveholding whites, their confidence in the slave knew no bounds. Spratt was certain that slaves could easily be trusted to work expensive machinery, nor did he doubt that the "couple-working" system would produce the desired results. Most important of all, he and his followers dismissed the main argument of their opponents in the most cavalier manner.

For the principal concern of those who condemned his plan was with its impact on the slave himself. Sometimes this took the form of a concern for his moral and physical well-being. A fall in the price of slaves, it was contended, would make the slave too cheap and create an incentive for the master to abandon current practice and treat the bondsman with cruelty instead of kindness. According to Judge Peter Gray of Texas, the slaves "would become mere brutes – animals of labor. Instead of the patriarchal institution we now boast, it would become a mere matter of work and profit." In case this appeal to humanitarian values missed its mark, Gray added that "one of our strongest arguments against abolition fanaticism would fall." But behind this concern lay an issue of even greater magnitude. Writing in *De Bow's Review* former senator Walker Brooke of Mississippi warned that reopening would mean that "every semblance of humanity would have to be blotted out from the statute-books." The result would be that "the slaveholder would become – instead of the patriarchal friend and master of his slave – a bloody, brutal, and trembling tyrant." Here the key word was "trembling," for it was not only the slave who would have to live in constant fear.[139]

The opponents of the slave trade argued that an influx of Africans would increase the danger of servile insurrection to unacceptable levels.

139. *Address of Judge Peter W. Gray to the Citizens of Houston, on the African Slave Trade* (n.p., n.d.), p. 26; *De Bow's Review*, xxvii (1859), p. 361.

They wondered whether the "savage" slaves might not instead contaminate the "civilized" ones, turn them into heathens and, finally, as the *Charleston Courier* put it, "introduce the insurrectionary element among our now orderly and contented slaves . . . ." A report of the Louisiana State Legislature said the same, while the *Richmond Enquirer* in 1856 observed that slave revolts originated in the "blind passions of the ignorant and brutal mass – a mass to which it is the interest of the South to make no addition from the savage wilds of Africa." In discussions of the African slave trade, its opponents were wont to refer to Nat Turner's revolt, and, still more alarmingly, to the experiences of Santo Domingo.[140]

Spratt and the other slave trade advocates had no answer to this other than bland assurances. Once again no-one knew what the actual effect of importations of Africans would be. Of course if the numbers remained small, the danger of disturbances would have been correspondingly reduced, but then so would the alleged benefits. Some of Spratt's opponents argued that the numbers entailed must run into millions, and then threw up their hands in horror as they contemplated the effect on the existing, "civilized" slaves. Not for the first time, proslavery southerners were trapped by their own arguments. Claiming much for the influence they had had upon their slaves, they could not help but conclude that the African was "barbaric." What they never managed to show, however, was how a barbarian could become a member of the family.

We have now come full circle. Both the advocates and the opponents of the African slave trade sounded warnings to their fellow southerners. But where the former concentrated on the dangers posed by the non-slaveholding whites, the latter were struck instead by the potential danger of the master–slave relation. In a deeper sense, however, both groups were concerned with the weaknesses of slavery. Spratt recognized that without the support of the non-slaveholders, slavery was doomed: the master needed a positive commitment from the non-slaveowning whites. His opponents feared that an influx of new slaves would more directly undermine the institution. It is impossible to say who was right. But it is clear that neither group had an effective answer to the questions posed so starkly in the debate over the African slave trade.

140. Charleston *Courier*, Sept. 4, 1858; Takaki, *Pro-Slavery Crusade*, pp. 125–126; Richmond *Enquirer*, Dec. 16, 1856. See also *Speech of Wade Hampton*, p. 18.

Race and class in the Old South

I

The history of the proslavery argument is one of irony and paradox. It came into existence principally to combat the antislavery virus in the North and to ensure that it did not infect the South or the federal government. To resist a determined and militant antislavery movement – whether aiming at immediate abolition or a slower strangulation by way of free soil – slaveholders needed to believe in their own cause. The older "necessary evil" argument would no longer suffice. Yet antislavery itself came to prominence in the North as a result of slavery's weaknesses, weaknesses which, I have already argued, were to a large extent not merely perceived but real. In this way a set of doctrines glorifying slavery's triumphs was born out of slavery's failures.

Northern opponents, whether Republicans or abolitionists, denounced the South's failure to diversify, her inability to keep pace with the North in population, in manufacturing, in urbanization. There is ample reason to believe that these criticisms were valid, and that slavery was indeed the cause. As we have seen, many southerners believed that slaves ought not to be placed in cities or in industry; many also doubted the wisdom of encouraging a large white urban or industrial population. This constraint in turn helped to deter immigration, in the absence of which southern population growth failed to match that of the North. A vicious cycle was created in which industrialization, urbanization and immigration were all retarded. The slow pace of development inevitably alarmed northerners while at the same time apparently confirming the superiority of their own free labor economy.

The South's reaction to antislavery, however, from the 1830s onwards, served only to place more doubts in more northern minds. The curtailment of free speech and civil liberties laid the groundwork for the attack upon the "Slave Power" which was employed in the early years of the abolitionist crusade but which culminated in the Republican appeal of the 1850s. Once again southern anxieties about the stability of their system were crucial. Antislavery propaganda, like the growth of cities and industry, might have damaging effects upon their slaves. In each case the danger arose because of the delicacy of the relation between master and slave. It would be threatened either by the slave himself or by non-slaveholding whites but either way the problem, as the masters viewed it, was the slave's gullibility, his inability fully to recognize that enslavement was his proper condition in life. The task of the proslavery theorists was to convince the South that the enslavement of black men, women and children was in conformity with the will of God and was of incalculable advantage to both blacks and whites.

At this point, however, the proslavery argument ironically repudiated the very force that had brought it into existence. For while southerners attributed the danger to the gullibility of the blacks, modern scholarship explains it instead in terms of black resistance, the slave's desire for freedom, his refusal to accept that enslavement was his natural or normal condition. Resistance and conflict are endemic in the relationship between master and slave. The proslavery theorist had been driven to enunciate his doctrines by the consequences of that inevitable conflict but it was a conflict whose inevitability he could never acknowledge.

Instead he insisted that the relation between master and slave was, or could easily be made, harmonious. Drawing upon biblical and historical precedent, his arguments showed little sign of guilt. Nor was he a hypocrite. But his theories were weak nevertheless. In the final analysis his argument was incoherent. He could not solve the problems of the South partly because he could not even recognize their origin.

In this complex and curious manner, class conflict between master and slave suffused the South but (via its effects upon northern antislavery opinion) prevented its own recognition. Proslavery theorists would frequently address the problems consequent upon that conflict but always they would be led away from an accurate diagnosis. Hence the proslavery argument, even in its failure, registered the needs and failures of the slaveholders of the South. Its fascination is that an important proslavery spokesman or group of thinkers was frequently able to fix on and illuminate a key weakness in the South and present unanswerable arguments in favor of a certain strategy – while at the same time failing to rebut the equally powerful arguments in favor of a different and incompatible one.

The defenders of slavery had three groups of potential antagonists to consider. First were the northerners who, by controlling the federal government, might launch an attack upon slavery in the South. Closer at home were the non-slaveholders of the South, who might either aid such an attack or, by virtue of their numerical strength, launch an assault of their own. Closest of all were the slaves themselves, whose potential for misbehavior the proslavery theorist could not afford to overlook. These three groups formed concentric circles surrounding the slaveholder and limiting his political and intellectual freedom of movement.

II

For Calhoun the crucial problem facing the slaveholders was the federal government and its susceptibility to the control of a hostile northern majority. No-one saw this danger more clearly; no-one failed so utterly to comprehend it. The South had become a minority not because the federal government had illegitimately conferred favors upon the North but because the South's population could not keep pace. In his search for allies Calhoun also encountered, again without recognizing or understanding, the weaknesses of slavery. His attempt to forge an alliance with northern radicals failed because he could not endorse, even at state level, their democratic and egalitarian aspirations. The uneven ownership of slaves in the South made Calhoun distrustful of the white majority, even in his own state. Hence this alliance foundered on the different class position of slaveholders and non-slaveholders in the South. In his attempts to combat the potential hostility of the North, Calhoun was here defeated by the potential hostility of the non-slaveholding whites in the South. When he sought instead to create a defensive alliance with northern conservatives, the initiative failed because he could not accept their aspirations for the federal government. Here an interesting asymmetry was apparent. Despite their reservations about democracy and popular government, northern conservatives did not fear that federal power could effect the ruin of their labor system. Calhoun, by contrast, based his entire career (after 1830) on the need to prevent the federal government from uprooting the labor system of the South. Once more he responded to the weaknesses of slavery, while failing to recognize them. Unable to see the conflicts within the South, but needing to combat their consequences, he ended by predicting social revolution in the North. In so doing he emphasized the problem of the subordinate classes there, the very problem which existed in the South in a more intense form but which he was utterly unable to confront. Like many other proslavery theorists Calhoun claimed that the southern social system was peculiarly stable; his entire career – its successes as well as its failures – after 1830 testified to its peculiar instabilities.

Those who sought instead to rest slavery on the supposed equality of whites in the South were no more successful in grasping the true nature of their society or charting a course that would bring them to safety. An intense racism answered many of the needs of the South. Dissatisfaction with the slave's economic performance together with fears that he might be unable to recognize the diabolical intent of abolitionism reinforced the tendency to emphasize the inferiority of blacks. Even more important, the need to reach out for the support of the non-slaveholder promoted an emphasis on the racial superiority of all whites. Yet once again reality defeated these theories. The differences between slaveholders and non-slaveholders were too great. When the racist egalitarian sought to describe the labor process he needed to be able to show that the slave's labor was entirely different from both the master's and the non-slaveholder's. But the more he stressed the advantages of slavery the more his analysis confirmed that a gulf separated the master from the non-slaveholder. Even more alarmingly, the more details he gave of the labor process, the more the labor of the non-slaveholder seemed to resemble that of the slave. The reality was that slaveholders constituted a different class from non-slaveholders and racial solidarity could not disguise this fact.

In a sense, those who advocated the reopening of the African slave trade grappled with this problem. They knew that slave ownership did not correspond to race lines in the South. But their arguments exposed the difficulty of all who claimed or who sought to create an equality of whites in the South. The attitude of the non-slaveholders would not have been a problem at all if the loyalty of the slaves had been complete. If the slaves had indeed been happy as slaves, the masters could have afforded to ignore the non-slaveholders. But the advocates of reopening added a further twist to the problem. In demanding the importation of thousands of blacks from Africa, they risked aggravating the problem that had indirectly called forth their campaign. In responding to the danger posed by the non-slaveholder, the advocate of reopening proposed a program that not only ignored but actually aggravated the danger posed by the slave himself.

George Fitzhugh by contrast focused attention onto the class nature of slavery in the South. In effect he posited a three-class South – of slaves, non-slaveholders and masters – and did not shrink from the inegalitarian tendencies of his analysis. But the analysis failed utterly in that, while celebrating class distinctions, it resolutely ignored class conflict. Fitzhugh ignored the dangers posed by the slaves or the non-slaveholders and even (on some occasions) by the North. While he was able to score some telling points against the advocates of a white egalitarianism, he missed the fact that racism was needed both to rationalize slave behavior and to secure the loyalty of the non-slaveholder. He sought to base slavery squarely on class but failed utterly to see the dangers of this strategy.

Finally, those who looked at the economics of slavery were subject to similar conflicting and contradictory pressures. When they looked to the North they were tempted to argue that slave labor was highly productive and hence would not retard the development of the West. But at the same time it was difficult to concede that slaves worked especially hard (and were thus oppressed) or worked especially well (and thus should not be enslaved). The only way out of this impasse was to stress the control of the master and his role in slavery's economic success story. But with this control and its effects, did the masters not form an aristocracy? When they looked to the non-slaveholders the defenders of slavery were on the horns of another dilemma. If the slaves were racially inferior and congenitally lazy why should they not be removed from the nation, as northern colonizationists urged, in the interests of economic growth and development? But if the South were indeed prospering, how had this prosperity been achieved? The argument about climate was attractive in this context but it raised more problems than it solved. There was no acceptable answer. When they looked at the slave himself, different pressures were present and another dilemma emerged. A slave who was told he worked well might entertain aspirations about his status; in particular his success might antagonize the non-slaveholding whites. But a slave who was assumed to be unproductive might thereby receive a license for poor work, for slowdowns and for malingering, to the detriment of the economy as a whole. Such were the pressures on the proslavery theorist who sought to analyze the southern economy.

Each of these groups or individuals managed to grasp at least one of the major weaknesses of slavery but without being able to diagnose the central problem: the endemic nature of conflict within southern society. That same conflict created the need to defend slavery but at the same time ensured that the resulting theories would be, in the final analysis, incoherent.

III

Let us end by considering the role of class conflict more systematically. As previously observed, the slaveholder's enemies (real or potential) were arranged in concentric circles. Closest to home were the slaves themselves, next came the non-slaveholders of the South, most distant were northerners. In fact the slaveholders would meet their doom at the hands of the North. Yet the largest problem was posed by the slaves themselves. Only because their loyalty and contentment could not be taken for granted did the attitude of the non-slaveholders become a major difficulty. And only because the loyalty of both slaves and non-slaveholders was problematic did southerners need to register their alarm at the growth of antislavery in the North. Although the challenge from each group was important and interdependent (because mutually reinforcing), the interdependence was asymmetrical. The conflict with the slaves, alone, would have existed in the absence of the others.

This conflict, I have already argued, is in the most fundamental sense, a class conflict, a struggle brought into existence because of one class's attempts to exploit another, by appropriating the fruits of its labor. In a slave society this exploitation takes a form different from that found in free labor societies. From this fact the weaknesses of slavery, as registered in the proslavery argument, ultimately derive.

Class conflict thus suffused southern slave society and wreaked havoc with the proslavery argument. We should note, however, that this (Marxist) conceptualization of class differs sharply from that found in the work of most historians. There is no claim here that, at the level of consciousness, class was primary. The argument advanced here does not depend on the claim that class bulked larger than race in the minds of southerners (and would not be strengthened if the converse were found to be true). Indeed it would be unaffected by the discovery that all southerners were more race conscious than class conscious. Of course the existence or absence of class consciousness in any society is an important issue, but it does not affect the argument for the primacy of class as presented here. Indeed I have suggested that the reality of class conflict actually limited the extent to which class itself could be perceived as the central problem.

Nor is class in this sense to be equated with stratification. The extent to which there was mobility into and out of the ranks of the slaveholders is an important one. The extent of inequality within southern society is also important. But the class analysis offered here in no way depends on the claim that the Old South was an especially stratified society. Finally, my argument departs from that of Eugene Genovese in rejecting the notion that a writer like George Fitzhugh, who set about a class analysis of the South, himself possessed a higher form of consciousness and was thus able in his writings to expose "the logical outcome of the slaveholders' philosophy." As I have indicated, Fitzhugh's arguments are important but for another reason.

Instead I have argued that class is to be understood as a real structural relationship, existing whether or not it is recognized or acknowledged, playing an important role in creating inequalities, but not constituted solely by those inequalities. This was the southern reality, simultaneously provoking the proslavery argument and condemning it to register, in its very incoherence, the problems of the slave mode of production.

PART III

The second party system

5

Whigs and Democrats

"Jacksonian Democracy"

Although never used by contemporaries, "Jacksonian Democracy" has been a favorite term of historians. From the time of the so-called Progressive school of American history, the second quarter of the nineteenth century was celebrated as "the era of the common man," the time when a triumphant democracy, led by Andrew Jackson, conquered the nation and transformed its institutions irrevocably. The culmination of Progressive history came as late as 1945 with the publication of Arthur M. Schlesinger Jr.'s *Age of Jackson*. Schlesinger hailed Jackson as a great democratic leader and applauded the achievements of the Democratic party.[1]

Schlesinger's book was itself a great achievement, unquestionably one of the most important works in American history in the twentieth century. Its strength was the author's ability to empathize with the Democrats. As a result he was aware of, and able brilliantly to communicate, their sense of urgency, their conviction that they were the special champions of the people locked in a desperate struggle against the "aristocracy." Moreover, Schlesinger realized, as his critics did not, that there was an anti-capitalist animus in the Jacksonian movement. The Democratic party was, he argued, hostile to the claims of "the business community."[2]

1. On Jacksonian historiography see Alfred A. Cave, *Jacksonian Democracy and the Historians* (Gainesville, Fla., 1964); Edward Pessen, *Jacksonian America: Society, Personality and Politics* (rev. ed. Homewood, Ill., 1978); Charles G. Sellers, Jr., "Andrew Jackson *versus* the Historians," *Mississippi Valley Historical Review*, XLIV (1958), pp. 613–634; Don F. Flat, "Historians View Jacksonian Democracy: A Historiographical Study" (Ph.D. dissertation, University of Kentucky, 1974); Ronald P. Formisano, "Toward a Reorientation of Jacksonian Politics: A Review of the Literature, 1959–1975," *Journal of American History*, LXII (1976), pp. 42–65; Sean Wilentz, "On Class and Politics in Jacksonian America," in Stanley I. Kutler and Stanley N. Katz (eds), *The Promise of American History: Progress and Prospects* (Baltimore, 1982), pp. 45–63.
2. Arthur M. Schlesinger, Jr., *The Age of Jackson* (Boston, 1945), pp. 318–321, 263, 521–523.

Ironically, it was here, where Schlesinger had, if anything, understated his case, that the attacks came. Despite a paucity of evidence to support the claim, other historians argued that the Democrats, so far from being anti-capitalist, were themselves incipient capitalists desiring merely to widen entrepreneurial opportunities for small businessmen. The Age of Jackson witnessed above all the "rise of liberated capitalism." While the Jacksonians may indeed have been "democrats," their democracy was one that sought merely to further the interests of the "rising entrepreneur."[3]

Even if Schlesinger had in fact underestimated Democratic hostility to capitalism, his book was nonetheless open to damaging criticism. His identification with the Democrats was a source of weakness too. Writing as a confirmed New Dealer, he undoubtedly found too many parallels between the 1830s and the 1930s. He ignored the Democratic commitment to limited government (repudiated of course by the New Deal) and exaggerated the role of labor and indeed the non-agricultural sector in the politics of the 1830s and 1840s (again reflecting the experience of the 1930s). None of these weaknesses, however, should obscure the great merits of his work.

A final problem in *The Age of Jackson* was its tendency to overlook Democratic racism. Schlesinger ignored the Democrats' expropriation of the Indians and underestimated their complicity in slavery in the South. These issues, however, were also largely ignored by his critics – at least until the 1960s – and indeed the relationship between Democratic ideology and slavery remains as a question requiring the most careful consideration.[4]

Other historians have advanced different interpretations of the Jacksonian era. An "ethnocultural" school has come into existence, with its claim that ethnic, religious and cultural differences, rather than disagreements over the fundamentals of capitalism and democracy, were central to Jacksonian politics.[5] (Since I have already attempted a critique

3. Richard Hofstadter, *The American Political Tradition and the Men Who Made It* (N.Y., 1948), chapter 3; Bray Hammond, "Jackson, Biddle, and the Bank of the United States," *Journal of Economic History*, vii (1947), pp. 1–23; Joseph Dorfman, *The Economic Mind in American Civilization* 2 vols (N.Y., 1946); Marvin Meyers, *The Jacksonian Persuasion: Politics and Belief* (Stanford, 1957). The main error of these historians lay in the ahistorical assumption that *laissez-faire* is invariably a capitalist doctrine.
4. See below this and the next chapter.
5. The principal works (for the Jacksonian era) are Lee Benson, *The Concept of Jacksonian Democracy: New York as a Test Case* (Princeton, 1961); Ronald P. Formisano, *The Birth of Mass Parties: Michigan, 1827–1871* (Princeton, 1971). For a critique see John Ashworth, *"Agrarians" and "Aristocrats": Party Political Ideology in the United States, 1837–1846* (London, 1983). See also (for a critique of Benson), Michael A. Lebowitz, "The Significance of Claptrap in American

of this school, I shall not discuss it in detail here.)[6] On the other hand, the work of Charles G. Sellers has, in my view, brilliantly re-emphasized Democratic agrarianism as a central determinant of political conflict in these years. With this interpretation I am very much in sympathy.[7]

Several problems remain, however. Even if we accept – as I shall argue we should – the central claims of the Sellers school, the relationship between the Democratic party and slavery requires further elucidation. As we shall see, this issue raises difficult conceptual problems. But before these can be tackled, we need to re-examine the principal features of Democratic and Whig ideology.[8]

Parties and political theory

I

American political thought had inherited many of the assumptions and ideals current in the mother country. In the eighteenth century, of course, a central tenet of the English political faith had been the emphasis on constitutional balance and harmony. Originally Americans like Englishmen had assumed that the balance should be between different orders: monarchy, aristocracy and democracy. But developments before and immediately after the Revolution quickly made such notions obsolete. Yet the goal of constitutional balance by no means disappeared; instead it underwent a significant change and re-emerged in the thought of Republicans like John Taylor of Caroline. We have already examined some features of Taylor's thought but it is of great importance not merely

History," *Studies on the Left*, III (1963), pp. 79–94. Among more general critiques of this school are J. Morgan Kousser, "The 'New Political History': A Methodological Critique," *Reviews in American History*, IV (1976), pp. 1–14; Richard L. McCormick, "Ethno-Cultural Interpretations of Nineteenth-Century Voting Behavior," *Political Science Quarterly*, LXXXIX (1974), pp. 351–377.

6. I shall in fact examine the conflict over immigration and temperance in the 1850s in the sequel to this volume.

7. Charles G. Sellers, Jr., *James K. Polk, Jacksonian* (Princeton, 1957), *James K. Polk, Continentalist* (Princeton, 1966), "Who were the Southern Whigs?" *American Historical Review*, LIX (1954), pp. 335–346, *The Market Revolution: Jacksonian America, 1815–1846* (N.Y., 1991). Very much in the Sellers mold is James R. Sharp's excellent study, *The Jacksonians versus the Banks: Politics in the States after the Panic of 1837* (N.Y., 1970). See also Michael A. Lebowitz, "The Jacksonians: Paradox Lost?" in Barton J. Bernstein (ed.), *Towards a New Past: Dissenting Essays in American History* (N.Y., 1969), pp. 65–89.

8. I believe Sellers to be mistaken about the relationship between slavery and the party system. What I shall seek to show is that his interpretation of "Jacksonian Democracy" does not entail his view of the "Southerner As American" – Sellers, "The Travail of Slavery" in Sellers (ed.), *The Southerner As American* (Chapel Hill, 1960), chapter 3.

in its own right but because the Democratic party of Andrew Jackson and Martin Van Buren adopted many of his ideas unchanged.[9]

Taylor's *magnum opus*, his *Inquiry into the Principles and Policy of the Government of the United States*, was written to refute the political theories of John Adams. Adams, still locked into eighteenth-century patterns of thought, argued strongly for a separate chamber for the aristocratic elements within American society (in part, it should be added, to protect the rest of the community against this aristocracy). Taylor argued even more strongly that such provision was not only unnecessary but positively dangerous. But he did not entirely repudiate the idea of constitutional balance or rather of a balance in society, maintained and preserved by constitutional structures. Rather than a balance of orders, Taylor insisted upon a balancing of individuals within society; indeed he assumed that white males would naturally, in the absence of governmental intervention, balance one another. None would be able successfully and persistently to exploit the rest. "It was reserved for the United States," he observed, "to discover that by balancing man with man, and by avoiding the artificial combinations of exclusive privileges, no individual of these equipoised millions would be incited by a probability of success, to assail the rest." The result would be that "the concussions of powerful combinations, and the subversion of liberty and happiness, following a victory on the part of the one, would be avoided." The task of government for Taylor – and one might add, for Andrew Jackson and his followers – was to maintain this politically underwritten social balance.[10]

Taylor, as we have already seen, feared that this equilibrium would be threatened not by the poor but by a rich and aristocratic minority, which would seek to use the power of government to further its own interests. He argued that this threat was to be resisted by harnessing the power of the majority, itself incapable of exploiting the minority, and employing it defensively to combat the predatory aristocracy. Many years after Taylor's death, Martin Van Buren, for a quarter of a century a key figure in the Jacksonian movement, wrote a history of American politics which bore the rather Taylorean title, *An Inquiry into the Origin and Course of Political Parties in the United States*. The resemblance did not end here. What Van Buren did was to extend Taylor's thought and to use it to

9. Taylor's thought has not received the attention it merits. See, however, Eugene T. Mudge, *The Social Philosophy of John Taylor of Caroline: A Study in Jeffersonian Democracy* (N.Y., 1959); Robert E. Shalhope, *John Taylor of Caroline, Pastoral Republican* (Columbia, S.C., 1980).
10. John Taylor, *An Inquiry into the Principles and Policy of the Government of the United States* (new ed. London, 1950), p. 373.

provide what Taylor himself had not attempted: a justification for party organization and permanent party conflict.[11]

Like Taylor, Van Buren argued that the danger from the wealthy minority was acute. Unlike Taylor, however, he was able to survey the history of American politics over a lengthy period. He reached the conclusion that the danger was ever present and could be reduced but never entirely eliminated. For "to be allied to power, permanently, if possible, in its character and splendid in its appendages, is one of the strongest passions which wealth inspires." In England the "grandeur of the Crown and of the landed aristocracy" illustrated the effects of this "passion." But in the United States, where both monarchy and titled aristocracy were unknown, this tendency took a different form. Rather than formal titles, the holders of great wealth craved instead "the establishment of a moneyed oligarchy, the most selfish and monopolizing of all depositories of moneyed power." How had they set about this task? Predictably Van Buren now focused his attention upon the old Federalist party. But he added that despite its defeat at the hands of Thomas Jefferson and the Republican party, and its apparent collapse in the first decades of the nineteenth century, the "seed" of Federalism had "never been eradicated." Indeed "it seems not susceptible of eradication." Like many Democrats he insisted that the National Republican party, and later the Whig party, had been the Federalist party reincarnated. Of course such a charge was a potent vote winner, since the Federalists were irrevocably identified with hostility to democracy and the "common man." But there is no reason to doubt that Van Buren and most other Democrats who employed this terminology were sincerely convinced of its accuracy.[12]

The task of politics in general, therefore, and the task of the Democratic party in particular, was to mobilize the majority to resist the encroachments of the wealthy "aristocratic" minority. Most of the political changes inspired by the Jacksonians can be understood in these terms. We have already examined the theory that underlay Democratic innovations in the theory of party, which allowed them to set aside traditional reservations about party conflict. Let us also consider three

11. Van Buren *An Inquiry into the Origins and Course of Political Parties in the United States* (N.Y., 1867).
12. Van Buren, *Inquiry*, pp. 166, 267. See also Washington *Globe*, Aug. 3, 1838; *Proceedings of the Convention of Pennsylvania to Propose Amendments to the Constitution* 14 vols (Harrisburg, 1837–1839), I, p. 116; *Congressional Globe*, 26 Congress, 1 Session, Appendix, p. 590; *Speeches of Messrs Weller, Orr, Lane, and Cobb Delivered in Phoenix and Depot Halls, Concord New Hampshire, At a Mass Meeting of the Democratic Party of Merrimac* Co. (n.p., n.d.), p. 2.

other issues: the growth of presidential power, the role of government and the locus of sovereignty.[13]

II

All histories of the American presidency attach great importance to the Jacksonian era. Andrew Jackson remade the office and converted it into the focal point of the federal representative system. Yet the power accruing to the presidency was a negative one. It was demonstrated above all in the vetoes used by Jackson and his Democratic successors in the White House. Not only did Jackson employ the veto more than all his predecessors combined, he also claimed the right to reject legislation that he deemed inexpedient or impolitic rather than simply unconstitutional. Jackson presented the president as the especial representative of the entire people, charged with maintaining the rights and interests of all Americans. Although John Taylor had in no way anticipated and would indeed have repudiated the Jacksonian conception of the presidency, his theories and general outlook were easily reconciled with the new practice. So long as the danger was from government legislation, passed by the "aristocracy," then the veto power could be defended on majoritarian grounds. Democrats argued that legislators were all-too-liable to promote their own interests or the narrow interests of the minority whom they represented. Alliances struck and bargains made within Congress would thus allow legislation to pass which actually sacrificed the interests of the majority. Democrats condemned this process of "logrolling" as it has come to be known. President Polk explained that the veto "arrests for the time hasty, inconsiderate, or unconstitutional legislation." The veto would be wielded in the interests of the majority by the President, the man in whom "the popular will is most potently concentrated." Hence Democrats continued, long after Jackson's departure from the White House, to champion executive power in general and the

13. Good surveys of Democratic political thought include Lawrence Frederick Kohl, *The Politics of Individualism: Parties and the American Character in the Jacksonian Era* (N.Y., 1989); Rush Welter, *The Mind of America, 1820–1860* (N.Y., 1975). See also Robert V. Remini, *The Legacy of Andrew Jackson* (Baton Rouge, 1988), pp. 7–44. Among the major recent works which shed light on the Democratic party are Donald B. Cole, *Martin Van Buren and the American Political System* (Princeton, 1984); John Niven, *Martin Van Buren: The Romantic Age of American Politics* (N.Y., 1983); Robert V. Remini, *Andrew Jackson and the Course of American Freedom, 1822–1832* (N.Y., 1981), Remini, *Andrew Jackson and the Course of American Democracy, 1833–1845* (N.Y., 1984); Major L. Wilson, *The Presidency of Martin Van Buren* (Lawrence, Kan., 1984). The interpretation given here is advanced in greater detail in my *"Agrarians" and "Aristocrats": Party Political Ideology in the United States, 1837–1846* (London, 1983).

veto in particular. "I love the Veto power," Joseph Holt announced to a party gathering in 1852.[14]

At the same gathering, Holt also announced that he was hostile to governmental power in general. It was not a contradiction. He himself correctly restated Democratic theory when he observed that "the Democratic party . . . have insisted and insist, that all government is, at best, but a necessary evil, and that, as a general rule, that nation is the best governed which is governed the least." Similarly the *Washington Globe*, the newspaper set up by Jackson himself, had as its motto the adage "the world is too much governed." Horatio Seymour of New York had "but one petition to our law-makers – it is to be let alone" while, according to the St Paul *Pioneer and Democrat*, "the truth" was that "men legislate too much; they make too many laws." "The laws of nature," it was claimed, "are better than the laws of men." The Democratic demand for limited government underwent significant changes as the Civil War neared but in Jackson's era it was based on the reasoning which Jefferson and Taylor had employed a generation earlier: an active government was exploitative and "aristocratic".[15]

These same hopes and fears were reflected in Jacksonian theories of sovereignty. It is quite wrong to assume, in the fashion of historians who adopted a "consensus" view of the American past, that after the demise of the Federalists, general agreement had been reached on fundamental questions like sovereignty. The Democrats in the 1830s and 1840s advocated a highly populistic political system, one that empowered adult white males and championed their rights against many of the social and political elites in the nation. The Democrats emphasized the dangers of power and, in keeping with their emphasis on the need to mobilize the majority interest against the minority, sought to recruit even the propertyless white male. The result was that most Democrats insisted that such citizens possessed an inherent right to vote.[16] (Whigs by contrast usually

---

14. James D. Richardson (ed.), *A Compilation of the Messages and Papers of the Presidents, 1789–1897* 10 vols (Washington, D.C., 1899), IV, p. 375; *Speech of Joseph Holt, Delivered at a Democratic Meeting Held at the Court House, . . . Louisville . . . 19 October 1852* (Louisville, 1853), p. 7. See also Washington *Globe*, Dec. 29, 1840; Leroy P. Graf and Ralph W. Haskins (eds), *The Papers of Andrew Johnson* (Knoxville, Tenn., 1967–), I, p. 93; John B. Moore (ed.), *The Works of James Buchanan* 12 vols (Phil., 1908–1911), V, pp. 604–605.

15. *Speech of Joseph Holt, Louisville, 19 October, 1852* (Louisville, 1853), p. 3; Thomas M. Cook and Thomas W. Knox (eds), *Public Record: Including Speeches, Messages, Proclamations, Official Correspondence, and other Public Utterances of Horatio Seymour* (N.Y., 1868), p. 5; Washington *Globe, passim*; St Paul *Pioneer and Democrat*, Jan. 14, 1858. See also *Democratic Review* motto and I (1837), p. 4. Theodore Sedgwick, Jr. (ed.), *A Collection of the Political Writings of William Leggett* 2 vols (N.Y., 1840), II, p. 273.

16. For additional evidence of Democratic populism see *Democratic Review*, IX (1841), p. 435, XXIX (1851), p. 520; *Journal of the New Hampshire Senate* (Concord, 1842),

claimed that the suffrage was a privilege rather than a right.) But while the parties in the states frequently differed on the suffrage question, they were even more divided on the nature of sovereignty. The crucial test case came in Rhode Island when in 1842 after several years of failed attempts at constitutional reform, advocates of a more liberal suffrage boldly set aside the existing constitution and, invoking the original rights of the people, submitted to them a new constitution. When this constitution was ratified by a large majority there were two governments in the state. The Democrats demanded that the new constitution, the new government and the new Governor, Thomas W. Dorr, be recognized. But this raised the vexed question of sovereignty. In keeping with his often-stated commitment to majority rule, Jackson, in retirement in Tennessee, declared that "the people" were "the sovereign power" and hence had "a right to alter and amend their system of Government when a majority wills it, as a majority have a right to rule." On this issue there was (outside the ranks of the Calhounites) complete agreement within the Democratic party. As we shall see, there was an equally complete agreement among Whigs – but to the opposite effect. Democrats espoused a highly populistic view of sovereignty.[17]

Democratic political theory was in fact not only populistic but remarkably egalitarian – so far, at least, as adult white males were concerned. While party spokesmen were quick to concede that such men were different one from another, the political system which they sought either ignored such differences or sought to combat their inegalitarian effect. The tasks of government were simple and straightforward; as Jackson himself had observed in the early years of his presidency, they were such that "men of intelligence" might easily perform them. Hence there was no need for the "natural aristocracy" so beloved not only of Federalists but also of Republicans like Thomas Jefferson (though not, it should be noted, of John Taylor of Caroline). Some Democrats stated quite unreservedly that they did not desire to see those with great talents in government. Thus even though they acknowledged the differences between men,

p. 4; George Bancroft, *Oration Delivered Before the Democracy of Springfield and Neighboring Towns, 4 July 1836* (Springfield, 1836), p. 4; Robert J. Ker (reporter), *Proceedings and Debates of the Convention of Louisiana* (New Orleans, 1845), p. 150; Benjamin F. Shambaugh (ed.), *Fragments of the Debates of the Iowa Constitutional Conventions of 1844 and 1846 along with Press Comment and Other Materials* (Iowa City, 1900), pp. 120, 222–223; Washington *Daily Union* March 16, 1849.

17. On the events in Rhode Island see Arthur M. Mowry, *The Dorr War* (Providence, R.I., 1901); Marvin Gettleman, *The Dorr Rebellion, A Study in American Radicalism* (N.Y., 1973). For Democratic responses see John B. Rae, "Democrats and the Dorr Rebellion," *New England Quarterly*, IX (1936), pp. 476–483; Washington *Globe*, 13 May, 1842.

Democrats sought a political system which in no way relied upon such differences, and which would indeed have functioned just as well – and probably better – if all men had been precisely the same.[18]

Two further points are important. First, we should note that Democrats were able, as a result of these theories, to extol the democratic process itself in ways that were quite controversial in the 1830s and 1840s. As we shall see, for good reasons most of their opponents did not share their faith in democracy and were indeed alarmed by Democratic exuberance on this subject. Closely linked with their confidence in democracy was the Jacksonian faith in the virtue of the people. We shall consider the role of virtue in Democratic thought later but it is important to note that Jackson, Van Buren, Polk and the other leaders of the party went out of their way to emphasize their confidence in popular virtue. In a letter written in 1841 Jackson himself announced that "a long and intimate acquaintance with the character of the American people inspired me with the most implicit faith in their disposition to pursue and maintain truth, virtue, patriotism and independence with a single purpose." These sentiments were common among Democrats, uncommon among their opponents.[19]

III

It is scarcely too much to claim that the Whig party owed its existence to the desire to challenge the populistic tendencies of the Democratic party. Indeed the party's name implies its *raison d'être*: the need to resist Jackson's alleged executive usurpations. Without doubt Whigs were genuinely dismayed at the growth in executive power over which Jackson and his Democratic successors presided but this was part of a much wider

---

18. Richardson (ed.), *Messages of Presidents*, II, p. 449. See also *Congressional Globe*, 25 Congress, 1 Session, Appendix, p.21, 2 Session, p. 251; Washington *Globe*, Sept. 24, 1840; *Western Review*, I (1846), p. 18; *Democratic Review*, XXI (1847), p. 202; Ely Moore, *An Address on Civil Government* (N.Y., 1847), pp. 23, 15; George Sidney Camp, *Democracy* (N.Y., 1845), pp. 54, 139; *Young Hickory Banner*, Aug. 17, 1844; John P. Tarbell, *An Oration delivered before the Democratic Citizens of the North Part of Middlesex County, at Groton, July 4, 1839* (Lowell, 1839), pp. 27–28; *Kendall's Expositor*, II (Jan. 20, 1842), p. 18. See also Michael J. Heale, *The Presidential Quest: Candidates and Images in American Political Culture, 1787–1852* (London, 1982), chapters 8 and 9.

19. Jackson to J. P. Hardwicke *et al.*, Oct. 20, 1841 in *Niles Register*, LXI (1841), p. 151. See also Van Buren to Jackson Oct. 17, 1837 in John S. Bassett (ed.), *The Correspondence of Andrew Jackson* 7 vols (Washington D.C., 1926–37), V, p. 516; Washington *Globe*, July 5, 1837, June 28, Aug. 24, 1840; George Bancroft, *The Principles of Democracy: An Address at Hartford . . . Feb. 18, 1840* (Hartford, 1840), p. 4.

concern with the changes in American government generally. The innovations upon which Democrats enthusiastically embarked were deplored by the Whigs.[20]

They emphasized, of course, that a concentration of power in the hands of a single individual was necessarily unhealthy. Calvin Colton, for example, writing as "Junius," warned that "power, and such power [as the executive had acquired]" was "a giddy elevation," was "sweet" and was such as to "nourish aspiration." But as Colton's career clearly demonstrates, the fear was not so much of the president alone, or even of the president and the officeholders whom he had appointed, but instead of the populistic appeal to the majority that was the stock-in-trade of Democratic presidents.[21] Most Whigs looked instead to Congress, the deliberative body of the Republic, dependent upon, but somewhat removed from, the will of the people. They believed such detachment essential if those in government were to be able to employ their wisdom and superior judgment in the interests of all. Hence, as one New Yorker put it, "there must be no short cut or side path to the will of the people." The Senate, in particular, must retain considerable autonomy; in the words of Alexander Stephens, future vice-president of the Confederacy, it must be "free from the influence and control of sudden changes in popular opinion." Such reasoning made Whigs highly suspicious of populistic devices such as pledges. Campaigning for the presidency, Zachary Taylor refused to give pledges on the grounds that "one who cannot be trusted without pledges, cannot be confided in merely on account of them."[22]

20. After over a century of total neglect the ideas of the Whigs have at last received adequate attention. The best single work is Daniel Walker Howe, *The Political Culture of the American Whigs* (Chicago, 1979). See also Thomas Brown, *Politics and Statesmanship: Essays on the American Whig Party* (N.Y., 1985). Many insights are to be found in Welter, *Mind of America*. In my view, however, historians continue to underestimate Whig hostility to, or at least suspicion of, democracy (largely because they misconstrue Democratic ideology). See Ashworth, *"Agrarians" and "Aristocrats," passim.*
21. "Junius", *One Presidential Term* (N.Y., 1840), p. 5; Alfred A. Cave, *An American Conservative in the Age of Jackson: The Political and Social Thought of Calvin Colton* (Fort Worth, 1969), p. 57.
22. Daniel D. Barnard, *A Discourse delivered before the Senate of Union College* (Albany, 1843), p. 48; Stephens quoted in Donald A. Debats, "Elites and Masses: Political Structure, Communication and Behavior in Ante-Bellum Georgia" (Ph.D. dissertation, University of Wisconsin, 1973), pp. 226–227; Zachary Taylor to J. S. Allison, April 22, 1848 reprinted in Arthur M. Schlesinger and Fred L. Israel (eds), *A History of Presidential Elections 1789–1968* 4 vols (N.Y., 1971), II, p. 913. See also "Junius", *Democracy* (N.Y., 1844), p. 6; Frank H. Severance (ed.), "The Millard Fillmore Papers" 2 vols, *Publications of the Buffalo Historical Society*, X (1907), II, p. 174; Allan Nevins (ed.), *The Diary of Philip Hone* (N.Y., 1936), p. 349; Lynn L. Marshall, "The Strange Stillbirth of the Whig party," *American Historical Review* LXXII (1967), pp. 445–468.

A Democrat would have replied that the dangers of power were so great that pledges and other formal commitments were essential. But in Whig eyes it was important that the representative be given the opportunity to discuss issues fully and dispassionately with other representatives and to change his views if the need arose, all the time remaining accountable to his constituents. Moreover, Whigs argued that the representative was charged with the welfare not merely of his own constituents but of the entire nation. Deliberation and compromise were thus essential. Prior to Jackson's election, "Junius" observed, "Congress had been independent, and the dominant power in the republic, as the immediate representatives of the people ever ought to be." According to the *Arkansas Whig*, the party had "an abiding faith in the power and strength of law, and of the moral and intelligent functions of the government," believing that "the Representative qualifiedly impersonates a moral power, representing not the aggregate, but the unity, the one-mindedness, in a moral sense of the whole American people."[23]

Though they could agree on the need to curb presidential power, the Whigs were not unanimous in their attitude to democratic government. Those on the more conservative wing of the party were wont to lament the degeneration from republic to democracy. Such men made no secret of their distaste for mass politics and would in fact have been entirely at home in Alexander Hamilton's Federalist party.[24] Others were far more liberal and were occasionally capable of delivering encomiums on the nation's democratic system that could rival those of the Democrats.[25] But neither group represented mainstream Whig opinion. Most Whigs were political conservatives, not wishing to return to the early decades of

23. *The Junius Tracts* (N.Y., 1844), p. 64; Arkansas *Whig*, May 22, 1851. See also *National Intelligencer*, Jan. 12, 1836; R. McKinley Ormsby, *A History of the Whig Party* (Boston, 1859), pp. 67, 363, 370.

24. For examples of conservative Whig utterances see *Proceedings of the Whigs of Chester County, Favorable to a Distinct Organization of the Whig Party* (n.p., n.d.), pp. 17–18; [William R. Watson], *The Whig Party; Its Objects – Its Principles – Its Candidates – Its Duties – and Its Prospects, An Address . . . by "Hamilton"* (Providence, R.I., 1844), p. 4; Cincinnati *Gazette*, March 19, 1841; *John, The Traitor, or, The Force of Accident . . .* (N.Y., 1843), pp. 11, 13; NewYork *Courier and Enquirer*, May 19, 1845; [Calvin Colton], *A Voice from America to England by an American Conservative* (London, 1839), pp. vii, 3, 57–58, 216–217, 220–227, 244, 265, 347; Washington *Independent*, Feb. 4, 22 , March 8, 22, April 22, 29, May 17, 27, June 3, 21, 1841.

25. For illustrations of this more progressive brand of Whiggery see Milo M. Quaife (ed.), "The Convention of 1846," *Publications of the State Historical Society of Wisconsin, Collections*, XXVII (Madison, Wis., 1919), p. 588; Boston *Atlas*, Aug. 4, 1840; Harriet A. Weed (ed.), *The Autobiography of Thurlow Weed* (Boston, 1884), I, p. 360; Albany *Evening Journal*, March 31, May 28, 1838; *New Yorker*, May 12, 1838; George E. Baker (ed.), *The Works of William H. Seward* 5 vols (Boston, 1884), II, pp. 197, 312, III, pp. 17–18, 148, 209–210, 213, 263, 394; Frederick W. Seward (ed.), *William H. Seward: An Autobiography* (N.Y., 1891), p. 547.

the Republic but equally concerned to rebut or reject Democratic claims for the common man.[26]

They looked with suspicion on the Democratic conception of the presidency, not simply because it undermined Congress but also because it was closely allied to the Democratic demand for limited government. The Whigs instead wanted a talented elite to administer what was for the mid-nineteenth century at any rate an interventionist government. This applied at state level and in the federal government; Whigs repudiated outright Democratic theories of *laissez-faire* and limited government. As Horace Greeley put it, "the best government is *not* that which governs least." An active government was needed to guide the development of the American economy but before it could play this role it had to be viewed by the citizen as a support for, rather than a potential threat to, liberty. Individual citizens could only be secure if the majesty of the law were respected. Here was a principal cause of Whig dissatisfaction with the Jacksonian regime. As late as 1856 a pamphlet specifically directed to "Old Line Whigs" rehearsed the objections which many in the party had always had to the politics of conflict pursued by the Democrats. "There can be no condition of society so perfect, or the administration of its laws so impartial," the writer warned, "but that some classes of the people will have apparent grounds of complaint against the unequal burdens which seem to rest upon them." Such complaints were always likely to be "directed against the ruling power as the nearest *perceivable* cause." Yet the real cause was all too likely to be elsewhere, "not necessarily in the government" but instead resulting from "the frail and corrupted condition of the nature of man himself, both the governors and the governed." Here was the scope for the demagogue and here too the reason the great majority of Whigs did not compete with Democrats in heaping praise upon the people. Extravagant claims for them would undermine the true function of the representative and subvert the true role of government.[27]

These priorities were evident when the Dorr rebellion broke out in Rhode Island. All Whigs, from the most conservative to the most liberal, joined in condemning the Dorrites, just as Democrats hastened to offer support. Many of them had some sympathy with the goal of suffrage reform but all recoiled from the theory of sovereignty underlying Dorr's

26. The differences between the two wings of the Whig party are discussed at length in Ashworth, *"Agrarians" and "Aristocrats,"* pp. 111–125, 147–170.
27. Horace Greeley, *Hints Towards Reforms* (N.Y., 1850), p. 126; Greeley, *The Whig Almanac and United States Register for 1843* (N.Y., 1843), pp. 29–30; *The Great Fraud upon the Public Credulity in the Organization of the Republican Party: An Address to the Old Line Whigs of the Union* (Washington, 1856). See also *Whig Review*, I (1845), pp. 3, 275, II (1845), pp. 446–467.

action and the Democrats' response. In 1848 a test case came to the Supreme Court, *Luther* v. *Borden,* which raised once again the key issues of the Dorr rebellion. Appearing for Luther, Benjamin Hallett, a well-known Democratic statesman, argued that it was "the right of the people to change, alter, or abolish their government, in such manner as they please; a right, not of force, but of sovereignty." But Borden's lawyer was still more illustrious: the "Godlike" Daniel Webster. In the course of his defense Webster enunciated classic Whig doctrine. He insisted that republican government be anchored in something more stable than the shifting opinions of a mere majority. There had to be, he argued, "some authentic mode of ascertaining the will of the people, else all is anarchy." The danger was that government would degenerate into "the law of the strongest, or, what is the same thing, of the most numerous for the moment." Once again the Whigs were sceptical about a populistic democracy. As the *National Intelligencer,* the leading Whig paper in the nation, observed: "it too often happens, that the multitude acts first, and deliberates afterwards, when inquiry and reasoning are perhaps of no effect but to induce an unavailing repentance."[28]

As a result many Whigs were equally unhappy about the role of political parties in the Republic. Some of them would clearly have preferred to do without parties altogether but the need to combat the Democrats, quite apart from any other considerations, made this a difficult position to sustain. Yet even as they plunged into party organization – and on occasion fought fire with fire – many of them continued to express doubts. At the minimum they refused to invest any party, even their own, with the sanctity with which the Democracy was surrounded. In Iowa in the mid-1840s one Whig newspaper noted the "harmony" that seemed to characterize the Democratic party and contrasted it with the "difference of opinion" within Whig ranks. "That party," the newspaper continued, "is not formed of the right material to be drilled and marshalled by aspiring leaders." A few years later, in North Carolina United States Senator William A. Graham was reminded that "The Dem [sic] party have ties of affinity to which we are Strangers." In general, Whigs

28. Arthur M. Schlesinger, Jr., *The Age of Jackson* (Boston, 1945), p. 413; *National Intelligencer,* July 16, 1836. See also John Whipple, *Substance of a Speech Delivered at the Whig Meeting Held at the Town House, Providence, Rhode Island, August 28, 1837* (Providence, 1837), p. 4; Samuel G. Brown (ed.), *The Life and Writings of Rufus Choate* 2 vols (Boston, 1862), II, p. 288. For other Whig responses to the Dorr controversy see *National Intelligencer,* May 9, 1842; Boston *Atlas,* April 12, 1842; Hartford *Courant,* July 2, 1842; Allan Nevins and Milton H. Thomas (eds), *The Diary of George Templeton Strong* 4 vols (N.Y., 1952), I, p. 180; *Letter of Mr. Cuthbert Powell, to the People of the Fourteenth Congressional District of Virginia* (n.p., n.d.), p. 11; Natchez *Daily Courier,* Oct. 3, 1844; Albany *Evening Journal,* June 1, 1842, Oct. 29, 1844. See also the voting in Congress in *Journal of the United States House of Representatives,* 28 Congress, 2 Session, pp. 182–183.

did not seek, and were not able, to match Democratic enthusiasm for political parties any more than they could match Democratic enthusiasm for American democracy.[29]

Democrats and capitalism

I

An obvious problem confronts the historian who wishes to understand the place of capitalism in Democratic (or Whig) thought. What is "capitalism"? Few terms are so commonly used by historians and social scientists but there is no agreement on its meaning. For some scholars a "capitalist" society seems to be one whose members display a significant degree of acquisitiveness; a widespread desire to possess or, perhaps, to consume, is the key characteristic. For other scholars a different, though by no means incompatible, definition centers upon more narrowly economic phenomena and concerns itself above all with the purpose for which production is intended. On this basis a society becomes capitalist as its members cease to produce for their own consumption and begin to produce for the market. Such a definition, which in effect equates capitalism with commerce, is perhaps the most commonly accepted, in practice if not in theory. Throughout this work, however, I have adopted a more restrictive definition derived from Marxist theory, according to which capitalism requires not merely production for the market, but in addition a market for wage labor. I have also emphasized the relationship between wage laborer and capitalist as one of especial importance in determining the structure of the society in question as well as its political and ideological practices and its future trajectory of development. On this definition, therefore, capitalist societies are necessarily commercial, but commercial societies need not be capitalist.

When we examine the Democratic social philosophy, however, we shall consider the extent to which it is either commercial or capitalist, and the extent to which Jacksonian man was thought to be acquisitive. Some difficulties, however, are immediately apparent. The party underwent major changes both in its principles and in its practice in the 1850s,

29. Bloomington *Herald* in Shambaugh (ed.), *Iowa Constitutional Conventions*, p. 395. Robert Hall Morrison to William Graham, Feb. 3, 1852, in J.G. de Roulhac Hamilton and Max R. Williams (eds), *The Papers of William Alexander Graham* (Raleigh, 1960–) IV, p. 246. See also *New York Review*, II (Jan. 1838), p. 48; *Congressional Globe*, 25 Congress, 2 Session, Appendix, pp. 581–582, 29 Congress, 1 Session, Appendix, p. 64; [John P. Kennedy], *A Defence of the Whigs By a Member of the Twenty-Seventh Congress* (N.Y., 1844), p. 22; New York *Courier and Enquirer*, Sept. 27, 1842.

primarily, of course, as a result of the growing sectional tensions within the nation. In that decade it saw its northern strength severely weakened. Similarly in the early years of Jackson's presidency, party principles had not yet been hammered out. Only after the bank war had been launched did Democratic social thought crystallize. Indeed it was only in the years following Jackson's departure from the White House that Democratic principles were most clearly enunciated. We must remember, therefore, that the party principles were not unchanging.[30]

Equally we must note that the party was never monolithic. To begin with, those who followed John C. Calhoun, as we have already seen, differed in their views from those in the party mainstream. Moreover, there was an equally fundamental split between radical and conservative Democrats. In their attitudes to commerce and to capitalism the two groups disagreed sharply.[31] We shall consider the impact of these differences upon the sectional controversy later, but for the moment we shall concentrate on the radical wing, which was dominant in most of the states and also at federal level until at least the mid-1840s.

II

Democratic thinking placed a heavy emphasis upon the role of the farmer in the nation's economy, society and polity. At a time when agriculture employed over 80% of the nation's labor force and accounted for almost 70% of commodity output this emphasis is perhaps not in itself remarkable. Yet as we shall see, the Whigs did not address the agricultural interest in quite the same way. Moreover, the Democratic appeal was to a particular kind of agriculture. Echoing Jefferson's famous passage in the *Notes on Virginia*, the *Democratic Review*, quasi-official publication of the party, announced that it was "the cultivators of the earth" who "must be looked upon as the great and perennial fountain of that Republican spirit which is to maintain and perpetuate our free institutions." One might think that all who worked on the land were included in this classification but such was far from the case. Slaves were certainly excluded as far as the *Democratic Review* or any other mouthpiece for Democratic opinion was concerned, just as they had found no place in Jefferson's rural arcadia several decades earlier. Nor was the tenant farmer especially worthy of esteem. Instead it was the freeholder who was most admired. "What possible mode could you adopt," one

---

30. The evolution of the Democratic party and the development of its ideology are the subject of the following chapter.
31. I have examined the ideas of the conservative Democrats in *"Agrarians" and "Aristocrats,"* pp. 132–146.

Missouri Democrat asked Congress, "so well calculated to develop all that is great and noble in the character of a people, as that of making every citizen of the country a freeholder and the lord of the soil on which he lives?" In the words of the *Mississippian*, the leading Democratic newspaper in Mississippi, "an independent yeomanry" was "a country's pride and bulwark of defence." Here the key word was "independent". The freeholder was independent in a way that neither the slave nor the tenant could ever be. The superiority of the freeholding farmers derived from the "peculiar adaptation of their occupation to the cultivation of the independent spirit of man."[32]

Independence, however, is itself a slippery concept. Even if we restrict the term so that it denotes a lack of dependence on other humans or human institutions (rather than, for example, on the land or the climate) then the ultimate form of independence might be one in which citizens produce only for their own consumption. The result would then be an absolute independence of the market. It is not easy to determine whether this is what the Democrats meant. So far as I am aware, no Democrats ever expressed disapprobation of subsistence farming in the way that the Whigs did. Nor were doubts cast upon the subsistence farmer as they were upon the tenant. Yet purely subsistence agriculture was becoming rather uncommon in the United States by the time Andrew Jackson took office, and it did not occupy a central place in Democratic thought. More important was the kind of semi-subsistence farming which was common throughout the nation in 1830 and still fairly common in the South as late as the Civil War. Here production might be principally for subsistence needs but with a small yet significant surplus used to buy other goods in a local market. The locality itself might be almost entirely cut off from the wider regional, let alone national and international economy, but within its boundaries some trade would occur. The next position along what we might call the commercialism/subsistence spectrum is one in which production is in large part for the market, for distant, even international markets as well as for local ones, but with the important proviso that the produce of the farm also meets, to a considerable degree, personal and family subsistence needs. Such a proviso is indeed crucial since it allows a degree of protection and shelter from the vicissitudes of trade

---

32. Douglass C. North, *Growth and Welfare in the American Past* (Englewood Cliffs, N.J., 1966), pp. 19–22; *Congressional Globe*, 25 Congress, 2 Session, Appendix, p. 293; *Democratic Review*, VI (1839), pp. 500–502; *Mississippian*, Jan. 12, 1838; Edmund Burke, *An Address Delivered Before the Democratic Republican Citizens of Lempster, New Hampshire* (Newport, N.H., 1839), p. 17.

at the same time as it frees the farmer to create and increase what historians and contemporaries have termed the "marketable surplus."[33]

It is probable that Democrats welcomed agriculture that was as or less
commercialized than this. But they were reluctant to admit what in retrospect we may see as the next stage. For a variety of reasons American
farmers, certainly by the later part of the century, had been forced into an
almost total dependence upon the market so that land ownership itself
bestowed no greater autonomy than any other form of capital.

If the Democratic ethos can be termed commercial, then we must
acknowledge that it was a highly restricted commercialism. What the
Democrats wanted was a system of farming that would preserve a
close relationship between effort and wealth; the function of the market
should be to strengthen, not to supersede this relationship. What they
wanted, in other words, was risk-free commerce. It was not the kind of
commerce they observed in their own times. Merchants received much of
the blame. "The profession of a merchant," complained the Washington
Globe, the newspaper set up by Andrew Jackson to promote the party's
views, was "with many honorable exceptions, a succession of throws of
the die." Merchants were too willing to go into debt and thus were too
often bankrupted. If, instead, their high-risk enterprises were successful,
then the result would be great wealth, itself a grossly excessive reward for
the effort invested and, moreover, a direct threat to the social equality
upon which a democratic government rested. One Democrat spoke dis-
paragingly of "the large sums of money which they accumulate without
much bodily toil" but which enabled them to live "in ease and splendour
not enjoyed by any other large class or community." Instead merchants,
who were clearly indispensable if there were to be any international trade,
should conduct themselves in precisely the way that the virtuous farmer
operated. What Democrats wished to see were "the slow, sure, and silent
gains of a business prudently conducted, requiring years of cautious
sagacity, and, above all, a character as clear as the sun, to build up an
independency."[34]

In the 1830s and early 1840s, however, Democrats believed that social
practices had degenerated so far that rather than the merchant emulating
the independent farmer, the farmer had instead been seduced by the

33. Jeremy Atack and Fred Bateman, "Self-Sufficiency and the Origins of the Marketable
Surplus in the Rural North, 1860," *Agricultural History*, LVIII (1984), pp. 296–313;
Steven Hahn, "The 'Unmaking' of the Southern Yeomanry," in Steven Hahn and
Jonathan Prude (eds), *The Countryside in the Age of Capitalist Transformation*
(Chapel Hill, 1985), pp. 179–203.
34. Washington *Globe*, July 1, 1839; *Congressional Globe*, 25 Congress, 1 Session,
Appendix, p. 46.

high-risk ventures adopted by so many merchants. In 1837 a Panic struck
the nation's financial and banking system and it was soon followed by a
recession from which the economy did not recover until 1843.[35] At this
time Democrats voiced deep grievances about the condition of their country. Its commercial practices were closely scrutinized – and found wanting. Debt, for example, was perceived as a major problem. Too many
Americans had been tempted into debt and had paid a severe penalty.
"Individual debts, state debts and national debts," a group of New York
Democrats complained in 1840, "are productive of a condition of dependence destructive of equality among men and freedom of action among
States and nations." There were obvious implications for policy: laws
which offered corporations limited liability, for example, immediately
fell under suspicion since they encouraged risk taking and indebtedness.
For the same reason, lenient bankruptcy laws were anathema: a severe
penalty was needed as a deterrent.[36] But by far the most important issue
for the Democrats in these years was the banking question. The
Democrats voiced many criticisms of banking and paper money but
none was more fundamental than the tendency of banks to accentuate
the trade cycle by enticing men into speculative ventures so that wealth
became the product of chance rather than labor. President Martin Van
Buren in 1838 complained that in recent times bank expansions had
"seduced industry from its regular and salutary occupations by the
hope of abundance without labor, and deranged the social state by tempting all trades and professions into the vortex of speculation on remote
contingencies." As the *Democratic Review* explained, "a sudden increase
of currency" and a "consequent rise of prices," were likely to "seduce
thousands of industrious individuals to abandon their regular employment under the expectation of realising speedy fortunes by speculation."
The problem was, in the words of another Democrat, that "rural occupation, steady habits, moderate living are cast into such eclipse, that few can
endure their lot, contrasted with the glare of sudden fortune." These were
the commercial practices which Democrats could not tolerate. High-risk
schemes, venture capital, the reward for labor disrupted by the trade
cycle – such were the dangers that an excessive haste for commercializa-

---

35. On the Panic of 1837 and the subsequent recession see Peter Temin, *The Jacksonian
    Economy* (N.Y., 1969); Marie Sushka, "The Antebellum Money Market and the
    Economic Impact of the Bank War," *Journal of Economic History*, xxxvi (1976),
    pp. 809–835.
36. *Address to the Democratic Republican Electors of the State of New York*
    (Washington, D.C., 1840), p. 19. See also *Congressional Globe*, 26 Congress, 1
    Session, Appendix, p. 91; *Journal of the Senate of New Hampshire* (Concord,
    1840), p. 5; Washington *Globe*, July 18, 1837; *Democratic Review*, v (1839), p.
    84, viii (1840), pp. 101–102, x (1842), pp. 48–50; Theophilus Fisk, *A Vindication
    of the Rights of Man* (Portsmouth, Va., 1838), p. 14.

tion entailed. The Washington *Globe* observed that since "we are, notoriously, a moving, striving people," there was "more danger that we should do too much than that we should do too little." "Enterprise," according to its editor, was "a good thing." But "prudence and honesty are better."[37]

Many Democrats thus entertained profound doubts about prevailing commercial practices and did not hesitate to open fire upon those engaging in them. We may note once again that they offered no criticisms of those engaging instead in subsistence agriculture; such farmers were honored and praised. This surely places a question mark against the Democratic commitment to commerce and consequently, according to one definition of the term, against the Democratic commitment to capitalism. Nevertheless it is also important to note that Democrats hoped to tame and control commerce. They wanted the increased prosperity the market offered but without the loss of that form of independence which they cherished and which, with hindsight, we know to have been a casualty of commercial progress. Hence it would be misleading and an oversimplification to label them either "commercial" or "anti-commercial."

The Democratic view of wage labor also requires examination. At the time when Jefferson became president, it has been estimated, only 12% of Americans were employed for wages; by the time of Lincoln's election the figure had risen to 40%.[38] The Democratic party in the Jacksonian era took a Jeffersonian, rather than a Lincolnian view of wages. Not surprisingly, a party that was unhappy with the dependence entailed by tenant farming was unenthusiastic about the relationship between employer and worker. The dismay with which Democrats viewed prevailing commercial practices, as we have seen, played a major role in generating the controversy over banking. Similarly, those who were most implacable in their hostility to the banking system tended also to be those who were most distrustful of wage labor. At the furthest reaches of the Democratic party was Orestes Brownson who, as is well known, in 1840 proposed that the party prohibit the inheritance of property. Less well known, however, is the view of wages that he expressed at the same time. Brownson's goal was to "combine labor and capital in the same individual" and he argued that it was agriculture, more than any other pursuit, which could achieve this. But even in the agricultural sector, the

37. Richardson (ed.), *Messages of Presidents*, III, p. 494; *Democratic Review*, IV (1839), p. 97; *Congressional Globe*, 27 Congress, 1 Session, Appendix, p. 409; Washington *Globe*, Dec. 8, 1837; Sharp, *Jacksonians versus Banks*, passim.
38. Stanley Lebergott, "The Pattern of Employment Since 1800," in Seymour Harris (ed.), *American Economic History* (N.Y., 1961), pp. 281–310.

situation was deteriorating since "the distance between the owner of the farm, and the men who cultivate it" was "becoming every day greater and greater." Yet this problem shrank into insignificance beside the scene in the towns and manufacturing villages where "the distinction between the capitalist and the proletary" was "as strongly marked as it is in the old world." For Brownson the ultimate threat to individual autonomy was the wages system. Wages were "the cunning device of the devil" and the wage system had to be eliminated "or else one half of the human race must forever be the virtual slaves of the other."[39]

Brownson was an unusual Democrat and an erratic partisan. More measured in his utterances was New York Senator Silas Wright who was known to speak for the Van Burenites, in the late 1830s and early 1840s the dominant group within the party. Wright focused attention upon manufacturing and complained of "the great power which the manufacturing capitalist must hold over the employee, and, by necessary consequence, over the living, the comfort, and the independence of the laborer." Similarly, Amos Kendall, one of Andrew Jackson's closest collaborators, urged the sons of farmers to remain on the farm rather than to seek employment in factories.[40]

For Kendall the worthy citizen was either a farmer or an "independent mechanic." Here he perhaps left the way open for a modest amount of wage labor. What did he mean by "independent"? Unfortunately it is difficult to answer this question. An "independent" mechanic, according to Kendall, was one who could refuse "to sell his services to any man on other conditions than those of perfect equality – both as citizens and men." Kendall may have meant here the self-employed craftsman, who sold his services not to an employer but instead to the consumer. Or he may have meant a wage worker, whose terms of employment were not such as to produce large inequalities of wealth, power and esteem. How were such terms to be attained? Kendall did not specify.[41]

Other Democrats had trouble with wage labor. Like Kendall, they believed that independence was essential, but like him they were unsure whether it was compatible with employment for wages. The Washington *Globe* referred approvingly to, in effect, two kinds of mechanic or artisan and had no difficulty in defining the first. He was none other than the self-employed craftsman. But a string of subordinate clauses was

39. *Boston Quarterly Review*, III (1840), pp. 475, 467–71, III (1840), pp. 370, 374.
40. Ransom H. Gillet, *The Life and Times of Silas Wright* 2 vols (Albany, 1874), II, pp. 1487–1488; *Kendall's Expositor*, II (May 31, 1842), p. 163. See also *Democratic Statesman*, May 10, 1845; *Young Hickory Banner*, Aug. 24, 1844.
41. *Kendall's Expositor*, II (May 31, 1842), p. 163.

necessary to offer even an approximate definition of the second. The newspaper spoke of

> the healthy mechanic or artisan, who works for himself at his own shop, or if he goes abroad, returns home to his meals every day, and sleeps under his own roof every night; whose earnings are regulated by the wants of the community at large, not by the discretion of a pernicious master; whose hours of labor depend on universal custom; who, when the sun goes down, is a freeman until he rises again, who can eat his meals in comfort, and sleep as long as nature requires.

The problem was that the *Globe*, like Kendall and like other Democrats, did not explain how the conditions necessary for acceptable forms of wage labor were to be obtained.[42]

Alongside Democratic doubts about commerce we should therefore place Democratic suspicions of wage labor. But what of the third criterion for a capitalist society: did the Democrats assume a large measure of acquisitiveness on the part of the citizen and rest their social theory upon it? At this point it may be helpful to refer to the debate which historians have pursued in recent years about the relative importance of liberalism and republicanism in early American thought. Liberal thought takes as its starting point the self-interested individual and attaches great importance to the market as an instrument through which individual self-interest promotes the general good. Hence merely to advance his own interest, the citizen buys and sells on the market and in so doing increases both the efficiency of the economy and the total wealth created. He thus promotes the welfare of others, even though such may not have been his motive. Classical republican thought, by contrast, rests upon a notion of civic virtue and civic virtue is defined, in turn, as the capacity to subordinate one's own interest to that of the community. Republicanism by no means denies the existence of markets, but it does suggest that market signals will not, by themselves, be sufficient to ensure social harmony and tranquility. Restraint is also necessary; without it society will degenerate in a frenetic scramble for wealth and power with anarchy the likely political outcome.[43]

---

42. Washington *Globe*, Jan. 11, 1842. See also *Democratic Review*, XIX (1846), p. 86.
43. The historiographical debate over classical republicanism and liberalism has concentrated on the Jeffersonian era. Important statements of the "classical republican" interpretation include J. G. A. Pocock, *The Machiavellian Moment: Florentine Political Thought and the Atlantic Republican Tradition* (Princeton, 1975); Lance Banning, *The Jeffersonian Persuasion: Evolution of a Party Ideology* (Ithaca, 1978). An alternative approach is provided by Joyce Appleby, *Capitalism and a New Social Order: The Republican Vision of the 1790s* (N.Y., 1984), which emphasizes the liberal tenets of the Republican faith. For an assessment of this controversy see John Ashworth, "The Jeffersonians: Classical Republicans or Liberal Capitalists," *Journal of American Studies*, XVIII (1984), pp. 425–435.

Democratic thought shared many of the characteristics of liberalism. Most important, it emphasized the role of individual self-interest. Men were necessarily self-interested, Democrats believed, and to deny it was not merely foolish but also dangerous. As we have already seen, the Whigs claimed that for the benefit of the entire community, an elite should be allowed to wield a degree of power, both in the economy and in government, that was incommensurate with its numbers. Democrats replied that the members of this talented elite, if such it were, should not have power conferred upon them since they would use it for their own benefit, precisely as other men would. A failure to recognize the elemental force of self-interest would thus jeopardize the nation's political future. This conviction played a major part in fueling the bank war. Bankers enjoyed the power to determine who should and who should not receive credit. Even more alarmingly, they were able to print bank notes which would then circulate as legal tender, and which, moreover, would help determine the price level and the real value of debts and loans throughout the economy. Here was a constant temptation – and it was one which human beings, necessarily self-interested, could not resist and should not be expected to resist. Who was fit to exercise this fearsome power? "Do the banks," one partisan inquired, "choose men who are more honest, faithful and capable than the people?" "Does a bank stamp upon men as it does upon paper," he continued, "change their qualities, value, worth and character?" The answer was a sobering one: "the history of banks and corporations is the blackest page in the history of fraud and violated trust." Another Democrat reasoned that if a banker were able to print as much money as he chose, and he stood to gain more by printing more, then "the chances are ten, ay, a hundred to one against the man so situated." While men did exist who "might stand the united temptation of opportunity and impunity," these men "come like angel visits – few and far between."[44]

Again and again Democratic theory emphasized the importance of self-interest. "The love of wealth," it was asserted, was "a universal propensity of mankind;" "the love of money" was "one of the strongest passions of the human heart." These convictions had many implications both for the structure of government and for the kinds of policy which government should pursue. They bred a suspicion of all legislation in the economic sphere: the legislators were too likely to further their own interests,

---

44. *Congressional Globe*, 25 Congress, 2 Session, Appendix, pp. 123, 228; Washington *Globe*, Dec. 9, 1840. See also *Address to Working Men, on the Low Price of Wages, by a Mechanic* (n.p., n.d.), p. 4; *Democratic Review*, II (1838), p. 10, XI (1842), p. 258.

or the interests of those whom they represented, to the detriment of the rest of the community.[45]

Moreover, while the self-interest of the rich and powerful was a threat to the nation and its democratic institutions, the self-interest of the majority was seen as its most important bulwark. As we have seen, Democratic theory, following Jefferson and, more precisely, John Taylor of Caroline, sought to pit the self-interest of the majority, expressed above all through their votes, against that of the equally self-interested minority elite, expressed all too often in self-serving legislation. The votes of the majority would thus block schemes hatched by the privileged minority for its own aggrandizement. The Democrats infused a populism into American politics which had not hitherto been present and which their opponents found highly disturbing. They wished to bring the power of an egalitarian democratic system to check the inegalitarian tendencies of the emerging social order.[46]

The implications for morality and for moral legislation were equally important. Democrats in general had many reasons for resisting attempts to legislate on the subject of temperance, for example, but amongst the most important was the belief that society could adequately rest upon the self-interest of its members. The *Democratic Review* advanced a highly secular view of society when it took issue with Alexis de Tocqueville's assessment of the role of religion in maintaining American democracy. The *Review* flatly contradicted Tocqueville when it asserted that "its [religion's] influence is . . . subsidiary to that of the enterprise and industry which form . . . the actual basis of good moral habits." If men were guaranteed an adequate reward for labor, their moral well-being was assured. Only under an inferior form of government, where such a reward was not guaranteed, would religion play a larger role. In these circumstances, "its office would be to resist the moral plague, which would then flow in upon society from the highest places, to furnish new motives for good conduct, in lieu of the worldly prosperity which might then not so uniformly follow it." The function of religion would then be "to preserve as much as could be preserved of the principles of truth and virtue." This was a major departure from traditional republican demands for a self-sacrificing citizenry.[47]

---

45. Washington *Globe*, Dec. 9, 1840. See also *Congressional Globe*, 25 Congress, 2 Session, Appendix, p. 123; Robert Rantoul, *An Oration Delivered Before the Democrats and Antimasons of the County of Plymouth, 4 July, 1836* (Boston, 1836), p. 7.
46. Washington *Globe*, Dec. 29, 1840, March 4, 1841; Richardson (ed.), *Messages of Presidents*, IV, p. 375; *Papers of Andrew Johnson*, I, p. 93; Ker, *Proceedings and Debates of the Constitution of Louisiana*, p. 302.
47. *Democratic Review*, I (1838), pp. 350–352.

That the *Review* was not alone in these opinions can be seen from an examination of the views expressed by George Sidney Camp in his work *Democracy*. Camp, a committed Democrat, also emphasized the role of self-interest in maintaining the republic. He thus followed John Taylor of Caroline and in language which Taylor might himself have used, took issue with those who claimed that republics required an especially virtuous people. "The general opinion that republican government requires for its basis an unusual amount of virtue," he asserted, "is one that adds but little to the energy of benevolent efforts for the promotion of good morals . . . , while it has a strong negative influence in deterring enlightened minds from favouring liberal efforts, and nations from making the experiment of freedom." The virtue which a republic required, he concluded, was "the virtue which almost necessarily results from our having a moral nature." To those among his readers who were wondering how much virtue this was Camp answered that it was "a degree so low, that no state nor nation can, under any circumstances, be supposed to be destitute of it." Moreover, he explicitly denied that self-restraint on the part of the citizenry was necessary. "A republic," he assured his readers, "expects no more than other governments of its citizens." It relied not "upon the state of the public morals, but upon the combination of the virtuous impulses of a moral nature, with the strong motives of a personal interest."[48]

Democrats like Camp thus called attention to the role of self-interest in sustaining the republic. As a result, it is tempting to assume that theirs was a quintessentially liberal outlook. Such a view requires careful qualification, however. Much liberal thought assumes that the pursuit of self-interest, so long as it does not lead to illegal activities, is acceptable. Individual aggression in the economy is defensible; if it leads to the creation of new economic units or the replacement of old ones this can be justified – or even celebrated – in the name of efficiency and increased productivity. In extreme cases, liberal thinkers might wish to exclude from the political arena consideration of such questions as the resulting distribution of wealth, or the moral purpose to which production is put. Each of these matters would be for the individual rather than the political community to consider and act upon.

This variant of liberal thought was not present in the Jacksonian era, least of all among the Democrats. For one thing, the need for an egalitarian distribution of wealth was a constant preoccupation.[49] For another, they expressed, as we have seen, a clear preference for agricultural over

48. Camp, *Democracy* (N.Y., 1845), pp. 94–104.
49. I have discussed Jacksonian notions of equality in "The Jacksonian as Leveller," *Journal of American Studies*, XIV (1980), pp. 407–421.

all other forms of production and did not hesitate to proclaim the moral superiority of the farmer. Even more important, they assumed that individuals would be anything but aggressive in their economic activities. Above all, they believed that the pursuit of self-interest should itself foster virtue and even altruism in society.

If we are not simply to dismiss Democratic thinking as contradictory and confused, then these beliefs require careful analysis. Although they wished to rest government and society upon self-interest, Democrats still emphasized the role of virtue and still condemned in the strongest terms, greed and avarice. Thus William Leggett complained that too many Americans displayed "a feverish avidity for sudden wealth," while Roger Taney, writing to Andrew Jackson, sadly noted that "speculation and the desire of growing rich suddenly without labor, have made fearful inroads upon the patriotism and public spirit of what are called the higher classes of society." Jackson himself declared that "a long and intimate acquaintance with the American people inspired me with the most implicit faith in their disposition to pursue and maintain truth, virtue, patriotism and independence with a single purpose." He added that, "at this late day of my life, it gives me joy to say that this faith is unabated."[50]

Perhaps the key phrase here was Taney's reference to "growing rich suddenly without labor." The Democrats believed that self-interest would impel men to labor and the market would send a clear signal to those who wished to sell some of their produce. It would encourage the production of cotton, or corn or wheat. Or it would direct a blacksmith to set up shop where his services were needed. And the laws of supply and demand would ensure that everyone received a fair reward for his labor, neither too high nor too low. Wealth would then be acquired slowly and painstakingly and there would be a strong and growing conviction that the government under which men lived, and the society of which they formed a part, were fair and just. The resulting distribution of wealth would be approximately equal. Charles Jared Ingersoll of Pennsylvania cited with approval Montesquieu's belief that "love of equality" was "the patriotism of Republics." "Paper money," according to Ingersoll, "extinguishes that patriotism." Other Democrats in effect explained the process. "A man is fitted," Robert Strange of North Carolina told the Senate, "by a gradual increase or reduction of his means," to bear the small fluctuations in his wealth that he might experience. But "sudden reverses either way" would "bring in their train the loss of content, and with it, happiness" since "in either case the passion of avarice is stirred to madness."

50. Sedgwick (ed.), *Political Writings of Leggett*, II, p. 325. Roger Taney to Andrew Jackson, Oct. 18, 1843 in Bassett (ed.), *Correspondence of Jackson*, VI, p. 235.

Democrats assumed that men possessed what we might term a natural sociality; if government encouraged them to labor and gave a fair reward for that labor, this sociality would flourish. Men needed to remain alive to the dangers posed by the rich and powerful minority; despite this, or even because of it, they would show care, compassion and understanding in their dealings with other men. Thus although society rested upon self-interest, Democrats expected altruism to predominate over greed.[51]

This process of reasoning allowed Democrats with one breath to insist upon the role of self-interest and with the next to complain about greed and avarice. According to the *Globe*, "every measure of policy should be estimated by its effects" upon "the morals of the people" rather than "the sordid, miserable standard of profit and loss." The *Globe*'s objection to the banking system was that it had "undermined and prostrated to the earth that mutual confidence between man and man, which forms the great cement of society." Similarly President Van Buren objected to the banks on the grounds that they had nourished "a craving desire for luxurious enjoyment and sudden wealth." On the other hand, in a properly democratic society and under a properly democratic government men would be "less regardful of self, and more mindful of the welfare of the many." According to Edward Barber of Vermont, "the laws" would then be "general in their provisions and impartial in their operation; neither oppressing one, nor granting favors to another." As a result, "independence" would be "in every breast – industry and contentment [would] go hand in hand to their toil, and frugality" would be "the companion of gain." The alternative system, the one now prevailing, marked instead "the triumph of the *selfish* over the *social* principle." Hence the Democratic emphasis upon the role of self-interest in society in no way precluded a deep concern with morality. Samuel McRoberts of Illinois in 1840 expressed a view that was common to many within his party when he claimed that American democracy "has done more, in fifty years, to elevate the moral and political condition of men, than has been effected by any other civil institutions since the Christian era."[52]

We have now come full circle. For Democratic attitudes to virtue and self-interest are only comprehensible in the light of Democratic views of commerce. Commerce depended upon markets and the markets must

---

51. *Congressional Globe*, 27 Congress, 1 Session, Appendix, p. 409, 26 Congress, 1 Session, Appendix, p. 235. See John Zvesper, *Political Philosophy and Rhetoric: A Study of the Origins of American Party Politics* (Cambridge, UK, 1977), pp. 103–104, for a similar view of the Jeffersonians.

52. Washington *Globe*, Nov. 7, 1839; Richardson (ed.), *Messages of Presidents*, III, p. 554; *Address of the Democratic Republican Young Men's Central Committee of the City of New York, To the People of the United States* (N.Y., 1840), p. 3; Edward D. Barber, "Oration at Montpelier, July 4, 1839" in (Vermont) *North Star*, Aug. 10, 1839. Samuel McRoberts, *To the General Assembly of Illinois* (n.p., n.d.), p. 7.

operate, Democrats insisted, in conditions close to those which economists term perfect competition. Yet Democrats also assumed that this would be a tranquil, placid economy, in which changes in production would occur slowly and unthreateningly, and where there would be increased prosperity but without the restless striving for change, the process of decay and regeneration, the turbulence that characterize modern capitalism. In such a society the laws of supply and demand would play a key role and in this sense the economy would be a competitive one. But the individuals participating in it would feel no competitiveness toward one another.

How are we to characterize the Democratic social philosophy? Clearly it would be highly misleading to term it "capitalist." Indeed there is at least as much reason to call the Jacksonians "anti-capitalist." No single term can do justice to the subtlety of Democratic thought. Nonetheless the phrase "pre-capitalist commodity production," inelegant though it may be, is again one that commends itself. Sometimes known as "simple commodity production," it has been defined as follows:

> Simple commodity production is a system in which there are no relations of personal dependence. Each producer owns his own means of production, and there is no wage labor. Furthermore, there are no *classes* as in capitalism. Individual producers work on their own account, and sell their commodities on a competitive market.[53]

Plainly this is not precisely the social order which Democrats desired, since they did not attempt to dismantle the wage system, for example. But there is a close resemblance. It is also interesting to note that in the theoretical model of pre-capitalist commodity production commodities are exchanged on the basis of the labor embodied in them. Again this was a goal to which the Democrats would have been highly sympathetic. We should note that simple commodity production may give rise to capitalism proper, but is nevertheless quite different from it. And slavery? It remains to explore the links between the Democratic social ethos and slavery. But first we need to revert to Whig ideology in order to examine the prevalent anti-Democratic attitude to commerce and to capitalism.

Whigs and capitalism (1)

If the Democrats' attitude to commerce was complex, that of the Whigs was not. Common to all in the party, at least after the departure of

---

53. M. C. Howard and J. E. King, *The Political Economy of Marx* (Harlow, 1975), p. 48.

Calhoun and his small band, was a deep appreciation of commerce and a
desire to maintain or even accelerate its development. The Whigs rallied
to the defense of the nation's banks in the belief that, by so doing, they
were simultaneously defending its commerce. "If we restrict our business
to the exclusive use of specie," Henry Clay warned, "we must cease to be
a commercial people; we must separate, divorce ourselves from the commercial world." For Clay the prospect was frightening: to do so would be
"to throw ourselves back for centuries." John Quincy Adams similarly
extolled commerce. He took strong exception to Jefferson's characterization of commerce as "the handmaid of agriculture," since it clearly
implied a subordinate role. In reality the two were equal. Some Whigs
went even further. In the words of one Tennessee Congressman, commerce was "the main source and fountain from which all our prosperity
and greatness flow."[54]

These sentiments underlay many Whig policies. Eager to promote commerce, the Whigs accurately perceived a chronic shortage of capital in the
United States and concluded that future commercial development
required measures to encourage capital formation. Since credit played a
vital role, the party was driven to resist the Democrats' attacks on the
banking system. According to Daniel Webster, "we owe more to credit,
and to commercial confidence, than any nation which ever existed." The
banks, of course, were the principal suppliers of credit. In addition, the
Whigs defended corporations and also the privilege of limited liability as
spurs to capital formation. When one Indiana Whig senator argued that
capital was needed "to give impetus to the industry and enterprise of our
citizens, to enable them to develope [sic] the immense resources of the
West," the economic development he envisaged was clearly commercial.
It was not that he expected agriculture to disappear from his state and
section; rather that an increasingly commercialized agriculture would
emerge. Horace Greeley, in criticizing many features of the farmer's
life, in effect described the kind of agriculture the Whigs wished to promote:

> [The farmer] is now too nearly an isolated being. His world is a circle
> of material objects he calls his own, within which he is an autocrat,
> though out of it little more than a cipher . . . . Of the refining, har-

---

54. *Congressional Globe*, 25 Congress, 1 Session, Appendix, p. 181; John Quincy
    Adams, *Parties in the United States* (N.Y., 1841), pp. 39–40; *Congressional Globe*,
    25 Congress, 1 Session, Appendix, p. 311. For typical Whig statements about the
    interdependence of commerce and agriculture (and manufacturing), see "Letter of
    Henry Clay to Messrs. L. Bradish, Erastus Root etc., 15 April, 1842," in *Kennebec
    Journal*, May 6, 1842; Severance (ed.), *Papers of Fillmore*, II, p. 238. It should
    perhaps be noted that Adams had some anxieties about prosperity.

monizing, expanding influences of general society, he has little experience . . . . Not until the solitary farmhouse, with its half-dozen denizens, its mottled array of mere patches of auxiliary acres, its petty flock and herd, its external decorations of piggery, stable-yard, etc. . . . shall have been replaced by some arrangement more genial, more expansive, more social in its aspects, affording larger scope to aspiration and a wider field for the infinite capacities of man's nature, may we hope to arrest the tendencies which make the farmer too often a boor or a clod, and the cultivation of the earth a mindless, repugnant drudgery.

Here Greeley agreed with the Democrats that contemporary agriculture promoted autonomy. But what they celebrated he condemned.[55]

Finally, in extending a warm welcome to commercial development, the Whigs were mindful of the vital role played by merchants. Once again they had to rally to the defense. "Who have done more than they," it was asked, "to extend the commerce, the wealth, the honor, and the glory of the nation?" In defending the merchants, the Whigs explained that they were to be honored and praised for engaging in high-risk ventures. For "it is the merchant who risques his all to bring us the comforts and luxuries of foreign climes, and finds a market for our surplus produce, who ought to be encouraged." Once again Whigs extolled the very activities which Democrats condemned.[56]

The high-risk ventures upon which merchants were engaged meant the prospect of huge gains as well as huge losses. Robert Winthrop, addressing a group of Boston merchants in 1845 reminded them that, while a large number might fail, a minority would become very rich. As such they were "to become responsible for the exercise of that vast social power, on which the comfort and happiness and prosperity and even bread of so many thousands of your fellow citizens will depend." He then exhorted them to remember to "regard wealth as mainly valuable as an instrument of philanthropy." Great riches, according to Edward Everett, were the reward of successful merchants. But he too told them that "wealth is ennobled only in its uses."[57]

55. *Congressional Globe*, 25 Congress, 2 Session, Appendix, p. 606, 25 Congress, 3 Session, Appendix, p. 352; Horace Greeley, *Hints Towards Reforms*, pp. 66–68. See also *Congressional Globe*, 25 Congress, 2 Session, Appendix, p. 589; *Jeffersonian*, March 17, 1838; *Kennebec Journal*, May 1, 1841; *Whig Almanac* (N.Y., 1843), p. 30; Henry T. Tuckerman (ed.), *The Collective Works of John P. Kennedy* 10 vols (N.Y., 1871–1872), IV, p. 138.
56. *Congressional Globe*, 25 Congress, 2 Session, Appendix, p. 513, 25 Congress, 1 Session, Appendix, p. 284; *New Hampshire Statesman*, Jan. 7, 1837.
57. Robert Winthrop, *Addresses and Speeches on Various Occasions* (Boston, 1852), p. 53; Edward Everett, *Orations and Speeches on Various Occasions* 4 vols (Boston, 1850), II, p. 311.

These expressions of confidence in the merchant class reveal another vital Whig assumption. Men should not be ruled by self-interest. And in the right kind of society and under the right kind of government, they would not be. Thus the merchant could be trusted with great wealth, since he would not use it to oppress those who were less prosperous. Similarly bankers could be given the power to print money. Of course the Whigs were not so naive as to deny the need for checks and controls. Indeed one of the principal reasons most of them favored a central bank was to provide such checks over the local and state banks. The key point is that where Democrats were likely to argue that no-one could be trusted with this power and even to conclude that it should not exist, the Whigs instead argued that the power should be used creatively and for the social good. They therefore looked for a different ethic, a different set of values within the community and particularly among its natural leaders.

While Democrats emphasized individualism and self-interest, Whigs hoped to temper self-interest with restraint. Democrats held that the sense of community would flourish *after* self-interest had operated, but the Whigs believed that such a sense should guide, moderate and harmonize the many self-interests that were at work within society. In their view, Democratic individualism was highly dangerous. It was dangerous politically. As we have seen, the Whigs were sceptical of Democratic claims both for the people and for the nation's democratic institutions and a key reason was their fear that such claims would undermine individual self-restraint. The *Republican Review*, an early Whig rival to the *Democratic Review*, acknowledged that "the people are and ought to be sovereigns." But the editor then placed a typical Whiggish emphasis on the need for restraints. "That sovereignty," he continued, "is to be regulated and restrained by laws and constitutions, or it becomes the force of the mob." Even more significantly, he then expressed a view of human nature that contrasted sharply with that of the Democrats. "Isolated man must be restrained by laws human and divine, and when he associates into the body politic, the necessity of that restraint becomes more apparent." To the Whigs self-interest, though a vital force, was also a dissolvent one. It had to be tempered by self-control. The *Whig Review*, a later and more long-lasting rival to the *Democratic Review*, in 1845 showed the contempt which many Whigs had for Democratic claims that self-interest could be "enlightened":

> An enlightened self-interest indeed! Has not all experience shown that this term is a contradiction, that self-interest is ever blind, that selfishness is darkness, and has no light . . . and that this is even more apt to be the case with blind and unmeaning masses than with individuals.

Thus the Whigs sought to give power and influence both in the economy and in government to those who were able to take a view that transcended their own self-interest and that instead reflected the wider social interest. According to the *American Quarterly Review*, the "personal feelings and interests" of those in government "should be lost sight of in the nobler consideration of the public good."[58]

Here the Whigs were, of course, echoing classical republicanism. They wished to foster the kind of virtue which classical republicans had desired: a willingness to place, on certain occasions at least, the common good ahead of private and personal gain. They hoped to find legislators who would be capable of this. More important, they feared Democratic political appeals to the self-interest of the masses. In particular they resented Democratic attempts to array either the self-interest of the farmers against merchants and manufacturers, or, more simply, that of the poor against the rich. For the counterpart of the enlarged vision of the ruling elites was a spirit of mild deference on the part of the ruled. It was this which Democratic rhetoric threatened. "Our business," said Webster, "is not to array our various interests into a belligerent and hostile state, not to inflame our own passions or others' concerning the measures of government for the protection of our particular interests; but let us make the whole government a national, I may say a family, concern." The comparison between society and a family was one that came easily to the Whigs. It suggested a collective interest, one identified and supervised by the wise paternalist. For the Whigs those in government should be an elite, able to play a fatherly role in the development of the nation. And like a harmonious family the nation should be bound together by ties of interdependence. "We are all," Henry Clay declared, "- People – States – Union – banks, bound up and interwoven together, united in fortune and destiny, and all, all entitled to the protecting care of a parental Government."[59]

It is by now, perhaps, apparent that the social order that the Whigs desired bears a much closer resemblance to "capitalism" than the one to which Democrats were committed. The Whigs gave an almost wholehearted welcome to commercial development; they applauded the actions of merchants; they hastened to the defense of banks and bankers.

58. Lyman Beecher, *A Plea for Colleges* (Cincinnati, 1836), p. 92; *Republican Review*, I (1839), p. 224; *Whig Review*, II (1845), p. 340; *American Quarterly Review*, XX (1836), pp. 240–241.
59. J. W. McIntyre (ed.), *The Writings and Speeches of Daniel Webster* 18 vols (Boston, 1903), XIII, p. 184; *Congressional Globe*, 25 Congress, 1 Session, Appendix, p. 182. See also *Congressional Globe*, 25 Congress, 1 Session, Appendix, p. 272; *Jeffersonian*, Sept. 22, 1838; William G. Brownlow, *A Political Register* (Jonesborough, Tenn., 1844), p. 10; George E. Badger, *Speech Delivered at the Great Whig Meeting in the County of Granville (N.C.), 3 March 1840* (Raleigh, 1840), p. 15.

Moreover, as we shall see, they were sympathetic towards manufacturing and, on occasion, enthusiastic about wage labor. Yet we should remind ourselves that they displayed considerable reservations about individualism[60] and were reluctant to rest society squarely upon the self-interest of its members. In the twentieth century we naturally associate commerce and capitalism with individualism and self-interest. But in Jacksonian America these configurations simply did not exist. The Democrats were more individualistic, more accepting of self-interest. But the Whigs were the defenders of commerce, of wage labor (in the North), and in this sense, of capitalism.

The defense of manufacturing was a major Whig concern in all parts of the nation, although not surprisingly it had a higher priority in the North than in the South. For Clay and Webster the tariff was useful chiefly for its effect in stimulating manufactures by protecting them from competition with Europe and especially Britain. In New England the manufacturing interest was already by 1830 highly vocal and even in as agricultural a state as New Hampshire the Whigs called for the development of manufacturers. "It is absurd and useless in contemplation of the future," the *New Hampshire Statesman* asserted in 1841, "to suppose that the people of New England are to be a community of farmers. It cannot, it will not be so." The editor argued that the natural endowments of the region precluded an exclusive reliance on agriculture. "No portion of the country," he insisted, "offers less facility to the farming interests or greater to the manufacturing or mechanical." In the West too the Whigs argued that manufacturers should be developed. At the Iowa Constitutional Convention of 1846 an exchange occurred which neatly illustrated the party differences on the question. Democratic representative Stephen Hempstead asked rhetorically, "What was the condition of the laborer in factories in Massachusetts?" The answer was an alarming one: "it was the condition of serfs and slaves." For "the laborers went to their dinners at the tap of the bell, and they returned at the tap of the bell." Hempstead concluded that "they were not like free American citizens, but were more like Southern slaves." But Joseph D. Hoag, a Whig, made an immediate rejoinder. He argued that "manufactures were of unquestionable advantage to a country, and it was to its interest to encourage them." But like other Whigs Hoag did not simply claim that the community benefited from manufacturing; he also insisted that the laborers were among the primary beneficiaries. Announcing that he had spent twelve years in manufacturing, he reassured the convention about the conditions of the

---

60. This point, it seems to me, vitiates one of the central theses of Kohl, *Politics of Individualism*. The Whigs had at least as many doubts as the Democrats about individualism, but of a different kind.

operatives who, he said, "often made more than the owners." He then made the classic Whig defense of wage labor in terms of mobility. "Common hands who were stronger and careful," he declared, "would in a comparatively short time be able to buy small farms, or otherwise go into business for themselves." Since "they did not leave the factory with the mark of the branding-iron on their cheeks, nor of the whip on their back," then "was this like the slavery the gentleman had referred to?"[61]

This powerful reply illustrated two of the principal concerns of the Whigs. When combating Democratic accusations, they stressed both the prosperity of the worker and his extraordinary opportunities for betterment. The result was a dual emphasis upon social mobility and high wages, with each reinforcing the other. Neither played a significant role in Democratic thought. Democrats assumed a society of independent yeomen who would begin and end their working lives as farmers having gradually acquired a "competence" for their old age.[62] But Whigs envisaged a large degree of mobility, with changes of status, of condition and even of rank, facilitated by the supply of credit, and encouraged by economic diversification. A high wage rate supplied a necessary social lubricant. The departure of the upwardly mobile into the ranks of the self-employed or of the employers then functioned so as to preserve the wage rate. All would benefit, even those who did not cease to be wage laborers. "High wages," according to John P. Kennedy of Maryland, "are the peculiar blessing of our country." Kennedy explained their role and in so doing described the material and moral improvements they promoted:

> It is through high wages that we make the laboring man a partner in the gains of the rich. They are the principal ingredient of that American system of which the scope and end are to secure the physical comfort of the working man, by affording him a full remuneration for his toil, yielding him time for mental and moral improvement, by which he shall be progressively lifted up into a higher scale of social respectability and usefulness; and identifying him with the prosperity and happiness of the nation, by causing him to feel that in promoting that prosperity he promotes his own.

Here it was the gains of wage labor, both moral and material, rather than the opportunities to cease to be a wage laborer, that were emphasized. Kennedy was not alone in taking this approach.[63]

61. *New Hampshire Statesman*, Sept. 23, 1842, April 18, 1843; Shambaugh (ed.), *Iowa Constitutional Conventions*, p. 146. See also John J. Berrien, *Speech on the Tariff* (Washington D.C., 1844), p. 16; Brown (ed.), *Life and Writings of Choate*, II, p. 213.
62. Democrats did, however, demand geographical mobility, in the form of access to western lands.
63. *Collective Works of Kennedy*, IV, p. 292. See also Thomas R. Hazard, *Facts for the Laboring Man* (Newport, R.I., 1840), p. 30.

Other Whigs, however, dwelt instead upon upward mobility. According to John Aiken of Massachusetts "he who five years ago was working for wages, will now be found transacting business for himself; and in a few years hence, will be likely to be found a hirer of the labor of others." But the fullest and most interesting discussion of wages by a Whig spokesman came from Calvin Colton, author of the widely read "Junius" Tracts in the 1840s. Of all Whigs he came closest to anticipating the Republican appeal of the 1850s. Colton, as "Junius," struck an exultant note when describing American society. "This is a country," he announced in 1844, "of self-made men, than which nothing better can be said of any state of society."[64] Four years earlier he had written a pamphlet entitled *American Jacobinism* in which he pilloried Orestes Brownson for the doctrines he had put forward that year and in particular for his attack upon wage labor. Colton's words are worthy of careful analysis:

> It is a libel on our state of society, the vital principle and moving spring of which is, labor at wages, in its various forms. Nine-tenths of the people of the Northern and Eastern States, begin life and rise to independence, some to great wealth – and all the industrious and frugal to a social importance – on the principle of wages. This constitution of the machinery of our society is its felicity and chief glory.

Two features of this passage are noteworthy. First is the absence of the South. The society which Colton describes and which, he believes, discredits Brownson's analysis, is northern and eastern. It is not southern; slavery is entirely absent. We shall return to this question later. Second, it does not quite go as far as Abraham Lincoln did in the next decade when wages and social mobility were identified with democracy and the nation itself. Other Whigs were still further from making this identification. As we have seen, there was a widespread alarm in Whig ranks in the 1830s and the early 1840s about the new populism of the American republic. Democratic encomiums on the people and on democracy were a source of deep concern. Indeed the Whigs deplored all appeals to the passions of the people. "How often do we see," asked Sargent S. Prentiss of Mississippi, "in this country that the employer of to-day is the laborer of tomorrow, and the laborer, the employer." "When such is the evidence," he continued, "how dare any man rise up and address himself

---

64. John Aiken, *Labor and Wages, At Home and Abroad* (Lowell, 1849), p. 16; "Junius", *Labor and Capital* (N.Y., 1844), p. 15. Curiously the passage from Colton was quoted by Richard Hofstadter to bolster his "entrepreneurial" interpretation of the Democrats. Hofstadter ignored the fact that Colton was a Whig. In fact his interpretation fits the Whigs well, the Democrats not at all. Note also that Hofstadter also cites Webster – Hofstadter, *American Political Tradition*, pp. 65–66.

to the passions of different classes of the community and declare there is a distinction between them." Here was the classic Whig fear of a crass appeal on the part of the demagogue to the passions of the electorate. The danger was that men were not yet sufficiently confirmed in their social roles to withstand such an appeal.[65] As a result mobility was often cast in a defensive role. According to a group of Massachusetts Whigs, "the high reward for labor in all its branches . . . is the best security for the permanence of our free institutions." It is also significant that Calvin Colton held a private view of democracy that was sharply at odds with his public utterances as "Junius." In an anonymous work he wrote that "Christian morality and piety" were "the last hope of the American people, and the only adequate means of bridling and holding in salutary check that rampant freedom which is so characteristic of the American people." In the apt words of his biographer, Colton throughout his career hoped "that capitalism might conceivably make democracy safe for America." The fusion between the two, as a result of which democracy would be extolled in terms of capitalism and of a wage labor system, still lay in the future.[66]

Democrats and slavery

I

Of all problems confronting the historian of American politics in the antebellum years, the relationship between the Democratic party and slavery is probably the most difficult. This is not generally recognized because those who have studied "Jacksonian Democracy" have not normally concerned themselves with the sectional controversy and *vice versa*. But those historians who have been willing to confront the question have presented what are in effect diametrically opposed views. As we shall see, the issue cannot be resolved by accumulating additional evidence; the key questions are theoretical rather than empirical.

Most of the seminal interpretations of Jacksonian Democracy have in fact given little attention to the slavery question. Arthur Schlesinger Jr.'s urban labor thesis relegated the South – and the West – to a subordinate role in the Democratic movement. Although he argued that "the group which took the lead on the political stage in combating the slave power were the radical Democrats in the straight Jacksonian tradition," he insisted that until the mid-1840s slavery was far less important as an

---

65. "Junius," *American Jacobinism* (N.Y., 1840), p. 5; Prentiss in *Kennebec Journal*, Aug. 22, 1841.
66. *The True Whig Sentiment of Massachusetts* (n.p., n.d.), p. 7; [Colton], *Voice from America to England*, p. 60; Cave, *An American Conservative*, p. 62.

issue than, for example, banking or the tariff. Schlesinger claimed that most of the slaves were held by Whigs (or Calhoun Democrats). The Democrats neither owned slaves in large numbers nor made the defense of slavery a central concern.[67]

The historians who sought to replace Schlesinger's thesis with the "entrepreneurial" interpretation of Jacksonian Democracy gave scant attention to slavery. In their view Democrats, the small, incipient capitalists, were pitted against the larger established capitalists and the South was distinctive in this respect only because large amounts of capital were invested in slaves. The debate over Jacksonian Democracy initiated by Schlesinger's work was thus conducted without much reference to the slavery issue. In a sense this emphasis was continued in the work of Richard P. McCormick who declared that the function of the political parties was to amass votes. This they could only do if slavery, clearly the most explosive of all questions, were kept outside the political arena. Like Schlesinger, McCormick noted that other issues were uppermost; unlike Schlesinger, he pronounced these issues "artificial."[68]

In 1966, however, Richard H. Brown published an important article entitled "The Missouri Crisis, Slavery and the Politics of Jacksonianism." Brown argued, essentially on the basis of a letter from Martin Van Buren to Thomas Ritchie, that the Democratic party had been founded in the 1820s with the explicit purpose of protecting slavery. Van Buren, the party's chief architect, was so successful in this enterprise that "until the Civil War the South was in the saddle of national politics." In the Jacksonian era according to Brown, the Democratic party's *raison d'être* was the defense of slavery. As some historians have since pointed out, Brown was reviving the charge of John Quincy Adams who attributed his defeat at the hands of Jackson in 1828 to the votes of southern slaveholders and the aggressions of the "Slave Power." Since Schlesinger's view of the clash between the two men was essentially that of Jackson himself, one might argue that historians were still fighting the election of 1828.[69]

---

67. Schlesinger, *Age of Jackson*, p. 433.
68. Richard P. McCormick, *The Second American Party System* (Chapel Hill, 1966), p. 352. For a critique see my *"Agrarians" and "Aristocrats,"* pp. 260–267.
69. Richard H. Brown, "The Missouri Crisis, Slavery and the Politics of Jacksonianism," *South Atlantic Quarterly* (1966), pp. 55–72; John Quincy Adams, *Address to Constituents, at Braintree, Sept. 17, 1842* (Boston, 1842), pp. 15–25 ; Leonard L. Richards, "The Jacksonians and Slavery," in Lewis Perry and Michael Fellman (eds), *Antislavery Reconsidered: New Perspectives on the Abolitionists* (Baton Rouge, 1979), pp. 99–118. See also Brown, "'Southern Planters and Plain Republicans of the North': Martin Van Buren's Formula for National Politics" (Ph.D. dissertation, Yale, 1955).

While some historians have endorsed and refined Brown's thesis, Jackson himself has not been without defenders. Robert Remini, who has written the definitive multi-volume biography of Jackson and who probably knows more about him than anyone has ever known, has done much to revive Jackson's reputation. (He has even attempted a qualified defense of his Indian policy.) So far as slavery is concerned, Remini rejected Brown's interpretation in its entirety, claiming that it had sent historians off on "a totally wrong tack." Remini argued that "the Jacksonian movement as it began had nothing to do with the desire of Southerners to protect slavery" and dismissed as "nonsense" the idea that the Democratic party was proslavery.[70]

This debate has been a fruitful one. Each side, as we shall see, has scored some telling points without, however, being able to dispose of the arguments of the other. Nevertheless, as I shall attempt to show, this question is resolvable. While doubt hangs over some evidence – specifically Van Buren's precise meaning in the letter to Ritchie, more "facts" will not remove the impasse. The problem is essentially a conceptual and theoretical one.

II

We may begin with the evidence presented by those following the "Adams/Brown" interpretation. As Leonard Richards has pointed out, Jackson ran extremely well in the South, winning over 70% of the southern vote in 1828. Although this sectional imbalance was less apparent by the late 1830s and the 1840s, by the 1850s, of course, the Democracy was once again leaning heavily towards the South. Moreover, on the race question, Democrats were more tainted with prejudice than their National Republican or Whig opponents. And when the abolitionists tried to send their pamphlets to the South in the mid-1830s, Jackson was adamant in resisting. He even encouraged northerners to break up their meetings. But the clearest evidence of Democratic support for southern slaveholders in the 1830s came over the attempt to impose the "gag" law, designed to prevent all discussion of abolitionist petitions. A typical vote in the 24th Congress found each party in the North achieving over 80% unity on this question. But where the northern Whigs opposed the "gag," northern Democrats supported it.[71]

70. Pessen, *Jacksonian America*, p. 301; Remini, *Legacy of Jackson*, p. 83.
71. Richards, "Jacksonians and Slavery," p. 112; Thomas B. Alexander, *Sectional Stress and Party Strength: A Study of Roll-Call Voting in the United States House of Representatives, 1836–1860* (Nashville, 1967), pp. 130, 133.

Similarly, Jackson's Indian removal policy, which not unnaturally won a disproportionate amount of support from Democrats, was an attempt to respond to southern rather than northern land hunger. Such opposition as it provoked came from Whigs and National Republicans. In the 1840s the annexation of Texas, opposed by the vast majority of Whigs, especially in the North, was another policy designed primarily to meet southern demands. When it produced a northern challenge in the form of the Wilmot Proviso, it was northern Whigs, not northern Democrats, who displayed the greater antislavery sentiment notwithstanding the Democratic affiliation of David Wilmot himself.[72]

One must take care not to reduce these votes to mere jockeying for position. Those Democrats who followed Jackson in excoriating the abolitionists were not merely seeking temporary political advantage. Their views should be seen in a longer and wider perspective. As the voting analysis of Thomas Alexander demonstrates, northern Democrats from the mid-1830s to the Civil War were more likely to take a pro-southern position than their National Republican, Whig or Republican counterparts on a whole range of issues. These included, in addition to the "gag" law and the extension of slavery into the lands of the Mexican cession, the question of slavery in the District of Columbia, the colonization of free blacks, the recognition of Haiti, the imprisonment of northern black sailors in South Carolina, the capture of fugitive slaves, and the repeal of the three-fifths compromise. The voting patterns revealed by these issues foreshadowed the alignment of the 1850s when the Democratic party would be increasingly identified with the interests of the slaveholding South.[73]

To demonstrate these voting patterns, however, is not to explain them. Here Martin Van Buren's letter to Thomas Ritchie of January 13, 1827 assumes great importance. Without question Van Buren's role in the formation of the Democratic party was second only to that of Jackson himself – and may even have been greater than Jackson's. Between the election of 1828 and the introduction of the Texas issue into presidential politics in 1843, Van Buren, head of the Albany Regency, benefited enormously from an alliance struck with Thomas Ritchie, editor of the *Richmond Enquirer* and moving spirit of the "Richmond Junto." The New York–Virginia axis was vital to the success of the Democratic party nationally, as well as to the personal fortunes of the two leaders.[74] On January 13, 1827 Van Buren wrote to Ritchie and set forth his reasons for favoring the revival of a national two party system and for supporting

---

72. Richards, "Jacksonians and Slavery," p. 113.
73. Alexander, *Sectional Stress*, p. 73 and *passim*.
74. Remini, *Martin Van Buren and the Making of the Democratic Party* (N.Y., 1959).

Jackson in the forthcoming presidential election. For Richard Brown (and for John Quincy Adams if he had been allowed to read the letter!), the crucial lines were those in which Van Buren explained the link between party conflict and sectional controversy:

> We must always have party distinctions and the old ones are the best of which the case admits. Political combinations between the inhabitants of the different states are unavoidable and the most natural and beneficial to the country is that between the planters of the South and the plain Republicans of the north. The country has once flourished under a party thus constituted and may again. It would take longer than our lives (even if it were practicable) to create new party feelings to keep those masses together. If the old ones are suppressed, geographical divisions founded on local interests or, what is worse, prejudices between the free and slave states will inevitably take their place. Party attachment in former times furnished a complete antidote for sectional prejudices by producing counteracting feelings. It was not until that defence had been broken down that the clamour agt. [sic] Southern Influence and African Slavery could be made effectual in the North. Formerly, attacks upon Southern Republicans were regarded by those of the north as assaults upon their political brethren and resented accordingly. This all powerful sympathy has been much weakened, if not destroyed by the amalgamating policy . . . . It can and ought to be revived.

This letter, Brown concluded, proved that the Jacksonian coalition had been formed to protect slavery in the South. Little wonder, therefore, that Democratic partisans even from the North defended southern interests whenever they reasonably could.[75]

III

Yet Van Buren's letter proves rather less than one might suppose. Democrats, including Van Buren, wrote many other letters in which they explained what they took to be the *raison d'être* of their party. As we shall see, James K. Polk and Andrew Jackson, to say nothing of northern Democrats, as far as their writings indicate, certainly did not believe that their primary task was to protect slavery in the South. Their priorities were entirely different. In the case of Van Buren himself, it is important to note that he was identified with the economic principles of Jefferson from the very earliest period of his life and we have already seen that in his *Inquiry into the Origins and Course of Political Parties in the*

---

75. Van Buren to Ritchie, Jan. 13, 1827 reprinted in Remini (ed.), *The Age of Jackson* (N.Y., 1972), pp. 3–7.

United States, written at the end of his life, he cited as the primary
purpose of the Democratic party, the need to curb the inegalitarian tendencies of Federalism. The defense of slavery did not feature here. Why,
one might ask, should this single letter of 1827 be privileged above all his
other writings? And why has so little evidence of this type come to light?
Are we to believe that Democratic partisans somehow suppressed all
references in public correspondence, and removed from posterity's eye
all private references to the slavery issue? Moreover, it is not entirely clear
that the letter to Ritchie is as unambiguous or unequivocal as one might
suppose. As Remini points out, Van Buren in the letter gave six reasons
for reviving the party system and the protection of slavery was not one of
them. The "antidote for sectional prejudices" he cites was an effect,
highly desirable to be sure, but not a cause of the political division.
The letter itself is quite ambiguous but, read this way, it is entirely compatible with the views contained in the *Inquiry* as well as those expressed
by Van Buren at other times, and also with those held by other prominent
Democrats.[76]

Brown's interpretation has the great merit of drawing attention to one
of the Democratic party's discernible functions, the defense of slavery, but
it has the disadvantage of making a mystery of their often avowed primary aim, which was to protect and extend the political and social equality of adult white males. Their first object, as they saw it, was to prevent
the subjugation or, as they often put it, the "enslavement" of whites by
other whites, not to facilitate the enslavement of blacks. Hence the concern, found in the private as well as the public utterances of leading
Democrats, for the financial questions of the era. Even in the 1820s,
before the party's war with the banks had fully defined its character,
the reason which men like Van Buren usually gave for the formation of
the Democratic party was, as Remini points out, "to reaffirm a political
ideology that they believed was in jeopardy on account of Monroe's
'Amalgamation policy'." Historians are plainly wrong to dismiss all
such concerns as "artificial." But the question is why, in pursuing these
goals, Democrats simultaneously protected the interests of southern slaveholders. We need to ask what the relationship is between slavery and
the so-called "Jacksonian" issues?[77]

To answer this question we need to understand the Democratic view of
slavery. Not surprisingly there was within the Democratic party no single

---

76. Remini, *Legacy of Jackson*, p. 87; John C. Fitzpatrick (ed.), "The Autobiography of
    Martin Van Buren," *Annual Report of the American Historical Association for the
    Year 1918* (Washington, D.C., 1920), pp. 198–199. Van Buren's reputation as a
    trimmer probably derives above all from his tendency to straddle on the tariff ques-
    tion.
77. Remini, *Legacy of Jackson*, p. 87.

position on this issue. Changes over time were of great importance: the party's relationship with slavery, slaveholders and the South was not in the 1850s what it had been in Jackson's day. At no time was there unanimity within the party. A spectrum of opinion existed, ranging from neo-abolitionism to proslavery. Between these two poles there were many positions but it is reasonable to identify at this stage only three: those which had developed prior to the controversy over Texas and the Mexican cession. Let us consider them one by one.

The first is the neo-abolitionist position. William Leggett is the Democrat in whom, according to Arthur Schlesinger, "social radicalism and antislavery feeling united most impressively" and in the last year or two of his life Leggett converted to abolitionism. But while Schlesinger takes this as an illustration of the natural affinity between radical Democracy and antislavery, Leggett's career actually demonstrates the opposite. For the conversion to abolitionism marked the end of any hope Leggett might have entertained of advancement within the party. At around the same time (the late 1830s), Thomas Morris, United States Senator from Ohio, astounded the Senate when he denounced the "Slave Power" and pledged himself to the cause of emancipation. Morris had been an orthodox radical Democrat, enthusiastic in his support of the Jackson and Van Buren banking policies, but his attack on slavery meant that he met the same fate as Leggett. He was denied re-election to the Senate.[78]

Morris gravitated towards the Liberty party. The same path was taken by James Birney who also found continued membership of the Democracy incompatible with abolitionism. Another key figure in the Liberty Party was Salmon P. Chase, later of course to become a leading radical Republican. Chase was responsible for the Republican interpretation of the Constitution, according to which slavery should be entirely a creature of local law, but his views are of interest here because of their similarity, in most respects, to those of orthodox Democrats. He was wont to argue that the federal government should be separated from slavery precisely as Democrats had succeeded in separating it from the "Money Power." This use of Democratic terminology was quite deliberate on his part. As he himself put it, his party "demand the divorce of the National Government from Slavery as sternly and uncompromisingly as Gen. Jackson demanded its divorce from the Banks." In the 1840s and early 1850s Chase claimed that he was faithful to Democratic principles,

---

78. Schlesinger, *Age of Jackson*, p. 426; Sedgwick (ed.) *Political Writings of Leggett*, II, pp. 289, 335; Stanley N. Worton, "William Leggett, Political Journalist (1800–1839): A Study in Democratic Thought" (Ph.D. dissertation, Columbia, 1954), pp. 30–31; Eric Foner, *Free Soil, Free Labor, Free Men: The Ideology of the Republican Party before the Civil War* (N.Y., 1970), pp. 90–91.

more faithful to them, indeed, than orthodox Democrats. Unlike them, he declared, he was prepared to "push out" his "democratic principles to their anti-slavery application." Writing to Preston King, Chase announced that he "sympathized strongly with the Democratic Party in almost everything except its submission to slaveholding leadership & dictation." Yet there was no room for Chase within the party. Such was the fate of the abolitionist or neo-abolitionist, however orthodox his views might be on other questions.[79]

One must be careful to define the views of antislavery Democrats. Many within the party wished that the United States had never imported slaves and many looked forward to the day when every state would be a free state. Such opinions were entirely acceptable provided they did not influence policy or the distribution of national patronage. It was when he sought to politicize his antislavery that the Democrat encountered, at the minimum, resistance or, more likely, expulsion from the party.

Thus while an outright antislavery (as opposed to free soil) position is identifiable within the Democracy, its influence was virtually negligible. At the opposite pole, and of greater importance, were the proslavery Democrats, those who believed slavery superior, overall, to free labor. If these proslavery Democrats had actually formed the second party system, then Brown's interpretation would be absolutely correct, for their central concern in politics was indeed the protection and perpetuation of slavery. But prior to the 1830s their views were relatively uncommon, certainly outside South Carolina, the state, it might be worth noting, that was least well integrated into the party system. As we have seen, John C. Calhoun and his supporters developed the theory of nullification to combat not merely the protective tariff but also the prospect of an increasingly antislavery northern majority in the federal government. After his break with Jackson, Calhoun spent several years acting with the Opposition. But in 1837 he rejoined the Democratic party, where he and his supporters remained.[80]

How much support did Calhoun enjoy within the South and how widespread was proslavery sentiment within the Democratic party? In the mid- and late 1840s the situation began to change so let us confine our discussion to the years before the annexation of Texas and the Wilmot Proviso. When he returned to the Democracy, Calhoun brought with him only a dozen or so congressmen (though it is fair to point out that a few more who shared many of his views remained in the Whig

79. *Politics in Ohio: Senator Chase's Letter to Hon. A.P. Edgerton* (n.p., n.d.), p. 8; Albert Bushnell Hart, *Salmon Portland Chase* (reprint: N.Y., 1969), p. 113; "The Diary and Correspondence of Salmon P. Chase," *Annual Report of the American Historical Association 1902*, Vol. II (Washington, D.C., 1903), p. 121.
80. See below, Chapter 6.

party until the Tyler crisis of 1841). At that time the South elected approximately one hundred congressmen. While it is possible that some proslavery Democrats had never followed Calhoun into opposition, it is also possible that some who acted with him did not fully endorse his proslavery principles.[81]

A brief glance at the southern states allows an assessment of Calhoun's influence in these years. His support, as might be expected, was greater in the Deep South than in the Upper or Border South. Indeed in states like Tennessee and Missouri the slavery issue was rarely raised politically. In North Carolina, each party tried to make capital out of the nullification episode – but by branding the other as its supporters.[82] The situation in Virginia, however, was different. In the coastal regions of the state men like R. M. T. Hunter adopted many Calhoun doctrines and their influence was boosted following the Tyler defections from the Whig party in the early 1840s. It is doubtful, however, whether these proslavery ideologues could match the power within the state of Thomas Ritchie, Van Buren's foremost southern ally.[83]

In the Deep South Calhoun's support was most impressive in the states of Alabama, Mississippi, Georgia and South Carolina. As far as Alabama is concerned, one may safely endorse the findings of J. Mills Thornton III who concluded that "until the final decade of the ante-bellum period, the men who had followed [Calhounite] Dixon Lewis out of the Whig party in the summer of 1838 . . . made few converts to their extreme strict constructionist outlook within the Democracy, and thus remained a small minority whose numbers were, however, relatively stable."[84]

The case of Mississippi is especially interesting, since it would become in the 1850s a secessionist stronghold. In the 1830s and early 1840s, however, the position was different. Calhoun certainly had his admirers

81. As usual Charles Wiltse (in an otherwise admirable biography) grossly exaggerates Calhoun's influence within the Democratic party. See *John C. Calhoun, Nullifier, 1829–1839* (N.Y., 1949), *passim*.

82. Charles G. Sellers, Jr., *James K. Polk, Jacksonian* (Princeton, 1957), p. 251 and *passim*; Robert H. White (ed.), *Messages of the Governors of Tennessee, 1845–1857* (Nashville, 1957), p. 269; J. G. de Roulhac Hamilton, "Party Politics in North Carolina, 1835–1860," *The James Sprunt Historical Publications*, xv (Durham, N.C., 1916), p. 38; Clarence C. Norton, "The Democratic Party in Ante-Bellum North Carolina," *The James Sprunt Historical Publications*, xxi (Chapel Hill, 1930), p. 103; Henry M. Wagstaff, *State Rights and Political Parties in North Carolina, 1776–1861* (Baltimore, 1906), pp. 50–54; Clarence H. McClure, *Opposition in Missouri to Thomas Hart Benton* (Nashville, 1927), p. 22.

83. Charles Ambler, "Virginia and the Presidential Succession, 1840–1844" in *Essays in American History Dedicated to Frederick Jackson Turner* (N.Y., 1910), pp. 165–202, esp. 176; Richard E. Ellis, *The Union at Risk: Jacksonian Democracy, States' Rights and the Nullification Crisis* (N.Y., 1987), pp. 123–140.

84. J. Mills Thornton, III, *Politics and Power in a Slave Society: Alabama, 1800–1860* (Baton Rouge, 1978), p. 132. See also *Democratic Gazette*, Dec. 27, 1843.

but the climate of opinion as late as 1844 was probably shown by an editorial in the Jackson *Mississippian*, the leading Democratic newspaper in the state. The editor first complained that "the slavery question is being very unnecessarily agitated in the South," a clear reference to the Calhoun school, and then went on to condemn extremists North and South alike, an archetypal Jacksonian response. Moreover in the same year the State Democratic party adopted a resolution which asserted that "the people are sovereign and supreme, having the right to alter and abolish governments whenever they see proper." Although this declaration did not refer to the slavery question, it was utterly opposed to the doctrines championed by Calhoun and his closest supporters and thus tends to confirm their failure to dominate the state. Once again this was sound Jacksonian theory.[85]

In Georgia politics were extremely complex, partly as a consequence of the nullification crisis. Of all the other southern states Georgia was the one in which South Carolina nullifiers found most support. The Georgia States Rights party did not, as a whole, support nullification but nevertheless expressed great hostility to Jackson's handling of the crisis. In 1843 Calhoun won the nomination of the Georgia state Democratic party for President only to have it withdrawn after the party sustained a heavy defeat at the subsequent local election. Proslavery sentiment was, however, a major force in Georgia. But only in South Carolina did the proslavery forces exert unchallengeable control over the Democratic party. Although there were factions within the South Carolina Democracy, Calhoun enjoyed a personal power in the state that no other statesman could match anywhere in the Union.[86]

The influence of the Calhounites in the South was probably greater than mere numbers would suggest, for most represented powerful groups of elite planters. Nevertheless, it is clear that the overtly proslavery Democrats were not dominant even within the South in the 1830s and early 1840s, let alone in the nation as a whole. In the late 1840s and still more in the 1850s proslavery Democrats would receive considerable accessions of strength when the controversy over free soil began to polarize opinion. In the aftermath of the annexation of Texas and the Mexican war, what might be termed free soil and anti-free-soil positions gathered strength. But neither had been apparent in the 1830s. At that time the preponderant view of slavery was the one held by, among others, Andrew

---

85. *Mississippian*, July 19, 5, 1844; "Address of the State Central Committee of the Democratic Party, to the People of Mississippi," in *Mississippian*, Aug. 16, 1844. See also Natchez *Free Trader*, May 6, 1843.

86. Ellis, *Union at Risk*, pp. 102–122; William W. Freehling, *Prelude to Civil War, The Nullification Controversy in South Carolina, 1816–1836* (N.Y., 1965), pp. 203–204, 265; Wiltse, *Calhoun, Nullifier, passim.*

Jackson, Martin Van Buren and James K. Polk, the Democratic presidential triumvirate. Since Van Buren's views were heavily modified in the 1840s it will be convenient to treat them later. And though Polk's views were extremely close to those of Jackson, it will also be convenient to defer consideration of them. We shall concentrate therefore on Jackson himself, and his closest supporters.

IV

It is said to have been one of Jackson's greatest regrets that during the nullification crisis he lost an opportunity to march into South Carolina in order to hang John C. Calhoun. Anyone who believes that there was unanimity within the ranks of southern Democrats on the slavery question would do well to consider the relationship between Jackson and his closest supporters on the one hand, and Calhoun and his followers on the other. Men like Francis P. Blair and Thomas Hart Benton, together with Jackson himself – slaveholders all, it might be noted – hated Calhoun with a venom rarely seen in American politics. It is well known that Democrats despised abolitionists but in Jackson's White House hatred of nullifiers was even more intense.

The Jacksonian position on slavery was a simple one. As Blair put it in the *Globe*, "there is no debatable ground left upon the subject." The reason was equally simple: the constitution had made specific and explicit provision for slavery, as a result of which there was nothing left to discuss. Jackson and his closest supporters did not merely assert this to be true; they assumed that all men of good faith instantly perceived it to be true. Hence it followed that those who attempted to agitate the slavery question, knowing that it had in the past threatened the stability of the country, must be traitors. Little wonder then that Jacksonians reacted so fiercely to nullifiers and abolitionists alike.[87]

In the 1820s, notwithstanding Van Buren's letter to Ritchie, fears for slavery were not uppermost in the minds of most Jacksonians. To be sure, there were doubts about the Adams administration's use of federal power and some southerners saw federally sponsored internal improvements as a pretext for assaults upon slavery. But the Adams administration was not antislavery; Adams's career as an opponent of slavery and the "Slave Power" only began after his eviction from the White House. Jackson's major concern in these years was the restoration of the purity of the government, corrupted, as he believed, not by abolitionists or proslavery theorists but by the intriguers whose "corrupt bargain" had denied the

---

87. Washington *Globe*, May 1, July 10, 1833.

people their choice in 1824. This crusade against "aristocrats" in government was not a temporary concern. Indeed it became ever more central to "Jacksonian Democracy." In the next decade Jackson and his supporters would see not only the struggle with the Bank of the United States but also controversies over slavery in this light.[88]

The emergence of a militant abolitionism in the 1830s did not escape the attention of the Jacksonians. They saw the followers of Garrison, the Tappans, or Weld as, at best deluded, at worst treasonous. Writing to Nathaniel Macon of North Carolina, Martin Van Buren referred to abolitionism as a device "of evil disposed persons to disturb the harmony of our happy Union." In his Farewell Address, Jackson warned that all attempts "to cast odium upon the institutions of any state and all measures calculated to disturb the rights of property or the peace of any community are in direct opposition to the spirit in which the Union was formed, and must endanger its safety." This, of course, was identical to the warnings that Calhoun frequently issued. But Jackson's next words immediately distinguished his position from Calhoun's. "Everyone," he affirmed, "upon sober reflection, will see that nothing but mischief can come from these improper assaults upon the feelings and rights of others." The danger was slight; the people could be trusted to discountenance abolition as soon as they were told of its dangers.[89]

Calhoun might in 1837 have agreed that abolitionism was weak numerically. But he expected it to grow, in part because he feared unscrupulous party leaders (who would pander to abolitionism in the quest for votes) and in part because he had grave doubts about free society anyway. Jackson, however, had unlimited confidence in the majority, was by now fully converted to Van Buren's pro-party position and refused to enter into comparisons between free and slave society. Thus he believed that all good men would scorn abolitionists. And if abolitionism were self-evidently pernicious, it followed that the South was not under threat.

Once again Jackson and his followers believed that all men of good faith would instantly recognize the truth: abolitionism, thanks to the good sense of the majority, did not pose a real threat to slavery or the South. The constitution had removed all cause for anxiety. "Has it ever been pretended," Blair wrote in the *Globe*, "that Congress has any power to subvert the basis on which the Constitution itself was founded?" "Has any statesman," he continued, "ever suggested the idea that the general government has authority to subvert not only the rights guaranteed to

88. Leonard L. Richards, *The Life and Times of Congressman John Quincy Adams* (N.Y., 1986), pp. 99–101; Remini, *Legacy of Jackson*, p. 13, *Jackson and Course of American Democracy*, pp. 343, 349.
89. Van Buren to Nathaniel Macon, Feb. 13, 1836 quoted in Remini, *Legacy of Jackson*, p. 105; Richardson (ed.), *Messages and Papers of Presidents*, III, p. 298.

individuals by the Constitution but rights recognized as appurtenant to the state institutions, and on which their ratio of representation is made to depend?" The danger was slight.[90]

It might become greater, however, if the flames of sectional animosity were fanned by unscrupulous southerners. When the Jacksonians saw men like Calhoun claiming that abolitionism justified the break-up of the party system, their suspicions were aroused. What was the real purpose? Unfortunately for Calhoun his often expressed fears of the majority simply confirmed the Jacksonians' darkest suspicions. Calhoun, like Clay and Webster (with whom he had recently been acting), was an "aristocrat" who had no faith in the people and who, unable to gratify his ambition by winning the presidency in a free election, was seeking to unite the South behind him by agitating the slavery question. The result would be either the presidency for Calhoun, or the creation of a southern confederacy – headed, of course, by none other than John C. Calhoun. According to Jackson's followers, it was Calhoun's great crime that he was prepared to weaken the Union merely for his own personal advancement.

At first, Jacksonians noted, Calhoun had risked the Union merely to lower the tariff. After the nullification crisis, Jackson predicted that "the next pretext" on which to assault the Union "will be the negro, or slavery question." As Blair put it, the nullifiers in 1833 now "counterfeited newborn terrors about dangers, about the security of their slave property." They were prepared to take this reckless action despite knowing – as all knew – that agitation of the slavery question "would be mortal, at once, to our glorious Confederacy and all its political benefits." Sure enough, after nullification, Calhoun's actions began to confirm Jackson's prediction. Calhoun insisted on debating the right of petition, when the prudent course was merely to table the abolitionist petitions with as little discussion as possible. His resolutions of 1837 were yet another attempt to agitate the slavery question and, by breaking down attachment to party, weaken the Union. By 1840 men like Jackson, Blair and Benton had not the slightest doubt that the creation of a southern confederacy, with himself at the head, was Calhoun's goal. Final confirmation, if any were needed, came when Calhoun set about annexing Texas. Writing to Jackson, now in retirement in the Hermitage, Blair told him that the purpose of Calhoun's Pakenham letter (in which he advocated annexation on proslavery grounds) was "to drive off every Northern man from re-annexation" and give "a pretext to unite the whole South upon himself as the champion of its cause." According to Blair, Calhoun did not even want the treaty of annexation to be ratified. Though favoring annexation

90. Washington *Globe*, May 1, 1833.

himself, Jackson agreed with this estimate of Calhoun's motives. Such was the animosity between Jackson's followers and Calhoun's.[91]

V

Those Democrats who shared the opinions of Jackson were explicitly neither proslavery nor antislavery. So far from their primary goal being the protection of slavery, they were adamant that slavery should play no part in federal politics. Without any doubt Jackson's priority was to protect the American masses from falling under the control of the "aristocratic minority," to prevent them as he often put it, from becoming "hewers of wood and drawers of water" to a privileged elite. Jackson's enemies, whether bankers, abolitionists or nullifiers, he viewed as potential "aristocrats" and he pinned his faith on the majority of (white) Americans, who by their votes, would sustain the Union and American democracy.[92]

To say this is to endorse the views of Robert Remini who has done more than any historian to restore Jackson's reputation as a democrat (albeit a highly racist one.) Yet Remini's interpretation is not entirely satisfactory. His words are worth close analysis:

> Jacksonian Democracy did not represent a defense of slavery. Jacksonian Democrats *believed* they were defending the notion of majority rule and that the abolitionists and nullifiers and Whigs abhorred the notion of democracy and entered any sort of political alliance to discredit the new political system [emphasis added].

This passage gives a clue to Remini's thinking. He assumes that because Jackson and his followers did not *believe* the defense of slavery to be one of their purposes, it was not a function of Jacksonian Democracy. But this is a *non sequitur*. As we have already seen, interests may be furthered in ways that are neither intentional nor random. Such was the process by which Jacksonian Democracy furthered the interests of American slaveholders. Although Jackson took a quintessentially middle view of slavery, this mainstream attitude was not neutral towards the institution. Exactly like that of Thomas Jefferson, it bore the imprint of the class power of the slaveholders and as a direct result functioned to protect their vital interests. Like Thomas Jefferson, Jackson may have wished to preserve the

---

91. Jackson to A. J. Crawford, May 1, 1833 in Bassett (ed.), *Correspondence of Jackson*, v, pp. 70, 56; Washington *Globe*, May 1, 1833, April 24, 1838; Blair to Jackson, May 2, 9, 1844, Jackson to Blair, May 11, 1844 quoted in Remini, *Legacy of Jackson*, pp. 106–107.
92. Jackson to E. G. W. Butler, date uncertain, in Bassett (ed.), *Correspondence of Jackson*, v, p. 524.

status quo but it was a *status quo* in which slaveholders predominated. Though no proslavery apologist, Jackson, like Jefferson, had views that were *functionally* proslavery.[93]

To understand this process, we must recur to Democratic ideology. To Jackson and his supporters the Union, American democracy and the Democratic party itself were insolubly linked. Blair in the *Globe* credited democracy with developing the "resources, both physical and moral" of Americans "in a degree and with a rapidity which are almost incredible" and expressed doubt whether "the history of the world" presented "a similar example." American democracy, in the words of another party spokesman, was "perhaps the greatest achievement of modern times." What had been the role of the anti-Democratic parties since the time of Jefferson? They had played no part at all. Democrats reviewed the past and recalled that they had been responsible for the Louisiana Purchase (as they would be responsible for the acquisition of territory from Mexico). They had been the champions of popular government, despite the objections of Federalists and the reservations of most Whigs. They had destroyed the second national bank (and would largely dismantle the protective system). The Democratic party, for most of its supporters, was synonymous with Union, nationhood, and democracy. It was in these years akin to a church.[94]

The result was a view of history that was curiously conservative, even as it embraced change and progress. As late as the end of the nineteenth century William Jennings Bryan often remarked that he had learned all he knew of government from the writings of Jefferson; in the Jacksonian era such reverence was widespread. The task of politicians, and of Democrats especially, was to extend and purify Jefferson's legacy. Hence more territory would be acquired, more offices would be made elective, more people would enjoy the benefits of American democracy. Progress there would be, but it would be along tracks already laid down. Thomas Hart Benton in 1851 announced that all the great issues of politics had been resolved. Addressing Charles Sumner, he told him that he had "come upon the stage too late:"

> Not only have our great men passed away, but the great issues have been settled too. The last of these was the National Bank, and that

93. Remini, *Jackson and Course of American Freedom*, p. 343.
94. Washington *Globe*, Dec. 15, 1837; Samuel McRoberts, *To the Members of the General Assembly of Illinois* (n.p., n.d.), p. 7. See also Benjamin Butler, *Representative Democracy in the United States* (Albany, 1841), p. 16; George Bancroft, *The Principles of Democracy* (Hartford, 1840), p. 9; Hugh A. Garland, *The Principles of Democracy Identical with the Moral Improvement of Mankind* (N.Y., n.d.); *Democratic Review*, XVII (1845), p. 172.

has been overthrown forever. Nothing is left you, sir, but puny
sectional questions and petty strifes about slavery and fugitive
slave-laws, involving no national interests.

The path that the nation must follow had been charted for all time by
Jefferson and his party and reaffirmed by Jackson. Hence the enormous
irritation experienced by so many Democrats when sectional issues
intruded into politics. The task of the statesman was instead to remain
loyal to the priceless heritage.[95]

It was a heritage from which the slave was excluded. Like that of
Jefferson and Taylor a generation earlier, Democratic social philosophy
as exemplified by Jackson ignored the existence of slavery in the South.
When American society or the American economy were being considered
the slave once again simply disappeared from view. Let us return to
Thomas Hart Benton and the paean to agriculture in which he paid
homage to "the cultivators of the earth" as "the great and perennial
fountain of that Republican spirit which is to maintain and perpetuate
our free institutions." Slaves, of course, were "cultivators of the earth," at
least as much as the free men of the South. Jacksonians, of course, knew
this. But what is remarkable is that Benton simply excluded them from
consideration. What is still more remarkable is that he gave no reason for
doing so. Most remarkable of all is that he, and the many other
Democrats who spoke in identical terms, knew that those to whom
their remarks were addressed would not need, or expect a reason. The
slave had disappeared and no-one searched for him.[96]

The slaveholder, however, had experienced a different fate. Indeed if,
as was likely, he owned a plantation, he was addressed as a "cultivator of
the earth." He possessed the prized quality of "independence," upon
which Democratic thought placed such heavy emphasis. Many slaveholders, and especially those who owned only a few slaves, did indeed
work on the land and were cultivators of the earth. Those who owned
large numbers of slaves often would not, indeed in some parts of the
South they were absentee landowners (though this was less common
than in other slaveholding societies). Although orthodox Democrats frequently insisted that manual labor should be performed by all, they never
acknowledged that slave ownership presented a problem in this connection and they never acknowledged that any plantation owners were other
than "cultivators of the earth."[97]

95. Merrill D. Peterson, *The Jefferson Image in the American Mind* (N.Y., 1960), pp.
    259, 69–87; Benton quoted in Welter, *Mind of America*, p. 372.
96. *Congressional Globe*, 25 Congress, 2 Session, Appendix, p. 293.
97. Within some of the southern states there was occasionally hostility directed towards
    the slaveholding elite. More often than not, however, it came from Whigs seeking a
    more commercialized agriculture and a more diversified economy. A figure like

Moreover, the "independence" of the slaveholder was never explained. As Hegel remarked, it is the paradox of slavery that the master comes to be dependent upon the slave, even while his rhetoric maintains that it is the slave who is the dependant. The freeholding slaveholder was simply assumed to display the independence of the freeholding farmer. In this restricted sense only, the slaveholder was present in Democratic thought. He was not interpellated directly. As in the thought of Jefferson and Taylor, the plantation for Democrats had become the farm writ large and the master had become a farmer. The slave, meanwhile, had become nothing at all.

From a study of the thought of all but the tiniest number of Democrats in the 1830s and early 1840s, one would conclude that even the wealthiest slaveholders did not challenge the egalitarianism professed by so many within the party. The *Montgomery Advertiser* spoke in classic Jacksonian terms of the struggle between capital and labor:

> There is an incessant war waging in every commercial country between the moneyed interest and the rights of labor. In European governments the former have prevailed, and the people are reduced to penury and want while their masters roll in luxurious ease. All laws in these countries favor wealth and grind poverty. Hence the incessant wars, revolutions and massacres that occur.

The writer then added that in the United States a similar danger was developing. But not in the South. Instead it was "in the Northern and Eastern States," where "this system is taking deep root." As a result "in the cities of Boston, New York and Philadelphia, a frightful proportion of the population are paupers!" The South, however, and especially the Southwest, was the haven of American democracy. "With us of the Southwest," the writer boasted, "nineteen twentieths of the freemen are agriculturists" and "labor is the great controlling interest." Yet "even here," he warned, "we find men so blinded to the true interest of the State and the people that they are ready to legislate for capital and against labor."[98]

We need to be clear about what the writer meant when he spoke of legislation that was "for capital and against labor." Without any doubt he had in mind laws which the Whigs favored, and which would promote commercial development, using the resources of government. In only two ways might the slaveholder pose a threat to democracy or "the true interests of the state". One was by championing such laws. If he voted

---

Andrew Johnson, who directed Jacksonian arguments against the slaveholders, was a rarity, at least outside the Upper South.

98. Montgomery *Advertiser*, Dec. 19, 1849.

Democrat, this threat disappeared. The other was by challenging the political equality upon which Democrats (outside the ranks of the Calhounites) insisted. Some radical Democrats in the South argued strongly that the so-called "white basis" should be used in state elections, in order to eliminate the advantage conferred on slaveholders by the three-fifths rule. We should not underestimate the importance of these demands but we should also recall that even if they were met, they left slaveholders in an extraordinarily powerful position.[99]

Let us return once again to Democratic ideology. The demand was that all men be allowed to receive the full fruits of their labor. However, slaves were not defined as men at all for these purposes. Hence the slaveholder was allowed to retain not merely the fruits of his own labor, but in addition the fruits of the labor of his slaves. The existence of slavery in the South, the distribution of slaves there and the inequality within the white race that was consequent upon that distribution were not subjects of political debate or of economic analysis. All were absent from the writings of mainstream Jacksonian Democrats, precisely as they had been absent from the work of John Taylor of Caroline. This inequality was one that the typical Jacksonian Democrat, however egalitarian, never even recognized, let alone combated.

The Jeffersonian legacy was heavily implicated. The Jeffersonian tradition had an in-built tendency to emphasize a certain kind of inequality, in practice that defended by Federalists, at the expense of another, in effect that conferred by slaveownership. All white men were equal, socially and politically, in that all must be given the right to the fruits of their labor together with the political power to maintain that right. But some would enjoy in addition the right to the labor of one or more black workers. If all white men were equal, some were more equal than others.

Hence when Jackson, Blair and Polk insisted on keeping slavery out of politics they were, unwittingly perhaps, helping to confirm the slaveholders in what I shall argue was their position as the dominant class in the Republic. The tradition of Jefferson and of the Democratic party was one that obscured the social power of the slaveholder, by merging him with the farmer, even as it ignored the plight of the slave. Thus merely by continuing with what he took to be the traditions of the party, the Democrat helped perpetuate the dominance of the slaveholding elite.

99. See, for example, Montgomery *Advertiser*, July 16, 1851 as quoted in Thornton, "Politics and Power in a Slave Society: Alabama 1806–1860" (Ph.D. dissertation, Yale, 1974), p. 56.

VI

The Jeffersonian legacy not only functioned to obscure the social power of slaveholders and the suffering of the slave, it also succeeded in mystifying antislavery sentiment. Just as Jefferson himself in 1820 had seen northern attacks on slavery as a mere front for "Federalism" and all its social and political ambitions, so most Democrats in Jackson's time immediately leapt to the same conclusion. New York labor leader Ely Moore, a committed Democrat in the late 1830s, reviewed in Congress the tactics that "Federalists" (among whom he included the Whigs) had employed against the Democracy. "It has always been the policy, the aim and object of the Federal aristocracy of this country," he announced, "to impoverish, depreciate, and degrade the Democracy; and especially that portion who, in obedience to the mandate of Heaven, eat their bread in the sweat of their face." To achieve their goal "the Federalists," he continued, "have availed themselves of every means in their power." What were these means? They included scurrilous political attacks, bribery, corruption and, most important, "unequal, unjust, and exclusive legislation" to "defraud the Democracy of their equal political rights." But now, he warned, another tactic was being used. Moore introduced a theme that would become the stock-in-trade of northern Democrats in the 1840s and 1850s, indeed until the slaves had been emancipated. Federalism and abolitionism had fused:[100]

> And now, in order to render the condition of the laboring classes of the North and East still more depressed, the Federal party have joined the Abolitionists, for the purpose of conferring upon the black laborer *nominal freedom*, and upon the white laborer *virtual bondage*! Yes, sir, for the essential purpose of humbling and degrading the Democracy, have the Federal party of the North and East joined in the Abolition crusade; and whenever their object shall be attained, and the Southern negro shall be brought to compete with the Northern white man in the labor market, the moral and political character, the pride, power and independence, of the latter are gone forever, and Federalism will have realized its fondest and most cherished hopes.

Moore was on the outermost fringe of the Democratic party. But we should not conclude that such rhetoric was confined to a minority of labor leaders. In a speech at Nashville in 1840 Andrew Jackson himself warned that the abolitionists had been manipulated in a "false direction" by those who favored the "doctrines of the federal party." Some years

---

100. *Congressional Globe*, 25 Congress, 3 Session, Appendix, p. 241.

earlier, Frank Blair in the *Globe* had argued that the northern Democrats were entirely trustworthy on the abolition question, since they did not wish to have to compete for work with "myriads of half-famished blacks." The Whigs, on the other hand, as befitted neo-Federalists, "would not hesitate to liberate the blacks with a view of reducing the whole laboring classes to their level . . . depriving the great mass of the people of all political rights and build up the aristocracy upon the sacrifice of the principle of free suffrage." Nor should we believe that such statements were merely for public consumption. Silas Wright in a private letter to Daniel Dickinson showed the ease with which Democrats equated abolitionism with Federalism. Wright represented the radical (Barnburner) wing of the New York Democracy, while Dickinson was an arch-conservative (Hunker) but they clearly shared the same view of abolitionism. "You are doubtless right," Dickinson was told, "that the next phase of federalism is to be, to drop the names of 'Whig' and 'Abolitionist' and adopt that of 'Liberty Party,' and try us under a banner of black and white, that is, if we beat them now." Another group of Democrats explicitly stated that the slave question had had its origin as a party issue with the Hartford Convention, had re-emerged – again as a Federalist ploy – during the Missouri controversy and was now being used by antislavery Whigs for the same purpose. There was a grain of truth in these charges, at least insofar as antislavery sentiment was quite widespread within the ranks of northern Whigs and former Federalists but the reality was, of course, far more complex. Democrats, however, believed that their party was destined always to be combated by "Federalism" and it was apparently difficult for many of them to see antislavery in any other light.[101]

Similarly, Democratic orthodoxy lent invaluable support to the slaveholders by virtue of its racism. As we have already seen, the polity which Jacksonian Democrats desired did not depend at all on the differences between man and man. The same is true of the Democratic economy, which would have functioned perfectly if men were precisely the same. Yet this egalitarianism, which one would have thought might have triumphed over even the most virulent racism, was instead itself deeply racist.[102]

The Democrats viewed the citizenry – the majority in whose name they purported to act – as an undifferentiated mass. Each citizen was, in

---

101. Jackson in *Nashville Union*, Oct. 15, 1840; Washington *Globe*, May 5, 1835; Wright to Dickinson, Oct. 9, 1844 in John R. Dickinson (ed.), *Speeches, Correspondence, etc., of the Late Daniel S. Dickinson of New York* 2 vols (N.Y., 1867), II, p. 372; *Address and Proceedings of the Democratic State Convention, August 1849* (Albany, 1849), pp. 4–5; David Brion Davis, *The Problem of Slavery in the Age of Revolution* (Ithaca, 1975), p. 184.
102. Ashworth, *"Agrarians" and "Aristocrats,"* pp. 221–223.

political and social terms, equal to the rest; this was the theoretical foundation for the demand for "equal rights." Women and children were excluded from the citizenry, but immigrants were not. Democrats took pains to stress that they had precisely the same political and social rights as the native-born. But ironically, the process by which political equality was explicitly founded upon social equality and "equal rights" had the effect of confirming the second-class status of blacks (and Indians) in the North as well as in the South. Democratic theory could not tolerate a class of secondary or inferior voters. As one New Yorker put it, "you could not admit the blacks to a participation in the government of the country, unless you put them on terms of social equality." In Michigan another Democrat avowed that he would oppose the enfranchisement of blacks "until we [can] consent to treat them as equal with us in all respects."[103]

Could the blacks be so viewed? Only a tiny minority of northern Democrats entertained such opinions. For one thing, they operated so as to legitimate abolitionism. As a result the alliance with the planters of the South, the protections of the Constitution, the territorial expansion of slavery, the Democratic party itself – all would immediately fall into disrepute. The notion of racial equality would have turned the Democratic world upside-down.[104]

Hence in the North Democrats took the lead in disfranchising blacks, even as they lowered the franchise requirements for whites. The *Cincinnati Daily Enquirer* praised Ohio's legal discriminations against blacks, "framed for the purpose of keeping beyond our borders the whole negro race." Such laws were "well and wisely . . . framed, since, as a mass, that population is of the most undesirable and vicious character." Blacks were "ignorant, degraded, and vicious." Many other Democrats made similar statements. Indeed it was probably northern Democrats, rather than southern proslavery theorists, who made the most virulently negrophobic statements of the antebellum years. A leading exponent of such ideas was Dr. J. H. Van Evrie, of New York city, whose best-known work was entitled *White Supremacy and Negro Subordination; or, Negroes a Subordinate Race, and Slavery its Normal Condition*. This book contained chapter subheadings entitled "The Negro Incapable of Standing Upright," "The Relative Approximation of the Ourang Outang to the Negro," "The Beard of the Caucasian indicative of Superiority and the Negro and other Races

---

103. Bishop Perkins quoted in Ernst P. Muller, "Preston King, A Political Biography" (Ph.D. dissertation, Columbia, 1957), pp. 379–380; Harold M. Dorr (ed.), *The Michigan Constitutional Conventions of 1835–1836* (Ann Arbor, 1940), p. 157.
104. Similar considerations blocked the recognition of the rights of Indians.

have not the Flowing Beard of the Caucasian", "Inability of the Negro Features to express the Emotional Feelings peculiar to the Caucasian," and "The Negress, after a certain period, loses all Love for, or Interest in, her Offspring." Van Evrie was a committed Democrat.[105]

Such intense racism had its effects on the universalism of the American creed, as understood by Democrat partisans. Although they could agree with Theophilus Fisk that "the Christian and the Patriot look upon all mankind as brethren – made of one blood – and all equally welcome to this glorious heritage of uncontrolled freedom," in practice, they, like him, made it clear that they excluded blacks from humanity. In the 1850s this process would reach its culmination when Democrats like Stephen A. Douglas would flatly state that the Declaration of Independence was not intended to apply to blacks at all. But already in the Jacksonian era, Democratic egalitarianism rested on an explicit racism.[106]

Yet this should not be viewed as a problem of ideology divorced from material interests. If Democrats even in the North had repudiated and combated racism, the power of the slaveholding class would instantly have been brought to bear upon them, as the cases of William Leggett and Thomas Morris illustrate. Some northern Democrats did, of course, come to resent the aggressions of the "Slave Power" in the 1840s, when they followed Martin Van Buren out of the party, and again in the 1850s when the Kansas–Nebraska Act was the occasion for a larger and more permanent defection. But the traditions of the party discouraged such action and indeed inhibited the thought processes that it required. Democrats had long since made their peace with the Constitution, they had ample reason to venerate "states' rights" and they not only accepted but glorified the "Union" under which so much national progress had been made. As Frank Blair's *Globe* insisted in 1838, slavery agitation "would be mortal, at once, to our glorious Confederacy and all its political benefits." In Daniel Dickinson's estimation "the question" at the time the Union was formed "then was, and still is [in 1848], whether we should have a Union with slavery, or slavery without a Union."[107]

105. Cincinnati *Daily Enquirer*, Feb. 14, 1845; J. H. Van Evrie, *White Supremacy and Negro Subordination; or, Negroes a Subordinate Race, and Slavery its Normal Condition* (N.Y., 1868), pp. x–xiii; Washington *Globe*, Feb. 4, 1839; Dickinson, *Speeches, Correspondence* . . . , II, p. 299. Racism united the two wings of the New York Democracy as few other questions could – see Judah P. Ginsberg, "TheTangled Web: The New York Democratic Party and the Slavery Controversy, 1844–1860" (Ph.D. dissertation, University of Wisconsin, 1974), p. 105.
106. *Democratic Expositor*, Aug. 16, 1845. I shall discuss the views of Stephen A. Douglas at length in the sequel to this study.
107. Washington *Globe*, April 24, 1838; Dickinson, *Speeches, Correspondence* . . . , I, p. 255; John Ashworth, "The Democratic-Republicans before the Civil War: Political Ideology and Economic Change," *Journal of American Studies* (1986), pp. 375–390.

Thus by the time of Jackson's election, the middle position on slavery favored by the president was one that confirmed the privileged status of the slaveholder. States' rights, racism, party traditions, the perception of the federal constitution – all converged to undermine any prospect of a Democratic variant of abolitionism. Merely by adhering to traditional party principles, Democrats were led to support the class power of southern slaveholders with which the party ideology was inscribed. Theirs was not an explicitly but a functionally proslavery position.

VII

We are now able to appreciate that the slaveholders were the dominant class in the antebellum Republic. Let us compare their situation with other elites. During the second party system one could dislike manufacturers, merchants, banks and bankers and take one's hostility into politics. One could get into the White House on the basis of policies that were recognized by their advocates and opponents alike as detrimental to those groups. Andrew Jackson destroyed the Second Bank of the United States, by far the largest commercial institution in the land; in many of the states Democrats sought to rid themselves of all banks; in some they succeeded.[108] Despite the claims of manufacturers that tariff reduction would mean ruin, Democrats lowered the tariff, in some instances actually hoping that the predictions would prove correct.[109]

One could also dislike slavery. But until the mid-1840s it was hard to take this hostility into politics, and make it a vital, animating principle. It might be attempted, but there was no hope of high office if one pursued policies that were seen by all concerned to be adverse to slavery. The greatest hostility to slavery (within the major parties) came, as we shall see, from northern Whigs. But Whig leaders knew that an attack on slavery would turn the whole South over to the Democratic party, which, with its additional strength in the North, would then rule unchallenged.

But most Whigs, even in the North, did not wish to challenge slavery in the way that Democrats challenged banking, for example. As we shall see, Whigs in the mainstream of their party defended social and economic elites, and viewed the slaveholding interest as one among many that was to be cherished. Here was a vitally important asymmetry within American antebellum politics. As good conservatives, the Whigs rallied to the defense of the propertied elites, both north and south of the

108. See below, Chapter 6.
109. *Congressional Globe*, 27 Congress, 2 Session, Appendix, p. 484; Washington *Globe*, Jan. 11, 1842; *Young Hickory Banner*, Aug. 24, 1844.

Mason-Dixon line. Democrats were wont to challenge those interests, with a single exception: the slaveholding interest. As a dominant class, the slaveholders wielded power not by claiming that they were specially suited to rule, but instead by the exercise of hegemony. Let us remind ourselves of the significance of "hegemony." As one writer has explained, without referring to the Democratic party, antebellum politics, or the United States at all: "what a dominant hegemonic ideology can do is to provide a more coherent and systematic world view which not only influences the mass of the population but serves as a principle of organization of social institutions." As I have sought to demonstrate, this applies to Democratic ideology, the dominant ideology in the Age of Jackson.[110]

Let us review Democratic principles in the light of a Gramscian notion of "hegemony." Before doing so, however, it is important to reiterate that many of these ideas had their roots in the European past and had been highly visible in societies that had no slaves. This means that they are not *reducible* to the class interest of slaveholders. Yet this in no way precludes the possibility that they operated in the United States to the advantage of slaveholders to maintain what Gramsci termed "hegemony." What were they? First Democratic insistence upon limited government, and especially on the limited extent of federal power operated to reduce the threat from antislavery sentiment generated outside the South. The threat was by no means eliminated but the doctrine of states' rights undoubtedly provided a considerable measure of protection. Second, the emphasis on agriculture permitted the slaveholders to reach out into areas of the South in which slaveless farms predominated, as well as into the North, and launch a powerful appeal on the basis of shared interests and values. Third, the emphasis on racial differences, which had always characterized the Democratic tradition, operated to disable the forces of abolition (though not of free soil) and to cement loyalty to the slaveholders' governments in the South. Fourth, the appeal to a highly egalitarian individualism – provided it was understood to exclude racial minorities – offered a genuine appeal to white Americans faced with threatening social and political developments. Again this appeal could be made not merely to southerners but also to northerners. Fifth, the Democratic emphasis on individual moral autonomy – provided once again that blacks were excluded – served to empower each individual to choose whether or not to hold slaves, uncoerced by the views of others. Again the effect was to disable the opposition to slavery.

110. A.S. Sassoon in Tom Bottomore *et al.* (eds), *A Dictionary of Marxist Thought* (Oxford, 1983), p. 203.

When we recall that the Democrats were able to cast themselves as the special custodian of the Union, of American nationality and indeed of American democracy itself, it becomes apparent that party principles indeed operated to the slaveholders' advantage. Gramsci argued that hegemonic classes were able to maintain their dominance by exerting a moral and intellectual leadership. Such, we may argue, was the role of the Democratic party from Jackson's time (and indeed of the Republican party under Jefferson) until the 1850s. Some additional points are, however, in order. As we have already noted, a class that rules hegemonically may well need to make compromises with a variety of allies who are unified in a social bloc of forces. As we have already seen, Gramsci termed this a "historic bloc." The slaveholders of the South were able to make such compromises quite easily, with the other groups who voted Democratic in the North as well as the South. As research into voting behavior indicates, this meant farmers living in subsistence or semi-subsistence areas, the Catholic Irish and other immigrants, together with certain labor groups who responded favorably to the Democratic assault upon, for example, the banks. This Democratic coalition was the dominant force in American politics until the late 1850s.

What had happened, in effect, was that a pre-capitalist radical tradition had come to prominence in the United States because it was quite compatible with the maintenance of the rights of an extraordinarily powerful and determined social group: the slaveholders of the South. In other countries that radicalism remained outside politics in normal times; it required war, social revolution or both.[111] In the United States, however, this radicalism, at the center of which lay a demand for a society of equalized, atomized power, was admirably suited to the needs of slaveholders. Indeed the most remarkable feature of its triumph in the United States was that it was not amended to reflect even the existence of slavery, let alone the dominance of slaveholders. As we have seen, the political economy of Jefferson, Jackson and John Taylor simply ignored the existence of the slaves. Only the emphasis on race, not found in its European antecedents, betrayed the social character of the dominant class.

As we have already noted, the existence of this "historic bloc" was vaguely recognized by those contemporaries who spoke of the alliance between planters of the South and "plain republicans of the North." Nevertheless many Democratic partisans did not recognize – and would have indignantly rejected the suggestion – that the party functioned to perpetuate the dominance of southern slaveholders. Here was

---

111. As I hope to show in a future publication, the attitudes of the Jacksonians were remarkably similar to those of the Levellers at the time of the English Civil War. There are also many similarities with the views of the *sans-culottes* during the French Revolution.

the strength, but also the weakness, of this "bloc." Its strength was that a
set of principles so valuable to slaveholders was instead perceived as part
of the natural order. Thus northerners – and even southerners – who
might have opposed slavery were likely to find themselves faced with
an appealing and egalitarian creed which point by point undercut that
opposition. If the creed had explicitly defended or privileged slavery in
the South, the support or acquiescence of these groups might well have
been jeopardized. But the absence of any explicit support created problems of its own. Could southerners continue to assume that the creed
would afford sufficient protection? In effect Calhoun was the first major
Democratic party leader who began to doubt it. As we have seen, he came
to feel that northern opinion could not in the long term be trusted and he
demanded overt recognition of the rights of southern slaveholders. He
demanded, in effect, cast-iron constitutional guarantees for slaveholders
rather than the loose, hegemonic control afforded by Jacksonian
Democracy. The result was to call forth great indignation from some of
those who had enlisted under the Democratic banner but without
acknowledging the privileged position of slavery. Such outbursts punctu-
ated the history of the Democratic party from the time of nullification
onwards. In 1832 the party *en masse* repudiated Calhoun and his efforts,
though at the cost of some defections to the Whigs. In the 1840s, however, the attempt to acquire lands in the Southwest, made by Calhoun
(and others) on explicitly proslavery grounds, created stresses and strains
as the party endorsed the attempt (though not the proslavery rationale).
The Van Burenite defection of 1848 was the direct consequence.[112]

Indeed, when some Democrats combated the Calhounite influence
within the party, they employed egalitarian principles *against* the slaveholding class. Here was the second problem for slaveholders. It was
always possible to redirect Jacksonian arguments. If the federal government must not be allowed to fall into the hands of the "aristocratic"
minority, could one allow its power to be used expressly to secure additional territory for slaveholders? This was never the mainstream position
but it was the position of the defectors of 1848 as well as those who
followed Thomas Hart Benton of Missouri. Moreover, racist sentiment
now rebounded on slaveholders: the more the anti-Calhoun Democrat
accepted black inferiority, the more he resented attempts to carry black
slaves into western territories. In the 1840s these tensions within the
Democratic party proved damaging but containable; in the 1850s they
would be ruinous.[113]

112. See below, Chapter 6.
113. I shall consider this process in the sequel to this volume.

VIII

We must take care, however, not to assume that those who did not own slaves but who nevertheless responded favorably to Democratic rhetoric were mere dupes.[114] To begin with, in the case of the North, there was a real threat to many Americans posed by the commercial changes against which the Democracy inveighed. An alliance with southern Democrats was difficult to resist and if the price was acquiescence in southern slavery, we need not wonder that so many northerners were prepared to pay it. We shall return to this question later. In the South, however, the situation is more complex. Did the southern slaveholder exploit the non-slaveholder? It may be worth noting that there is no exploitation according to the Marxist or the Jacksonian definition of the term: the non-slaveholder was to be allowed to keep the full fruits of his labor. While there might well be contact between them, especially in the low country areas of the South, the two groups need not come into conflict. So long as the non-slaveholder defined freedom as the right to enjoy the fruits of his labor, then if he owned the land he worked, as hundreds of thousands did, he was indeed free. So long as the slaveholder was secure in his right to exploit the slave, he could afford to view the non-slaveholding white man as his friend and ally.[115]

Moreover this notion of freedom was one with deep roots in western thought. It flourished for example in seventeenth-century England, where there were no slaves at all, as well as in Antiquity, where there were. Indeed the example of the Roman world is a telling one. Christianity, at the time of its inception, like Jacksonian Democracy, looked askance on commercial and mercantile wealth, even as it abstained from criticism of the slaveholder. We should not, of course, assume that all southerners were profoundly versed in history but it would be strange if popular consciousness had been untouched by these traditions.[116]

Most fascinating of all is the relationship between the upcountry areas of the South and the plantation belts. Here we can appreciate the subtlety of Democratic thought. The emphasis on local and indeed individual autonomy met perfectly the needs of many farmers who were engaged in only a modest amount of commodity production and who feared the

114. Such people were no more duped than historians like Schlesinger and Remini, who have also responded favorably to Democratic rhetoric.
115. Although I share his enthusiasm for the concept of "hegemony," I am employing it in a very different way from Eugene Genovese. I shall discuss these questions more fully in the sequel to this volume. See Genovese, "Yeomen Farmers in a Slaveholders' Democracy," in Elizabeth Fox-Genovese and Eugene D. Genovese, *Fruits of Merchant Capital* (N.Y., 1983), pp. 249–264.
116. G. E. M. de Ste. Croix, *The Class Struggle in the Ancient Greek World* (London, 1983), *passim*.

loss of independence that greater subjection to the market might entail. Yet Democratic thought also encompassed the production of huge amounts of cotton as well as other cash crops. As long as he did not seek to challenge the political rights of the slaveless community, or to levy taxes upon it to build roads, establish banks, or aid merchants, the wealthy slaveholder could remain the partner of the subsistence or semi-subsistence farmer. Here was the social basis for the assimilation, in Democratic rhetoric and ideology, of the plantation to the farm and of the wealthy slaveholder to the yeoman farmer.[117]

Whigs and slavery

I

Just as the Democratic party contained within it several different views of slavery, so Whig opinion on the subject was varied. Yet while the Whig spectrum of opinion was of approximately the same width, it was a different spectrum. Whigs on the proslavery side were fewer in number than Democrats and they were positioned closer to the middle; conversely on the antislavery side there were more Whigs than Democrats and they were more extreme in their views. But from its formation in 1833–1834 until the advent of the territorial question some ten years later the party was able to contain these differences. At this time, and even after the annexation of Texas had become a vital question, Whig politicians were able to continue recruiting support from all sections of the Union.[118]

The dominant Whig views of slavery at this time were probably those of Henry Clay and Daniel Webster. Although they were not by any means in full agreement, the points of convergence were many and the two men represent mainstream Whig opinion north and south of the Mason-Dixon line. In later years each would come under pressure from the militants on either side of the sectional controversy, Clay primarily from southern proslavery militants, Webster from northern abolitionists and free-soilers. The Compromise of 1850 was a triumph for the two aging statesmen and their attempts to resolve sectional differences; by then, however, Whig (and Democratic) differences on slavery were endangering party unity.[119]

117. James A. Henretta, "Families and Farms: *Mentalité* in Pre-Industrial America," *William and Mary Quarterly*, 3rd series, xxxv (1978), pp. 3–32; Steven Hahn, *The Roots of Southern Populism: Yeoman Farmers and the Transformation of the Georgia Upcountry, 1850–1900* (N.Y., 1983), p. 29.
118. There is no single work on the Whigs and slavery. See however Howe, *Political Culture of Whigs*; Brown, *Politics and Statesmanship*.
119. On Clay and Webster, see, in addition to the works already cited, Glyndon G. Van Deusen, *The Life of Henry Clay* (Boston, 1935); Clement Eaton, *Henry Clay and the*

As we shall see, Clay and Webster perceived slavery primarily as a major national interest. Ironically, however, at the beginning of their careers, well before the formation of the Whig party, each had questioned the legitimacy of this interest. Before he even entered Congress, Webster in 1819 wrote a memorial in which he objected to the admission of any new slave states on the grounds that "we have a strong feeling of the injustice of any toleration of slavery." Like many other northerners, especially those of a Federalist persuasion, he objected strongly to the three-fifths clause and sought its repeal, partly on humanitarian grounds but primarily, one suspects, because it politically disadvantaged the North – and especially the Federalist party. Clay meanwhile had launched his own career in Kentucky as a severe critic of slavery, stressing both the suffering endured by the slaves and the vices encouraged in the master. He introduced a proposal for the emancipation of the children of existing slaves, without, moreover, insisting that they be colonized.[120]

Yet both men moved away from these early positions. Clay became an enthusiastic supporter, a founder member and ultimately president of the American Colonization Society. He now doubted whether race prejudice in the United States could be overcome. It may also be worth noting that he had by this time begun to acquire slaves in ever-increasing numbers. At the time of the Missouri Crisis, when Webster was opposing the creation of any new slave states in the West, Clay, like many other southerners who professed antislavery sentiments, was recommending the "diffusion" of slavery. Indeed the different positions the two men took in 1819–1821, together with the obvious fact that Clay was himself a slaveholder, go far to account for the much greater hostility that Webster, until the very end of his career, encountered in the South. Yet by the time he had achieved national fame, Webster had moderated his antislavery considerably. In his celebrated debate with Robert Hayne in 1830 he restated his view that slavery was "one of the greatest evils, both moral and political." He also insisted that the state of Kentucky, for example, would have been far more populous and far more prosperous without it. But he then stressed

Art of American Politics (Boston, 1957); Merrill D. Peterson, *The Great Triumvirate: Webster, Clay and Calhoun* (N.Y., 1987); Henry Poage, *Henry Clay and the Whig Party* (Chapel Hill, 1936); Norman D. Brown, *Daniel Webster and the Politics of Availability* (Athens, Ga., 1969); Irving H. Bartlett, *Daniel Webster* (N.Y., 1978); Robert F. Dalzell, Jr., *Daniel Webster and the Trial of American Nationalism, 1843–1851* (Boston, 1973); Sydney Nathans, *Daniel Webster and Jacksonian Democracy* (Baltimore, 1973); Richard N. Current, *Daniel Webster and the Rise of National Conservatism* (Boston, 1955). I have, of course, made extensive use of Calvin Colton (ed.), *The Works of Henry Clay* 10 vols (N.Y., 1904), McIntyre (ed.), *Writings and Speeches of Webster,* and Charles M. Wiltse *et al., The Papers of Daniel Webster* 8 vols (Hanover, N.H., 1974–).

120. Wiltse, *Papers of Webster,* I, pp. 58–59; Brown, *Politics and Statesmanship,* pp. 137–141.

that the issue lay entirely outside his control. "The domestic slavery of the Southern States," he announced, "I leave where I find it, – in the hands of their own governments." For "it is their affair and not mine." By now he no longer advocated the repeal of the three-fifths clause. Indeed the constitution's provisions for slavery, like all other clauses in that document, had come to acquire for him a transcendental importance and he asserted that according to the constitution, "slavery, as it exists in the States, is beyond the reach of Congress." Since it was "a concern of the States themselves" and "Congress has no power over it," Webster avowed that he would "concur, therefore, in no act, no measure, no menace, no indication of purpose, which shall interfere or threaten to interfere with the exclusive authority of the several States over the subject of slavery as it exists within their respective limits." To this extent he had made his peace with slavery.[121]

The militant abolitionism that sprang up in the 1830s was viewed with scant sympathy by either Clay or Webster. Clay deprecated the pamphlet campaign and favored the outright rejection of abolitionist petitions that called for immediate emancipation in the States. He was willing, however, to receive petitions calling for abolition in the District of Columbia, even though he opposed this policy. In 1839, and with one eye perhaps on southern support in the forthcoming presidential election, he made a major speech in the Senate on abolitionism. The speech is important, not merely because it shows his attitude to immediatism but because it exemplifies his fundamental approach to political questions. Once again he acknowledged the evil of slavery; once again he expressed deep misgivings about the possibility of a biracial society in the United States; now, in addition, he confirmed that abolition would mean the end of the Union. Moreover, if freed, he predicted, ex-slaves would either flood the North and drive wages down or precipitate a race war. "Their liberty," he concluded, "if it were possible, could only be established by violating the incontestable powers of the States, and subverting the Union;" "beneath the ruins of the Union would be buried, sooner or later, the liberty of both races."[122]

Clay here made a set of claims that the abolitionist could not concede. The disagreement was in part over the feasibility of immediate emancipation but, in a larger sense, it was a clash over moral absolutism. An abolitionist like Garrison, for example, believed that evil was unitary. It could be combated unambiguously and unqualifiedly. Clay insisted, however, that evil could not always be eradicated without the creation

---

121. Brown, *Politics and Statesmanship*, pp. 140–142; *Annals of the Congress of the United States*, 15 Congress, 2 Session, pp. 1187–1188; Colton (ed.), *Works of Clay*, VI, pp. 328–340; Wiltse, *Papers of Webster*, I, pp. 293–296, II, p. 130.
122. Colton (ed.), *Works of Clay*, VIII, pp. 158, 151, IX, p. 387.

of still greater evil. Moreover, he rejected Garrison's argument that Americans, by tolerating slavery, were themselves guilty of sinfulness. The slavery of blacks in the United States, he asserted, "forms an exception – an exception resulting from a stern and inexorable necessity – to the general liberty in the United States." Americans, he continued, "did not originate, nor are we responsible for, this necessity."[123]

It followed that the task of the statesman was to further the public good not by fanatical crusades against evils – real or imagined – but by carefully drawing up a balance sheet of the advantages and disadvantages of various courses of action. Thus Clay condemned abolitionism because "it is a power that mounts the hobby of one principle to rule over all others – a sword that cuts all ties, however sacred, for the sake of cutting one admitted to be bad." The balance of advantage lay with the maintenance of slavery in the states where it existed, at any rate as long as this was the favored policy of those states themselves.[124]

Clay believed that statesmanlike action required calmness, prudence and caution. "All legislation," he once observed, "all government, all society, is formed upon the principle of mutual concession, politeness, comity, courtesy." It was this which abolitionism threatened. The danger was of an appeal to the passions. In 1850, seeking support for his compromise measures, he declared that it was "passion, passion" that he "dread[ed]." The abolitionist claimed, of course, to be addressing the conscience of his reader or listener but for Clay a passionate zeal for or against slavery threatened the normal, natural deliberative processes of Congress, of government and thus of the Union itself.[125]

Webster's engagement with the abolitionists was more dramatic. In the 1830s he believed that all their petitions should be received, and, as befitted one with his Federalist antecedents, argued that it was indeed constitutional to abolish slavery in the District of Columbia (though he did not suggest that it was expedient to do so). But he had little respect for abolitionists. Echoing the southern view that "they have done nothing but delay and defeat their own professed object," he dissociated himself from them entirely: "they have never received any encouragement from me, and they never will."[126] But it was not until his famous "7 March" speech in 1850 that he brought the full force of his rhetoric to bear upon them. This speech earned him great acclaim from many southerners and some northerners but it also led to vilification and charges of treason from large numbers of antislavery campaigners in the North and

123. Colton (ed.), *Works of Clay*, VIII, p. 158.
124. Colton (ed.), *Works of Clay*, VIII, p. 158.
125. Colton (ed.), *Works of Clay*, IX, p. 418, III, p. 304, IX, pp. 563ff.
126. Wiltse, *Papers of Webster*, II, pp. 198–293, 482.

especially New England. The most controversial part of the speech was that which offered concessions to the South but his remarks on abolition were highly significant. He offered a series of characterizations of the abolitionists. They were "men with whom every thing is absolute; absolutely wrong or absolutely right," "men who, with clear perceptions, as they think, of their own duty, do not see how too eager a pursuit of one duty may involve them in the violation of others, or how too warm an embracement of one truth may lead to a disregard of other truths equally important," and finally "men who, in reference to disputes of that sort, are of opinion that human duties may be ascertained with the exactness of mathematics." Webster not surprisingly condemned their perfectionism, their belief that "nothing is good but what is perfect" as well as their tendency to reject all compromises "in consideration of difference of opinion or in deference to other men's judgment." Finally he stressed that abolitionists failed to understand that progress had always been, and would necessarily continue to be, gradual:

> They are impatient men; too impatient always to give heed to the admonition of St. Paul, that we are not to "do evil that good may come;" too impatient to wait for the slow progress of moral causes in the improvement of mankind. They do not remember that the doctrines and the miracles of Jesus Christ have, in eighteen hundred years, converted only a small proportion of the human race.

Thus abolitionism grossly underestimated the practical difficulties standing in its way, its moral absolutism threatened the normal deliberative processes of government, its perfectionism generated intolerance and a fanatical refusal to compromise.[127]

These priorities were of course identical to those revealed when Clay and Webster took their stand against Andrew Jackson and the Democratic party. Though Jacksonians and abolitionists were mortal enemies they both threatened the kind of politics that the two leading Whigs espoused. In language that Henry Clay might have used, Webster condemned Democratic appeals to the populace on the grounds that they threatened to make Americans mere "slaves to their own passions." As we have seen, both men viewed abolitionism in identical terms. Democrats and abolitionists alike ignored the need for statesmanship.[128]

Both Clay and Webster were thus profoundly ambivalent towards slavery. Both continued to insist that it was a blemish on American society, in Clay's words "the darkest spot in the map of our country." Undoubtedly the two men were sincere in these views. As late as 1850,

127. Wiltse, *Papers of Webster*, II, pp. 521–522.
128. McIntyre (ed.), *Writings and Speeches of Webster*, VI, p. 266.

when his stance on the Compromise brought him praise in the South and vilification in the North, Webster emphasized in his private correspondence the "injustice" of slavery, the fact that it was "opposed to the natural equality of mankind," that it was founded "only in the power of the strong, over the weak." "Slavery," he affirmed, "has proved itself every where, a great social & political evil." Clay for his part had the preceding year brought his career in Kentucky state politics to a close where he had begun it: calling for emancipation. Though his plan was almost extreme in its gradualism, he courageously demanded that it be made public. The result was to call forth a barrage of criticism from southerners and even from Kentuckians. When elections were held for a constitutional convention, the emancipationists failed to elect a single delegate. Some observers claimed Clay could no longer carry the state. By 1850 both Clay and Webster were finding their moderate antislavery under threat from extremists.[129]

But more important than their antislavery was their insistence that slavery, at least in the states where it existed, was a legitimate interest. Clay throughout his career tried to create a harmony of interests between labor and capital, between agriculture and industry, between slave and free labor. Webster also sought to extend the hand of friendship to the slaveholders of the South. In a speech at Rochester in 1843 he welcomed them into the family whose protection was the primary task of government:

> We have a vast country, a variety of climate, and various pursuits. We have agricultural States and we have plantation States. We have manufacturing interests and we have commercial interests. And our business is not to array our various interests into a belligerent and hostile state, not to inflame our own passions or others concerning the measures of government for the protection of our particular interests; but let us make the whole a great national, I may say a family, concern.

As we shall see, the rise of the free soil issue would put Whig claims of a harmony of interest to a severe test.[130]

II

Henry Clay's views on slavery commanded wide respect within the ranks of southern Whiggery. The *Richmond Whig*, for example, espoused a moderate antislavery in the early 1830s and continued to advocate

129. Wiltse, *Papers of Webster*, VII, p. 9; Peterson, *Great Triumvirate*, pp. 378, 452.
130. McIntyre (ed.), *Writings and Speeches of Webster*, XIII, p. 184.

colonization even after Nat Turner's revolt. Like Clay too, the newspaper's editors charged abolitionists with having retarded the progress of emancipation in the South. By the mid-1840s, however, the *Whig* had ceased to discuss slavery as an abstract question. Such a stance was not uncommon. The *Arkansas Whig*, nevertheless, continued to voice the standard criticisms. "No-one," its editor remarked quite inaccurately, "will deny that the institution of slavery encumbers the South." He added that "it will, in our opinion, always do so." As late as 1850, Edward Stanly, a Whig congressman from North Carolina, acknowledged that "slavery is an evil . . . an evil to the white man," while John M. Botts of Virginia right up to the Civil War was prepared to avow himself "one of those who think slavery, in the abstract . . . much to be deprecated," once again on the grounds that it retarded economic growth.[131]

Some southern Whigs, however, took Clay's antislavery much further. Until the emergence of Hinton Helper in the 1850s by far the most prominent southerner who could be described unambiguously as antislavery was Cassius Clay, ironically cousin of the Whig leader and also based in Kentucky. Beginning in 1840 Clay, having freed his own slaves, indicted the peculiar institution for having retarded the state's development. If abolitionism meant Kentucky ridding herself of slaves, then, he announced in 1843, "I am an abolitionist." Clay was prepared, however, to offer compensation to slaveholders. But his most controversial utterances were those in which he endorsed northern condemnations of the southern elite as a "Slave Power." Clay admired the economic development of the North; he did not hesitate to express a wish that Kentucky become more like Massachusetts. Cassius Clay now became the target for vilification and physical intimidation in the State.[132]

Neither the Clays nor other Whig critics of slavery came from the Deep South. There were two reasons for this. First, after the loss of Calhoun and his little band, the party did not find it easy to recruit in the states of the Deep South. Second, those southern Whigs who were from these states did not usually endorse even the moderate antislavery of Henry

131. The Arkansas *Whig*, June 5, 1851; Robert H. Tomlinson, "The Origins and Editorial Politics of the 'Richmond Whig and Public Advertiser', 1824–1865" (Ph.D. dissertation, Michigan State University, 1971), pp. 72, 84; *Speech of Edward Stanly, of North Carolina, Exposing the Causes of the Slavery Agitation* (Washington, D.C., n.d.), p. 10; *Speech of John Minor Botts at a Dinner at Powhatton Court-House, Virginia, June 15, 1850* (n.p., n.d.), p. 2.

132. Horace Greeley (ed.), *The Writings of Cassius Marcellus Clay* (N.Y., 1848), pp. 91, 370. See also *ibid.*, pp. 129, 163, 176, 187, 189, 224; *The Life of Cassius Marcellus Clay, Memoirs, Writings, and Speeches* (N.Y., 1886), pp. 26, 110; William W. Freehling, *The Road to Disunion: Secessionists at Bay, 1776–1854* (N.Y., 1990), p. 462.

Clay, let alone that of his kinsman. More common was the position of Henry Hilliard of Alabama who merely avowed that he had "never sought to vindicate slavery by a single quotation from the scriptures." Hilliard came under considerable pressure in his own state in the late 1840s for being disloyal to slavery and the South. He denied that slavery was a moral evil where it already existed.[133]

If we wish to understand the predicament facing Whigs from the Deep South, the career of Alexander H. Stephens is instructive. Stephens announced in 1845 that he was "no defender of slavery in the abstract." As one historian has observed, "Stephens defended slavery apologetically where it already existed, in much the same manner as [Henry] Clay." It is possible that he shared Clay's desire for colonization and as late as 1850 he noted that the condition of southern slaves was "certainly not a good one." Yet by this time Stephens was experiencing the same pressures as Hilliard and these statements were now reserved for private correspondence. They clashed with his far more militant public utterances. As we shall see, Stephens was unable to remain within the Whig party at this time and his discomfort illustrates in microcosm the difficulties experienced by the entire party in the Deep South.[134]

By this time a small number of Whigs from the Deep South were subscribing to the view that slavery was a positive good, though they frequently hedged this claim with reservations or qualifications of one sort or another. William Alston of Alabama denied that slavery was either a violation of divine law or a sin. He also extolled the role of women in slaveholding societies and contrasted it with their situation in the North. More typically, Edward Cabell of Florida argued that slavery was highly desirable in "tropical or warm climates" and claimed that it created a "purer" spirit of "freedom and true republicanism" than would otherwise be possible.[135] Yet such utterances were unusual from Whig partisans. They were no more typical than the antislavery outbursts of Cassius Clay. Until at least the mid-1840s, and probably later, it was the more moderate views of his kinsman that prevailed. Hence, like Henry Clay, southern Whigs urged that slavery, as an interest, be protected. John P. Kennedy of Maryland in a letter to his constituents declared that he wished to extend the protective hand of government around every interest in the State:

133. *Congressional Globe*, 31 Congress, 1 Session, Appendix, pp. 179, 485; Carlton Jackson, "A History of the Whig Party in Alabama, 1828–1860" (Ph.D. dissertation, University of Georgia, 1962), pp. 109–131.
134. *Congressional Globe*, 28 Congress, 2 Session, 190, Appendix, pp. 309–314; Howe, *Political Culture of Whigs*, p. 245.
135. *Congressional Globe*, 31 Congress, 1 Session, Appendix, pp. 465–466, 241. See also Charles C. Langdon, *Reply to the Twenty-Seven* (Mobile, 1850), p. 6.

> If I were asked, what is the chief object of Government and what its first duty, I would answer, protection. I do not mean the protection of manufacturers and mechanical industry only; I mean the protection of every interest in the State.[136]

Yet Kennedy had no policies that were specifically intended for slaveholders (other than a tariff to protect some of the products of slave labor). Instead, like other Whigs, he wished to keep slavery out of national politics. Southern Whigs were adamant on this point not least because they feared its impact upon party unity. They were right to harbor these fears. But it was not the differences within the party at the South that were the object of concern. These were easily contained. Instead it was the alarming strength of antislavery elements within northern Whiggery.

III

By the time of Andrew Jackson's election to the presidency no northerner advocated the reintroduction of slavery into the North or wished to encourage its spread into the West. But northerners differed in the extent to which, and the means by which, they would oppose it. Northern Whigs were, in general, more hostile to the South and to slavery than northern Democrats. But unanimity existed in the ranks of neither party. Until the crisis produced by the annexation of Texas and the war with Mexico, most northern Whigs took a position that resembled that of Daniel Webster.

Like Webster they made it clear that they objected strongly to abolitionism. Abbot Lawrence, on the grounds that he was "in favor of maintaining the compact as established by our fathers . . . the Union as it is," announced that he had "no sympathy with the abolition party of the North and East" which, he believed had "done mischief to the cause of abolition in several States of the Union." The constitution made "the abolition of slavery in the States . . . exclusively a State question and one with which I do not feel that I should meddle or interfere in any shape or form." The New York patrician Philip Hone likewise feared that abolitionism would overthrow the institutions of the country and fellow New Yorker George Templeton Strong as late as 1850 opined that the abolitionists "deserve to be scourged and pilloried for sedition or hanged for treason."[137]

136. *Collective Works of Kennedy*, IV, p. 306.
137. Abbot Lawrence to Cassius M. Clay, March 12, 1845 quoted in Kinley J. Brauer, *Cotton versus Conscience: Massachusetts Whig Politics and Southwestern Expansion, 1843–1848* (Lexington, Ky., 1967), pp. 23–24; Herbert Kriedman, "New York's Philip Hone: Businessman – Politician – Patron of Arts and Letters" (Ph.D. dissertation, New York University, 1965), p. 230; Nevins and Thomas (eds), *Diary of Strong*, II, p. 22.

Like Webster and Clay these Whigs objected not merely to their policy of immediate abolition but also to their appeal to conscience. When abolitionists insisted that all men must do their duty unhesitatingly, unflinchingly and regardless of consequences, Calvin Colton as "Junius" replied that "the very question of duty depends in part on a consideration of consequences." Similarly Horace Greeley observed that "it is the easiest thing in the world to shove off all responsibility by saying do your duty and let the results take care of themselves." Yet "considering consequences and choosing the best way to do a thing is the prerogative of human reason." The *Princeton Whig* chided reformers who, like the abolitionists, believed that "a change of heart was a change of purpose, which a man could effect as easily as change his route on a journey." Abolitionists were men and women who threw themselves into a frenzy by failing to see that while slavery was a sin, a virtuous slaveholder could still exist. As a result they were forced into "the most unnatural exaggeration of what they call the crime of slaveholding, in order to satisfy their conscience, and justify them to themselves, in their hatred and denunciation of good men." A good Whig, with his respect for order and prudence, would have nothing to do with such reckless agitation.[138]

Or would he? Some northern Whigs felt differently. Although never a thoroughly reliable party member, former president John Quincy Adams was, until at least the mid-1840s the most conspicuously antislavery Whig in the North. While a presidential aspirant Adams had courted southern support in the manner of all northern candidates and he had no real record of opposition even to the extension of slavery. As one historian has remarked, Adams in the White House had "carefully avoided" the slavery question. But as we have already seen, he attributed his defeat in 1828 to the influence of what would later be termed the "Slave Power" and began to harbor doubts about the ability of the Republic to contain sectional differences. With the growth of abolitionism Adams, who had decided to re-enter politics as a humble Congressman, found his niche. He did not endorse immediate abolition and he believed that compensation should be offered but he shared the abolitionist conviction that slavery was grossly immoral. The petition campaign of the mid-1830s soon attracted his attention and support. Skillfully manipulating the issue to show the threat which slavery presented to republican institutions, Adams succeeded in infuriating southerners and drawing attention to the antislavery cause. He became by a considerable margin the leading opponent of the "gag," from its introduction in 1836 to its repeal in 1844.[139]

138. *Junius Tracts*, pp. 79, 72; New York *Tribune*, Dec. 9, 1843; Princeton *Whig*, Supplement, Jan. 31, 1845.
139. Mary W. M. Hargreaves, *The Presidency of John Quincy Adams*, p. 323; Richards, *Congressman Adams*, *passim*.

Adams had a small band of supporters, the most influential of whom was Joshua Giddings of Ohio. If Adams himself was in many respects highly pessimistic about the future, Giddings by contrast believed that progress, both material and moral, was the order of the day. He was a committed evangelical and like most evangelicals had broken entirely with Calvinist notions of predestination. Indeed he explicitly compared the slavery of the South with that of Calvinism: both denied individual free will. Similarly, he argued that slavery was a drag on economic progress; it blocked the division of labor in the South and obstructed the development of a home market for American products. Antislavery was therefore, he concluded, implicit in Whiggery, which as all its supporters knew, aimed at diversification, and a home market as well as commercial "progress."[140]

If Giddings had had his way, the Whig party would have been directly associated with antislavery and with the project of abolition if not the tactics of the abolitionists. Though he disagreed with the Garrisonian wing fundamentally over the question of the constitution, he agreed with Garrison himself that slavery would not be able to survive without northern support. His goal therefore was identical to that of Salmon P. Chase: the divorce of the federal government from the "Slave Power." Accordingly he worked, largely unsuccessfully, to move the Whig party closer to antislavery principles.

Prior to the emergence of the Texas question, the biggest sectional issue which Giddings confronted came in 1842 with the slave rebellion on board the slave trading vessel, the *Creole*. Giddings argued that slavery had no legal existence outside the jurisdiction of individual states and thus the rebellion was justified. The resolutions he introduced were condemned by southerners in the most violent manner and Giddings was formally censured by the House. He then resigned his seat, returned to his constituents and was triumphantly re-elected.

Giddings and Adams were not the only members of the Whig party to oppose slavery in these years. William Slade of Vermont was one of the most antislavery of all members of Congress, though his influence was small if only because southerners had given up on the state of Vermont. But a much larger number – and probably a majority – of northern Whigs assumed that the onward march of progress would probably result in the marginalizing of slavery in the United States. If this were indeed so, then northerners should be patient. In the meantime slaveholders should

---

140.   On Giddings see James B. Stewart, *Joshua R. Giddings and the Tactics of Radical Politics* (Cleveland, O., 1970) and the incisive discussion in Howe, *Political Culture of Whigs*, pp. 167–180.

be welcomed into the coalition of propertied, commercially minded elites in whose name the party would continue to act.

Whigs and capitalism (2)

Having examined Whig views of slavery, we are now in a position to reconsider the Whig attitude to capitalism. Until at least the mid-1840s the slavery issue was subordinate to the need to defend the nation's commercial system, challenged by the Democratic party in the name of an agrarian creed that placed a heavy emphasis on the equality of all adult white males. As we have seen, the Whigs looked with favor upon commercial development, upon banks, credit, manufacturing, roads, canals and railroads.

The essentially defensive character of Whiggery is important. Although many Whigs believed that progress was the hallmark of the nineteenth century they also believed that the Democratic party threatened it. In its heyday the Whig party represented a coalition of interests, each looking to the "fostering" care of government, each to be considered by the benign and prudent statesman elected by a discerning and self-restrained people. The coalition was of those benefiting from, or expecting to benefit from, the commercial development of the American economy.

The threat to these Whig ideals came from both North and South. Democratic egalitarianism and Democratic agrarianism were prominent on both sides of the Mason-Dixon line; the attack on the banks, for example, was carried on by northerners and southerners alike. Commercial development, so many of whose effects Democrats feared, was itself a national and not a sectional phenomenon.

This was one reason why the Whig party never managed to generate a fully fledged appeal to "free labor," as the Republicans would in the 1850s. The need to rally to the defense of commercial interests throughout the nation blocked the full development of a "free labor" ideology. It did appear in the writings of Whig propagandists like Calvin Colton, but, as we have seen, it was cast in an essentially defensive mold and it largely ignored the South.[141]

It was not, however, merely the needs of the southern wing which inhibited the formulation of a more aggressively "free labor" appeal. Even many northern Whigs feared what they took to be an excessive individualism (whether the abolitionist or the Democratic variant) on the grounds that men were not yet sufficiently confirmed in their roles

---

141. I shall consider Republican ideology in the sequel to this volume.

and institutions not yet sufficiently well established to be left without the fostering hand of government.

An outstanding example was western land. Whigs objected to Democratic plans to make western lands freely available (via graduation and pre-emption) on the grounds that this would diminish the supply of laborers in the East. The Republicans in the 1850s would advocate homesteads on precisely the same grounds, but confident that a reduction in the number of laborers would strengthen eastern capitalism not weaken it. Republicans knew, as Whigs did not, that the supply of wage workers in the East was quite adequate to the needs of northern capitalism; as we shall see, Republican ideology reflected the greater maturity of northern capitalism in the 1850s.[142]

Similarly most Whigs were alarmed at the prospect of immigrants exercising full political rights. A high proportion of eastern wage workers were of immigrant stock and many Whigs doubted whether they had sufficient understanding of the American political system to cast their votes in a discriminating manner. More precisely, they feared that immigrants would respond all too easily to the demagogic appeals of Democratic politicians. Licentiousness and anarchy were the anticipated results.[143]

The Whigs did not, of course, seek to curtail immigration. On the contrary, they welcomed the increase in the labor supply provided by the immigrants. But they fretted about the compatibility between wage labor and democracy with a workforce that was ethnically and religiously divided. (Even the Republicans experienced these doubts, though it should be noted that the levels of immigration were far higher in the late 1840s and early 1850s than previously.)

For these reasons the Whigs emphasized paternalism, order and self-restraint. They clung to an organic view of society, one in which ties of interdependence were to be welcomed and strengthened. They were also, as Daniel Howe has pointed out, quick to assume moral responsibility for others, in a way that classic liberalism would denounce, just as orthodox Democrats denounced it. This was the task of the statesman, but it was also the task of the educator and the social reformer, both of whom were

---

142. For Democratic and Whig policies on the disposal of the public lands see Richardson (ed.), *Messages of Presidents*, III, pp. 386–389, IV, p. 503; Roy M. Robbins, *Our Landed Heritage: The Public Domain 1776–1936* (Princeton, 1942), pp. 75, 85, 94; *Collective Works of Kennedy*, IV, p. 605; New York *Tribune*, April 18, 1842; *Congressional Globe*, 25 Congress, 3 Session, Appendix, p. 307.

143. I shall consider the issue of immigration (seen by some historians as crucial to Jacksonian politics) in the sequel to this volume. However, for an argument that immigration largely reinforced existing divisions between Whig and Democrat, see Ashworth, *"Agrarians" and "Aristocrats,"* pp. 179–193.

conspicuously identified with the Whig party rather than the Democracy.[144]

It was even the task of the capitalist. As Howe also observes, the town of Lowell, showpiece of early New England industrialism and founded by Nathan Appleton, a successful merchant turned industrialist, was to be run like a large family. The workers themselves were women, whose moral welfare would be safeguarded by the wise paternalists who owned and managed the mills. Indeed "the model that influenced the founders of Lowell most of all was the pre-industrial New England village, with its traditional patterns of deference made more rigid by a corporate table of organization." This paternalist scheme gradually disintegrated, as the employers shifted to Irish immigrant labor but the heyday of paternalist Lowell was the heyday of the Whig party. Its frankly experimental character and the tentativeness with which even the most committed Whigs viewed the growth of the factory system are apparent in a remark of Henry Clay. "Lowell," Clay predicted (as late as 1843), "will tell whether the Manufacturing system is compatible with the social virtues."[145]

Appleton was a significant figure not merely for his role in founding Lowell but also as a pioneer in banking and as the moving spirit of the Boston Associates. The Boston Associates were a group of business and professional men whose purpose, again in Howe's words, "was to consolidate control of the textile industry and related economic activities like insurance [and banking]." They established the "Suffolk System" which required all banks to keep contingency funds at the Suffolk Bank in Boston. The system was a response to the fragility of the nation's commercial system even in Massachusetts, the most developed state in the Union, and it sought to overcome that fragility by restricting competition and "retaining control of New England banking in the hands of a few well established capitalists." The curtailment of competition was no misfortune, so far as Appleton and his associates were concerned. "Excessive competition," in the words of his pastor, "generates fraud. Trade is turned into gambling, and the spirit of mad speculation exposes public and private interest to a disastrous instability."[146]

Appleton and his associates provided the leadership for the party in Massachusetts, a banner Whig state. Men like Daniel Webster, Rufus Choate, Edward Everett and Robert Winthrop shared most of their views and were indeed the spokesmen for the same merchant–industrialist

---

144. My debt to Howe here, and indeed throughout this section, is, I hope, apparent. In particular I have found his discussion of the "Entrepreneurial Ethos" (pp. 96–112) invaluable.
145. Howe, *Political Culture of Whigs*, pp. 104, 105–106.
146. Howe, *Political Culture of Whigs*, p. 138.

interests. Appleton and his circle had much in common with some of the large southern planters who were their contemporaries. Both groups inclined to paternalism; both stressed the ties of kinship among themselves. Neither had accepted the liberal norms which in future generations would dominate American political and social thought. This was the basis of their union – and of the intersectional appeal of the Whigs. While "Appleton and his associates brought modern industrialism to the United States, . . . they themselves were not fundamentally modern in their outlook. They were paternalists and *rentiers* who regarded their factories much as old-fashioned gentry might regard their estates." In their suspicion of excessive competition, in their desire to employ government rather than trust exclusively to market forces, they represented a transitional era in American capitalism, one just before the traditional merchant was supplanted by the aggressive entrepreneur. In future generations the supply of wage workers would be too large to be threatened by agrarian-based egalitarianism, the supply of capital would be too great to need the intervention of government to raise additional sums. A less paternalistic, more liberal political economy would be in place.[147]

It was no coincidence that the supply of both labor and capital seemed problematic to the Whigs or that by the 1850s there seemed to be a shortage of neither. With the emergence of larger units of production in the 1850s, profits were sufficient to allow venture capital to be raised without recourse to the mixed public–private enterprises so favored by the Whigs. The availability of wage workers thus simultaneously ended the shortage of labor and capital as well as paving the way for the Republicans' exuberant celebration of free labor and their triumphant reconciliation of wage labor and democracy.

Conclusion

Let us conclude by restating the principal features of the second party system. Neither the Democratic nor the Whig party was monolithic; neither party was impervious to change even in the decade following the establishment of the two party system, let alone when the conflict over slavery began to assume greater proportions. Nevertheless one cannot, it seems to me, deny the Progressive interpretation of the struggle between Democrat and Whig as one over democracy and capitalism in the United States.

But two important points must be added. First these struggles, though they involved key issues as well as vitally important economic interests, were conducted within a political system and an ideological universe

---

147. Howe, *Political Culture of Whigs*, p. 108.

which privileged and sheltered the slaveholder of the South. While Democratic egalitarianism challenged banks and factories, the building of canals and the construction of railroads, it left untouched the inequalities of wealth and power effected by slaveownership. Indeed it obscured the origins as well as the effects of these inequalities and, especially before the mid-1840s, it disabled rather than facilitated all attempts to combat them. For this and for other reasons the Democratic commitment to democracy was flawed by the assumption that only adult white males were fit to participate in the political system.

Second, the ability of the Whig party to recruit in all sections of the Union ironically reflected the relative immaturity of American capitalism. Since northern conservatives were not yet confident of a stable relationship between worker and employer (the hallmark of mature capitalism), they sought a defensive alliance with southern conservatives, also eager to defend their major interests and their commercial future against the onslaught of Democratic egalitarianism. Hence Whiggery was not linked to specific relations of production but instead rested upon an alliance of manufacturers, market-oriented farmers and slaveholders together with their dependants. In his insistence that different systems of production were valid and worthwhile, the archetypal Whig was a merchant rather than a manufacturer. With its suspicions of *laissez-faire*, its rejection of disorderly individualism and its stress on the harmonizing and facilitating role of government, Whiggery reflected not the new liberalism of (wage labor) capitalism but the older paternalism associated with the dominance of merchant capital. The second party system thus pitted the defenders of a merchant-capital-based elitism against the advocates of a racially flawed, functionally proslavery, egalitarianism.[148]

---

148. Here I am seeking to extend and modify the conclusions presented in *"Agrarians" and "Aristocrats."*

6

Slavery, economics and party politics, 1836–1850

The alignment of 1850 (1)

On the seventh day of September, 1850, the city of Washington celebrated. A hundred-gun salute was fired, skyrockets were launched, and bands began to play "The Star-Spangled Banner," and "Yankee Doodle." Bonfires, processions, and serenades followed and word went round that it was the duty of every patriot to get drunk. The remarkable events were in response to the actions of Congress; for once Americans with a high degree of unanimity applauded the actions of their federal representatives.[1]

The occasion was, of course, the final passage of the measures that made up the Compromise of 1850. Observers realized that the nation had come close to disaster and the celebrations in Washington and elsewhere expressed the relief of millions. It seemed as if the explosive issues separating North from South had been finally resolved and the nation looked forward to a lasting sectional peace.

The settlement proved ill-fated. Within less than five years, tensions were greater than ever; within little more than a decade a still more profound crisis would engulf the nation, despite the renewed efforts of men eager once again to find a lasting settlement. The Compromise of 1850 proved little more than a truce or armistice. In yet another way the future would be unkind to the Compromise. Although it has been thoroughly studied by many historians, there are two questions that have not yet been satisfactorily answered. The first is the most obvious question of all: why had party loyalties been subordinated to sectional feelings. The comparison with 1840 could not be sharper. At that time party issues dwarfed sectional considerations. A decade later the position was reversed. These growing sectional antagonisms, of course, and the process by which they supplanted the issues of the second party system have

1. Allan Nevins, *Ordeal of the Union: Fruits of Manifest Destiny 1847–1852* (N.Y., 1947), pp. 343–344; Holman Hamilton, *Prologue to Conflict: The Crisis and Compromise of 1850* (N.Y., 1960), p. 160.

been studied by all those scholars who have investigated the origins of the Civil War. Nevertheless there is reason to doubt the conclusions which historians have presented.[2]

The second question, by contrast, has hardly been posed at all. Why did the alignment of 1850 take the form it did? At first glance the sectional division was as expected. Many southerners feared that too much was being surrendered to the North and voted against the Compromise measures; many northerners refused to support them on the grounds that they conceded too much to the South. Moderates within each section, however, managed to combine to pass each measure separately. Such is the nature of compromise settlements. But the problem for historians has been to explain the relationship between party and sectional loyalties in the alignment of 1850.

The crisis erupted at a time when the party battle between Democrat and Whig was still a feature of the political landscape. Each party was, as it had been for over a decade, quite strong both north and south of the Mason-Dixon line. Neither had been formed to fight over the slavery question and there were slaveholders within the ranks of each. Yet party loyalties were apparently still present in the voting on the Compromise of 1850. A complex and puzzling alignment had become visible. Support for the Compromise measures came principally from two groups: northern Democrats and southern Whigs. Opposition came from northern Whigs, on antislavery grounds, and from southern Democrats on what might loosely be termed proslavery grounds. Although it is tempting to seek the explanation in the specific events of that year, this temptation must be resisted.[3] The alignment was in no sense unique to that year. Indeed it was as old as, perhaps even older than, the second party system itself. Moreover it would persist even after the demise of one of the parties.[4] The year 1850 was merely the occasion when it was most visible. Though many historians have noticed this alignment, none has satisfactorily explained it.

There are several reasons for this failure. One is quite simply a consequence of the high degree of specialization within the ranks of American historians: in general those who have concerned themselves with the sectional controversy have not studied the party battles of the

---

2. I shall not consider the historiography of the Civil War until the sequel to the present volume.
3. This is the interpretation offered in Michael F. Holt, *The Political Crisis of the 1850s* (N.Y., 1978), pp. 88, 91. Though I disagree with his view, it is nevertheless important to acknowledge that he is almost the only historian to confront this question.
4. Former Whigs remained less militant on sectional questions long after their party had disappeared. See Thomas B. Alexander and Richard E. Beringer, *The Anatomy of the Confederate Congress: A Study of the Influences of Member Characteristics on Legislative Voting Behavior, 1861–1865* (Nashville, 1972), p. 17.

Jacksonian era and *vice versa*. Another is the refusal of some scholars to take party ideology seriously. But the third is the difficulty of reconciling two different approaches to the politics of the era. Let us examine this in more detail.

The first approach to the politics in this period might, if only for convenience, be termed a "party" interpretation. According to its adherents, politics until at least the late 1840s revolved around the same issues north and south of the Mason-Dixon line. These issues were both political and economic, just like those of the first party system in the 1790s and the early years of the nineteenth century. Slavery was at best a subordinate question, and each party was as a consequence able to command an impressive degree of support in both sections. Northerners and southerners alike, worshipped at what one scholar has aptly termed "the shrine of party."[5]

The second approach emphasizes instead the growing sectional division within the nation. Some scholars have argued that the South, for example, was absorbed with "the politics of slavery;" others have argued that the party battle, in the North as well as the South, was artificial in that it ignored the real sectional cleavages which were the most prolific source of political conflict and which in a comparatively short time would overwhelm the political system. If the first is a "party" interpretation, the second approach is a "sectional" one.[6]

Not surprisingly both sides in this debate can score some telling points. As we have already seen, the political parties did indeed subscribe to different and opposing ideologies or world views, and the antagonism that this difference generated was sufficient to unite northerners and southerners within the same parties. In short, northerners and southerners divided over some fundamental questions that did not directly relate to slavery. No more than the first party system, then, should the second be dismissed as artificial.

On the other hand those who point to sectional differences have been able to demonstrate that in the South, especially, the politics of slavery

---

5. Of great importance here are the works of Charles G. Sellers, Jr. See especially Sellers, "Who Were the Southern Whigs?" *American Historical Review*, LIX (1954), pp. 335–346 and also Sellers *The Market Revolution: Jacksonian America, 1815–1846* (N.Y., 1991). See also Joel H. Silbey, *The Shrine of Party: Congressional Voting Behavior, 1841–1852* (Pittsburgh, 1967); Arthur C. Cole, *The Whig Party in the South* (N.Y., 1914). In my earlier work – *"Agrarians" and "Aristocrats": Party Political Ideology in the United States, 1837–1846* (London, 1983) – I endorsed this interpretation. Here I am presenting a modified view.

6. William J. Cooper, *The South and the Politics of Slavery* (Baton Rouge, 1978); Avery O. Craven, *The Coming of the Civil War* (Chicago, 1957), *The Growth of Southern Nationalism* (Baton Rouge, 1953); Richard P. McCormick, *The Second American Party System* (Chapel Hill, 1966), p. 353.

were of vital importance. There each party tried to prove that the other, certainly in the North and perhaps even in the South itself, was unsound on this key issue. In the North too, the parties were frequently forced to confront slavery-related issues; in this sense the collapse of the second party system was merely the final failure of northern statesmen to keep these issues out of the political arena.

The problem is that each view appears to be negated or at least weakened by the evidence presented in support of the other. If slavery and sectional issues were indeed uppermost, then how do we account for the relatively persistent ideological stances which cut across sectional lines and united northern Whigs and northern Democrats with their colleagues south of the Mason-Dixon line? But if party issues were predominant, what was the role or function of debate and disagreement over slavery in these years? The impasse is apparent when we examine the voting pattern of 1850. Each of the rival schools can explain half of the alignment. Those who emphasize slavery can show that many southerners were ready to break up the Union at this time because of the slavery issue. But they cannot show why the party division was as it was. Conversely those who stress party can point to the persistence of partisan loyalties but can offer no reason why southern Democrats, for example, should be more militant than southern Whigs. After all if parties were founded on the great financial questions, why should they now clash on apparently unrelated issues concerning slavery? Common to both views is a crucial weakness: in neither is the relationship between slavery and the mainstream party questions elucidated.

These two questions are not unconnected. By understanding the nature of the alignment of 1850, we shall be better able to understand the process by which sectionalism first challenged, then undermined and finally destroyed the second party system. We shall then be able to consider a key question, one that is all too easily obscured by a concentration on political maneuvering: what was the role of class and class conflict in bringing sectional issues into the political mainstream. First, however, we need to examine the relative importance of, and the interaction between, party ideology and sectionalism in the 1830s and 1840s. The starting point, therefore, is the years of Jackson's presidency.

Toward the second party system, 1828–1836

I

The creation of the second party system was completed only in the early 1840s; until then the Whig party lagged considerably behind the Democracy both in the techniques of electioneering and in the development of a coherent program to place before the voters.[7] By the end of Jackson's second administration, however, Democratic principles had been firmly established. Although the party was not monolithic, it was as united as it would ever be. Its appeal would never be clearer. Yet in Jackson's years in the White House, issues that related to slavery, and on which there was no single party stance, were always present; they defied any easy resolution and they threatened to undermine the foundations of a party system before it had even been properly constructed.[8]

Prior to Jackson's departure from the White House, four episodes or themes were vital to the process of party development. First was the outcome of the election of 1824. Although Jackson's plurality gave him no legal or constitutional right to the White House, he and his supporters believed the voters had spoken in the most unequivocal terms. The process by which Jackson was set aside and Adams installed had a number of major effects. It provided, of course, the rallying cry of "corrupt bargain" that would prove so effective in 1828 and which would periodically return to haunt Henry Clay. More important, it sowed the seeds of Jackson's suspicion of Congress, seeds which would flower in his vetoes, and his attempts to appeal over the heads of elected representatives to the people themselves. Most important of all, it confirmed Jackson's majoritarianism (despite his failure to obtain a majority of the votes cast). Believing that the electorate had been cheated, he now began to assume a natural conflict between the people and the elites of the nation. In the words of Robert Remini, the "corrupt bargain" was "the single event that drove men – Jackson especially – to a more pronounced democratic position and ended forever the notion that representatives are somehow free agents to decide by themselves the public good." In 1824 the elites which aroused Jackson's wrath were political rather than economic. By 1836 they would be both.[9]

---

7. In this discussion I shall not consider the important franchise reforms at state level that preceded Jackson's election, nor the constitutional changes of the era – the direct election of presidential electors, the emergence of single-member districts, etc. This is not because I believe them unimportant. See McCormick, *Second American Party System*; Chilton Williamson, *American Suffrage from Property to Democracy,1760–1860* (Princeton, 1960); Fletcher M. Green, *Constitutional Development in the South Atlantic States, 1776–1860* (Chapel Hill, 1930).

8. Richard B. Latner, *The Presidency of Andrew Jackson* (Athens, Ga., 1979) covers the ground well. See also Robert V. Remini, *Andrew Jackson and the Course of American Freedom, 1822–1832* (N.Y., 1981), *Andrew Jackson and the Course of American Democracy, 1833–1845* (N.Y., 1984).

9. Remini, *The Legacy of Andrew Jackson: Essays on Democracy, Indian Removal and Slavery* (Baton Rouge, 1988), p.14. Remini has done a great service to historians by re-emphasizing the role of the election of 1824 and the "corrupt bargain." See also Michael J. Heale, *The Presidential Quest: Candidates and Images in American Political Culture, 1787–1852* (London, 1982), pp. 37–63.

The second event or set of events that played a key role in the creation of the party system concerned the American Indians. By the time Jackson came to office, the Indians in most parts of the country no longer presented a barrier to the expansion of white America. In the South and Southwest, however, they did – or so men like Jackson believed. The new president wished to secure large and valuable tracts of land currently held by Cherokees, Creeks, Choctaws, Chickasaws, and Seminoles in the states of Alabama, Mississippi, Georgia, North Carolina and Tennessee. These "Civilized Tribes" were not nomadic but had formed settled communities resembling in many respects those of white Americans. However, the pattern of land tenure differed sharply from that of white America: land was held in common rather than by individual owners and could thus not be commodified in what for Americans was the normal way. This together with basic racial prejudice disposed large numbers of southerners and southwesterners to desire the complete removal of the Indians.[10]

Events were most dramatic in Georgia, where the discovery of gold led to invasions of Cherokee territory and wholesale violence. Without federal aid the Indians were at the mercy of white aggression and cupidity. At this point Jackson suggested the "voluntary" removal of Indians in Georgia and elsewhere in the South beyond the Mississippi. The scheme was tantamount to forced relocation, since the pressures on those who chose to remain would soon become unendurable. During his administration, Jackson and his officials signed dozens of treaties with the Indians, obtaining in the process some 100 million acres of land.[11]

In its impact on the Indians themselves this dispossession and forced relocation constituted one of the greatest tragedies of the entire antebellum era, such was the suffering endured by its alleged beneficiaries. As far as the second party system was concerned, the effect was less dramatic but still significant. Indian removal was enormously popular in the South and it contributed to the great strength which Jackson enjoyed in most of the states concerned. When allied to his personal popularity (resting in part upon his earlier military victories against Indians as well as

10. Ronald N. Satz, *American Indian Policy in the Jacksonian Era* (Lincoln, Neb., 1975); Michael P. Rogin, *Fathers and Children: Andrew Jackson and the Subjugation of the American Indian* (N.Y., 1975); Michael D. Green, *The Politics of Indian Removal* (Lincoln, Nebr., 1982).

11. William G. McLoughlin, *Cherokee Renascence in the New Republic* (Princeton, N.J., 1986); Mary E. Young, "Indian Removal and Land Allotment: The Civilized Tribes and Jacksonian Justice," *American Historical Review*, LXIV (1959), pp. 31–45; Grant Foreman, *Indian Removal: The Emigration of the Five Civilized Tribes of Indians* (Norman, Okla., 1953). For a defense of Jackson's policy see Francis P. Prucha, "Andrew Jackson's Indian Policy: A Reassessment," *Journal of American History*, LXVI (1969), pp. 527–539 and Remini, *Legacy of Jackson*, pp. 45–82.

Englishmen), it made his presidency almost, but not quite, unchallengeable in the states most directly affected. While in the North some criticism
of the administration's policy was offered, for the Opposition it was a
poor issue electorally. On balance Indian removal was a tremendous vote
winner for the Democratic party in general and for Jackson in particular.
Moreover, it operated so as to reinforce a cardinal tenet of the
Democratic creed: the party would advocate "equal rights" – but not
for those whose skin was the wrong color.

The third major event of Jackson's presidential career concerned the
politics of slavery. In the early and mid-1830s the slavery question was
being agitated both by those demanding immediate abolition and by
those insisting that slavery was perpetual in the Union, guaranteed by
the constitution, and, as such, deserving of special protection. We have
already examined the motives of abolitionists and nullifiers alike,
together with the Jacksonian response to them. But the impact on party
formation was complex and needs to be carefully traced.[12]

Jackson's reply to the nullifiers was couched in the most acerbic language. Utterly unable to see any real threat to slavery, and concluding
that Calhoun was driven by the basest of motives, the President condemned nullification as treason. "The power to annul a law of the
United States, assumed by one State," he asserted in his Nullification
Proclamation, is "incompatible with the existence of the Union, contradicted expressly by the letter of the Constitution, unauthorized by its
spirit, inconsistent with every principle on which it was founded, and
destructive of the great object for which it was formed." Jackson went
still further. Insisting that the Union was perpetual, he refused to
acknowledge that states possessed the right of secession. Indeed secession,
like nullification, he implied, was treason. To remove any possible ambiguity about his intentions Jackson asked Congress for a "Force Bill"
allowing him to use troops, if necessary, to collect the federal revenue.[13]

Here the President ignored the counsel of many of his most trusted
supporters. Van Buren had advised against discussing the right of secession and even Democrats like Silas Wright and Thomas Hart Benton, the
Senate's archetypal Jacksonians, balked at the Proclamation and
the Force Bill, even as they voted for them.[14] In the North the effect on
the party's fortunes was not serious; indeed many erstwhile enemies of

12. William W. Freehling, *Prelude to Civil War: The Nullification Controversy in South
     Carolina, 1816–1836* (N.Y., 1965) is the standard work on nullification. The impact
     on party formation, however, is covered in greater detail – and with great skill – in
     Richard E. Ellis, *The Union at Risk: Jacksonian Democracy, States' Rights, and the
     Nullification Crisis* (N.Y., 1987).
13. James D. Richardson (ed.), *A Compilation of the Messages and Papers of the
     Presidents, 1789–1897* 10 vols (Washington, D.C., 1899), ii, pp. 643.
14. Ellis, *Union at Risk*, pp. 156, 163.

the President now found his conduct highly gratifying. But in the South the result was very different. Neither the Proclamation nor the Force Bill was actually in contradiction of states' rights, as Jackson understood them. What needs to be remembered is that for Jackson states' rights was in no sense a minoritarian creed; on the contrary it was a part of the broader commitment to limited government, itself intended to combat the influence of the predatory minority. In other words, Jackson expected a majority to support states' rights and states' rights to reinforce the rule of the majority. Calhoun, of course, as we have already seen, viewed the matter quite differently and made states' rights the cornerstone of a minoritarian political theory. But other southerners had rallied to the states' rights banner without having fully resolved these questions. Without necessarily endorsing Calhoun's "positive good" theory of slavery, all those who had doubts about majority power were highly alarmed at the possibility of federal power being turned against slavery and the South at some future time. It was also unclear whether Jackson's views were compatible with the venerable Virginia and Kentucky Resolutions, now viewed as key statements of the states' rights creed. Many original Jackson supporters had not, of course, shared all his views; in the South they had had to choose between Jackson and Adams and for many this was no choice at all. But the Proclamation and Force Bill helped define Jacksonian principles and thus had a major impact on party formation.[15]

These effects were particularly apparent in Virginia where the states' rights creed had of course originated. Thomas Ritchie, probably the most important Democrat in the state, was extremely unhappy with Jackson's conduct during the crisis, though he was also adamantly opposed to nullification. Governor John Floyd, together with US Senators John Tyler and Littleton Tazewell, were still more dissatisfied and wanted the state to repudiate Jackson's actions entirely. Only after a protracted struggle were they defeated. Finally the Virginia legislature compromised by rejecting nullification but also reaffirming the right of secession. It was all Jackson's supporters could do to keep the state neutral in these years.[16]

The effect was to embolden the President's critics. His previously unassailable position now became vulnerable. An identical process occurred in Georgia where the Indian policy had made Jackson even more popular. The Proclamation and Force Bill now allowed his critics to come out into the open. Throughout most of the Middle and Deep South, where

15. As Richard Latner points out, Jackson was by now becoming increasingly convinced that the tariff should be seen as an instance of monopolistic and unfair legislation – Richard B. Latner, "The Nullification Crisis and Republican Subversion," *Journal of Southern History* XLIII (1977), pp. 19–38.
16. Ellis, *Union at Risk*, pp. 123–140.

Jackson had run so very strongly in 1828 and 1832, the results were similar. When the Force Bill went to the Senate it won the support of only three senators from these eight states. Here was a clear indication of southern opinion in the early 1830s. While most southerners applauded Jackson's view of nullification, many were extremely reluctant to endorse his view of secession, and in some cases the majoritarianism upon which it rested.[17]

Though the nullification crisis was soon over, the next few years continued to be plagued by agitation of the slavery question. These were the years of the abolitionist pamphlet campaign as well as the petition controversy and the gag rule. The result was to introduce a new set of problems for northerners and southerners alike. For northerners the problem would be to seek to accommodate southerners who were or who might become party allies but without appearing to surrender northern rights of petition and free speech. For southerners (other than the Calhounites) the problem was to secure what they took to be their own right to defend themselves against abolitionism, but without alienating their own supporters or potential supporters in the North. A statesman who appeared to stretch too far to accommodate the other section risked being stigmatized in the North a "doughface" or in the South an "abolitionist." If these labels stuck they were in the former case damaging, in the latter fatal. Moreover the existence of militants in each section – Calhounites in the South, abolitionists in the North – intensified these pressures since a bipartisan agreement on sectional moderation would leave both parties vulnerable to extremist denunciation. On the other hand, extremism itself risked not only undermining the bi-sectional alliance within the party but also incurring in the North as well as the South the charge of disunion – an especially damaging accusation. Politicians thus had to tread extremely warily whenever these issues arose. In his presidential election campaigns, Jackson had not had to contend with these difficulties but in 1836 they would pose a severe test for all parties and for statesmen on both sides of the Mason-Dixon line.[18]

The fourth event or set of events to exercise a major influence on the growth of the party system was, of course, the war with the Bank of the United States.[19] For many years historians were reluctant to acknowledge

17. Ellis, *Union at Risk*, pp. 102–122.
18. A very good discussion of the gag rule controversy and the pressures under which politicians labored in these years is in William W. Freehling, *The Road to Disunion: Secessionists at Bay* (N.Y., 1990), pp. 289–352.
19. Bray Hammond, *Banks and Politics from the Revolution to the Civil War* (Princeton, N.J., 1957); Robert V. Remini, *Andrew Jackson and the Bank War* (N.Y., 1967); Jean A. Wilburn, *Biddle's Bank: The Crucial Years* (N.Y., 1967); Michael A. Lebowitz, "The Jacksonians: Paradox Lost?" in Barton J. Bernstein (ed.), *Towards*

the basic – and, it should be said, obvious – fact that Andrew Jackson disliked all banks on ideological grounds. Yet it remains true that these sentiments were not prominent in his election campaigns of the 1820s. By the time of the Annual Message of 1829, however, Jackson was expressing serious misgivings about the bank and a year later he proposed important modifications to any new charter it might receive. But when, in an act of the most egregious folly, Nicholas Biddle applied for a re-charter in 1832 ahead of time, all Jackson's suspicions were confirmed. He not only vetoed the bill but expressed what would become classic Democratic hostility to "the rich and powerful," whose influence on government, he declared, posed an ever-present threat to the well-being of the masses. In 1832 Jackson was triumphantly re-elected; the masses seemed to have endorsed his view of the Bank of the United States.[20]

Though the Bank veto produced some defections from the original Jacksonian ranks, it is probably true to say that its fiercest critics were already vehemently anti-Jacksonian. Southerners in particular who had always been overwhelmingly behind Jackson, had often questioned the wisdom of the BUS and the implications for states' rights of its federal charter (even though that charter had received Madison's blessing), so relatively few dissented once Jackson had launched his veto. But Jackson's next move, the removal of the government deposits from the Bank, was another matter. Convinced that the Bank involved itself regularly in politics, the President feared Biddle might seek by bribery or other forms of "lobbying" to persuade enough Congressmen to override his veto. Removal of the government's funds, however, would leave the Bank too weak to launch a counterattack. All Jackson's cabinet except Roger Taney opposed this measure and indeed Congress had recently affirmed that the deposits were safe in the Bank. But Jackson made the unprecedented claim that the recent election had given him a popular mandate to crush the Bank. Once again the President expressed his suspicion of the nation's elites, now both commercial and political. Once again he prevailed, though now against a chorus of opposition from all sections of the Union.

Jackson placed the government funds in a number of state banks, soon opprobriously known as "pets." His goal was to require these favored banks in return to limit their emissions of paper money. Here the ultimate

---

a New Past: Dissenting Essays in American History (N.Y., 1969), pp. 65–89; Frank O. Gatell, "Sober Second Thoughts on Van Buren, the Albany Regency and the Wall Street Conspiracy," *Journal of American History*, LIV (1966), pp. 19–40; John J. McFaul, *The Politics of Jacksonian Finance* (Ithaca, N.Y., 1972).

20. On the election of 1832 see Remini, "The Election of 1832" in Arthur M. Schlesinger, Jr., and Fred L. Israel (eds), *A History of American Presidential Elections, 1789–1968* 4 vols (N.Y., 1971), I, pp. 495–516.

goal of the President and those who shared his views could be glimpsed. He wanted to force smaller bills out of circulation entirely. Although paper money would continue to be used in larger commercial transactions, many, perhaps most, Americans would encounter throughout their lives only specie. With the same goal in mind Jackson in 1836 required that government agencies receive only gold and silver in payment for the public lands.

To those who took the trouble to analyze these, Jackson's last, actions as president, the principles of Jacksonian Democracy were now apparent. In his Farewell Message he went far beyond attacks upon a single commercial institution, however large. Excoriating the "Money Power" and the "Paper System," the President warned that they engendered speculation, corruption, and inequality. In good times, he noted, the ready availability of paper money would foster an "eager desire to amass wealth without labor . . . and inevitably lead to corruption." The "great moneyed corporations," he declared, had "a crowd of dependants about them who hope to grow rich without labor by their countenance and favor, and who are therefore always ready to execute their wishes." If successful, they would undermine the political process and subvert the Republic itself. The only remedy was perpetual vigilance. Jackson posited an unending struggle between "the agricultural, the mechanical, and the laboring classes" on the one hand, and the "Money Power" on the other. Here was the pure milk of Jacksonian Democracy.[21]

This was not the discourse that all Jackson's original supporters wished to hear. Many Democrats were utterly opposed to the hard money policy and some of them left the party in disgust. A second group of dissidents would depart later, during Van Buren's presidency, while a third would remain within the party, though frequently voting on key issues with the opposition. But by the time of Jackson's Farewell Message, Democratic principles were as clear as they would ever be.

The situation of the opposition was, however, quite different. After Henry Clay's defeat in 1832 the National Republicans realized that a broader political base was required. They had run well in the North and in the Border South, but not in the Middle or Deep South (apart from Louisiana). Indeed in some states Clay had not even been on the ticket. So a wider appeal was needed. In the North large numbers of Antimasons were easily persuaded to join the National Republicans in opposing Jackson's ticket in the 1832 election.[22] But it was in the South

21. Richardson (ed.), *Messages of Presidents*, III, pp. 301–306.
22. I shall not discuss antimasonry here. See Michael F. Holt, "The Anti-Masonic and Know-Nothing Parties," in Arthur M. Schlesinger, Jr., *A History of U.S Political Parties* 4 vols (N.Y., 1973), I, pp. 629–636; Kathleen Smith Kutolowski, "Antimasonry Reexamined," *Journal of American History*, LXXI (1984), pp. 269–293.

that recruits were most needed. Fortunately for the opposition, the events of nullification and particularly Jackson's Proclamation and Force Bill had, as we have seen, created considerable dissatisfaction with the Administration. Moreover by 1836, the Indian "problem" had been largely resolved (though for the Indians the problems were only just beginning) and with it disappeared a major source of Democratic votes in the South. Likewise there were southern Democrats dissatisfied with the Jacksonian bank policy. Finally, Van Buren, the Democratic candidate in 1836, whatever his political skills, clearly lacked Jackson's overwhelming personal popularity. Moreover he was a northerner with a record on sectional issues that left him not entirely invulnerable to southern assaults. Thus by the time Jackson was ready to step down from office, new opportunities beckoned his opponents throughout the nation, but especially in the South.

II

The recently christened Whig party, however, was not yet ready to exploit them. Or perhaps it would be more accurate to say that the Whigs were not clear which opportunities should be seized and which ignored. The Indian question having all but disappeared from the political agenda, there were three sets of issues that the new party could take up, each growing out of the principal episodes or events of the Jackson years. Each had advantages; each entailed risks.

One concerned Jackson's bank policy. It had one enormous advantage: the administration had offended northerners and southerners alike and both could join in condemning it. Though it was not the source of the nullifiers' opposition to Jackson, other southerners of a states' rights persuasion were highly alarmed at the hard money policy as well as the removal of deposits. Ultimately the Whig party would grasp these issues and offer the electorate a program unambiguously based on the promotion of banks (as well as tariffs) and geared towards commercial expansion. This was not the strategy of 1836, however.

At this time there was no agreement among anti-Jacksonians on an alternative to Jackson's bank policy. Some northern Whigs had concluded that the bank was an electoral liability and should therefore be discarded. Some southerners continued to have constitutional doubts about a national bank. Above all, Jackson's bank policy still seemed popular. The electorate had, to the astonishment of National Republican leaders in 1832, vindicated the president's action. The party thus needed to look elsewhere.

It found in Jackson's expansion of presidential power a much needed issue. This development rested, it will be recalled, on Jackson's suspicion of Congress acquired in 1824 and periodically strengthened thereafter.

All anti-Jacksonians could agree in condemning this arrogation of power. Not surprisingly, therefore, the Whigs stressed executive usurpation in the election of 1836 and declared war on "King Andrew" as well as his hand-picked successor. Still there were problems. In dwelling upon Jackson's alleged departure from established constitutional practices, the Whigs risked losing sight of the success the president had enjoyed. Hoping to re-establish the style of government that had preceded Jackson's election, many of his opponents were slow to grasp that the new populism of American politics was there to stay. Moreover, the strength of this issue would also prove to be its weakness. As the party would find out in 1841, success in uniting discordant elements behind a bland political program risked a party split and thus defeat in the very hour of victory.[23]

The final set of issues inviting the Whigs was sectional. In the aftermath of the nullification proclamation, and fortified by the recruitment into the opposition ranks of John C. Calhoun and his disciples, many southerners wanted to create a states' rights party that would eschew Jacksonian majoritarianism, as well as Jacksonian radicalism. This was the goal of men like John Tyler of Virginia and Hugh Lawson White of Tennessee (though Calhoun himself was going through a phase of disillusionment with all parties). Without any formal nominating process occurring, White's name was put forward by his "friends." Tyler became his running mate. These southerners now turned upon Van Buren and charged that he was untrue to the South. At this point abolitionist agitation played a major role. Could Van Buren, a northerner who had sided with his own section at the time of the Missouri Crisis, be trusted on the slavery question? The vice-president tried with some success to overcome southern doubts by assuring them of his decided opposition to abolition in the District of Columbia. He refused, however, to pronounce it unconstitutional. To this extent, at least, the Whigs had triumphed.[24]

The triumph was hollow. In the North anti-Democrats had not the slightest desire to hand the presidency to White[25] and except in the state of Massachusetts, where Daniel Webster was nominated, they rallied to the cause of William Henry Harrison, like Jackson a military hero, and, like Jackson before his first presidential campaign, not closely identified with any set of policies. Harrison inclined, however, to the nationalism of Henry Clay, rather than to the states' rights philosophy of White

23. Lynn L. Marshall, "The Strange Stillbirth of the Whig Party," *American Historical Review*, LXXVII (1967), pp. 445–468. As we shall see, however, Whig unity in 1840–1841 was greater than many historians have believed.
24. Cooper, *South and Politics of Slavery*, pp. 76–90; Freehling, *Road to Disunion*, pp. 299–301, 305–307, 339–340.
25. Except, perhaps, in Illinois, where White was nominated.

and Tyler. The problem, of course, was that Harrison's northern supporters were also critical of Democratic policy on the slavery issue, but for the very opposite reason. They denounced Van Buren as the quintessential "doughface." As we have seen, Whigs who took their cue from either Daniel Webster or Henry Clay were more critical of slavery than Democrats, not less so. This applied with even greater force to other northern Whigs like John Quincy Adams, the mention of whose name was enough to create paroxysms of rage in Hugh Lawson White and all his "friends." So the slavery question, although it offered the prospect of electoral gain in the South, was a fragile foundation for a party aspiring to national pre-eminence.

The Democrats charged that the Whig goal in 1836 was to place the election once again in the House of Representatives. Historians have frequently endorsed this claim. It is more likely, however, that the Whig party was simply unable at this early stage to unite on a single presidential candidate. Many of its supporters, we should recall, had objected to the existence of party conventions, seeing them as an illustration of the baneful effects of faction as well as a symptom of the nation's descent from a republic into a democracy. Among their number was White himself. The Whigs were simply too diverse in 1836, and too reluctant to endorse the populism which Jackson had introduced into American politics.[26]

Van Buren's supporters in the Middle and Deep South, meanwhile, seeking to neutralize the sectional appeal of the White candidacy, replied in kind. Though White himself could scarcely be depicted as an enemy of slavery, Democrats were able to claim that support for him would result in a hung election and would allow the House of Representatives to install Harrison, who was untrustworthy on these matters, or even Daniel Webster, who was still more so. In these states, therefore, each party claimed the other was unsafe on the slavery question.

The result of the election was not surprising. Van Buren won, but narrowly. The most interesting results were in the South. Across the entire region Jackson had won 66 percent of the popular vote in 1828 and 60 percent in 1832. But in 1836 Van Buren received only 50 percent. Moreover the changes in the Middle and Deep South, where the party system had hitherto been weak or non-existent, were still more striking. Van Buren won only 51 percent of the popular vote where Jackson had polled over 70 percent or even 80 percent. The South was now beginning to fall into line with the rest of the nation; soon all the southern states

26. Richard P. McCormick, "Was There a Whig Strategy in 1836?" *Journal of the Early Republic*, IV (1984), pp. 47–70.

except South Carolina would have a properly organized and functioning Whig party, closely allied to the national organization.[27]

The selection of White, however, and the deployment of sectional issues by his supporters revealed that this time had not yet arrived. In the mid-1830s southern Whigs from the Deep South were more militant on the slavery question than Democrats. This reflected the absence of the Calhounites from the Democratic ranks (Calhoun himself refused to support either party in the election of 1836) as well as attempts by some southern Whigs to establish an alternative states' rights party. But Calhoun before long would rejoin the Democratic party and the states' rights Whigs would realize that they could only combat the Democrats by cooperating with northerners. By 1840 the pattern would be reversed and southern Whigs would be more moderate than southern Democrats. And this alignment would outlast the second party system itself.[28]

III

By 1836 each of the four principal events of the Jackson years had left its indelible mark on the political system. Together they had defined "Jacksonian Democracy." They had brought the Whig party to an understanding of what it opposed, if not as yet an agreement on what it proposed. Democratic disdain for established political elites, and the accompanying commitment to majority rule had brought one political triumph after another. It would continue to be a potent vote winner after 1836, even though it exposed the party to neat Whig counterattacks against a Democratic "elective monarchy." Jackson's Indian policy, despite its catastrophic effects on the Indians themselves, also proved enormously popular and confirmed the absence of non-white Americans from the Democratic temple. Once achieved, however, the removal policy itself largely removed the Indian question from the political arena. The slavery question, by contrast, had only begun to make its mark upon American politics and upon the second party system. In the early and mid-1830s it had a temporary muddying effect upon the political parties. Eventually the states' rights Whigs would be faced with a choice of either abandoning the Whig party or modifying their states' rights principles. The process would not be completed until the Tyler presidency in the early 1840s forced the southern Whigs to decide where their priorities lay. On the other hand, nullification, the most

27. Freehling, *Road to Disunion*, pp. 339–340.
28. Thomas B. Alexander, *Sectional Stress and Party Strength, A Study of Roll-Call Voting Patterns in the United States House of Representatives, 1836–1860* (Nashville, 1967), p. 26.

dramatic event concerning the politics of slavery, had a second legacy. South Carolinians, having failed to establish a specific constitutional guarantee for slavery and southern rights in the form of a state veto, now had to use other weapons if they were to break up the party system. They would now seek to force other southerners to take more extreme positions on the slavery question regardless of the impact on northern allies. This process began in the mid-1830s but not until the drive for the annexation of Texas would it enjoy any real success. Finally, Democratic hostility to banks and contemporary commercial practices had had a dramatic effect in creating a party system. Although the Democrats would never achieve unity on this question, it would ironically help – and had by 1836 already begun to help – unite the Whigs. This would be the story of the late 1830s and early 1840s.

The cumulative effect of these four issues was enormous. The legacy of 1824 was the creation of a populist, majoritarian political force, critical of established political practices and prescribed forms. The assault on the BUS demonstrated its growing suspicion of prevailing commercial norms and capitalist institutions as sources of inequality, moral corruption and "aristocratic" tyranny. The cupidity displayed in the expropriation of the Indians illustrated its racial intolerance, its insistence upon the commodification of the land and its responsiveness to the needs of southern slave-dominated agriculture. Finally its attempt to chart a course that would marginalize both abolitionists and proslavery theorists alike showed that while it would operate functionally in defense of slaveholders and the "peculiar institution," their needs would receive no explicit or formal recognition. Such was Jacksonianism. It was securely in place by 1836.

Zenith of the party system, 1837–1843

I

Writing to the editor of a party newspaper, Thomas L. Hamer, an Ohio Democrat, complained about the policies pursued by the party in his state. He referred scathingly to "hard money articles . . . and . . . speeches . . . made up from the crude generalities of John Taylor, of Caroline county, Va., whose 'INQUIRY' after a profound sleep of nearly thirty years, has been raked up from the rubbish of a past generation and made the standard for Ohio Democracy."[29] Hamer's observations were accurate in that Taylor's theories had indeed become Democratic orthodoxy

29. Letter of Thomas L. Hamer to editor of Ohio *Eagle*, May 9, 1842 printed in Ohio *State Journal*, June 2, 1842.

in Ohio. Moreover, although Ohio was in the vanguard of the struggle against the banks, similar policies were in evidence in almost every state of the Union in the late 1830s and 1840s. Despite or rather because of the earlier destruction of the Bank of the United States, the bank war now entered its most critical phase. It exerted a profound influence not only upon the Democratic party itself, but also on the Whigs. Until the mid-1840s it pushed sectional antagonisms between North and South onto the political margin. It even had complex and contradictory effects upon the other principal legacy of Jackson's presidency: the debate over the nature of representative democracy in the United States.

The bank war reached a crescendo in these years essentially for one reason. No sooner had Van Buren taken the oath of office in March 1837 than news of a financial crisis broke. By May a Panic had set in. Probably acting independently, banks as far apart as Providence, Rhode Island, and Mobile, Alabama, suspended specie payments. The inflation of the years since 1834 now abruptly ceased. After taking advice from different quarters, the new President made a crucial decision. He would follow Jackson's lead (and indeed Jackson's advice from the Hermitage) and refuse to rescind the Specie Circular. Moreover, since some of the pet banks were themselves in trouble, it was difficult to justify continuing to place government funds in them. Van Buren thus decided to establish an Independent Treasury, an institution which would hold and disburse government funds but which would not act like a bank in other ways. In effect the president was, as his supporters claimed, "divorcing" the government from the banks.[30]

In his first message to Congress, Van Buren blamed the Panic on "excessive issues of bank paper" and "other facilities for the acquisition and enlargement of credit." In his second Annual Message he complained that bank expansions had "seduced industry from its regular and salutary occupations by the hope of abundance without labor, and deranged the social state by tempting all trades and professions into the vortex of speculation on remote contingencies." By this time, however, the banks had resumed specie payments and it was widely hoped and believed that normal times had returned. But in the following year an even more serious suspension of payments occurred, followed by a prolonged period of deflation and recession, if not outright economic slump, from which the nation did not recover until the mid-1840s. In 1839 in his third Annual

---

30. Peter Temin, *The Jacksonian Economy* (N.Y., 1969), pp. 113–114. On Jackson's role in bringing about the Panic compare Temin with Richard H. Timberlake, Jr., "The Specie Circular and Distribution of the Surplus," *Journal of Political Economy*, LXVIII (1960), pp. 109–117 and Marie E. Sushka, "The Antebellum Money Market and the Economic Impact of the Bank War," *Journal of Economic History*, XXXVI (1976), pp. 809–835.

Message Van Buren condemned the banks as institutions whose "result, if not their object, to gain for the few an ascendancy over the many." Little wonder that Andrew Jackson was gratified by the actions of his hand-picked successor.[31]

The effect, as one partisan observer later remarked, was to place the banks against the President even if the President had little power to act directly against the banks. Moreover the Washington *Globe*, the foremost Democratic newspaper in the nation, in an effort to rally the entire party behind the President, sounded warnings about the future which echoed Van Buren's arguments. Blair pointed repeatedly to the dangers posed to the Republic by "the moneyed power" and even, more simply, by the rich, who were "naturally disaffected to a system which recognizes no personal distinctions, no inequalities of birth or condition." After the Whig triumph of 1840 Democratic radicalism did not abate. If anything it grew still more intense. At the end of 1838 the *Globe* had merely called for the gradual removal of notes under $20 but five years later Blair was looking forward to the "extinction of [all] banking institutions, as their present charters expire," while Van Buren was publicly condemning all forms of paper money. Jackson himself in 1840 urged that "ere long" no paper money be printed of a lower denomination than $100, a recommendation whose effect would have meant most Americans living their entire lives without coming into any contact with a bank or even seeing a banknote.[32]

Although the Independent Treasury did not pass both Houses of Congress until 1840, it swiftly became the principal test of party orthodoxy. Some Democrats left the party in protest. Others, unhappy with the course Van Buren was taking but reluctant to sever all ties, accepted the Independent Treasury but hoped that its antibank implications could be checked. Until economic recovery came, however, these Democrats were an unhappy and incongruous minority within the party, able to restrain the anti-bank, hard money wing only by voting with the Whigs. Most party members believed with Van Buren that the task at federal level was to "divorce" the government from the banks and thus give the states a free hand to reform, curtail, or even destroy, the banks within their borders. As Thomas Hart Benton put it, the Missouri legislature could

---

31. Richardson (ed.), *Messages of Presidents*, III, pp. 325, 494, 554.
32. Jabez D. Hammond, *A Political History of the State of New York* 3 vols (N.Y., 1852), II, p. 502; Washington *Globe*, Jan. 30, 1838, March 19, 1840, Jan. 11, 1843; Van Buren to the Democratic State Convention of Indiana, in Washington *Globe*, Oct. 12, 1843; Jackson to Blair, Feb. 15, 1840 in John S. Bassett (ed.), *The Correspondence of Andrew Jackson* 7 vols (Washington, D.C., 1926–1935), VI, p. 50. See also Jackson to Moses Dawson, May 26, 1837, Dec. 9, 1839 in John J. Whalen (ed.), "The Jackson–Dawson Correspondence," *Historical and Philosophical Society of Ohio*, XVI (1958), pp. 3–30, esp. 8, 17.

"save the state by excluding all paper money under twenty dollars (I had much rather say under one hundred); congress can save the general government by establishing the independent treasury system."[33]

The result was that the bank war now went into the states. These years mark the high point of agrarian radicalism, not only in the Jacksonian era but in the entire history of the United States.[34] They also signaled the eclipse of sectional hostilities. Banking overshadowed the slavery question throughout the nation.[35] And the differences between North and South on this question were insignificant. Far more important were those between East and West. As it would prove to be again in the 1890s, it was in the West that agrarian radicalism would record its greatest triumph.

II

In no region was antibank sentiment more intense than in the Southwest.[36] Although here as elsewhere Democrats had shown little hostility to state banks before 1837, in the Gulf states especially they more than made up for it after the Panic had struck. In Mississippi the essence of Democratic radicalism was captured in a single question posed by the editor of the Vicksburg *Sentinel*. Why, he asked, "should a few rich men be allowed the privilege of drawing interest on three dollars for every one they own." In the same state radical hard money Democrat Governor Alexander G. McNutt led a campaign not merely to abolish banking throughout the state but to repudiate the debts of some of the banks to which the state government was pledged. Repudiation horrified Whig opinion throughout the nation since it seemed to challenge the most fundamental principles of commercial intercourse. Only in 1846 or 1847 did the banking question subside in Mississippi.[37] In Louisiana despite having operated more conservatively, the banks were not spared from

33. Benton quoted in James R. Sharp, *The Jacksonians versus the Banks: Politics in the States After the Panic of 1837* (N.Y., 1970), p. 13.
34. William G. Carleton, "Political Aspects of the Van Buren Era," *South Atlantic Quarterly*, L (1951), pp. 167–185.
35. This is conceded even by Cooper, the most extreme proponent of the primacy-of-slavery thesis – Cooper, *South and Politics of Slavery*, pp. 149–181.
36. My discussion of state politics in these years rests primarily on my own research. However, my debt to Sharp is, I assume, so evident as scarcely to need acknowledgement. Perhaps I should add that I consider his work to be a major achievement in Jacksonian historiography.
37. Vicksburg *Sentinel* quoted in Dunbar Rowland (ed.), *Mississippi: Comprising Sketches of Counties, Town, Events, Institutions, and Persons* . . . 3 vols (Atlanta, Ga., 1907), I, p. 200; *Whig Reveiw*, I (1845), p. 17; Jackson *Mississippian*, May 5, June 9, July 7, 1837, Feb. 23, Aug. 17, 1838, Jan. 29, 1841, Aug. 17, Dec. 6, 1843; Sharp, *Jacksonians versus Banks*, pp. 55–88.

Democratic attacks. Radical sentiment gradually intensified after the Panic until at the Constitutional Convention of 1846 the chartering of all banks was forbidden and old ones were allowed to continue only until their charters expired. (In the same year a constitutional amendment was passed in Arkansas to the same effect.)[38] By that time there was only a single bank in Alabama and the Democrats looked forward eagerly to its demise. In his 1845 Annual Message Governor Benjamin Fitzpatrick expressed the hope that the banking system was "forever ended" in Alabama while another Democrat later in the decade argued that God had forbidden banks. "Banking and paper money," he argued, "is [sic] in conflict with justice, equity, morality and religion;" there is "nothing evil that it does not aid."[39]

In the border states of the Southwest economic growth had been less frenetic in the early 1830s, the banks had been more conservatively managed and, as a result, were better able to survive. In Missouri, for example, the Bank of the State of Missouri managed to withstand the crisis of 1839 without suspending specie payments. This did not prevent it arousing fierce hostility from Thomas Hart ("Old Bullion") Benton, the embodiment of hard money radicalism throughout the nation, and his supporters. Since Missouri had chartered comparatively few banks, it was flooded by the paper money of banks from other states; Benton's supporters introduced bills at every session of the state legislature between 1838 and 1843 to outlaw such notes from the state. In Missouri as in virtually every state in the Union a bitter struggle broke out between soft and hard money Democrats. While over 80 percent of the Whigs favored a liberalization of banking operations in the late 1830s and early 1840s, only 43 percent of the Democrats concurred. A compromise was finally reached as a result of which the state bank would be the only one allowed.[40]

---

38. Robert J. Ker (reporter), *Proceedings and Debates of the Convention of Louisiana* (New Orleans, 1845), p. 848; New Orleans *Democrat*, Oct. 11, 1840; Gene Wells Boyet, "The Whigs of Arkansas, 1836–1846" (Ph.D. dissertation, Louisiana State University, 1972), p. 124; Melinda Meek, "The Life of Archibald Yell," *Arkansas Historical Quarterly*, XXVI (1967), p. 230.

39. *Journal of the House of Representatives of the State of Alabama at the Session begun and held in . . . Tuscaloosa . . . Dec., 1845* (Tuscaloosa, 1846), p. 11; J. Mills Thornton III, *Politics and Power in a Slave Society: Alabama, 1800–1860* (Baton Rouge, 1978), p. 48; Sharp, *Jacksonians versus Banks*, pp. 115–117; Carlton L. Jackson, "A History of the Whig Party in Alabama" (Ph.D. dissertation, University of Georgia, 1962), p. 84.

40. Clarence H. McClure, *Opposition in Missouri to Thomas Hart Benton* (Nashville, 1927), pp. 18–21; Dorothy B. Dorsey, "The Panic and Depression of 1837–43 in Missouri," *Missouri Historical Review*, XXX (1936), pp. 132–161; Paul W. Brewer, "The Rise of the Second Party System: Missouri, 1815–1845" (Ph.D. dissertation, Washington University, St. Louis, 1974), pp. 415–416.

In Missouri the Democratic party was utterly dominant in these years; Kentucky by contrast was a Whig stronghold where Democratic radicalism made no headway. Tennessee like Missouri had a state bank and even a Van Buren Democrat like James K. Polk advocated its enlargement – in preference to a proliferation of privately owned institutions. Here anti-bank sentiment was more muted than in the Deep South but the Democrats nevertheless sought to force resumption on those banks suspending specie payments, to prohibit all notes of low value and generally to tighten the regulations under which the banks operated.[41]

In some of the states of the Northwest, Democratic radicalism matched the achievements of the Southwest. In the 1830s the Democracy had shared a general enthusiasm for internal improvements and most of the states of the region had at least one official state bank, chartered in part to fund such projects. Even in the immediate aftermath of the Panic the party was slow to adopt hard money doctrines but by 1840 the recession was hitting hard.[42] By the mid-1840s Illinois had no authorized bank within her boundaries and her Democratic Governor had reached the conclusion that, while banks were perhaps of value in a commercial community, "we must be satisfied that we, in the state of Illinois, are better without them."[43] In Michigan over the course of the same decade, the number of banks declined from twenty-eight to one; in 1845 the Democratic state platform announced that the party was "entirely opposed to the further incorporation of banks of issue in the state."[44] The newly created state of Iowa was meanwhile preparing to enter the Union with a constitution forbidding banks entirely, on the grounds, as one Democrat put it, that they were "a set of swindling machines." More vividly, another Iowan referred to banking as a "mad untameable beast;" it was "unchainable" and "the best policy" was "to cut its head off." Similarly in the state of Wisconsin, also seeking admission into the Union

41. Charles G. Sellers, Jr., *James K. Polk, Jacksonian* (Princeton, 1957), pp. 387–394; Sharp, *Jacksonians versus Banks*, pp. 197–200.
42. The Northwest's encounter with banking is covered very efficiently in William G. Shade, *Banks or No Banks: The Money Issue in Western Politics, 1832–1865* (Detroit, 1972).
43. Compare the attitude of the *Illinois State Register*, Aug. 25, 1837 with the same newspaper Oct. 16, 1846; Don E. Fehrenbacher, *Chicago Giant, A Biography of "Long John Wentworth"* (Madison, Wis., 1957), pp. 27–28, 34–35, 73; Rodney O. Davis, "Illinois Legislators and Jacksonian Democracy, 1834–1841" (Ph.D. dissertation, University of Iowa, 1966), pp. 144–191 esp. 147–150, 164–170, 177; Delva P. Brown, "The Economic Views of Illinois Democrats, 1836–1861" (Ph.D. dissertation, Boston University, 1970), pp. 63–70; Shade, *Banks or No Banks*, pp. 75–79, 101, 135–138.
44. Marshall *Democratic Expounder*, Oct. 30, 1846; Niles *Loco Foco*, Aug. 21, 1840; George N. Fuller (ed.), *Messages of the Governors of Michigan* 4 vols (Lansing, 1925–1927), I, p. 468; Floyd B. Streeter, *Political Parties in Michigan, 1837–1860* (Lansing, Michigan, 1918), p. 19; Shade, *Banks or No Banks*, p. 100.

at this time, antibank sentiment was rife. The *Milwaukee Courier* in 1846 claimed that one could "trace the artificial inequality of wealth, much pauperism and crime, the low state of public morals, and many of the other evils of society directly to this [paper money] system." Its "natural consequence," the paper continued, illuminating the central concerns of the hard money Democrats throughout the nation, was to "break up that social equality which is the legitimate foundation of our institutions, and the destruction of which would render our boasted freedom a mere phantom."[45]

In Indiana (as in Kentucky, though to a lesser extent) radical Democrats were frustrated by Whig strength within the state. At the high tide of antibank sentiment, half of Indiana's Democrats opposed all banks. In Ohio the parties were very evenly matched. But in no state of the Union were the principles of radical Democracy more enthusiastically trumpeted. In the United States Senate, William Allen was probably the most radical of all Democrats; within the state, newspapers like the *Cincinnati Advertiser* and the *Cincinnati Enquirer* launched savage attacks on the banking system. But soft money Democrats were also powerful in Ohio and so the radicals had considerable difficulty in securing their policies. The struggle with the banks persisted throughout the 1840s and reached a climax only in 1850–1851 when at a constitutional convention a large majority of Democrats voted to eliminate banks entirely. But a small group of conservatives defected, allied with the Whigs, and so frustrated radical hopes once more.[46]

45. Benjamin F. Shambaugh (ed.), *Fragments of the Debates of the Iowa Constitutional Conventions of 1844 and 1846 along with Press Comment and Other Materials* (Iowa City, 1900), pp. 70, 102; Milwaukee *Courier*, Nov. 18, 1846 in Milo M. Quaife (ed.), "The Struggle over Ratification, 1846–1847," *Publications of the State Historical Society of Wisconsin, Collections*, XXVIII (Madison, 1920), pp. 200–201. See also *Iowa Capital Reporter*, May 6, 1846 in Shambaugh (ed.), *Fragment*, pp. 336–337. Louis Pelzer, "The History and Principles of the Democratic Party of the Territory of Iowa," *Iowa Journal of History and Politics*, VI (1908), pp. 2–54, esp. 50–51. For good Whig defenses of banks see the letter of William Penn Clarke in Iowa *Standard*, July 20, 1846 in *ibid.*, pp. 347–365; Madison *Express*, Oct. 27, 1846 in Quaife (ed.), "Struggle over Ratification," p. 161; Milo M. Quaife (ed.), "The Convention of 1846," *Publications of the State Historical Society of Wisconsin, Collections*, XXVII (Madison, 1919), p. 92.
46. Shade, *Banks or No Banks*, pp. 139–140, 71–75, 119; Sharp, *Jacksonians versus Banks*, pp. 123–159; Cincinnati *Advertiser*, August 5, 9, 1837, Jan. 23, 1839; Cincinnati *Enquirer*, July 5, Nov. 26, 1845. For Whig views see Richmond (Ind.) *Palladium*, Nov. 28, 1840, May 29, 1844, Fort Wayne (Ind.) *Sentinel*, Feb. 29, 1840. Compare Ohio *State Journal*, May 24, 1839 (where the editor denies that the Whigs are a bank party) with the same newspaper April 8, 1843 (where the editor concedes that the party's task is indeed to defend the banks). An extremely valuable survey of Ohio politics in the 1840s is provided in Edgar A. Holt, "Party Politics in Ohio, 1840–1850," *Ohio State Archaeological and Historical Quarterly*, XXXVII (1928), pp. 439–591, XXXVIII (1929), pp. 47–182, 260–402.

In the East, Democratic hostility to banks was as visible as in the West (although it took a different form) and the divisions within the Democratic party were equally prominent. In the East too, conservative Democrats frequently voted with the Whigs in order to frustrate Democratic radicalism. But the experience of East and West was in other respects markedly different. In general the more mature economy of the eastern states (whether North or South) meant that the boom and bust cycle of the 1830s and 1840s was less marked. The banks were more stable, they had more – and more effective – defenders. Moreover, in the East most radical Democrats aimed at the reform, not the destruction, of banks. In some states they were successful but in none was banking eliminated entirely.[47]

Many of the states of the Northeast were bastions of Whig strength. Vermont and Massachusetts were two of the strongest Whig states in the Union. Within the Massachusetts Democracy a bitter struggle broke out between the supporters of David Henshaw, a conservative who was to receive a post in John Tyler's cabinet, and those who backed Marcus Morton. Although Morton was elected Governor on two occasions, he was faced with a hostile state legislature which blocked the radical program entirely. In Vermont the Whigs publicly defended the state's banks and though the Democrats disagreed they were powerless. In Rhode Island the Whigs were also strong; this together with the protracted fight for suffrage reform in the state diminished the importance of the banking question.[48]

The case of New Hampshire, was entirely different. The Democrats held power continuously but a bitter feud broke out between conservatives and radicals culminating in the overthrow of Isaac Hill, an original Jackson supporter and his replacement at the head of the party by Henry Hubbard, John Steele and Edmund Burke. Although attempts were made to curtail the privileges of the banks, more attention was given to the controversy surrounding the state's railroads. But behind the railroad issue lay the same issues that produced the struggle in other states over banking. The railroads were symbols of commercial development and

---

47. The opposite view is put forward in Arthur M. Schlesinger, *The Age of Jackson* (Boston, 1945), pp. 142, 263. Schlesinger erred because historians then too often neglected state politics and ignored the bank war in the states.

48. Arthur B. Darling, *Political Changes in Massachusetts* (reprint New Haven, Conn., 1968), pp. 174–181, 197, 216, 224, 284 and *passim*; Robert D. Bulkley, Jr., "Robert Rantoul, Jr., 1805–1852: Politics and Reform in Ante-Bellum Massachusetts" (Ph.D. dissertation, Princeton, 1971), pp. 179–182; Walter H. Crockett, *Vermont, The Green Mountain State* 4 vols (N.Y., 1921), III, pp. 304–305, 314; *Vermont Statesman*, Aug. 30, 1837, Jan. 10, 1838, Sept. 11, 1839; Danville, *North Star*, May 22, 1837; Edward Barber, "Oration at Montpelier, July 4 1839" in *North Star*, Aug. 3, 1839.

were defended as such by both Whigs and conservative Democrats. The radicals, however, viewed their privileges as an affront to true Democratic principles. Predicting an attack from the railroad owners on the recently established principle of unlimited liability, one Democratic Governor observed that "individual, as well as associated wealth, rarely, if ever, suffers an opportunity to pass without making strenuous exertions to retain, if not to gain, privileges denied to the mass of the community." These sentiments were identical to those which elsewhere fueled the bank war.[49]

In Maine and Connecticut events were similar to those in other states of the Northeast. Governor John Fairfield, a dedicated Van Burenite, conceded that Maine's banking system was "probably as free from imperfections as that prevailing in any State of the Union." Still he called for stricter regulations, limitations on small bills and higher specie requirements.[50] This was the typical radical program in the East. Yet in some parts of the Northeast, in particular the urban regions, there was a significant additional impetus behind the bank war provided by radicals who were, or had previously been, too extreme in their views to support the Democratic party at all. The Workingmen's movements of the late 1820s and early 1830s had expressed a decided hostility to banks and the Locofocos in New York city had separated from Tammany Hall regulars as a result of disagreements over banks, paper money and corporate charters. In the late 1830s and early 1840s these groups supported the Democratic party with greater enthusiasm than at any previous time. Undoubtedly they wished to push the party further in a radical direction but their presence alarmed conservatives within both parties and raised the possibility that the radical Democrats might embrace still more of the Workingmen's program.[51]

Such fears were rife in New York not merely among the Whigs but also among conservative Democrats. When the banks suspended specie

49. *Journal of the Honorable Senate of the State of New Hampshire, Session beginning June 4, 1845* (Concord, 1845), p. 19; Donald B. Cole, *Jacksonian Democracy in New Hampshire* (Cambridge, Mass., 1970), pp. 187, 188–192, 199–214; New Hampshire *Patriot*, Aug. 26, 1841, March 24, June 9, 1842, Feb. 29, 1844; *Hill's New Hampshire Patriot*, Feb. 2, 9, May 13, 1843, Feb. 8, 1844.

50. Message of Governor John Fairfield to the Legislature of Maine in Portland *Advertiser*, Jan. 7, 1842. Brownson's program of 1840 stoked conservative fears – see, e.g., Kennebec *Journal*, July 28, 1840. For Whig attitudes to the banks see *Address of Governor Kent to Both Branches of the Legislature of the State of Maine, January, 1838* (Augusta, 1838), pp. 7–9; *Address of Governor Kent to Both Branches of the Legislature of the State of Maine, January, 1841* (Augusta, 1841), pp. 4, 22–23; Hartford *Courant*, Oct. 14, 1837, Jan. 7, 1843.

51. This of course was precisely Schlesinger's claim – *Age of Jackson*, pp. 132–143, 209. By far the best work on New York's workingmen's movement is Sean Wilenz, *Chants Democratic: New York City and the Rise of the American Working Class, 1788–1850* (N.Y., 1984), pp. 240–241.

payments in 1837 the Democratic controlled legislature voted to legalize the suspension and waive all penalties. Some radicals within the party condemned this action unreservedly and even called for an exclusively hard money currency to be established in the state. The Democratic party was already split into radical and conservative wings, but now the division deepened and lifelong friendships were ended. Van Buren's closest allies in the party, the radicals (or Barnburners, as they were known) denounced the conservatives, whose most prominent spokesman was Governor William Marcy. "The cry is up against the banks," Marcy lamented, "and they must be surrendered to the hideous monster of Locofocoism." The sentiments of the radicals, by contrast, were voiced by John A. Dix, a lifelong Van Burenite, who denounced "all monsters in a monied shape, whether procreated by state or federal authority." When the party lost control of the state in 1837 each wing held the other responsible. The following year the Whig majority passed a free banking act which radical Democrats criticized on the grounds that it provided insufficient protection for noteholders and allowed the banks to operate with inadequate specie reserves. In New York the years of Whig and conservative Democrat control witnessed an increase of credit facilities in the state, but the process was halted when the radicals were in control. Simultaneously a struggle took place over the state's canals. As in New Hampshire with the railroad controversy, radical Democrats attached stringent conditions to the building program and the contest once again pitted radicals against an alliance of Hunkers and Whigs.[52]

The Whigs meanwhile were acting in New York state, as they were acting throughout the Union, as the defenders of the credit system. Despite the real divisions within the party on some questions, a real unity existed here. Although they did not undertake to justify the actions of every single bank or banker in the nation, they nevertheless made it clear that they championed the banking system itself. As the New York *Courier and Enquirer* put it in 1842, the United States offered "triumphant proof of the beneficial effects of credit."[53]

52. Ernest P. Muller, "Preston King: A Political Biography" (Ph.D. dissertation, Columbia, 1957), p. 158; Marcy to Albert Gallup, Sept. 23, 1837 quoted in Patricia M. McGee, "Issues and Factions: New York State Politics from the Panic of 1837 to the Election of 1848" (Ph.D. dissertation, St. John's University, 1969), p. 33; Dix to Silas Wright, Feb. 11, 1834 quoted in Sister Theresa Fournier, "The Political Career of Azariah Cutting Flagg, 1823–1847" (Ph.D. dissertation, Middle Tennessee State University, 1975), p. 101; McGee, "Issues and Factions," pp. 75–99; John D. Morris, "The New York State Whigs, 1834–1842, A Study of Political Organization" (Ph.D. dissertation, University of Rochester, 1970), p. 189. See also Wright to Flagg, Aug. 1, 1833 in Fournier, "Career of Flagg," p. 100.
53. New York *Evening Star*, Nov. 5, 1838; Whig "Address to the People" in New York *Courier and Enquirer*, Oct. 2, 1838.

Events in Pennsylvania were complicated by the presence of Biddle's bank, given a state charter after its mauling at the hands of Andrew Jackson. Radical Democrats were not in a position of great strength in the state but they had in Charles Jared Ingersoll the author of one of the most remarkable documents of the Jacksonian era. At the state's constitutional convention called in 1837 Ingersoll, a determined advocate of an entirely specie currency, insisted that "there is no other standard" for money. The attempt to substitute paper money he likened to an attempt to substitute "ardent spirits for solid food, as the substance of life." "It intoxicates and ruins," he warned. Dismissing all corporations as "unrepublican and radically wrong," he stunned his fellow delegates when he claimed that property was more unequally divided in Pennsylvania than in France. The laws establishing corporations, since they assumed inequality, were in reality "no more laws than the prescripts of a Roman Empire." Hence, he concluded, all charters were repealable. Ingersoll's views were not accepted even by a majority of his fellow Democrats and his report on banking caused a furore. But he represented an important strand of opinion within the state. Nevertheless, Senator James Buchanan, a moderate on the bank question, together with the even more conservative Governor David R. Porter, was able to ensure that the dissident factions within the Democracy did not split irrevocably. The attempts to subject the state's banks to more stringent control met with only limited success.[54]

The voting alignments in New Jersey have been subjected to close analysis. In the late 1830s a large majority of Democrats voted to penalize the banks for suspending specie payments, an even larger majority of Whigs opposed the move. In 1841 the question of full liability for bankers saw over 90 percent of Democrats voting against a completely united Whig party. In 1844 at the state constitutional convention Democrats called for stricter limits on bank charters and demanded the right to repeal existing charters. A party vote, however, defeated these proposals. The Whigs were strong enough in New Jersey to frustrate radical demands. In Delaware the Whigs were stronger still and the Democrats were unable to make any headway. Moreover even after the recession the state was not even in debt; not a single bank collapsed.[55] In Maryland the

54. *Proceedings of the Convention of Pennsylvania to Propose Amendments to the Constitution, 1837* 14 vols (Harrisburg, 1837–1839), I, pp. 358–359, 366–367. *Spirit of the Times and Daily Keystone*, Aug. 14, Oct. 9, 1847; Sharp, *Jacksonians versus Banks*, pp. 285–296. Henry Mueller, *The Whig Party in Pennsylvania* (N.Y., 1922), p. 38. On the splits within the Pennsylvania Democracy see Charles M. Snyder, *The Jacksonian Heritage, Pennsylvanian Politics, 1833–1848* (Harrisburg, 1958), pp. 50–67 and *passim*.
55. Peter D. Levine, "Party-in-the-Legislature: New Jersey, 1829–1844" (Ph.D. dissertation, Rutgers, 1971), pp. 194, 203–213; John Bebout *et al.* (eds), *Proceedings of the*

parties were far more competitive. Radical Democratic sentiment was exemplified by the *Democrat and Carroll County Republican* in 1840 when it dismissed the existing banking system as "fraudulent," operating to allow "a few overgrown speculators" to "faten [sic] on the necessities of the public." On the other hand John P. Kennedy for the Whigs asserted that the banks "have done much good and may do more." Indeed, he wrote at the end of 1836, the credit system was "the mainspring of that beautiful prosperity which adorns our land." Despite electing an anti-bank radical Governor in the person of William Grayson, the Democrats were able to do little more than force the banks to resume specie payments. Other measures foundered on the combined opposition of Whigs and conservative Democrats.[56]

In the Southeast the bank war took a form similar to that found in the Northeast. Once again the banks had acted more responsibly than in the West and were better able to withstand the shocks of the late 1830s and early 1840s. In Virginia, for example, not a single bank went bankrupt at this time, while in South Carolina no bank failed between 1783 and the Civil War. Nevertheless hard money Democrats were strong in all of these states except perhaps South Carolina. Thus Peter V. Daniel of Virginia held that "the utter extinction of all Banks throughout the world" would be "the greatest possible good which could be done to mankind" and his wing of the party was dominant in the post-Panic years. Yet in Virginia federal questions were of enormous importance and the question of the Independent Treasury bulked large. Indeed the most eminent Democrat defector in these years, William Rives, was a Virginian who hoped to carry much of the state with him. Although these hopes were not realized, Democratic governors were sympathetic to his views. Moreover, Thomas Ritchie, veteran editor and a key figure in the organization of the Democratic party in the state and the nation, was slow to accept the Independent Treasury. The more committed hard money Democrats campaigned for full liability for bankers, the curtailment of small notes, and the right to repeal bank charters. The suspensions of 1839 and 1841 strengthened their position but, as in so many other states, they were defeated by a combination of conservative Democrats and Whigs. By the end of 1842 the bank war was effectively over in Virginia.[57]

New Jersey State Constitutional Convention of 1844 (Trenton, N.J., 1942), p. 562; Sharp, *Jacksonians versus Banks*, pp. 316, 276, 283; John Thomas Scharf, *A History of Delaware, 1609–1888* 2 vols (Philadelphia, 1888), I, p. 320.

56. *Democrat and Carroll County Republican*, Feb. 20, 1840; Henry T. Tuckerman (ed.), *The Collective Works of John P. Kennedy* 10 vols (N.Y., 1871–1872), IV, p. 182; Sharp, *Jacksonians versus Banks*, pp. 280–282.

57. Sharp, *Jacksonians versus Banks*, pp. 215–246, esp. 224, 277. On the conservatives in Virginia see Raymond C. Dingledine, Jr., "The Political Career of William Cabell

In the Carolinas the struggle was also muted. But as ever the differences between North and South Carolina were striking. In South Carolina there was some criticism of the State bank, and some of the state's Governors expressed standard Democratic criticisms of banking in general. But the highly oligarchic political system in the state, which allowed Calhoun extraordinary influence and power, meant that it was unresponsive to any popular antagonism towards the banks. Calhoun himself was eager to see the state united in order the better to resist the federal government and while he was a keen supporter of the Independent Treasury he had not the slightest desire to embark upon a crusade against the banks in South Carolina. The Democrats, of course, controlled the state.[58] In North Carolina, by contrast, the Whigs were dominant. Here the political alignment was closer to the national norm, especially after the state's Whigs fell into line behind Henry Clay. In 1838 Whig Governor Edward D. Dudley asserted that "an increase in banking capital in our own State is certainly necessary to meet the wants of industry." In the sharpest possible contrast Democratic leader Bedford Brown, a United States Senator, urged the merits of an exclusively specie currency. Although the Democrats were able to mount a challenge to the Whigs, a combination of Whigs and conservatives prevented them from advancing the cause of hard money.[59]

In Georgia, the state where conditions most resembled South Carolina, the second party system was slow to develop. Nevertheless in 1841 Governor Charles McDonald urged a return to hard money and demanded stiff penalties against banks that had suspended specie payments. The Democrats (or rather, those who would later become Democrats) had been for many years closely identified with the Central Bank of Georgia and some of them were disposed to defend it against the

Rives" (Ph.D. dissertation, University of Virginia, 1947), *passim*; Charles H. Ambler, *Thomas Ritchie, A Study in Virginia Politics* (Richmond, Va., 1913), *passim*.

58. Alfred G. Smith, Jr., *Economic Readjustment of an Old Cotton State: South Carolina, 1820–1860* (Columbia, S.C., 1958), pp. 202–205, 217; Sharp, *Jacksonians versus Banks*, pp. 277–279; *Journal of the Proceedings of the Senate and House of Representatives of the General Assembly of South Carolina at its Regular Session of 1839* (Columbia, S.C., 1839), p. 9; *Reports and Resolutions of the General Assembly of South Carolina, At its Regular Session of 1840* (Columbia, 1841), pp. 81–91.

59. *Journals of the Senate and House of Commons of the General Assembly of the State of North Carolina, at its Session in 1838–1839* (Raleigh, 1839), p. 281 (see also p. 277); "Message of the Governor of North Carolina to the General Assembly of the State . . . Session of 1840," in *North Carolina Public Documents, 1838–1840* (n.p., n.d.), pp. 7–11; Clarence C. Norton, "The Democratic Party in Ante-Bellum North Carolina," *The James Sprunt Historical Publications*, XXI (Chapel Hill, 1930), p. 56; Harry L. Watson, *Jacksonian Politics and Community Conflict: The Emergence of the Second American Party System in Cumberland County, North Carolina* (Baton Rouge, 1981), pp. 260–266 – an outstanding study.

claims of the privately owned banks in the state. Yet in 1836 the *Federal Union* criticized the Central Bank on the grounds that it "has a direct tendency to make the rich man richer and the poor man poorer." Eight years later, Democratic Congressman Mark Cooper, in an Address to his Constituents, denounced paper money as "an evil, an unnecessary evil, demoralizing to the people, and destructive of free government." On the other hand the Whigs, or those who would later become Whigs, defended the banks. "The banking capital of Georgia," the Milledgeville *Southern Recorder* observed in 1838, "is too small."[60]

In almost all the states of the Union[61] politics in these years was dominated by the bank question. Where the Whigs were in control, the Democrats made little progress in reforming the banks or in advancing the cause of hard money. Similarly where the banks had been prudently managed, and the state's economy had not experienced sharp fluctuations, Democrats aimed at reform, rather than destruction. In almost all the states they had to combat an alliance of Whigs, who with extraordinary unanimity defended the banks, and soft money dissidents from within their own ranks. Only in the West did the goal of an exclusively specie currency prove attainable and only in some of the western states did the Democrats manage to outlaw banking entirely. Nevertheless in almost all the states of the Union the struggle over the banks infused a new radicalism into American politics. The hard money Democrats, the heirs of Andrew Jackson, brought the Jacksonian era to its culmination, even though their hero was no longer in the White House.

III

In the midst of the struggle over banking came one of the most famous presidential campaigns in American history. The election of 1840 has acquired a unique reputation. It has been viewed as illustrative of the unprincipled nature of the Whig party which, it is alleged, fought an issueless campaign around the bland symbol of the "log cabin." It has also been seen as demonstrating the pragmatism of American politics, the

---

60. Donald A. Debats, "Elites and Masses: Political Structure, Communications and Behavior in Ante-Bellum Georgia" (Ph.D. dissertation, University of Wisconsin, 1974), p. 293; *Federal Union*, Aug. 30, 1836 in *ibid.*, p. 305; *Federal Union*, April 2, 1844; Milledgeville *Southern Recorder*, Nov. 13, 1838 – see also Oct. 2, 1838; Message of George R. Gilmer in *ibid.*, Nov. 6, 1838; Thomas P. Govan, "Banking and the Credit System in Georgia, 1810–1860," *Journal of Southern History*, IV (1938), pp. 164–184, esp. 165.

61. On the bank war in Florida in these years see Arthur W. Thompson, *Jacksonian Democracy on the Florida Frontier* (Gainesville, Fla., 1961), pp. 23–24, 15, 30–31; Herbert J. Doherty, Jr., *The Whigs of Florida*, pp. 9–10; Florida Tallahassee *Sentinel*, Oct. 22, 1841.

absence of real ideological differences between the political parties, the agreement on the need to use hullabaloo to court a mass electorate, and the final acceptance of democracy (for adult white males) by both major parties. Only recently has this interpretation been challenged.[62]

There is just enough truth in the traditional view to explain its widespread acceptance. The Whigs were not as united on policy as the Democrats, nor as united as they would be within the next two or three years. They did indeed take their case to the people, dwelling on the virtues of "hard cider", to be consumed, if possible, in, or at least in celebration of, "log cabins." Some Whigs now abandoned, or at least set aside, their reservations about the techniques of mass persuasion pioneered by the Jacksonians and to that extent the election did indeed herald the arrival of a consensus in American politics on the need both for political parties and for mass electioneering. But the election of 1840 was more complex than this. As we shall see, the Whigs were far more united than this model would suggest; moreover, Whig doubts about democracy were by no means absent after 1840. In fact the election of 1840 came at a moment when the differences between the major parties were probably starker than they would be for another century.[63]

The decision to adopt Harrison as their candidate, however, owed something to the divisions within Whig ranks. Those who argue that the Whigs were united on nothing except the desire to oust the Democrats from office can find no better evidence than a private letter written by future president Millard Fillmore in February 1839. Fillmore had concluded that his favorite for the party nomination, Daniel Webster, was unelectable (or "unavailable," as the contemporary euphemism had it) and he commented on the heterogeneity of the Whig coalition:

> It must be recollected that we have got to cement the fragments of many parties and it is therefore very important that we get a substance to which all can adhere, or at least that presents as few repellent qualities as possible. Into what crucible can we throw this heterogeneous mass of old national republicans, and revolting Jackson men; Masons and anti-Masons, Abolitionists; pro-Slavery

62. Whig heterogeneity is exaggerated in Robert G. Gunderson, *The Log Cabin Campaign* (Lexington, Ky., 1957) pp. 11, 36–40; Edward Pessen, *Jacksonian America: Society, Personality, and Politics* (rev. ed. Homewood, Ill., 1978), pp. 168–169, 190–191. A corrective is supplied in Sydney Nathans, *Daniel Webster and Jacksonian Democracy* (Baltimore, 1973), p. 147; Richard Carwardine, "Evangelicals, Whigs, and the Election of William Henry Harrison," *Journal of American Studies*, xvii (1983), pp. 47–75; Watson, *Liberty and Power*, pp. 220–222.
63. Alexander, *Sectional Stress and Party Strength*, p. 38; Herbert Ershkowitz and Willam G. Shade, "Consensus or Conflict: Political Behavior in the State Legislatures during the Jacksonian Era," *Journal of American History*, lviii (1971), pp. 591–621.

men; Bank men and anti-Bank men with all the lesser fragments that
have been, from time to time, thrown off from the great political
wheel in its violent revolutions, so as to melt them down into one
mass of pure Whigs of undoubted good mettle?[64]

Undoubtedly the choice of Harrison as standard bearer in 1840 reflected
the widespread Whig belief that both Clay and Webster were too closely
identified with the policies of the old National Republicans to be acceptable to all shades of opinion within the party.

But to understand the Whig victory of 1840 we must return to the
defeat of 1836. This had driven home to many Whigs the fact that the
party of Andrew Jackson was not after all based simply on the huge
popularity of a single individual but instead had a life of its own. The
Democratic convention of 1836 marked, according to the *National
Intelligencer*, the foremost Whig newspaper in the nation, "AN ERA in
the history of the country." The editors' verdict was confirmed by the
verdict of the electorate that November, as Van Buren, the archetypal
party politician, won the right to succeed Jackson. Henceforth many
Whigs realized that party conventions (which Hugh Lawson White, a
Whig candidate in 1836, had himself opposed) were essential. Between
1837 and 1839 the Whig party, as one historian has observed, "became a
political organization dedicated to victory." Some prominent anti-
Democrats lamented what they saw as a drift toward demagoguery but
the need for victory after three successive defeats in presidential contests
weakened the force of these objections. As the Whig Executive
Committee, charged with overseeing the national campaign, reminded
the party faithful in 1840: "hitherto you have been beaten . . . by the
force of the superior drill and discipline of your opponents." It followed
that the Whigs must meet fire with fire.[65]

Organization, however important, was not the sole key to success.
Policy changes were also needed. Many Whigs now concluded that a
national bank was an electoral liability. Joseph Gales and William
Seaton, editors of the *National Intelligencer*, announced in 1837 that
they would no longer agitate the question. In November 1839 they conceded that the public mind was not yet ready for another Bank of the
United States. It needed, as they put it in February 1838, "a necessity

---

64. Fillmore to G. W. Patterson, Feb. 6, 1839 in Frank H. Severance (ed.), "The Millard
     Fillmore Papers," 2 vols *Publications of the Buffalo Historical Society*, x (1907), II, p.
     185.
65. *National Intelligencer* quoted in Edward L. Mayo, "The National Intelligencer and
     Jacksonian Democracy" (Ph.D. dissertation, Claremont, 1969), p. 124; Nathans,
     Webster and Jacksonian Democracy, p. 104; *To the Whigs and Conservatives of
     the United States* (Washington, D.C., 1840), p. 1.

stronger than any that now exists;" indeed the editors acknowledged that they were unlikely to live to see another BUS.[66 ']

Similarly, Henry Clay, the embodiment of what might be termed Whig orthodoxy, in these years made some significant policy retreats. Rather than emphasizing the need for protection, he reaffirmed his support for the Compromise tariff (which he had himself, of course, played a major role in negotiating). More significantly he renounced the Bank of the United States, at least until public opinion requested it. Since funds were no longer available either for federal internal improvements, or to be distributed to the states, it seemed that much of the American system had been dismantled.[67]

At this time, Clay also delivered a ringing attack on the abolitionists. The combined effect was to remove most of the doubts that southerners had entertained about him. When a Whig national convention met at Harrisburg in 1839 all the southern delegates voted for him on the first ballot (though it should be noted that not all the southern states were represented). But in the North, the conviction was widespread that Clay was, alas, "unavailable." On the other hand, Harrison or Winfield Scott, according to Whig managers like Thurlow Weed, were highly available; indeed Harrison, the Hero of Tippecanoe, it transpired, was availability personified. In part Weed, and those who thought like him, were aware of the need to conciliate recent Democratic defectors, many of whom had spent an entire career combating Clay and his American system; in part the feeling was that Clay was too closely identified (and Webster still more so) with a political style that shunned direct appeals to the masses. Hence Clay was pushed aside, and Harrison nominated. To please the South, John Tyler, a Virginian states' rights Whig who had been alienated from the Democracy as a result of nullification, was made Harrison's running mate. Tyler was known to be a "friend" of Henry Clay. The convention adjourned without adopting a platform, though the chairman did recommend a single term for the president as well as endorsing the now largely irrelevant policy of distribution.[68]

In the campaign itself, the Democrats emphasized the Independent Treasury, in which Van Buren had invested so much political as well as financial capital, and generally sought to make banking the crucial election issue. The Whigs preferred to concentrate on artefacts like the "log

66. *National Intelligencer*, Dec. 21, 1837, Feb. 27, 1838, Nov. 19, 1839; Mayo, "National Intelligencer and Jacksonian Democracy," pp. 123–129.

67. Cooper, *South and Politics of Slavery*, pp. 121–122 (though Cooper perhaps exaggerates this development).

68. Cooper, *South and Politics of Slavery*, pp. 124–126; Glyndon G. Van Deusen, *The Jacksonian Era* (N.Y., 1963), p. 153; *Proceedings of the Democratic Whig National Convention ... For the Purpose of Nominating Candidates for President and Vice-President of the United States* (Harrisburg, 1839), p. 14.

cabin" in which Harrison had allegedly been born (though in reality had not). Undoubtedly they pushed the techniques of mass electioneering – parades, campaign songs, badges – further than the Democrats had taken them in earlier years. But the election was not quite so issueless as is sometimes claimed. Harrison himself made a major speech at Dayton, Ohio, in September 1840. He complained of the growth of executive power and once again pledged that he would seek only a single term in the White House. On the question of a national bank he argued that the constitution gave no "express grant of power for such purpose." From this he concluded that "it could never be constitutional to exercise that power," unless – and here he entered a crucial rider – "the powers granted to congress could not be carried into effect, without resorting to such an institution." In all events, he added, he would respect the views of Congress on this question. Harrison thus left the way open for another Bank of the United States.[69]

Clay meanwhile, in the course of a campaign speech in Taylorsville, Virginia, was more explicit. He argued that a BUS should be established by a Whig Congress, and authorized by a Whig president. Webster himself also endorsed this plan. Hence the three Whig leaders in 1840 advocated a national bank, at least as a last resort. As we shall see, however, Harrison's equivocation was important, especially in the South, where many of his supporters were able to present him as an anti-BUS candidate.[70] But Whig unity existed at a deeper level. Historians who have concentrated on federal politics, and who have been all-too-aware of the Whig split in the early 1840s on the bank question, have missed the agreement among all the Whigs on the need not for a national bank specifically, but for banks and credit in general. Indeed this agreement was vital to the entire Whig effort of 1840. When it is recalled that in most of the states of the Union, the party was embroiled in a fierce battle with hard money Democrats, Whig tactics become more understandable. To beat back Democratic radicalism, the Whigs could afford to submerge their differences on some policy questions. True to their traditional political conservatism they could agree that Congress should be allowed to decide on matters like a national bank, precisely as it had before Jackson had revolutionized American politics. They could plausibly claim that even a question like the Bank of the United States paled into insignificance when banking and credit *per se* were being challenged.[71]

69. *Niles Register*, Oct. 3, 1840 (p. 71); William N. Chambers, "The Election of 1840" in Schlesinger and Israel (eds), *History of Presidential Elections*, I, pp. 643–684. Harrison's important Speech at Dayton is reprinted in *ibid.*, pp. 737–744.

70. Nathans, *Webster and Jacksonian Democracy*, p. 147.

71. This has been missed, one suspects, because of the traditional over-concentration on federal issues, once common among political historians.

Viewed in this light, Whig utterances in 1840 acquire a different meaning. In the same speech at Dayton, Harrison was as unequivocal about banking in general as he was evasive about the BUS in particular. Paper money and credit, he announced, "are the only means, under Heaven, by which a poor industrious man may become a rich man without bowing to colossal wealth." Placing a characteristic Whig emphasis on the need for social mobility, he declared that "a properly devised banking system alone, possesses the capability of bringing the poor to a level with the rich." Using language similar to that employed by Whigs in every state as they battled against Democratic radicalism, he denounced as "the vilest imposture ever attempted upon the credulity of the public mind," the attempt "to array the poor of the country under the name of Democrats against the rich, and style them aristocrats."[72] Here was classic Whig doctrine.

Not surprisingly such sentiments suffused the Whig campaign in the North. Here the party's populism had been established in states like New York, where William Henry Seward, Weed's *alter ego*, had already won the governorship. But the most interesting developments came in the South. In much of the border South, where Whiggery was already well established (and was in effect National Republicanism under a new name)[73] there was little change from 1836 or even 1832. But in the Middle and Deep South the situation was different. Here many Whigs were unenthusiastic or apologetic about a national bank, a protective tariff and federal internal improvements. In a pamphlet explicitly addressed to southerners one partisan conceded that Harrison had indeed supported the odious tariff of abominations in 1828 but claimed that he had at least done so in an open and manly way, unlike the scheming Van Buren. The same writer claimed that Harrison followed Madison on the question of a national bank and insisted that, however distasteful such an institution might be, the Independent Treasury, a "government bank," was even worse. Another southern propagandist claimed that the Nullification proclamation had demonstrated that the Democrats were in fact more "Federalist" than Alexander Hamilton himself. This writer voiced his approval of a national bank, while at the same time expressing a decided opposition to the tariff and to federally sponsored internal improvements.[74]

72. Harrison, "Speech at Drayton," in Schlesinger and Israel (eds), *History of Presidential Elections,"* I, p. 741.
73. See for example, *The Campaign*, published in Frankfort, Kentucky, at the time of the election of 1840. Henry C. Reed (ed.), *Delaware, A History of the First State* 3 vols (N.Y., 1947), I, pp. 150–152.
74. *The Northern Man with Southern Principles, Or the Southern Man with American Principles* (Washington, D.C., 1840), pp. 28, 38; John L. Dorsey, *The Spirit of Modern Democracy Explained* (St. Louis, Mo., 1840), pp. 9, 19–20, 38, 49.

The complexities of the situation become more apparent when we look at some of the individual southern states. In Kentucky and Missouri, the party was unambiguously committed to a national bank and indeed to the American system in its entirety. More surprisingly, perhaps, in Tennessee the party took a similar stance, despite the past hostility of Hugh Lawson White and many of his supporters, who had previously espoused a states' rights commercialism.[75] But in North Carolina, Virginia and Georgia the Whigs were unable to achieve this degree of unity. In North Carolina the most popular Whig issue was undoubtedly distribution, by which the state hoped to pay her debts and also improve her infrastructure. William Shepard in 1840 termed the failure of distribution in the 1830s the biggest misfortune to afflict the state since the Revolution and many party members were prepared to tolerate an increase in the tariff if it would supply the funds for distribution. Nevertheless the Whig state convention placed itself on record against either an increase in the tariff or in the scale of federal internal improvements. On the subject of a national bank party opinion was divided.[76] The state convention did endorse a new BUS but a major party leader like George E. Badger claimed in an election speech that Harrison was opposed to a re-chartering. Badger also took pride in denying that Harrison favored a protective tariff. But he in effect demonstrated why he was a Whig supporter when he boasted that Harrison, once elected, would not be "like an evil spirit seeking to divide the different portions of society and array them against each other." The spirit of North Carolina Whiggery was caught in a Message delivered by Governor Edward B. Dudley in 1838. Dudley voiced his opposition to the high tariffs of the 1820s but affirmed his support for a Bank of the United States. He added that "an increase of banking capital in our own State is certainly necessary to meet the wants of industry." Then he offered a classic Whig vision of future economic development:

> We must extend the credit system; afford the means to erect manu-
> factories, to build ships, to improve our navigation, open canals and

---

75. Richard A. Wire, "John M. Clayton and the Search for Order" (Ph.D. dissertation, University of Maryland, 1971), p. 102; John V. Mering, *The Whig Party in Missouri* (Columbia, Mo., 1967), p. 7; Sellers, "Who Were the Southern Whigs," *passim*; Thomas B. Alexander, "Thomas A. R. Nelson as an Example of Whig Conservatism," *Tennessee Historical Quarterly*, xv (1956), pp. 17–29, esp. 27–28.

76. William B. Shepard in the North Carolina Senate, quoted in the Raleigh *Star and North Carolina Gazetter*, Dec. 30, 1840; *Journals of the Senate and House of Commons of the General Assembly of the State of North Carolina, at its Session in 1838–1839* (Raleigh, 1839), p. 436; J. G. de Roulhac Hamilton, "Party Politics in North Carolina," *The James Sprunt Historical Publications*, xv (Durham, N.C., 1916), pp. 56–57.

construct turnpikes and railways, to improve and use our water power, and to work the mines of ores and minerals with which our State so richly abounds.

It was a message which Clay or Webster would have warmly applauded. Once again, beneath disagreements over the proper role of the federal government lay a consensus on the need for commercial development.[77]

In Virginia the political situation was complicated by the presence of William C. Rives and his small but significant band of recent "conservative" defectors from the Democracy. Originally they had claimed to differ from the Democrats on a single question, the Independent Treasury, but after it became apparent that this was now the crucial test question such a claim became meaningless. In the state's House of Delegates the conservatives managed to hold the balance of power for a time but nevertheless experienced great difficulties in remaining united, with some leaning toward the Democrats, others inclining in the direction of the Whigs and others advocating independence. The two most important conservative leaders were James Garland and Rives himself. Both wrote significant public letters in 1840. Rives complained that Van Buren was seeking to destroy the credit system to which "every candid and well informed mind must admit that the unparalleled development of American prosperity and civilization has been mainly owing." As far as the tariff was concerned, Rives pointed out that Van Buren had supported the tariff of 1828; Harrison could be no worse. On federal internal improvements Van Buren's record was bad; Harrison would use "forbearance." On the bank question, Rives noted, Harrison was unfortunately pledged to sign a bill for re-charter in some circumstances but this was far better than the Independent Treasury, a government bank. Hence Harrison was to be preferred to Van Buren. These sentiments were shared by Garland. If anything he was still more hostile to a national bank than Rives but he also avowed a belief that "the banking system" was "among the highest inventions and noblest results of modern civilization" without which "no country can ever reach a high degree of commercial greatness."[78]

Although many Virginia Whigs were more orthodox than these men, the need to propitiate both conservatives like Rives and states' rights Whigs like Tyler would have made it difficult for the party to endorse

77. George E. Badger, *Speech Delivered at the Great Whig Meeting in the County of Granville, [N.C.], 3 March 1840* (Raleigh, 1840), pp. 4, 15; *Journals of Senate and House of North Carolina, 1838*, pp. 269–270, 275–281.

78. Ashworth, *"Agrarians" and "Aristocrats,"* p. 140; *Letter from the Hon. William C. Rives, of Virginia* (n.p., n.d.), pp. 3, 12, 13; Garland, *Letter of James Garland to His Constituents* (n.p., n.d.), pp. 17–18; *The Essays of Camillus, Addressed to the Hon. Joel Holleman* (Norfolk, 1841), pp. 69, 72, 84 ,85–86, 89.

a candidate fully committed to the American system. Harrison's equivocations were thus most welcome. An official Address by the state party in 1840 claimed that the bank, the tariff and internal improvements were not issues. The implication was that Harrison was hostile to a national bank but that in all events, he could scarcely be worse than Van Buren. This lukewarm attachment to Whig policies foreshadowed a deep split within the Virginia party in the early 1840s. Of all states Virginia would be most damaged by the breach between Clay and Tyler.[79]

In Georgia politics were still more fluid. Here the Whig party scarcely existed in 1836 and instead the opposition to Jackson derived from the nullification crisis. The so-called States Rights party was far closer in views to Calhoun than it was to Clay; Jackson's supporters described themselves as Unionists rather than Democrats. When Calhoun returned to the Democratic party over the Independent Treasury some members of the States Rights party followed his example. The Unionist-Democratic party now sought to make the Independent Treasury the crucial test question but the States Rights party resisted this, claiming instead that federal power was the paramount issue, in comparison with which banks and credit were insignificant. In the late 1830s both the Milledgeville *Southern Recorder* and Alexander Stephens, destined to be the foremost representative of Georgia Whiggery, reviewed the claims of both Van Buren and Clay (who was expected to oppose him in the forthcoming presidential election). According to the *Recorder*, Van Buren was "obnoxious to the South," since he accepted the constitutionality of abolition in the District of Columbia and because of his stance over the Missouri Compromise. A victory for Clay, meanwhile, would be "no less unjust than injurious to the best interests of the South." Webster, of course, was still more suspect, and the newspaper rounded off its analysis by rejecting the claims of Harrison too. Constantly referring to the evils of the Force Bill and the Nullification Proclamation, the editor urged southerners to rely only on themselves for the defense of their vital interests. Similarly Stephens in July 1839 dismissed Van Buren as a "known enemy" and Henry Clay as "a traitor to our cause." Only in 1840 or 1841 would he become an orthodox member of the Whig party.[80]

To some of the States Rights party Harrison's candidacy in 1840 was advantageous in that it allowed a *rapprochement* with the Whigs without

79. *Address of the Whig Convention for the Nomination of Electors, To the People of Virginia* (n.p., n.d.), p. 11.
80. Milledgeville *Southern Recorder*, April 3, July 24, Dec. 4, 1838; Paul Murray, "The Whig Party in Georgia," *The James Sprunt Historical Publications*, XXIX (Chapel Hill, 1948), pp. 89, 93; Richard M. Johnston and William H. Browne, *Life of Alexander H. Stephens* (rev. ed. N.Y., 1971), p. 75; Columbus *Enquirer* quoted in Debats, "Elites and Masses," pp. 101–102.

the loss of face that a capitulation to Henry Clay would have entailed. The party sent no representatives to the convention at Harrisburg. But John J. Berrien, Robert Toombs and others argued that Harrison's candidacy should be endorsed fully. The Milledgeville *Southern Recorder* reversed its previous recommendations and acquiesced. In June the Georgia state convention formally endorsed the Whig ticket. Yet as an address by Georgia's States Rights–Whig congressmen demonstrated, there was only lukewarm support for orthodox party principles. The congressmen consoled themselves by arguing that Harrison's position on the Bank was identical to that which Madison had held and that the Hero supported the Compromise tariff. Within a comparatively short time Georgia's Whigs would be supporters of both Clay and the American system, but in 1840 this moment had not yet arrived.[81]

IV

The Whig triumph of 1840 marked the high point of the party's fortunes. Carrying 19 out of 26 states, the Whigs won 53 percent of the two-party vote. Even in 1840, however, they were stronger in the North than in the South. Among northern states, only New Hampshire and Illinois supported Van Buren whereas he managed to hold five southern states. When it is remembered that in some of the southern states, the Whigs were not yet fully aligned with the national party, this imbalance is the more striking. Nevertheless, Harrison ran well in all parts of the Union.

Historians will never know how a Harrison administration would have fared, since the Hero of Tippecanoe died exactly one month after taking office. This brought John Tyler to the White House and the Whigs now paid the price for the obfuscation they had perpetrated. The significant underlying agreement throughout the party on the need for banks and paper money in general could not itself resolve the question of a national bank. At the outset Tyler agreed to approve such a bank provided that its powers were limited and did not prejudice what he took to be the vital interests or impair the sovereignty of individual states. But he offered this as a maximum concession and a proof of his desire to co-operate with the party in Congress, now subject to the increasingly overbearing leadership of Henry Clay. Clay and the Congressional Whigs, however, felt that they had waited a long time and suffered a great many political reverses at the hands of the Democrats and understandably wanted to introduce a full

81. *Address of J. C. Alford, William C. Dawson, Richard W. Habersham, Thos Butler King, E. A. Nesbit, and Lott Warren, Representatives from the State of Georgia, in the Twenty-Sixth Congress of the United States, to their Constituents, May 27, 1840* (n.p., n.d.), pp. 16–17; Cooper, *South and Politics of Slavery*, pp. 127–128.

Whig program. After all, they had a majority in both Houses of Congress and, as they had insisted in their addresses to the electorate, the power of Congress, held in check by Jackson and Van Buren, should be restored. Hence they passed a bill for a more traditional bank in the hope that, in the event of a presidential veto, they could fall back upon the more limited institution to which Tyler had already consented. But the president viewed this as an attempt at coercion and now retreated into his original opposition to virtually any national bank and vetoed not only the first but both bank bills. This apparent breach of faith sealed his fate and he was soon read out of the Whig party.[82]

Superficially this signaled a crisis of Whig unity; in reality it marked the high point of party stability and cohesion. For Tyler was able to take with him only a tiny number of Whigs either north or south of the Mason-Dixon line. In the Senate he had at best two supporters, in the House approximately a half dozen. Of 55 southern Whigs, only three stood by him after the second veto. Temporarily he enjoyed the support of Daniel Webster, who remained as Secretary of State after the second veto and who in 1842 was predicting a break-up of the entire party system. But as ever Webster betrayed an inadequate understanding of the role of parties and of party loyalties and had to limp back to the Whig ranks later that year. Over the next two years or so the party rallied behind Henry Clay and the American system as it had never done in the past (and would not do again). Quickly one state after another confirmed him as its choice for the presidency in 1844; most states, moreover, now fully endorsed the American system. Clay himself entered the campaign of 1844 confident that the victory of 1840 would be repeated.[83]

The fate of the states' rights Whiggery represented by Tyler and his small band of supporters requires consideration. Undoubtedly the key factor was the economy. In the entire history of the antebellum South the early 1840s was the time when the program of economic diversification, as championed by Clay, seemed most appealing. With cotton prices low, many southerners believed that the South must emulate the North and establish manufacturing on a greater scale than hitherto. Moreover the economic recession had, as we have seen, had its effect on the

82. George R. Poage, *Henry Clay and the Whig Party* (Chapel Hill, N.C., 1936); Nathans, *Webster and Jacksonian Democracy*, pp. 163–195; Lyon G. Tyler, *The Letters and Times of the Tylers* 3 vols (Richmond, Va., 1894–1896), esp. ii; Ashworth, *"Agrarians" and "Aristocrats,"* pp. 171–174.

83. Nathans, *Webster and Jacksonian Democracy*, p. 171; Poage, *Clay and the Whig Party*, p. 106 and *passim*. Nathans makes the point that the Whigs may have been misled by John M. Botts into thinking Tyler would accept the compromise bank bill. Then, when unity was achieved, it was maintained after the second veto. It should also be noted that Tyler signed the Tariff bill of 1842 out of an urgent need for revenue.

Democratic party too. The Whigs needed to be united in order to resist antibank radicalism. Finally, the Whig tariff of 1842 did not bring ruin to the agricultural interest, as its opponents had charged. An obstacle to the espousal of protection by southern Whigs was thus removed.[84]

If we look at the states of the South East, where the Whigs had been most heterodox before 1840, these changes are apparent. In North Carolina, Tyler's defection had little effect on the party either at home or in Congress. Senator Willie P. Mangum in 1838 boasted that he had never voted for any bank, state or federal or any federal internal improvement or for a protective tariff; in 1842 he was prepared to support the Whig protective tariff as well as a national bank. By the time the Democrats (in 1846) were in a position to introduce a lower tariff, North Carolina Whigs were defending the tariff of 1842.[85] In Virginia a similar process was in evidence. United States Senator William Archer, who had been a firm opponent of a national bank, now reversed himself and argued that there was no alternative since the pet bank system had been discredited (by the bank failures in the late 1830s) and the Independent Treasury repudiated (by the electorate in 1840). The *Richmond Whig*, meanwhile, was championing a program of economic diversification and applauding the growth of the tobacco industry in, for example, Richmond and other cities, and arguing that a protective tariff was required to prevent the thousands employed in manufacturing from returning to farming, to the obvious detriment of the entire agricultural interest. Even William C. Rives, Tyler's staunchest supporter in the Senate, was defending the tariff of 1842 by the time of the election of 1844. Moreover, by the early 1840s states' rights Whigs like R. M. T. Hunter had followed Calhoun back into the Democracy. Little wonder then that even in Virginia, Tyler's home state and the state in which he had most support, the Clay Whigs were utterly dominant.[86]

84. Douglass C. North, *The Economic Growth of the United States, 1790–1860* (N.Y., 1966), pp. 202–203. Recovery began in agriculture from around 1843 – though the part played by the Whig tariff was very limited.
85. de Roulhac Hamilton, "Party Politics in North Carolina," pp. 80, 71, 85; Robert N. Elliot, *The Raleigh Register, 1799–1863* (Chapel Hill, 1955), p. 83; Henry M. Wagstaff, *State Rights and Political Parties in North Carolina, 1776–1861* (Baltimore, 1906), p. 74.
86. *Congressional Globe*, 27 Congress, 1 Session, Appendix, p. 338; Robert H. Tomlinson, "The Origins and Editorial Policies of *The Richmond Whig and Public Advertiser*, 1824–1865" (Ph.D. dissertation, Michigan State University, 1971), pp. 105–115; Dingledine, "Career of Rives," p. 453; Lynwood M. Dent, Jr., "The Virginia Democratic Party, 1824–1847" 2 vols (Ph.D. dissertation, Louisiana State University, 1974), II, p. 358; Charles H. Ambler, "Virginia and the Presidential Succession, 1840–1844," in *Essays in American History Dedicated to Frederick Jackson Turner* (N.Y., 1910), pp. 165–202.

In Georgia the situation was once again more complex. The Congressional elections of 1842 marked the final step in the amalgamation of the old Troup-States-Rights party with the national Whig party. Nevertheless Clay was still at this time widely presented as a candidate favoring a revenue tariff (with incidental protection) and the tariff of 1842 was defended in these terms. As late as 1843 the *Southern Recorder* claimed that the Whigs of Georgia advocated a tariff for revenue and "in no instance for protection." Yet the paper argued also for economic diversification and denounced Democratic proposals for tariff reduction on the grounds that they would not raise sufficient revenue. At the same time Alexander Stephens was placing himself on record in favor of the tariff of 1842; he had already called for economic diversification in Georgia and the South. Nevertheless Stephens was less enthusiastic in his advocacy of a tariff than John J. Berrien who announced in 1844 that he had changed his mind on this question. "The march," he declared, of "the manufacturing spirit," was "still onward and southward" and Georgia was "awakening to the conviction that a portion of her productive labor may be better employed" than in agriculture. The state, he claimed, "was becoming more and more convinced of a division of labor." As elsewhere in the South, former opponents of protection voted against the Walker tariff of 1846 on the grounds that it effected too great a reduction in rates. Moreover in Georgia too disagreements on tariff policy concealed major agreements in other areas. The *Southern Recorder* rallied to the defense of a BUS, supported distribution and demanded an equal currency throughout the Union, to be achieved in defiance of "agrarian" attacks, launched by Democrats, against the nation's banks.[87]

Analysis of congressional voting patterns confirms this analysis. Throughout the years between 1837 and 1844 when the question of a national bank was frequently raised, the Whigs generally supported it by huge majorities, normally at least 90 percent of the party. This figure conceals, however, the growth in party unity, since in the late 1830s some southern states scarcely had an organized Whig party. By 1841 when the House of Representatives voted on a BUS charter, every Whig from the Southwest (together with virtually every northern Whig) favored the proposal. Eighty-seven percent of party members from the Southeast approved the plan. Some of the remainder were Tylerites and some of these left the party with him. It was not surprising, therefore, that in 1844

---

87. Murray, "Whig Party in Georgia," pp. 101–105, 109, 200; *Congressional Globe*, 27 Congress, 2 Session, Appendix, pp. 679, 815; Thomas Brown, *Politics and Statesmanship: Essays on the American Whig Party* (N.Y., 1985), pp. 198–199; John M. Berrien, *Speech on the Tariff* (Washington, D.C., 1844), p. 16; *La Grange Herald*, Sept. 28, 1843.

Clay and the Bank were taken up by the party throughout the nation. By that time party unity on the question was complete.[88]

A glance at party voting on the tariff question reinforces the analysis suggested by events in Georgia, North Carolina, and Virginia. In 1841–1842 the Whig party was united in the North behind the tariff. Southern Whigs, however, were somewhat divided on the question: in the House 21 can be classified as favoring a high tariff, 11 a moderate tariff and 12 a low tariff. By 1844 the entire congressional party had fallen into line and two years later with a single exception (Hilliard of Alabama) every Whig in the House of Representatives voted against the Walker tariff. Instead the party rallied behind the tariff of 1842, the highest (at that point) in the nation's history.[89]

V

The election of 1844 would thus see a united Whig party take the field committed to an economic program not unlike that which the National Republicans had offered in 1832. The differences between Whig and Democrat were there for all to see. On economic questions, like the BUS and the Independent Treasury, the alignment could not have been clearer. On the tariff, despite some crosscurrents (some southern Whigs claiming Clay was for a revenue tariff, some northern Democrats advocating protection) the party positions were as definite as they would be in any presidential election in the antebellum Republic.[90] Moreover, there were still vitally important differences between the parties on the question of political democracy. As we have already seen, the Dorr rebellion of 1842 demonstrated that even after the "Log Cabin" campaign a wide gulf separated the two parties on the question of political democracy. All agreed, of course, in celebrating the American republic, in maintaining a wide suffrage, in requiring public accountability of officeholders. But the Whigs clung to a view of the polity that differentiated them sharply from the Democrats and the Dorr rebellion exposed and widened the gap between the parties. Most Whigs remained reluctant to engage in the eulogies of the people and of American democracy that characterized Democratic political addresses. The "Log Cabin" campaign was no

---

88. Alexander, *Sectional Stress and Party Strength*, pp. 38, 158, 162; Ashworth, *"Agrarians" and "Aristocrats,"* pp. 231–232 and appendix.
89. Silbey, *Shrine of Party*, pp. 241, 71; Ashworth, *"Agrarians" and "Aristocrats,"* pp. 252–255 and appendix.
90. See Henry Clay's Letter to the *La Grange Herald* Sept. 13, 1843. Clay here denied he favored a high tariff and denied that the tariff of 1842 (which he approved) could be so described. It was generally acknowledged, however, that a Democratic administration would reduce the tariff.

exception. In an election speech in 1840 Harrison himself warned that, contrary to Democratic claims, republican governments never turned into aristocracies. The real danger was of a descent into a pure democracy, such as the French Revolution had witnessed. Democrats (apart from Calhounites) did not speak this way.[91]

Each party had now come to maturity. Neither, however, was monolithic. The Democrats, even before the advent of the territorial question, were divided, especially within the states, on the banking question. Agreement on the Independent Treasury coexisted with profound disagreement on the question of banks and paper money *per se.* Conservative, soft money Democrats, although as yet a minority within the party, were on this question closer to the Whigs than to the hard money elements within their own party. Equally important, however, was the division within Whig ranks. Despite the highly public disagreement between the congressional Whigs and President Tyler over federal economic policy, the main source of division within Whig ranks was as yet evident primarily at state level and arose over political rather than economic questions. Just as Democratic agreement on the evils of a national bank did not preclude deep disagreements about banking, so Whig agreement on the nature of sovereignty did not mean unanimity on all questions concerned with political democracy. Most Whigs were still more conservative on these matters than is generally thought. But there were important divisions. For example the Whig members of the Massachusetts legislature in 1840 declared flatly that the suffrage was not a natural right and Henry Clay believed that "the mass" was "very liable to deception." Little wonder then that like most Whigs he wanted a republic rather than a democracy.[92] Others within the party were more liberal. Men like William Seward of New York were willing, as most Whigs were not, to refer critically to an American "aristocracy," to

91. Harrison, "Speech at Drayton," in Schlesinger and Israel (eds), *History of Presidential Elections,"* I, p. 743.
92. *Answer of the Whig Members of the Legislature of Massachusetts . . . to the Address of His Excellency Marcus Morton* (Boston, 1840), pp. 27–28; Clay to Francis Brooke, Nov. 3, 1838 in Calvin Colton, (ed.), *Life and Works of Henry Clay* 10 vols (N.Y., 1904), V, p. 429. For other examples of conservative Whig political thought see Fillmore to Weed, Dec. 6, 1838, in Severance (ed.), *Fillmore Papers,* II, pp. 176–177; John Whipple, *Substance of a Speech Delivered at the Whig Meeting Held at the Town House, Providence, R.I., Aug. 28, 1837* (Providence, 1837), p. 4; Providence *Daily Journal,* Nov. 2, 1841; *National Intelligencer,* July 16, 1836; *Whig Review,* II (1845), p. 446, IV (1846), p. 29; Bloomington *Herald,* May 15, 1846 in Shambaugh (ed.), *Fragment,* p. 385; *John, The Traitor, or, The Force of Accident . . .* (N.Y., 1843), pp. 11, 13; Ashworth, *"Agrarians" and "Aristocrats,"* pp. 111–125 and *passim*; James T. Horton, *James Kent, A Study in Conservatism, 1763–1847* (N.Y., 1939), p. 318.

speak of the need to extend American democracy and to publicize and deplore the powerlessness of large numbers of American citizens.

Just as the Whigs were most divided over questions of federal policy in some of the southern states, so intra-party divisions over political democracy were sharpest in the Northeast and especially in the key states of New York and Massachusetts. In Massachusetts the problem would not erupt until later in the 1840s when the slavery controversy created a deep fissure within the party, pitting so-called "Conscience Whigs" against "Cotton Whigs." Although slavery was the vital issue here, the conflict between the two groups also entailed sharply divergent views of political democracy. We shall return to the Massachusetts Whig party later. In New York a similar alignment placed "Silver Grays" against "Woolly Heads," the former being in the later 1840s far more conservative on the slavery question. But here the division was much older; indeed it had been present since the inception of the party. There were several reasons. Immigration into New York city made the question of political representation an urgent one. Should immigrants be allowed to vote? How much autonomy should the representative enjoy? These questions were problematic in all states but the large immigrant presence in the Northeast and especially New York city posed a dilemma for the Whigs. Conservatives who were in any case sceptical about democratic government were utterly convinced that immigrants were unfit for the suffrage. Seward and his supporters were equally convinced, however, that the nation required immigrants and could assimilate them comparatively easily. Enfranchisement in his view would facilitate this process (as well as providing a source of Whig votes!). Furthermore the Democrats in New York state had, under Van Buren and the Albany regency, pioneered new methods of party organization. To compete, Seward and his closest ally Thurlow Weed believed, the Whigs had to develop a genuine mass appeal. Finally, the radicalism of the Democratic party (and earlier the Workingmen's parties) had frightened many conservatives into believing that concessions or changes of the type Seward was recommending, would pave the way for revolution. Hence they resisted the reformism of the Sewardites.[93]

By the mid-1840s the differences between the two wings of the New York Whig party were acute. In 1842 Seward decided not to seek re-election as governor. "My principles," he lamented, "are too liberal . . . -

---

93. On Seward see the discussion in Ashworth, *"Agrarians" and "Aristocrats,"* pp. 160–167; Howe, *Political Culture of American Whigs*, pp. 197–209. The best biography is Glyndon G. Van Deusen, *William Henry Seward* (N.Y., 1967). A good analysis of Whig divisions in New York state is provided in Lee H. Warner, "The Silver Grays: New York State Conservative Whigs 1846–1856" (Ph.D. dissertation, University of Wisconsin, 1971).

for my party;" hence he would be unable to run for the governorship with a united party behind him. A year earlier he had observed that because "it sympathized not with the masses," the Whig party "was always held at bay." The conservatives, however, held a very different view of the problem. The *New York Express* also pondered the reasons for repeated Democratic successes in the State but came to the opposite conclusion:

> Now there is no reason why the Whig party in this State should not always be in power, as it is in Massachusetts, Vermont or Rhode Island, or generally, as in Connecticut, but except that it is demoralized by such [liberal] principles. We have more Whig interests in property at stake than any Whig State in New England, or in the Union – *but this New York is the only one where in the Loco-Foco party there is nearly, if not quite as large an amount of property as there is in the Whig party* – and the cause of this is that such principles as the Albany Evening Journal and its slavishly following echoes in different parts of the State promulgate and defend, keep back from us men of property in the Loco-Foco ranks and divert from us men of property in the Whig ranks.

On this reasoning Seward did not possess the solution to the problem. Instead Seward *was* the problem.[94]

The conservatives, the "Silver Grays," were utterly opposed not only to Democratic but also to Whig populism. Daniel D. Barnard, a prominent Silver Gray, believed that the Seward wing threatened "the structure of civil society." Weed he dismissed as a "demagogue." While the Sewardites in many ways anticipated the appeal of the Republican party of the 1850s (Seward himself would become the foremost Republican leader prior to 1860), the Silver Grays would have been quite comfortable in the world of John Jay and Alexander Hamilton. Indeed Philip Hone, the prominent merchant and conservative Whig in New York city, complained of the absence from Whig tickets of any "leading federalist" name.[95] The New York *Courier and Enquirer*, edited by James Watson Webb, a leading conservative, in 1845 asked whether a "barrier" might be interposed "to stay this perpetual descent into the vortex of Democracy" and reviewed the nation's history since 1776:

> We started into existence as a *Republic*, with suitable guards and checks against the outbursts of popular passion; but have unfortu-

94. Seward to Christopher Morgan in Frederick W. Seward (ed.), *William H. Seward: An Autobiography* (N.Y., 1891), p. 547; New York *Express*, Aug. 25, 1845.
95. Sharon H. Penney, "Daniel Dewey Barnard: Patrician in Politics" (Ph.D. dissertation, State University of New York at Albany, 1972), p. 117; Herbert Kriedman, "New York's Philip Hone, Businessman – Politician – Patron of Arts and Letters" (Ph.D. dissertation, New York University, 1965), pp. 228–229.

nately degenerated into a *Democracy*, in which the majority claim the right to trample down all checks upon their *will*, and in which the minority have no rights. The fabric of our government was, in all its parts, based upon a solid foundation, which was none other than a judiciously restricted elective franchise . . . . In its place we have substituted *universal suffrage*. Between the one and the other, there is no more affinity than between a foundation of rock and one of sand.

As Webb was writing, Andrew Jackson, far away in Tennessee, was close to death. But he was still a forceful presence in American politics. "Since 1828," Webb concluded, "the downward tend of our Govt has been more rapid than during any previous period of our national history."[96]

As we have seen, many Whigs feared Democratic atomism and the appeal to individual self-interest, the rejection of all forms of deference and the disregard for the force of precedent. They wished to emphasize the prescriptive force of the past and the need for community values, the majesty of the Law and the need for restraint. Conservative Whigs were most committed to these goals. As we have also seen, these priorities implied a deep suspicion of abolitionists, who advocated a form of individualism which differed sharply from that of Democrats, but one which presented an equally striking challenge to conservative Whig assumptions. In short, the organic society cherished by Silver Grays and those who shared their beliefs was threatened equally by Democratic radicals and antislavery militants of the Seward stripe.

Before the eruption of the sectional controversy in the mid- and late 1840s, therefore, the seeds had been sown for significant disagreements within the Whig party on the slavery question. It would be no coincidence that those most suspicious of Seward's attempts to court the immigrant vote, for example, would be most reluctant to endorse his brand of antislavery. Of course, all northern Whigs opposed slavery in the sense that none believed that slavery could match free labor, either economically or morally. But the conservative emphasis upon the Union and upon property rights would in the late 1840s make conservative Whigs – in New York and elsewhere – more willing to compromise with the South when national unity appeared to be threatened.

96. New York *Courier and Enquirer*, April 28, 1845. See also *Courier and Enquirer*, April 16, 1844, March 19, May 19, Aug. 5, 1845; James L. Crouthamel, *James Watson Webb, a Biography* (Middletown, Conn., 1969), p. 104.

VI

It is vital to recognize that this Whig division had no connection whatever with the crisis that erupted after John Tyler's ensconcement in the White House. Conservative Whigs like Hone were staunch Clay supporters and were among the most enthusiastic devotees of the American system. Sewardites, meanwhile, welcomed the tariff, waxed lyrical about internal improvements and had reservations about a national bank only as long as it seemed an electoral liability. Moreover, Sewardites made no secret of their profound hostility to slavery and found Tyler's states' rights principles entirely alien. The divisions within the Whig party could thus not be exploited by the Tyler administration.

It was thus a grim predicament confronting John Tyler after his vetoes of the BUS re-charter bill. Despite all appearances, the Whig party was in fact more united on policy than it had ever been and ready to rally behind Clay and his American system. Indeed by 1844 the Whigs were as united on economic questions as any major party in the history of antebellum America. Ironically, however, the one significant voice of dissent came from the highest and most visible office in the nation.[97]

Having broken with the Whigs, Tyler and his small band of supporters toyed with the idea of a third party, one that would avoid the dangerous extremes of the two major parties and unite moderate opinion throughout the nation. But as the hopelessness of this scheme became apparent, Tyler began to move back toward the Democratic party. Clearly he needed a new issue on which to bid for support. After Webster left the Cabinet, the President replaced him with Abel P. Upshur, a proslavery theorist from Virginia. Upshur himself did not last out even the remainder of Tyler's term of office: he was the unfortunate victim of a steamboat accident. By now determined to rejoin the Democratic party, and even entertaining hopes of becoming its presidential nominee in 1844, Tyler now invited the other great outsider in American politics into his Cabinet. John C. Calhoun continued where Upshur had left off. With first Upshur then Calhoun at the State Department, the Tyler administration was able to devote its energies to a new issue, one destined to send a shock wave throughout the political system. This was the annexation of Texas.

The eruption of sectional animosities consequent upon the annexation of Texas and the Mexican war sharply differentiated the mid- and late 1840s from the period immediately preceding. Sectional tensions had been under Van Buren, Harrison and all but the last year of the Tyler administration at a low ebb. In these years the gag rule continued to be debated at each Congress and the activities of zealots like John Quincy

---

97. Once again the traditional over-concentration on federal, and indeed presidential, politics resulted in an exaggeration of Whig differences in the early 1840s.

Adams, Joshua Giddings and Henry Wise continued to attract consider-able attention.[98] But overall the slavery issue was quieter than it had been in the early and mid-1830s or than it would be after the advent of the Texas question. In the North the Liberty party challenged for the pre-sidency in 1840; it garnered only 6,000 votes and failed to carry even a single county. In the South that year (as in 1836) both parties tried to claim that the other's nominee was unsound on the slavery question. Van Buren was said to be disloyal to the South, Harrison to be a supporter of colonization and, in addition, the standard bearer of a party which in the North contained large numbers of abolitionists. In reply the Democrats pointed to Van Buren's record in office (which had been void of attacks upon slavery), while the Whigs claimed that Harrison had favored its spread into the old Northwest as long ago as 1804 and had favored the South during the Missouri crisis. In 1840 even the rhetoric of section-alism was invaded by the banking question, with each party claiming that its favored fiscal scheme (a BUS or an Independent Treasury) better safe-guarded states' rights.[99]

There is additional reason to question the importance of sectional issues in 1840. Even John C. Calhoun became a committed partisan. Having rejoined the Democratic party in 1837 he quickly converted the entire state to the Independent Treasury, in effect ruining the careers of those who dared to oppose him. The state endorsed Van Buren as Democratic candidate in 1840. To be sure Calhoun's goals had not changed. He still saw politics in sectional terms; he was still searching for a way of making the Union safe for slavery and the South. But the primacy of party questions in the late 1830s (together with his hope of succeeding Van Buren in 1844) meant that this strategy itself was to be pursued within the party system.[100]

With the containment of sectional issues, the increasing unity of the Whig party and the intensification of Democratic radicalism, the Jacksonian era in a sense came to a culmination in the years immediately after Jackson's retirement from politics. American politicians continued to dance to the tunes composed in his two terms of office. Although the Indian issue had disappeared and sectional animosities were dormant, the legacy of Jackson's assault upon the banking system dominated

98. On the gag rule in these years see the discussion in Freehling, *Road to Disunion*, pp. 289–352.
99. Cooper, *South and Politics of Slavery*, pp. 132–140.
100. *Journal of the Proceedings of the Senate and House of Representatives of the General Assembly of South Carolina at its Regular Session of 1840* (Columbia, S.C., 1841), p. 17; J. Franklin Jameson (ed.), "The Correspondence of John C. Calhoun," *Annual Report of the American Historical Association for 1899* (Washington, D.C., 1900), p. 445; Laura M. White, *Robert Barnwell Rhett: Father of Secession* (N.Y., 1931), p. 46.

politics – to the great dismay of his enemies. Moreover Jackson's populism continued to haunt the Whig party even after the success of 1840. Whig doubts about democracy had been diminished but not extinguished and important divisions remained, especially within some northern states.

From the mid-1840s a different agenda would begin to dominate American politics. The annexation of Texas and the war with Mexico would place new stresses and strains upon the political system. The parties would seek to respond and would initially manage to hold their ranks. But the new sectional currents unleashed by the Tyler administration and reinforced by the economic recovery that was beginning in these years, would take hold of each party and accentuate the differences not only between its northern and southern wings but also between the factions contending even within a single state. By the time this process was complete the second party system would be no more.

Advent of the territorial question, 1843–1847

I

The presidential election of 1844 marked the transition between the politics of Jacksonian America and those of the sectional controversy. The Log Cabin campaign four years earlier had centered on the question of social mobility. Behind the enormous emphasis on Harrison's supposedly humble origins lay the Whig concern for upward mobility challenged, as all Whigs agreed, by Democratic antibank radicalism. Thus even though the Whigs were somewhat equivocal about the question of a national bank, the election of 1840 raised key issues, issues on which the major parties took sharply opposed positions. In 1848, by contrast, the large issue would be the question of the territories. In that year neither party had a clear policy. Or rather the Whigs had no policy at all, the Democrats one shrouded in ambiguity, whose effects no-one could predict. Most observers had believed that the election of 1844 would be one even more directly concerned with the Jacksonian issues than those in which Jackson himself had participated. Henry Clay was the unanimous choice of the Whigs, the Democrats were expected to nominate Martin Van Buren. Neither party could have selected a more strictly orthodox candidate.[101]

Instead the election probably turned on a new issue: territorial expansion. The Democratic party embraced the annexation of Texas (as well as the occupation of Oregon), threw over Martin Van Buren for James K.

---

101.   The best single account of politics in these years is to be found in Sellers, *James K. Polk, Continentalist* (Princeton, 1966), *passim*.

Polk and won the election. The old issues were by no means absent; in some states the bank war had not yet reached a culmination and the Texas question was subordinate. Nevertheless Clay's vacillations on the question of immediate annexation, compared with Polk's unqualified enthusiasm for the enterprise, probably ruined his chances. Once in office Polk would reintroduce the Independent Treasury and effect a significant tariff reduction (the Walker tariff). Nevertheless his presidency would be overshadowed by the territorial question, one that neither he nor his party would be able to resolve.

II

For the Democratic party these were years of transition. In May 1843 William Seward turned a dispassionate eye on the party he had spent his career combating. He assessed the relative strengths of the two wings of the party in New York state. "The barn burners," he judged, were "now incalculably stronger than those who have come under the reproached banner of conservative." But Seward even now saw that the days of radical victories were numbered. For "the former are building upon quick sand." "The season of pecuniary calamity," he noted, "is passing away, the business and industry of the country" were "reviving, and within a very short period, the memory of the radicalism of this day" would be "held in fear." This was a shrewd assessment and it would prove to be valid not merely for his own state but for the entire nation.[102]

Economic recovery began in the mid-1840s. It helped transform American politics in precisely the way Seward suggested. Yet the recession of the late 1830s and early 1840s also had unexpected implications for the political agenda. In addition to polarizing the political parties and revitalizing the bank issue, it raised disturbing questions about the demand for American agricultural goods. Overproduction seemed to have become a pressing problem. The Whigs, of course, had always had a solution. They continued to advocate economic diversification. Hence the tariff of 1842. The Democrats, however, continued to question the growth of manufacturing; indeed the recession actually deepened these fears. They needed a different solution. Harking back not to Jackson (who had not needed to confront this problem) but to Jefferson and Madison, some party members believed that the acquisition of new overseas markets was the answer. An expanded commerce was the order of the day. With Madison they concluded that the United States would be able to avoid the perils of industrialization by expanding her

102. Seward quoted in Muller, "Preston King," pp. 251–252.

exports.[103] Here the thinking of the *Democratic Review* was typical. In 1844 the journal observed that protective tariffs were quite unacceptable since they "enhance the natural concentration of wealth in the hands of the few, and . . . leave the masses impoverished." Since "the chief products of the United States" were – and quite properly – "agricultural", the level of consumption within the economy "depends entirely upon the foreign market for their surplus." As President Polk put it in his second annual message, "the home market alone is inadequate to enable" farmers and planters "to dispose of the immense surplus of food and other articles which they are capable of producing, even at the most reduced prices." The United States should therefore look to overseas markets. For a number of reasons this meant looking westward. Oregon, and still more, California beckoned.[104]

If the United States were able to take possession of much of the west coast then a base could be established for trade with Asia. According to Stephen A. Douglas, the "great point at issue" in the dispute between Britain and the United States over Oregon was "the freedom of the Pacific Ocean, . . . the trade of China and of Japan, of the East Indies, and . . . maritime ascendancy" in East Asia. David Wilmot in 1846, before he had given his name to the famous free-soil Proviso, pointed out that exports to Europe were always vulnerable to trade restrictions. Asia, by contrast, offered "a field for commercial enterprise, more vast and valuable" than any other region, "a market for our grain and staple manufacturers beyond our power to glut."[105]

But acquisition of territory bordering the Pacific would not simply add ports and natural harbors to the national domain. When the United States eventually annexed Texas, together with New Mexico, Utah and California the national territory would increase by approximately 50 percent. This, of course, was for Democrats an unmixed blessing, indeed it was another glorious triumph achieved for the nation by the Democratic party. Thomas Jefferson had told Americans that they possessed "a chosen country, with room enough for our descendants to the thousandth and thousandth generation" but as Thomas Hietala has aptly observed, Democratic expansionists of the 1840s "feared that Jefferson had erred in his calculations – by about 999 generations." They believed in fact that population growth together with the ominous development of

103. The key work on this aspect of Madison's thought is Drew McCoy, *The Elusive Republic: Political Economy in Jeffersonian America* (Chapel Hill, 1980).
104. *Democratic Review*, XIV (1844), pp. 291–293; Richardson (ed.), *Messages of Presidents*, IV, p. 501; Thomas R. Hietala, *Manifest Design: Anxious Aggrandizement in Late Jacksonian America* (Ithaca, 1985), pp. 55–94.
105. *Congressional Globe*, 29 Congress, 1 Session, 916, Appendix, pp. 259, 186. On this subject, Hietala's work is of great importance. See also Norman A. Graebner, *Empire on the Pacific: A Study in American Continental Expansion* (N.Y., 1955).

the factory system in some of the northeastern states demonstrated that the United States needed yet more land to preserve its agrarian economy and social structure. Once again the *Democratic Review* enunciated classic Democratic doctrine. Displaying the fear that wage labor all too easily entailed subservience, the writer (probably John L. O'Sullivan) complained bitterly that Whig policy enslaved free men by chaining them to "the steam engine and the loom." Democratic policy, by contrast, sought "to favor the settlement of the land, spread the bounds of the future empire, and to favor, by freedom of intercourse and external commerce, the welfare of the settlers ... men of simple habits and strong hands, looking to mother earth for their only capital, and to their own labor as the sole means of making it productive." Little wonder that the phrase "Manifest Destiny" was coined at this time.[106] It was "manifest" (though apparently to Democrats and not to Whigs) that the United States' "destiny" was to take possession of the entire continent. The originator of the phrase was none other than John L. O'Sullivan.[107]

Yet the rationale for this expansionist program was highly problematic. A contradiction was present. It was arguable (if unlikely) that trade across the Pacific might end the depression and it was also arguable (and more likely) that the acquisition of territory on the Pacific might be necessary to promote this trade. But would additional territory not aggravate the problem of overproduction? In other words, by taking steps to facilitate the disposal of existing surpluses the nation would be creating yet greater surpluses for the future. No Democrat ever confronted this problem.

The reason was that by the mid-1840s territorial expansion had become a goal which few if any of them questioned. It was all too easy to assume that additional land would be absorbed as the lands of the Louisiana Purchase had been absorbed, and to ignore the problems that had surfaced in 1819–1821 over Missouri. The nation would expand, it would spread the benefits of American democracy and it would preserve its agrarian base. If, in addition, trade across the Pacific would be encouraged, did this not make America's continental destiny still more manifest?

106. Hietala, *Anxious Aggrandizement*, p. 109; *Democratic Review*, XIX (1846), p. 86. For a discussion of the ideology of the *Democratic Review* see John Ashworth, "The Democratic Review: A Radical Jacksonian Journal" (M.Litt. dissertation, University of Lancaster, 1973). On "manifest destiny" see Reginald Horsman, *Race and Manifest Destiny: The Origins of American Racial Anglo-Saxonism* (Cambridge, Mass., 1981); Frederick Merk, *Manifest Destiny and Mission in American History: A Reinterpretation* (N.Y., 1963); Albert K. Weinberg, *Manifest Destiny, A Study of Nationalist Expansionism in American History* (Baltimore, 1935).
107. Julius W. Pratt, "John L. O'Sullivan and Manifest Destiny," *New York History*, XXXI, (1933), pp. 213–234.

Yet the principal cause of the expansionism of the 1840s was not the desire to spread democracy, nor the need to promote trade with Asia, nor the fear of overpopulation and industrialization in the existing states. Instead it was the vulnerability of slavery. As we shall see, the Democratic party, in both its institutional structure and its agrarian ideology, was once again the agent for the slaveholders of the South. In the early and mid-1840s their hopes and fears centered on the newly independent Republic of Texas.

III

In 1821 Mexico had won her independence from Spain. On two occasions rejecting American offers to purchase Texas from her, she nevertheless welcomed American settlers into the area provided they agreed to abide by her laws. One of those laws, passed in 1829, emancipated all slaves. But the American settlers were mainly southerners, many of them slaveholders, and they refused to countenance such legislation. In 1830 came an abrupt change of policy and Mexico prohibited the further immigration of Americans into Texas. This law too was ignored.[108]

By now there were approximately twenty thousand American whites and a thousand American slaves in Texas. A change of government in Mexico brought to power General Santa Anna who, despite a previous promise to give Texas separate statehood, now engaged in a program of centralization that threatened to rob her of all vestiges of self-government. The American settlers quickly drew a parallel with the struggle of 1776.

Early in 1836 Texans declared independence. A short war ensued but in April, at the Battle of San Jacinto, the Texans under the command of Sam Houston defeated the Mexicans, took Santa Anna himself prisoner and forced him to concede Texan independence. The Mexicans subsequently denounced this "agreement" but made no further attempt to reassert their authority. In September 1836 the Republic of Texas submitted its new constitution to the voters for ratification. The constitution was approved but the voters also expressed overwhelming support for annexation to the United States. President Houston accordingly began negotiations with his old chum, Andrew Jackson.[109]

108. On Texas see Norman A. Graebner, *Texas Annexation and the Mexican War: A Study of the Old Northwest* (Palo Alto, 1978); Frederick Merk, *Slavery and the Annexation of Texas* (N.Y., 1972); Justin H. Smith, *The Annexation of Texas* (N.Y., 1911).
109. On Houston see Llerna Friend, *Sam Houston: The Great Designer* (Austin, 1954); M. K. Wisehart, *Sam Houston, American Giant* (Washington, D.C., 1962).

Jackson, however, perceived problems. Much as he liked the idea of taking Texas, he was alert to the danger of impairing Van Buren's chances in the forthcoming presidential election, given the level of opposition predicted in the North. This of course was the era of the abolitionist petition campaign and Jackson was fully aware of the explosiveness of the slavery issue. For this reason he even delayed recognition of the Lone Star Republic until his final day in office. Van Buren, even more mindful of the dangers of an attempt to extend slave territory, refused to recommend annexation. Accordingly Houston turned to Europe for recognition and aid.[110]

At this point chance intervened. The Whig triumph of 1840 brought Harrison to the White House and Webster to the State Department. Undoubtedly a Harrison administration would have had no more – indeed probably less – enthusiasm for the annexation of Texas than Van Buren had displayed. But the unfortunate death of the president changed the complexion of the federal government entirely. As we have already noted, Tyler made Abel P. Upshur his Secretary of the Navy then, when Webster finally resigned, his Secretary of State. After Upshur's death in 1844 he was replaced by John C. Calhoun. Upshur and Calhoun, with the full blessing of the president, set about annexing Texas to the United States.

Tyler, as a president without a party, needed an issue on which to build a new party, or alternatively upon which to ride triumphantly back into Democratic ranks. But the annexation of Texas had deeper causes. Calhoun had, of course, for more than a decade been preoccupied with the threat posed by abolitionism. A clue to the priorities of Upshur came when as Secretary of the Navy he sent his first annual report to Congress. He warned of the danger to the nation of a large black population in the South that could be manipulated by her enemies in wartime. An enemy could, he warned, all too easily take up the "promising expedient" of "arraying what are supposed to be the hostile elements of our social system against one another." In case there was difficulty in identifying these supposedly "hostile elements," Upshur spelt out the danger: foreign invasion together with a revolt by slaves and freed blacks would create an "intolerably harassing and disastrous" war. He recommended a huge build-up of the American navy. Like Calhoun, Upshur was a zealous advocate of slavery. Under the guidance of these two ideologues American foreign policy would be overtly based on the need to protect slavery in the South.[111]

110. Smith, *Annexation of Texas,* pp. 52–62; Freehling, *Road to Disunion,* p. 368.
111. *Report of the Secretary of the Navy* quoted in Hietala, *Anxious Aggrandizement,* pp. 13–14.

At this point the story moves across the Atlantic to London. Realizing that his small nation needed to increase its population quickly, Houston launched a policy which would have the most far-reaching consequences. He knew that the uncertain status of Texas and her vulnerability to assault from Mexico deterred immigrants; hence he determined to use Britain as an intermediary to secure a lasting peace with Mexico. Houston himself was probably fairly indifferent as to the future of slavery in Texas but he was fully aware that the British government was committed to promoting abolition wherever it could safely be accomplished. Here then was an incentive for Britain to aid Texas. In return for abolition, Britain might offer loans to Texans, or encourage her own citizens to migrate to Texas, or put pressure on Mexico to come to terms. If all this failed, the project might well alarm the United States into action, in which case annexation, Houston's preferred outcome from the start, would result.

Accordingly Houston allowed Americans to conclude that he was willing to negotiate slavery out of existence in Texas. He also had his ambassador in Washington ensure that Calhoun and Tyler, as well as prominent Democrats like Robert J. Walker, were aware of his overtures to Britain. As early as January 1843 an article appeared in the *Madisonian*, the administration newspaper, advocating the annexation of Texas. Meanwhile in Texas, abolitionist pressure was present, in the form of Stephen Pearl Andrews, who was claiming that slavery was lowering land prices and generally stunting economic growth. Andrews, however, was forced out of Texas. He went to London. At precisely this time a World Antislavery Convention was meeting there to celebrate the tenth anniversary of abolition in the West Indies. Andrews now teamed up with Lewis Tappan, the New York abolitionist, and the two set about investigating the possibility of compensated abolition in Texas.[112]

Tappan and Andrews went to visit the British Foreign Secretary, Lord Aberdeen. Aberdeen declared that emancipation in Texas was certainly "desirable" and indeed worth "all legitimate means" to secure a "great consummation." Andrews now leapt to the conclusion that British aid was a certainty and before long rumors to this effect were circulating in London. They reached the ears of Duff Green, a long-time supporter of Calhoun and defender of slavery, in London to negotiate trade

---

112. *Madisonian*, Jan. 23, 1843; Freehling, *Road to Disunion*, pp. 372–382, 394–395. On these events see Ephraim D. Adams, *British Interests and Activities in Texas, 1838–1846* (Baltimore, 1910); George P. Garrison (ed.), "Diplomatic Correspondence of the Republic of Texas" *Annual Report of the American Historical Association for the Years 1907, 1908* 3 vols (Washington, D.C., 1908–1911); David M. Pletcher, *The Diplomacy of Annexation: Texas, Oregon and the Mexican War* (N.Y., 1973).

agreements. Green reported back to Upshur, now Secretary of State. If Upshur had had any lingering doubts about the urgency of the situation they were quickly dispelled. In August 1843 Aberdeen was asked in Parliament if the British government would seek to promote abolition in Texas by suggesting Mexico make it a condition of recognition. The Foreign Secretary replied that "every effort on the part of Her Majesty's Government would lead to that result." Within a month the Tyler administration was reading reports of the debate. The annexation of Texas now rose to the very top of the political agenda.[113]

As far as Upshur was concerned, the immediate task was to rouse the South into action. Like Calhoun he believed that regardless of party affiliation southerners must unite in defense of slavery. After his death, when Calhoun took over, the same strategy was pursued. Calhoun moreover set about defending annexation on the narrowest of grounds. Rather than seek to enumerate all the reasons for the policy and couch it in terms of "Manifest Destiny" – the strategy the Democratic party would later successfully employ – he boldly rested the case on the need to protect slavery from British influence in Texas. But Calhoun went still further. Not content with asserting the right of the South to determine the future of slavery independent of all outside interference – a policy that even those who disliked slavery might endorse – he urged annexation on classic proslavery grounds. In his famous letter to the British diplomat Richard Pakenham he confirmed the danger of a free-soil, British-dominated Texas. He added that only slavery had raised blacks to their present, unprecedented level of "civilization."[114]

The effect was to make it far more difficult for northern Democrats, and even border state southerners like Frank Blair to support the policy. Andrew Jackson himself was contacted. He immediately lent the project of annexation his enormous prestige. But his case rested not upon proslavery thought (of which he had none) but instead upon the Anglophobia which had marked his entire military and political careers

113. Freehling, *Road to Disunion*, pp. 397–398. It should be quite apparent that I am heavily indebted to Freehling's brilliant discussion of Texas annexation.

114. The Pakenham letter is to be found in Richard K. Crallé (ed.), *The Works of John C. Calhoun* 6 vols (Columbia, S.C., 1851–1855), pp. 333–339. Calhoun's motives in urging annexation on proslavery grounds are the subject of some controversy. Freehling argues that this was no blunder, merely a necessary corollary of Calhoun's suspicion of northern power and his conviction that the South must rely above all upon herself. Nevertheless Freehling is on more shaky ground, it seems to me, when he suggests that Calhoun was seeking to convert southerners who, in their millions, he implies, still yearned to "diffuse slavery away." Rather it was an attempt to force them to determine their priorities, to make them see that they could not both retain slavery and remain indifferent to the fate of Texas. Only because diffusion was not so widely desired – out of the upper South at any rate – did Calhoun succeed. See Freehling, *Road to Disunion*, p. 409.

and which had been rekindled by the prospect of a British presence on the southwestern frontier. Van Buren, however, saw matters differently and refused to support the demand for immediate annexation. This sealed his fate so far as the Democratic presidential nomination was concerned. It also marked the beginning of the unraveling of the Democratic consensus on slavery.[115]

IV

Gideon Welles later wrote that the year 1844 signified the beginning of the "ultimate downfall of the Democratic party." From that year, he declared, "confidence and united zeal never again prevailed." Of course, Welles did not mean that electoral victories ceased in 1844 or that Democratic administrations in Washington were henceforth unable to implement their chosen policies. Rather he had traced the discomfort of the party with the territorial question – on which it was torn apart in 1860 – to the year 1844.[116]

By the time of the election of that year there were at least three views of the Texas question within the Democratic party. One was that of Calhoun, Upshur and their followers, who believed and openly avowed that the purpose of annexation was to protect slavery, an institution of incalculable benefit to the nation. Texas, if it were to fall under British control or influence, would become, as Calhoun himself later put it, "an exposed frontier," one that could not be defended against "the aggressions of the abolitionists." And if abolition were indeed effected in Texas it would produce a racial war in the South "of the most deadly and desolating character to be terminated in . . . the ascendancy of the lowest and most savage of the races and a return to barbarism." Once again Calhoun was responding to the weaknesses of slavery.[117]

On the opposite wing of the Democratic party were the Van Burenites. Van Buren's refusal to entertain the annexation of Texas in the late 1830s was based in part on the accusations leveled against him by northern Whigs. For most of his long political career Van Buren was assailed by his enemies as a "doughface," a northern man with southern principles. The climate of the mid- and late 1830s, with abolitionist pressure calling forth an attack on northern civil liberties, made this a particularly damaging charge. Moreover, as early as 1838 John Quincy Adams had claimed

---

115. It is true, however, as Freehling points out, that Van Buren came out against Texas before seeing the Pakenham letter – *Road to Disunion*, pp. 409–411.
116. Howard K. Beale (ed.), *The Diary of Gideon Welles* 3 vols (N.Y., 1960), II, p. 387.
117. Calhoun to William R. King, Dec. 13, 1844 in *Correspondence of Calhoun*, II, p. 632. See the exchange between Webster and Calhoun in the Senate in Charles M. Wiltse *et al.* (eds), *The Papers of Daniel Webster, Series 4: Speeches and Formal Writings* 2 vols (Hanover, N.H., 1988), II, p. 532.

in Congress that a vast conspiracy was afoot, as a result of which slaveholders had moved into Texas, disregarded her laws, perpetrated a rebellion and applied for incorporation into the Union. Adams even claimed that the Jackson administration had orchestrated this conspiracy, a move intended as he believed so many Democratic policies were to further the interests of the slave power. In many parts of the North, therefore, there was considerable sensitivity to charges that the Democracy was soft on the slavery question.[118]

Van Buren indeed in 1842 before the Texas imbroglio wrote an important letter to Frank Blair, editor of the *Globe* and one of his most dedicated supporters, describing the pressures under which the alliance with the South had placed New York's Democrats:

> The truth is that the Democrats of this State have suffered so often, and so severely in their advocacy of Southern men and Southern measures, as to make them more sensitive in respect to complaints of their conduct from that quarter, than I could wish. They say, that they were broken down entirely by the support of Mr Crawford, that they were next brought to death's door by their efforts to sustain the Indian policy of Genl [sic] Jackson from which the South and West have derived such incalculable advantages, and that their party has suffered in every limb by the abolition question, and all this is undoubtedly true.

Although the Van Burenite opposition to Texas was well established by the early 1840s, an accommodation might still have been reached by adding a plank for Oregon to the party platform. Oregon might then in effect offset Texas and northern sentiment be propitiated. Indeed this was the strategy actually adopted when the party convention met. But by then it was too late. The grounds upon which Upshur and Calhoun placed the demand for Texas reduced the prospects for unity within the party. Many northern Democrats who objected to the annexation of Texas explained that they would have accepted the policy had it been defended without reference to slavery.[119]

But it was not merely the defense of slavery that alienated them. It was also the perpetrator of that defense. In the entire nation there was not a single figure whose actions were regarded with greater suspicion by Van Burenites than John C. Calhoun. Calhoun's pursuit of Texas annexation merely confirmed the fears that men like Frank Blair and Thomas Hart

118. *Speech of John Quincy Adams on Resolutions of Seven State Legislatures Relating to the Annexation of Texas* (Washington, D.C., 1838).
119. Van Buren to Blair, Sept. 12, 1842 quoted in William E. Smith, *The Francis Preston Blair Family in Politics* 2 vols (N.Y., 1933), II, p. 157; Henry D. Hunt, *Hannibal Hamlin of Maine, Lincoln's First Vice-President* (Syracuse, N.Y., 1964), p. 30; Muller, "Preston King," pp. 301–302.

Benton had entertained for years. According to Blair, Calhoun was deliberately out to frighten northern men away from annexation in order to further, yet again, his "favorite scheme of a southern confederacy." "I sincerely believe," he wrote to Jackson, "that Calhoun and his old Junto of conspirators are more than ever anxious to separate the South from the north. They want Texas only as a bone of contention." In these circumstances the Van Burenites were bound to resist the proposal. On April 20, 1844 Van Buren wrote a public letter declaring himself opposed to the immediate annexation of Texas. From that moment on his chances of returning to the White House disappeared.[120]

Jackson, however, was for once at odds with both Blair and Van Buren. He too believed that the British might excite a servile war by "abolitionizing" Texas and indeed he regretted bitterly his failure to annex Texas at the end of his administration. Jackson's grounds for taking Texas would have been far more acceptable to northern opinion than Calhoun's since he made no controversial claims for the superiority of slave labor. Nevertheless, he too wanted to defend slavery in Texas and such a goal was not calculated to recruit the needed northern votes for annexation.[121]

At this point Robert J. Walker stepped forward and presented what was in effect the third (and most important) Democratic response to the Texas question. Originally from Pennsylvania but now representing Mississippi in the United States Senate, Walker was exceptionally well placed to present policies relating to slavery to a northern audience. He was an ardent expansionist, like Calhoun and Upshur, but unlike them had no proslavery opinions. In February 1844 he wrote a public letter on the annexation of Texas. It had a circulation of millions; no letter in the entire antebellum era had greater significance. Walker's achievement was to present Texas as a policy which antislavery northerners and southerners might adopt. In this sense he did much to undo the damage to Democratic unity done by Calhoun and Upshur.[122]

Walker made a series of preliminary claims concerning Texas. He presented the rather dubious argument that Texas really belonged to the United States anyway, since it had been a part of the Louisiana Purchase, but then had been returned to Spain during the Monroe

---

120. Washington *Globe*, May 27, 1844; Blair to Jackson, July 7, 1844 in Bassett (ed.), *Correspondence of Jackson*, VI, pp. 299–300.
121. Bassett (ed.), *Correspondence of Jackson*, VI, pp. 201–202, 224, 230, 249, 272, 278, 290, 294, 299, 351.
122. *Letter of Mr Walker, of Mississippi, Relative to the Annexation of Texas . . .* (Washington, D.C., 1844) – which is conveniently reprinted in Frederick Merk, *Fruits of Propaganda in the Tyler Administration* (Cambridge, Mass., 1971), pp. 125–128; James P. Shenton, *Robert J. Walker, A Politician from Jackson to Lincoln* (N.Y., 1961).

administration – an act, he contended, of doubtful constitutionality. He also emphasized the potential profits available to northern merchants and capitalists if Texas joined the Union and compared this prospect with an alternative scenario in which Texas became independent and so powerful that other southern states, faced with economic stagnation, seceded from the Union to join her. But at the heart of Walker's argument were his predictions about slavery in the South. Slavery, he argued, ruined the soil. Hence new territory was needed. If Texas were annexed it would allow unwanted slaves throughout the South to be drained away into these newly acquired and fertile lands. Although this meant the acquisition of a new slave state, the "diffusion" of slavery encouraged by annexation would complete the process by which the border states would rid themselves of slaves. Moreover, since the land of Texas itself would eventually become unsuitable for slavery, the same process would recur and the slaves in Texas (and the Deep South generally) would be drained away into Latin America, the areas most suited to black men and women. Annexation would thus speed the arrival of the day when slavery would disappear from the United States.[123]

Without annexation, however, the process of soil debilitation would have very different results. Walker now stressed the dangers to the North of a huge migration of freed blacks competing for work with northern labor. Thus annexation offered a solution to the problem of slavery, and a solution to the problem of race relations. By annexing Texas, Americans would be furthering the prospect of a white Republic, with white Americans able to rejoice in the absence of all blacks, slave or free.[124]

Although Walker's argument may strike the modern reader as fanciful in the extreme, it impressed many contemporaries and seemed to them highly plausible. Slavery after all did seem to be slipping southward. Since 1776 the North had abolished it; more recently Delaware and Maryland were losing slaves, the Deep South was acquiring them. The key feature of the Walker argument was that it allowed Americans and especially Democrats to respond to the needs of the slaveholders, as perceived by men like Calhoun and Upshur, while at the same time allowing them to believe that their actions were compatible with antislavery prejudices or convictions. Little wonder then that the Walker pamphlet received such a joyous welcome.

Other Democrats endorsed his arguments quickly. Charles Jared Ingersoll, George Bancroft and David Henshaw, all northerners, voiced their approval, as did the *Democratic Review*. The *Review*'s attitude was

---

123. *Letter of Walker*, pp. 5–6, 10, 11–12, 14–26.
124. *Letter of Walker, passim*.

particularly important since it would soon become the leading expositor of "Manifest Destiny" doctrines. It now became possible for even northerners to claim that the acquisition of Texas was in conformity with the nation's "manifest destiny" to spread democratic institutions.[125] As far north as Massachusetts, in the very heartland of antislavery, Benjamin Hallett claimed that annexation of Texas by the United States rather than Britain would mean the "extension of democratic instead of monarchical institutions." The Van Burenites, of course, remained unmoved by these arguments but for most northern Democrats Texas, the favored scheme of overtly antidemocratic defenders of slavery like Calhoun and Upshur, had become a project designed to spread freedom and democracy.[126]

Yet the party was merely storing up trouble for the future. At the Baltimore party convention in 1844 Van Buren had a majority of delegates pledged to him. Some of them could claim, however, that the electoral process had been completed before the Texas question had been adequately debated, and certainly before Van Buren's position was known. At Baltimore the annexationists quickly seized control of the convention and rammed through a requirement that the nominee receive the support not of a simple majority but instead two-thirds of the delegates. Van Buren's chances now disappeared entirely. Of course for many radical Democrats the key questions were still the financial issues of the Jacksonian era and it was all these delegates could do to prevent the nomination of Lewis Cass, an avowed conservative. James K. Polk became the Democratic standard bearer because he combined a Van Burenite stance on the financial questions with a Jacksonian enthusiasm for the annexation of Texas. The Oregon plank was then added as a counterweight to Texas.[127]

Despite their relief at having destroyed the Cass candidacy, the bitterness of the Van Burenites knew no bounds. Moreover, though the Calhounites were delighted to have committed the party to the annexation of Texas, they were unenthusiastic about Oregon and in no way committed to "Manifest Destiny." Indeed, the forces of expansionism now unleashed would quickly develop their own momentum and reopen the slavery question in a way that would be still more destructive to party unity.

125. *Democratic Review,* XV (1844), pp. 11–16. Merk, *Fruits of Propaganda,* pp. 232–236. See also *Congressional Globe,* 28 Congress, 1 Session, Appendix, pp. 543, 722.
126. Benjamin F. Hallett, *Speech on Bunker Hill, July 4, 1844* (n.p., n.d.), pp. 5–8. Hallett also endorsed the diffusionist argument.
127. On the events of the Baltimore convention see Sellers, *Polk, Continentalist,* chapter 2. See also Sellers, "The Election of 1840" in Schlesinger and Israel (eds), *History of Presidential Elections,*" I, pp. 747–798.

V

For Robert J. Walker 1844 was an extremely busy year. Not only did he write his famous letter on Texas, he also played a key role at the Baltimore convention in overthrowing Van Buren. Moreover when the election was under way he wrote – anonymously this time – another pamphlet of some importance. This one was directed at southern Whigs. The Whig party had been thrown into turmoil by the Texas issue. No less than for the Democrats, 1844 was the year in which sectional tensions threatened to wreck party unity.[128]

Walker's anonymous pamphlet was entitled "The South in Danger." It suggested that his earlier effort, however persuasive it might have been to its readers, might not have entirely persuaded its writer. For Walker now attacked Clay as a proto-abolitionist and urged all southern Whigs who wished to preserve slavery to vote for Polk, largely on the grounds that the annexation of Texas was clearly in the slaveholder's interest. The fact that this claim did not easily square with Walker's earlier argument that Texas would expedite the removal of slavery from the United States was not lost on northern Whigs who now juxtaposed the two in order to embarrass the Democrats.[129]

So far as Texas was concerned, northern Whigs were not seriously divided. Without exception they opposed immediate annexation and few of them wanted annexation under any conditions. In part this was a reiteration of standard Whig hostility to territorial expansion. Webster, for example, declared that he had "on the deepest reflection, long ago come to the conclusion, that it is of very dangerous tendency and doubtful consequences to enlarge the boundaries of this country, or the territories over which our laws are now established." For "there must be some limit to the extent of our territory, if we would make our institutions permanent." This was standard Whig policy. The *National Intelligencer* advanced as one "conclusive reason" against the annexation of Texas the fact that American territory was already large enough. "It is infinitely more important," the newspaper insisted, "that we should people and improve what we have than grasp after more." As we have seen, these priorities were apparent when Whigs responded to issues like the disposal of western lands. The desire to diversify and "improve" led the party to frown upon policies that promoted migration to the West at the expense of the older states and it was this same desire that militated against the acquisition of more land, even when slavery was not involved.[130]

128. Merk, *Fruits of Propaganda*, pp. 31–32.
129. [Robert J. Walker], *The South in Danger* (Washington, D.C., 1844). For proof of Walker's authorship see Washington *Globe*, Oct. 3, 1845.
130. Wiltse (ed.), *Papers of Webster, Series 4* , II, p. 357; *National Intelligencer*, March 16, 1844.

In the case of Texas, of course, slavery was very much involved and this raised northern Whig opposition to crisis proportions. Although Webster, as we have seen, had dropped his earlier hostility to the three-fifths clause, this was on the grounds that the compromises of the constitution must be strictly honored. So far as the acquisition of new states was concerned he did not feel so bound and indeed the possibility of an additional over-representation of slave property and slaveholders continued to rankle with northern Whigs whenever the Texas question arose. More generally, however, they voiced strong objections to annexation simply on the grounds that it would tend to strengthen and perpetuate slavery. Charles Francis Adams, son of the former president, in the Massachusetts State Senate declared that annexation would make it "unequivocally certain" to the entire world that the United States government was dedicated to the protection of slavery. Without annexation, he argued, slavery would die out; with it, nine or ten new slave states would give the institution a new lease of life.[131]

Adams at this time was keen to remain within the Whig party but even more keen to see it become an active force for antislavery. His wing of the Massachusetts Whig party, soon to become known as the "Conscience" wing, threatened to withhold support from Clay if he did not oppose Texas. Joshua Giddings, meanwhile, in Ohio was predicting in 1844 a dissolution of the Union if Texas entered and was soon speculating about the demise of the Whigs and the rise of a purely antislavery party. In New York state at the same time William Seward was announcing to abolitionist Gerrit Smith that abolition should be "the first, the leading, the paramount question of the day."[132]

Most of these men would later be in the vanguard of the struggle for free soil. But the more conservative elements in the northern Whig party were in 1844 at any rate, equally firm on the Texas question. Robert Winthrop, who would later be associated with the conservative "Cotton" wing of Massachusetts Whiggery, avowed himself opposed to the annexation of Texas because it was unconstitutional, because it was a danger to the Union but "above all" because he was "uncompromisingly opposed to the extension of Domestic Slavery, or to the addition of another inch of Slaveholding Territory to this Nation." Millard Fillmore, a conservative New York Whig, made similar utterances. Little wonder then that when resolutions favoring the Texas project

131. Adams quoted in Kinley J. Brauer, *Cotton Versus Conscience: Massachusetts Whig Policies and Southwestern Expansion, 1843–1848* (Lexington, Ky., 1967), pp. 62, 71. My discussion of the divisions within Massachusetts Whiggery rests heavily on Brauer's very valuable work.

132. Giddings to Oran Follett, Nov. 18, 1844 in "Selections from the Follett Papers," *Quarterly Publications of the Historical and Philosophical Society of Ohio*, x (1915), p. 21; Van Deusen, *Seward*, p. 119.

were brought into the state legislatures of Indiana, Illinois and Ohio, the Whigs were found to be overwhelmingly opposed. As the Ohio *State Journal* had observed as early as 1842, "as a party, in the free states, the Whigs are opposed to the acquisition of Texas."[133]

Nevertheless, until Van Buren was thrown over by the Democrats, everyone believed that the presidential election would be fought on the old issues. At the same time as Van Buren announced his opposition to immediate annexation, Clay wrote his famous "Raleigh letter", in effect attaching impossible conditions to the project. Only if Mexico would not go to war would he entertain the idea. Yet "annexation and war with Mexico," he explained, were "identical." At this time Clay believed the Texas question of little significance. Alexander H. Stephens of Georgia concurred. Annexation, he announced, was "a miserable political humbug got up as a ruse to divide and distract the Whig party at the South.[134]

Though this was scarcely the purpose of the annexationists, Stephens was entirely correct as to the effect of their policy. Whereas northern Whigs united in opposition to Texas and were pleased with Clay's initial stance, in the South and especially the Lower South the party experienced grave difficulties. Stephens himself favored the eventual admission of Texas and the Georgia state party in June 1844 passed a unanimous resolution that "we are in favor of the annexation of Texas to the United States, at the earliest practicable period consistent with the honor and good faith of the nation." In Mississippi similar resolutions were passed. Felix Huston, a committed Whig, actually announced he would be supporting Polk purely for the sake of Texas.[135]

Other southern Whigs reacted differently. United States Senator Alexander Barrow, together with Waddy Thompson, a Clay Whig from South Carolina, in effect stood Walker's argument on its head. They claimed that since Texas would indeed drain slaves away from the upper South and the South East, this was a decisive objection to its annexation. They added that the fertility of Texan soil would merely compound the problem of overproduction of southern staples and thus depress the southern economy. But these efforts merely underlined Whig

133. Robert C. Winthrop, *Addresses and Speeches on Various Occasions* (Boston, 1852), p. 459; Severance (ed.), *Fillmore Papers*, II, p. 255; Holt, *Political Crisis of the 1850s*, p. 45; Ohio *State Journal*, March 16, 1842; Brauer, *Cotton Versus Conscience*, pp. 43–44.

134. The Raleigh letter is reprinted in Schlesinger and Israel (eds), *History of Presidential Elections*, I, pp. 814–817; Stephens to James Thomas, May 11, 1844 quoted in Merrill D. Peterson, *The Great Triumvirate: Webster, Clay, and Calhoun* (N.Y., 1987), p. 359.

135. These reactions are well covered in Cooper, *South and Politics of Slavery*, pp. 210–211.

difficulties; throughout the South they were soon reporting that the Democrats had found a vote-winner, indeed an election-winner.[136]

Clay himself realized that his southern support was ebbing and in the course of the election campaign issued further statements on the Texas question. In the second of his so-called "Alabama letters," while confirming that the time had not yet arrived to acquire Texas, he added that he had "however, no hesitation in saying that, far from having any personal objection to the annexation of Texas, I should be glad to see it." Whether this statement had the desired effect in the South is difficult to say, but it certainly produced consternation in the North where, as we have seen, many of his supporters were opposed to the acquisition of Texas on any terms and under any circumstances. Since the Liberty party also had a candidate in the field, northern Whigs were under some pressure; indeed Whig defections in New York state may have cost Clay not merely that state but the election itself.[137]

The campaign was by no means exclusively concerned with Texas. Although Oregon attracted little attention outside the Northwest, the older issues were not absent. The tariff in particular remained highly controversial. Here Polk wrote a letter which allowed Democrats in Pennsylvania, where pro-tariff sentiment was extremely strong, to claim quite disingenuously that he would not cut duties. Some southerners, by contrast, sought to maintain that Clay was not a high tariff candidate. Yet since southern opinion had, to some degree, shifted on this issue, Clay's long-time advocacy of protection was not the liability it once would have been. In most states the electorate was presented with a clear choice: Clay wanted to use the tariff to build up American manufactures, Polk wanted a revenue tariff, which would provide at best only incidental protection.[138]

In some states, like Missouri, the currency issue was more urgent than the Texas question. Even in the lower South, committed expansionists went out of their way to announce that they would not support a candidate who did not espouse orthodox Democratic policies on the older issues. Equally, as far north as Massachusetts, many Whigs continued to stress the importance of the tariff and even adduced, as an argument against Texas, the fear that more southwestern states would mean more votes for free trade. Yet overall the Texas issue was probably crucial. Some northern Democrats, especially the Van Burenites, were reluctant to

---

136. Cooper, *South and Politics of Slavery*, p. 212.
137. This letter is reprinted in Schlesinger and Israel (eds), *History of Presidential Elections*," I, pp. 855–856; Sellers, "Election of 1844," p. 798.
138. The Kane letter is reprinted in Schlesinger and Israel (eds), *History of Presidential Elections*," I, p. 853. See also David M. Potter, *The Impending Crisis, 1848–1861* (N.Y., 1976), p. 26.

support party policy, even though they were prepared to campaign for Polk. But the greatest effect was almost certainly on the Whigs. Not only did Clay's vacillations erode his northern support, he also ended with a lower percentage of the southern vote than either Harrison had obtained in 1840 or than Taylor would garner in 1848. He lost every state of the future confederacy except North Carolina and Tennessee. Nevertheless the election was extremely close, Clay trailing Polk by a mere 38,000 out of a total of over two and a half million votes cast. For the Whigs it was a shattering defeat. Henry Clay, a statesman "whom every nation on earth would be proud to call her own," had been rejected by the electorate in favor of James K. Polk, "a partizan of the lowest order." What would be the fate of the Republic?[139]

VI

The mere "partizan" who had been elected to the White House enjoyed considerable success as President. He managed to reintroduce the Independent Treasury and to reduce the tariff, as promised. So far as Oregon was concerned, his administration negotiated a compromise with Britain that averted all danger of war, even though it roused the ire of some northwestern expansionists within the party. Their wrath intensified when the President vetoed various internal improvements measures that would have benefited the West. But Polk was able to claim he was acting according to the strictest Democratic orthodoxy.[140]

The anger of northwestern Democrats was intensified when they contrasted the handling of the Oregon question with the administration's attitude to expansion into the Southwest. The annexation of Texas was virtually completed by Tyler in his last days in office but this proved to be only the beginning of the expansionism of the 1840s. The President, it gradually became apparent, had set his heart not merely on Texas but also, and far more significantly, upon the acquisition of additional territories from Mexico, particularly California.[141]

When the United States annexed Texas, Mexico broke off all diplomatic relations. But there were boundary disputes yet to be resolved. Polk ordered General Zachary Taylor to take his troops into the disputed area and subsequently to the Rio Grande. The Mexican government not surprisingly viewed this as yet another aggressive act and was outraged to

139. Mering, *Whig Party in Missouri*, p. 115; *Mississippian*, May 22, July 5, 1844; Rufus Choate, *Addresses and Speeches of Rufus Choate* (Boston, 1878), p. 344; *The Whig Text Book, or Democracy Unmasked* (n.p., n.d.), pp. 30–31.
140. Robert W. Johannsen, *Stephen A. Douglas*, (N.Y., 1973), pp. 183–184; Van Deusen, *Jacksonian Era*, pp. 206–207.
141. Polk's designs on California did not become clear until 1846.

learn of an American offer to purchase New Mexico and California. As far as Polk was concerned the rejection of this offer together with the Mexican refusal to negotiate other points of contention was a sufficient cause of war but on April 25, 1846, Mexican troops crossed the Rio Grande and had a skirmish with the American soldiers there. Since Polk claimed this territory as American soil he was able to portray Mexico as the aggressor and obtained on May 11 from Congress a declaration of war. Military success in the war resulted in a brief flirtation with the idea of taking all of Mexico but in the end Polk contented himself with California, New Mexico and the Rio Grande boundary. The nation had acquired an additional half-million square miles of territory and had suddenly become a major power on the Pacific ocean.[142]

To swallow California and New Mexico was relatively easy; to digest them would be far more difficult. The key issue would of course be the status of slavery in these new territories. Even before Polk took office the nation had plenty of evidence that territorial expansion would generate severe sectional animosities. This was the lesson of 1819–1821; it was also the lesson of 1843–1844. The Whigs were constantly warning that additional territory would produce renewed sectional strife. Yet the Polk administration pressed on regardless. The result was precisely as the Whigs had predicted. The Van Burenites were adamant that slavery should not go into the new territories and accordingly introduced the Wilmot Proviso; the Calhounites were equally adamant that no act of Congress should exclude the South from its share of the spoils of war and threatened secession. Both parties split hopelessly on the issue. The result was a political crisis such as the nation had never before experienced. Not until the summer of 1850 would it be resolved.[143]

We need to ask why the Polk administration pursued this course. Undoubtedly the President was impressed with the commercial possibilities available in California. Undoubtedly he wished to augment national power and glory. But why did he risk such calamitous consequences at a time when the economic recovery was under way and when there was still an enormous amount of land available in the nation, both North and South? To answer this question we must recur once again to Democratic ideology and the mainstream Democratic attitude to slavery.

Polk believed with Jackson that the slavery question had no place in national politics. He also believed with Jackson that men of good faith,

142. On the Mexican war (and the opposition to it) see K. Jack Bauer, *The Mexican War 1846–1848* (N.Y., 1974); Robert W. Johannsen, *To the Halls of the Montezumas: The Mexican War in the American Imagination* (N.Y., 1985); John H. Schroeder, *Mr Polk's War: American Opposition and Dissent, 1846–1848* (Madison, Wis., 1973); Otis A. Singleton, *The Mexican War* (Chicago, 1960).

143. See the *National Intelligencer*, March 16, 1844 for a typical Whig prediction of sectional strife.

both north and south of the Mason-Dixon line, would not seek to agitate the question. Since he was convinced that the new territories to be acquired from Mexico were unsuitable for slavery anyway, it followed that there was no scope for sectional controversy. Indeed in his view a concerted national effort to acquire more territory ought to diminish sectional antagonisms by bringing northerners and southerners together in a common purpose. The slavery issue would thus remain outside national politics and the nation could rejoice in the acquisition of its new empire.[144]

Like Jackson, Polk had in the middle 1830s condemned abolitionists and nullifiers alike. As president he easily slipped into the (Andrew) Jacksonian assumption that all good men would recognize this truth. Once again the corollary was that those who professed to believe otherwise were concealing nefarious purposes. Thus, writing in his diary, Polk dismissed the Wilmot Proviso as "a mischievous and foolish amendment." On one occasion he actually expressed incredulity that anyone could link slavery with the Mexican war. "What connection slavery had with making peace with Mexico," he remarked, "it is difficult to conceive." But Polk was equally critical of the Calhounites, whose leader, he believed, was merely out to secure the presidency for himself. "I now entertain," he confided to his diary, "a worse opinion of Mr Calhoun than I have ever done before." The South Carolinian was "wholly selfish, and I am satisfied has no patriotism." Polk recalled that "a few years ago he was the author of Nullification and threatened to dissolve the Union on account of the tariff." But during the current [i.e. Polk's] administration, "the reduction of duties which he desired has been obtained, and he can no longer complain." Yet still Calhoun was not satisfied. "No sooner is this done than he selects slavery upon which to agitate the country, and blindly mounts that topic as a hobby."[145] Not for nothing was Polk known as "Young Hickory."

In the North meanwhile, Polk continued, the Van Burenites, Democratic supporters of the Wilmot Proviso, had "as unpatriotically . . . shown by their course that they desire to mount the same hobby . . . and hope to be successful in their opposition to slavery." Both groups, he concluded in classic Jacksonian manner, "forget that the Constitution settles these questions which were the subjects to mutual concessions between the North and the South."[146]

144. Sellers, *Polk, Continentalist*, p. 214. On this aspect (as on every other) of Polk's thought, Sellers's work remains invaluable. Allan Nevins (ed.), *Polk, The Diary of a President, 1845–1849* (N.Y., 1929), Jan. 5, 1847 (p. 183), Jan. 23, 1847 (pp. 189–190).
145. Sellers, *Polk, Jacksonian*, p. 314; Nevins (ed.), *Polk, Diary* (N.Y., 1929), Aug. 10, 1846 (p. 138), April 6, 1847 (pp. 210–211).
146. Nevins (ed.), *Polk, Diary*, April 6, 1847 (pp 210–211).

Both sides, Polk believed, were prepared to agitate the slavery question in order to secure the presidency for their favored candidate. A few weeks before the end of his presidency he again confided his thoughts to his diary:

> The agitation of the slavery question is mischievous and wicked, and proceeds from no patriotic motive by its authors. It is a mere political question on which demagogues and ambitious politicians hope to promote their own prospects for political promotion. And this they seem willing to do even at the hazard of disturbing the harmony if not dissolving the Union itself.

Like Jackson himself, Polk never defended slavery in the abstract; he assumed that the subject should, and quite easily could, be kept outside the federal arena. Events of course were to give the lie to this assumption in the most dramatic manner.[147]

The initial impetus to protect slavery in Texas thus produced a significant outcome. Calhoun's strategy of linking annexation with a proslavery position had in effect been rejected by the Democratic party. But Calhoun's specific objective – the taking of Texas – had been fully endorsed. Once again Democratic ideology had come to the aid of the slaveholders. It was relatively easy to legitimate the drive for Texas by citing historical precedent. Once again the Democratic party was expanding the nation's boundaries. Once again it was responding to the needs of agriculture, with the slaveholder reconstituted as a mere farmer. Once again it was spreading the benefits of American democracy over the American continent. When Oregon was added, it became even easier to present "Manifest Destiny" as a crusade owing little or nothing to the existence of slavery or the needs of slaveholders.

The exponents of "Manifest Destiny" were engaging in no hypocrisy here. John L. O'Sullivan, originator of the phrase, was a Van Burenite with no desire to strengthen slavery; as we have seen he fully endorsed the Walker view of Texas annexation. President Polk himself was undoubtedly sincere in his view of the relationship – or rather non-relationship – between slavery and expansionism. Such sincerity was of great importance. It enabled the Democrats to present a compelling case to the electorate and in the process defeat the opposition's most eminent leader. Expansion had in this sense broken loose from its moorings in southern proslavery thought.[148]

147. Nevins (ed.), *Polk, Diary*, Dec. 22, 1848 (p. 359).
148. O'Sullivan would later become a southern sympathizer but not in the 1840s. Schlesinger, *Age of Jackson*, pp. 496–497; Sheldon H. Harris, "The Public Career of John Louis O'Sullivan" (Ph.D. dissertation, Columbia, 1958), *passim*.

The nation would never have tolerated an attempt to acquire Texas on strict Calhounite grounds. Thus the slaveholders who feared the rise of an antislavery Texas gained considerably from the manner in which the policy of annexation was promoted. Democratic ideology legitimated and strengthened the slaveholder's desires. But this newly acquired strength was soon to become a fatal weakness. The very people who could sincerely defend annexation as a policy unrelated to slavery were now in control. Their own logic made them zealous imperialists, eager to acquire yet more territory and, of course, oblivious to the effects it would have on the relations between North and South. The crisis of mid-century would be the direct result.

VII

If all Americans had shared the administration's view that slavery and expansionism were entirely separate matters, the nation would have absorbed the territories acquired from Mexico with a single, painless gulp. Such was not the case however and dissent quickly emerged. In August 1846 the President requested an appropriation of two million dollars to negotiate with Mexico. At that moment an unknown congressman from Pennsylvania, David Wilmot, moved that the bill be amended to make it "an express and fundamental condition to the acquisition of any territory," that "neither slavery nor involuntary servitude shall ever exist in any part of said territory." So was born the Wilmot Proviso, the key issue in the sectional crisis of the late 1840s. The amendment failed and for the remainder of 1846 reaction in the South was muted. But before long it became apparent that while the Proviso would command the support of a large majority of northerners, the South would secede rather than accept it. Only after another five years of debate and recrimination would the conflict over the acquisition of the new territories be resolved. And this resolution would itself prove highly fragile.[149]

What had happened to the Jacksonian issues, those which had been dominant in the 1830s and early 1840s? The Indian question had long since disappeared from the political arena. The banking controversy, though still raging in some states, was of only moderate importance in most and the Polk administration's successful reintroduction of the Independent Treasury removed it from federal politics for the remainder of the antebellum years. A key factor here was the return of prosperity from the mid-1840s. The Democrats' espousal of political democracy, though still of considerable importance, was no longer quite so divisive

149. I shall return to the question of the Proviso in the next section of this work.

as it once had been. The end of the recession and the waning of Democratic radicalism removed some of the anxieties of those most troubled by the new populism. Under these circumstances a political vacuum was being created. Little wonder, then, that sectional issues were becoming increasingly prominent. Yet these explosive issues did not merely replace the older questions. Instead they deepened some of the existing divisions within the parties even as they created new sectional alliances across party lines. By the end of 1846 the controversy over the Wilmot Proviso was about to erupt. Such were the fruits of the expansionist policies pursued by Presidents Tyler and Polk.

Although the change in the political agenda cannot be explained by a single factor, three considerations were clearly crucial. First, the recovery of the economy both removed the older Jacksonian issues like banking and the tariff as well as strengthening the commitment of each section to its preferred labor system. In the South the advocates of diversification away from cotton and agriculture would lose the initiative which the recession had (albeit briefly) given them; fortified by the acquisition of land from the Indians and from Mexico, the defenders of slave-based agriculture, especially in the Deep South, would continue to dominate. In the North the waning of Democratic radicalism and the continuing triumphs of a free-labor economy would confirm the superiority of "free institutions" and deepen the resolve of those hostile to slavery in the South and its prospective extension into the West. Thus, just as the recession brought the conflict between Whig and Democrat to a culmination and at the same time promoted intersectional harmony within each party, so its ending narrowed the gap between the parties but pushed the two sections further apart. This process, a long-term and continuing consequence of commercial development within the nation, would end only with the outbreak of the Civil War.

Secondly, we should note the key role played by the Democratic party in presiding over this changing agenda. It is tempting, following the example of the revisionist historians,[150] to blame Democratic politicians for their short-sightedness, their inability to predict the consequences of the expansionism they had themselves set in motion. But the whole process was initiated by the South and the Democracy's responsiveness to southern interests was one of the key features of antebellum politics. Only if we fail to see the structural connection between slavery, the Democratic party and the South will we be tempted to reduce the failures of the American polity to the weaknesses of individual statesmen. Once again the key fact was the functionally proslavery orientation of Democratic

150. I shall discuss revisionism in the sequel to this volume.

ideology and thus even of Democrats who rejected out of hand all explicitly and overtly proslavery arguments.

Finally, the vulnerability of slavery as perceived by Calhoun and Upshur was of the utmost importance. Whether they were right about the danger to be feared from British influence in Texas is something, of course, that historians will never know. It is clear, however, that the relationship between slave and slaveholder was seen even by its most zealous defenders as being so delicate as to require dramatic political action at the highest level. Undoubtedly many southerners believed that their hold over their slaves would be threatened by the emergence of a free-labor Texas. In effect what they were responding to, (though they would have indignantly and sincerely repudiated the proposition), was the hostility of the slaves to their enslavement, a hostility without which abolition in Texas, in the District of Columbia, or even in the black belt coastal regions of South Carolina would have been a hopeless and thus harmless prospect. Although northerners were equally Anglophobic when they contemplated the prospect of a British Oregon they did not fear for the relationship between employer and worker in the North. The importance of this asymmetry between the labor systems of North and South cannot be exaggerated; it was an asymmetry which left southern slaveholders obsessed with the effects of the class conflict endemic in their cherished but, as it would soon transpire, doomed labor system.

The search for compromise, 1847–1850

I

In the late 1840s sectional questions became of paramount importance in federal politics and in most of the states too. At Washington a number of controversial issues began to divide northerners and southerners. One of these concerned fugitive slaves. In 1842 the Supreme Court in *Prigg* v. *Pennsylvania* ruled that the return of fugitives was a federal matter. State and local officials could not be required to assist. Many northern states then passed Personal Liberty laws which actually forbade their officials from intervening. Since the federal government lacked the manpower to recapture fugitives, southerners felt that a new law was required but since many northerners viewed the fugitives as heroes, any effective legislation was sure to be enormously controversial.[151]

151. Norman L. Rosenberg, "Personal Liberty Laws and Sectional Crisis, 1850–1861," *Civil War History*, XVII (1971), pp. 25–44; Larry Gara, "The Fugitive Slave Law: A Double Paradox," X (1964), pp. 229–233; Gara, *The Liberty Line: The Legend of the Underground Railroad* (Lexington, Ky., 1961).

The antislavery sentiment that produced the Personal Liberty laws also created growing pressure to rid the District of Columbia at least of its notorious slave depots, if not of its slaves entirely. Outsiders brought their slaves into the District in order to sell them and the spectacle was extremely offensive to many northerners. Most southerners of course resented any interference by Congress with the rights of slaveholders and were determined to resist this proposal. Here was a second controversial question.

But the key issues dividing North and South had arisen, of course, as a result of the territorial acquisitions of Tyler and Polk. The most important question of all concerned the right of the federal government to legislate for the new territories and the expediency of doing so. There were many different opinions here, and the situation was further complicated by the fact that some were highly ambiguous, admitting of both a "northern" and a "southern" interpretation. In addition, we should note that some politicians changed their views in response to pressure either at home or from the other section. Nevertheless it is reasonable to suggest that there were four principal views of the territorial question.[152]

The first was what might be termed the free-soil position. Its adherents maintained that the federal government had the power to legislate over the territories and saw no reason why this power should not be exercised as a congressional majority saw fit. Since the North had a clear majority in the House of Representatives and could cast more presidential ballots than the South (despite the three-fifths clause), this left open the possibility that unless the Senate intervened, a majority could act so as to outlaw slavery in each and every territory acquired by the nation. In such an eventuality the balance between free and slave states in the Senate would soon disappear and northern preponderance throughout the government would grow. For many northerners the key to a peaceful and gradual abolition of slavery was the prohibition of slavery in new territories; for this very reason many, indeed most, southerners viewed free soil as a particularly insidious form of abolition and reacted accordingly. By the 1850s it was scarcely safer to be a free-soiler in the Middle or Deep South than to be a Garrisonian abolitionist. The free-soilers in the late 1840s rallied, of course, behind the Wilmot Proviso.[153]

The second position was the antithesis of the first and its adherents were almost exclusively southern. They denied that Congress had the

152. Here I am following the analysis in Potter, *Impending Crisis*, pp. 54–62. See also Allan Nevins, *Fruits of Manifest Destiny*, pp. 26–33; Robert Russel, "Constitutional Doctrines with regard to Slavery in Territories," *Journal of Southern History*, XXXII (1966), pp. 466–486.

153. This view was, of course, held also by those who took the more extreme position that the federal government should discountenance slavery wherever possible (and not merely in the territories). This would become the radical Republican position.

power to regulate slavery in the territories, which, they claimed, were the property of the entire nation. The federal government had no power to discriminate in favor of certain citizens and their property. Just as a northerner could take his horse or plough into a new territory, so a southerner could take his slaves. Since the federal government had no power to prevent this, did it not follow that the territorial governments, the creation of Congress, lacked the power too? In February 1847 John C. Calhoun introduced a resolution to this effect; it stood diametrically opposed to the Wilmot Proviso.[154]

The third and fourth views were attempts at compromise. An obvious way of disposing of the lands acquired from Mexico was to extend the imaginary line at 36° 30', drawn across the Louisiana Purchase during the Missouri Crisis, to the Pacific. The proponents of this solution in effect acknowledged the right of Congress to legislate upon slavery in the territories but implied that the power should be exercised in a spirit of conciliation and forbearance. In the late 1840s James Buchanan was perhaps the principal advocate of this strategy, but it also had the backing of the Polk administration. As David Potter has observed, this solution was utterly unambiguous. But its lack of ambiguity was a liability rather than an asset. In this respect it contrasted sharply with the fourth position, which rested squarely upon the "popular sovereignty" formula.[155]

Popular sovereignty meant congressional non-interference with slavery in the territories. The inhabitants of the territory themselves would be left to determine whether slavery would or would not be allowed. But a crucial ambiguity was present. At what stage would the decision be made? Since no-one denied that a state could abolish or introduce slavery as it pleased, it followed that from the moment of entry into the Union the inhabitants of a territory-becoming-a-state could take the fateful decision. But this left the earlier phase shrouded in doubt and ambiguity. Could a territorial assembly exclude slavery? Clearly this question was of some importance since if slaveholders were absent during the territorial stage there would be no proslavery constituency when statehood was granted. In the 1840s this difference was deliberately left unresolved; northerners tended to the view empowering the territorial legislature, southerners to the opposite view. In the late 1840s the principal exponents of the doctrine were Lewis Cass, Daniel Dickinson and, above all, Stephen A. Douglas.[156]

154. Charles M. Wiltse, *John C. Calhoun, Sectionalist, 1840–1850* (N.Y., 1951), pp. 303–305.
155. Potter, *Impending Crisis*, p. 57.
156. Johannsen, *Douglas*, pp. 227–228, 137–138.

One should not exaggerate the distinctiveness of these various positions. In the 1840s no-one could know whether or not slaveholders
would enter the new territories, whatever the congressional rulings.
No-one could be certain whether the land and climate were suitable for
slavery or not. As a result many northerners, including Douglas himself,
were able to claim that the effect of popular sovereignty would be free
soil. Equally some of those who believed in the southern interpretation of
his doctrine held that it would facilitate the spread of slavery just as surely
as Calhoun's strategy. Ambiguity and uncertainty bedeviled the debate
over the Mexican cession.

Precedents could be cited to different, even contradictory effect. Some
evidence suggested that there were doubts in the minds of some of the
Founding Fathers about congressional power over the territories. One of
Madison's letters could be so construed and, in addition, the Supreme
Court's decision in *US* v. *Gratiot* in 1840 decreed that federal authority
over territories extended only to disposing of the land within them.
Nevertheless there was an enormous body of precedent for the opposite
view. The Northwest Ordinance had been reaffirmed by Congress in
1789 and repeatedly thereafter with the organization of many other territories. Washington, Adams, Jefferson, Monroe and Jackson (amongst
others) had all acknowledged Congress' power over slavery in the territories. Indeed until the acquisition of Texas, few national leaders ever
questioned it.[157]

On the other hand, there were many precedents for the view that this
power should not be exercised except in particular circumstances.
Congress had accepted land ceded by some of the southern states with
the stipulation that antislavery regulations not be imposed. The Missouri
Compromise had strengthened this tradition. Experience thus suggested
that while Congress did indeed have the power, it would employ it with
great forbearance in southern latitudes.

In a sense therefore, the most obvious solution to the territorial problem of the 1840s was the extension of the Missouri line. The advocates
of popular sovereignty, on the other hand, were reduced to the vague
claim that during the Revolutionary era, the colonists had acted like
"squatter sovereigns." It was thus ironic that the first of the solutions
to be discarded in the late 1840s was the extension of the Missouri line,
while the strategy that began to consume the time and energies of the
entire nation, and which dominated the debate over the territories until
1860, was popular sovereignty.

As we shall see, one reason was the congruence between popular sovereignty and Democratic ideology. Here as so often, party considerations

157. Nevins, *Fruits of Manifest Destiny*, pp. 26–28.

interacted with sectionalism.[158] Indeed in the late 1840s and during the crisis of 1850–1851, party and sectional loyalties jostled for supremacy. As Potter has observed, attachment to party prevented the emergence of a clear and unified sectional majority while loyalty to section undermined the power which either party, when in a majority, might command. Hence the years between the introduction of the Wilmot Proviso and the passage of the Compromise measures in 1850 were marked by considerable confusion and uncertainty.[159]

II

Let us now turn to the Democratic party in these years. As we have already noted, when sectional issues were discussed there were in effect three groupings within the party. One was a northern, free soil group who rallied to the Wilmot Proviso and who would with a few exceptions desert the party in 1848 to support Martin Van Buren, the Free Soil candidate, against the regular party nominee, Lewis Cass. The second group were the followers of John C. Calhoun, as heavily concentrated in the South as the free-soilers were in the North. The third group were the moderates, many of whom began by supporting an extension of the Missouri line, but who ended by endorsing popular sovereignty. As we have seen, this doctrine allowed significantly different interpretations; it was thus able to attract support from all sections of the nation.[160]

It was the Democratic free-soilers, however, who commanded most attention in these years. Martin Van Buren and his northern disciples had been archetypal Democrats in many cases since the 1820s and we have already noted his key role in creating the party. Clearly Van Buren, a man who placed a high premium upon party and party loyalty, must have had powerful motives for deserting the Democracy in 1848 and accepting the Free Soil nomination.[161]

---

158. With hindsight the extension of the Missouri line might seem to have offered the best chance of sectional reconciliation. It failed for many reasons, one of which was the tendency to reduce, rather than augment, the power of the federal government in these years. The abandonment of congressional power over slavery in the territories was not unrelated to the abandonment of congressional power over the nation's banks. Both derived their force from Democratic notions of *laissez-faire* and from Democratic localism.
159. Potter, *Impending Crisis*, p. 90.
160. Chaplain Morrison, *Democratic Politics and Sectionalism* (Chapel Hill, 1967); James C. N. Paul, *Rift in the Democracy* (Philadelphia, 1951); Richard H. Sewell, *Ballots for Freedom: Antislavery Politics in the United States, 1837–1860* (N.Y., 1976).
161. Donald B. Cole, *Martin Van Buren and the American Political System* (Princeton, 1984), pp. 407–426; John Niven, *Martin Van Buren: The Romantic Age of American Politics* (N.Y., 1983), pp. 566–589; Herbert D.A. Donovan, *The Barnburners* (N.Y., 1925).

To some extent the Van Burenites were motivated by sheer revenge. They had been outraged by events at the Baltimore convention and were, as ever, convinced that the sinister figure of John C. Calhoun was responsible for the treachery perpetrated against their leader. More generally they wanted retribution against the South. Thus Benjamin F. Butler, a Barnburner (as the Van Burenites were termed in New York state), in 1848 proposed the creation of a new northern Democracy which would teach the South a lesson and "thus render a great and lasting service to the country and the world." But it was not merely the events at Baltimore that generated the Van Burenites' hostility. As we have seen, they had repeatedly complained about the demands made over many years by the southern allies. They felt they had made sacrifices time and again for the sake of party unity and had incurred the damaging charge of "doughfaces" in the North. In this context the attempt to take Texas on explicitly proslavery grounds was the final straw and for this reason Silas Wright, Van Buren's first lieutenant, after his leader had been overthrown refused to accept the nomination for President or for Vice-President.[162]

Yet although the annexation of Texas was given a ringing endorsement in the party's platform in 1844, it was, as we have seen, presented as a crusade for "Manifest Destiny" rather than for the defense of slavery. Some of the Van Burenites could, albeit with difficulty, swallow this. Others during the election campaign sought to ignore the question. In New Hampshire, for example, John P. Hale, who disagreed with the party over Texas, nonetheless worked hard for Polk. Even those who publicly criticized the platform were relatively pleased that the candidate was Polk. John A. Dix remarked that "if we could not have Mr Van Buren, certainly they could not do so well as to give us Col. Polk" and Silas Wright observed that after Van Buren "Governor Polk was by very, very far my first choice over all the other candidates." Indeed Polk's nomination was viewed as a partial triumph, since it meant that Cass and his supporters had been denied. One Van Burenite reported that he and his friends were "weeping with one eye while we smile with the other at the overthrow of the intriguers and traitors."[163]

162. Butler to Van Buren, May 29, 1848 quoted in McGee, "Issues and Factions," p. 183; Sellers, "Election of 1844," pp. 769–770, 772.
163. Richard H. Sewell, *John P. Hale and the Politics of Abolition* (Cambridge, Mass., 1967), p. 49; Dix to Flagg, June 14, 1844 quoted in Martin Lichterman, "John Adams Dix, 1789–1879" (Ph.D. dissertation, Columbia, 1952), p. 131; Wright to Butler, June 3, 1844 quoted in Judah P. Ginsberg, "The Tangled Web: The New York Democratic Party and the Slavery Controversy, 1844–1860" (Ph.D. dissertation, University of Wisconsin, 1974), p. 41; O'Sullivan to Van Buren, May 29, 1844 quoted in Sellers, *Polk, Continentalist*, p. 98. Schlesinger, *Age of Jackson*, p. 438 points out that some prominent Democrats endorsed Polk while repudiating the Texas plank in the platform.

Within a short time, however, the Van Burenites were utterly disillusioned with Polk. In part the problems arose over the patronage. Control of patronage was of vital importance since it gave a great boost not simply to the party in power but also, and perhaps more importantly, to the faction of the party that was favored. The Barnburners believed themselves the only true Democrats in New York state. Their conservative opponents, the Hunkers, led by such men as Daniel S. Dickinson and Horatio Seymour, and (though less consistently) by William Marcy, they thought more or less corrupt. Since they identified Polk with the radical wing of the party, they expected him to confer all federal patronage upon them in order to build up Barnburner power within the state. But Polk's priorities were rather different. He sought above all unity. "I will do, as I have done, Mr Martin Van Buren's friends full justice in the bestowal of public patronage," he observed in his diary, "but I cannot proscribe all others of the Democratic party in order to gain their good will." Hence he conferred federal patronage upon Barnburners and Hunkers alike.[164]

Polk's problems were compounded by the fact that while the Barnburners were his natural allies on economic questions, it was the Hunkers who were most amenable to the territorial expansion upon which he had set his heart. In these circumstances an attempt at even-handedness in the distribution of patronage made good sense. The result, however, was that both sides were left feeling embittered. Moreover, the Barnburners felt that Polk, in favoring the Hunkers, was responding to southern pressure and intimidation. For the Hunkers were not only conservatives on the great financial issues; they were at the same time more conciliatory towards the South.

The Barnburners, by contrast, and the Van Burenites in other northern states, were both radical on the old economic questions and more inclined to adopt an antislavery, free soil position. The northern Democrats who defected from the party in 1848 over the slavery question came disproportionately from the radical wing of the party. Historians have noted this correspondence frequently; they have been less successful in accounting for it.[165]

Only by recurring to Democratic ideology can the pattern be explained. Pressure from Calhoun and other southerners in effect exposed the extent to which the Democratic party functioned to support slavery and created

164. Joseph G. Rayback, "Martin Van Buren's Break with James K. Polk: The Record," *New York History*, XXXVI (1955), pp. 51–62; Polk quoted in Schlesinger, *Age of Jackson*, p. 445.
165. Undoubtedly this failure owes something to the fragmentation of American history, as a result of which those who have studied the Jacksonian era have not concerned themselves with later sectional controversies and *vice versa*. Only recently has this trend been reversed.

the possibility of a redirection of Jacksonian arguments. The latent support which Democratic principles had always given to slavery allowed southerners to fasten onto them when antislavery sentiment from the North (or from Britain) threatened. But by the 1840s the price was a high one. As southerners seized upon and modified Democratic principles, the party's southern orientation became ever more apparent. What had previously been covert support became increasingly overt. The consequence was the Van Burenite defection. For the Van Burenites now employed the traditional radical Democratic arguments against the "aristocracy" but turned them against the slaveholders themselves.

The common theme in Van Burenite hostility both to grasping bankers and aggressive slaveholders was the commitment to equality. As we have seen, Democratic social thought, and especially that of radical Democrats, pitted the self-interest of the majority against that of the predatory minority. They followed John Taylor of Caroline in his assumption that "it would be as unnatural for majorities to fatten upon minor interests, as for pastures to eat the herds grazing on them." Yet as Taylor implied, it was as natural for the minority to fatten upon the majority as for herds to eat the pasture. In Taylor's thought the aristocratic minority was the interest that defended banks, paper money, tariffs and the funding system. This was the aristocracy which Jefferson had denounced too. As we have also seen, while Jefferson had also made antislavery utterances and had inspired some antislavery legislation, in particular the Northwest Ordinance, he had nevertheless managed to keep these concerns not only subordinate to, but separate from, his activities as a member and indeed the founder of the Republican party. In effect what the Van Burenites did was to take the social philosophy of Taylor and Jefferson and do what neither Virginian had done: differentiate the slaveholder from the yeoman farmer and pronounce the former the enemy of the latter. In a word, northern free soil Democrats reconstituted the "aristocracy" as an alliance of predatory slaveholders. Jeffersonian free soil principles, as enunciated in the Northwest Ordinance, were then invoked and the departure from established party tradition was explained as a defensive reaction against southern aggression.[166]

For the Van Burenites the acquisition of Texas was bad enough. But at least Texas already contained slaves. If more territory were to be taken from Mexico, this would be land from which slavery had by Mexican law been outlawed. When David Wilmot introduced his famous Proviso, he was seeking to prevent the spread of slavery into hitherto free territory. For the Barnburners this was a disgraceful prospect. John Van Buren, son

166. John Taylor, *Arator* (new ed.: Indianapolis, 1977), pp. 94–95.

of the former President, found "the idea of marching, in the nineteenth century, with the immense power of this free republic, upon an enfeebled and half civilized people and forcing upon them the institution of slavery" to be "so repugnant" that if he "could be satisfied that this war is prosecuted to plant human slavery in Mexico," he "would join the Mexicans tomorrow in resisting such oppression." The Proviso, of course, was an attempt to prevent such an outcome. It was the product of a growing distrust of the Polk administration and, above all, a growing suspicion of the political ambitions of the South.[167]

The outrage with which almost all southern Democrats denounced the Proviso merely confirmed these suspicions. Indeed if southern Democrats had set out to antagonize the Barnburners they could hardly have performed the task more effectively. First had been the demand for the annexation of Texas, explicitly recommended (by some of them) as a means of strengthening slavery. Then at the Baltimore convention they had flouted the majority principle (by passing the two-thirds rule). Next, by repudiating the Wilmot Proviso, they had denied the right of the federal government to prevent the spread of slavery. Finally they had corrupted enough northern Democrats (Hunkers) to threaten the purity of the party even in the North. Little wonder that Benjamin Butler wished to teach them a lesson.[168]

From 1847 onwards radical Democrats in the North rang the changes on this theme. In April 1848 an Address of the Democratic members of the New York state legislature, much of it written by Martin Van Buren himself, was a classic statement of Democratic free soil principles. It began with sentiments that might have been from the pen of John Taylor of Caroline. "From the first institution of government to the present time," the report announced, "there has been a struggle going on between capital and labor for a fair distribution of the profits resulting from their joint capacities." In the 1830s and the early 1840s radical Democrats would have followed this assertion with a denunciation of banks, merchants or manufacturing elites – again in the tradition of John Taylor. But gradually the address redirected attention onto the slaveholders of the South. "In the early stages of society," it continued, "the advantages was [sic] altogether on the side of capital; but as education and intelligence are diffused the tendency is stronger towards that just equality which all wise and good men desire to see established." But slavery obstructed this process. For "the wealthy capitalists who own slaves disdain labor, and the whites who are compelled to submit to it,

---

167. Van Buren quoted in Muller, "Preston King," p. 422.
168. John Ashworth, "The Democratic-Republicans before the Civil War: Political Ideology and Economic Change," *Journal of American Studies*, xx (1986), pp. 375–390, esp. 379–380.

are regarded as having fallen below their natural condition in society." The non-slaveholders could not "act on terms of equality with the masters for those social objects which, in a community of equals, educate, improve, and refine all its members." By degrading manual labor, slavery introduced unacceptable inequalities into society.[169]

In New York city the *Evening Post* developed these themes with great skill. Edited by William Cullen Bryant, it had been in the vanguard of radical Democracy since the time of Jackson's presidency. On April 27, 1848, it noted that whereas, in a free society, "social equality" was the natural tendency, in the South "a few slave owners exercise a vast influence in a community with a small population and control its political destiny." "They are as powerful at the south and west," the paper continued in a telling comparison, "as the manufacturers at the east." A week later the comparison with bankers and manufacturers was made still more explicit. The advocates of protection, Bryant noted, had tried everything to retain their privileges – "but in vain." For "like the paper money interest," the tariff interest was "in conflict with equal political rights and it could not be sustained." Now for a third time the struggle was being waged:

> The slave interest at the South appears now to be acting this part. It claims to be the whole south, instead of a mere interest that extensively prevails there. It looks up to the constitution of the United States as its shield and as pledged to be the instrument of its diffusion across the continent. It threatens terrible things. It will not allow us to have a President unless of its own selection. So talked the paper money interest. But Andrew Jackson came into office for a second term, like a mighty conqueror. It is no new thing for a sectional interest to set itself up for the sole interest, not only of its own section, but of the whole country.

The categories of thought which radical Democrats had employed for many years were here very evident. Slaveholders, however, had now been inserted into the place previously occupied by bankers and manufacturers.[170]

Hence southern slaveholders attracted precisely the distrust which bankers had aroused earlier. They were an aristocracy: according to David Dudley Field, "the most stupendous aristocracy of land-holders which the world contains." Especially distasteful to free soil Democrats was the three-fifths clause, by which slavery, in the words of a

---

169. "Address of the Democratic Members of the Legislature, [April 12, 1848]," in New York *Evening Post*, April 20, 1848. This Address is a classic statement of what would later become the principles of the Democratic-Republicans.
170. New York *Evening Post*, April 27, May 4, 1848.

Barnburner Mass Meeting in 1847, "denies to the masses that equality of suffrage which is an inherent element in the Democratic system." While the constitution required northerners to tolerate this arrangement they were in no sense required to extend it. John Niles of Connecticut in a letter to his state's Free Soil Convention argued that "like all other exclusive and monopoly interests, the slaveholding interest is jealous and restive, and constantly seeking to strengthen and fortify its own power." "In these respects," he continued, "its spirit and tendency are the same as an aristocracy, which is another form of privilege or exclusive interest." Niles concluded that "history abundantly proves that, in a confederacy of States, some of which are democratic, and others aristocratic, the latter have been ambitious, restive, intriguing and selfish, to the disturbance, and in the end to the ruin of the confederacy."[171]

The defection of 1848 was thus, as far as the free soil Democrats were concerned, an attempt to check the growing, "aristocratic" power of the South. Although without exception they supported the Wilmot Proviso, they had not sought to make it a plank in the Democratic platform, still less a test of party orthodoxy. According to Gideon Welles of Connecticut, it was preposterous to seek "to make Connecticut conform to the views of South Carolina on the subject of permitting or excluding slavery in the territories," while David Wilmot agreed that Democrats who supported his Proviso were quite willing to have the party remain neutral on the question.[172] In a letter to the Buffalo Convention which nominated him for president, Martin Van Buren explained that the founders of the Republic had limited the role of slavery within the nation by abolishing the international slave trade. Slavery was to depend on state laws, not repealable by the federal government. Thus all good men would display "a spirit of considerate forbearance towards the institution, where it was placed under the control of Congress." Nevertheless the Northwest Ordinance, together with the progress being made towards emancipation in the North at that time, had ensured a majority of states would become free. Why had this expected preponderance, "with knowledge of which" the non-slaveholding states had "assisted in investing the institution of slavery with the privileges and guarantees of the Constitution," failed to materialize? According to the former president, it had been "annihilated" by aggressive slaveholders with the result that there were now as many

---

171. David Dudley Field, *Speeches, Arguments, and Miscellaneous Papers of David Dudley Field* 3 vols (N.Y., 1870), III, p. 22; "Mass Meeting at Herkimer, 26 Oct., 1847," in New York *Evening Post*, Nov. 4, 1847; "Letter of John M. Niles to the Free Soil State Convention of Connecticut," in *The Barnburner*, Aug. 12, 1848.
172. Welles quoted in Eric Foner, *Free Soil, Free Labor, Free Men: The Ideology of the Republican Party before the Civil War* (N.Y., 1970), p. 152; letter from David Wilmot in *Barnburner*, Aug. 5, 1848.

slave as free states. By preventing the spread of slavery into the new territories of the West the free soil Democrats would restore the earlier compromises of the constitution and "neutralize the injurious tendencies" of slavery, "our one element of discord, more difficult to deal with than any to which our free institutions are exposed." For Van Buren and indeed the Van Burenites as a whole, the task in 1848 was to restore the traditional compromises of the constitution.[173]

The problem for southerners, of course, was that Democratic neutrality on the question of slavery in the territories would allow a bipartisan northern majority, unfettered by party ties, sooner or later to pass the Proviso. As unequivocal majoritarians, northern radical Democrats saw nothing wrong here. Formerly southern Democrats (apart from the Calhounites) had shared this faith in the majority but the days of sectional harmony within the party were already numbered. In fact both the northern and the southern wing were in the process of revising the principles of the 1830s. Northern Democrats were modifying their commitment to agriculture, for example,[174] southern Democrats were reexamining their attachment to majoritarianism.[175] But even where there was ideological unity, problems abounded. Most of the Democratic defectors of 1848 shared the traditional party prejudice against blacks. Wilmot himself, who became the dominant figure among Pennsylvania's Free-Soilers, ignored or refused to acknowledge the evil done to blacks by slavery. Moreover he was concerned to keep all blacks, whether slave or free, out of the new territories. Indeed he explained to Congress that in introducing his Proviso he had not been impelled by any "squeamish sensitivity upon the subject of slavery," or any "morbid sympathy for the slave." Instead his concern was to "plead the cause and rights of the free white man." This racism was standard among Democrats, both north and south of the Mason-Dixon line. As we have seen, it tended to undermine abolitionism (unless it could be coupled with colonization). But by the same token the desire to rid the territories of blacks, whether slave or free, promoted the cause of free soil.[176]

The Democratic defections in 1848 were, as one would have expected, greatest in New York state. The Barnburners were joined, however, by illustrious party members from other northern states. In most of the South of course, they commanded no support. Missouri, however, was

173. Letter of Martin Van Buren to the Committee of the Buffalo Convention in *Barnburner*, Aug. 26, 1848.
174. I shall return to this question in the sequel to this volume. I have attempted a preliminary analysis in "Democratic-Republicans before the Civil War," pp. 386–390.
175. I shall also examine this development in the sequel to this volume.
176. *Congressional Globe*, 29 Congress, 2 Session, Appendix, p. 317, 30 Congress, 1 Session, Appendix, pp. 1076–1079.

a partial exception. Here Thomas Hart Benton, a leading figure in the Democratic party and a senator for almost thirty years, did not actually vote for Van Buren in 1848. But he made it clear that he shared the views of the Barnburners on almost every issue. On the one hand Benton argued that the Wilmot Proviso ought instead to be referred to as the "Jefferson Proviso." If passed it would be an entirely constitutional act, resistance to which would be treason. In view of the esteem in which Benton held Jefferson, one would have thought this constituted a wholehearted endorsement of the Proviso. On the other hand, however, he believed it unnecessary, since the territories in question would become free anyway. But Benton presented another, a "stronger reason to claim forbearance." Opposition to the Proviso was Calhoun's "last card." It was the latest and last in a series of ploys intended either to make Calhoun president or to break up the Union. "Take that last card from him," Benton exulted, "and his game is up; – bankruptcy comes upon him – political bankruptcy." As usual Benton believed that the slavery question should be kept out of national politics but, unlike southern militants, he had "seen no danger to the slave property of any state in this Union by the action of Congress." Hence he could not "contribute to alarm the country by engaging in discussions which assert or imply danger." Such discussions were, of course, the stock-in-trade of the Calhounites.[177]

Although Benton advised against the bolt of 1848, he fully shared the Barnburners' desire to see the western territories become free. In a sense, his position was even more threatening to slaveholders than that of the northerners since he was himself a southerner and a slaveholder. He explained that, though a slaveholder, "my personal sentiments . . . are against the institution of slavery, and against its introduction into places in which it does not exist." "If there was no slavery in Missouri to-day," he declared, "I should oppose its coming in; if there was none in the United States, I should oppose its coming into the United States; as there is none in New Mexico or California I am against sending it to those territories, and could not vote for such a measure."[178]

Benton was not the only prominent Missouri Democrat to hold such sentiments. In a remarkable *Address to the Democracy of Missouri* written around 1849, a group of party members (who included two of Frank Blair's sons) complained that a group of slaveholders acting in combination had controlled the federal government for years. In this they resembled the banking interest. "But as the people did at last succeed in taking their government out of the hands of banks, so we anticipate,

177. *Speech Delivered by Hon. Thomas Hart Benton at Jefferson . . . Mo., . . . 26 May, 1849* (n.p., n.d.), pp. 16–17.
178. *Speech of Benton*, p. 17.

that while the slave-holders will be left undisturbed in their possessions, that [sic] the policy of the government will not hereafter be dictated by them." Needless to say, the guiding spirit of the slaveholding cabal was John C. Calhoun, whose "subtle and ingenious intellect has been the source of all the artful and numerous obstacles which have been thrown in the way of the Jefferson Proviso." Nevertheless these Missourians felt that the danger was passing "of alienating the Democracy of Missouri from the Radical Democracy of the North, with whom they have been so long associated."[179]

But the Blairs and their colleagues were not content to excoriate Calhoun. In addition they launched a searing attack on the social and political systems of South Carolina and Virginia. "The restricted suffrage which a property qualification imposes and the rotten borough systems which exist in Virginia and South Carolina, by which the poor white man is placed exactly upon a footing with the negro, and is actually less considered in the legislation of the country than the slave," the report announced, "do not make them model republics for Missouri." The slaveholders in these states constituted an aristocracy in whom "all political power and social consideration" was vested. As a result "the laboring class" was "a degraded class," precisely as in England. In Missouri the number of slaveholders was smaller and the ease with which land could be acquired made this effect "less sensibly felt." Yet many Missouri Democrats were prepared to throw in their lot with the South and already "the wishes of even the few Slaveholders in Missouri are more regarded than those of every body else, although they are not as one in a hundred of our population." The solution was a simple one: "so far . . . from permitting the extension of this institution, according to southern policy, the contrary policy – the Northern democratic policy – is the true one for us." This was "to keep free territories free; free not only to all within the Union, but free to every lover of freedom throughout the world."[180]

This Address contained the most explosive sentiments, sentiments which would not even have been allowed expression in the Deep South. The fascination of Missouri politics, of course, was that the opposite view, an overt proslavery, was also in evidence in the state. Hence in the 1850s Missouri would witness a dramatic confrontation between the advocates of free labor and the defenders of slavery. It was prefigured in the events of the late 1840s, events triggered by the territorial acquisitions of the Polk presidency.[181]

179. M. Blair, M. R. Fitzpatrick *et al.*, *Address to the Democracy of Missouri* (n.p., n.d.), pp. 4, 12.
180. Blair *et al.*, *Address to Democracy of Missouri*, pp. 12–13.
181. In the sequel to this volume I hope to look in greater detail at the politics of Missouri in the 1850s – a subject of the greatest importance.

III

At the opposite wing of the Democratic party stood John C. Calhoun and his followers. Just as Van Buren and Calhoun had been rivals to succeed Jackson, so the two men now found themselves at the head of the two antithetical groups within the party. Until his death in 1850 Calhoun remained the leading opponent of compromise with the North and the leading, though not the most extreme, advocate of southern rights. But whereas Van Buren's New York was deeply divided, with both a vigorous Whig party and a powerful conservative Democrat (Hunker) faction, Calhoun was able to carry almost the entire state of South Carolina with him. There was a small number of Whigs to contend with but they posed no threat and the old division between Unionists and nullifiers was by the early 1840s virtually healed. The only real opposition to Calhoun would come from those who wanted more extreme action, men like Robert Barnwell Rhett who already yearned for secession. These radicals chafed under his leadership and occasionally rebelled but there was no doubt who controlled the state.[182]

Unlike his northern rival, therefore, Calhoun was not really constrained by the need to retain moderate support in his home state. Nevertheless, he faced real constraints elsewhere. He was confronted in the 1840s with his old dilemma. Should he bid for national support within the Democratic party or should he seek to obliterate party lines entirely and try to create a united South? The former strategy was highly tempting. Not only did it offer the prospect of the White House, but a Democratic party under his control would be able to beat back abolitionism, together with free soil, and at the same time lower the tariff. A strict construction of the constitution would then become party orthodoxy, states' rights would be safeguarded, and the slaveholders of the South would be able to breathe again. Whenever there were signs that this strategy might be workable, Calhoun's thoughts turned once again to the Democratic party and the presidency.

Yet the strategy brought problems. As we have seen, Calhoun explained the growth of abolitionist sentiment in the North in part by reference to the baneful effects of party. Indeed he was highly suspicious of parties even in the South, since they seemed to him to threaten the rule of the elite. Moreover his analysis of the problems facing the South (over Texas for example) made it difficult for him to engage in the normal processes of bargain and compromise which were mandatory in an organization like the Democratic party. Finally his past record, together with his antidemocratic views, made him simply unacceptable to large numbers of Democrats not merely in the North but in the South too.

---

182. Wiltse, *Calhoun, Sectionalist*, p. 51.

One reason for this "unavailability" was his pursuit of the second strategy – the creation of a southern *bloc* in Congress. If he could not in fact control the Democratic party, the only alternative was to seek to break down the party system and, by a show of southern strength, force the North to choose between an end to agitation of the slavery question and an end to the Union itself. This strategy had obvious attractions too. If a solid South were able to repel northern agitation then slavery would be safe. And if a significant minority of northerners could be attracted to the southern banner then perhaps the White House could still be within reach. But the problems were enormous. Not only were most southerners highly attached to their parties, they also had to contend with the charge of treason leveled against them if they threatened secession. And without such a threat how could leverage be applied against the North?[183]

Not surprisingly, Calhoun never resolved his dilemma. In the mid- to late 1830s he was advocating the dismantling of the parties. But by 1840 and for a few years thereafter he hoped to lead the Democracy. In the late 1840s he swung back once again to the hope of united southern action. Indeed in 1848 he stood aloof from the presidential campaign and endorsed no candidate. This inconsistency itself aggravated the problem. It opened the way for his critics – most notably his arch-enemy Thomas Hart Benton – to claim that he was utterly selfish and unreliable, prepared to co-operate with his fellow Democrats only when they gave him everything he demanded and otherwise out to sabotage the party.

As we have seen, Benton, together with Frank Blair and others, were certain that Calhoun was forever plotting secession. In fact Calhoun still hoped to make the Union safe for the South by resisting what he took to be northern aggression. In 1844 South Carolina, after the collapse of his presidential candidacy, sent no delegates to Baltimore but Francis Pickens from the gallery endorsed Polk's nomination and, after receiving assurances from Polk on the tariff, Calhoun whipped the state into line. At this time a secession campaign – the Bluffton movement led by Robert Barnwell Rhett – was gathering momentum in South Carolina but Calhoun successfully snuffed it out. The Walker tariff, while not giving all that might have been asked, nevertheless met with his approval and, of course, by this time Texas had been annexed to the United States. Another threat had been removed.[184]

Yet Calhoun soon broke with the Polk administration. Ironically in view of the South Carolinian's key role in the annexation of Texas, it was Polk's plans for territorial expansion that caused the rift. "Manifest

183. Calhoun has often been regarded as a statesman of great intellectual power. While it is not surprising that his southern followers so viewed him, it is curious that so many historians have endorsed the judgment.
184. Wiltse, *Calhoun, Sectionalist*, pp. 180, 183, 187–198.

Destiny," insofar as it purported to extend the domain of American democracy, had little appeal to one who disdained majority rule and disavowed the name of democrat. Expansion into the Northwest moreover meant more free states – a most unappealing prospect – and threatened relations with Britain. Calhoun believed that the movement towards free trade would be greatly impeded if relations with Britain deteriorated. But expansion into the Southwest was equally unattractive. Calhoun was adamant that the demand for all of Mexico be resisted partly on the grounds that the Mexicans themselves were utterly unfit to be brought within the Union. Hence he was only a lukewarm supporter of the war and a firm opponent of Polk's expansionist policy.[185]

Given his priorities, these were sensible reactions. But they once again exposed his dilemma. He had done as much to bring Texas into the Union as any man but he balked at the bi-sectional alliance which linked Texas and Oregon and which in effect legitimated the former. As far as his critics were concerned, he had once again helped whip up a crisis over slavery and then betrayed those who had battled valiantly to resolve it. He was acting at one moment as the loyal Democrat, at the next as the sectionalist who scorned party.

In the mid-1840s he flirted briefly with a third strategy, one that had occasionally tempted him in the past. In 1845 he attended the Memphis Commercial Convention and made a bold bid for western support. Hoping now for an alliance with agrarian interests in the West (which might naturally support the cause of tariff reduction), he realized that westerners needed and demanded internal improvements at federal expense. The difficulty here, of course, was that no man in public life had spent so much time and energy warning of the dangers to be feared from an expansion of federal power. The solution would only have occurred to John C. Calhoun. He now discovered that the Mississippi was in fact an "inland sea" and as such entitled to federal expenditures. This was too much even for the Charleston *Mercury* but within a year Calhoun was complimenting himself on having effected a union between South and West.[186]

But in truth no such alliance could materialize. On the slavery question there scarcely was a West. Instead there were antislavery Democrats and antislavery Whigs in the Northwest, proslavery zealots in the Southwest, moderates from both parties throughout the region. When the territorial question arose the alliance between South and West, if it had ever existed at all, melted away and Calhoun was left to lead and inspire those southerners who rallied to the clarion call of "southern rights."

185. Wiltse, *Calhoun, Sectionalist*, p. 283.
186. Wiltse, *Calhoun, Sectionalist*, p. 239; Calhoun to Thomas G. Clemson, July 11, 1846 in Jameson (ed.), *Correspondence of Calhoun*, pp. 700–701.

Northern Democrats who advocated the Wilmot Proviso held Calhoun and his disciples responsible for the emergence of the territorial question and thus for the Proviso itself. Calhoun himself, however, had a very different explanation. For him it was merely the next stage in the inexorable growth of northern antislavery agitation. (This indeed had been why he had not stopped to consider the effect of the annexation of Texas: northern aggression would continue and intensify anyway.) But how to combat the Proviso? In a major speech delivered in the Senate in February 1847 Calhoun criticized the Missouri Compromise as "highly injurious to the South, because it surrendered, for mere temporary purposes, those high principles of the constitution upon which I think we ought to stand." Nevertheless he avowed himself willing to extend it, as a workable compromise between North and South. In fact, as he explained on another occasion, non-intervention would result in a dividing line between slave and free territory that approximated the Missouri line.[187] Northerners, however, rejected this offer. The following month, in an Address at Charleston, he repeated his old analysis of abolitionism as a cause for whose support both parties in the North were compelled to bid. He now recommended an alliance of southerners regardless of party. At first he wondered whether Taylor, as a southerner, a slaveholder and a cotton planter, might not be an acceptable candidate. But it soon became apparent that the General's priorities were not the South Carolinian's. Calhoun also recommended that his followers stay away from the Democratic Convention at Baltimore on the grounds that it was tainted with free soilism and because he did not want South Carolina to be committed to the nominee. Cass's nomination probably gave Calhoun some grim satisfaction since he had denounced Cass's popular sovereignty doctrine as one that would surely exclude the South from the territories. Hence he advocated neutrality in the 1848 presidential election, seeing as he put it, "much to condemn and little to approve in either candidate." But others in South Carolina disagreed and Cass carried the state quite comfortably.[188]

By now Calhoun was convinced that southerners had to choose between resistance and abolition. As he himself put it, we must either "give up our slaves, or give up all political connection & association with either of the existing parties at the North, and rely on ourselves for protection." But this still left the perennial problem of rallying southerners in support of slavery. The only hope was for the South "to present with an unbroken front to the North the alternative of dissolving the

187. Wiltse, *Calhoun, Sectionalist*, pp. 304, 348.
188. Crallé (ed.), *Works of Calhoun*, IV, pp. 382–396; Wiltse, *Calhoun, Sectionalist*, pp. 319, 359; letter from Calhoun in Charleston *Mercury*, Sept. 5, 1848.

partnership or of ceasing on their part to violate our rights and to disregard the stipulations of the Constitution." In 1849 Calhoun drafted a lengthy document entitled the Southern Address. Faced with continuing northern demands for the Wilmot Proviso, as well as bills in Congress for abolition in the District of Columbia, forty-eight southerners signed the Address. It called for united action against the North and insisted on southern rights in the territories, not, Calhoun was careful to point out, because southerners insisted on extending slavery, but because a denial of these rights would immediately reduce southerners "from being equals, into a subordinate and dependent condition." Calhoun by now wanted a southern convention to further the unification of the South.[189]

In his final speech to Congress, written a short time before his death and read by Mason of Virginia, Calhoun summed up his case against the North. The admission of California into the Union, he declared, would be "the test question." If she were admitted in defiance of established procedures, it would demonstrate that the northern majority was intent on excluding the South from the territories, and, it followed, intent on "destroying, irretrievably, the equilibrium between the two sections." "We would be blind not to perceive in that case," he concluded, "that your real objects are power and aggrandizement, and infatuated not to act accordingly."[190]

In this speech Calhoun reviewed the history of the Union and set out to demonstrate that the federal government had been used to benefit the North to the detriment of the South. Three classes of measures, he claimed, had destroyed the balance between the sections. One was the exclusion of slaveholders from the West by the Northwest Ordinance, the Missouri Compromise and, if passed, the Wilmot Proviso. Another was iniquitous financial legislation, and in particular the tariff. The third was a change in the government itself leading people to believe that the majority was supreme at Washington. But here the old problems that always seemed to dog the proslavery theorist surfaced once again. As we have seen, Calhoun himself had claimed that in the absence of federal legislation the dividing line between slavery and freedom (as determined by nature and climate) would be similar to the Missouri line itself. If this were so the Northwest Ordinance and the Missouri Compromise could not be cited as causes of southern inequality. Still less, of course, could the Wilmot Proviso, which had not only never even been passed, but posed a

189. Wiltse, *Calhoun, Sectionalist*, p. 359; Calhoun to J.H. Means, April 13, 1849 in Jameson (ed.), *Correspondence of Calhoun*, pp. 764–766; "Address of the Southern Delegates in Congress to their Constituents," in Crallé (ed.), *Works of Calhoun*, VI, pp. 285–313.
190. Crallé (ed.), *Works of Calhoun*, IV, pp. 542–573.

threat only because the South was already in a minority. The tariff had indeed been a source of grievance for many years but the problem had now largely been resolved. Moreover many southerners, especially in the Southwest, believed that they were prospering as never before. Finally the change in the role of government and the threat of the majority in Washington was also a problem only because the South was already a minority. It could not in itself be adduced as a cause.

Oblivious as ever to these difficulties, Calhoun advocated a constitutional amendment to restore the sectional balance. Perhaps he had in mind the proposal for a dual executive, a President from the North and one from the South, which he had put forward in his recently completed *Discourse on the Constitution*. No-one took up this suggestion, however, and four weeks later, before the Compromise was effected but not before the Southern Convention on which he had set his heart had been planned, Calhoun was dead. A few days before his death he had begun to doubt whether a reconciliation between North and South was possible; with great foresight he predicted the break-up of the Union within three presidential terms.[191]

IV

Throughout the 1840s the actions of Calhoun and his followers served merely to confirm the analysis of the Van Burenites. Indeed the activities of each group strengthened the resolve of the other by validating its predictions and underlining the need for action. In these circumstances the task facing a reconciliation became impossible; the two extremes within the party could not meet. The best that a moderate could hope for was that a program could be found which would detach as many northerners from Van Buren and southerners from Calhoun as possible. Hence on the territorial question the need to find a middle way soon became overwhelming.

Many northern Democrats were attracted to the Wilmot Proviso. Indeed had they had a free choice, few would have hesitated. But southern pressure meant that the options were quite different. It soon became apparent that the Proviso brought with it at least the threat and perhaps the reality of disunion (precisely as the motion to exclude slavery from Missouri had done over a quarter of a century previously). A compromise on the territorial question, however, might restore sectional harmony yet still result in only free states in the West. The benefits of the Proviso

---

191. Calhoun, "A Disquisition on Government and a Discourse on the Constitution and Government of the United States," is in Crallé (ed.), *Works of Calhoun*, I, see p. 392; Wiltse, *Calhoun, Sectionalist*, p. 473.

would come without the Proviso. Such was the promise of popular sovereignty in the North.

In New York state the Hunkers, long-time enemies of the Barnburners, adopted the doctrine in precisely this spirit. One of the first Democrats to espouse it was United States Senator Daniel S. Dickinson, who might well be described as an arch-moderate within the Democratic party. He was staunchly conservative on financial and sectional issues alike. Dickinson's problem was one that would plague northern Democrats right up to the outbreak of the Civil War: how to maintain unity within the party nationally without appearing to have capitulated to the South. The northern electorate wanted to reserve the new territories for free labor; what remained unclear was the cost and whether the voters would pay it. Dickinson's stance left him vulnerable to the charge that he was a defender of slavery. That such criticism was damaging may be inferred from his reaction. "I have never favored the institution of slavery nor its extension, either immediately or remotely," he insisted, "and whoever charges and insinuates the reverse, originates a base and deliberate, and, unless he is ignorant of my sentiments, a wilful calumny." Indeed he confirmed that northerners of all parties "regard with disfavor" the prospect of slavery entering the territories. Similarly at a State Convention held in January 1848 the Hunkers acknowledged that "we make no issue" with the Barnburners "on their proposed end." Instead "our issue is as to their means." To combat the charge that they were doughfaces, they stressed that the land in question was unsuited to slavery anyway, from which it followed that the Proviso was superfluous.[192]

Some of the Hunkers also doubted whether it was constitutional and these doubts naturally inclined them to favor popular sovereignty. More generally, an attempt to devolve the problem of slavery in the territories onto the inhabitants of those territories accorded neatly with the Democratic emphasis on decentralization and localism. According to Dickinson, even if Californians adopted slavery – which they would not – no outsiders would have the right to complain. Other features of Democratic ideology reinforced popular sovereignty's appeal. With a traditional lack of concern for the plight of blacks, Dickinson could not take seriously those who professed moral outrage at slavery. Antislavery was, he declared, "a spurious philanthropy" and slavery a "miserable question." But popular sovereignty promised to resolve it. Like Stephen A. Douglas in the 1850s, Dickinson in the 1840s refused to grant that the passions generated by sectional issues were genuine.

192. John R. Dickinson (ed.), *Speeches, Correspondence, etc. of the late Daniel S. Dickinson* 2 vols (N.Y., 1867), I, pp. 303, 342, see also pp. 279, 310; *The New York State Democratic Convention, January 26 and January 27, 1848* (n.p., 1848), pp. 7, 16.

Once again the weight of Democratic tradition bore down upon these partisans. Their view of the past made it difficult for them to recognize that issues other than those over which the parties had traditionally fought were authentic. Antislavery or proslavery militants were simply stirring up groundless fears. "It is the political agitators in both sections," Dickinson told the Senate in 1850, "who have made all the mischief." Then he claimed that if one could "take a small number of men out of the Northern and also out of the Southern sections of this Union, or silence their clamor," then "this accursed agitation could be settled in less than a single week." The promise of popular sovereignty was that it would take the slavery question out of the halls of Congress and place it beyond the reach of demagogues and agitators. Or so it was hoped.[193]

These Democrats claimed that the alternative policy of free soil would be "fatal" to the Democratic party's "ascendancy." Indeed it would jeopardize the Union itself. The Free-Soilers were engaging in "an agitation which, for a purpose comparatively trivial, sports at a game where the destiny of the world's freemen is the hazard." Was it not obvious to all that "the question . . . is, whether we should have a Union with slavery, or slavery without a Union"? But antislavery zealots were prepared to "risk the destruction of this Union to prevent the doubtful prospect of a few slaves being carried from the northern slave States to California." Clearly such agitation was "solely to furnish a hobby for demagogues to ride."[194]

Here of course Dickinson and his colleagues were bowing to southern threats. Indeed, having announced his desire to have the territories become free, Dickinson declared that rather than see the Union divided, he "would see every member of this unfortunate race, bond and free, well provided and provisioned for the journey, in one dark and mighty cloud, march from the old States to the new Territories, or any other section of the Union, there to reside, if the inhabitants would permit them." Though Dickinson was admirably forthright here, such declarations, despite his protestations and disclaimers, left him highly vulnerable to the "doughface" epithet.[195]

According to the Hunkers, the Democratic party was neither a slavery nor an antislavery party. The slavery question must not become "a test of party faith." Indeed "if there is one feature for which the National Democratic party is distinguished beyond another, it is that of antago-

193. *Address and Proceedings of the Democratic State Convention, August, 1849* (Albany, 1849), p. 10; *Speeches of Dickinson*, I, pp. 348, 300, 289, 330–331, see also pp. 228, 290.

194. *New York Democratic State Convention, January, 1848*, p. 7; *Speeches of Dickinson*, I, pp. 359, 255, 279, see also pp. 274, 289.

195. *Speeches of Dickinson*, I, p. 343.

nism to the slavery agitation in every form."[196] This of course was precisely the position occupied by the Barnburners. Indeed the Calhounites also longed for the day when slavery agitation would be beaten back. In this sense all three groups wanted the Democratic party to be neutral on the slavery question. Yet neutrality conveyed different meanings for the three factions. Each perceived the problem differently. The Calhounites believed that agitation – which was infecting even the Democratic party – was a consequence of the northern social and political systems; to resist it and re-establish a balance might require the kind of action which Calhoun himself had engaged in over Texas. For the Barnburners, by contrast, abolitionism posed no great threat to the South. Hence it was instead the very counter-measures taken by Calhoun and his disciples, including their threats to break up the nation, which were the real source of slavery agitation. The Hunkers meanwhile condemned extremists and agitators on both sides.

For the Barnburners the solution was for the party to remain neutral on the slavery question but to allow northern Democrats to vote for the Proviso, if they so wished, as a non-party issue. The Hunkers instead wanted an explicit neutrality that would defuse the slavery question by bringing the weight of the Democratic party itself onto the scales in favor of compromise. And popular sovereignty was to be the compromise position.

The Hunkers differed from the Barnburners principally because they did not fear the emergence of an "aristocracy." Neither bankers (whom they were prepared to tolerate) nor slaveholders threatened American democracy. The Hunkers were less committed to an egalitarian view of human nature than the Barnburners; hence they were less disposed to attribute inequality to the fraudulent actions of the aristocratic minority.[197] In this way the alignments of the Jacksonian era – the intra-party battles as well as the interparty struggles – persisted into the late 1840s and indeed the 1850s.

Initially many northern states, and many Democratic state parties in the North adopted the Wilmot Proviso. But when southern threats revealed the consequences that might follow from its passage, they drew back. Indeed Dickinson and his close friend, Lewis Cass, had themselves followed precisely this course. Despite once having voted for the Proviso, Cass in a famous public letter to A. O. P. Nicholson in December 1847 committed himself fully and unambiguously to popular sovereignty. Now doubting the constitutionality of the Proviso, Cass noted that the essence of American federalism was that it left the citizens of each state

---

196. *Address and Proceedings of Democratic State Convention, August, 1849*, pp. 4, 8.
197. See Ashworth, *"Agrarians" and "Aristocrats,"* pp. 132–146.

"to regulate their own concerns in their own way." The inhabitants of a territory, he argued, were "just as capable of doing so, as the people of the states." For good measure Cass added first that the territories in question were unsuitable for slavery and second that even if slaveholders and slaves did migrate to them the total number of slaves in the nation would be unaffected. Cass believed that popular sovereignty was in the finest traditions of American democracy. "By going back to our true principles," he concluded, "we go back to the road of peace and safety." For these sentiments he was rewarded with the Democratic presidential nomination.[198]

Undoubtedly the retreat from the Wilmot Proviso placated many southerners. By 1848 Democratic State Conventions in Virginia, Georgia, Florida and Alabama had pledged that they would support no candidate who was not on record against it. Repudiation of the Proviso was a triumph for southerners in that it removed the fear that a dangerous precedent was being established for ever-widening congressional action on slavery. Moreover it also removed what was felt to be a slur on the South. On the other hand popular sovereignty, as least as advocated in the North, could have done nothing to placate southern fears that a rapid increase in the number of free states was in any case imminent. If the North possessed the political power to assail the South, was it a consolation to know that the power had been acquired by popular sovereignty rather than the Wilmot Proviso? Such of course was Calhoun's reasoning. Southerners who did not accept it were forced to hope either that slavery would indeed be able to compete in the West or that a future northern majority could be trusted.[199]

The other problem, of course, was that the nomination of Cass was the last straw for the Barnburners and other free soil Democrats. Cass was the *bête noir* of the Barnburners, his defeat had been a top priority in 1844 and his nomination now seemed to confirm that the party had fallen under southern control. He himself was, of course, a northerner, but he represented the doughface faction against which the Free-Soilers inveighed. And there was much truth in these accusations. In repudiating the Wilmot Proviso and in questioning Congressional power over slavery in the territories, the Democratic party was, once more, stretching to accommodate the South. The fact that this accommodation could be made by reference to traditional party principles was, of course, no coincidence. Those principles had always borne the mark of the social power of the slaveholders of the South.

198. "Letter from Lewis Cass to Alfred O. P. Nicholson, December 24, 1847," in Schlesinger and Israel (eds), *History of Presidential Elections*, II, pp. 908–909, 911–912.
199. Morison, *Democratic Politics and Sectionalism*, pp. 33–51, 93–120; Holt, *Political Crisis of the 1850s*, p. 59.

V

The Whigs meanwhile were faced with a similar set of problems. The party managed to unite behind the demand that no territory (other than Texas) be taken from Mexico. Northerners and southerners alike rallied to this proposal and indeed leading Whigs like Webster warned of the dangerous consequences of any further territorial acquisitions. But the actions of the Polk administration quickly doomed this policy and deep divisions over the slavery question immediately surfaced. When the Wilmot Proviso was first introduced, it commanded all but universal approval from northern Whigs, but in the year or so that it took the South to respond it became clear that the great majority of southern Whigs were implacably opposed. In some of the border states the response was muted. Kentucky's Whigs, for example, agreed that if the Proviso passed Congress the President should sign it. They denied that such an event would furnish a just cause of secession. Senator Underwood avowed that he wanted "the Union, Sir, even with the Wilmot Proviso."[200]

But even Kentucky's Whigs denounced the Proviso as both needless and insulting to the South. Most southern Whigs went further. Though many of them denied that slavery could go into the new territories, they were incensed at the denial of southern rights implicit in the Proviso and at the precedent it established for a direct assault on slavery in the states. A further problem was the growth of northern power in Washington consequent on the admission of more free states. For all these reasons Robert Toombs and Alexander Stephens of Georgia, for example, made it clear that the Proviso must be resisted at all costs. The Milledgeville *Southern Recorder* stated quite unequivocally that enactment of the Proviso would mean a dissolution of the Union.[201]

The reaction of these Georgians was predictable given the intense sectionalism that had always characterized their state. More alarming was the response of a North Carolina Whig like Willie P. Mangum who had been in the 1840s a highly orthodox Clay supporter and of a newspaper like the *Richmond Whig*, which had been a still firmer advocate of Whig nationalist policies. Both Mangum and the *Whig* insisted on southern

---

200. A good indication of northern Whig support for the Proviso is provided in Alexander, *Sectional Stress and Party Strength*, p. 196 (roll call 18); Harry A. Volz III, "Party, Section and Nation: Kentucky and the Coming of the Civil War" (Ph.D. University of Virginia, 1982), p. 54. A good survey of the Whigs in these years is provided in Michael F. Holt, "Winding Roads to Recovery: The Whig Party from 1844 to 1848," in Holt, *Party Politics and American Political Development from the Age of Jackson to the Age of Lincoln* (Baton Rouge, 1992), pp. 192–236.
201. Toombs to Stephens, Jan. 24, 1845 in Ulrich B. Phillips (ed.), "The Correspondence of Robert Toombs, Alexander Stephens and Howell Cobb," *Annual Report of the American Historical Association for the Year 1911* (Washington, D.C., 1913), pp. 61–62; Milledgeville *Southern Recorder*, Feb. 16, 1849.

unity in order to repel the threat from the North in the form of the Proviso. By 1848 it was becoming apparent that if the North passed the Wilmot Proviso, there would be a real risk of disunion.[202]

Of course, the southern Whigs were to some extent forced into this position by pressure from southern Democrats. They simply could not allow themselves to be branded traitors to the South. A serious dilemma confronted them. They could either seek an accommodation with their northern allies and suffer damaging accusations at home, or they could secure their home base but at the cost of a disruption of national party ties. This dilemma would haunt southern Whigs for the remainder of their party's existence – and even beyond its grave.

We shall return to the southern Whigs later. In the North, party regulars faced an equally grave problem. Should they maintain party unity and repudiate the Wilmot Proviso or should they adhere to their principles and sacrifice their southern wing? As we shall see, the party would split on this question. But so far as the 1848 presidential election was concerned, strategists thought they had found a way out of the dilemma. By nominating General Zachary Taylor, hero of the late Mexican war, the party could appease both its northern and southern wings. Northern Whigs could present themselves as an antislavery party; southern Whigs could appear as committed defenders of the South. The key lay not in Taylor's policies but in the lack of them. The General had never even cast a vote in a previous election, had only a tenuous link with the Whig party and had expressed no views on the Wilmot Proviso. On the one hand, he was a southerner, now resident in Louisiana, and the owner of a hundred slaves. Could he not then be relied upon to veto the Wilmot Proviso? On the other hand, he had announced a traditional Whiggish dislike of the veto and of presidential power generally. Did it not then follow that he would *not* veto the Proviso? At the national Whig convention Taylor won the nomination and, appropriately, a motion to commit the party to the Proviso was ruled out of order.[203]

As a result the major parties went into the election of 1848 with candidates whose policies on the territorial question were either highly ambiguous or non-existent. Cass's popular sovereignty doctrine could be given a northern or southern construction while Taylor's silence and political neutrality could be interpreted to suit either section. But ambiguity did not satisfy the most zealous opponents of slavery. We have already seen that the nomination of Cass provoked a reaction from the

202. Cooper, *South and Politics of Slavery*, p. 240.
203. On Taylor see Holman Hamilton, *Zachary Taylor, Soldier of the Republic* (Indianapolis, 1941); Hamilton, *Zachary Taylor, Soldier in the White House* (Indianapolis, 1951); Brainerd Dyer, *Zachary Taylor* (N.Y., 1946); Elbert B. Smith, *The Presidencies of Zachary Taylor and Millard Fillmore* (Lawrence, Kan., 1988).

Van Buren Democrats; a comparable reaction among free soil Whigs followed Taylor's nomination. The split in the ranks of northern Whigs revealed a major disagreement within the party, one that had existed for many years and one that went far beyond disagreements over specific policies. Just as the conservative Democrats in the North were most enthusiastic at the nomination of Cass so conservative Whigs were most committed to the regular Whig ticket.[204]

VI

Whereas New York was the key state for Democratic defections, Free Soil Whigs probably made the greatest impact in Massachusetts. The more conservative Whigs were not themselves united, with some supporting Clay and others his arch-rival Webster. But all the conservatives feared driving off the southern Whigs. In the mid-1840s they were especially solicitous for the tariff. The conservatives, many of whom were linked with cotton factories – hence the name Cotton Whigs – were fearful that the acquisition of more southern states would mean more votes to repeal the Tariff of 1842. On the other hand they also feared the effect upon their southern allies of an extreme antislavery stance. Indeed southern Whigs made it clear that they would withdraw their support for the tariff if northerners pressed their antislavery views too hard. As a result the Cotton Whigs in Massachusetts, having opposed the annexation of Texas, accepted the measure once it was accomplished. At the same time, although denouncing the Mexican war, they were willing to vote supplies for the armies. Finally, while initially welcoming the Wilmot Proviso, some of them, including Webster himself, would later retreat from it.[205]

Such retreats were too much for their more ardently antislavery colleagues, the so-called "Conscience" faction. Their opposition to the annexation of Texas continued after the Cotton Whigs had acquiesced in it, they repudiated the Mexican war utterly, refusing to vote supplies for the army, and most of all they insisted upon the Wilmot Proviso and refused to countenance any compromise. The Conscience Whigs would in the 1850s become Republicans; with few exceptions they would be radical Republicans. Throughout the late 1840s and 1850s their goal would be to keep their party pure, to rest it upon a clear appeal to the "conscience" of the voters, and to resist any dilution of its antislavery principles.[206]

---

204. This is not to say that many of them would not have preferred Webster or Clay as their candidate, but rather that the defectors came from the ranks of liberal Whiggery.
205. Brauer, *Cotton versus Conscience*, pp. 68, 70, 95, 126, 207, 230.
206. Brauer, *Cotton versus Conscience*, p. 207 and *passim*.

In the mid-1840s Conscience Whig leaders actually co-operated with immediatists like Garrison as well as the more politically involved abolitionists in the Liberty Party. Charles Francis Adams believed that the Whig party was in danger of capitulating to the Slave Power. By 1845 he was seeking support from any quarter for opposition to Texas annexation. A short time later he was announcing that he would not support a slaveholder for the Presidency. Just as the Van Burenites were disgusted at the spectacle of northern Democrats truckling to the South, so Adams and the Conscience Whigs were contemptuous of the Cotton Whigs for bowing to southern pressure. Robert Winthrop was an eminent Massachusetts Whig, closer to Webster than to the Conscience wing, and he was in December 1847 a candidate for the Speakership. But John Gorham Palfrey, a Conscience Whig, together with Joshua Giddings of Ohio, refused to support him and, for a time, denied him the needed votes for victory. Winthrop had been willing to vote supplies for the armies in Mexico. Although he subsequently triumphed, the Cotton Whigs wanted recriminations. But as far as Adams was concerned, Winthrop's election was ominous. "I think," he wrote, "the election of Winthrop means the victory of the Slavepower among the Whigs, the granting of supplies, the smothering of the Wilmot Proviso, and the ultimate settling down upon either Mr. Clay or Mr. Taylor, as circumstances shall dictate." Such an outcome could not be tolerated; "those of us who will not subscribe to these terms must prepare the way for a separation from the Whig party."[207]

By now Adams, together with other Conscience Whigs like Palfrey, Henry Wilson and Charles Sumner, was in close correspondence with militant antislavery Whigs in other states as well as Liberty party men like Salmon P. Chase. When Taylor was nominated the stage was set for the unification of the Conscience Whigs, the Van Buren Democrats and the Liberty party. Thus was born the Free Soil party.[208]

The Conscience and Cotton factions did not simply clash over the slavery question. The former resented what they took to be the latter's concern with money rather than principle. In particular they resented the way the manufacturing interest seemed to control the party. In July 1846 the *Boston Whig* published a letter which, as one historian has pointed out, "comprised the manifesto of the Conscience Whigs:"

---

207. Brauer, *Cotton versus Conscience*; Adams to Palfrey, Dec. 11, 1847 quoted in Brauer, *Cotton versus Conscience*, pp. 114–134, 220–222.

208. See on the events of the Buffalo convention Frederick J. Blue, *The Free Soilers: Third Party Politics 1848–1854* (Urbana, Ill., 1973), pp. 70–80; Sewell, *Ballots for Freedom*, pp. 153–169.

Everywhere out of New England we are heartily despised for this greediness of gain, this selfishness of the manufacturing interest, now so identified with the Whig party. But we protest against this union. The great Whig party is capable of higher, nobler purposes than the worship of mammon. We hold that monopoly of the Whig party by the manufacturing interest to be the worst kind of monopoly. It has no right to the party . . . . Our object is to elevate our party to its true position, to give it nobler views and a nobler aim.[209]

Charles Sumner offered a similar indictment of the conservatives when he complained of their willingness to substitute monetary gain for principle. In the nomination of Taylor Sumner detected a "conspiracy" and he explained that it had involved "the politicians of Louisiana and Mississippi and the cotton-spinners and traffickers of New England." In Sumner's immortal phrase it was an alliance between "the lords of the lash and the lords of the loom." The Conscience Whigs wanted to inaugurate the reign of humanity, justice and freedom; compromise with slavery or slaveholders was anathema to them.[210]

Their differences with the Cotton Whigs become more apparent when we contrast the views of Sumner with those of Webster. For Webster, as we have seen, the role of government was to mediate, to harmonize the various interests, to resist the currents of radicalism wherever they flowed. The ultimate horror was an event like the French Revolution. Sumner, on the other hand, referred to it as "that great outbreak for enfranchisement" which triumphantly proclaimed the equality of man. Massachusetts, he declared on another occasion, ought to adopt and learn from its slogan "Liberty, Equality and Fraternity."[211]

Webster viewed such utterances as the rankest demagoguery and a dangerous incitement of the masses. The Conscience Whigs in fact were in many respects closer to the abolitionists than to his brand of Whiggery.[212] They were, as their name implied, wont to emphasize the role of conscience. Indeed their principal objection to the acquisition of Texas was that it tended to corrupt the conscience of the nation, to involve the American people in the perpetration of sin and evil. Sumner attacked Winthrop in precisely these terms for voting supplies for the armies in Mexico. As Boston's representative he had implicated the city in the destruction caused by the war; as a result guilt, Sumner charged, "reddens the hands of your constituents." Winthrop had polluted the

---

209. Boston *Whig*, July 31, 1846. See also August 4, 7, 1846.
210. Charles Sumner, *The Works of Charles Sumner* 15 vols (Boston, 1870–1883), II, p. 81.
211. *Works of Sumner*, II, pp. 334, 87.
212. I shall return to the radical Republicans (and consider their differences with both Whigs and abolitionists) in the sequel to this volume.

entire city. This emphasis on guilt and conscience was closely akin to that of William Lloyd Garrison and the immediatists.[213] Indeed while making clear their differences with the abolitionists, the Conscience Whigs sometimes went out of their way to praise and honor them.

They also shared the abolitionists' confidence in the untrammeled individual.[214] Where Webster feared the force of self-interest and sought restraints, the Conscience Whigs believed that the individual conscience itself would be an adequate restraint. Their view of slavery was paradoxical. On the one hand, they believed it utterly unnatural and alien; left to itself it would surely wither and die. On the other hand, they believed that the large slaveholders who constituted the Slave Power were extraordinarily determined and prepared to stop at nothing to maintain their evil system. It followed that the task of the North was to resist. The Slave Power needed northern compliance to maintain slavery in the South. Hence secession was an idle threat, "a political stratagem," as Palfrey put it, to force concessions out of the North. Yet in truth "there is and has been no danger to the Union whatever." Firm action on the part of the North would allow the natural demise of slavery to occur; concessions, by contrast, would only prolong its life and, since its eventual collapse was inevitable, merely create further crises in the future. The task of the statesman was to resist all pressure from the South, to reject all attempts to reach a compromise between good and evil.[215]

One problem for the Conscience Whigs and indeed all the Free-Soilers in 1848 was that both parties in the North, but especially the Whigs, claimed their policies would in fact promote free soil. Thus sincere and dedicated opponents of slavery, men who would in later years become radical Republicans, remained in the Whig party in 1848. While Joshua Giddings of Ohio defected, Benjamin Wade did not. Even Thaddeus Stevens, destined much later to become the embodiment of radical Republicanism, stayed loyal to the Whigs in 1848. Moreover in New York, prominent antislavery Whigs like William Seward and Horace Greeley endorsed Taylor (though in Greeley's case, it should be said, with little enthusiasm). Most of these men were soon to join the Free-Soilers in their opposition to compromise.[216]

---

213. See Sumner's Letter to Winthrop, Oct. 25, 1846 in *Works of Sumner*, I, pp. 317–329.
214. See above, Chapter 3.
215. [John G. Palfrey], *Five Years Progress of the Slave Power* (Boston, 1852), pp. 57–59; George Julian, *Speeches on Political Questions* (N.Y., 1872), pp. 47, 48; Joshua Giddings, *Speeches in Congress* (Boston, 1853), pp. 343, 345, 347. Conscience Whigs fully endorsed the economic critique of the South put forward from the 1830s by the abolitionists and in the 1850s by the Republicans.
216. Hans L. Trefousse, *Benjamin Franklin Wade: Radical Republican From Ohio* (N.Y., 1963), p. 56; Ralph Korngold, *Thaddeus Stevens: A Being Darkly Wise and Rudely Great* (N.Y., 1955), pp. 79–80.

VII

The campaign itself was relatively uneventful.[217] The most interesting feature was Taylor's reply to the letters of inquiry he received. Since no-one had been entirely sure of his political allegiance, he had been offered and had earlier accepted presidential nominations not only from the Whigs but also from some Native Americans groups and even some local Democratic gatherings. He quickly denied that he had any hostility to immigrants. But demonstrating his Whiggery proved more difficult. In the first of two public letters addressed to his brother-in-law John S. Allison he avowed that he was "a Whig but not ultra Whig." "If elected," he continued, he would "not be the mere president of a party" but would instead "endeavor to act independent of party domination" and "should feel bound to administer the Government untrammelled by party schemes." But this sounded ominous to orthodox Whigs; would the General even turn out Democratic officeholders? To meet these anxieties Taylor wrote his second "Allison letter" in which he neatly recast his views so as to conform to Whig principle without, however, repudiating his previous utterances. He was not, he now asserted, a party candidate "in that straitened and sectarian sense which would prevent my being the President of the whole people." Here was the traditional Whiggish suspicion of parties. "I understand," he added, that "this is good Whig doctrine – I would not be a *partisan* President; and hence should not be a party candidate, in the sense that would make one." In some measure, therefore, Taylor would be the candidate of the anti-party party.[218]

Taylor also explained that he would use the veto only against legislation he believed either unconstitutional or hasty. For northern Whigs, saddled with a slaveholding president, this was a life-saver. Writing to Thurlow Weed, Seward's *alter ego* in New York state, Washington Hunt reminded him that "the mass of our northern Whigs are deeply imbued with anti-slavery sentiments." Hunt admitted that "what plagues me most of all is to think how I, after all I have said about slavery and its extension, am to look the Wilmot Proviso people in the face and ask them to vote for a southern slaveholder." Nevertheless there was "one, but one, door of escape." Taylor's supporters would be able to claim that he was "strongly in favor of peace," that he would take less territory from Mexico than any other candidate "that is strong enough to be

217. A good, brief account of the election is to be found in "The Election of 1848," in Schlesinger and Israel (eds), *History of Presidential Elections*, II, pp. 865–896. See also Blue, *Free Soilers, passim*; Hamilton, *Taylor, Soldier in the White House*, pp. 98–116; Nevins, *Fruits of Manifest Destiny*, pp. 189–216.
218. Taylor to John S. Allison, April 22, 1848 and Sept. 4, 1848 in Schlesinger and Israel (eds), *History of Presidential Elections*, II, pp. 913–915, 915–917.

elected," and, "more than all that, will leave all legislative questions to the decision of Congress." The primary "legislative question," he did not need to add, was the Wilmot Proviso.[219]

Other Whigs fastened on Taylor's remarks about the veto. In New York city, the *Grapeshot*, a Taylor campaign sheet, insisted that electing a president and choosing congressmen were entirely different processes. Drawing upon standard Whig doctrine, the newspaper argued that "the great feature of the opening contest" was to be "POPULAR RIGHTS against Executive Privilege and official power." A victory for Taylor would ensure "the independence of Congress" and "the supremacy of the will of the people." At first the *Grapeshot* tended to cite Taylor on the veto and leave its readers to draw the obvious conclusion regarding the Wilmot Proviso. But perhaps as a result of the pressure imposed by the Free Soil party, more explicit declarations were made. Since it was "only through the *Veto* that the President can rightfully control the legislation of Congress," it followed from Taylor's declarations "that resident as he is of a slave State, and connected with the interests of Slavery – he is much more safely to be trusted upon this question of free soil, than such an inconsistent politician as Mr Van Buren." Indeed it was "Congress and not the President" who should "determine these high interests" and "it must be by legislative enactment and not by Executive action, that a soil now free is to be maintained in freedom, or to be polluted with slavery." The newspaper concluded that "the whole topic is necessarily extraneous to the Presidential election, since the President can have little or no voice and should neither have nor desire any personal influence in its settlement."[220]

Similarly Abraham Lincoln, who also remained a Whig in 1848, stressed that Congress rather than the president should determine the fate of the Wilmot Proviso. He too began by merely hoping Taylor would not use his veto, but ended by asserting both that he would not and that the Whigs were unambiguously a free soil party. Even Webster, whose antislavery was more moderate than Lincoln's, when he eventually got round to giving the Taylor ticket a reluctant endorsement, claimed that the Whigs were the only party that had in the past or could in the future resist the aggressions of the slave power. According to Thomas Corwin of Ohio, a committed opponent of slavery but no radical, Taylor would not have won a single electoral vote in the North if it had been thought he would veto the Wilmot Proviso.[221]

219. Hunt to Thurlow Weed, Jan. 1, 1848, in Thurlow W. Barnes (ed.), *Memoir of Thurlow Weed* (Boston, 1884), p. 165.
220. *Grapeshot*, July 20, 27, 1848.
221. Roy P. Basler (ed.), *The Collected Works of Abraham Lincoln* 9 vols (New Brunswick, N.J., 1953), I, pp. 504–505, II, pp. 3–4; *Speeches and Formal Writings*

In the South, meanwhile, Whigs like Alexander Stephens, for whom the passage of the Proviso would constitute grounds for secession, were strong supporters of Taylor. Indeed Stephens had been among the first to rally to the General. He and other southern Whigs now re-dedicated themselves to loyalty politics. Cass, it was said, had once voted for the Proviso. Could anyone be certain that he would not do so again? Might he betray the South precisely as Van Buren had betrayed her? The Democrats responded in kind. In the North they claimed that popular sovereignty would create free states galore and at the same time warned that intransigence on the slavery question would jeopardize the Union. In the South they were able to point to the many antislavery utterances of northern Whigs.[222] But the Van Burenite defection clearly damaged them in the North. New York itself went to the Whigs and the Free-Soilers beat the Democrats into second place. In the South Taylor's status as a slave-holder proved difficult to challenge. In addition to running well in the Whig strongholds in the Upper and Border South, Taylor also carried Georgia, Florida and Louisiana. In fact each of the major parties carried fifteen states but Taylor's victories in New York and Pennsylvania, the largest states, were conclusive. Taylor outpolled Cass in popular votes but thanks to Van Buren's 290,000 he had a plurality and not a majority.

The election was utterly inconclusive. No-one as yet knew how Taylor would handle the sectional crisis. Indeed his northern and southern supporters continued to harbor entirely contradictory hopes and expectations. His victory was in this sense a shallow one; he was almost certain to antagonize one wing of his party. Once again the Whigs had triumphed in a presidential election; once again success would bring only trials and tribulations.

VIII

Taylor's victory settled nothing. The one proposal that seemed to have been repudiated was popular sovereignty, the very formula that would eventually underpin the settlement of 1850. The campaign itself had done nothing to ease sectional tensions, despite each party's success in garnering votes from both sides of the Mason-Dixon line. Indeed the electioneering had actually encouraged sectional extremism, which had flourished under cover of the deliberate ambiguity of the party plat-

of *Webster*, II, p. 503; Josiah Morrow (ed.), *The Life and Speeches of Thomas Corwin* (Cincinnati, 1895), p. 356.
222. Cooper, *South and Politics of Slavery*, p. 245. On the campaign in the South, see *ibid.*, pp. 246–268.

forms.[223] In the immediate aftermath of the presidential election it was still unclear what the president would do.[224]

In the face of hardening northern opinion and in particular proposals from northern congressmen to abolish slavery in the District of Columbia, Calhoun's attempts to unite the South seemed more likely to succeed than at any previous time. As we have already noted, in December 1848 a large group of southern congressmen and senators assembled and it was this meeting that empowered Calhoun to write his Southern Address. In fact only forty-eight southerners (out of 121) signed the Address, even after it had been softened to appease more moderate opinion. One reason was that northerners had retreated somewhat from the demand for abolition in the District. Another was the distrust which Calhoun invariably aroused. Most important was the confidence felt by southern Whigs in the new administration. Calhoun for party purposes, it seemed, was trying to whip up the crisis. According to Robert Toombs of Georgia, it was a "perfectly desperate move" by Calhoun and the Democrats, a "bold stroke to disorganize the Southern Whigs and either destroy Genl [sic] Taylor in advance or compel him to throw himself in the hands of a large section of the democracy of the South." Alexander Stephens in January 1849 wrote that he and the southern Whigs "feel *secure* under General Taylor."[225]

Calhoun and the large number of southern Democrats prepared to follow his lead desired a Southern Convention. The southern Whigs were never as keen on this proposal but the events of 1849 made them increasingly responsive. As early as December 1848 some of them began to suspect that Taylor would not in fact veto the Proviso, precisely as his northern supporters had claimed. Moreover they soon observed with dismay that none other than William Seward, the personification of free soil Whiggery, was high in the President's confidence. Taylor's inaugural did nothing to resolve the uncertainty about his plans but it gradually became apparent that while he wished to avoid the Proviso, he was prepared to admit California into the Union immediately, bypassing the

223. Though I shall delay consideration of the collapse of the second party system until the sequel to this volume, we should note that there is no reason to believe that this ambiguity on slavery (which reached a peak in 1848) actually strengthened the parties, as Michael Holt believes – Holt, *Political Crisis of the 1850s, passim*.

224. My account of the events leading up to the Compromise has been heavily influenced by Nevins, *Fruits of Manifest Destiny*, pp. 219–345; Potter, *Impending Crisis*, pp. 82–120 and Holman Hamilton, *Prologue to Conflict: The Crisis and Compromise of 1850* (N.Y., 1964).

225. Toombs to Crittenden, Jan. 3, 22, 1848, Stephens to Crittenden, Jan. 17, 1849 in Phillips (ed.), "Correspondence of Toombs, Stephens and Cobb," pp. 139, 141. See William Graham to James Graham, March 24, 1850 in J.G de Roulhac Hamilton and Max R. Williams (eds), *The Papers of William Alexander Graham* 5 vols (Raleigh, N.C., 1957–), III, pp. 318–319, for a typical southern Whig response to Calhoun.

territorial stage entirely. Without doubt this meant that California would become a free state. Moreover, Taylor told an audience at Mercer, Pennsylvania, that "the people of the North need have no apprehension of the further extension of slavery." Finally he may have made a statement (the record is not entirely clear here) to the effect that he would not in fact veto the Wilmot Proviso if it were passed and warning that he would regard resistance from the South as treason.[226]

As a result southern opinion hardened in 1849. As early as January Calhoun was gleefully noting that the South was "more aroused than I ever saw it on the subject [of slavery]." A sign of the times came when at the opening of the Thirty-First Congress, Stephens and Toombs asked the congressional Whigs to drop the Wilmot Proviso. When they refused Stephens told them "distinctly and positively that I should hold no connection with a party that did not disconnect itself from these aggressive abolition movements." He and Toombs, along with six other southern Whigs, now left the party. They would never act with it again.[227]

There were other signs of growing southern militancy. In January 1849 the Virginia legislature adopted a resolution to the effect that if the Wilmot Proviso were passed, the governor should convene a special session to consider redress. In Alabama and Georgia the state Democratic parties were on record as favoring the same course of action. The Florida and Missouri legislatures likewise affirmed their loyalty to the South and welcomed the call for a southern convention. In October a large convention at Jackson, Mississippi, called for the state to send delegates to the southern convention, now scheduled to meet the following year in Nashville. That same month Mississippians declared that passage of the Wilmot Proviso, or abolition in the District or a prohibition of the domestic slave trade would constitute grounds for secession. In South Carolina, of course, secessionist feeling was rife. Indeed throughout the South the possibility of disunion was now being discussed more widely than at any time since the Missouri Crisis and perhaps at any time in the nation's history.[228]

Meanwhile northern opinion was also hardening. No longer constrained by the need to support Cass and popular sovereignty, many northern Democratic state parties reverted to the Wilmot Proviso. In some states – Vermont, Massachusetts, Connecticut – the coalition that

---

226. Richardson (ed.), *Messages of Presidents*, v, pp. 4–6; Hamilton, *Taylor, Soldier in the White House*, p. 202; Chapman Coleman, *The Life of John J. Crittenden with Selections from His Correspondence and Speeches* (Phil., 1873), pp. 364–365; Potter, *Impending Crisis*, p. 86.
227. Calhoun to Mrs. T. G. Clemson, Jan. 24, 1849 in Jameson (ed.), *Correspondence of Calhoun*, pp. 761–762; Nevins, *Fruits of Manifest Destiny*, p. 251.
228. Potter, *Impending Crisis*, p. 88; Nevins, *Fruits of Manifest Destiny*, pp. 219–220.

472   *Slavery, economics and party politics, 1836–1850*

had formed the Free Soil party in 1848 survived, albeit in a looser form. In addition, there were now nine Free Soil congressmen, elected in 1848. The northern Whigs were if anything still more adamantly for the Proviso.[229] From the New York assembly came a resolution that opposed the extension of slavery into any territory now free and that expressed hostility to slavery in the District of Columbia. The Governors of Michigan, Pennsylvania and Illinois stated quite bluntly that slavery should never go into areas now free. Before the end of the year every northern legislature except Iowa had insisted on the power and the duty of Congress to exclude slavery from the territories. In these circumstances it seemed that North and South were irretrievably set on a collision course.[230]

By this time, one of the territorial policies that might have produced a compromise had already been discarded. In August 1848 Stephen A. Douglas had proposed the extension of the Missouri line to the Pacific. The Senate with its strong southern representation approved the measure but in the House, where there was a clear northern majority, it was rejected. Those northerners who might otherwise have been sympathetic were faced with the need to head off the incipient Free Soil party and so could not afford to make concessions to the South. Moreover southerners could not prevent the organization of Oregon, where slavery was abolished. From this point onwards, the North had nothing to gain from an extension of the Missouri line and the proposal was doomed.[231]

If Taylor hoped to carry the South with him in his plans for the territories, these hopes were quickly dashed. The President believed that slavery should be protected in the states where it already existed but had no desire to see it extended. He hoped that southerners would be able to tolerate the outcome of a free California so long as they had not had to swallow the Wilmot Proviso. But southerners now wanted a broader sectional adjustment that would end their fears of northern antislavery agitation as well as facilitate the return of fugitive slaves. In these circumstances Taylor's plan was simply inadequate: it offered them nothing. By the beginning of 1850 Taylor would not have been able to carry a single state of the future confederacy.

Nor could he carry with him either house of Congress. After a bitter wrangle the House had finally elected as Speaker Howell Cobb of Georgia, a Democrat noted for the moderation of his views on the slavery question. In the Senate there was a clear Democratic majority. In a special message of January 1850 Taylor repeated his proposals. California was to bypass the territorial stage and it was possible that New Mexico would

229. Holt, *Political Crisis of the 1850s*, p. 72; Nevins, *Fruits of Manifest Destiny*, p. 246.
230. Nevins, *Fruits of Manifest Destiny*, pp. 220, 255.
231. Potter, *Impending Crisis*, pp. 75–76.

do likewise. In California gold had recently been discovered; this made the organization of the territory or state imperative but also meant that free settlers outnumbered slaveholders by a huge margin. In New Mexico it was unclear whether Mexican law, barring slavery, had actually been repealed, so here too there was little prospect of slavery expanding. Southerners' alarm was intensified when they recalled that California would be the thirty-first state of the Union and the sixteenth free one. It would thus destroy the balance between the sections in the Senate; the future course of New Mexico and the absence of any additional territory suitable for slavery seemed to offer little prospect that the balance could ever be restored.[232]

At this point Henry Clay, veteran architect of the Compromises of 1820 and 1833, stepped forward. At first he claimed to be acting in compliance with the wishes of the administration but it soon became apparent that he and Taylor were at odds. Clay introduced a set of measures, each of which he believed desirable in itself but which he hoped would be accepted or rejected as a package. They would be debated for the next six months. Some of them were to be incorporated into the settlement that was finally reached in 1850, others would be modified. The core of the settlement was the arrangements made for the territories and the Fugitive Slave recommendations. California was to enter the Union on her own terms with respect to slavery – hence as a free state – and the remaining territory acquired from Mexico would be organized without restriction or condition regarding slavery. Though some southerners had hopes for slavery in these territories, these provisions were regarded as favorable to the North. On the other hand, the passage of a more stringent Fugitive Slave law was universally viewed as a measure for the benefit of the South. (Its only southern critics were those who argued that the North would not enforce it.) In addition Clay proposed the abolition of the slave trade (or, rather, aspects of it) in the District of Columbia. This proposal too would become a part of the final settlement.[233]

Clay also planned to reduce the boundaries of Texas and take away from her an area claimed by New Mexico. Texans were to be appeased by the United States assuming her public debt. He also affirmed the legality of the interstate slave trade and the need to obtain the consent of slaveholders in both Maryland and the District of Columbia before

---

232. Richardson (ed.), *Messages of Presidents*, v, pp. 26–30; Nevins, *Fruits of Manifest Destiny*, pp. 251–252. See also *Congressional Globe*, 31 Congress, 1 Session, Appendix, p. 1533.
233. Nevins, *Fruits of Manifest Destiny*, pp. 253–285; Poage, *Clay and the Whig Party*, pp. 191–205; Van Deusen, *Life of Clay* (Boston, 1937), pp. 396–398; Potter, *Impending Crisis*, pp. 96–108.

slavery was abolished in the nation's capital. These measures were either modified or dropped in the course of the debates that followed. In fact most of Clay's proposals had already been introduced, and most at the instigation of Stephen A. Douglas, Democratic Senator from Illinois. Clay's idea was that they should be bound together; in fact time would show that they could only be passed separately, as Douglas had always believed.[234]

In the course of the debates Clay insisted, as he always had, that slavery was an evil and refused to legislate to extend it. On the other hand he left open the possibility that in a new territory popular sovereignty might allow slavery to be established. Without a doubt the principal strength of his measures was their avoidance of the Wilmot Proviso. This mollified many southerners; northerners on the other hand were encouraged in the belief that the outcome would be precisely as if the Proviso had been enacted. Throughout the debates uncertainty as to the true meaning of "popular sovereignty" continued.[235]

Taylor, however, refused to throw his support behind the Compromise measures. Indeed he seemed willing to send federal troops against Texas, where feelings on the boundary question were running high. On July 3 he saw Toombs and Stephens who sought to explain the South's opposition to his actions. But the President refused to budge and argued that if he had to sacrifice one wing of the Whig party it would have to be the minority southern wing. To Thurlow Weed he described the two Georgians as traitors. But Taylor's views soon became an irrelevance. A week later he was dead and Millard Fillmore was President of the United States.[236]

Fillmore had been perceived as a typically antislavery northern Whig, placed on the ticket to balance a southern slaveholder. His brand of Whiggery had always been close to that of Daniel Webster and it soon became apparent that he would throw the entire weight of the administration behind the compromise proposals. (Seward immediately lost all influence in the administration and a fierce struggle broke out in New York state between supporters of the President and the Senator.) Nonetheless an alliance between northern and southern opponents of the compromise measures made their passage extremely doubtful. At the end of July the Omnibus bill – so called because it contained all the

234. Nevins, *Fruits of Manifest Destiny*, p. 266.
235. This of course is the standard judgment. It has, however, been challenged by Robert Russel, "What was the Compromise of 1850?" *Journal of Southern History*, XXII (1956), pp. 292–309. But see Potter, *Impending Crisis*, pp. 116–117 for a more accurate evaluation. A reading of the debates in Congress, in my opinion, supports Potter's view.
236. Nevins, *Fruits of Manifest Destiny*, pp. 330–331.

resolutions pertaining to the compromise – failed in the Senate. Clay left Washington, his strategy in ruins.[237]

Now it was the turn of Stephen A. Douglas to seize the initiative. Mindful of the way in which the Missouri Compromise had been achieved, Douglas proposed to separate the various measures and have them voted on one by one. In the House of Representatives no measure commanded the support of a majority of both sections and in the Senate only one measure, and that a relatively unimportant one – was so favored. (This was the bill organizing New Mexico.) But one by one the various measures went through. Despite the opposition of a majority of southerners, California was admitted as a free state and the slave trade was abolished in the District of Columbia. Against the wishes of a majority of northerners, a new and as it would prove, enormously contentious Fugitive Slave Act was passed. As Douglas had anticipated, on some key votes, opponents simply abstained in the hope that a satisfactory overall settlement might be obtained. A key factor may have been the attitude of Daniel Webster. Webster made a number of concessions to the South, which although they may not have changed the votes of any congressmen, undoubtedly suggested to southerners that the North was not irredeemably corrupted by abolitionism. They helped turn back the rising tide of southern militancy. Though the Nashville Convention in June voiced its opposition to the compromise measures, it was noticeable that dissenting voices were heard. Moreover some states had sent no delegates. Most important of all, calls for secession were conspicuously few. The forces of Unionism in the South were in the ascendant. By mid-September the Compromise measures had been passed and rejoicing had begun.[238]

Yet this success had been purchased at a high price. The Fugitive Slave law was denounced as an outrage in much of the North and would be enforced only with the utmost difficulty. The crucial ambiguity over the doctrine of popular sovereignty remained as a future source of difficulty and disturbance. Most important of all, perhaps, a large tract of territory, lying between Missouri and California, a part of the Louisiana Purchase, remained unorganized. It could scarcely remain so for long if California were to be properly integrated into the Union but would southerners allow the creation of yet more free states, as the terms of the Missouri Compromise stated? Northerners assumed they would; a shock awaited

237. On Fillmore see Robert J. Rayback, *Millard Fillmore* (Buffalo, 1959); Smith, *Presidencies of Taylor and Fillmore*.
238. For Webster's speech see Wiltse (ed.), *Papers of Webster, Series 4*, II, pp. 513–551. On the Nashville Convention see Thelma Jennings, *The Nashville Convention: Southern Movement for Unity, 1848–1851* (Memphis, 1980); Freehling, *Road to Disunion*, pp. 481–486; Nevins, *Fruits of Manifest Destiny*, pp. 315–318.

them in 1854. But these problems lay in the future. Despite the opposition of extremists North and South the nation seemed to have found peace. Most hoped it would last.[239]

The alignment of 1850 (2)

I

Although sectional considerations were obviously uppermost when congressmen voted on the measures of 1850, party influences, as we have seen, were also present. In the North the Democrats, apart from the Van Buren sympathizers, were inclined to favor the Compromise measures. A similarly high proportion of northern Whigs were hostile. Here the exceptions came from the Webster supporters. Northern Whigs like William Seward, who had campaigned for Taylor in 1848, as well as former Whigs like Charles Sumner, who had supported the Free Soil cause that year, expressed a decided opposition to the Compromise. In the South, however, the pattern was reversed in that the most enthusiastic supporters of the Compromise were Whigs, its fiercest opponents Democrats.

The task, however, is to explain this alignment. It is remarkable that in all the literature on the sectional controversy there has been only one explanation offered. Only Michael Holt has sought to explain the voting patterns of that year. He argues, correctly in my view, that the parties had indeed been fighting over financial questions in the 1830s and 1840s. He then asserts, incorrectly I believe, that because of "the dynamics of inter-party competition" Whigs and Democrats made "the national issues concerning slavery" "grist for interparty conflict at the state level." In other words, since they needed to be different on this issue one party in each section opposed the Compromise while the other supported it.[240]

It seems preferable, however, to claim that the stances taken over slavery were in fact determined by ideology. Yet a problem immediately arises. The parties were not formed over the slavery question, they had both been able to recruit north and south of the Mason-Dixon line, and they had been engaged in a highly acrimonious struggle over banking and currency, issues that did not separate North from South at all. What then is the relationship between slavery and the financial issues of the Jacksonian era? If parties in fact took shape as a result of the banking question, why should there be any other than a random alignment on questions relating to slavery? As we shall see, it is only by returning to the

239. I shall discuss the fate of the Compromise in the sequel to this volume.
240. Holt, *Political Crisis of the 1850s*, pp. 88, 90. Most surveys simply note that southern Whigs and northern Democrats were the moderate groups.

role of slavery in Democratic ideology that the alignment can be explained.

II

Let us briefly confirm the alignment of 1850. Joel Silbey has shown that while southern Whigs were unanimously in favor of the Compromise, southern Democrats were deeply divided. He classifies 44 percent of them as "in favor," with 13 percent "moderate" and 43 percent "opposed." This is also the conclusion reached by Thomas B. Alexander in his study of roll-call voting in the House of Representatives. There is, moreover, evidence to show that this pattern was visible outside of Congress. According to David Young, in Mississippi "the Whig press solidly endorsed the Compromise, whereas the Democratic press was almost uniformly against it." Another study finds that "the North Carolina Democrats in the main disliked the Compromise" while in Tennessee the major issue of the 1851 gubernatorial campaign was the Compromise with the Whigs condemning the Democrats for not support-ing it. Perhaps the most dramatic indication of party differences over the sectional question came in Arkansas at this time when a resolution was introduced into the lower house asserting that "Arkansas will abide the fate of the majority of the Slaveholding States and will seek their destiny." As many as 86 percent of the Whigs but less than half the Democrats voted to table this resolution. Clearly the southern Whigs gave the main-tenance of the Union a higher priority, and were less militant in their defense of slavery, than southern Democrats.[241]

In the North support for the Compromise came disproportionately from Democrats. According to Silbey, 68 percent of northern Democrats in the House of Representatives can be classed as "pro-com-promise" but only 31 percent of northern Whigs. Approximately 15 percent of northern Democrats were "anti-compromise" as opposed to over 34 percent of northern Whigs. Thomas B. Alexander similarly finds 80 (out of 95) northern Whigs, but only 14 (out of 52) northern Democrats taking a strongly anti-compromise view.[242]

---

241. Silbey, *Shrine of Party*, p. 114 (though it should be noted that Silbey's data refers to the House of Representatives; he finds a different pattern in the Senate); Alexander, *Sectional Stress*, p. 72; David N. Young, "The Mississippi Whigs 1834–1860" (Ph.D. dissertation, University of Alabama, 1968), p. 142; de Roulhac Hamilton, "Party Politics in North Carolina," p. 139; Robert H. White (ed.), *Messages of the Governors of Tennessee* 4 vols (Nashville, 1957), IV, p. 413; Gene W. Boyet, "The Whigs of Arkansas, 1836–1865" (Ph.D. dissertation, Louisiana State University, 1972), p. 353.

242. Silbey, *Shrine of Party*, p. 114; Alexander, *Sectional Stress*, p. 72.

Yet this alignment, although at its most visible in 1850–1851, was not the product of these years. Instead the tendency of northern Democrats and southern Whigs to favor moderation on sectional questions was as old as the party system itself. In the South *throughout* the period of the second party system and even beyond it, Whigs and Democrats differed over slavery. The Whigs were from the late 1830s (when the party fully took root in the South) always less militant. In other words the pattern of 1850 was in no sense unique to that year or even to the era of the second party system. It is hard to see how "the dynamics of interparty competition" can explain this especially since ten years later, when the Whig party had no organization at all and was to all intents and purposes defunct (and quite uncompetitive), former Whigs were still far more reluctant to endorse secession than former Democrats. According to a study of voting in the Confederate congress there was a clear tendency for Democrats to favor secession and for Whigs to be Unionist. Indeed "four-fifths of the 206 members for whom party and secession stand are known fit into one of these two categories." Moreover this correlation almost certainly existed as early as the 1830s. Roll-call analysis shows that over a wide range of issues, including the gag rule, the return of fugitive slaves, black enlistment in the army, the imprisonment of black sailors in southern ports, and colonization, southern Whigs were more moderate in their attitudes than southern Democrats. At the time when Calhoun was acting with the southern Whigs this tendency was obscured, since the Calhounites were more militant on sectional questions even than most Democrats. But from 1839 onwards southern Whigs were less insistent upon the gag, less rigid in their defense of racism, more inclined to favor colonization. Of course this was a difference of degree: southern Whigs were not voting with northern antislavery groups here. The point is simply that the alignment of 1850 had precedents in the 1830s and 1840s just as it would recur in the 1850s and during the secession crisis. This alone is sufficient to suggest that there were important principles, and principles in some way related to the mainstream party questions, involved.[243]

Similarly in the North. The tendency of northern Democrats to side with the South in fact predated the second party system itself. We have seen that at the time of the Missouri Compromise northern Jeffersonians provided the crucial votes for compromise; Federalists were both more antislavery and anti-southern. The tendency of northern Democrats in the 1850s – and even during the Civil War and Reconstruction – again to

243. Alexander and Beringer, *Anatomy of Confederate Congress*, p. 17; Alexander, *Sectional Stress*, pp. 33, 38, 46, 53, 59, 72, 87, 93, 101, 106. Holt himself observes this phenomenon but without relating it to his interpretation of the alignment of 1850 – Holt, *Political Crisis*, p. 29.

side with the South is too well known to require further comment. And during the 1830s and 1840s, the same roll-call analysis confirms that on the gag rule, the return of fugitive slaves, black enlistment in the army, the imprisonment of black sailors in southern ports, and colonization, northern Democrats were more inclined to a moderate position than northern Whigs. We cannot therefore explain the alignment of 1850 by reference to party maneuvering at that time. Something more than short-term political considerations was at work.[244]

I have throughout this work argued for an alternative explanation for the alignment in the North. If the principles of Jeffersonian and Jacksonian Democracy indeed functioned to support slavery in the South, it is scarcely surprising that a disproportionate number of northern Democrats were sympathetic to the southern viewpoint. To repeat: northern Democrats had not joined their party to support slavery in the South, nor did they doubt that free labor was superior to slave labor. Instead they had enlisted with a party that advocated states' rights, and limited government, doctrines which implied hostility to the BUS and a protective tariff but which also protected slavery in the South and (via their extension into "popular sovereignty") facilitated compromise in 1850. Their desire for an egalitarian and agrarian society fueled the bank war but also fed their suspicions of antislavery when it came from commercially oriented northerners who could be accused of plotting to use the labor of free blacks to degrade northern whites. Their emphasis on racism enabled them to emphasize the equality of all white men (including immigrants) but it also blinded them to the plight of the slave. Finally their insistence on individual moral autonomy allowed them to make bold claims for the ordinary citizen but (since blacks were excluded from the human family), it also encouraged them to concede the right of all individuals to hold slaves if they so wished and thereby robbed antislavery of its cutting edge. The support which northern Democrats offered the South did not derive from an explicit proslavery, still less from any desire to make slavery a primary political question. But nor was it an accident. It derived from their functionally proslavery outlook.

We need to look more closely, however, at the South. And here we encounter an important claim about Jacksonian politics. According to William Cooper, the South was preoccupied with the politics of slavery throughout the time of the second party system, except perhaps in the

---

244. Glover Moore, *The Missouri Controversy, 1819–1821* (Lexington, Ky., 1953), p. 105; Alexander, *Sectional Stress*, pp. 33, 38, 46, 53, 59, 87, 93, 101, 106. Moore notes that on the decisive vote fourteen northerners supported the South and all but three (two of whom were neutrals) were Jeffersonians.

early 1840s, when the banking question was primary. This, however, was very much an "aberration." Moreover, according to Cooper "each party maintained an identical and wholehearted commitment to the politics of slavery." Yet the roll-call analysis already cited casts doubt upon this claim. Moreover, Cooper cannot simply pronounce the early 1840s aberrant in this way. If slavery were indeed the key question, why were the two parties in the South, at both state and federal level, aligned on the banking question as they were? In effect Cooper has sought to add together rather than synthesize a slavery and a party interpretation.[245]

In the late 1840s many Whigs as well as Democrats in the South insisted that the passage of, for example, the Wilmot Proviso would and should produce a dissolution of the Union. Yet the Whigs were more moderate. The reason is not hard to find. It was simply that they believed it would not happen. According to Edward Stanly, a North Carolina Whig, it was "wrong to suppose that the great body of our Northern people, who believe slavery to be an evil . . . are therefore disposed to interfere with the Southern States, or are 'enemies of the South'." In May 1851 the *Arkansas Whig* offered a prognosis which clearly illustrates the attitude of southern Whigs to the sectional controversy. "We are sure," the editor announced, "that conciliation will be met with conciliation, concession with concession, compromise with compromise, if the South will take a high and independent stand upon the doctrine of Union and nationality." Similarly an address by the Whigs of Tennessee explicitly refused to threaten action against the North if the Compromise were violated on the grounds that such violations would simply not occur. The southern Whigs accepted the Compromise as a final solution, confident that the North would not betray it. They viewed the North sympathetically.[246]

Most southern Democrats, on the other hand, were far less sanguine. Their fears were clearly voiced by Senator Albert Gallatin Brown of Mississippi who predicted that the North would abandon the Compromise as soon as it ceased to benefit northern interests. Hence for Brown the first act of aggression committed by the North against the South would justify secession even if that act did not touch vital southern interests:

> At the first moment after you consummate your first act of aggression upon slave property, I would declare the Union dissolved; and for this reason: such an act perpetrated after the warning we have

245. Cooper, *South and Politics of Slavery*, p. 148.
246. *Speech of Edward Stanly of North Carolina, Exposing the Causes of the Slavery Agitation, Delivered in the House of Representatives March 6, 1850* (n.p., n.d.), p. 5; *Arkansas Whig*, May 22, 1851; "Address to the People of Tennessee by the Whig State Convention," in White (ed.), *Messages of Governors of Tennessee*, IV, p. 407.

given you would evince a settled purpose to interpose your authority in the management of our domestic affairs . . . . Do not mistake me; I do not say that such an act would, *per se*, justify disunion; I do not say that our exclusion from the territories would alone justify it; I do not say that the destruction of the slave trade in the District of Columbia, nor even its abolition here, nor yet the prohibition of the slave trade among the states would justify it. It may be, that not one, nor two, nor all of these combined would justify disunion. These are but the initiative steps – they lead you on to the mastery over us, and you shall not take these steps.

Brown expressed this view more vividly and succinctly some years later when he declared that it was "better to die defending the door-sill than admit the enemy and then see the hearth-stone bathed in blood."[247]

This was the reasoning behind the southern Democrats' hostility to the Compromise. They condemned the abolition of the slave trade in the District of Columbia as an unwarrantable interference by Congress and a precedent for further acts of governmental aggression. Southern Democrats were wont to argue that "its first great purpose was, to condemn and stigmatize, by a national vote, the transfer of slaves from one owner to another upon slave soil," while "its second great end was to establish a precedent for emancipation." Such an act was "encouraging and inviting further aggression." According to one Georgia newspaper, it would be acceptable for the South to renounce all the land in the Mexican cession if this would "purchase . . . future peace." But "no sane man" could "anticipate such a result." Instead "if the South submits now to the exactions demanded of her, she will soon be called to submit to other and still more exorbitant demands."[248] The Raleigh *Standard*, the foremost Democratic newspaper in North Carolina, likewise asserted that northern demands for a free California together with the abolition of the slave trade in the District of Columbia, were "but the entering wedges to complete a universal emancipation." In similar vein the *Mississippian* predicted that the next step would be abolition in the District, then abolition of the interstate slave trade, then the removal of the three-fifths clause. All that was needed for these usurpations was a few more free states in the West. This was also the official message of the Nashville Convention, dominated of course by southern Democrats. The Address was drafted by Robert Barnwell Rhett, an ardent secessionist, but it was toned down in

247. M.W. Cluskey (ed.), *Speeches, Messages and Other Writings of the Hon. Albert G. Brown* (Phil., 1859), pp. 169, 477, see also p. 190.
248. Raleigh *Standard*, June 26, 1850, quoting Milledgeville *Union*.

order to placate more moderate opinion. Its essence was the claim that one concession would simply lead to more.[249]

Those southern Democrats who voiced deep suspicions of the North were not in full agreement in their diagnosis of the current problem. Some of them believed that northern opinion was already irredeemably corrupted by antislavery sentiment. William B. Shepard in the North Carolina State Senate was among those who doubted whether a majority of northerners actually favored the Compromise. Those who followed his reasoning were not placated by the passage of the Fugitive Slave law. For "the public sentiment of the North is against its enforcement."[250] Many from the Deep South in particular expected little from the Act for precisely this reason[251] and thus concluded that all the real gains from the Compromise were going to the North. Some southern militants went on to contrast the attitude of the better northern congressmen with that of their constituents. They doubted whether, with the best of intentions, these congressmen could honor their promises. For it was "the force of public opinion and not the want of good will upon the part of leading statesmen at the North, that constantly drives the government into acts of hostility to the South." In these circumstances an agreement with northern congressmen, even if their sincerity and integrity were unimpeachable, was of little value.[252]

Other southerners instead dwelt on the utterances of the more hostile antislavery congressmen. But once again the problem was traced to the state of public opinion in the North. The *Mississippian*, for example, warned that the present agitation could not be attributed merely to the antics of unscrupulous demagogues or party spoilsmen. Rather than being "merely to subserve a present partisan end," the agitation against,

249. Raleigh *Standard*, June 20, 1849; *Mississippian*, May 3, 1849; Address of the Southern Convention to the People of Delaware, Maryland, Virginia . . . " in Mobile *Advertiser*, semi-weekly June 29, 1850.
250. Speech of Mr. William B. Shepard in the North Carolina Senate, Nov. 27, 1850 in Raleigh *Standard*, Dec. 14, 1850; *Address of the Hon. Jacob Thompson of Mississippi to His Constituents* (Washington, 1851), pp. 8, 10; *Reply of the Hon J. McRae to the Speech of Senator Foote* (New Orleans, 1851), p. 17; *Speeches of Brown*, p. 593. It should perhaps be added that in the states of Georgia, Alabama and Mississippi the situation around 1850 was rather different in that Southern Rights parties here faced Unionist parties. Yet the alignment was much the same since the Southern Rights parties were almost exclusively composed of Democrats while virtually all the Whigs (plus a minority of Democrats) joined the Unionist ranks. In these states sectional feeling was too strong to allow southern Whigs to continue to act with northern Whigs. Yet the Whigs remained less militant than the Democrats. I shall return to this issue in the sequel to this volume.
251. Here I am in disagreement with William Freehling. *Address of the Southern Delegates in Congress, to their Constituents* (n.p., n.d.), p. 1; *Mr. Soule's Speech at Opelousas, La. Delivered 6 Sept. 1851* (New Orleans, 1851), p. 6. Here great concern was shown for the fugitive slave issue.
252. *Speeches of Brown*, p. 593.

for example, the Fugitive Slave law "proceeds from a fixed and unalterable principle in the religious, the moral, and social creeds of millions at the North." The widespread northern conviction was that "slavery is an evil in the sight of God – a dark spot upon our character as a nation, and ought by every means consistent with prudence and the dictates of wisdom, to be abolished."[253]

These southerners thus had the gravest doubts about the current state of northern opinion. Even more widespread among southern Democrats, however, were fears about its future condition. As Calhoun had been doing for more than a decade, many southerners now measured the progress that antislavery doctrines had made in the North and projected the same rate of development into the future. The (Democratic) Governor of Arkansas pointed out that while few might now endorse Seward's "higher law" doctrines, in the past a similarly small number had advocated abolition or free soil. Did it not follow that time was against the South? In the words of another Arkansas Democrat, "the constitution will not protect us in ten years."[254] On this reasoning, it was no consolation for the South to find that many northerners, in or out of Congress, were sincerely committed to the Compromise. As Albert Gallatin Brown pointed out, there was every possibility that in the future they would be replaced by men whose antislavery convictions were stronger and deeper. In such circumstances the need for action was urgent.[255]

Thus we can explain the differing southern responses to the Compromise in terms of the parties' contrasting views of the North. But this of course merely displaces the question. We now need to ask why they viewed the North differently. At this point the connection between party and sectional issues becomes apparent. It would surely have been extraordinary if Whigs in the South, holding standard party views on economic issues, had not been sympathetic to the North. When they turned their gaze northwards they liked much of what they saw. Governor Neill Brown of Tennessee in the late 1840s (a Whig) found much for Tennesseans to admire in the North, and especially in New England, the most developed region of the country. He claimed that "the same spirit of internal improvement and education which has blessed, and enriched, and adorned New England, would make Tennessee the first state in the Union and in the world." Similarly a writer in the *Richmond Whig*, the foremost Whig paper in Virginia, complained of "the woful absence" in the state "of the energy and industry" that were "the

253. *Mississippian*, Nov. 8, 1850.
254. Message of Governor John S. Roane of Arkansas, Nov. 5, 1851 in Washington (Ark.) *Telegraph*; Helena (Ark.), *Southern Shield*, July 12, 1851; *Address of* [congman] *Robert W. Johnson of Ark to his Constituents, Jan. 29, 1850* (n.p., n.d.).
255. *Speeches of Brown*, p. 170.

distinguishing characteristics of our Yankee brethren." Such respect and even admiration for the North shaped southern Whig attitudes to every event in the sectional conflict of the late 1840s (and also the 1850s). The *Arkansas Whig*, for example, dismissed the southern Democrats' claim that the "loss" of California to the North was a result of fraud by the northern majority in Congress. Instead it was attributable to the failure of the South. While southerners were stupidly talking of disunion, "the hearty freemen of the West and North were on their march to plant their empire and fix the destiny of California."[256]

To put it simply, southern Whigs admired the North, or at least certain features of the North, because they were those which they hoped to promote in the South. It followed that there was no necessary conflict between such features and slavery. Southern Whigs, like their allies in the North, championed the cause of economic diversification. In 1851 the *Arkansas Whig* complained that the South was "too dependent on cotton" and warned of "the general colonial dependence into which producers of the raw material, in a remote and half-civilized community, depending on the one profit of production for their wealth and without manufacturing resources, must necessarily fall." Such a dependence, the paper warned, "must necessarily" produce "a moral, an intellectual and a pecuniary subordination." Similarly the *Richmond Whig* asked whether it was not "rather humiliating, that a country like Virginia, boundless in its resources, and capable of producing every thing which can conduce to human comfort and pleasure, should so frequently resort to other markets for even the necessaries of life?" To the *Whig* the lesson of the crisis of 1849–1850 was that the equality between the sections should be restored: the South should be made equal to the North. This was the end and no good Whig doubted the means. The newspaper called for internal improvements, more manufactures, and greater attention to commerce. This was the orthodox Whig outlook – both north and south of the Mason-Dixon line. [257]

Many southern Whigs thus wanted to propel the South along the road the North had already taken. They felt that, in many respects, the North was simply more advanced. Similarly, they continued to place a Whiggish emphasis on the interdependence of the various interests in society. As late as 1860 ex-Whigs would be insisting that there was no basis for the conflict between North and South since "the prosperity of one section is

256. White (ed.), *Messages of Govs of Tennessee*, IV, p. 182; Richmond *Whig*, Sept. 19, 1850; Arkansas *Whig*, June 5, 1851.
257. Arkansas *Whig*, May 29, 1851; Richmond *Whig*, Aug. 29, Dec. 16, 1850. It is true that some proslavery southern militants also wished to promote diversification. This, however, was calculated to complete the separation from the North and thus perpetuate sectional differences – the opposite of the southern Whig view.

intimately blended with that of another." There were "reciprocal interests of vast magnitude, and a mutual dependence of one section upon the other." This view would be universal within the Constitutional Union party, which of course in 1860 would nominate John Bell for president. The party was composed almost exclusively of former Whigs.[258]

At the heart of the differences between southern Whigs and southern Democrats, however, lay a different perception of slavery itself. We have already considered the views of Democrats like Jackson and Polk, who never claimed or even believed that a slave society was superior to one based upon free labor. As we have also seen, such claims were commonly made by Calhoun and his followers. In South Carolina, of course, the proslavery argument was well established more than a decade before the crisis of 1850. But we need to determine where other southern Democrats stood on this question. In the normal course of events no test questions arose; it is thus difficult to locate the majority position. But the very fact that men like Jackson and Polk were able to command the Democratic party nationally suggests that southern Democrats, apart from Calhoun and his supporters, either did not endorse the proslavery argument or did not insist on politicizing it. By 1850, however, the situation was changing. Of course, those southerners who had always shared Calhoun's views were inevitably opposed to the Compromise, just as their leader was. But the mainstream southern Democrats had now moved much closer to a proslavery position than ever before. Jefferson Davis of Mississippi, after Calhoun's death perhaps the leading southern opponent of the Compromise, acknowledged that slavery was wasteful. But he also noted that there was less "cruelty" in the master–slave relation "than in any other relation of labor to capital." According to the *Mississippian*, whose importance as an indicator of Democratic opinion in the state can hardly be exaggerated, "our negroes . . . are cared for, prayed for, and labored for in spiritual things as much as the whites are; and so far as temporal matters are concerned, their condition is not only agreeable but happy when compared with thousands of the whites and nine-tenths of the blacks in the free States." In 1850 Albert Gallatin Brown, Mississippi's other Senator, avowed that slavery was a blessing to slave and master alike. This was the purest proslavery orthodoxy.[259]

Nevertheless, it is difficult to demonstrate that such views were dominant even in the Deep South in 1850. More common, perhaps, was what might be termed an embryonic proslavery. Such an outlook undoubtedly fueled the opposition of many southern Democrats at mid-century. As we

---

258. Ex-Governor Morehead of Kentucky in *Union Guard,* Oct. 10, 1860. I shall consider the Constitutional Union Party in the sequel to this volume.
259. *Congressional Globe,* 31 Congress, 1 Session, Appendix, pp. 149–157; *Mississippian,* May 23, 1849; *Speeches of Brown,* p. 166.

have seen, many believed that the northern social and political systems
inevitably generated a fraudulent and disreputable antislavery movement.
Why was this? They had been led to compare the northern and southern
social orders and so huge a flaw in the North suggested that the South
would not suffer from the comparison. Such a comparison and such a
conclusion were the staple foods of the proslavery diet. Moreover, the
logic of the southern Democratic position required that they at least
threaten secession in the event of further northern aggression, even if
they did not necessarily advocate or recommend it. They were compelled
to argue that the South would not suffer unduly from a break-up of the
Union. Jefferson Davis, for example, insisted that disunion would
damage the North far more than the South.[260]

In these ways then, southern Democrats were led to disparage the
northern social order and simultaneously to stress the advantages enjoyed
by the South. Of course this did not necessitate a claim that the South's
advantages were the consequence of slavery, or that a free labor society
necessarily contained these flaws. But it was not easy to find any alternative explanation. The views of North Carolina state Senator William B.
Shepard may have been shared by many southern Democrats, especially
those from the Upper or Border South. Shepard in effect distanced himself
from the proslavery theorists when he argued that it was "worse than
idle" to ask whether slavery was good or evil. Moreover he acknowledged that slavery impoverished the soil. With no outlet for her slaves,
North Carolina would face a bleak future. On the other hand he insisted
that the state had derived great benefits from slavery. Shepard then urged
an extension of the Missouri line as the most workable solution to the
current problem over the territories. But the most important part of his
speech perhaps came when he referred to slavery as "an institution"
which in North Carolina was "forming the substratum of our social
system, which no legislation can remove, and with which all tampering
produces more evil than good." Here the key phrase was "the substratum
of our social system." Just like the proslavery theorist, but in sharp contrast to Thomas Jefferson, Andrew Jackson or James K. Polk, Shepard
argued that slavery was the foundation of the southern social order. It
produced the vital differences separating North from South. Even if
Shepard shrank from the conclusion that slavery was better than free
labor, he had defended a South which differed from the North primarily
because of its labor system.[261]

Here was the key to southern Democratic hostility to the North. In its
"Address to the People of the Southern States" the Nashville Convention

260. Once again I am in disagreement with Freehling here.
261. Speech of Mr. William B. Shepard in the North Carolina Senate, Nov. 27, 1850 in
Raleigh *Standard*, Dec. 14, 1850.

argued that "the great difference – the *one* great difference – the greatest
which can exist among a people, is the institution of slavery." "This
alone," the Address continued, "sets apart the Southern States as a peculiar people." Of course, such opinions had been held by the Calhounites
for many years, but the Address was endorsed by southern Democrats
who had not previously followed the South Carolinian leader. We should
note that these sentiments once again did not necessitate the claim that
slavery was superior to free labor (though many of those who assembled
at Nashville as well as Rhett, the author of the Address, would certainly
have made this claim). The crucial claim was that slavery was at the
foundation of southern society.[262]

We are now in a position to understand the differences between southern Whigs and southern Democrats on the slavery question. A clear
majority of both were dedicated to its defense. Northern assaults were
anathema to both groups; both derided and feared the abolitionists. Yet
there was a crucial difference. Southern Democrats viewed slavery as the
foundation of the southern social order, southern Whigs instead viewed it
as an interest. Undoubtedly it was a large interest, without much doubt
the largest in the South. But still it was an interest, to be placed alongside
other interests in a relationship of mutual interdependence.

It is unfortunate in this connection that, when discussing southern
ideas on slavery, historians have generally been at pains to contrast
those who viewed it as a "necessary evil" with those who thought it a
"positive good." This distinction, important though it is, does not fully
capture the disagreement between southern Democrats and southern
Whigs. Both might say that slavery needed to be defended. Even some
militant southern Democrats, in common with virtually all southern
Whigs, might shrink from asserting the superiority of slavery. Nor is
the difference revealed when we measure southern hostility to abolitionism – a hostility which both parties shared. It is instead the relationship
between slavery and the developmental features of a commercial order –
features most visible in the North – which is crucial.

This did in fact produce one difference over abolitionism in that
whereas many southern Democrats saw it as a more or less spontaneous
and inevitable product of a free labor economy, southern Whigs marginalized and dismissed the movement. They even blamed southern secessionists for driving northern opinion against the South. Thus the Whig
editor of the *Mobile Advertiser* claimed that "Southern agitators have
magnified the power and influence of the Abolitionists, and, by their
violence and threats, have done more during the last fifteen years to excite

262. "Address of the Southern Convention to the People of Delaware, Maryland,
Virginia, . . . " in Mobile *Advertiser*, semi-weekly, June 29, 1850.

opposition to slavery and the South than the Abolitionists, by themselves, could have done in a century." He added that "but for the ultraism of the Southern disunionists, abolition would have died out of itself long ago." Since the great majority of southern Whigs rather approved of the North and indeed believed that the South should follow its example, they did not, virtually could not, believe that antislavery was inherent in its social structure. Economic development, which all Whigs applauded, was thought by southern Whigs to be quite compatible with slavery. Slavery would be a major interest in the South just as manufactures would be a major interest in the North. The two would be linked, to their mutual advantage.[263]

These principles necessarily meant that in the South it would be the Democrats who would take the lead in attacking the North. It was they who were heirs to a politics of conflict. The assumption that the federal government was a threat to the liberties of the people was central to Democratic ideology. It was then easy to dismiss antislavery as a pretext for northern attacks upon southern interests. As we have seen, Jefferson had frequently made these allegations and, as we have also seen, some northern Democrats repeated them. But whereas in the mouths of northerners these words implied sympathy for the South and a desire for sectional compromise, in the mouths of southerners, they produced a militant opposition to the North and a reluctance to countenance compromise. The *Mississippian* argued that northerners, with "their love of political power over us; their desire to make the national treasury a conduit by which the resources of the government can be drawn off to build up gigantic systems of internal improvement; their desire for national banks and high tariffs," had effectively dissolved the Union already. The editor concluded that "every thing in the North socially and politically, is opposed to a Union with the South."[264]

As the words of the *Mississippian* remind us, the tradition upon which Democrats had been nourished emphasized the superiority of agriculture. This suspicion of urban and manufacturing interests, in conjunction with the fear of federal power, helped provide a straightforward and clear explanation of the behavior of the North. In 1851 Jacob Thompson of Mississippi, reviewing the events of the recent past, told his constituents that "there can be no doubt that the commercial and manufacturing interests of the North have encouraged these assaults and aggressions upon the South because there was found the great agricultural interest that refused to favor class legislation, conferring bounties upon one pursuit, and burdens upon another." This was Jacksonian language used

263. Langdon, *Reply*, p. 13. See also Arkansas *Whig*, May 22, 1851; Tuscaloosa *Independent Monitor*, May 28, 1859.
264. *Mississippian*, July 5, March 13, 1850.

against the North. Hence many southern Democrats reaffirmed the orthodox Jeffersonian and Jacksonian faith in agriculture and once again gave vent to the fear that the agricultural interest was vulnerable to predatory attacks from naturally hostile interests. In the 1830s and early 1840s Democrats North and South had seen this threat in the policies promoted by Whigs throughout the nation. In the late 1840s and the 1850s the southern Democrats plausibly located the threat in the North as a whole.[265]

The corollary of southern Democrats' fears of the federal government was an attachment to states' rights. Here again their views had strong precedents within the Democratic and Jeffersonian tradition. Indeed they pushed the emphasis on states' rights beyond the limits which Jackson had established during the nullification crisis. Thus in 1850 in the North Carolina Senate a resolution asserting the right of a state to secede from the Union won the support of only two Whigs but of fourteen Democrats. (Ten Democrats and twenty-one Whigs opposed it.) Jackson himself had of course denied the right of secession and Jefferson's legacy was at best ambiguous. But this does not alter the fact that the Democrats had generally denounced Whig policies in the name of states' rights while orthodox Whigs had favored a more powerful central government. This was another sign of the continuity in ideology between the Jacksonian era and the years when the sectional controversy was dominant.[266]

It is of course true that southern Democrats had not always been skeptical of the Union. When Andrew Jackson crushed South Carolina's attempt at nullification in the 1830s many southerners, Democrats included, had applauded him. At this time Democrats, regardless of regional loyalties, tended to be majoritarians; they were confident about democracy. But as the 1840s progressed so Democrats in the South, hearing the growing clamor in the North for free soil and abolition, had their faith in the majority shaken. In effect their majoritarianism clashed with their attachment to slavery. They chose to keep their attachment to slavery and in so doing began to turn states' rights into the minoritarian creed which it had been for Calhoun but never for Jackson.[267]

This was an ideological adjustment whose importance should not be underestimated. But once he had made it the southern Democrat easily became the southern militant. He had always expected to see a tyrannical aristocracy attempting to subvert liberty and states' rights so the northern antislavery phalanx was easily understood. He liked agriculture; the South was the agricultural section. In other ways Democratic ideology

---

265. *Address of Thompson*, p. 11.
266. Hamilton, *Party Politics in North Carolina*, pp. 144–145.
267. See above, Chapter 4.

promoted a pro-southern viewpoint in the South, precisely as it did in the North. The refusal to allow moral reform movements into politics undercut the antislavery movement throughout the nation. In the North the resulting hostility towards the antislavery crusade encouraged sympathy for the South; in the South it intensified hostility to the North.

Hence it is quite wrong to claim that the two parties in the South viewed slavery similarly. It is true that both excoriated the abolitionists. It is also true that each accused the other of harboring abolitionists or free-soilers. Such was the "loyalty politics" that characterized every presidential election from 1836 onwards. But the rhetoric of the two parties was different. As we saw when considering their view of abolitionism, southern Whigs frequently attacked southern Democrats for being too extreme on the slavery question and thus for giving ammunition to antislavery fanatics. They also attacked southern Democrats for fomenting the spirit of disunion. Typical was the 1851 Address of the Tennessee Whigs which branded as "formidable conspirators, deliberately plotting the destruction of the greatest and wisest government ever formed for the happiness of men" all those who were "the open advocates of Secession and Disunion." The Tennessee Whigs then mentioned not only "the Garrisons, the Hales and the Tappans of the North" but also "the Cheveses, the Rhetts, and Quittmans [sic] of the South." It was no accident that all the southerners named were Democrats. This even-handed denunciation of extremists on both sides of the slavery question was characteristic of southern Whigs.[268] But southern Democrats rarely if ever leveled these charges against southern Whigs. They often denounced southern Whigs for disloyalty to slavery and the South, but not for an excessive attachment to their section or their labor system. So when Professor Cooper claims that "each party maintained an identical and wholehearted commitment to the politics of slavery," he is, quite simply, wrong.[269]

268. "Address to the People of Tennessee by the Whig State Convention," in White (ed.), *Messages of Governors of Tennessee*, IV, p. 407; *Journals of the Senate and House of Commons of the General Assembly of the State of North Carolina, at its Session in 1850–1851* (Raleigh, 1851).

269. Cooper, *South and Politics of Slavery*, p. 148. For southern Whig attitudes to their opponents see, for example, the campaign sheet for 1852, *The Signal*. It may be worth noting that Professor Cooper's Prologue, intended to show the potency of the slavery issue in politics, also shows the tendency of southern Whigs to go for moderation. He also finds that the northern Democrats generally opposed the Compromise of 1850 while the Whigs supported it and that "no equivalent of William Henry Seward walked among the northern Democrats" (p. 332). I would suggest that the evidence in Professor Cooper's book supports the view offered here rather than his own interpretation. Cooper also, I believe, errs when he asserts that the two parties took the same view of political democracy. Nonetheless, I do not wish to deny that his work has been a major contribution to southern political history in these years.

We are now in a position to appreciate why, even though not all southern Democrats adopted a proslavery position, southern Whigs virtually never did so. The proslavery theorist either remained aloof from both parties or he supported the Democracy (or in Calhoun's case did both!). A southern Whig advocated commercialization and diversification. He perceived that the North had traveled further along this road. So how could slavery be better than free labor overall? If free labor were indeed inferior, where was the evidence? If northern society were on the verge of a breakdown what was the point of an alliance of interests north and south? If the North was in fact poorer than the South, why seek to emulate it? Such was the implicit reasoning of the southern Whig.

Whiggery was, of course, in no way incompatible with slavery or even with a strong commitment to slavery. The southern Whig could be a large slaveholder, utterly hostile to the abolitionists, and utterly dedicated to the retention of slavery in the South. He was almost certain to believe that the South was better served by having millions of slaves than by having millions of freed blacks. He could even argue that the South was better than the North. But he could scarcely derive this from the superiority of slavery over free labor. More characteristic of southern Whigs was a disinclination to stress or even examine the different labor processes.

The corollary was the proslavery theorist's distrust of Whig policies. If slavery were indeed better than free labor, then it almost inevitably followed that the wage workers of the North were grossly exploited. Hence northern successes in diversification, industrialization and urbanization must be viewed skeptically. Indeed did it not follow that the North was unstable and that there was an acute danger of its numerical power being turned against the South? If so the Whig program was dangerous in the extreme. Such was the implicit reasoning of the proslavery theorist.

III

We can explain the alignment of 1850 by reference to the economic changes taking place throughout the nation in the Jacksonian era. Those most keen on the emerging commercial order, North and South, tended to be Whigs. The Whig party was an alliance between commercial and capitalist groups in the North and those in the South who perceived no necessary conflict between slavery and capitalism. The party could recruit in all sections of the Union but its heartland, as historians have recognized, remained the North and especially New England, the most developed region economically. In the early 1840s all Whigs, north and south of the Mason-Dixon line, could agree on the need for banks and credit. But when the sectional controversy erupted, the northern orientation of the party simultaneously made its northern supporters highly militant, but pushed its southern supporters in the direction of compromise. The Democrats, by contrast, had throughout the nation been the critics of this emerging social order. They too were powerful in each section but the Democratic creed was inscribed with the values of the slaveholders of the South, even when it professed indifference to southern slavery itself. This did not mean that the Democrats were unable to win support in the North or the Whigs in the South. The debate over banking and the disagreement over such fundamental questions as the extent of popular control over government were issues which produced a competitive party system in each section and in every region. Moreover, when the sectional controversy first emerged, the party that might otherwise have been disadvantaged in each section by its social philosophy (the Democrats in the North, the Whigs in the South) was able, as the party of sectional moderation, to launch a powerful appeal on the basis of national harmony and the Union. Only in the 1850s would this appeal fade. By then the party system, and the Republic itself, would be on the verge of collapse.

Conclusion: Economic development, class conflict and American politics, 1820–1850

The growth of an increasingly market-oriented economy was a dominant feature of the second quarter of the nineteenth century. In a country as large and economically diverse as the United States, the development of commercial structures and commercial practices had complex and contradictory effects. In the North, and especially New England, the most developed region, it accelerated the growth of wage labor which in turn posed a challenge to traditional republican notions of virtue and independence. I have argued that abolitionism, though clearly of appeal to only a small minority of northerners, was a response to these economic changes. The abolitionist redefined the role of conscience and family in accordance with the needs of a society in which wage labor was increasingly prominent. The resulting view of the proper northern social order implied a deep hostility to slavery everywhere, but especially in the United States. In the South, however, the same processes of commercial development had an opposite effect in that they tended to reinforce and perpetuate the section's dependence on, and attachment to, slavery. The strong commercial bonds connecting slave produce with the markets of Europe generated economic growth in the South just as in the North, but growth ironically widened the gap between the two sections. Even in parts of the South that were suffering from competition from more fertile lands, like South Carolina, the successes of some planters, combined with the sheer numbers of blacks involved, made the prospect of emancipation increasingly unimaginable.

From the early 1830s the twin forces of proslavery and abolitionism began to take their toll on the American political system. They hindered the efforts of statesmen to create national political parties. Nevertheless as yet the major problems with which statesmen grappled were national rather than sectional. How should the nation respond to the development and extension of market forces? In a sense even John C. Calhoun and William Lloyd Garrison were involved in this debate, the one aiming at universalizing the northern response, the other at building barriers against the political, economic and cultural imperialism implied by that process.

Yet the most commanding solution was offered by the Democratic party. Until at least the late 1830s a Whig solution was not on offer, though Whigs made it clear that they objected to the Democratic solution, and individual leaders had ideas of their own. The Democratic solution was to seek to maintain traditional republican ideas, those of Thomas Jefferson and John Taylor, modifying them in important though minor ways (the revised view of the presidency and of the political party) and strengthening some elements at the expense of others. This offered a solution, racially flawed but electorally commanding, to the problems of the American polity and American society.

The impact of the economic recession, however, in the late 1830s brought the party battles of the Jacksonian era to a climax. The key effect was in strengthening Whig unity. In resisting the anti-commercial animus that fueled the bank war both nationally and (what is more important) in the states, the Whig party was able to offer by the early 1840s a viable alternative solution to the problems of American government and society. As the progressive historians recognized, the Whigs were less enthusiastic about political democracy for white men, more enthusiastic about the process of commercial development that had been under way throughout the nation but which was faltering in the late 1830s and early 1840s. The result was the creation of a two-party system that was remarkably well balanced in both sections. Since the democratization of the American polity and the commercialization of the American economy were national phenomena, the two parties were each able to recruit both north and south of the Mason-Dixon line.

Nevertheless, by 1850 the gap between the parties had narrowed, while that between the sections had widened. The resumption of economic growth in the mid-1840s caused the views of more northern Whigs to resemble those of the abolitionists, not necessarily in the demand for immediate abolition but rather in the insistence upon an individualism nourished within the domestic circle and fettered only by the ties of "conscience." As northerners in increasing numbers were moving towards a legitimation of northern society in terms of social mobility, wage labor and diversification they would be driven to emphasize the unslave-like qualities and attributes of northern labor. In the 1850s the Republicans would seek to equate these with the nation itself and while the equation did not necessarily imply abolition it undoubtedly implied free soil and a strictly subordinate status for slavery. The conservative strand of northern Whiggery represented by Daniel Webster, which clung instead to a more organic view of society, had previously been dominant in the North, but the economic recovery of the 1840s strengthened the more liberal antislavery wing. The role played by Webster in 1850 was in a sense a last gasp of the old northern Whiggery, that which called for forbearance towards the slaveholder, and a cautious calculation of the advantages and disadvantages of specific political strategies and moral demands.

In the South, on the other hand, economic recovery restored confidence in the economic prospects of a slave-based agriculture. The Whig party, the champion of economic diversification, would pay a price for this recovery. Moreover, the need to combat antislavery propaganda propelled more southerners towards a view of the North that re-emphasized the servile status and the allegedly deplorable living conditions of the wage worker. Once again it is important to recognize that the process of economic growth had both stimulated this propaganda in the North and strengthened the resolve of slaveholders to resist it. Finally, the success of the slave regime in responding to commercial opportunities as well as antislavery pressure in the Southwest was responsible for the injection of the Texas question into national politics. This too would snap some of the ties binding North and South.

These economic developments damaged the political parties. Democratic ideology had always functioned to promote the interests of southern slaveholders. But the need to combat antislavery in the North meant that, as Calhoun was quick to see, this loose, hegemonic control was insufficient. The attempts to secure additional protection for slavery produced strains within the Democracy and, given the growing antislavery sentiment among northern Whigs, within the Whig party too. When southerners reached out for additional territory, or even demanded a share of the territory acquired by the nation's armies, they found in the North a minority of Democrats and a majority of Whigs unwilling to accede to their demands. As a result much of the controversy over slavery was focused on, and even displaced into, the struggle over the territories, a struggle that threatened the unity of each party. The Compromise of 1850, which allowed both parties to maintain their existence, even as it permitted the continued co-existence of North and South, showed that these disruptive processes, however ominous, were not yet fatal to the nation and its political institutions.

II

Let us now attempt a preliminary assessment of the role of class conflict in these developments. (I shall argue in the sequel to this volume that such conflict played a vital role in bringing about the American Civil War.) It is important to consider our terms. If class conflict means conflict resulting from purposive action undertaken by class conscious individuals in pursuit of known class interests, then its role is only a minor one. But we must widen our categories. If we include behavior which, whatever its intention, generates conflict with another class, then class conflict will become more important. And if we recognize that neither of these contending classes need necessarily have any awareness (or understanding) of class itself, then the role of class conflict will again expand. If we further accept that class conflicts often generate highly complex processes of action and response, and that their effects may be registered in specific ideologies, then once again we will assign them a larger role. And finally, if we recognize that their effects may be visible only in the attempt to suppress other (and more damaging) effects, then we will at last be in a position to attempt a true evaluation of the part they played in producing the American Civil War.

This means that so far as the South is concerned we should focus on the resistance of the slave. History presents no example of a people desirous of enslavement, and the work of social historians has confirmed that (at the minimum) a large proportion of American slaves earnestly desired their freedom. Though this desire only occasionally produced outright rebellion and induced only a minority to attempt flight to the North, we should not think that the aspiration to freedom – or slave resistance in general – was otherwise inconsequential. To assess its impact, let us try to imagine an alternative scenario, one in which American blacks were truly reconciled to slavery.

In such circumstances it is, as I have suggested, possible to doubt whether southerners would have been so reluctant to diversify, to encourage town-building, or to engage in manufactures. While more research is clearly needed to resolve this question (despite its long history), an explanation of the relative lack of southern economic development in terms of the constraints produced by slavery is still very viable. And, as I have also suggested, these constraints derived in turn from the structural antagonism endemic in the master–slave relation. The political effect of this lack of development can scarcely be exaggerated. It helped make northerners highly critical of the South and strengthened the conviction of all, from the most doughfaced Democrat to the most militant abolitionist, that free labor was superior to slavery. And at a time when the nation was expanding its territorial boundaries, the importance of this conviction in turn can scarcely be exaggerated.

But of course this was only one of many effects of the antagonism between master and slave. If the slaves had indeed been fully reconciled to slavery, the entire fugitive slave question would scarcely have arisen. Nor would there have been any need to worry about the "exposed frontier" in Texas, the existence of which, as we have seen, played so huge a part in the drive for annexation and thus in the eruption of the territorial controversy. Moreover there would have been little need for slaveholders to institute a blockade against the antislavery propaganda of the North, a blockade that produced considerable disquiet even among northerners indifferent to the fate of the slave. Indeed if slaveholders had actually had a completely pliant work force, they would have been able to view with considerable indifference the activities of northern antislavery groups. Even more fundamentally, would the abolitionist crusade even have come into existence if the slaves of the South had not wished to be liberated?

To say that this counterfactual is opposed not only to the historical record but to any remotely conceivable past is merely to confirm that class conflict suffuses slavery. We should note, however, that in tracing its consequences, we sometimes find ourselves dealing with economic factors, sometimes with ideological developments, sometimes with social and political movements. In some cases we are concerned with direct purposive action intended to promote class interests but in most the actors are not so self-aware. Indeed one of the most subtle effects of class conflict in the South was to render itself partly invisible even to those who (in developing the proslavery argument, for example) were responding to its dictates.

Similarly in the North. In the sequel to this volume I shall suggest that the Republican party needed to combat and thus revise older views of wage labor, which would have been utterly inappropriate and indeed highly dangerous in an economy where free labor was increasingly taking this form and in a regime which enfranchised the wage worker. Abolitionists in the 1830s, and later some Whigs in the 1840s began this process, though it was far from complete by 1850. As they defined wage labor in contradistinction to slavery (by emphasizing the work ethic, social mobility, and the gains accruing to all in a developing and diversifying economy), these northerners were constructing an ideology whose political appeal and thus socially integrative effect was extraordinarily powerful. But the cost was an increasing disenchantment, and finally a repudiation of all affinity, with the slave South. Here northerners were responding to the potential for disruption contained within the employer–worker relation, just as southerners so often responded to the potential for disturbance inherent in the relationship between slave and master. Such is the stuff of class conflict. As we shall see, each elite could contain its subordinate class quite easily – but only at the cost of alienating the elite in the other section. The result would be war, emancipation, social upheaval – and the consolidation of capitalist relations of production in the United States. In other words the result would be a bourgeois revolution.

Appendix: A review of some major works on the economics of slavery

The contribution of Fred Bateman and Thomas Weiss to the debate over slavery and industrialization has been a considerable one, given the data they have unearthed and their skill in manipulating it. But their conclusions are not valid and warrant a brief review. They argue that "by market dictates, industrial expansion should have occurred." Aggregate levels of demand were satisfactory, savings and investment were more than sufficient, markets in the South in general operated adequately. So why the "deplorable scarcity" of industry? "The answer," they argue, "appears to lie with the planter class, specifically in its members' entrepreneurial attitudes and decisions, especially their behavior toward risk." Yet they immediately discount the risk factor: "even after risk is taken into account, the manufacturing returns should have been judged superior by shrewd investors." Only if southerners were especially averse to risk can this factor provide the key. Why should southerners be so risk-averse? Bateman and Weiss end by pointing to "the conservative, cautious and slow-moving southerner of literary tradition." Despite market signals, "it seemed to take more evidence and more time to convince southerners to enter the murky waters of the American Industrial Revolution."[1]

What is curious is their reluctance to interpret this behavior in terms of the constraints imposed by slavery. They recognize that some planters doubted whether industrialism and slavery were compatible and acknowledge that the effect of these doubts "may have been sufficiently real to have discouraged some planters from investing in manufacturing enterprises." Yet "many of these fears seem exaggerated." And "exaggerated" is the word they frequently employ when discussing the claim that slavery constrained industrial development. Since some poor whites and some slaves did work in manufacturing, the traditional arguments, they conclude, "appear to have been exaggerated." Similarly, they claim that "there is good reason to believe that slavery's impact

1. Fred Bateman and Thomas Weiss, *A Deplorable Scarcity: The Failure of Industrialization in the Slave Economy* (Chapel Hill, 1981), pp. 159–163.

on immigration has been exaggerated," and point to the large number of immigrants in New Orleans to support the claim. But here as elsewhere a curious logic is being invoked. No-one denies that there was some industry in the South, that some slaves and some white workers were employed there and that some immigrants came to the region. But it is the *relative* weakness of southern manufacturing and the *relatively* small number of immigrants which are to be explained. (As they themselves point out, the South in 1860 had only 10 percent of the nation's foreign-born.) It must follow that *any* factors adduced to explain these deficiencies can only be tendential in their operation. To look for rigid, unyielding constraints is illogical: no factors, including those which they emphasize, can have played such a role. Of course it may be that some historians have overstated their own case for one or other of these constraints but this is not a reason to deny or minimize their explanatory power. The fact that their constraining power was not complete does not exclude the possibility that they offer a complete explanation for the scarcity of southern manufacturing.[2]

To clarify the argument, let us consider one of the concluding paragraphs of the Bateman and Weiss volume. It raises many important points:

> That there was not more industry reflects the decisions of planters, acting individually and without legal constraints, to shun manufacturing opportunities. Some planters may have avoided them, giving great weight to the potential long-run social costs of further industrialization when they calculated the benefits of such economic progress. Yet it seems unlikely that this attitude checked industrial development on a wide scale. Few planters would have felt that their particular investment would mean the demise of slavery. Nor is it probable that most recognized the problem of the fallacy of composition. At the individual level, the pecuniary gains would have dominated these nebulous social costs. Such concerns cannot explain widespread anti-industrial behavior unless coupled with a more personal cost, one not appearing in an income statement or balance sheet: the industrial maverick might have been ostracized by the agricultural society if the planter ethos placed industrial wealth in low esteem.

The authors begin by referring to the constraints imposed by slavery but then, once again, seek to minimize their importance. Next comes the vital assertion as they give what is probably the key reason for their reluctance throughout the book to accept the power of these constraints. The probability of gains accruing to the individual, they maintain, would have triumphed over the possibility of a loss, shared among a collectivity. But what does this assertion rest upon? It rests upon the assumption that individual slaveholders were profit-maximizers. Yet the task the authors have set themselves is to explain the failure of so many slaveholders to respond to the opportunities available in manufacturing. As already noted, there can be only one conclusion: in certain important circumstances they

---

2. Bateman and Weiss, *A Deplorable Scarcity*, pp. 161, 160, 90.

were not profit-maximizers. Rather than resort to some alleged and unexplained southern behavioral characteristic (risk-aversion), it is surely more reasonable to argue that the slaveholders were extremely sensitive to activities that might threaten their regime. To put it another way, they were highly conscious of their class interests and actions which threatened slavery itself were likely to be discountenanced. Self-interest was mediated by the need to safeguard their slave-based society. Not all southerners, of course, perceived the danger in the same way and some industrialization accordingly occurred. As long as the numbers were not excessive no action needed to be taken. How might pressure to conform be exerted? Bateman and Weiss see one mechanism, only to misinterpret it. The tendency to "ostracize" the "industrial maverick" need not be seen as yet another unexplained social practice. For it surely served to reinforce this collective self-interest in the best way imaginable, not by force of law (which would be divisive and might set dangerous legal precedents concerning the power of the master), but instead by "custom."[3]

Such "customs" are frequently used to maintain collective and specifically class interests. To make this claim, however, is not to postulate a conspiracy. A subtle process may have been at work. Let us suppose that only a minority of southerners believed that industrialization threatened their regime. But if these southerners believed in "ostracizing the industrial maverick" and their values were adopted by many who had not even stopped to consider the role of industry in the South then it would be right to conclude that it was slavery that played the key role. Its effects would have been twofold: first to generate the original hostility of the minority, and second to confer the prestige upon this minority necessary for its opinions to hold sway.

The central weakness in the Bateman and Weiss view is their inability to free themselves from the confines of neo-classical theory. They have taken as natural behavior patterns observed in a society where the wage relation, not the master–slave relation, is the norm. In the wage labor economies of the developed world it is plausible to believe that self-interest cannot be legally pursued and at the same time threaten the maintenance of the wage relation itself. But in a slave society, there was reason to believe that the legal pursuit of self-interest might jeopardize the master–slave relation. The overriding point is that it is dangerous to generalize about human behavior in a slave society on the basis of unconscious assumptions drawn from experience of a wage labor economy.

(2) Claudia Goldin

Though a valuable contribution to the debate on the economics of slavery, Claudia Goldin's book *Urban Slavery in the American South 1820–1860* nevertheless illustrates once again the dangers of an excessive and uncritical reliance upon neo-classical economics. In general she follows the Fogel and Engerman approach to the study of slavery and consequently ends by endorsing the view that slavery did not really constrain urbanization in the South. Yet what is

---

3. Bateman and Weiss, *A Deplorable Scarcity*, p. 162.

remarkable in this study is the amount of data presented to show that masters had good reasons indeed for being suspicious of cities and of slaves living in them. First, she notes the hostility of white labor. "The white artisans and tradesmen," she writes, "were an effective propaganda machine in the cities, who searched for ways to remove their black competitors from the market." Indeed, she acknowledges, "examples of these artisan petitions are legion." Second, she stresses the importance of hiring out, living out and self-hire in the cities and even makes it clear that the laws against self-hire were unenforced and probably unenforceable; "many slaves," she concludes, "hired out their own time." Third, she agrees that slaves in the cities had greater opportunities to behave in ways that alarmed many masters, whether by mingling with whites or free blacks in backroom bars and gambling or by buying liquor with goods obtained illegally. Indeed stealing, although also a feature of plantation life was "reported as being especially easy for slaves in urban areas, for many of them worked in stores and on the docks." Fourth, she concedes that the urban environment was generally hospitable to fugitive slaves. "Runaways from plantations," she observes, "flocked to the towns, where free blacks and slaves harbored them and, on occasion, helped them to flee to the North." She concludes that "the problem of runaways seems to have been a relatively greater one in the cities than in the rural community." Finally, she notes that many city authorities tried to control their slaves by requiring passes if they were out at night, or were to be allowed to buy and sell goods, or badges if they had been hired out. But such regulations were often highly inconvenient to the owner or hirer as well as being impossible to enforce. In many cities the courts simply gave up.[4]

The obvious conclusion is that these problems of control impeded the process of urbanization. Yet Goldin rejects this verdict on the basis of a single assumption: only if the problem of control affected the profits of the individual master could it have had any real effect in deterring urban slavery. Since license fees, court costs and local taxes imposed on slaveholders were of only modest proportions, it follows that they had no great impact:

> The main conclusion of this monograph is that slavery and Southern cities were not incompatible during the period 1820–60. Although there were some forces unique to urban areas which created an inhospitable environment for slavery, they were relatively weak. The additional costs that were imposed on urban owners and hirers amounted to only a small percentage of the yearly hire rate and do not appear to have increased over time.

She also notes that whenever artisans challenged the master's use of slaves, the authorities supported him "over and over again." And the fear of runaways could

---

4. Claudia Goldin, *Urban Slavery in the American South 1820–1860: A Quantitative History* (Chicago, 1976), pp. 28–30, 35, 38–40, 32, 47, 48, 108, 38. A recent restatement of her views (with only minor changes) is to be found in Goldin, "An Explanation for the Relative Decline of Urban Slavery: 1820–1860," in Robert Fogel, *Without Consent or Contract: The Rise and Fall of American Slavery: Markets and Production*, Technical Papers, Vol I (N.Y., 1992), pp. 95–131.

not have been a significant concern since it did not reduce the demand for slaves in the cities. The conclusion is that "the issue of control raised in the traditional literature was clearly not important in impeding the progress of urban slavery."[5]

But this conclusion only follows on the same neo-classical assumption we have previously encountered: that the slaveholders were profit-maximizers. If they were not, if they took account of a general interest, common to all slaveholders, in securing the long-term stability of the institution, then they might be deterred from cities even though the profits were as high as, or higher than, on the land. There was a shared interest in retaining the support of urban labor for the regime and a shared concern that opportunities for runaways not be increased. The problem of runaway slaves is illustrative. Insofar as the cities attracted runaways from the rural areas (as Goldin notes), they encouraged the slave in his initial decision to flee. But who would bear this cost? Not the urban slaveholder. It would not appear in any profit and loss account we might construct for him. Instead we may surmise that the city's hospitality to the runaway would strengthen the customary anti-urban sentiment in the South. Such "customs" can often be an important way of maintaining a collective self-interest.

As we have seen, slaveholders had other reasons to be skeptical about cities. Hiring and self-hiring were, as we have seen, common practice. Goldin argues that hiring was "probably the most important contribution to the economic survival of slavery in its urban environment," while living out, she maintains, "provided additional flexibility which enabled slavery to compete effectively with a free labor system in the city." But she will only accept that these practices suggest any tension between slavery and urban life if a mechanism can be found which will explain how such practices reduced profits and thus the urban demand for slaves. Again this is far too narrow an approach. Slaveholders were faced with great problems in the final antebellum decades; in particular they had to contend with the growth of an increasingly militant anti-slavery movement in the North. They developed a proslavery ideology in order to combat it. At the core of this ideology was the assertion that the slave needed the supervision of his master (or the overseer, his master's representative). An image of paternalism was projected. Even if the reality on many plantations was very different, there can be little doubt that thousands of slaveholders believed that blacks needed the paternal care of the master. Hiring out, living out, and especially self-hire, challenged this relationship. These urban practices resembled those of a wage labor system and were therefore hard to reconcile with the proslavery argument, which derived much of its power from an assault upon the relationship between employer and wage laborer. Thus one may question Goldin's interpretation of hiring-out. One might argue that, rather than demonstrate the flexibility of slavery, it suggests instead the tension between urban life and slavery. Only by weakening the ties with the master could the South sustain even a small proportion of its slaves in an urban environment (never more than 10 percent).[6]

For these reasons then, many slaveholders were surely less likely to want to see their slaves in an urban environment and less likely to welcome urbanization in

5. Goldin, *Urban Slavery in the American South*, pp. 123, xiv.
6. Goldin, *Urban Slavery in the American South*, pp. 35, 42.

the South. To repeat: such behavior is not in itself "non-economic," since it was premised on the need to safeguard slavery, the source of the master's income and wealth. But it was not the profit-maximizing self-interest, pursued according to an individualist calculus, which neo-classical theory assumes.

This is not the only problem in the Goldin analysis. When one considers slavery and urbanization, there are in fact three different questions which, though apparently closely related, need to be kept separate. First, could existing southern cities accommodate some slaves? This is an easy question: they could. Second could those cities accommodate a high proportion of slaves among their inhabitants without suffering severe problems of control or incurring unacceptably high social and political costs? This is a much more difficult question. Third, could the South with its slave labor base, urbanize? This is much the most important question. An affirmative answer to the first question does not imply an affirmative answer to the other two. A small number of slaves in a small number of small cities plainly does not show that a large number of slaves could function in the cities of an urban society. But Goldin concentrates on a fourth question, apparently in the belief that this will answer the others too: why did the slave population of various southern cities fluctuate considerably from decade to decade in the antebellum years?[7] But to explain variations around a low norm is not to explain why the norm itself is low. It follows that an explanation for the lowness of the norm need not explain variations around it. Let us consider an analogy. The temperature of the earth is determined chiefly by the sun. We do not challenge this view by showing that the sun may not explain why one room in a house (which perhaps has electric heating) is warmer than another. Claudia Goldin, however, assumes that an answer to the large question about slavery and cities must also answer her more narrow question. After having reviewed the arguments of those who claimed that slavery was unsuited to cities, she concludes:

> The general difficulty with all the explanations outlined above is that they are too sweeping; they do not explain the considerable variation in the course of urban slavery. They do not help the investigator explain why slavery declined in some cities while it increased in others, and why slavery declined in certain decades while it increased in others. What is required then is an explanation flexible enough to cope with all of the experiences in the cities between 1820 and 1860.

But we may well be skeptical about her answer to the narrower question concerning the fluctuations in slave populations. She emphasizes the highly elastic urban demand for slaves, as compared with the relatively inelastic rural demand. In cities where this high elasticity prevailed, then in a period of rising slave prices

---

7. She is not entirely consistent in her claims here. On one occasion (p. 7) she writes that the question whether "the existence of slavery could have retarded southern urbanization" forms "a much larger problem . . . than can be tackled here." But elsewhere (p. 10) she declares that "although focusing on changes in urban slave populations, this research also explores the role of slavery in determining the level of urbanization." And in her conclusion she asserts (p. 128) that "slavery was adapted to the urban milieu."

free labor would be substituted and slaves would be moved into rural areas. The free labor would be supplied principally by immigrants. And the explanation for the differing elasticities of demand? Immigrants wished to live in cities, and could thus do the work of slaves. But the gang labor system on the plantations repelled them; only slaves could be induced to do this work. Yet this analysis is perfectly consistent with a different explanation: immigrants were put off southern cities by slavery; when they did enter a southern city, an exodus of slaves would generally follow. If this explanation is correct, the conclusion would be that slavery deterred immigration and, in so doing, retarded urbanization. This, of course, is the traditional view. Here, as elsewhere, it can withstand the cliometric challenge with surprising ease.[8]

(3) Gavin Wright

Special reference must be made to the work of Gavin Wright, in my view by far the most gifted economic historian working on southern history.[9] Wright's contribution to the debate over slavery has been immense. He has, moreover, advanced a novel and intriguing view of the economics of slavery which warrants the most careful consideration. The neo-classical approach to economic history emphasizes profit-maximization; the approach I have taken, derived from Marxism, instead stresses the relations between the exploiting and exploited groups. Wright, by contrast, focuses upon individual wealth, its maintenance and augmentation, and the effect upon economic development of different types of wealth. He argues that the incentives of slave property were not such as to encourage town building, and that, as a consequence, southerners did not emulate northerners in attracting immigrants, or in diversifying out of agriculture. Southerners were "laborlords," with a high proportion of their wealth in slaves (whose value was independent of "townbuilding"), while the northern economy was one of "landlords," in which the maintenance and augmentation of land prices was accorded the highest priority.

Wright's approach, in my view, marks many advances upon neo-classical orthodoxy. It can offer a plausible explanation for the slow pace of urbanization and industrialization in the South and it accords with the observed behavior of the rural majority, both North and South, for whom the maintenance of the family

---

8. Goldin, *Urban Slavery in the American South*, p. 7. This criticism has also been made at greater length in Gavin Wright, *Political Economy of the Cotton South: Households, Markets, and Wealth in the Nineteenth Century* (N.Y., 1978), pp. 122–125. For a good critique of Goldin, with a somewhat different emphasis from that offered here, see Barbara J. Fields, *Slavery and Freedom on the Middle Ground: Maryland During the Nineteenth Century* (New Haven, 1985), pp. 49–57.

9. The principal works are *Political Economy of the Cotton South; Old South, New South: Revolutions in the Southern Economy Since the Civil War* (N.Y., 1986), "Prosperity, Progress, and American Slavery," in David (*et al.*), *Reckoning With Slavery*, pp. 302–336, "Slavery and the Cotton Boom," *Explorations in Economic History*, XII (1975), pp. 439–451, "The Efficiency of Slavery: Another Interpretation," *American Economic Review*, LXIX (1979), pp. 219–226, "Cheap Labor and Southern Textiles Before 1860," *Journal of Economic History*, XXXIX (1979), pp. 655–680.

farm was of paramount importance. Moreover, Wright recognizes the importance of the non-slaveholder's loyalty to the slaveholders' regime and draws attention to the resulting constraint upon economic development. It is interesting that the emphasis on wealth yields an analysis that is often quite compatible with the Marxist approach.

Yet there are important differences. As we shall see, Wright remains, in the final analysis, wedded to the individualism of the neo-classical approach even as he leaves behind its preoccupation with profit-maximization. In fact he offers what might be termed a neo-Beardian, rather than a Marxist interpretation; the emphasis on property types is highly reminiscent of Charles Beard's analysis of the politics of the antebellum Republic with its contrast between landed wealth (realty) and other forms of property (personalty). The similarity ends, however, when we remember that for Beard it was the South in the decades before the Civil War which was the society of landowners, while in the northern economy other forms of wealth, commercial and industrial, were acquiring increased importance.[10] And this offers a clue to one of the deficiencies in Wright's interpretation. Is it not a little perverse to describe northern society as one of "landlords," when its chief characteristic, and the one we are most concerned to explain, is a diversification away from agriculture, and a relative diminution in the importance of the rural sector and of landed wealth? Indeed one may press this point further. Owning land itself scarcely encourages townbuilding. On the contrary, one might much more plausibly argue that, across the entire developed world, it was when men no longer had the opportunities for landownership that the process of urbanization really got under way. In the United States, such a diminution in opportunities was precisely the reality that confronted thousands of northerners, especially in the East, following the opening up of western land. Urban development and economic diversification were the consequences both before and after the Civil War.

Is Wright asserting that the incentives of landownership furnished a necessary condition for urbanization? The argument is plausible for the United States though, I shall suggest, mistaken. Can it be applied elsewhere? The British case is instructive. In Britain land was, of course, much more difficult to acquire. Hence the incentives which Wright describes simply did not operate on any significant scale. And yet the process of urbanization was almost a century further advanced. One of two conclusions must follow. Either the United States and Britain urbanized for utterly different, indeed contradictory, reasons or Wright's argument is incorrect. Perhaps there is an alternative interpretation which can explain the similar outcomes in the two countries but which can also do justice to the different circumstances and the different rates of change.

Let us take a critical look at Wright's argument. We may begin by noting that one need not own any land at all to want to encourage townbuilding. A doctor or storekeeper, even a local merchant, might want to see his locality built up even if he were quite indifferent to the effect on the value of any land (or real estate) he

---

10. See Charles A. Beard, *An Economic Interpretation of the Constitution of the United States* (N.Y., 1913); Charles A. Beard and Mary R. Beard, *The Rise of American Civilization* 2 vols (N.Y., 1933), II, pp. 3–54.

might own. A local population meant a local market and local customers, and its principal effect might be on levels of income, rather than on the stock of wealth. Moreover, eastern industrialists had a strong interest in seeing the development of western agriculture (so long as they could be sure that migration from east to west would not divert from them the manpower needed for their factories).[11] Long before the Civil War, large areas of the North were in food deficit and western agriculture offered the prospect of a cheapening of food prices. Many easterners welcomed and encouraged the development of the West for precisely this reason. Moreover, while townbuilding may have benefited some farmers, it surely had an adverse effect on others. Did landowners in New England, for example, stand to gain from western townbuilding, if one of its principal effects was to introduce damaging competition from the new lands now brought into cultivation? This process, of itself, surely tended rather to reduce the value of their land.[12] It follows that one would need to assess the disincentives as well as the incentives before coming to any conclusion about the overall importance of capital gains on land.[13]

Nevertheless for western farmers, land speculators and others, the incentives to engage in townbuilding might well have operated as Wright describes them. Here the effect on the value of the land might be very considerable indeed. Wright is therefore correct to emphasize the incentives operating in the North, since they differed significantly from those found in the slave South. Where he errs is in failing to recognize that these incentives are themselves the consequence of deeper structural forces. Let us take the case of those northerners who did indeed encourage the process of townbuilding in order to reap capital gains on land. When they were successful, the enhanced value of the land was a reflection of the increased opportunities available to them as landowners. In the North this meant the opportunity to sell the produce of the land to, and perhaps to buy from, others who themselves were either not farmers or who, alternatively, were farmers producing different crops or livestock. The consumers might be either locally based or might be some distance away, perhaps in the case of western produce, in the East. The capital gains derived from an increase in land values were thus ultimately a product of the increased commercialization and specialization in the northern economy.

Northern economic development took the form of an ever-increasing specialization which first occurred within a locality on a modest scale, with local markets and relatively little trade outside the locality. Then came specialization within a region with substantial intra-regional but only modest inter-regional trade. Finally inter-regional trade and specialization developed. By 1840 the final stage was under way.[14] For example, the East was by this time in substantial food deficit

---

11. By the 1850s industrialists had reached this conclusion. In general it is safe to claim that the northern Whigs had this fear, the Republicans did not.
12. This is not to claim that land prices in the North were falling, merely that such economic effects exerted downward pressure on them.
13. One might also wonder about the effect on urbanization of those who "gambled" on land in a certain locality and lost. Did the loss of productive capital here not impede the process of townbuilding?
14. This process is very ably discussed in Diane Lindstrom, *Economic Development in the Philadelphia Region, 1810–1850* (N.Y., 1978).

and it depended for its food for the rest of the antebellum years, indeed for the rest of the century, upon western agriculture. Increased land values in the North thus reflected, and depended upon, the constantly deepening division of labor in the North either in the immediate locality, or, in the case of western lands, in the East as well.

In the South, however, the process operated differently. Although crops like cotton were grown almost entirely for commercial purposes, they were sold outside the South. Moreover the self-sufficiency of the plantation impeded the process of specialization that was occurring in the North. So while commercialized agriculture meant both specialization and a deepening division of labor in the North, in the South these trends were either much weaker or entirely absent.

The key difference involved the growth of wage labor. For a deepening division of labor both entails and is entailed by, the growth of wage labor. Let us examine this process. Let us imagine an economy whose principal sector is agriculture and in which a hundred farmers each produce exclusively for their own (and their families') needs. Nothing is produced for the market. But gradually specialization begins and goods are exchanged. If, as is likely, efficiency increases, the process accelerates. Soon there are ten different kinds of farming, with each sector comprising ten farms, and almost all output is produced for the market. But some farmers are more industrious or more talented or perhaps simply more fortunate than others. They prosper accordingly. If land is freely available, they may be able to expand their farms and thus their crop output. The consequent price reduction may well cause further injury to their competitors. Alternatively, if an economic recession strikes, the more prosperous farmers will be better able to ride out the storm. And, finally, it is possible that the more prosperous farmers will be able to invest in machinery (whose construction is itself encouraged by their growing wealth), which further improves their competitive advantage. In each and all of these cases, pressure on the less successful farmers will tend to force some of them to sell their lands or retreat into self-sufficiency. Such a retreat of course halts the processes of commercialization and specialization. Disposing of the land implies, however, one of several outcomes. Perhaps more land can be bought, in which case the process begins again. More often, the outcome is likely to be tenancy. The tenant may continue to produce for the market but when the advantages accruing to the large farms become too great, even tenancy will be difficult to sustain. At that point the tenants will join the other dispossessed farmers in the ranks of wage labor. Thus specialization means commercialization and dependence on the market. If this dependence is complete and all, or almost all, output is marketed, then commercialization means the possibility that the land itself will be lost. Such an outcome was precisely the danger confronting almost every landowner in the antebellum United States. And the fear of losing one's land entirely – a fear which Wright more than any other economic historian has emphasized – was to prove well founded indeed. The process by which the landowner, or the landowner's child, became the wage worker, was repeated over and over again in the nineteenth century and beyond, both in the United States and elsewhere.

We are now in a position to explain the role of landed property in the process of urbanization. Landownership and the incentives of landed property are not, as the British example implies, necessary conditions for townbuilding. In the United States, indeed, the relative ease with which land could be obtained almost certainly at first impeded the process of urbanization. However, the widespread ownership of landed property meant that when the deeper forces for urbanization could no longer be contained, they generated the incentives among many landowners which Wright describes. So whereas Wright wishes to argue that the incentives of landed property made northerners townbuilders, we may ask whether the causal process ought not to be reversed. Did not the fact that northern society was urbanizing create an added incentive to invest in land? A dispersed population of landowners now stood to gain from townbuilding. But it was not the ownership of land that set the process in motion. Rather landownership in the United States played a mediating role, affecting the pace and pattern of urban development, rather than generating the process itself.

Of course, to the individuals themselves these underlying forces may not have been apparent. The incentives which Wright describes may well have been the motive for townbuilding. The crucial point is, however, that individuals are not necessarily aware of all the processes operating upon them. In this case, they may have simply responded to the incentives without perceiving the underlying forces. What Wright has described is at best the process as it appeared to the participants. His stress upon individuals serves him badly in that it results in an interpretation that makes a mystery of the parallel developments in other countries, slights the other causes of urbanization in the United States and overlooks the countertendencies created by landownership. The alternative view suggested here, derived instead from a relational approach, can explain the perceptions and the incentives which Wright emphasizes, but it can also explain the underlying urbanizing process in general.

Index